The Diary and Letters of Edward Irving

The Diary and Letters
of Edward Irving

Edited by
Barbara Waddington

PICKWICK *Publications* · Eugene, Oregon

THE DIARY AND LETTERS OF EDWARD IRVING

Copyright © 2012 Barbara Waddington. All rights reserved. Except for brief quotations in critical publications or reviews, no part of this book may be reproduced in any manner without prior written permission from the publisher. Write: Permissions, Wipf and Stock Publishers, 199 W. 8th Ave., Suite 3, Eugene, OR 97401.

Pickwick Publications
An Imprint of Wipf and Stock Publishers
199 W. 8th Ave., Suite 3
Eugene, OR 97401

www.wipfandstock.com

ISBN 13: 978-1-62032-270-3

Cataloging-in-Publication data:

> Irving, Edward, 1792–1834.
>
> The diary and letters of Edward Irving / edited by Barbara Waddington.
>
> xiv + 450 p. ; 23 cm. Includes bibliographical references and index.
>
> ISBN 13: 978-1-62032-270-3
>
> 1. Irving, Edward, 1792–1834. 2. Catholic Apostolic Church. I. Title.

BX6593.I7 W126 2012

Manufactured in the U.S.A.

Cover image: Edward Irving, by Andrew Robertson, 1823.

For Elizabeth, Nick, Matthew, and Thomas.

Contents

Preface | ix
Acknowledgments | xi
Abbreviations | xii

Part I: The Diary
1 The Diary: 18 July to 31 August 1810 | 3

Part II: The Letters
2 The Letters: 1814–1821 | 59
3 The Letters: 1822–1824 | 124
4 The Letters: 1825–1826 | 209
5 The Letters: 1827–1828 | 232
6 The Letters: 1829–1831 | 259
7 The Letters: 1832–1833 | 293
8 The Letters: 1834–1835 | 379

Bibliography | 437
Index |

Preface

We know how Edward Irving looked and in *The Spirit of the Age* William Hazlitt informs us that he possessed 'a broad northern dialect,' so with this in mind when I read the letters I was anxious to catch the rhythm and idiosyncrasy of his silent speech.

Many of the letters are personal and Irving, being the man he was, expressed himself with honesty and affection. In addition it should be remembered that he was using the language and idiom of his age. Recognizing this, I resisted the obvious temptation of heavily editing his grammar, style of expression, even the variations of date and address to try and retain something of his personality; perhaps also to get to know and understand him a little better.

Barbara Waddington
Archivist, Lumen United Reformed Church[1]
April, 2012.

---

1. Formerly known as Regent Square United Reformed Church.

Acknowledgments

I should like to take this opportunity of thanking Tim Grass, Rev Geoffrey Roper, Church Secretary of Lumen, and my husband Richard Waddington, for their invaluable help in preparing these letters for publication. I should like to further acknowledge the help and assistance from others. To the staff of libraries: the British Library, National Library of Scotland, New College Library of the University of Edinburgh, the University of Edinburgh Library, Westminster College Library, Cambridge, Fife Council Museums: Kircaldy Museum and Art Gallery, and the Trustees of The Lambeth Palace Library. In addition, the staff of *The Banner of Truth*, Edinburgh. The letters of the Drummond Family by the kind permission of His Grace the Duke of Northumberland and also the Strutt letters and papers by the kind permission of the fifth Baron Rayleigh. Further, the encouragement and donations of papers by Miss Penny Howell, the Martin family and Manfred Henke of Germany and the support of Professor Rosemary Ashton and Dr. Timothy Stunt.

Abbreviations

ANAC	Archives of the New Apostolic Church, North Germany, Hamburg. Folder 'Irving.'
BL:	British Library.
BT:	Letters held at the *Banner of Truth,* Edinburgh.
CL:	*The Collected Letters of Thomas and Jane Welsh Carlyle.* General editor, Charles Richard Sanders. Durham, NC: Duke University Press, 1970.
CSD:	*Concise Scots Dictionary.* Edited by Mairi Robinson. Edinburgh: Edinburgh University Press, 2005.
CW:	*Christian Weekly.*
DCM:	Grimal, Pierre, *Dictionary of Classical Mythology,* ed Stephen Kershaw from the translation by A.R.Maxwell-Hyslop, London, Penguin Books, 1986.
DFP	Drummond Family Papers at Alnwick Castle. DFP: C/9/1–51: The Archives of the Duke of Northumberland.
EIL:	Archives of Regent Square United Reformed Church, London.
ML:	Letters from a private source.
MSND:	*A Midsummer-Night's Dream* by William Shakespeare.
NCL:	New College Library, The University of Edinburgh.
NLS:	National Library of Scotland.
OCEL:	*The Oxford Companion to English Literature.* 5th ed. Edited by Margaret Drabble. Oxford: Oxford University Press, 1987.
ODA:	*Oxford Dictionary of Art.* Edited by Ian Chilvers and Harold Osborne. Oxford: Oxford University Press, 1998.
ODCC:	*The Oxford Dictionary of the Christian Church.* 3rd ed. Edited by F. L. Cross and E. A. Livingstone. Oxford: Oxford University Press, 1997.
ODNB:	*Oxford Dictionary of National Biography.* Edited by H. C. G. Matthew and Brian Harrison. Oxford: Oxford University Press, 2004.
Strutt:	Archives of Lord Rayleigh of Terling.

Abbreviations

UEL: University of Edinburgh Library.

WCL: Westminster College Library, Cambridge.

Part I

The Diary

The Rev Edward Irving when a Young Man, David Wilkie (1785–1841)

1

The Diary

18 July to 31 August 1810[1]

Editor's Introduction

The only regret concerning Edward Irving's Diary is that there is not more of it. Though he clearly records his intention of continuing it, what we have ends with blank pages to spare at the 31st August 1810. In these seven weeks he records his thoughts and feelings, his daily activities, and the people and friends with whom he spends his time, evoking the manners and society of a small Scottish town in the early nineteenth century.

Edward Irving was born in Annan (Dumfries and Galloway) on the 4th August 1792. His father Gavin was a tanner, his mother Mary a daughter of a 'bonnet laird,'[2] said to be of Huguenot descent. He had two brothers, John and George, both of whom became surgeons and died rather young. Four sisters also reached maturity. Initially he was taught to read and write at a small local establishment run by one Peggy Paine; then, until he was twelve, he was instructed in the elements of mathematics by Bryce Downie, a blind teacher,[3] and Adam Hope[4] at Annan Academy. At thirteen he went up to Edinburgh University, admission to which was easy at that time with no entrance examination and modest fees. The fact was that for some it was a more attractive

---

1. Source: ML 09.jpg-148f.jpg
2. A small landowner.
3. See George Blair, *Biographic and Descriptive Sketches of Glasgow Necropolis*, 224.
4. Apparently a kind, spare, middle-aged man, possessed of a logical mind and strong Calvinistic views, with a skeptical attitude towards the world. He imposed discipline on his charges with his 'Cat' strap. See a long passage about Hope in Carlyle's *Reminiscences*, 204–12.

Adam Hope had closed his school in 1803 to join the Rev. William Dalgleish's newly opened Annan Academy. Edward Irving transferred to the Academy at the same time where he stayed until he left to go to Edinburgh University.

alternative than going on to a secondary school.[5] On graduation, he took a teaching post in Haddington (East Lothian) to support himself while pursuing Divinity studies on a part-time basis. He had not determined to become a minister at first but received his 'call' during his time as an Arts degree student.[6]

While at Edinburgh University he had come to the attention of Sir John Leslie (1766–1832), then Professor of Mathematics, who had recommended him to the post of schoolmaster at the newly established school of mathematics at Haddington. 'When Irving first came to Haddington,' writes one of his pupils, 'he was a tall, ruddy, robust, handsome youth, cheerful and kindly disposed; he soon won the confidence of his advanced pupils, and was admitted into the best society in the town and neighborhood.'[7]

Irving supplemented his income with a tutorial post to the children of General Lord William Schaw Cathcart, 1st Earl Cathcart. The family were in residence at Salton Hall,[8] and it is here that we first meet him. He describes a scene worthy of Jane Austen. He is completely ignored by the haughty mistress of the house, forty-four year old Lady Cathcart; while disdaining to speak to him directly, she communicates her displeasure at his behaviour via the French governess Miss Brame. This was a daunting task for her because, as Edward observes, although she 'has been most of her life in England, she speaks the language rather indifferently, and as I never attempt to talk in French, we are not infrequently at a loss to understand each other.'

We are privy to Edward's thoughts and opinions, and introduced to his family, friends, and social life. What emerges is a picture of a serious, upstanding young man, already committed to his vocation and already practising his life-long habit of self-examination of any perceived weakness. This does not preclude the occasional youthful indulgence, and he was demonstrably a sociable character and popular. Through him we are introduced to the inhabitants of this small, rural community and to his daily round of work and relaxation. His commendable gravitas is expressed in his theological and classical reading, his contemplation of the meaning of faith, and his striving towards honourable and decent behaviour.

---

5. Saunders, *Scottish Democracy 1815–1840*, 19.
6. See Grass, *The Lord's Watchman*, 10–11.
7. Oliphant, *Life*, 1, 36.
8. Salton Hall [or Saltoun] was situated five miles south west of Haddington. 'Salton Hall, the seat of the family of Fletcher . . . has been much ornamented in late years. It was formerly a place of considerable strength, possessing all the appurtenances of an old fortress.' Forsyth, *The Beauties of Scotland*, 462.

Haddington. Wednesday, 18 July 1810

This day being Wednesday I went up as usual to Salton Hall, nothing material occurred on my Journey. After teaching the younger part of the family, as usual during their dinner hour I went up to the Drawing room to teach Miss Cathcart.

Upon entering the Room, her Ladyship[9] did not as usual turn about to Salute me; I took no notice of it but proceeded to my business. We finished the first Book of the Elements and I read out for our next Wednesday's task the three first propositions of the Second. Word having come that they were ready in the School Room, or at least that dinner was removed, I went down without having exchanged a single word or look with Lady Cathcart. Finding the School Room empty, I was beginning to ruminate upon the Cause of the dryness. Then Miss Brame, the French Governess arrived, to take her work as usual while I taught Miss Mary & Miss Augusta.—Miss Brame is a native of Lille and left her own Country for the reestablishment of her health at the Commencement of the last war with France about the end of 1792 or the beginning of 93. She was then a young girl (as near as I can learn from her conversations about 10 years old) and was intended as a Companion to Miss Blinny, daughter to Lady Blinny. Being prevented by the war from returning to her native Country, she continued in the same family after the Restoration of her health. Upon the death of Miss Blinny she was engaged to teach Miss Cathcart French and continued in the family till that young lady had no further want of her. I believe she then returned to Maison Blinny's or to some other situation untill [sic] she was again requested to resume her occupation in Lord Cathcart's family for the education of the two younger Ladies, in which situation she has continued ever since.—Miss Brame is a woman about the middle size, rather inclining to fatness: her features though not the most regular contain a good deal of expression. A nature fairly tempered by good sense appears very strikingly in her countenance. A frank cheerful and open disposition is strongly marked upon her face, and almost in every action. But her appearance not as is too frequently the case especially among young Ladies assumed from a desire to appear agreeable, it seems, so far as I yet know, to be a true Index of her mind. From the conversations I have had with her and from a circumstance which I am about to relate, she is a woman of a good heart and the improvement of her understanding has I think, occupied a good deal of her attention. Of her knowledge she is not at all vain; but is possessed of a good deal of modesty. Though she has been most part of her life in England, she speaks the language rather indifferently, and as I never attempt to talk in French we are not infrequently at a loss to understand each other.

After coming in to the Schoolroom and making some remarks upon the weather she observed that she had something to inform me of and that she told it as a very good friend. She said the young Ladies had told Lady Cathcart that I very frequently read books during the teaching hours, that her Ladyship was very ill pleased and desired

---

9. Lady Elizabeth Cathcart (née Elliot), born before 1764, died 1847.

her, Miss Brame, to let me know that she by no means liked it. Miss B replied that she did not like, and observed that it was not from Lady Cathcart's desire but out of pure friendship that she now had mentioned the circumstance. After returning her my most grateful thanks, we were interrupted by one of the young Ladies coming to her Lesson, but I resolved within my own mind, and I here Confirm that Resolution, that no person should ever have to find fault with such an action again. With regard to the degree of blame that might be attached to the circumstance I was then, and am yet of the opinion, that it was by no means so great as I am like to suppose her Ladyship considers it. The nature of Arithmetic is such that the teacher of it neither might nor can be always looking over and speaking to his pupils, when the scholar knows that there is always one on hand to correct them, he is apt to become less attentive, than he would be if he was forced to discover these errors himself, and, if the teacher speak to him while he is working, it is very apt to turn his attention from the operation, the worst thing which can happen to an Arithmetician. It therefore appears that when the number of pupils is small, the master must be at times unemployed with them; and during this time I used sometimes to look upon a Book. I must either have done so, or remained idle or have entered into some Conversation with the Governess which would have been a great deal worse for, from politeness, Conversation cannot always be interrupted whereas reading can. I do not mention these Circumstances to palliate the offence, I only wish to place it in a true light. Her Ladyship in my opinion has been wrong informed—Miss Mary, who of late has appeared a little displeased that I do not always look over her Questions when she desires it, has very probably misrepresented me.—I cannot however sufficiently admire Miss Brame's delicacy in refusing Lady Cathcart's request, or be enough grateful for her kindness in privately making me acquainted with it—I can thus remedy the Cause of Complaint with a better grace than I could otherwise have done.

After returning from his Lordships I went over to sup with my friend Mr Alexr Reddoch, in the Company of Mr Lowrie from Dunbar and Mr Lamb his Landlord. During the conversation after supper the Subject of Ambition was introduced. I observed that the passion when carried to excess was peculiarly dangerous in a statesman, or general. Mr Lowrie remarked that Q. Cincinnatus the Roman General was certainly devoid of it; the conduct of that patriot being explained, Mr Reddoch said there might be perhaps as much pride in such a character as in one who accepted of all the honours proposed him. This observation led him to relate the story of Diogenes the father of the Cynic philosophy. He being one day invited to an entertainment at Plato's house which was as usual very splendid, entered in his rags and trampling upon the sophas [sic] and other rich ornaments of the apartment exclaimed, 'Behold how I trample upon the pride of Plato.' 'Yes,' answered Plato, 'and with more pride Diogenes.'– I returned from supper at about half past eleven o'clock.

Thursday, 19 July 1810

After teaching, the most of the time till 4 o'clock I prepared before Tea to finish a Letter to my Sister Jenny.[10] A few days before I had ordered James Robertson Bookseller Edin*r* to send her a copy of Coelebs[11] elegantly bound and writing her at present, my attention was to desire her acceptance of Coelebs and to press the designs for which that Book appears to have been written. I made some observations upon the manner in which the present system of private education was managed—upon its consequences—upon the difference in point of Enjoyment between a woman of an uncultivated mind and a friend who had improved her understanding and who was possessed of religious principles—upon the influence of bad or ignorant and foolish company—upon what Books she ought to read—upon the inutility and dangerous consequences of novells [sic]—and lastly upon the advantages to be derived from a careful perusal of her Bible.—Recommended to her & Elizabeth a private course of Mathematics and promised to speak to my father upon the subject when I came to Annan.—Mr Reddoch called, asked him to stop and eat Cheese & Bread and drink a bottle of ale with me.—Conversation turned principally upon the folly of youth in following the pursuits of debauchery even after they knew that they led only to misery and ruin—this subject was introduced by the discourse which had passed between R and a young man from Dunbar on the road to Phantassie.[12] Lent him the 2nd volume of Haüy's Nat. Philosophy[13]—parted a little after ten.

Friday, 20 July 1810

As I returned from the School at one o'clock I was accosted by Mr George Banks who after making some apologies for his not having seen me up in his house before this time, very politely asked me to sup with him that evening. I answered that it was not from want of invitations that I had not called upon him sooner, but was extremely sorry an expected Engagement in the Country in the Evening prevented me from waiting

---

10. 'Janet Irving, sister of the late Rev. Edward Irving, and wife of Robert Dickson, Esquire, late of Annan, Dumfriesshire, who died at Glasgow on 29th August 1849. Aged 55 years': Blair, *Biographic and Descriptive Sketches of Glasgow Necropolis*, 222.

11. More, *Coelebs in Search of a Wife*. Hannah More wrote a sequel five years later entitled *Coelebs Married*, which ends with an observation that clearly illuminates Irving's wish to direct his sister into the correct ideals and behavior for young women as expounded by these books. See also Jones, *Hannah More*, 191.

12. A village about six miles east of Haddington, near East Linton.

13. Haüy, *Elementary Treatise on Natural Philosophy*. Natural philosophy is a term applied to the study of nature and the physical universe. It was regarded as one of the precursors of physics. Moral philosophy was the other hand concerned with ethics and how we conduct ourselves in life.

on him. This was to see Mr Finch assistant to Mr Graham, Teacher of the Grammar School, forward to Prestonpans, he intended to have left this day but found that he could not get away so soon as he expected.

Natural Philosophy. The plan which I have adopted is this, after teaching and thoroughly understanding a paragraph, I turn over to the end of the Book and mark upon the Blank leaf such words and notes as will enable me to recollect the substance of it. When I sit down to peruse the Treatise the first thing I do is to look to my notes and not only recollect but also repeat the part which I have already read. This will no doubt in time become troublesome and very much retard my progress, but in my own opinion the loss of time is far more than compensated by the advantages in point of memory, and a thorough and connected knowledge of the Treatise.—In the evening Mr Reddoch called to see if I would accompany him to the drill club.[14] Being a little fatigued with Study I had no objections to go for a relaxation.—The conversation chiefly consisted of anecdotes, lengthy stories from the two old men & some observations upon the practicability of a parliamentary reform at all times and in every state of the Country. The majority of the members seemed to believe that it was not always practicable, and as an instance brought forward the conduct of Mr Pit[15] [sic] who before he got into power was a violent advocate for Reform, and yet when he was able to have effected it was prevented by the state of the public mind. I gave it as my own opinion that neither Mr Pit nor any other man in power would, by voluntarily pushing a reform cramp their own power, that I thought it must proceed from some one to be greater than the Minister. Came home at ten.

Saturday, 21 July 1810

In company with Mr Graham I left Haddn about one o'clock for White Kirk[16] to dine with Mr Ker, after a very pleasant journey of about nine miles we arrived there at four o'clock. The party consisted principally of farmers; and in addition to them of Mr Millar, Clergyman of the parish. He has more the appearance of a young Beau than of a Minister, his behaviour however both at and after dinner was perfectly consistent with his profession. The conversation turned chiefly upon farming and I therefore joined very seldom in it.

---

14. An establishment where young men could practice army drill with musket and bayonet. An invasion of Scotland and England by Napoleon seemed a real threat at this time, so the existence of such an establishment would have served a vital purpose. Great Britain was officially at war with France between 1793 and 1815.

15. William Pitt the Younger (1759-1806). Prime Minister from 1783-1801 and 1804-1806.

16. North East of Haddington.

We returned betwixt eleven and twelve, an hour certainly too late on any, but especially, Saturday night.

~

Sunday, 22 July 1810.

After breakfast Mr Farish called upon me, and after resting a little I proposed, as the Parish Church did not meet till two o'clock, to go and hear a Sermon from Mr Jackson, English Clergyman. When we arrived at the Chapel[17] door we found it so much crowded with soldiers as completely blocked up the passage. We then resolved to go to Mr Chalmers[18] the Antiburgher,[19] but were rather surprised to see the door with a padlock upon it. We asked a boy what was the reason, and received for answer that Mr C. preached during the forenoon in another place. Musing upon the two disappointments and beginning to think that it was not intended we should hear sermon this forenoon, Mr Reddoch beckoned us up as we passed his lodging.

We found him at breakfast, and sat down till he finished his meal. The conversation turned upon Mr R's paintings and among others upon those of Dr Sibbald[20] and his wife; from which the transition to his family becomes very easy. So I paid Mr William Sibbald some compliments which I thought he did not merit. With regard to the pictures I agreed with him, but in point of mind I gave it as my opinion that he was very deficient, and differed from Mr S in his belief that he would figure as an advocate. Mr R then pointed to one of his pictures (Mr Brodie) and observed that he would raise himself to prominence at the Bar, because he was possessed of a very strong ambition to excel and also of a good deal of pedantry.—This introduced a conversation upon pedantry and I was asked for a definition of the word. With an author whom I have now forgot, I replied that Pedantry consisted of speaking upon Subjects and in a manner in which the rest of the Company could not sympathize. Mr R thought this definition inaccurate as it made the term arbitrary and dependent upon the opinions of the persons you were speaking with and who perhaps were not capable of judging.

From this subject the Conversation changed to pride, and from that again to the present system of female education. Mr R. thought it was highly absurd as the improvement of the mind was totally neglected and because, in general, the Ladies of

17. Holy Trinity Chapel, Haddington, built in 1770. It was a Scottish Episcopal Church.
18. Rev Robert Chalmers of Haddington.
19. Antiburgher. In the 'Burgess Oath,' the burgesses were to swear to uphold to 'the true religion confessed within the realm'; this was required of all holding civic office in Scotland. In 1747 the Secession Church divided over the legitimacy of this oath, those who accepted it becoming known as the Burghers or Burgher Seceders, and those who refused to subscribe to it becoming known as Antiburghers. See *ODCC s.v* 'Antiburgher.'
20. William Sibbald (1760–1833), minister from 1808 of the Church of Scotland's second congregation in Haddington. See Scott, *Fasti*, 1.357.

the present day were wholly unacquainted with the principles of religion. And what could be expected of a wife destitute of piety, who would tend to destroy every good impression existing upon her husband's mind and her children would only hear religion mentioned in ridicule; what could be expected from a partner devoid of judgment and understanding—could she sympathize in her husband's misery, could she bear the half of his troubles. She might augment but never could alleviate them. If doomed to suffer from the pinching hand of poverty, her adverse comparisons between her former & present circumstances would multiply his woe and give an additional pang to his breast. From this and other conversations upon the same subject which I have had with my friend Reddoch & also from my own reflections upon the advantages & disadvantages of the matrimonial connection, I have *almost* formed the resolution never to mary [sic] except I can find a woman of wholly religious principles and a Consistent practice, as well as a sound judgment, who is willing to join her fortune to mine.

At two o'clock went to Church, it was Dr Sibbald's turn to preach. As usual after singing psalms & praying, he read a Chapter in the Acts of the Appostles [sic], it was the 8th.[21] When the Doctor came to that part which was an account of the Baptism of the Ethiopian Eunuch, he made some observation upon *infant Baptism*. It appeared to be the practice of the Appostles [sic] and primitive Christians for three reasons— 1st, because it is said of the former that they Baptised *whole* houses, 2ndly, because our Saviour says, 'Suffer little children to come unto me and forbid them not: for of such is the Kingdom of heaven,'[22] and 3dly, because this Sacrament was instituted in [the] room of the rite of Circumcision which was usually performed upon the *Eighth* day, and hence it appears from Scripture that the children of believing parents may be admitted into the Church of Christ at any period of life. And also nothing can be more *reasonable* than to dedicate the first fruits of our body as early as possible to the Lord.

– After singing a second Psalm he proceeded to his sermon, the subject of which was from Isaiah IX v 6 'For unto us a child is born unto us a Son is given: and the government shall be upon his shoulder: and his name shall be called Wonderful, Counsellor, The mighty GOD. The everlasting father. The prince of peace.' What the Doctor proposed chiefly to insist upon was—'and he shall be called the mighty God.'—He divided his discourse into three heads.

Ist. "To refute some of the objections brought against the Divinity of Christ.— Having considered this last Sunday when I was in Edinburgh, he only recapitulated; and observed 1st. That it had been objected to, because it was incomprehensible how the Divine & Human natures could exist in the same man at the same time. 'We don't deny it,' replyed [sic] the Doctor, 'but it does not follow from hence that it is impossible.' There are many things inconceivable which we know have every evidence to exist.— For example the union of the Soul with the Body and their mutual dependence upon

---

21. Dr Sibbald was here following the custom in English-speaking Reformed churches of giving an exposition of the chapter read as something separate from the sermon.

22. Mark 10:14, Luke 18:16.

each other. The existence of the Soul independent of the Body in a future state and its acting without it. The formation of Matter out of nothing which we know exists and which must have had a beginning. 2nd. It was objected that those passages which speak of Christ as God were forgeries and interpolations. Shall we, replied he, have the presumption to call those things falsehoods which the Appostles [sic] and primitive of Christians living 1800 years nigher the time of their origin, believed to be genuine—also forgeries & interpolations bear some internal Evidence that they are such, & may easily be recognised by their want of connection with what precedes and what follows them—whereas no such want of relation can be perceived in the passages or questions but on the other hand, they receive corroboration from thousands of other parts, both in the Old and the New Testaments.

II. To prove from Reason that none except God could have executed all the offices which were taken upon himself by Christ, the offices VIZ of setting us a pure and full pattern of those duties which God expected from his creatures[,] of redeeming us from our sins, of making intercession for us and at last of judging the world,—God might have formed a *man* who was able to execute the first of these offices but as every man must of his Nature be imperfect, he could have no additional merit to bestow upon his fellow Creatures and was therefore unable to perform the second of them.—2ndly. An Angel of the highest rank was also unable to become the Saviour for Sinners, for as Angels are created beings their life and every action of it was due to that being who formed them and therefore they had not any moral behaviour. But if we suppose the person to have been God—He being an independent & self existent being, by submitting to the frailties and sinless miseries of our nature, had merit to bestow, which merit being infinite, was sufficient for all the sins of the human race.

IIIdly. To prove that he was God from scripture. Thus the Doctor deduced a great many passages of Scripture completely establishing the truth to be proposed—among others I remember John I.1 & 3, Phil II v 6, I Tim III v 6, Rom I.3 & 4, I Tim II.5.

The Doctor then observed that he did not reprobate these persons who were unable to see the necessity of any part of revelation, he pitied them and prayed for them but certainly those men who gave their spirit to revelation but in a mutilated form, were deserving of the greatest wrath which God could inflict upon them. The Improvement[23] is reserved for a future discourse. After church was dismissed I went up to drink tea with Mr R when we conversed principally upon the sermon we had heard. At six o'clock returned to the Kirk and heard a sermon from Dr Lorimer[24] upon John VII v 46 'The officers answered, never man spake like this man.' The Doctor considered our Saviour superior to every other Teacher. I. Because he was better acquainted with his subject. The Prophets very frequently knew not fully the import of the Prophecies

---

23. The 'improvement' or 'application' showed the difference, which the truths expounded, should make to the lives of the hearers.

24. Robert Lorimer, (1765–1848) minister of the Church of Scotland's first charge in Haddington. See Scott, *Fasti*, 1:370.

Part I: The Diary

which they delivered. II. In the Superior excellence of the Subject and doctrines which he came to reveal. He might have explained the most eminent levels of the natural world but of what use were they compared with the precepts he delivered & the objects he set up for man's attainment. The Dr concluded with an Improvement which seemed very unconnected with the discourse, so much so that I could not follow it. Came home, went out to take a walk but not for pleasure.[25]

∽

Monday, 23 July 1810

This day took leave of Mr Farish at 2 o'clock, he is going into Edinburgh & from there to Dumfriesshire with the intention of standing trials before the Presbytery of Lochmaben; after that of returning again to Haddington.[26] He made a similar attempt last year but from some want of qualification (I believe deficiency in classical knowledge) was remitted back to his studies, if the Examiners [*sic*] be at all strict it is my opinion that Mr Farish will again be rejected upon the same score; as a friend of his I should not wish it; but as a person who afterwards intends to become a member of the Church I scarcely desire his admission.—Before tea I employed myself in writing up my Journal which had fallen a day back and during Tea I read a paper in the Spectator[27] upon the unnatural means which were not infrequently employed by tragic writers to seek in the audience those feelings and emotions which the Sentiments and language alone should produce.

During a walk which I took afterwards fell in with Mr John Walker, he began as usual by relating some of his anecdotes of which to use his own words 'he has a great fund.' They were mostly of a smutty nature and were very disgusting from the mouth of a man of Eighty.—Heard him very impatiently because they had grown stale from frequent repetition. Got quit of him as soon as possible and took a solitary walk but was prevented from proceeding far by a small thick shower which began to fall. After my return I prepared to turn the Introduction to Bonnycastle's Algebra[28] into

---

25. 'But not for pleasure.' Edward Irving is at pains to explain that he took this walk to clear his head after Dr Lorimer's confusing improvement and not, as some might judge, as a misuse of the Sabbath.

26. After obtaining a degree, if a graduate wished to become a minister of the Scotch Church it was required that he should obtain the necessary training. This was achieved by undergoing a series of probationary trials. See Saunders, *Scottish Democracy 1815–1840*, 348; Mechie, *Education for the Ministry* 14, 115–33, 161–78, and 124–25.

27. '*The Spectator*, periodical conducted by Steele and Addison, from 1st March 1711 to 6th December 1712, which was regarded as the best issues. However, Addison revived it in 1714, when 80 numbers (556–635) were printed. In the late 18th and 19th centuries, bound into 8 volumes, it was sold and read by many, particularly the rising middle class. The contents were considered to be a laudable, accessible and an amusing mixture of sound moral advice and manners.' See *ODCC*.

28. Davis, *Bonnycastle's Algebra*.

Latin in order to send it on Friday to my dear friend James Brown.[29] Although found it more difficult than I had expected principally from the want of Latin words. This defect arises chiefly from not having read much of the Classics for a long time intend therefore as soon as I get my hands a little emptied to revise some parts of Plato and Virgil.—Supped upon Bread and Butter, went to bed at 11 o'clock.

Tuesday, 24 July 1810

This day I employed my leisure time betwixt one and two and betwixt four and five o'clock in arranging the letters which I had received in 1809 & 1810 and also in the order of their dates and in Marking them.—Went out with the Boys to examine whether there was a rood[30] in the property purchased by the town for the intended manse.— Could not get it properly done on account of a Hay-stack which stood in the way and the potatoes which Mr Walker did not wish us to injure. Resolved after this never to undertake the measurement of any ground which I have not previously examined, or of any particular plot unless there is some person along with me to point out the several circumstances connected with it.

An unfortunate Clerk of the name of Robert Waugh called upon me begging charity; he had left the service of a Mr Ker in Edinburgh on account of an asthma under which he had laboured and was intending to go up to London to his Brother who was a Bookseller there. The man had an honest appearance and told a pretty consistent story. Gave him an old hat & a shilling.—After Tea employed myself in my Latin version—find it still very troublesome, mostly from the difficulty of obtaining proper Latin words—about 9 o'clock went to the Club[31] but I scarcely know for what reason. I cannot attribute it to a Love to the Ale—as that I could have got in my own house. My two principal reasons were the want of more agreeable Society and a desire for a little relaxation. What a great loss to a young man the friendship and company of agreeable families are; with none else almost can he associate in Safety[;] if he go to his equalls [sic], he too generally finds them desirous to engage in all the follies of youth, if to select Clubs he is apt to Contract bad habits. Conversation turned upon Local subjects and particular Characters altogether uninteresting to me.—Supped upon Bread and Butter, went to bed at 11 o'clock.

---

29. James Brown (1786–1830) replaced Irving when he left the Mathematical School at Haddington in 1812. In 1813 the Mathematical School and the English School were amalgamated with Brown as headmaster; the resulting establishment later became known as James Brown's Public School. See, *CL*, 1, 3, n.

30. A unit of measurement.

31. Presumably the 'drill Club' Edward mentions in his entry of 20 July.

Wednesday, 25 July 1810

About 12 o'clock set out [on] my Journey to Lord Cathcart's. Took with me my Bible and my observation Book; and when out of the Town began to consider the 22nd verse XVth Chap to I Corinthians. 'For as in Adam all die, even so in Christ shall all be made alive.' As I always do when examining a passage of scripture, I endeavoured first to discern what was the object of the writer, this the context soon shewed me was to prove the resurrection of the Lord. I next desired to see whether the passage was to be understood literally, or in a spiritual sense, whether as referring to natural death entailed upon his descendents by Adam's fall and future existence proved by Christ's resurrection; or to the bondage of original Sin, and the removal of it by Christ's sufferings and death. In order to the proper solution of this question it became necessary to understand thoroughly the meaning of the Context.—It seemed all very clear except the word *firstfruits* which occurs in verses 20 and 23. The original is ἀπαρχη signifying primitive.

I could not see how Christ could be the firstfruits or indeed how he could be properly said to be the fruits of them that slept.

After returning home I consulted my Lexicon and from a hint which I received from it was enabled to obtain a more clear understanding of the word. I then saw that the same word was used in Lev XXIII, 10 and in Deut XXVI and 2nd by the Septuagint.[32] I found that it was employed in these passages to denote that portion of the fruits of the promised land which was presented to the priest and dedicated to the Lord in an offering of thanks and as an acknowledgement of Gratitude for his mercies towards them as well as in the expectation of a full harvest. I considered that Christ in hope of the life derived from his death, had the same relation to them that slept as the firstfruits set apart for holy purposes had to the harvest. That as a prosperous & plentiful crop was expected to succeed that part presented to the Lord, so the resurrection to eternal life would follow that of Christ. Did not clearly see whether the passage under consideration was to be understood in the first or last sense, but have resolved to give it a more full consideration during some of my future journeys. Marked down the following notes of an Introduction.

Resurrection of the dead [is] a question in every age and country—especially in Greece. Socrates in doubt—Paul proves it in this Chap[ter]—how—supposes both orders of the question—consequences of the negative—of the affirmative—sums up the whole in the words of the Text.

---

32. 'Septuagint ('LXX'). Greek translation of the Hebrew Scriptures. According to Jewish tradition Ptolemy Philadelphus (285–246 BC) commissioned seventy-two scholars (hence 'Septuagint' from the Greek for 'seventy') to translate it from Hebrew into Greek for his library at Alexandra. See *ODCC*.

The Diary

Arrived safe at Salton Hall, felt during the whole of this and the end of last week, and especially now, a strong desire for an opportunity to remove the Cause of complaint mentioned in the last Wednesday's Diary; paid therefore all my attention to the young people and was always, except now and then when chatting with Miss Brame, employed in looking upon their work or asking them questions. Found Miss Cathcart in a very pleasant humour but with her task not well prepared. Upon returning to the School room Miss B presented me a Letter and begged that I would look over it and tell her whether the language was correct or not.—It was to a Mrs Baxter, confectioner in Edinburgh, through the medium of whose husband Miss B. expected to get a letter conveyed safe to her mother in Lille, she has had no word from that place these five years and is at present uncertain whether her parents are living or not. Returned home and was engaged after tea in finishing the version of the first paragraph of Bonnycastle's Introduction to his *Algebra*. About 9 o'clock Mr & Mrs Sibbald called & introduced to me Mr Grierson from Dumfries, who brought me word from Mr Preacher, Governor of the Hospital there.[33] While he was in the house I received a visit from Mr Reddoch who stopped and ate a piece of Cheese & drank a bottle of ale with me. He left my room about eleven when I went to bed.

Thursday, 26 July 1810

Before Tea employed myself in making up yesterdays Diary and after my meal went out to enquire at Mr Cunningham's for my friend Mr Brown's watch: fell a cracking[34] with Mr C. and heard for the first time that two wheels of an unequal number of Teeth can be driven by the same person the one lying above the other. Of the two concentric wheels the one had 57 and the other 59 teeth. Being drawn by the same pinion it is necessary that the size of each tooth should be nearly the same and the radius of the wheels must be very nearly equal. Now I understood that being very close together the teeth of the pinion were of such a breadth as to enter those of both wheels, and to turn them with an equable motion[.] But in this case it would be necessary that the teeth of the wheels should differ in size in order that a smaller part of the pinion tooth might lap the tooth of the lap wheel in the same time that a thicker part of the pinion tooth past a tooth of the larger wheel. However I can only see that this circumstance might be with difficulty allowed for. The use of the two wheels was to shew the respective motions of the sun and moon. The dial plate of the clock is divided into twice twelve hours so that the hour hand performs a complete revolution in a day upon the hollow axis through which the [axel bar?] holding the hour hand passes is placed another hand

---

33. The Moorhouse Hospital opened in 1753 as a workhouse for the old, orphaned and destitute inhabitants of Dumfries. See McDowell, *History of the Burgh of Dumfries*, 657.

34. 'cracking,' i.e., talking.

which also points to the 24 hours upon the dial plate.—The hour hand being placed upon the wheel with fewest teeth and the other upon the wheel with the most teeth it follows that when the first Index has made a complete revolution the cogs then will want something of a full circuit or will appear to fall back upon the dial plate. This retrograde motion will be 2/57 of the time in which the hour index makes one revolution or 2/57 of 24th = 50 10/19 minutes being nearly the mean daily retardation of the moon. The clock had some other apparatus which I had not time to examine. Came away after promising to drink tea with Mr Cunningham some evening.

Having forgot my watch in the School I went down to get it and seeing some person in the bowling green I entered it and was desired to play. Lost 6 pence including the price of the green. Came home about nine o'clock wrote a letter to Brown, enclosing a version of the first paragraph of Bonnycastles Preface to his Algebra. Went to bed at 11 o'clock.

∽

Friday, 27 July 1810

As I was preparing after Tea to call upon Dr Lorimer, one of our Haddington clergymen, I received a visit from Mr Sheriff [of] Drem. He wished to know what my account for his two sons Frank & John amounted to. I presented it to him, and after looking at it he noted my charge per quarter. I answered that as the account shewed 10/-[35] for teaching arithmetic, and all other Branches not connected with mathematics for which it was one additional 5/-. Is it the same, replied he, when they attend the half of the day as when they attend the whole? I have as yet made no difference nor do I intend to do it. But they are at liberty to come the remaining two hours in the afternoon if convenient. It would be very hard said he if Mr Graham should also charge the full amount of his quarter, and had I known of these circumstances before sending them they should have come to you the whole of your teaching hours; but Mr Graham told me he would be very easy and from that I understood he would not have made the full charge but, added he, I intend to speak to him upon the subject to-morrow.—It does indeed Mr Sheriff appear very hard but I have been repeatedly informed by a person a good deal connected with the Mathem.[36] School; and indeed I always understood

---

35. 10 shillings. There were 20 shillings in the old pound; the sign /- denoted a proportion of it. Thus, 10/- meant ten shillings and no pence.

36. Until 1809 there were two schools in Haddington, the grammar school and the English school, when because of the 'overburtherened state' of the English school it was decided to open a Mathematical School. On consulting Professor Leslie at Edinburgh University, he recommended one Edward Irving, who was appointed on 27 March 1809. His salary was £20 per annum with additional quarterly fees of 15 shillings for mathematics and 10 shillings for geography. However, at this point the fees were raised by 8 shillings per term and encroaching on the curriculum of the grammar school, it was agreed that the teaching of English should be added at the rate of 5 shillings per term. See Miller, *The Lamp*

so myself, that my charge was regulated by the subjects the pupil was learning and not by the number of hours per day he was attending. He observed that he paid my account with pleasure. It was Mr G's fee charge that he grudged.—Upon reviewing this conversation and coolly reflecting upon it, it appears that my answers were correct. Though it must be confessed the plan of charging as much for a half day as for a whole one appears a little unfair; yet when it is considered that the pupil has the liberty of attending all the teaching hours; that it is the custom in all public schools which I know and especially that the opposite system would be far more unfair to the Teacher than the present one is to the parent; the justice of the plan will appear evident and my resolution to persevere in it correct. What! Shall I only charge half a crown for teaching the Elements of Euclid[37] per quarter? No, never, sooner will I give up the Mathem. School and try another way of living. Do I care how the Grammar Teacher acts? I tell a man flatly my terms, no dubious expressions shall disgrace my lips, no sentiments of favour towards any persons shall ever stain my Conduct. Went afterward and called upon Mr Reddoch who informed me that he saw Dr Lorimer riding into the country—took a turn in the Bowling Green and after playing two games single handed with Mr R, winning one, we joined a party which was formed. Passed the door of the Club house without entering it—was afterwards well satisfied with my conduct as it shewed that I had the resolution to prefer my Books at home to any conversation which I might have there and even though entertained with a glass of ale. Employed myself principally during the remainder of the evening in studying Haüy on Electricity. I still persist in my plan of taking short sentences or hints in order to bring under one view what I have formerly read. A great advantage which I derive from this method is that it tends to improve me in speaking upon subjects of Science, for from these notes I make it a frequent practice to express the same Ideas in the same order as they were given in the Book and in as full a manner.

Sent away this Evening my Letter to Brown and expect an answer in a week.

Went to bed about 11 o'clock.

Saturday, 28 July 1810

Rose this morning as usual at about half past 6 o'clock. Mr Wm Clarke did not wait upon me from 7 to 8. Went to the School from 8 to 9 and taught Geography.—Breakfasted between 9 and 10 and took my usual walk through the Town up by the Tollbar Lane by the Irongate. From 10 to 12 was engaged in the School teaching, writing, and

---

of Lothian, 455–56.

37. The author of *Elements* was the mathematician Euclid, active between 323 and 283 BC. The *Elements* consists of thirteen books and covers the development of geometry and other branches of mathematics. Book 1 covers geometry.

preparing my pupils upon arithmetic for the examination, and in examining their instruments. Between 12 and 1 heard the lesson in Euclid's Elements. After I returned home, I was preparing to take some Rust & tarnish from the Sextant by help of an Emery and a piece of Buff Leather, when Mr Reddoch called. He went to call upon Dr Lorimer but was so unfortunate as not to find him at home. After Dinner I read Haüy upon the apparatus by which Coulomb[38] proved that the action of Electricity was as the squares of the distances. Drew with my pencil a copy of the Instrument in order to fix it more firmly in my memory. In the afternoon Mr K. took me to pay a visit to Mr Walkers garden, we received from him as much fruit as we could eat, amused ourselves with observing the great variety of colouring exhibited by nature in the different species of the same flower. Drank Tea with Mr R and had a Conversation upon matrimony: I was pointing out the almost unclouded prospect of happiness which he had in the married state. The woman to whom Mr R. has promised himself is called Miss Ann Paul but receives in general from himself when speaking familiarly of her, the name of Jenny McGie, she lives at Linlithgow & is an only daughter. Of her mind I may perhaps give a more full description afterwards. Mr R had an appointment in the evening at Mr Lang's and would not go unless I accompanied him. The Conversation turned upon the advantages of early marriages. All seemed to agree that they were very good & therefore in order to start an argument, I took up the Cudgells [*sic*] on the other side. Four of us drunk three bottles of Port returned home about half past eleven and was in bed before twelve.

Sunday, 29 July 1810

From my last nights debauchery I did not rise this morning till half past ten o'clock, and was therefore too late to attend any place of worship before the meeting of the Church. During and after breakfast employed myself in reading the Westminster Confession of faith[39] upon covenants, and among the proofs found the verse which engaged my thoughts last journey to Salton Hall, and which I have mentioned in that day's Diary,

---

38. Charles de Coulomb (1736–1806), French physicist best known for the formulation of Coulomb's law, and in today's atomic science is one of the principal forces in atomic reactions. See University of St. Andrews, *Biography of Charles Augustin Coulomb*, www. britannica.com, accessed 25 November 2008.

39. The puritan Westminster Assembly, at the behest of Parliament, completed the Westminster Confession of Faith in 1646. It has remained the benchmark for Presbyterian teaching and all ministers in the Church of Scotland were at this time expected to subscribe to it. Irving was probably reading Ch. VII. 'Of God's Covenant with Man,' which teaches that God made a covenant of grace' to offer life to sinners through Christ and promised to give them the Holy Spirit to enable them to repent and believe. However, 1 Cor 15:22 is not cited as a proof text here, though it is in the previous chapter, 'Of the Fall of Man of Sin, and of the Punishment thereof.'

used in a sense signifying not only death temporal and other terrestrial ills but also death spiritual and the Consequences of Sin introduced by our first parents.—About twelve o'clock necessity called upon me to take a walk which I did with very great injoyment [sic]. Returned before the forenoon churches dismissed, and until 2 o'clock, the time of them meeting in the afternoon, read one or two of the last Chapters in the Acts of the Appostles [sic]; and among other things was forcibly struck with the Christian forgiving wish of Paul annotated in the XXVI Chapter the 29th verse when Agrippa having told the Apostle that he almost persuaded him to be a Christian was answered 'I would to God that not only thou, but also all that hear me were both almost and altogether such as I am *except these bonds*.'—Went to church where Dr Sibbald after reading the tenth Chapter of the Acts of the Appostles [sic] gave out for the Subject of his Lecture Matthew V, v 38th–43rd—'Ye have heard that it hath been said an eye for an eye and a tooth for a tooth, but I say unto you that ye resist not evil whosoever shall smite thee on thy right cheek, turn to him thy other also. And if any man will sue thee at the law, and take away thy Coat, let him have thy Cloak also, And whomsoever shall compel thee to go a mile, go with him twain. Give to him that asketh [thee] and from him that would borrow [of thee] turn not away.'—The Doctor is Lecturing[40] regularly through our Saviours Sermon on the Mount and therefore very properly introduced his discourse by repeating those duties in the Law of Moses which Christ had in the final part of the Chapter informed and extended. The Crimes of murder & adultery, he observed, had been already described and those of perjury and swearing which last engaged our attention, our Lord had also condemned. 'Swear not at all' that is, to change the figurative expression for what is intended, swear only when the taking of an oath is very necessary to your own and the preservation of Civil Society or advantageous to the Religion of Jesus. All other criminals offending of the Law of God have some excuse for their Conduct; the habitual swearer alone has not any, he does it solely for the sake of committing sin or of serving the Devil. The thief's proffessed [sic] object is the desire of gain; the Father's is the prospect of a future comfortable and elegant establishment; that of the sensualist, the indulgence and pleasure of animal gratification; The savage is the only volunteer in the service of the Devil. Some men could *very prettily* lay their hands upon their hearts and swear upon their honour to the truth of what they had said; whatever may be the Case with the world in general, it is always the practice with myself, continued the Doctor, that whenever I hear a man in Company vouching for the truth of what he has said by an oath, it is then and not till then that I begin to doubt his veracity and scrupple [sic] all he has said. After thus recapitulating what he had inculcated on a former occasion he proceeded to consider the subject of this present Lecture. After reading the 38th verse he referred to the parts

---

40. A 'lecture' when given would precede the sermon, and it would concentrate more on elucidation of the text, leaving application to the sermon. The practice of lecturing enabled ministers in churches belonging to the Reformed tradition to work their way through a book of the Bible, following the pattern set by Huldrych Swingli (1484-1531) in Zürich and Jean Calvin (1509-64) in Geneva.

of Scripture in which it was commanded, *viz*, to, Exodus XXI v 24, Leviticus XXIV v 20, Deut XIX v 21. He then read the remaining verses and comparing them with the first observed that our Lord in the former part of the Chapter only strengthened and enlarged the Law of Moses and that in these verses he seems for the first time to go in direct opposition to them. This appearance only results from a superficial reading of the passage and vanishes when we began to consider more thoroughly what is meant and referred to. The persons to whom the Commandment is delivered in the Old Testament are the Judges only, it is to those men alone who have been raised to the rank of administering impartial justice that it is said an eye for an eye, a tooth for a tooth blemish for blemish etc. The Jews however interpreting the words literally and considering them as applicable to the great bulk of the nation, not only gave free vent to their passions of revenge but even thought it a meritorious action and that they were performing God's will to punish those who went in opposition to their Sentiments in religion. It was to counteract these erroneous and dangerous notions that our Saviour addressed them in the words of three following verses.

The Dr then observed that we ought to read these words with Caution, he did not mean with distrust, God forbid. We should understand them in the same sense in which our Lord intended them and in which they were easily understood by those to whom he addressed himself, not in a literal sense of having that meaning which His words now convey but as expressive, bold and beautiful figures used to convey the strength of what he delivered, and the importance of Christian meekness so far opposite to the former principles of the Jews.—As an instance of the same proverbial language we were referred to the Prophecies concerning our Saviour contained in Isaiah L v 6, Lamentations III v 30. He then passed on to verse 42 and after making a similar observation upon it, he said that, though Children of the same just father, our situations in life were widely diffuse, we observe the man of righteousness exposed to all the wiles of the world and buffeting every storm of adversity, while the man who disregards God and his Commandments was loaded with every favour the world can bestow. We have represented in Scripture a man who was dressed in fine linen and fared sumptuously every day living and afterwards miserable in hell, while a beggar laid at his gate and covered with sores also dies and is immediately conveyed by Angels to the bosom of Abraham. External circumstances in life are neither to be considered as marks of God's approbation or displeasure. The humble spirit which adversity might break, prosperity may cherish, the ambitious man who might run riot in affluence, may in a less elevated sphere live upright & correct. Some men are entrusted with the things of this world in order to increase the sphere of their utility, while others are deprived of them that they might not abuse them. There must on these Accounts be always a part of the world dependent upon the bounty of others, and these it is our peculiar duty to support. The care of our families and relations ought to be our first object and after them, attention to the poor. There are few persons in the world whose circumstances will not allow them to extend their bounty to their suffering brethren.

An hour earlier up in the morning, an hour later up at night, time saved from our meals which are frequently made unnecessarily tedious, the retrenchment of some useless expense, these may all be converted into sources of revenue for the relief of the indigent.

The Dr then proceeded to make some Improvement of the Subject:

1st We ought to hew out that corruption of our nature which prompts us to twist and distort passages of Scripture from their true meaning in order to support those Erroneous opinions which the evil dispositions of our own mind have adopted—can Scripture be misapplied? Yes, my friends, it can.—Satan quoted Scripture in his temptation of our Lord. Every sect of Christians however different in doctrine adduces Scripture in support of their tenets and we find in this Chapter the whole nation of the Jews misunderstanding texts of Exodus, Leviticus & Deuteronomy.

2ndly We ought not to take upon ourselves the execution of duties with which we have not been vested. After making some more observations upon this head the Doctor added—We leave it to the Church of Rome and the disciples of Mahomet to propagate their doctrines by fire, by faggot, by scaffold and gibbet, the measures which we use are argumentation, prayer, and perhaps the most powerful of any, holy lives.

3dly Even in personal Injuries, we ought not to take upon ourselves the punishment of the offender: we ought to deliver them up to the law of the Land and to those persons who are raised by their country to execute them. We view the crimes of those who have wronged us, through a false witness. Our minds are very apt to magnify their guilt and to diminish our own Errors. It is not on these accounts proper that we ourselves should pass sentence, we ought to refer the case to those men who from their Education and Uprightness as well as from their easy circumstances in life have been raised to the rank of Judges and who are therefore bound to give eye for eye, tooth for tooth etc. who standing aloof from the quarrel and patiently & coolly investigating both sides of the quarrell, [sic] will give an honest and conscientious verdict.

4th We ought never to be the aggressors—pressed from the example of our Saviour and from his precepts.

5th But ought to live quiet and peaceable lives.

The Doctor observed when enforcing charity that though we had not the comforts of life to bestow—we had hearts, souls, lips & knees to kneel for them, we ought to cause our prayers to ascend on their behalf.

And upon [the] 2nd head of the Improvement, that God very seldom employed good men to be the instruments of his vengeance upon the bad part of the human race. They were in general the most abandoned characters[;] the very besoms[41] of the Earth.

I liked this Lecture very well and thought it in general very correct. I cannot completely trace the relation which the 2nd Head in the Improvement had with the rest of the Discourse.

---

41. 'low women.'

Part I: The Diary

At Six o'clock returned to church and heard a Sermon from Dr Andrew Stewart,[42] Bolton upon Hebrews X v 23?[43] 'Hold fast the proffession [*sic*] of your faith without wavering.'

The Discourse he gave us was a very excellent one but as this day[']s Diary has already extended to such a length, I am rather sorry that I cannot give a full account of it.

During Church time received an Invitation from Mr Graham to sup with him, accepted it though contrary to my own inclination and what was infinitely more, though contrary to my duty as a Christian—Of all natural inclinations which I ought to guard against, nothing [is] so strong as a desire to please—it is undoubtedly the sin that doth most easily beset me.—Our conversation was uninteresting, Mr G committed a very great blunder in supposing that a meteorological appearance which was seen throughout the greater part of Europe in 1783 was a comet.

Returned from supper about eleven and went immediately to bed.

Monday, 30 July 1810

Rose this morning at 7 o'clock and except from 9 to 10 and from 1 to 2 was engaged in teaching till 4. As I was finishing my yesterday's Diary Mr Jas Sibbald[44] called but would not stop to Tea. He spent Wednesday Evening last with Messrs Farish & Charteris in Edinburgh who left it for Dumfriesshire the morning following. From the accounts which he gave me they had passed a very riotous evening, having nearly got a night's quarters with the Police. Mr Sibbald terminated his visit with an Invitation to come and sup with the Drs family, spent a very pleasant Evening—his father was not at home. Came home about half past two. Lent Mr Graham La Place's System of the World—Vol. 1st.[45]

---

42. Mrs. Oliphant writes: 'Irving also made the acquaintance of Mr. Stewart, then Minister of Bolton, afterwards Dr Stewart of Erskine, who was himself the subject of a sufficiently romantic story . . . In this Manse of Bolton Irving was in the habit of spending his Saturdays': Oliphant, *Life*, 1:45. The story was that Andrew Stewart had trained as a doctor and fallen in love with one of his patients, whom he married, and that he changed his profession for that of minister.

43 The question mark was possibly a reminder to Irving to check the quotation, which was indeed wrongly remembered. It should read: 'Let us hold fast the profession of *our* faith without wavering.'

44. James Hope Sibbald (1787–1853), minister of Cranshaws, 1813. See Scott, *Fasti*, 2:7.

45. La Place, *System of the World*. The book put forward various theories about the creation of the Universe, and he is principally known for his investigations into the stability of the solar system.

Tuesday, 31 July 1810

After teaching as usual till 4 o'clock went up to Mr Reddoch's lodgings and after sitting some time we took a walk towards the Signal post and for exercise amused ourselves with putting or throwing the stones. He beat me the Common way by about half a foot and I beat him over the head[land]. Returned to my room about 7 o'clock and after Tea went over to Mr R's. Upon our road to the Club we past by Mr Samuel's door who very courteously asked us to drink a bottle of ale with him; we accepted his invitation and were introduced to his wife. She is a very pretty woman but so far as may be judged from the short conversation we had, her mind seems uncultivated. Drank three bottles of ale and returned home a little before eleven.

Received no additional knowledge all this day—Very ill satisfied with myself.

Wednesday, 1 August 1810

This being the first day of a new quarter we had no teaching—Mr Reddoch and I went out before breakfast to take a walk and as he intends leaving here for Dundee tomorrow I wrote two introductory Letters, one to Mr George Little, the other to Mr John Holliday. At 12 o'clock set out for Salton Hall as usual and arrived there before 2. While teaching Miss Cathcart in the drawing room her ladyship entered from the library and though there passed no signs of any kind between us, I felt myself very disagreeably situated from the consciousness that she thought I had not discharged my duty. Upon my Journey I met with Dr Stewart who very kindly asked me to come and see him—as he has done this repeatedly and as he is a man I should like to be acquainted with I mean to accept of it. Could study none from the intolerable heat either during the time of my going or returning.—Being fatigued I did very little after my return.—Received Haüy Vol 2nd from Reddoch.

Thursday, 2 August 1810

Mr Clarke waited upon me at 7 o'clock and when he was about to leave me at 8 I observed that as this was the beginning of a new month and as he had attended between 7 and 8 during July he would, according to the agreement between his mother and me, come for the Arithmetic to the School from 8 to 9 the Geography hour; he answered that he intended to do so. I replied that as the examination[46] was approach-

---

46. These yearly oral examinations (required by the Education Act, 1803) of the pupils on the curriculum at Irving's school were to be conducted by local clergymen including Drs Stewart, Lorimer,

ing I would be unable at that time to give him proper attention; but said he, I can attend during the same hour as last month and accordingly we agreed to do so. Had his mother Mrs Marchbanks been in town she should have been consulted but as she is gone to England it was impossible to have this reversed and as my fee for a private hour per month is more than 6 times that of a public hour, I am conscious that this action may be received as proceeding from a love of money.—I am conscious however that this view is an incorrect one and that the motives from which I acted in this case were pure.—Could I have done my duty to the Class of Geography and at the same time also to Mr Clarke? Besides, the proposition of continuing the same hour through August as through July proceeded from himself.—After the Geography called to see if Mr Reddoch was gone, and found him getting out of bed, but resolved to leave town after Breakfast. Took leave of him after obtaining his promise to write from Dundee—considering that Mr R has occurred so frequently in my Diary I feel myself somehow bound to give some account of him. His dispositions are excellent; professes himself of an open mind; he expects the same in others; from instances which I know his human feelings, especially charity, exceed almost the bounds of propriety, and are exerted towards objects whose conduct even at the moment is undeserving of it: by nature sociable he soon acquires a great many acquaintances but as he informed me the other day retains very few intimates. His ambition though considerable is kept within proper bounds, and will very easily yield to the more powerful desire of happiness. An acquaintance with mankind and a variety of scenes have served considerably to mature his judgement; his resolutions are generally formed with propriety and executed with firmness. Naturally Mr Reddoch possesses strong mental abilities but these abilities from a neglect of Education have not been properly cultivated; and hence the reason why his knowledge is so extensive and yet sometimes so confused; he expresses himself with ease and energy and his observations are in general apropos as they are original. I have frequently been surprised that a man so little acquainted with the Elements of Science should yet understand so well the more general and useful applications of it.— His notions of religion are rather peculiar—I know no sect with which his Sentiments agree, they approach nearest to those of the baptist Congregation in Edin of which Mr McClean[47] is the pastor. I have heard him frequently say that were he perfectly convinced that a clergyman was a Scriptural profession he would, in spite of all the labour of reviving his languages, turn to that line of life. His Ideas of a Pastor are that he should not be set apart to the office but during the week should employ himself with some calling, that he should be completely a layman and recommended to the office only by superior sanctity, more extensive acquaintance with the Scriptures and a more

and Sibbald.

47. Archibald McLean (1733–1812), Scotch Baptist leader. A printer by trade in 1767 he took a position as overseer to an Edinburgh printer and was elected as an elder in a new Baptist congregation in the city. See Bebbington, ed., *The Baptist in Scotland*, 15, cf. 21–14. The Scotch Baptists were noted for their belief that a plural eldership rather than one minister, their rejection of ministerial training and ordination, and their weekly celebration of the Lord's Supper should lead congregations.

general knowledge than his brethren.—He is well acquainted with the Scriptures and with the Doctrines of Christianity in general, he knows the necessity of a Correct walk, although he is equally guilty with myself, in not properly practising it.—What in my opinion serves to distinguish Mr Reddoch more than any other thing is that almost inconceivable facility with which he Contracts acquaintances, he will do more to form an intimacy in one night than I would in a month. This perhaps arises from his easy and rather blunt manner of addressing a person, it goes so far sometimes as to be mistaken for impertinence or rather improper freedom. Under these circumstances it appears that Mr R was pointed out almost by the hand of nature for a proper acquaintance. His plainness tended to counteract my uneasy manner, his judgment served in many points to assist mine and though upon Religion our sentiments were at variance, he communicated to me 'a strong desire to draw religion from my Bible alone.'[48] His abilities as a Painter are of the first rank—as his pictures declare, his Genius for this art is altogether natural not acquired. He is a native of Stirling and about 27 years old.

After breakfast took my usual walk and upon my return from School received from Mrs P. Dods the present of a pint of gooseberries, gave the boy two pence & after he was gone shared them with my Landlady. A little after received from Mr & Mrs Dods Clerking town[49] a present of Eleven very fine Peaches. Gave James a shilling for his trouble in bringing them down. Gave the children one and sent four in a Compliment to Mrs Graham. Before and during Tea read my notes from Paley's Evidences[50] and after it received two letters one from Mr Brydon[,] Tranent,[51] concerning the Schoolmaster's widows fund, the other from my sister acknowledging the receipt of Coelebs and giving an account of Mrs Ridicks wedding.

As I was going out to take a walk went into Neil's shop, had a crack with Lieutenant Wickham principally upon the wars. Returned home about 9, supped upon a Welsh Rabbit[52] & a glass of ale. Went to bed at 11.

---

48. It was to be Irving's insistence upon appealing to the teaching of the Bible (as he understood it) over against that of the Westminster Confession, which would bring him into controversy as a minister. The germ of this approach may be evident here.

49. A district just south west of Haddington town centre.

50. William Paley, *A View of the Evidences of Christianity,* 1794. This influential work brought together the standard eighteenth-century arguments for the truth of Christianity and the divine creation of the universe. See *OCEL*.

51. Located 7 miles west of Haddington.

52. Welsh rarebit is a dish of grated cheese melted with milk, wine, or beer, seasoned with mustard, salt, pepper, and/or a little cayenne and served on toast. 'Welsh rabbit' was the original name for the dish, first recorded in 1725. McLagan, *Fat,* 46.

Part I: The Diary

Saturday, 3 August 1810[53]

This day did not rise till half past seven o'clock which was certainly very improper as I was awake at half past six. Drest quickly but Mr Clarke did not arrive, dont [*sic*] suppose he had been at the door before the time of my rising as Mr Morton my landlord who was not sleeping at 7 did not hear him. As I came out of school, Mr Graham gave me the 'Couriers de Londres'[54] which occupied my attention before tea. Perused the 'affaires publiques' and although some of the Company's vessels were announced as having arrived safe in England nothing was mentioned of the Lord Minto, the one my Brother is a board of.[55]—After Tea took a walk and as I had no companion I supplied the want by putting Virgil in my pocket, began to read the first Book of the Aeneid but found myself very much deficient in the knowledge, not of the construction but of the words of the language, in order however to make myself still better acquainted with my Grammar I began upon my return to revise my Rules of Syntax and in a space of half an hour was completely master of the first 38.

Went to the Club and for the first time renounced the ale for whisky. Conversation chiefly turned upon particular but not public characters, at last talking of General Hitchens Taste, it was observed by one that he displayed very little in painting his mahogany white, I asked might not the Gentleman's taste be correct if he was induced to do this from a desire for uniformity? for I knew that the wainscoat [*sic*] was white, some replied some one thing and others another. Baillie[56] Johnston gave the only one *a propos* that Beauty did not consist in uniformity. I answered that it was a principle [*sic*] ingredient in it and put the Question if Dr Blair was not of the same opinion. The Baillie believed not. Came home about half past ten and went to bed at eleven.

∽

Saturday, 4 August 1810

This morning Mr Clarke waited upon me a little after 7 and told me that he had not been able to attend the preceding morning. This information as it may be conjectured from yesterdays Diary gave me a good deal of easiness, but did not at all diminish my regret for the impropriety of my yesterdays conduct or tend in any degree to weaken the resolution which I had formed of being always punctual to my hour. Mr Bail called

---

53. Edward slipped a day here—Friday in 1810 was the 3rd not the 4th of August.
54. A political newspaper for émigrés published in French twice weekly until 1826.
55. His brother John (1790–1822) was a medical officer in the East India Company and died of a fever on Irving's birthday in 1822. Lord Minto was at that time Governor General of India from 1809 to 1813.
56. 'A town magistrate next in rank to the provost,' *CSD*. Irving's father was a Baillie in Annan.

while at Breakfast with a new pair of shoes when I settled his account 17/6 but fool that I was, forgot to ask a receipt. –

After Dinner I took a walk as far as Tranent woods to see what had become of my pupil Thos Hood and settle with Mr Brydon for the widows fund. After receiving Mr B's receipt for the money I thought as the evening was not far advanced of taking a step to Preston Pans [sic] to see Mister Sibbald.—Went to Mr Bruce's Inn and wrote him a line desiring his company there soon.—He came immediately and after drinking a Bottle of ale together I asked Mr Sibbald to come up to Hadn and take share of a Birth Night bottle of Gin which I had in the house. He declined my Invitation because tomorrow is their Sacrament[57] at Preston Pans but accompanied me about three miles upon my way and gave me directions about the remainder of it. I found it out and after having walked about 19 miles since 9 o'clock in the afternoon came home about 10. I was perspiring very much and in order to prevent cold and ensure a good nights rest, as also to drink the health of all my family & my future success in the world, I indulged in a Rummer of Gin Tody.[58] [sic]

This being my Birthday and having now completed my *Eighteenth* year, I am of opinion that I can scarcely employ an hour better than in marking the present state of my mind as also the Improvement which I have made since the 4th of August 1809 and as it is the most important.

Ist *of religion*. It is at present my intention to become a Clergyman of the Church of Scotland—and with this view I have studied at the University four successive winters and attended partially at the Divinity Hall one season. I came to Edinburgh long before I was able to judge the inclination of my own mind at the age of 13. I had previously received a Classical Education, first under Mr Hope, and then under Mr Dalgliesh.[59] The first of these Teachers I shall remember while I have the remembrance of any thing, if were I [to] rise to any eminence in this world which it is scarcely my wish and much less my hope to attain or if ever I am useful in my future passage through life which I sincerely expect and most anxiously desire, it shall, be attributed totally to Mr Hope whose Instructions it may have pleased the Almighty to prosper and from whose care of my early Education I have derived that activity of Mind, which I know how to value and which I hope will accompany me through life. I was also before I left Annan well acquainted with arithmetic and Practical Mathematics and under Mr Fisher, had gone through first six Books of Euclid's Elements in 17 days. With this Instruction I set

---

57. Communion was usually celebrated once or twice a year in Church of Scotland's parishes with preparatory services during the days before and a thanksgiving service the day after. It was a great social as well as religious occasion, often attracting numbers from neighboring parishes.

58. A rummer was a large, stemmed drinking glass. The basic ingredients of a gin toddy are gin, sugar, and water.

59. Rev. William Dalgleish (1771–1846). It is unclear whether or not he was related to Edward Irving at the time he was teaching him at the Annan Academy. However, Edward Irving's sister Janet (1794–1849) married Mr. Robert Dickson, brother to Mr. Dalgleish's second wife. See Miller, *A Bibliography of the Parish of Annan*, 42.

out for Edinburgh on the 7th Novr 1805 in company with Willm Irving[60] with whom I was intended to lodge during the winter.—We were committed to the charge of Mr John Mc Whir[61] then a preacher & private Teacher in the town and now clergyman of the Chapel of Ease at Dunfermline.—This plan was suggested to my parents by Miss Johnstone, Dumfries[,] Sister to Dr Bryce Johnstone[,][62] my mothers uncle[,] a man whose early death I shall ever regret as Dispensation of Providence which deprived me of a well wisher and friend united in the person of a near relation. A person so well Calculated and so much disposed to give a good advice, to Correct your Errors and direct your Studies I never expect to meet with. I am particularly interested in his death from another circumstance. About that time it was always a part of my morning and evening prayers that my father might receive the means of compleating [sic] my Education.—Dr B Johnstone died and left my mother about £500.—My Desire was granted but at a very dear rate.—Let this teach me to pray for Gods direction in those things we ask from him.

To be continued.

From the fatigue of my yesterday's Journey I did not rise till a little after ten. After breakfast I sat down to write that day's diary and as it was my Birthday I was induced to attempt some delineation of the present state of my mind and of the Improvement I had made since Aug 4th 1809. In putting that plan into execution a more extensive one struck my mind[,] namely to take a short retrospect of my life since I came to the University first, from doing this I promise myself a good deal of enjoyment, it will give me an opportunity of observing the gradual improvement of my mind, the circumstances which have been most favourable and those which have been most adverse to its advancement, as also to point out those Errors in my former conduct which if I had the time again should have been corrected.

At two o'clock went to Church and heard from Dr Sibbald a Lecture on Matthew V 43–48 Ye have heard that it hath been said, Thou shalt love thy neighbour, and hate thy enemy etc. After making a general remark upon the disposition of the Jews to neglect the spirit of the Law while they most rigorously conformed to its Letter and even at times to go so far in their blinded and rigid Zeal as to misinterpret its meaning. He observed that our Saviour once more quotes it in order to restore its true import to strengthen its hands and to extend the precepts contained in verse 44th.—We were then referred to Lev XIX v 18 and to another passage which I have now forgot perhaps Deut VII v 16 as the places of the Mosaic writings in which these precepts were delivered. The word neighbour is used in the old Testament to signify a person who

---

60. Edward Irving's cousin, born 1751. From a private source.

61. John McWhir, tutor to the family of David Welsh, Esq. of Earlhaugh and Tweedshaws. See Scott, *Fasti*, 2: 307.

62. Rev Bryce Johnstone (1747–1805), minister of Holywood near Dumfries: his father John was provost of Annan and his sister Elizabeth was Edward Irving's maternal grandmother. See *ODNB*, 393, and Scott, *Fasti*, 2.276.

has done us favours & laid us under obligations and expressed what is now meant by a friend, a well wisher & Benefactor—as a confirmation the Doctor read our Saviours description of it in the beautiful parable of the good Samaritan as recorded in Luke 10 v 25.

He then proceeded to explain what was meant by 'hate thine enemy.' The Jews understood that as they were bound to love their neighbour so they had a title also to hate their enemies personally, this belief was founded upon those passages in the old testament in which God commands them to destroy the inhabitants of the Promised Land to which their forefathers journeyed. They have as usual neglected the spirit of the injunction, they forgot that they were only instruments employed by the Almighty to punish those nations for their vices, and by these means set an example to the nations with whom they were surrounded. That God never intended them to hate the persons much less the Souls of their Enemies they might have gathered from the Moabites being allowed to remain tributary to David after they had been conquered and from Ruth being persuaded to settle in the land of Judea though one of the nation of the Moabites as recorded severally in 2 Sam VIII v 2, Ruth I. But even, continued he, had the Jews passed over these circumstances they might still have gathered the true import of those Commands from other passages in Scripture as Isaiah XIX v 9 & 10, Job XXXI v 29, 36. He then passed on to verse 44 and the remaining verses but made upon them no remark very worthy of notice.

After Church dined with Mr James Burn, in consequence of a promise I had inadvertently made yesterday.—His intention was to reprove Adam [Mr Burn's son?] for his carelessness, in my presence; and to see whether it would produce any better effects upon him. Heard from Dr Lorimer a Sermon in the Evening from John VIII 10 & 11. The Dr remarked that the passage had been always considered as spurious by the *fathers of the early* Church & that it had been marked in asterisks as being a doubtful passage and worthy of rejection, this however displayed a false timidity and [he] observed that God was true, that ten thousand were liars. It was necessary to take into Consideration the Several circumstances with which the passage stands connected. He shortly summed up the matter of the preceeding [sic] Chapter, the ineffectual attempt which the Pharisees had made to cite Jesus before the bar of their tribunal, ineffectual though they were armed with all the insignia of power and had the disposal of effective force while he was unarmed, implicated by the Law and exposed to all the Rage of popular fury. He made some very biting and pertinent observations upon Verse 1st of Chap VIII and then proceeded to relate the Circumstances of the story under consideration. That our Lord went up into the temple to instruct and was immediately surrounded by a Concourse of people. The Pharisees brought to him a woman Caught in the act of adultery and after mentioning the punishment inflicted in the law of Moses upon such an offence and with all the appearance of sincerity and even as if they believed him to be a person commissioned from above asked to know what he said. Their intention however was of the blackest kind, their plot was of the deepest design; it was to ruin

Jesus that they now asked his advice. They knew that if he declared against the law of Moses he would incur the hatred and perhaps the vengeance of the Sanhedrin,[63] if he presumed to pass sentence upon her they would report him to the Roman Governor as a person interfering with the discharge of Justice & the Law which it is well known that nation had then engrossed to themselves; and thus they imagined that they had him fairly intangled [sic]. Our Saviour makes no immediate reply but by a particular action endeavoured to shew them that He was already engaged—they importune him for his Counsel [–] he answered[,] 'He that is without sin among you, let him first cast a stone at her'[64] the word sin may be considered here as thus meaning the same sin and the Dr was rather inclined to follow that opinion. Upon this being convicted by their own conscience they all, that is all the accusers, went away and left him alone with the woman in the midst of the Crowd He had been formerly instructing.—Jesus answered to the womans reply Verse ll, Neither do I condemn thee: that is neither do I take upon me the discharge of Judicial power.—The Doctor then proceeded to make some Improvement of this story, one remark he made worthy of notice namely the immense advantage our Lord possesses over his accusers & enemies by his intimate acquaintance of character and knowledge of man, so much so that he answers to men's thoughts as other persons do generally to their words. Instance his first conversation with Nicodemus John III 3 where our Lord makes an answer quite unconnected with what the Pharisee had said but quite in union with the thought which Nicodemus might be conjectured to have had and which he would not have uttered namely how he might attain the Kingdom of Heaven.—Found upon my return from Church a letter from James Hope, my old school fellow and found nothing in it particular—not answering it till I can say when I will be at Annan—nor my Sister's till the same time for the same reason. Went to bed at a little past ten.

∽

Monday, 6 August 1810

This morning got up about half past six o'clock, and received Mr Clarke's visit a little after 7. Between 2 and 3 o'clock met with Dr Lorimer upon the street who after asking what had become of me so long said that when young men were seldom seen he always began to suspect that there were something wrong. I answered that there really was something not right for I had been very idle for two months past—but was kept very busy at present preparing for the examination.—He hoped I would call down some evening soon, intend to do it tomorrow night or Thursday at the farthest. After Tea, put my Virgil in my pocket and went to take a walk by the North side of the town

---

63. The Sanhedrin was the supreme court of the Jewish nation.
64. John 8:7.

amongst the plantings. My Enjoyment was greatly heightened by the band of the 25th Foot Regiment lying in the Barracks. It was most delightful—I was in the midst of a plantation walk upon the side of the same hill the Barracks are placed on and at a considerable elevation above them. The strains were most exquisite and floating up the eminence struck upon my ear quite unexpectedly. Instantly I felt one of those thrilling sensations, which words cannot describe, the Virgil imperceptibly dropt from my hand and for a few minutes I was riveted to the spot. Before I could restrain the wanderings of my mind, it had carried me to the seats of my youth and surrounded me with the Companions of other years. The association working upon an imagination which has been sometime feasted with the prospect of revisiting my native town and enjoying once more the conversation of relations and friends, produced one of those happy intervalls [sic] in which the pleasures of melancholy are most sensibly expressed.—Upon my return finished the Rules of Syntax and intend before engaging in anything of importance to commit to memory the principal notes attached to each.

Supped about ten went to bed a little after eleven

Revenir[65]—Continued from Saturday

On our Journey to the metropolis my father accompanied us to Moffat; and here it was that I felt for the first time those aggonizing [sic] pains which the Separation from a dear family occasions.—Though my absence was to be comparatively short to me who had never been above three days at a time from home it appeared almost an age. How my Heart swelled when I gave my father the parting farewell and received his advice and blessing[;] with what pain I last clasped his hand, & tore myself from his presence.—The disagreeable morning and the wild scenery tended to depress my spirits and made my Journey for some time heavy—it wore off by degrees and gave place to a peaceful kind of pleasure when from the summit of Erickstane [Ericstane] we looked into the deep glen below known by the name of the 'Marquis of Annandales Beef Tub.' My tender feelings were again excited when the carrier with whom we travelled pointed to the place where the Annan first Breaks Ground descending from the summit of the hill in an almost imperceptible rivulet it first formed its Bed in the vale below through which meandering it passes the small town of Moffat where it receives the water of the same source a more considerable stream than itself. Escaping through the plains of Annandale and communicating fertility to the Country through which it passes, after watering the Burgh of Annan it falls into the Solway. On the banks of this my native river, how oft have I returned after the School was dismissed[,] in thy Stream how oft have I stemed [sic] the flowing tide, and by thy side how oft have I tossed the heavy quoit.

Happy times! farewell never shall I again in such a manner experience your genial influence.

Rose this morning about half past six and after going through the examination of school found myself at 4 o'clock unnaturally depressed, produced perhaps by the

65. To come back.

Part I: The Diary

badness of the day. In order to prevent myself from falling asleep began to read Jonathan Wild and derived from it this important lesson 'Never to trust a person who hath reason to suspect that you know he had injured you.' Fielding[66] founds this rule upon the principle that though we may forgive a man an injury, he bears it still in his mind and misinterpreting our actions, considers our pardon as only feigned and that we are secretly Considering plans of revenge and that all our professions to the contrary are so many contrivances to lull asleep his attention and thus to make our punishment more complete. Whether this rule be of a general application and how it would answer if practised in this world appears somewhat doubtful. A rigid adherence to it would deprive Mankind of the benefits of reconciliation at least in a considerable degree and would prevent that confidence which should result from genuine repentance.—A little after 7 called upon the Dr Lorimer and found him in his Library. The conversation turned upon various topics. From speaking upon the use of the oriental languages to a Clergyman he passed to a Hebrew who is to preach on Friday the 17th and the collection to be appropriated to the Society for the Conversion of the Jews.[67] Thence we changed to the probability of the speedy accomplishment of that event. Bonaparte's endeavouring to unite the Jews in a body might encourage and put in action that spirit which every Hebrew possesses of returning to the country of their fathers.[68] The success which the society has already met with as conjectured from the opposition and seeming attention of the unconverted Jews, and a General Spirit of doubt prevalent among those of Jerusalem about the Coming of the Messiah, all declared that the eventful period was at hand—Old and New Testament Prophecies as far as their chronology can be determined point nearly to the present time.

Many other subjects were discussed.

Came home about 10 went to bed at 11.

66. Fielding, *The Life and Death of Jonathan Wild*; a story is based on the life of a real criminal. At the end of the book the author writes that his hero; 'laid down certain maxims as the certain methods of attaining greatness, to which, in his own pursuit of it, he constantly adhered.' There are fifteen of these principles and it is the fourth to which Edward Irving refers; 'Not to trust him who hath deceived you, nor knows he hath been deceived by you.' See Fielding, *The Life and Death of Jonathan Wild the Great*, 177-78.

67. The London Society for Promoting Christianity among the Jews, one of whose central figures was Joseph Frey (1771-1850), whom Irving was to hear preaching ten days after this entry. Frey turned out to be a very unreliable and dishonest person. He was caught forging a cheque and stealing silver plate belonging to Rev Lewis Way for whom he worked. Later it was discovered he was conducting a scandalous affair with a reformed prostitute. To cover their dismay, the London Society packed him off to New York where he continued his missionary work under the auspices of the American Society for Meliorating the Conditions of the Jews. See Endelman, *The Jews of Georgian England, 1714-1830*, 74-75.

68. Napoleon Bonaparte (1769-1821). By now Emperor of the French. Napoleon believed in freedom of worship and his attitude towards Jews was, by contemporary standards, extremely liberal. Indeed he had gone further and in 1797 expressed the opinion that Jews were entitled to a 'political existence' and during his reign did much towards their emancipation. See Horner, *The Age of Napoleon*, 15, 16, and 165.

Wednesday, 8 Aug 1810

This day went up to Salton Hall as usual but was prevented by the badness of the day and roads from reading or thinking upon my Journey. My mind however could not be totally unoccupied and somehow or other was led to the 14 Prop II Book of Lister's Geometry on the I Book of Euclid, and during my reflections a new method of deducing it presented itself to view and which will be found in my math. Place Book page [page number missing]. Upon my return called at Mr Ainslie of Begbie[69] in order to try the truth of his optic Square, we were not able to obtain an accurate Experiment for want of light.—In the Evening asked Mr Morton my landlord to come and drink a Glass of Gin with me. A little afterwards Mr Reddoch called and joined us. He has returned to Haddington in order to finish some pictures. Went to bed at 11 o'clock.

Revenir—continued from Monday.

After passing the Summit of Erickstane hill and taking a parting farewell of Annandale for a considerable time, we entered upon one of the most dreary wastes that my eyes had then or have since beheld. The sight was nowhere relieved from the view of the barren Mountains and inhospitable marshes; it was seldom delighted by one of those sublime prospects in which nature indulges even in her wildest aspect, and much less by any of those villages to which the Shepherd might return after the labours of the day and in the sweets of social intercourse forgot his trials and taste the pleasures of friendly communication.

When we passed Broughton the most considerable place upon the road the hills began to assume a verdant hue, the sheep pastured upon these summits and the hand of man became more visible. The remains of a harvest were now more plentiful and the houses from the hovells [*sic*] of Tweeddale changed to the more comfortable dwellings of Mid Lothian. As we approached the Metropolis, my heart beat with expectation, and my desire to behold the place which was now to become the scene of my studies increased.—We at length arrived after a Journey of a day and a half from Moffat; it was as pleasant as could be expected from the conveyance of a Carrier. We lodged at Broughton, and with Beds were not well accommodated. My Spirits were considerably depressed during the whole of the way which made everything assume an appearance more gloomy than I ever afterwards found them possess.

---

69. Situated four miles south west of Haddington.

Part I: The Diary

Thursday, 9 Aug 1810

At 1 o'clock went over to Mr Neil's Shop and met with Mr Sheriff [of] Mungo's Wells who asked me to dine with him on Sunday next, I had not the resolution at the moment to refuse it but upon reflection and considering the heinousness of the Crime, I sent an apology by Peter at night. Received at the same time an invitation from Mr Diddep to sup with him on Saturday night and to put my account in my pocket. This I intend to do and as one of his sons, Thomas, only attends one half of the day there may probably be some words upon the justice of a full charge. I have however resolved to act impartially and what I do to one nothing shall prevent me from also doing to another. It may be of temporary disadvantage to myself but will [be] of lasting utility to the Mathem: teaching of Haddington—at 4 o'clock Mr Reddoch called and desired that I would go down and play Bowls with him, this I consented to do and gained from him the price of the green. After Tea exchanged the two first volumes of Hume's History[70] at Mr Neil's Library with Heron's Tour through part of Scotland.[71] As I intend soon to travel I wished to make myself acquainted with the observations which are generally made and by that means to guard against errors and observe the Beauties of such works. Did not feel myself so much interested in Heron as I had expected. The objects he describes appear to be rather numerous instead of giving you a general description of the Country he seems more inclined to detail the particular seats with which it is adorned and thus leaves his reader surrounded by a mass of confusion—I will be better able to give an opinion of the Book when I have perused the whole of it.—I went to the kitchen and cracked till about half past eleven with my landlord—went to bed immediately after.

Friday, 10 Aug 1810

Returned as usual from the School at one o'clock and found a letter and parcel from my esteemed friend Brown [of] Abbey. It consisted of my Lecture or Homily which he had been perusing and the last number of L[e]ybourn's[72] maths repository of which he made me a present.—Was somewhat surprised he did not acknowledge the receipt of my letter of the 27th ult. He desired me to purchase him a Golfing club which I did, and paid for it & the ball 3/6; took them over to Mr Pringles and sent them by the Berwick Carrier. In his letter Mr B mentioned that he intended going down to

---

70. In 1754 appeared the first volume of Hume's subsequently popular *History of Great Britain*, devoted to the early Stuarts, followed by further volumes in 1757, 1759, and 1762. See *OCEL*.

71. Heron, *Scotland Described*.

72. Leybourn, *The Gentleman's Diary*; an Almanack for 1741. The first ever published of this kind, from 1741 to 1840.

Dumfriesshire at 3 or 4 weeks hence; this news I heard with the greatest pleasure and was almost Intoxicated with the idea of travelling such a distance with *such* a friend[:] of all young men that I have ever known my attachment to Mr B is the greatest and the roots of our friendship seem to be so deeply fixed in a similarity of dispositions, opinions, progress, studies, and pursuits that, though as yet of short duration, I have the firmest hope it will only be terminated by life.—He sent up a passage of Livy I Book—11 Chap last sentence, beginning '*sunt qui de*' for my consideration I found out the meaning of it after about an hours study, but of the pleasantest kind; it had baffled my friend's exertions, it was the desire of a friend, so that both the feelings of vanity and affection called upon me to do my utmost.—I wrote a letter to Brown mentioning that our examination took place about the 29th or 30th Inst and if convenient for him, we would undertake our journey immediately afterwards. Thought that I was entitled a walk but as I went to the Post-office met Mr Walker going to the Club—joined him and returned from it about 10 o'clock—went to bed about eleven.

Saturday, 11 Aug 1810

Did not rise this morning till half past seven o'clock and found Mr Clarke waiting in my sitting room, and after dressing had not above ten minutes to instruct him—desired him therefore to wait upon me any hour in the after part of the day from one to nine he fixed upon the time from one to two. Before he arrived Mr Red[doch?] called and asked me to come up & eat the *share* of a leg of lamb at his home with Baillie Johnston, did so after teaching Mr Clarke; our conversation after dinner was general & turned principally upon the present and former state of Europe particularly of France. They seemed all to agree that from its burdensome taxes and the smallness of its trade its condition was truly miserable. After returning from Mr R's I employed myself among other things in reading Heron's Tour. Speaking of the religion of Perth, he brings forward some arguments in favour of establishments in Religion. One which I now recollect is 'that as religion persuaded both the Sentiments and Conduct of men it was necessary that the government by fixing one species of belief in the Country, should prevent the inhabitants from receiving disloyal and dangerous principles from that religion they professed.' Mr James Sibbald called when I was going to Tea, and stopped to take a cup along with me. Our conversation turned principally upon Mr Farish and in conjecturing what fortune he had experienced with the Presbytery: from this we came to speak of the steps which he might take if again rejected and both agreed that were the Examinators [sic] to mix their refusal with a little flattery & a few fair promises, Mr F would return very pleasantly to his studies and wait calmly for another opportunity. As I was wishing to have a walk, I told Mr S that I would call down at the manse in about twenty minutes. Did so in about 40 and was received at the door by Thomas who informed me that he was in, but immediately there issued a voice from the parlour (which I easily recognised to be the Doctors) that James was not in. I turned upon my heel and came off very highly chagrined at the parson's conduct. Thought I, had he wished me to visit his house or had my company been acceptable he would certainly have invited me in and then told me that his son was out[;] in addition to this I reflected upon the small favour I had done for the Doctor, without the least acknowledgment on his part, and hath upon the principle of ingratitude and unpoliteness [sic] concluded that he had acted what I thought incorrectly. Reflecting upon this circumstance at home, three things appeared to justify his conduct; the first and principal was that being Saturday night he would be busy in preparing for next day—2ndly, as I was later than my appointment I could not expect to find everything right, 3rd, the Dr's natural avarice which is the source of almost every evil.

From this circumstance I was led to reflect upon the general behaviour of the heads of that family towards me.—My first introduction to them was slight[,] from a person who had not been intimate with the Dr for a considerable time, on the other hand James had been friendly treated at Annan, and Good Manners expected a return.—Instead of that, however, the greatest reserve in asking me back to the house was evident. I would never have gone, could I have answered James's importunities in any other way. This, however, I have resolved that until some more particular Explanation take place I will not appear in the manse. –

Walked betwixt 8 & 9 with Mr R and talked chiefly upon the conduct of a Mrs Bell & the bad pass into which she had brought her husband.—Went to Mr Diddep's at 9 and received from him the amount of my account.—The party consisted of Dr Williams, Mr Johnstone & myself. Conversation bad & disgusting—Came home before 12. -

Sunday, 12 Aug 1810

During breakfast was employed in reading the Westminster Confession of Faith and examining the principles and thought of going to hear a Sermon on the forenoon. Called upon Mr Reddoch and desired his company; we went to the tabernacle[73] and heard from Mr Hill a Lecture upon Luke III v 16 to the end. The subject was treated

73. The Tabernacle was a Congregational or Independent church established in Haddington from 1798 by the brothers Robert (1761–1842) and James Haldane (1768–1851). Having left the Church of Scotland, they carried on a vigorous itinerant ministry in various parts of Scotland, founding such Tabernacles in various towns. The first pastor of the Haddington Tabernacle was James Hill, who was ordained in 1804; when they adopted Baptist views they moved him and his flock to a house in the High Street, which was converted into a chapel, also known as the Tabernacle. See *BDGB*; Haldane, *The Lives of Robert and James Haldane of Airthrey*; Miller, *The Lamp of Lothian*.

in a very dreary and uninteresting manner. His Ideas both in point of arrangement & mutual connection had all the appearance of an extemporary discourse. He made an observation upon the nature of repentance, these were two kinds, the first consisted in a horror and remorse for our past conduct, such was that of Judas; the next and true kind proceeded not only from that source but also from a conviction that our former ways were bad and productive of the most dangerous consequences and also to a resolution to lead a life contrary to that we have formerly passed. Mr Hill made another remark upon the seeming contradiction between Matthew's and Luke's Genealogy of our Saviour and instanced one particular. The former of these Evangelists calls Joseph our Lord Saviours father, the son of Jacob and the brother of Heli.[74] He reconciled this apparent contradiction by supposing that Matthew speaks of Josephs natural father while Luke refers to his father as sons & to Mary's father, as an instance of a similar expression he referred us to Genesis XXXVI v 2 of which, however, I did not thoroughly see the application.—We came out of the Tabernacle nearly an hour before the Kirk met, this time Mr R and I employed in reading the beginning of Stewarts Outlines[75] and conversing upon them. Mr Reddoch was of opinion that the Author was wrong in endeavouring to draw a line of distinction between the philosophers and men of plain sense and judicious observation—we were both of opinion that their philosophy differed in degree, but could not with Mr S believe that there was any difference in the means of acquiring it. Mr R: whose mind is peculiarly fertile in familiar and apposite examples & illustrations, brought some to show that the deduction which is drawn in the outlines has no foundation in fact. I had occasion here to observe, in addition to the many times I have before noticed it, the great advantage which is derived from two reading together. Different minds must have somewhat different views of the same subject, these views lead to a train of Ideas which again produces a chain of reasoning and thus has a tendency to rivet in your mind the Subject you are reading.

Heard from Dr Lorimer a Sermon in the afternoon upon John VIII & 12—but made no observations worthy of a particular detail—after Church went over the way and ate Hotchpotch[76] with Baillie Johnstone and afterwards went & heard an evening

74. Luke 3:23–26.

75. Stewart, *Outlines of Moral Philosophy* (1753–1828). Stewart was educated at Edinburgh High School and at Edinburgh and Glasgow Universities. He became professor of mathematics at Edinburgh University and subsequently professor of moral philosophy there. See *OCEL*.

76. Hotch-potch is a mutton stew consisting of mutton, grated and sliced carrot, 'young turnips, young onions, lettuce and parsley.' Plus 'young green pease [sic].' In 1826 a review of a recently published cookery book, *Cook's and Housewife's Manual* by Meg Dods, prints from it a recipe in full with the following comments. 'There is but one other Scotch dish at all comparable to a haggis . . . and that, gentle reader, is Hotch-Potch. . . . Hotch-Potch, we cheerfully admit, is often met with in England—but it is of Scottish extraction. The truly delightful thing about Hotch-Potch is, that it comes in with the season of green pease [sic]. . . . It is redolent of summer-gardens . . . It is a dish that must have been best known in Paradise—nor do we doubt that Meg Dod's receipt is the same as Eve's.' The enthusiastic reviewer towards the end of his article discusses the evident healthy appetites of the Presbyterian clergy and finishes his piece thus: 'Before the arrival of Edward Irving's Millennium, in 1847, good eating in Scotland will have reached its acmé—and that will be celebrated by a Great National Festival, of which

Sermon from Mr Steel, Minister of Morham,[77] upon Hebrews IX and 27—'After death is the Judgment.'—The whole of what he proposed was to shew the probability of a future Judgement from the unequal distribution of good and evil which we observe in the world and which can only be reconciled with our notions of a just God by supposing that there is a state of retribution. This subject though an important one was certainly rather narrow in order to occupy a man for half an hour without frequent repetitions.—Accordingly there was a great degree of sameness both in Ideas and in Language.—His words were well arranged and upon the whole it was an elegant sort of a harrangue [sic]; but if utility is to be considered as the Criterion of pulpit Eloquence, Mr Steel's discourse would have rated very low. His application was included in about half a dozen words. Allusions are very good when introduced with Judgment; this observation holds in a very high degree, in Sermons. Mr Steel had one which appeared to me ill suited—'When the Curtain draws up.'—

Mr R called over in the Evening took a walk & Conversed upon religious subjects—after returning, Mr Lamb, his landlord, and he came up & ate cheese & bread & drank a bottle of ale with me.—For Conversation see Monday's Diary. Went to bed at 12.

∽

Monday, 13 August 1810

Our Conversation last night turned upon Character and to my utmost astonishment I was informed that the master of the Bugle inn had made an observation that I attended bad houses.[78] This false report I can account for in three ways he may have mistaken me for Mr G Irving, Mr Graham's present assistant who, I know, used to frequent such places. 2nd, as from Mr Irving Dumfriesshire militia or 3rdly. But having observed me once go in to the same entry to speak to Mr Preacher who had his School in that quarter. The effects which such a story produced upon my mind were greatly diminished by a consciousness of innocence, but this did not totally destroy them—I felt hurt that I should be suspected of such a thing, and also from the consequences which it might occasion to a person with my views. This leads me to reflect upon the advantage of public opinion—a man in whatever situation of life must be dependent upon some of his brethren upon whose good opinion his happiness in moving in this

---

the Cookery will be transcendental. Mr. Irving will preside, and we ourselves, if alive, will cheerfully accept the office of croupier': Dod's Cookery, *Blackwood's Edinburgh Magazine*, 657 and 660.

77. Morham is three miles South East of Haddington. John Steel (1760–1831) was a schoolmaster of Dunbar and a man of a sociable disposition. He took a great interest and encouraged he young men of the district with help and advice. He was not in very good financial circumstances, however, through a mis-placed trust in a friend. See Scott, *Fasti*, 1.379.

78. The Oxford Dictionary gives a definition for bad as 'immoral, wicked' therefore the implication would seem to be that 'bad houses' were 'houses of ill repute' (i.e., brothels).

world considerably depends. In these circumstances it is abundantly necessary that his external conduct should agree with that which is expected from him and though they be exactly in unison, he should endeavour to prevent every opportunity to mischievous beings of misrepresenting him.

Read Herries['] *Taxes*[79] before Tea and went after it to take a walk. Called at Mr Lamb's and found Mr Reddoch as usual and took a game at quoits; after which Mr R desired me to go to Laing's inn and bear him Company until he paid a chaise hire—did so and sat down with him to drink a bottle of porter when Mr Stewart the principal waiter brought in a pair of Bag pipes which had been given by Allan McLean formerly piper to Colonel McLean of this town at the Exhibition in Edinburgh.[80]—They were the head prize & no doubt he was wonderfully pleased with them. In him one might observe the characteristics of a true Highlander. Patriotic to a fault. Blunt but honest. Proud but not vain of the honours he had acquired. Came home after ten. I went to bed about 12.

Tuesday, 14 August 1810

After playing an hour or two with Mr Reddoch at Quoits; we came up to my room and sat down to our usual supper ale & cheese & bread. The conversation turned among other things upon the authenticity of Ossian's Poems.[81] He took the negative side of the Question and I the other. We did not enter into any argumentation upon the subject but merely suggested to each other our Ideas. On my side I observed that the simple Manners, the warm and honest feelings, the Religious belief of his persons were in perfect unison with that rude & early stage of society, and in addition to this it seemed to me quite inconsistent with human nature that any man should voluntarily renounce fame, that he should prefer the satisfaction of his own bread though of rather a higher nature to the praises of the world. Mr Reddoch opposed this as is usually his practice with arguments which appeared at the moment stronger, but still not convincing. Went to bed about 12.

---

79. Rt Hon John Charles Herries (1778–1855), was an English politician and financier and a frequent member of Tory and Conservative cabinets in the early to mid-nineteenth century. See Herries, *A Reply to Some Financial Misstatements*.

80. There were yearly exhibitions at the Royal Scottish Academy founded in 1763.

81. 'James Macpherson, born near Kingussie, the son of a farmer, was educated at Aberdeen and Edinburgh Universities. In 1759 he produced the first of his series of forgeries of early poetry purporting to be the writings of Ossian, the son of Finn, dating from a distant period of early Scottish history. The publications caused a sensation but almost at once led by Dr Johnson, their authenticity was questioned. However despite the revelation of their forgery they still continued to be popular.' See *OCEL*.

Part I: The Diary

Wednesday, 15 August 1810

Took my usual Journey to Salton Hall at 12 o'clock in company with Mr Reddoch who was going to Dr Stewarts to paint. Among other things Miss Brame was so kind as to invite me rather to press me to address her in French. And this I intend to do. It will no doubt make me appear for some time ridiculous in the eyes of my young pupils who speak the language so fluently, but of how insignificant a nature is this objection when compared with the numerous & important advantages that may result from such a practice. A knowledge of the French language is of all other modern tongues the most useful, there are no parts of Europe or even of the civilized world in which it is not spoken at least understood. No nation has produced more scientific and original authors especially in the mathematics—as the Empire extends its Boundaries, its language & manners must be more widely diffused. Amid the convulsions of Empires which Europe has for some time and still continues to experience, no human sagacity can determine how soon the French & British may be more intimately connected, and were peace again restored to these two Countries the communication between the two would become very general. England would be overwhelmed with a deluge of Continental Books and the Continent stocked with English travellers. The situation of a travelling tutor might then present itself and if I know my own mind nothing would be more eagerly accepted of. When these important advantages are considered and in addition to them, that such an easy cheap and excellent opportunity will probably never again occur I do think it would be very foolish in me not to accept Miss Brames invitation. After returning home and drinking Tea Mr Reddoch called and was wanting me to go up to his lodging but declined as I was all wet and could not be troubled to change—at the same time desired him to stop and sup with me. He did so and after faring as usual and cracking[82] mostly upon his rising prospect of changing his mode of life, he left me about 11 o'clock. Went to bed about twelve.

Thursday, 16 August 1810

Reflecting after school hours upon the Circumstance mentioned in my yesterday's diary, I came to the resolution of revising my French with the greatest avidity and of sacrificing for some time every other study in the prosecution of this Design. In order that my attention might be confined to this one object I returned to my press every Book except my French ones and immediately set to my French Grammar. I studied the articles, committed their declension to memory, and during a walk which I took in the long planting read eight pages of Charles the twelfth, and attended particularly to the use of the article; I found this exercise very simple but thought that in order to my

82. I.e., talking.

speaking the language with fluency it was not only necessary that I should be able to read it but also to write it. To attempt turning a piece of an English author into French appeared to me useless as I had no person at hand to correct it & also not to trouble Miss Brame, in order to supply this defect I adopted a plan which will I think answer all the purposes of this. In the prosecution of it I translated into my exercise Book nearly a page from the beginning of Voltaire's Charles the twelfth[83] and will after the construction of the passage has left my mind turn it again into French. By comparing this with the original I will soon discover my Errors and by finding out those parts in which I am most deficient will be able to guard against them in future exercises of the same kind. In the kitchen I had afterwards a pleasant crack with my landlord & landlady and a young lady Miss P. My Behaviour was rather too free and such as might insensibly lead to the most dangerous consequences. Women are fascinating and young men apt to be inflamed; I may hope however that upon that score I have my passions under complete subjugation. Went to bed about half past Eleven.

Friday, 17 August 1810

This day had a visit of Mr Jas Robertson & his brother Thos on their way to Gifford.—Had their company to dinner after which we went to hear the Jew preach. His name is Mr Frey.[84] His text was Job XIX v 21[:] 'Have pity upon me, have pity upon me, O ye my friends, for the hand of the Lord hath touched me.' He began by observing that there was no other rank of men in Britain who could utter those words accept the Jews. He then compared their Condition with that of Job and proposed 1st to shew the miserable state of the Jews. They were in a state of nature and believing not upon Jesus the condemnation of the Lord was upon them. They depended for salvation upon their being the posterity of Abraham but yet as Ishmael & Esau were deracinated from the source some of their Rabbis thought something else was necessary. The 8th day of every month they confess their sins upon the head of a fowl and after doing so eat him, they fast next day and are in the temple the following one from sunrise till the appearance of the stars. A person dying on the day of sacrifice was thought to go immediately to heaven, if between two of them he had to get through purgatory.—Their children prayed for their souls & went through some ceremonies.—Instead of sacrifices, set prayers had been appointed in this country by the Rabbi's, these prayers were not understood by most part of the people offering them, during their performance the synagogue was more like a stock Exchange than anything else.

---

83. Voltaire, *Histoire de Charles XII of Sweden*, (1731).
84. Joseph Samuel Frey CF (1773–1850). See entry for the 6 August 1810.

II. Causes of their miserable state. The hand of the Lord has touched them not so much for crucifying Christ as for denying the evidence of his resurrection. 2nd. They are not possessed of New Testaments, the Old Testament contained the most important truths but like a Castle full of Gold wanting a lock or key they were deprived of its treasures unless they possessed the new Testament also.—Common people have only part of the old Testament. The five Books of Moses & about Sixty Chapters of the Prophesies unconnected, however, with the coming of the Messiah. Did not understand the literal meaning of the Hebrew. 3rd. Want of Education—children were taught to repeat their prayers in Hebrew when from five to nine years old but generally by rote only—afterwards left to shift for themselves. 4th Want of hearing the scriptures preached.

III. Means of delivering them from their miserable condition. First, an asylum for those who professing Christianity or sending their children to Christian Schools, were excluded from gaining their bread among the Jews. 2nd. A School for the Education of such Children as may be sent to it gratis. This Establishment has been formed and already possesses 49 young people. 3rdly a Chapel in which they may hear Christianity in their native tongue, one has been already oppened.[85][sic]

IV. Arguments to induce us to aid the Jews. 1st. We receive the old Testament through their hands—they preserved it and excellent preservers they were—numbered the words in each Book in each page & also the letters in every line, lest there should be interpolations. 2nd. The writers of the new Testament were all Jews. 3rd. Christ lives as a Jew by the flesh and hence a Jew sits at the right hand of God. 4th. From the injuries that nation had suffered in this country at former periods.

Mr Freys sermon was rather unconnected, the Ideas might be proper & even tend in some way or other to establish the truth of his propositions, but it was difficult to trace the connection. It was delivered with earnestness & at times with a great deal of feeling.—It contained facts new and calculated to rouse the pity of his audience. It produced a better Effect as Mr F speaks English but indifferently and very much like a Highlandman. Messrs Robertsons & Mr Reddoch supped with me—Thos slept all night in my lodgings. Went to bed about half past eleven.

∽

Saturday, 18 August 1810

Then this morning in company with Messrs Robertsons I breakfasted with Mr Reddoch. Went in the afternoon in a chaise with the painter to Nunraw[86] stopped at

---

85. 'The Society [The London Society for Promoting Christianity among the Jews] had opened a chapel in Brick Lane, Spitalfields.' Endelman, *The Jews of Georgian England, 1713–1830*, 72.

86. About six miles south east of Haddington, the site of an Abbey.

Garvald[87] within half a mile of it in a Mr Foggus a shoemaker until Mr R went up with the chaise to make his Call. Had an opportunity of observing in Mr F another instance of the general knowledge diffused among every rank in Scotland. His information I found extensive, and of a liberal nature.—He expressed himself with care & correctness and seemed upon the whole a very shrewd man. Was much pleased with my jaunt. The Country in that quarter is more uneven than about Haddington & of course more picturesque. It has quite an undulated appearance—Continued in my application to the French—wrote out my lesson & compared it. Went to bed about half past eleven.

Sunday 19 August 1810

After breakfast Mr Reddoch and I went to the tabernacle and heard from Mr Hill a Lecture upon our Lords Temptation as recorded by Luke IV Chap. In the beginning of his discourse made some very good observations upon the intentions with which we should read the Bible. We ought not to peruse the sacred volume in order to gratify a vain curiosity or with the design to discover faults & expose them, for in this case we may find in every page something which our narrow and evil minds may cavill [sic] at, & which our limited capacities are unable to comprehend, but on the other hand our views should be directed to discover the will of God and the duty required of us we ought to read in order that we may profit and in this case we will find every page of sacred text fraught with the most important lessons, and calculated to produce the most beneficial Effects.—In the after part of his Sermon Mr Hill tells wonderfully of and handles in a very exact and dry manner, one of the finest subjects in the Sacred volume—

At 2 o'clock went to the Church and heard from Dr Lorimer a Sermon upon the same subject as last Sundays discourse. He began as usual very well and expressed in very fine figures in calling the Sun Moon & Stars the 'Apostles of Nature'; but towards the middle & end of his discourse he became very insipid.

If I may judge from the following remarks I would conclude both this and Mr Hill's discourse to be extempore. The Marks of an unstudied discourse are in my opinion the following. First. The great difference in point of connection and neatness between the beginning and the after part many men come to the pulpit without having arranged the whole of their Ideas but few without having thought over part of them. They have digested so much of their subject as their memory will conveniently have and for the remainder they trust to their reflections at the moment and hence the great inequality in discourses of this nature. Hence also 2ndly. Why they are in general longer than those which have been thoroughly arranged. The mind of man

---

87. Near Nunraw.

may be considered as a sort of quarry containing those materials from among which we must dig for our Ideas upon any particular subject it is this general repository of all our information and therefore a good deal of labour and judgment is necessary in order to select from this stock what is *apropos* for our sermon. And a man speaking extempore cannot give this requisite degree of labour and in however polished a state his mind may be, it will present the Ideas undivested of that unconnected matter with which they are surrounded, also words are not always at hand and instead of them circumlocutions must be used & from these circumstances arises the great [many?] of them. 3rdly. From the same thought being frequently repeated without a special intimation to the audience. The speaker when uttering Ideas just as they occur to his mind, and without having any distinct impression of them, very soon forgets what he has said. One paragraph destroys the recollection of the preceding one, and no wonder then that it should be again repeated—4thly. From the great want of connection in its different parts. A good discourse may be compared to a good machine, every wheel has a peculiar object and yet contributes in some degree to the general design of the whole—a bad discourse again resembles an ill contrived and badly regulated piece of mechanism, its parts have some connection with each other, but are so injudiciously placed as to produce no effect or at least no effect compared with what might have been obtained from a proper disposal of its parts a man speaking extempore is glad of anything that presents itself, he snatches at every twig how ever insufficient to aid him.

Next to a correct private life due attention to pulpit discourses is the first object of a Clergyman. They ought to be made level to the capacity of the weakest mind, and yet in such a manner as to be useful to all. To simplify is one of the most difficult part of Eloquence and in a preacher of the Gospel is absolutely necessary. He therefore who thinks himself in the list of Jesus's ministering servants, cannot be considered as discharging the duties of his important station unless he devote sufficient time to his discourses unless properly composed they can scarcely be expected to interest, they may disgust part of the audience but can never attract, they may tend to produce infidels and careless attenders on public worship but can never reclaim them. In this particular I do think Dr L is defficient [sic]; but from what cause his carelessness arises I do not yet know.

In the Evening we heard from Dr Sibbald the remainder of the Sermon upon Isaiah IX v 6 [See Diary 22 July 1810], on the second particular of the first division. He made the following additional observations. By whom could these interpolations be made? By this superstition answer some. Fear is known obviously to be the very soul of superstition & would persons of this nature lay themselves under the Curse pronounced against those who should add or take away from the Law, without any object to obtain? It was unprofitable to suppose it. By the Philosophers answered others.—It has always been a principle amongst this class of men to believe nothing which they dont [sic] understand and not a single instance has occurred in which any of them have believed the Divinity of Jesus except those who have had the humility to receive it from revelation.—It is not therefore probable that any of this Class would make these interpolations. Upon the Second Head the Dr summed up this reasoning with regard to our Saviour's attonement [sic] very elegantly. If we suppose our Surety to have been a divine person Him being subject to no law, obedience in him was meritorious this merit from the nature of the person was infinite & being infinite was sufficient to attone [sic] for the sins of the whole world. The Dr then proceeded to the Improvement of the Discourse and observed 1st. That the Divinity of Christ should be an Article of our creed. 2ndly. That we should worship him as such. 3rdly. That we should keep his Commandments. 4thly. That we should rely upon him alone for salvation.—This discourse, like the generality of Dr Sibbalds was neatly composed, very correct, and delivered with great energy. It was not however such a one as I would have written upon the subject. The arguments appeared to be too much clothed with ornament, and it required too great an exertion of the mind to free them from the trappings with which they were surrounded.

There appears to me to be two great distinctions in the Eloquence of the pulpit. The first and real kind draws the attention from the speaker to the Subject and keeps it steadily to this one object. The second sort which is of a spurious nature, tends to lead your mind from the matter of the discourse to the person who delivers it. The preaching of the Dr has this effect upon me, unless I be remarkably guarded, I am more pleased than benefited my mind is apt to settle rather upon the fine language in which it is clothed than on the Ideas themselves. The substance bears only a small proportion to the quantity of words. This feeling which his Eloquence inspires is rather analogous to that which is created upon men in general by a person in a fine Equipage and who possesses little mental superiority above the Rest of the Species. Received this day a letter from Brown in which he approves of my Translation, my version and my plan of keeping a diary. He thinks were he to adopt a similar one, his attention would be principally confined to the account of his own observations upon men and manners—Wrote my Diary after Tea and went to bed about half past eleven.

Monday, 20 August 1810

After School hours Mr Reddoch called and stopped to drink Tea with me; as the examination is fast approaching I have resolved to teach every night betwixt 6 and 7, began to night.

At 7 called upon Mr R to take a walk, after our walk I came home as he had a letter to write to his Jenny McGie as he calls her.—Oh that I had some Jenny McGie as worthy of my affection as she is of his—Oh that I possessed the affections & esteem of some religious well informed, well disposed & good tempered Girl. To meet with a person of such a description should be deemed the happiest circumstance of my life. An acquaintance of such a nature would be productive of the most happy consequences, it would guard me in a very strong degree from the sallies and passions of unguarded youth. When virtually betrothed to another I would consider myself as her own, and my passions would all be made subservient to this consideration.

At Mr R's invitation I went down and supped with him. Our conversation turned amongst other things upon the Haddington clergymen. We both agreed that they were all correct men & very fortunately so considering the prevalent disposition of the Haddington people. Possessed normally of a happy mediocrity they seem to pride themselves in their happiness, they are very apt to throw of [*sic*] all allegiance to God as the giver of every good, and to believe that their present comfortable circumstances arise solely from their prudence and carefulness. They are in general in that careless state which is, perhaps, the most dangerous. Their external conduct is not glaringly bad, but yet inconsistent. Like the Pharisees of old they make clean the outside, they attend on religious ordinances & partake of holy things but all within is rottenness and corruption –

Returned home about half past ten and went to bed a little after eleven.

Tuesday 21 August 1810

As the examination of the Schools takes place Wednesday the 29th I have left many things in order that we may be able to undertake every thing necessary I have fixed upon the hour between 6 and 7 in the evening as a kind supplement to the others. After 7 called upon Mr Reddoch who asked me to go along with him to Dr Lorimer. We found him in and at his dinner. Stopped to supper.—The doctor and Mr R entered into a crack[88] with thoughts upon several subjects but principally upon religion. During the whole conversation I hardly made a single observation. This would no doubt appear very singular and stupid to the rest of the Company but did not at all surprise myself. There are times when I can speak with candour upon any subject—there are others in which I speak with difficulty upon any subject. There are companies which produce very nearly the same effect—when conscious that I am upon an equality in point of intellect with the rest, or that we are of nearly similar dispositions and manners, my words and Ideas flow before men. My common sense, my judgment, my memory, are all recovered. I found myself to-night, from what cause I know not quite unhinged for conversation, my tongue and lips seemed unwilling to obey my mind even in uttering the mark of spirit 'yes' I enjoyed the conversation of the host with little satisfaction, I was in every respect a blank in the company—Mr Reddoch and Dr Lorimer were both

---

88. I.e., a conversation.

possessed of far more general Ideas, more general knowledge, and much more experience than I was—any remark which I could make would, I thought, be no additional information to them, and therefore it would be more wise to be silent—One sentiment I remembered to have uttered; that the first people were not the happiest people and as a support of my principles brought forward the state of savages: Mr R by a single observation returned me but did not satisfy me I felt unable as well as unwilling to defend my position and therefore allowed it to fall to the ground; if I had held my tongue it would have been much wiser.—Returned about twelve o'clock packed up a small Box for Annan bands of my cousins lace and accompanied it with a letter appologising [sic] for my conduct. Went to bed at 1.

Wednesday, 22 August 1810

Rose as usual before 7 and as I was going out of my lodging for Salton Hall met with Dr Lorimer. We walked arm in arm to his own door, and among other things began to speak about the examination, he said that they (the Clergymen) & I must have some *suitable* paragraph in the papers concerning my School as I knew from his way of uttering the sentence that the word suitable was used in a good sense, I observed that he should wait for the examinations & not pass sentence prematurely. Oh sir replied he I am fully persuaded that nothing can be taught better. I mention this circumstance merely as exhibiting a trait in Dr Lorimers Character namely, a strong desire to make himself agreeable or a great degree of politeness. This frequently in him appears to degenerate into a fault; and in this case he is apt to lower his dignity, servility, will, and not infrequently does take the place of politeness; it has occurred even within the sphere of my own narrow observation; I have observed young men and not infrequently grown up sensible persons follow from a mere desire to please, the tide of opinion and from the same motive indulge in the most disgraceful scandal. How absurd such conduct, how inconsistent with Beings possessed of reason & judgement; let it never be a part of my character '*jurare in verba magistri.*'[89] –

Nothing material occurred on my journey. I arrived there safe and after working my usual time returned by Bolton in order to call upon Dr Stewart. Did not find him in—after I came home wrote a letter to Brown in which there was nothing of consequence, except in my opinion of the reasons which created in Mr Farish such a strong desire to be preacher. This I forebear mentioning here as I may have some future opportunity of inlarging [sic] upon them—Indulged in a Glass of Ale & a Welsh Rabbit to supper and went to bed about eleven.

---

89. To swear to a master's word, to accept opinions upon authority.

Part I: The Diary

Thursday, 23 August 1810

According to an Engagement which I have made, went at four o'clock to dine with Mr Cockburn. Mr & Mrs C. are a very pleasant agreeable couple, possessed both of a considerable portion of common sense and also very polite—there is no house in Haddn in which I feel more at my ease, conversation is carried on in a fair manner and generally has a rational turn. Our company consisted of Mr & Mrs Graham and some people from the Country; our dinner was very splendid, and after it retired to teach my evening School—at 7 returned and found the company sitting. Left them about 9 o'clock.

The conversation had a more particular turn than I expected. The Jews came to be talked upon & the probability of their being speedily converted. Mr C. was of the opinion they would not and rested his judgment chiefly upon the punctuality with which they observed their sabbaths. I accounted for this from the nature of their religion. It rested their whole title to Salvation upon the observance of the rites of the Law and without a due attention to these it was thought a matter of impossibility that a man could be saved; upon this principle also I endeavoured to account for the superior attention which Roman Catholics, the Church of England etc paid to their external worship[;] their religion was more of a ceremonial nature than our own; it addressed itself more directly to the Jews and though their Clergymen might preach up the inutility of their observances if not produced by a godly mind yet the Common people[,] who are in general in their Countries incapacitated by their want of knowledge to make such discriminations[,] confound appearance with reality and transfer to the former all the Consequences of the latter.

Other Subjects were talked upon.—The accomplishments of a Lady were mentioned by one person to be principally; French, Drawing, Music and some such flimsy superficial trifles—Made some observation upon their inutility to wives. Came home went to bed at 11.

∽

Friday, 24 August 1810

Went out after School hours in company with Mr Thos Brough & two of my pupils to try the truth of Mr Ainslie's optic square and by an observation with the Theodolite as well as dimensions with the Chain, found it very accurate.

After setting fast the instruments and teaching between 6 and 7 came into Mr McIntyre's Shop and began to converse upon various subjects we were joined by Mr Jamieson by whom politics were introduced.

Whether it may arise from less ceremony or from superior information I am uncertain but I always find myself more informed, and better pleased with the observations of people in middling or even in what are generally reckoned inferior stations than by those of the highest ranks. How much more instructive, how much more rational and how much more correct was the conversation of these two Gentleman than what generally passes at the [dull?] or [irregular?] Clubs or even at the more genteel dinner parties. Divest the latter of smutty ribaldry and common place observation and what is left? It is impossible for a moment to introduce a conversation upon any subject on Science, upon any branch of religion or even upon the general politics of the world—without incurring the name of a pedant, of a superstitious enthusiast, or of a forward young man. Make an observation and it is received by a 'yes' or 'I don't know,' that false complaisance that foolish opinion about the nature of genteel behaviour prevents all argumentation and rational talk and, of course, precludes any chance of information. Supped with Mr Peter Dods, our Company was large, the conversation was an excellent confirmation of the above remarks; while the Ladies retained their seats it was correct but the instant that they retired, it broke out into the greatest obscenity that I have at any time heard. Came home about 1 o'clock.

Saturday 25 August 1810

As our Examination takes place next Wednesday, this day was fixed upon to go up to Salton Hall, which engagement interfering with my Mathem Class we met between 6 & 7 in the morning. At 12 took my Journey and amused myself with reading Frey's Narrative.[90] Noticed in Miss Brame to day for the first time a desire to quize; [sic] but as I usually do when I observe this disposition answered in her own manner as I thought succeeded tolerably well in this method of retaliation. Among other things the conversation turned upon the Methodists who Miss B observed, she thought calculated to produce very bad and dangerous consequences. I answered that I was of a different opinion, the disadvantages which were produced by such societies appeared, in my view to be trifling when compared with the benefits arising from them. They had no doubt a tendency to unhinge the minds of men, employed as they frequently are in religious controversies in disputes about the most insignificant trifles, in as it were, of splitting hairs: their minds become unsettled and their firmest resolutions wavering; fond of examining every thing with the greatest minuteness they are apt to become unwilling members of Society; but on the other hand the advantages arising from Methodist societies are of greater importance—Nothing is more dangerous to men than that listless aimless unheeding state in which the great Bulk of Mankind live. Nothing can therefore be of superior moment than to awaken persons from that Condition and in this point I believe, it will generally be acknowledged that the Methodists have

---

90. Frey, *Narrative of Joseph Samuel Frey*.

succeeded. Only awaken the minds of men and the highest object is attained; though they may from want of Experience and a consequent defficiency [*sic*] of Judgement go wrong at first, yet there is a greater probability of their finally attaining the true path than if they had continued in the listless path from which they were lead [*sic*]. Supped with [Mr Graham ?] & came home at half past eleven. Went to bed.

Sunday, 26 August 1810

Slept very long this morning. Heard at 2 o'clock a Lecture from Dr Sibbald upon the first four verses of the 6th Chapter of St Matthew. No remarks were made worthy of notice; in the evening at 6 o'clock we had a Sermon from Dr Lorimer upon Luke 10—41 & 42 but chiefly these words 'one thing is needful'[;][91] a very confused discourse it was as almost any I have heard from him. Took Cheese and Bread with Mr Reddoch and as I returned a little after 9 o'clock heard Mr Jameson a young man at the Book,[92] stood and listened and instantly began to reflect upon my own careless state, and to be grieved at my conduct. With my mind full of these Ideas I returned home & sung a psalm, read a chapter & prayed to God to increase my resolution to walk in the image of godliness. Went to bed at 11 o'clock.

Monday, 27 August 1810

After School hours received a visit from Mr Sheriff [of] Drem in order to settle about the School Wages for his two boys. In his behaviour I thought that I discovered some effects of my former firmness (27th June), no mention was made of reduced charge, no dryness was shown—he seemed to be very well satisfied and promised his company on Wednesday—after drinking Tea taught between 6 and 7 and then called upon Mr Reddoch—being joined by Mr Diddep we commenced a match at putting. Mr D was first, Mr R and I nearly equal. Employed myself after coming home in reading the Jew's Narrative. In the behaviour of the Missionary Society to Mr Frey[93] we have a very strong instance of Servility being desired instead of Gratitude. That two such opposite feelings should be expected to result from the same circumstances appears somewhat strange yet though far different in their nature, they are like those sudden changes

---

91. 'But one thing is needful': Luke 10:42

92. 'The Book' to which Irving refers must be the Bible. His remark that 'he stood and listened' implies that the young man is reading in the street to all that chose to listen.

93. He had broken away from the London Missionary Society and in 1809 had founded the London Jews' Society. See footnote to entry for 8 August 1810.

which the face of nature sometimes assumes separated by a narrow strait. Advance beyond Gratitude and you find your self unexpectedly upon the Side of Servility—After taking his Book went to bed about eleven.

Tuesday, 28 August 1810

I was somewhat surprised at the easy state of my mind the whole of this afternoon when I reflected that the Examination takes place tomorrow. To such height did this feeling sometimes attain that I was led to mistake it for carelessness. Upon a more thorough consideration I found it to proceed rather from a consciousness that my pupils were well prepared and that I had discharged a faithful duty to them; if the Judges be unsatisfied and my present hopes blasted—I may exclaim in the words of one of Addison's heroes 'Tis not in mortals to command success, But we'll do more, Simpronius, we'll (endeavour to) deserve it.'[94]

Read some of The Scottish Chiefs and admire in it principally the natural and yet distinct way in which Miss Porter[95] makes every Character declare itself by the incidents which occur & the sentiments they utter. Kirkpatrick's character is finely drawn—and so is Lord Andrew Murray's—Took the Book & went to bed about eleven.

Wednesday, 29 August 1810

This day at half past ten o'clock came in our Examination. My Scholars did not all turn out, owing to what they thought some fault in my distributing their places, but of such an ill founded belief I disdain to take any notice.

The Clergymen present were Dr Stewart, Dr Lorimer, Dr Sibbald, Dr Hamilton, Mr Ritchie & Mr Lumsden The pupils answered the questions put to them very well and all the Examinators seemed to be well pleased, and in their report gave a pretty good account of our Exhibition; an account however which was perhaps more satisfactory and flattering to some of the Teachers than to others—whether this difference proceeded from merit or not I am unable to know, as I was not present in the other Schools. Left Dinner at half past 7 o'clock & went to bed at 10.

---

94. Addison, *Cato*, Act 1 Scene.2.
95. Porter, *The Scottish Chiefs*. A story of William Wallace, which was successful and was translated into German and Russian. Kirkpatrick and Lord Andrew Murray are characters in the book. See *OCEL*.

Part I: The Diary

Thursday 30 August 1810

As I had promised to meet with my friend James Brown at Dunbar at 8 o'clock in the morning I rose a little before 5 and after taking a Cup of Tea set out upon my Journey. The morning was at that time pleasant a few light clouds hovered around but as I thought, would be quickly dispelled by the appearance and influence of the sun. My opinion was completely contradicted by the event. Before I had proceeded a mile upon my road the clouds began to gather, a thick gloom appeared in the East from which [part?] the [little?] wind that blew, came, and eventually fell one of the most drenching rains I have at any time felt. Dryanbender law[96] began to be enveloped in a mist & in clouds hung heavy over the Lismuir ridge, before I had passed Linton I was wet to the skin. The whole face of the Country bore a cheerless aspect. The corn ready in their stook would be completely drenched and that which was uncut would be flattened by the heavy rain.

As I approached the small village of West Barns the morning began to clear—within a mile of Dunbar I passed through a village of which I have now forgot the name,[97] it lies immediately upon the coast and the Barrack Huts in its neighbourhood declare that it was one of those places upon which the weight of the threatened invasion[98] might fall. After passing through this town I had a very good view of Dunbar—it is situated in the midst of a very fertile and highly cultivated country on the South & South East lies the coast of the Frith[99] and on the North it is flanked by some woods. The Town has a thriving aspect and being upon the high road between London & Edinburgh and possessing a tolerable harbour it seems probable that a good deal of business will be transacted in it. The principal street runs in the direction of North and South—upon the South it is terminated by the back part of Dunbar House the seat of Lord Lauderdale. Mr Brown did not arrive till half past eight and after getting breakfast we took a walk to view the old Castle. It is situated upon a rock which is surrounded on three sides by water and detached from the land on the fourth by a steep ascent. The ruins shew that it has been very extensive but hardly enough of these is left to shew its [sic] or inner structure. Several caverns open their now narrow mouths in different parts of it and lead probably to the Sea and also to the Land, as commanding the entry to the harbour it must in ancient times have been very important. About 20 or 30 small boats were busy fishing among the rocks for herrings which are here caught in such plenty during the Season as to supply almost the whole of the County of East Lothian.

From Dunbar we proceeded on foot towards Berwick; our road lay very near the Coast which rendered the walk most delightful; the harvest was pretty well advanced

---

96. Drylawhill?
97. Belhaven.
98. The feared invasion of Great Britain by the French under Napoleon.
99. An old spelling of Firth.

The Diary

and the Crops in this part of the country had the most flattering appearance; a great many rivulets flowed from the neighbouring ridge of Lammermuir, the woods upon their banks and the very elegant bridges over them served much to diversify the scene. The situation of one cottage in particular [drew] both my own and the attention of my friend, it was situated in one of the deep glens formed by a small stream; within a few hundred yards of the sea, and sheltered by a rising ground as well as the wood within which it was embosomed it received all the advantages without any of the inconveniences arising from the neighbourhood of the ocean; its neat clean appearance with the loaden cherry tree upon its end wall tended to increase its effect; upon the whole it was one of those delightful spots which I have rarely met with, which higly [sic] display the taste of the constructor and which I should select for the seat of my future life.—As we approached the Press Inn and ascended the hills which form the boundary between East Lothian and Berwickshire the country began to assume a wilder aspect, the golden plains of Haddington were exchanged for heathery uncultivated moors. No mark except the solitary milestone and a rudely engraven pillar marking the spot where a refractory deserter had been murdered appeared to relieve the eye. After refreshing at the Press Inn with a herring and a Glass of Gin we betook our staffs and again turned our faces towards Berwick though the appearance of the country began to improve it did not in that part which we traversed equal that which we had left. We arrived in Berwick about half past six[100] & I went to bed about ten.

Friday, 31 August 1810

Slept this morning very soundly till a Bell which we supposed to be the six o'clock one was rung. After dressing we went out to view the curiosities about Berwick. The Castle as being the most famous occupied the first part of our attention. It is situated on the West side of the town at the Entry from the Country upon high precipice very extensive at the top it is joined at present to the main land by a long isthmus about a hundred yards long upon which three men might stand abreast. This seems to have been fortified by a strong gate at both extremities a deep ditch has surrounded it on the greater part of which appears to have been supplied with water either from the River Tweed or a pond on the one side of it. On the remaining part the bottom of the rock is washed by the Tweed. The upper part of the rock seems to have been strongly fortified and contains about two acres. One of the Bastion towers seems now to have been converted into a wind mill and the pond mentioned above drives a water wheel nothing can in a more striking degree display the change of manner between this and

---

100. That means he had walked forty miles in about thirteen hours, as well as stopping for breakfast and a walk round Dunbar castle.

the times of Scotland's wars with her more powerful neighbour. Berwick Castle being then the head of power and strength would also be the seat of Gallantry. Its apartments would be the abode of the warriors & the fair; its squares would be crowded with armed Knights & their followers now no foot seemed to tread this once thronged spot, the cow and milkmaid would be perhaps its only regular visitors and the occasional traveller who came to visit its once noble and famed battlements. The ramparts upon which many a head has bled and many a fierce contest been decided now moulder unregarded into dust, and before the end of another century will probably have totally disapeared [*sic*].

Though the situation of the town itself is not by nature strong, every power of art has been executed to render it so. A massy wall surrounds it; its stand upon a piece of ground gently rising from the sea and terminating abruptly towards the upper part of the river and the castle by a steep precipice. The sea washes it on another side and to its inroads is opposed a Mass of building in some parts forty feet thick and generally twenty feet high. There the ramparts are mounted with cannon & a sentry paces his sober round, towards the Land the same wall is continued and its strength is increased by a deep ditch which appears to have been formerly supplied by the pond mentioned above or to have been lately drained into it.

Editor's Epilogue

A few months after the diary ends, Edward Irving, still in Haddington, became tutor to a local doctor's ten-year-old daughter, Jane Welsh. She was eventually to become the wife of Thomas Carlyle, and a significant emotional disturbance for Irving at the time of his marriage.

Towards the end of 1812, again through Sir John Leslie, he was invited to teach in the newly formed school at Kirkcaldy. Here he was to meet the Minister John Martin and his family, including their daughter Isabella. And when a rival school was set up in the town, the new young master, one Thomas Carlyle, became a life-long friend.

William Hazlitt's observed of Edward Irving's preaching that: 'To hear a person spout Shakespeare on the stage is nothing—the charm is nearly worn out—but to hear anyone spout Shakespeare (& that not in a sneaking undertone, but at the top of his voice, with the full breadth of his chest) from a Calvinistic pulpit, is new & wonderful.'[101] Could this theatricality have encouraged the fictitious account by William Leman Rede, writing the Records of a Stage Veteran, in the *New Monthly Magazine* of March 1835, and reported in *The Times* on the 2nd March, that: 'The Rev Edward Irving acted in Ryder's company, in Kirkaldy, a few miles from Edin-

---

101. Hazlitt, *The Spirit of the Age*, 84.

burgh, about 24 years ago, and was then passionately devoted to the stage.' There was certainly a Ryder's company, but there is no evidence of Edward Irving acting with them. Further, Mr Rede had already produced a publication called *Oxberry's Dramatic Biography*, the contents of which were 'entertaining, but intrinsically it has no merit, being correct in neither fact nor chronology.'[102]

There is, however, a true connection between Edward Irving and the stage. Richard Foulkes makes the observation that a young actor by the name of John Henry Brodribb chose for his stage name Henry Irving, 'adopted partly in honour of a celebrated preacher Edward Irving. . . . Obliquity of vision, strangeness of dialect and awkwardness of gait were physical characteristics which Henry Irving shared with his adopted namesake, as he did a fascination with the Satanic. Thus, for Henry Irving, the choice of his stage name may have extended beyond the popular association with preaching to a more powerful sense of identification and a determination to overcome his own physical disadvantages in the profession from which the preacher had been deterred.'[103]

And it is in 1813, at Kirkcaldy, that we next meet Edward Irving.

---

102. Rede, *New Monthly Magazine*, 104.
103. Foulkes, *Church and stage in Victorian England*, 212.

Part II

The Letters

2

The Letters: 1814–1821

Editor's Introduction

As well as the original letters and manuscripts transcribed for this publication, some for the first time, it also includes those that have already been reproduced in print. Mrs Oliphant obtained many original manuscripts from Irving's family, friends, and associates on which she drew for inclusion in *The Life of Edward Irving*, first published in 1862. The Journal and correspondence, except for one or two letters, no longer exist, so we do not know what Mrs Oliphant may have changed or omitted. However what does remain is both necessary and valuable.

'Cometh the man,' the slightly frivolous, adolescent tone of Edward Irving's first letter in this chapter to Robert Story is soon replaced by a more sombre and adult one when he corresponds with people who were to be significant and lifelong associations: the Martin family, Thomas Carlyle, and Dr Thomas Chalmers. The first were to become his in-laws, the second a greatly loved and intimate friend. Thomas Chalmers, whose assistant Irving became, was a remarkable figure in the theological history that was to lead the Disruption of the Scottish Church in 1843. Even Edward's handwriting changes from the script of the schoolroom to the hastier and individualistic fist of one more confident and self assured.

By the end of this budget of correspondence, we leave Edward Irving on the threshold of fame and influence in his life in London and what promised to be the fulfilment of his avowed vocation.

Part II: The Letters

Edward Irving to REV MR MARTIN

[Undated][1]

Dear Sir,

I am truly obliged by your kindness and the trouble which you have taken. Your references and suggestions I shall attend to with care. I think it may be shown with considerable success that the decree[2] was only designed for those of the gentiles who had formerly been proselytes of the Jewish church, and that obedience was required in order to preserve them in the possession of those political and religious privileges to which such according to the law of the Jewish state were entitled. If this were established, it would account for Paul's permitting so very soon after the decision of the Council,[3] the violation of those precepts to which he had then given his consent, and it would also fix precisely the extent, and the period of their continuance to have been till the destruction of the Jewish state. This is the plan which I was proposing to myself to pursue. There is one thing, however, by which I am much graveled.[4] The evidence of Church History on the subject. Tertullian[5] bears testimony to the universal practice of refraining from blood in his time. So do the churches of Lyons & Vienne in their epistle to their sister churches of Asia as preserved by Eusebius.[6] It was so in the time of Bede,[7] at the conversion of the Pomeranians etc. I do not see very well how to remove this stumbling block.

I returned the Bija Gannita[8] which I have not thoroughly examined, principally that it might be out of my reach, for by a singularly unfortunate mistake of my envoy or Chargé d'affaires at the seat of Theological Government I have been doomed unfailingly to prepare one discourse and if possible two before the 24th instant with no longer warning than from Sunday last. This is indeed overwhelming, but it must be done, and of course all less imperious engagements must give way. If it continue at the manse I may at some future period again look into it.

I do not remember whether Mr. Duncan used to call a meeting of the committee for such purposes as that to which the subject of my card [plan] would lead. Perhaps the subject would be attained with less trouble by sending round a notice upon the

---

1. ML, MSS 104a and b.

2. Irving is referring to the decree issued by the Apostles from Jerusalem, setting out the terms on which Gentile converts could be received into the church, and in particular to the requirement to refrain from eating blood (Acts 15:29, cf. 16:4).

3. Council of Jerusalem, which considered whether Gentile converts to Christianity, should be required to observe the Jewish Law. Acts 15.

4. I.e., confounded, perplexed.

5. Tertullian (*c.*60–*c.* 225), early Christian apologist.

6. Eusebius, (*c.*260–*c.*340), Bishop of Caesarea, the 'Father of Church History'.

7. Bede (673–735), historian and scholar. 'The Venerable Bede.'

8. 'Bija Gannita or the Algebra of the Hindus.' An article by Professor John Playfair (1748–1819), Scottish mathematician, extracted from the *Edinburgh Review*, 1813.

subject, if you should see this proper I would easily circulate it by means of the children if it were sent to me by Miss Isabella who by the bye has either a great deal of trouble or a great deal of honour[,] I do not know which she may reckon it, in being made the bearer of all my dispatches.

>I am,
>Dear Sir,
>Yours most truly,
>Edwd Irving

Friday Even^g.

~

Edward Irving to THE MEMBERS OF THE COMMITTEE OF THE KIRKCALDY SUBSCRIPTION SCHOOL

Kirkcaldy, Jany 1814[9]

Gentlemen,

Before the Christmas holidays there was mentioned to me a proposal to extend the basis of our seminary,[10] which, though at first I received it with diffidence, I came afterwards most cordially to approve. The grounds of this approbation, I had then an opportunity of mentioning to the Revd. President and one or two of the subscribers only. And, therefore, viewing the success of the scheme as of infinite importance to the institution, I should feel myself wanting in the confidence I owe to my employers, and in the exertions it becomes me to make for the interest of my charge, were I to refrain from laying before the Committee and, through them, before the subscribers in general[,] those beneficial consequences which, it appears to me, will flow from its being carried into execution.

In doing this, I shall mention in the first place those circumstances, which lead me to consider that some additional assistance is necessary; and then lay before you, as accurately as I can foresee them, those effects which the addition of a new assistant and 25 new scholars would produce.

In the literary department of the school, we have been employed hitherto in laying the foundation: to rear and finish the superstructure is a task of more delicacy and care. The rudiments of the language, when acquired, have to be diligently revised, and, in addition, their application is to be taught and new instruction to be communicated. For doing this last part of our duty, the time formerly devoted to the Class becomes

---

9. ML, MS 91a, b, c, d.

10. The school had been founded in 1812. See Edward Irving to Robert Story, Spring 1813: Oliphant, *Life*, 1:59–61 and footnote. At that time Irving was a master at the school in Haddington where he had tutored the ten-year-old Jane Baillie Welsh.

daily more and more insufficient. The correcting of the exercises written at home, the pointing out the reasons of these corrections, and the Comments upon the beauties and allusions of the authors, and many other things, so necessary towards forming taste and discernment, are things altogether superadded, and require additional time. The labour of retaining the acquisitions we have made is also an increasing burden; and indeed, so fully are my assistant and I engaged that at the present moment, this very important article, we are under the necessity of entrusting to boys—a mode of teaching at all times feeble, but more especially so when, as in our case, we have not time to inspect rigorously the way in which it is discharged. Besides[,] the number of our Latin classes has this year been increased; and there is every probability that before the end of it, another in French will be called for. It is also highly expedient if not absolutely necessary, that without delay a class for the Grammar and Composition of English should be begun. In the *Mathematical* department the same difficulties occur. The present class, as it advances, requires more time to teach it; the use of the instruments is to be explained, and their application taught, by taking the scholars out into the fields and enabling them to perform actual measurements and surveys. Before the end of the year, a respectable part of the school will be fit for forming a new class. In Geography another class will be afterwards called for, and though it is to be hoped that the present one will then be off our hands, yet its attention should be then, if it were profitable, turned to the study of History and the kindred branches of Knowledge. To meet this accumulated number of objects, to which our attention must necessarily be drawn, will be truly a difficult if not an impossible task; and has long been the subject of thought and anxiety to my mind. If they be not attended to, the progress of the seminary must remain in a considerable degree stationary, and, if it be attempted to embrace them all, being necessarily subdivided, and the labour the same, each object must be attained with less success; and therefore the character and utility of the Seminary may be expected to decline.

In anticipating the effects with which the projected extension of the school might be attended, it naturally occurs, first, that the addition of a third teacher would enable us to meet the increased demand for exertion, and, I doubt much, whether the additional assistance thus conferred would be more than adequate to that end. This remark acquires its full force, when it is known that the addition of 25 or 30 new scholars would be attended with an increase of labour proportionately small. This fact, at first sight so paradoxical, arises from the peculiar circumstances of the school which I shall now explain. A Latin class just begun would receive all those who had not already commenced, or had not advanced far in that study: and others whose progress was considerably in advance would join one of the two higher classes. An Arithmetic class also only commenced a week or two ago, and would take in such as might be judged fit for that study. Those who might wish to learn Geography, could, from the disunited nature of that study, join the class in any stage of its progress.—Such again as might be designed for Mathematics would obtain that object at no distant period; when the portion of the school to which I have already alluded are fit to commence. Nor is this a delay of which any person would complain, for so many new objects put into the hands of young people at once serve only to confuse, and the doing it can only be justified by necessity. Those who might wish to cultivate the study of French will meet the class which I have said, must speedily be called for.—There can therefore only be a few English scholars who can engage separate attention, and that only for a while, for it will not be long before they are brought into a state to join the other classes. Thus then it is not difficult to foresee that, except in the way of increasing the numbers of each class, which within the limitations to which it is in this case restricted I have no hesitation in pronouncing an advantage, the proposed alteration will place at my disposal a third more exertion without increasing in any sensible degree the work to be done; or, in other words, that it will be all gain to the institution.

In addition to these things, I am of [the] opinion, that were my time less fully occupied in the school, had I a few minutes occasionally to spare, I could by superintending more carefully than I am at present permitted, the operations going on in the different parts of the school give more vigour and effect to our exertions.—It seems also not impossible to arrange the teaching hours of the new assistant so that he might be at hand to aid the pupils in making out the difficulties of their tasks, an advantage which, if it could be attained, would be very considerable. These are the circumstances which lead me to approve of the proposed change; and I have been minute in detailing them as I conceive the object to be exceedingly important.

It is perhaps scarcely necessary to add to Gentlemen whose liberality I have so often witnessed and of which I would be understood to convey not the slightest suspicion, that I am most willing to undertake the additional charge without any increase of the salary allowed me by our original bargain.

I am,
Gentlemen,
With the greatest respect yours,
Edwd Irving

Kirkcaldy.
Jany 1814.

Mr. William Douglas
Mr. Alex^r Malcolm
Mr. Hugh Aiken
Mr. Robert Kirk
Mr. George Beveridge
Mr. Ebenezer Rutherford
Mr. Edward Lang

Kirkcaldy 17th Jany 1814. The subscribers to the school under the charge of Mr. Irving are respectfully requested to peruse & consider the representation contained in the preceding pages, that they may be fully prepared to judge of the subject of it, should it be thought expedient to call another general meeting for that purpose.—The subscribers whose names stand above, will be so good as to circulate this copy among themselves.

Jo[hn] Martin P[rincipal].

⁓

Edward Irving to REV JOHN MARTIN

Kirkcaldy, Monday, 25th December 1815.[11]

Dear Sir,

I did not receive your letter of Saty Evening till this morning—I think there is hardly one motive or consideration in it which I have not weighed with all the candour I could bring to the subject—and after all my resolution is the same. If the Academy be dissolved; the interests of my numerous charges will be grievously endangered—but if those interests weigh any thing, or the advantage conferred by my instruction be of any esteem, why should such a catastrophe be feared? And if there be so much unsound materials in the Academy as from the present circumstance to endanger its stability believe me, that though your efforts and those of my friends be able to prop it for the present, it must eventually and speedily fall. Why then attempt to support a thing which will not support itself? But supposing that there were in the institution sufficient vigour to remove all cause of alarm, and resist those attempts which are aired and then made against it; what better way in all the world can be taken to destroy even this, than that I should hear and respect all those complaints which disappointment in the progress of their children—disaffection to the prosperity of the institution or ill-grounded dissatisfaction of any man may prompt any one to make and this too though I myself be convinced of the utter groundlessness of such complaints. Why Sir[,] Mr. Greig has done the institution all the ill in his power. He has made the cause of his vexation known with as great an avidity as if the justice of his cause or its success depended upon the numbers that he could get to applaud his own conduct or reproach that of his opponent. He has spread it till I am persuaded that not only my Employers and my pupils do every one of them know it; but almost every one of the town to whom his influence or rather his voice can extend. I do not say that his own tongue has given it so extensive a circulation, but it can only be by his influence and agency. The question therefore is now no longer a private dispute between Mr. Greig and me, but a struggle for my authority in the school with my pupils, out of it with my employers, and every where for my publick character. All this from one who must have known that

---

11. Letter source: ML, MS 89a, b, c, d, e.

I had ample cause for refusing the satisfaction he demanded, to one who had been by him most grievously injured formerly in those very matters in which I doubt not that he may think, I have injured him, to one too who has borne the gross insults of his letter in silence and shewed them to no man living. All this too for the puny matter of pulling a boy's years [sic],[12] who did he receive the chastisement which would do him good, would receive more in one day than for some time back he has got in a week. At this moment when I write that boy, an original scholar of the Academy is asked by his Teacher the nom.[inative] pl.[ural] of *rex*, answer *regi*; again answer *regia*,[13] again nothing at all but obstinate silence. And yet forsooth all this must go for nothing in estimating the feelings and actions of a teacher—this the boy, whose safety is endang[er]ed by pulling his ears, and whose life must be guarranteed [sic] from a man 'destitute of Christian or human principle or feeling' by an express deputation of the general meeting—this same the creature who has excited a storm that threatens to blow into ruins an institution in which flourish the education of almost a hundred, and in which their future prosperity is in no small degree embarked—but this paragraph has drawn me from my duty to the school. Looking at the subject on Christian principles, I own at once that it is both my duty and Mr. Greig's to forgive each other, and make every sacrifice of personal feeling to maintain public peace and secure publick [sic] good. This as an individual is my duty; but as the head of an institution I question whether it does not receive some modification. What respectability can I retain, what influence can I command, not to say what enjoyment can I have in my life, if I do not take means to preserve them; nay if I take those steps which must have the very opposite tendency. By such a way of treating the subject, I might gain more of your esteem and of theirs who know the motives and at the same time know to appreciate them; but by the greater number it would be stigmatized as silliness or construed into an acknowledgment of a bad cause; which impression however false in fact is just as prejudicial to my interests [–] which are in the long return the very interests of my Employers—as if it were accurately true. I am sure you can see this remark to be dictated by regard to the interests of the Seminary, not by any courting of popular opinion, or any desire to screen improper conduct from exposure or shelter it when exposed—I scarcely know what a general meeting could do or has power to do if it were called—and I think truly that those of my Employers who may view a dissolution of the Academy [as] so much a matter of course, feel very little the strength in our country of positive engagements or can very easily indeed emancipate themselves from their obligations. If Mr. Greig has brought himself into an engagement and his pride or bad temper has made that engagement a dilemma, I do not think that he should be helped out of it at the expense

12. Irving means 'ears.' Mrs. Oliphant observes: 'A young man of twenty, with the full charge of a large number of boys and girls, in a limited space, and undertaking all the items of a miscellaneous education, no doubt needed the assistance of a somewhat rigorous discipline, and it is evident that he used its help with much freedom.... These severe measures, however, no means obliterate the pleasanter recollection with which Irving's pupils recall his reign at the academy.' Oliphant, *Life*, 1:52–53.

13. Correct answer, *reges*.

Part II: The Letters

of the institution or its teacher. It is folly to talk of security for the safety of his children, and it would have entered into the head of none but one whose ill-management of his family had brought him to pay for their education when they were absent, for a great part of last year. When he constituted me their Teacher or associated himself to that body which so constituted me did he not express confidence in me, and surrender the management of his children into my hand, in so far as it is surrendered according to the practice of other schools, and the support which the law of the country gives to that practice, or rather in so far as that management is yielded to me by the contract of which he is one of the principals—and to be informed of this—let him consult the first Article. I have just one objection to the referring of the matter, because it is making too much *fuss* about the matter and because it is too tedious and clumsy a way of settling every dispute that ill judging or ill disposed people may originate and because it affords too little publicity to the conclusion of a business which he has already made publick [*sic*], and too much room for misrepresentation and misstatement. It is with me indispensable that the proposal for such a mode of accommodation should come from him who has already thrown out the threat of a committee meeting and a general meeting and an action. None of which I shrink from for a moment, not that I wish to continue quarrel and prevent reconciliation—much less to endanger the stability of an institution in which surely I am most of all concerned—but because I wish to retain that attitude which is necessary for the security not of myself but of the institution—that degree of dignity which may place me above being the object of vulgar attacks—and believe me not an iota higher.—But I perceive that when I write I am apt to declaim. And at all events, I feel not the confidence which attends private conference. If you have not therefore done too much for one who is altogether unworthy of your services—would you do me the honour of conversing with me an hour or two [to] night, and of advising me in some matters regarding my future conduct. Mr. Pears[14] also has a load of anxieties to pour into your breast.—Would you do us the pleasure therefore of eating a salt herring with us to-night at 9 o'clock; [15] and, if you could come an hour or so sooner it would be an additional favour to

       Dear Sir,
       Yours with great Gratitude & Esteem,
       Edwd Irving

 Monday, 25th Dec 1815

  14. John Pears (1790–1866), who accompanied Irving and Carlyle on a walking tour through parts of Scotland in 1817. (Carlyle calls him Piers.) He is described as "Irving's house-mate or even landlord, Schoolmaster of Abbotshall, i.e., of *"the Links,"* or *southern extra-burghal* part of Kirkcaldy, a cheerful scatterbrained creature, who went ultimately as Preacher or Professor of something to the Cape of Good Hope." See Carlyle, *Reminiscences,* 230. In 1829 Pears accepted a call from a Scottish Church in South Africa. He became a professor of classics at South African College, Cape Town, where he taught for five years. In 1836 he joined the Dutch Reformed Church as a minister. The town of Pearston is named after him. See CL, 2:200 n.

  15. An invitation, which it would appear, Dr Martin did accept, judging by Edward Irving's letter dated the next day, which follows.

Addressed to: The Rev John Martin, Kirkcaldy.

Edward Irving to THE REV JOHN MARTIN

Kirkcaldy, 26th December 1815[16]

Dear Sir,

Again I return you my most unfeigned thanks for your most excellent letter.—But my mind is now made up. I have yielded till I can yield no longer—I am persuaded that in the Kingdom there is not a school in which so much good is done with less punishment, than has been in ours for the last year. A simple apology to Mr. Greig would have prevented all the consequences which may ensue, that apology I refused to give—both because I judged it unnecessary, and because it was asked in a most unbecoming tone.—Let the committee or general meeting be called, or let an action be raised, I shall abide the result. And whatever that may be, much rather receive it, than be doomed to receive the scurrilous abuse of every man who can take offence and vent it in a speech or a letter. I would send you Mr. Greig's letter but I do not wish that you who have had so much trouble should have any more on my account. I would like to see the sense of a general meeting regarding my conduct—it is indeed necessary that I should know it. Though I am conscious to myself of many defects, and it becomes me not therefore to boast, I am also conscious of the services that I have rendered to one and all of my Employers. And let the one be balanced against the other.[17]

> With the warmest gratitude I am,
> Dear Sir,
> Yours truly,
> Edwd Irving

Addressed to: Revd. John Martin,
Kirkcaldy.

---

16. Letter source: ML, MS 90a,b,c.

17. Whether there was a disciplinary meeting or not, the outcome of the complaint against Edward Irving must have been positive as he did not resign from the school until the summer of 1818 to move to Edinburgh so that he could pursue his ecclesiastical career. See Oliphant, *Life*, 1:77.

Part II: The Letters

Edward Irving to THE REV JOHN MARTIN

Duff's Lodgings, 35 Bristo Street, [Edinburgh].
31st March 1819[18]

My Dear Sir,

You will be surprised to find me where I was a year ago, bent upon a tour to the continent at my own charges and for my own behoof—that is to say, if the kind intention & exertions of your Brother-in-Law should fail of their object.—In that I have taken no steps since I saw you, except to write a letter to Mr. Walker declining the task which, in a manner, I had fixed for myself of removing the amiable but false delicacy of Sir Charles. On contemplating this more closely it appeared to me rather forward to take or to seem to take, any part in an arrangement with which I was perfectly unconnected, or rather more delicately situated still, by having a connection in prospect.—At the same time in declining this I shewed, in order that Mr. W might have it in his power to shew to others if he saw good, that I had thought upon the subject of a young Nobleman's tuition on a tour, and rapidly sketched, by the way of shewing what might be done, that which from feelings of delicacy I could not permit myself to fill up or formally to present.—To this letter I have had no reply, and am so full of business as never to have thought what may be the cause of the delay, or whether it may have any cause at all.

At present however my plan is this, to gather in all the ways and means I can raise and convert them into a Bank bill or Letter of Credit by the beginning of May; and sometime in that month to proceed to Paris by way of Rotterdam,—After dissipating amid the luxury & science of Paris six weeks to find myself at the Boulevards, my knapsack on my back, and my face to Geneva, either by way of Basle or Lyons—to pass there a week with the shades and recollections of the wise & the great & the free, and after standing upon the fields of Murat & Cappel & Sempach,[19] to descend by the Borromean Isles to Florence[,] that birthplace of modern literature and fine arts—thence to the 'Niobe of nations.'[20]—And to Naples—by sea to Sicily—and after looking into the Crater of Etna to take ship I reckon about the beginning of Nov either for Marseilles or Venice as I shall then judge it better, to study the winter in Paris or at a German University.—Once more next spring to disembark in Kirkcaldy bay & clasp friends endeared by time & distance—And what then? Without a penny in my

---

18. Letter source: ML, MS 100a,b,c,d.

19. The 'fields' Edward Irving is referring to are battlefields.

Joachim Murat (1767–1815) was one of Napoleon's generals. He conducted campaigns in Austria and Egypt, married Napoleon's sister Caroline and was King of Naples from 1808 to 1815. After Napoleon's fall he was eventually captured and executed by firing squad. See Cole, *The Betrayers*, 99, 250–51.

The battle of Cappel took place on 11 October 1531. During it Ulrich Zwingli (1484–1531), the Swiss Protestant reformer, was killed.

The battle of Sempach took place in 1386 during the emancipation of Switzerland.

20. I.e., Rome. 'The Niobe of nations! there she stands Childless and crownless, in her voiceless woe.' Byron, *Childe Harold's Pilgrimage*, 4th canto, verse 78, lines 1 and 2.

pocket, or still worse without having gained a single step upon a church what then? Why shortly to follow the teaching & the Student life no longer, but betake myself with heart and hand to the preaching of the Gospel, to seek for the first assistancy that is open, and to give myself to the only duty which is congenial to my mind, the preaching of the Gospel to a congregation of immortal beings.—This I think I shall not find it difficult to obtain, for I find it is very much slighted by our great men who here employ their greatness in curing the ignorance & brooking the insults of misguided children. But if that cannot be obtained[,] once more to join them in their noble calling. But by the aid of my friends, which I intend to lay in requisition before I embark, I shall obtain the object of my wishes to have the honour of preaching the Word, and obtaining along with that honour the wherewithal to exist.—And so I trust I shall be content to continue, till Providence sees meet to call me to a charge of my own that is to a higher salary and independence or the power of being idle without penalty—& if he see not meet there to abide until I be called, where surely the pious wishes of the soul shall need no patron to get themselves embodied in execution.

So, you perceive, the ends of my life are laid together, and in a manner which most would laugh at, which I cherish with much fondness. Some things it does not take in, and those the dearest to every heart, the happiness of a home to inhabit, of a companion to bless it—a great commission doubtless, and in no case more than in mine, for I am fond of domestic happiness to excess.—But His will be done—I must not, I cannot yield myself to the lowness of mind which has taken possession of my brethren—I can not live this life of inaction.—Something I must do—either flatter some great one's vanity & bear his contumely, swear by some powerful man's party—or pursue the course I have sketched.—This better part I have chosen—it is my own choice.—And I am happy in it.—And in despite of all the singleness & poverty which attend it, I must pursue till He shall see good to say it is enough.—And then my heart shall no longer be widowed of its dearest enjoyments.—Till then I must abide in the faithful discharge of duty though there be few earthly comforts to attend it.

Such is the *beau ideal* of my future live [*sic*][;] there is in it no high colouring of prosperity, no deep shading of adversity—it contains no objects of great ambition, and can suffer no keen disappointments.—All it calls for is force of character to maintain my opinion, and that calmly, that it is every way more honourable to maintain the integrity of ones mind and do for £70 or £80 a year that duty for which with suppleness or management one might have had £200 or £300.—I see difficulties in execution, I may have to bear the whim of some testy or regardless old man, whose self esteem has made every thing without that routine in which he has stayed all his life, appear as a deviation from what is right—but when the building up of the faith & consolation & piety of 8 or 900 people depends upon it, there is something for which to bear the humours of the most testy. –

The length of this letter shews you I know you are able to peruse it. Oh be careful of yourself for the sake of your family & your flock. I have not made use of your

Part II: The Letters

kind letter to Mr. Paul in the uncertainty of my long continuance. Pears writes me to get him some instruments & draw on you for the amount, but does not say for how much—and I cannot set the little money I have afloat.—Would you be kind enough to take the earliest opportunity of informing me. –

I desire to be remembered with all love to your household, and, however unworthy, to have an interest in your prayers.

Yours with the greatest esteem & affection,
Edwd Irving

Addressed to: Revd. John Martin,
Manse, Kirkcaldy.

~

Edward Irving to THOMAS CARLYLE

Edinburgh, 4th June 1819[21]

Dear Sir,

My apology for neglecting you so long is that I have been equally negligent of myself. By what fatality I know not, I have been so entirely devoted to idleness or to insignificant Employments since you left me that German, Italian & every other study useful or serious have been relinquished. Perhaps this renewal of our intercourse may be the date of my awakening from my slumber, as the breaking up of our intercourse was the date of its commencement. To speak of myself[,] that most grateful of topics, is therefore out of the question, as that would only be to expose the day-dreams of this my lethargy to one whose active mind has no sympathy with listlessness and drowsiness. And this subject being excluded where shall I find materials for this letter.

I could detail to you the mineralogy of the Campsey [Campsie] hills and tell you of the overlaying formation of porphyry above the green-stone, and of the horrizontal [sic] bed of limestone in the green stone which supplies the greater part of Stirling, Dumbarton & Strathearn. And of a curious quarry of stone which is carried far & near for building stoves & setting grates on account of its singular virtue of resisting heat—but well I know you are weary unto death of such jargons. And I could narrate to you one most sentimental incident that did befal [sic] me on that journey—whereby hangs a tale which might furnish matter for a novel or even a modern tragedy—but then I suspect you have already put me down for an adventure-hunter, which is too near a stage to a story-teller to fall in with my fancy. Now the truth is, to throw in a word in self defence, if I have a turn for the romantic, it is not for the vanity of being the actor of a strange part or the spouter of a strange tale in the various scenes of the great

---

21. Letter source: NLS, MS 665, fol. 20.

drama of this mortal state—but rather to be a spectator of those who are so, more especially if they be unfortunate withal, and occasionally I confess to have the privilege of the antient chorus of moralising a little or rather not a little upon the passing events—and occasionally to reach an admonition or consolation to the suffering hero or heroine of the piece. But see! I am letting you into some of the vagaries which came and went across my fancy during the interval of apathy which has passed away since I was separated from your conversation for which I have not yet found a substitute.

And I could dwell upon the rich harvest of insight into character which I gathered from the debates of the General Assembly,[22] and of the lack of genius and honesty which took from its value, and of the rankness and superfluity of vulgarity & bad-temper & party zeal which were as the thistles & rag-worts and tares of the crop—but that I know your mind is incurious of these things engaged as it is with much higher contemplations.

Of the men of Edin & their employments I know as little as of those of Canton in China—save that Christison[23] rather inclines to fall in with Lord Lauderdale's[24] views of the Bullion Question than the Committee's, and that he is sure as ever all men alive have mistaken the meaning of Aristotle which it seems is wonderfully wrapped up in the power of the particle EU. And that Galloway[25] is as ill-bred as ever, stares as full, and wears his hair hanging over the ample circumference globular skull, as usual, like the thatch of these round rustic Chinese-roofed cottages which Gentlemen sometimes plant at the outer gates of their grounds. As to Dickson,[26] he plays quoits with Charters and at times with me, and has got his mouth filled, always filled, with wit at me for admiring these beautiful lines of Milton's hymn on the nativity: 'It was no season then for her (nature,)[27] To wanton with the Sun her lusty paramour.'[28]

I need not tell you where the wit lies. And you know when he is primed any thing will do for a match. He is just in the predicament of a Spring-gun in a garden

22. The General Assembly is the highest court of authority in the Church of Scotland, meeting in Edinburgh each May.

23. Alexander Christison, a classics professor at Edinburgh University, had been one of Irving's referees when he successfully applied for the post of a master at the newly formed Mathematical School in Haddington in 1810.

24. James Maitland, 8th Earl of Lauderdale (1754-1839). He supported a report of a House of Lord's Secret Committee who was against a return to cash payments. Because of the high price of bullion in 1810 a House of Commons Select Committee was appointed to enquire into the matter. It was fund that the Bank was over-issuing notes and to resolve the situation it was advised that cash payment in gold suspended by Pitt in 1797 should be resumed. In 1819 the House of Commons agreed to this. See Briggs, *The Age of Improvement*, 168, 204.

25. 'He came in company with one Galloway—a small dogmatical teacher of Mathematics—a wrangler of the first order—of brutal manner, and a terror to those embryo philosophers which (or rather who) frequent the backshop of David Brown': Thomas Carlyle to Robert Mitchell, 27 November 1818. CL 1:149.

26. See 39n, page 73.

27. An editorial insert added by Irving.

28. Milton, 'Ode on the Morning of Christ's Nativity,' stanza 5, lines 35-36.

which has ropes in every direction. You cannot stir a foot—but twitching of one of its ropes—round it turns full-mouthed upon you, and hit or miss off it goes to the no small wonder if not dismay of the unfortunate wight.[29] Weary then not, My Dear Carlisle, of the Country. I am here in the midst of the busy world, and its business only interrupts me, and would vex me if I would let it fill up with the softness of rural beauty and the sincerity of rural manners, the contentment of rural life, those strong impressions of nature and of men which are already in your mind, till the pictures become more mellow and joyous and yield to yourself more delight in forming & to others more pleasure in viewing them. I would I were along with you to charm the melancholy of solitude & in your company to carry my eye into those marks of beneficence and love which every part of nature exhibits & win from the contemplation of them a portion of that beneficence so that the restless and evil passions of my heart might be charmed if not shamed into repose, and I might go forth again into the world of busy spirits, resolved to mar the enjoyment of no one, but in my little sphere to do all the good it would allow—to wish for a wider sphere, and to live in hope of that wider & better existence which when it is revealed I pray that you & I and all we love, and should love, may be prepared for. Don't be so tardy in writing me as I have been in writing you. Arrange the place of a correspondence which may be useful to us both. You proposed it first—and now I reckon myself entitled to press it. Remember me kindly to your Father and Mother and to Sandy[30] & the others—to your friends, Johnstone[31] & Mitchell,[32] and any you think take an Interest in

    Your faithful friend,
    Edwd Irving

29. Luckless creature.

30. Alexander Carlyle (1797–1876), brother of Thomas Carlyle.

31. James Johnstone, nicknamed the 'Targer.' Born before 1795, he died late in 1837. He was married to Carlyle's cousin Janet Carlyle, and was head of the parochial school at Haddington from 1826–37. See CL, 1:4 n.

32. Robert Mitchell (c.1795–1836). At this time he was living as a tutor with Henry Duncan, minister of Ruthwell, near Annan. Eventually he was elected classics master of the new Edinburgh Academy, where he taught until his death. See CL, 1:6 n.

Allen's[33] Kind Compliments & Dickson who has lately discovered Pym[34] & Hampden[35] & Hollis[36] & St. John[37] to be a pack of Scoundrels.

Addressed to: Mr. Thomas Carlyle,
Mr. James Carlyle,
Mainhill by Ecclefechan.

~

Edward Irving to THOMAS CARLYLE

35 Bristo St., [Edinburgh,] 16th July 1819[38]

Dear Carlyle,

You must not scold because I am irregular. I have been preaching at such a rate as to have excited no small speculation in this Mighty City, but as I have been dwelling on that Topick [sic] in a letter to Brown (honest fellow!) I have no patience with any more of it. So has Dixon.[39] By the bye, did you ever see another mind constituted like Dixon's—he seems to me to have no faculty of reasoning except through the medium of sensible representation. All reasoning is doubtless a series of comparisons, but not of similitudes which are commonly said (though incorrectly) to prove nothing. Now Dixon is similitude from beginning to end—and he seems to restrain no step of his process unless it either has a similitude to support it, or indeed he is content at any time to have a similitude for a step—this, I am convinced, is the true solution of the difficulty we have so often found in dealing with him in argument. You have no sooner stated the proposition than his mouth he opes—and out there flies a hope. Then when you are busy shewing its mal-application, before you are done, he opes again and out

---

33. Matthew Allen (1783-1845), a turbulent character who had been a troublesome youth and was about to be appointed apothecary to the York Asylum on the recommendation of his sorely tried brother Oswald. Later in life he met Tennyson and inveigled him to invest in his newly conceived idea of a wood carving machine. It was a disaster and they lost a great deal of money. See CL, 1:250 n.

34. John Pym, leader of the parliamentary group opposed to Charles I.

35. John Hampden together with John Pym headed a group who challenged Charles I authority in 1640 in the Long Parliament to raise money for him to purchase supplies for the army. See Fisher, *A History of Europe*, 652 and 653.

36. Thomas Hollis (1720-74), English political philosopher and author.

37. There are a couple of possible candidates for Dickson's disapproval: (1) John St John (1793), politician and fop; (2) Henry St John, 1st Viscount Bolingbroke, British Tory politician and political philosopher. He was foreign secretary 1710-14 and a Jacobite conspirator. His books, such as *Idea of a Patriot King* and *The Dissertation upon Parties*, laid the foundations for nineteench-century Toryism.

38. Letter source: NLS, MS 1764, fols. 153-56.

39. Frank Dickson, who Carlyle describes as 'a most quizzing, merry, entertaining, guileless and unmalicious man' but who eventually came to a sad end. See *Reminiscences*, 243-46.

comes another. And so it is like trying to bind Proteus[40] to reason him to a finale—it is not reasoning but a most laborious tasks of solving Enigmas, or which is worse of disentangling and exposing the hypothetical solution which another's ingenuity would torture into a true one. Add to this, the incongruity & ludicrousness of the similitudes, and their entire strangeness and foreignness to those which are naturalised in the republic of letters, and which raise the laugh so readily to incommode one in this business of deciphering these unnatural hieroglyphs, and you have a complete explanation of the utter unprofitableness of besieging him with argument, and the sense of weariness though never of discomfiture, with which you retire.

Pears has reappeared on this busy stage, and with as much business on hand as usual—he has again got-a-going at Kirkcaldy & Abbotshall, and after serving their turns is once more at work in the metropolis. I am happy to see him in such good trim after his hard service in the South—he is well mounted and equipped, has taken on none of the novelties of more favoured skies—but is to be found in the exact trim and condition in which we knew him with so much delight. I am really happy to find him in such good heart—about every thing. I am to give him a touch at the Italian—but he is so full of employment that I fear it will be hardly a touch. He looks for us at the Examination of his School, and I confess to you, I see nothing very unfeasible in the scheme—if it could be brought to bear I need not say how much delight it would afford me to coast along the border line, and visit the retreats of that people famed like Homer's heroes as 'tamers of Horses'[41] η/ο ιπποδαμοσ Νησος and issue upon the fat plains of Northumberland. But more of this when we meet.

Peter's Letters appeared yesterday, and they lie waiting my perusal. So you see the sacrifice I am making, nevertheless I shall fill every particle of this sheet. Three volumes 8vo.[42] Lockhart[43] is understood to be the author. It contains about a dozen or twenty etchings of our most notable savants and literary men—from Playfair down to Jameson[44] on the one hand[,] from W. Scott down to Hogg[45] on the other. Galloway is for having an immediate Syndic[46] appointed over the Edin press, it has become so licentious. Poor Playfair, by the way, is thought dying. The new tales seemed to be

---

40. Proteus was another 'Old Man of the Sea'. He was the son of Oceanus and Tethys, and his duty was to guard Poseidon's herd of seals. He also had oracular powers and to escape a captor could metamorphose into different shapes such as an animal, water, a tree. See *DCM*, 377.

41. The *Iliad*, Homer. See *OCEL*.

42. 8vo: the size of a book whose pages are made by folding a sheet of paper three times to form eight leaves—eightvo, octavo. www.thefreedictionary.com/8vo. Accessed 26 June 2012.

43. John Gibson Lockhart (1794–1854), a contributor to *Blackwood's Magazine*. From 1825 to 1853 he was editor of *The Quarterly Review*, and his nickname, 'The Scorpion,' reflected his acerbic criticisms. His sketches of life in Edinburgh and Glasgow, *Peter's Letters to His Kinfolk*, were published in 1919. See *OCEL*.

44. Robert Jameson (1774–1862), Professor of Natural History at Edinburgh University.

45. James Hogg (1770–1835), called the 'Ettrick Shepherd' as he had been a shepherd in Ettrick Forest. His literary talent was discovered by Sir Walter Scott who became his lifelong friend. See *OCEL*.

46. Delegate appointed to control the press.

already as a tale that is told—and Byron's Mazippa[47] seems to have made little or no diversion in the literary field. I never saw so much paper thrown away on such a subject. An adulterer taken in the act is stripped & lashed to a wild untamed horse, and the twosome set adrift upon the wide & desolate plains of Poland. They see no human habitation or human being but run till they fall down; both of them finished, & so finishes a poem of near 1000 lines.

I have been employed lately in reading Alfieri's[48] tragedies; his style is certainly very peculiar. Contriving in general to involve and disentangle the whole plot by the help of four or five characters. There are consequently no room for those necessary personages in the French Drama—le confident et la confidante.[49] Nor has he recourse much to the other alternative of soliloquies. There is accordingly not much intricacy, and they fail in exciting a great deal of interest—but in their composition they are very chaste and classical—have much more of freedom than the French school—but want the busy movement and the splendid poetry of Shakespeare. Indeed there is little or none of that abstract and lofty speculation upon the nature and vanities of our existence which gives such a charm to our great bard by shewing to every man who has thought at all—the living picture of his own thoughts & the reality of his own hallucinations, spread over with a light which gives them distinctness and glory without rendering them confused. But I am getting beyond my depth—this was introduced to say that you may have a vol[ume] when you please.

I mean to proceed by Glencoe and Staffa, Ferguson[50] will accompany me I think—then cross to Ireland and if I can get a vessel to the Solway firth come home that way—if not by Port Patrick. I will be home by the end of August. Write me, I pray, soon and let me know all the bearings of your thoughts. This was intended to have been the subject of this letter—but it never occurred to me till now. So it must be reserved. Kind respects to your Father's family and to our mutual friends

Your faithful friend,
Edw[d] Irving
Addressed to: Mr. Thomas Carlyle,
Mainhill by Ecclefechan.

~

47. Published in 1818.
48. Vittorio Alfieri (1749–1803), Italian tragedian and poet.
49. Keeper of male and female secrets.
50. John Fergusson (1792–1859), son of a farmer at Conachan, Glenalmond, Perthshire. He assisted Irving when he was teaching at Kirkcaldy. Like Carlyle, he did not enjoy teaching; nevertheless that became his career, teaching at both the Academy of Arbroath from 1821 to 1830 and then as rector of the Kelso Grammar School, Roxburghshire. See CL, 1:168 n.

Part II: The Letters

Edward Irving to THOMAS CARLYLE

Glasgow, 25th September 1819[51]

My Dear Carlyle,

I have written to Mrs. Duff and received her answer to-day in which she says—'the back room is empty, the rent is 6 shillings and 6d with coals—if your friend thinks of taking it I will thank you to let me know.' It is this which makes me so prompt in my correspondence; for, otherwise I should have been busy at my Sermon for to-morrow-week, having been so much fortunately relieved this first Sunday by Andrew Thomson who is to introduce Dr Chalmers.

I am fairly introduced to the Dr's duty, and certainly I never saw or heard of a parish[,] much less a town parish, organised and attended to in such a way before. He visits from house to house, and by acts of duty purely religious has contrived to establish himself in the affections of many of the very outcasts of human society whom I have visited along with him, and such a strength, as he is neither established in the admiration of the literary nor religious public. He has published the first number of his periodical work,[52] containing an exposé of the university affair, and of his disputings with the Glasgow institutions—he fears he has committed to the public too much of his private affairs—indeed you would be astonished how much of alarm he has on this head—he has little of the Stoic in him.

I have nothing at hand to say, and I dare not strike into any topic away from the immediate subjects of my present meditations of which my head is at present so full, and on which so much depends.

But I am looking about me and by & bye shall have to communicate anything peculiar about this capital. Meantime I shall be happy to hear from you on general matters. With regards to the room I think you had better correspond with Mrs. Duff directly.

With respects to all your family,
      I am, Dear Sir,
      Yours faithfully,

Edwd Irving
Glasgow—Mrs. McCall's, 34 Kent St.,
25th Sept 1819.
Addressed to: Mr. Thomas Carlyle,
Mainhill, Ecclefechan.

---

51. NLS, MS 1764, fol. 163–64.

52. Chalmers's new quarterly magazine *Christian and Civic Economy*. Together with his friend and church elder, William Collins, Chalmers had contributed to the finance of a new publishing house to promote the issue's quarterly circulation. See Stewart J. Brown, *Thomas Chalmers and the Godly Commonwealth in Scotland*, 145. Collins also encouraged Irving to publish his *Farewell Discourse to the Congregation and Parish of St John's Glasgow*. See Grass, *The Lord's Watchman*, 49.

Edward Irving to ROBERT LUNDIE[53]

Glasgow, 34 Kent St., 17th December 1819[54]

Dear Sir,

I am very much honoured by the confidence of your letter, and were any thing wanting to make the case of Mr. Herbertson's sister,[55] so affecting in itself, an object of attention and interest to me, that were supplied by the circumstance of its being recommended to me by one of whose benevolence and good-heartedness I have heard so much.

His sister's case, he will tell you, has turned out better than he anticipated, still however it may grow worse again, and in that case I have made a free offer of my counsel and aid to her, and I shall give it when called for in all the prudence I am possessed of. She is now in Dr Dewar's parish—to whom however I shall take it on me to make it known, and recommend it to his Christian Sympathy. Also I shall see, if possible, by my own private acquaintance with the Gentleman who directs that district of Sabbath Schools, to bring it about that the two children shall have religious instruction.

Our town is still in much fear though in great quietness. I am visiting the worst parts of it, and find more cordial entertainment[; I] would fain hope things have not passed out of the range of ordinary management and remedies. But the general fear is only equaled [sic] by the general ignorance.

I am happy to be remembered by Mrs. Lundie of whose further acquaintance I am exceeding ambitious. Meanwhile pray she may accept the best wishes of one who is almost a stranger—but who has to you and to her the honour of subscribing himself
An affectionate Wellwisher,
Edwd Irving

---

53 51 Rev Robert Lundie (1774-1832), Minister of Kelso from 1807. See Scott, *Fasti* New Vol 2.72.

54. NLS, MS 9848; fol. 143.

55. There is a letter of Thomas Carlyle's that mentions a scandal concerning 'Herbert-son and Caven.' The lady in question was Herbertson's sister about whom Carlyle comments 'She must have been *une chose tres piquante* [a very saucy titbit] who could kindle such a fire in Mr C's kidneys—a fire that was *roasting* his reins and pertinence before he fell—and I shall only add *Cave vel Caveto tu* [underscored twice; 'Take care or you shall have to take care']. Do you know any thing of what has been 'the holy lecher's' fate?—a wanderer on the face of the earth—every one that findeth him shall *geld* him!': Thomas Carlyle to Robert Mitchell, 24 October 1814: CL, 1:31-32.

A footnote to Carlyle's letter observes, 'Samuel Caven seems to have been Mitchell's predecessor at Ruthwell (where he was teaching the family and boarders of Dr. Henry Duncan) and to have got into some sort of scandalous liaison. Herbertson may be the woman involved in the scandal.'

For Robert Mitchell see letter Edward Irving to Thomas Carlyle, 4 June 1819: NLS, MS 665; fol. 20 n.

Part II: The Letters

>Addressed to: Revd. Rob Lundie,
>Kelso.
>Hand by Mr. Herbertson.

∼

Edward Irving to THOMAS CARLYLE

34 Kent St., Glasgow, 26th December 1819[56]

Dear Carlyle,

I think it right to write you in whatever trim I may be, lest you may think, that present friends make me forget those that are absent. I pray that you may prosper in your legal studies, and nothing can hinder you from prospering, provided only you will give your mind to take in all the elements which enter into the question of the obstacles. But remember it is not want of knowledge alone that impedes, but want of instruments for making that knowledge available. This you know better than me. Now, my view of this matter is that your knowledge[,] likely very soon to surpass in accuracy & extent most of your compeers, is to be made saleable not by the usual way of adding friend to friend in the usual way of society which neither you nor I are enough patient of—but by a way of your own. Known you must be before you can be employed. Known you will not be for a winning, attaching, accomodating [*sic*] man, but for an original, commanding & rather self-willed man. Now establish this last character and you take a far higher grade than any other. How are you to establish it. Just by bringing yourself before the public as you are. Find vent for your notions. Get them tongue. Upon every subject get them tongue. Not upon Law alone. You cannot at present get them either utterance or audience by ordinary converse. Your utterance is not the most favourable—it convinces but it does not persuade, and it is only a very few (I claim place for myself) that it fascinates. Your audience is worse—they are generally (I exclude myself) unphilosophical, unthinking drivellers who lay in wait 'to catch you in your words'[57] and who give you little justice in the recital—because you give their vanity or self-esteem little justice or even mercy in the encounter. *Therefore, My Dear, some other way is to be sought for*. Now Pause if you be not convinced of this conclusion—if you be, we shall proceed, if you be not, read again and you will see it just. And as such admit it. Now what way is to be sought for—I know no other than the press. You have not the pulpit as I have, and there perhaps I have the advantage. You have not good & influential Society. I know nothing but the press. Now of every department of the press, for your purpose—none are so good as these two, the

---

56. NLS, MS 1764; fol. 167–69.

57. 'to catch you in your words' reflects Mark 12:13, 'And they send unto him certain of the Pharisees and of the Herodians to catch him in his words.'

Edinburgh Review & Blackwood's Magazine.[58] Do not start away and say; the one I am not fit for, the other I am not willing for. Both pleas I refuse. The Edinburgh Review, you are perfectly fit for—not yet upon Law, but upon any work of Mathematics, Physics, General Literature, History & Politics, you are as ripe as the average of their writers. Blackwood's Magazine[59] presents bad company, I confess, but it also furnishes a good field for fugitive writing, and good introduction to Society on one side of the question. This last advice I confess is against my conscience, and I am inclined to block it out—for did I not rest satisfied that you were to use your pen for your Conscience, I would never ask you to use it for your living. Writers in the Encyclopedias, except in leading Articles, do not get out from the crowd, but writers in the Review come out at once, and obtain the very opinion you want, opinion among the intelligent and active men in every rank, not among the sluggish *savants* alone. It is easy for me to advise what many perhaps are as ready to advise, but I know I have influence, and I am willing to use it—therefore again let me entreat you to begin a new year by an effort continuous not for getting knowledge but for communicating it, that you may gain money & favour & opinion. Now do not disembark all your capital of thought & time & exertion out of others into this concern but disembark a portion equal to its urgency—and make the Experiment upon a proper scale—if it succeed, the Spirit of Adventure will follow, and you will be ready to embark more; if it fail, no great venture was made, no great venture is lost—the time is not yet come—but you have got a more precise view by the failure of the obstacle to be surmounted, and time and energy will give you what you lacked.

Therefore I advise as a very sincere friend, that forthwith you chuse [sic] a Topic, not that you're best informed on, but that you are most likely to find admittance for, and set apart some portion of each day a week to this object and to this alone—leaving the rest free for objects professional and pleasant. This is nothing more nor less than what I urged at our last meeting—but I have nothing to write I reckon so important. Therefore do take it to thought. Depend upon it you will be delivered by such present adventure, and its future return[,] from these harpies of your fear you are too much tormented with. You will get a class with whom Society will be as pleasant as we have found it together and you will open up ultimate prospects which I trust, no man shall be able to close. I am done with this—at present.

I think our town is safe for every leal[60] hearted man to his Maker and to his fellow-men, to traverse without fear of scathe[61]—such traversing is the wine and milk of my present Existence. I do not warrant against a radical rising, though I think it

---

58. *The Edinburgh Review (1802-1929)*. A quarterly periodical, established by Francis Jeffrey, Sydney Smith and Henry Brougham, and originally published by Archibald Constable. It's views were liberal and its literary reviews were highly influential. In 1831 Irving himself was to appear in the publication. See *OCEL*

59. *Blackwood's Magazine* (1817-1980) or 'the Maga,' was a monthly periodical presenting the Tory view as opposed to the Whiggish opinions of the *Edinburgh Review*.

60. Loyal, faithful, honest, true.

61. Harm, damage.

Part II: The Letters

vastly improbable—but continue these times a year or two, and unless you unmake our present generation, and unman them of human feelings and of Scottish intelligence, you will have commotion.[62] It is impossible for them to die of starvation, and they are making no provision to have them removed. And what on Earth is for them. God and my Saviour enable me to lift their hearts above a world that has deserted them though they live in its plenty and labour in its toiling service, and fix them upon a world which, My Dear Carlyle, I wish you and I had the inheritance and we may have, if we will. But I am going to preach else I would plunge into another subject which I rate above all subjects. Yet this should not be excluded from our communion either.

I am getting on quietly enough, and if I be defended from the errors of my heart, may do pretty well. The Doctor is full of acknowledgements. And I ought to be full to a higher source. I have no philosophical speculations that I think of—but it is past one, I have been talking all night—but I would write you, farewell. My love to kind and good Mrs. Duff, and my consolations to my esteemed friend John Ferguson.

Yours affectionately,

Edwd Irving

P.S. In your letter which I wish soon I would rather discuss this subject of our opening up the world than any other but most of all would I like that you were to acquiesce. Though I have taken no notice of it I had great sympathy & delight in your Letter. And may notice it when this is more of my mind. E.I.

Addressed to: Mr. Thomas Carlyle,
Duff's Lodgings,
35 Bristo St.,
Edinburgh.
Favd by Mr. Brown.

～

Edward Irving to THOMAS CARLYLE

Glasgow, 34 Kent St., 14th March 1820[63]

My Dear Carlyle,

---

62. There had been a riot in Glasgow on the 19th August, reported in *The Times* on 20 August 1819, together with other disturbances in Paisley and Hamilton on the 15th and 16th. In the case of Glasgow, however, the police with the aid of two troops of Hussars, managed to restore peace with 'some prisoners taken, brought to town, and lodged in the Police office.' See *The Times*, 21 September 1819.

63. NLS, MS 1764: fols. 173–74.

I would be culpable beyond all excuse if I did not seize the first moment I have unemployed in hard office, to acknowledge the debt which you have laid me under, and do the little I can to discharge it. These are debts which it is pleasing to owe, and your Epistles would be of this sort, but then I fear you would not go on to give me credit, though it does not become me at present to say so. Since I received your last epistle, which reminded me of some of those gloomy scenes of nature I have often had the greatest pleasure in contemplating, I have been wrought almost to death, by labour and kindness oft the more disagreeable of the two (I mean the kindness of our Citisens [sic], of which roast beef and Glasgow punch are the main ingredients) having had three sermons to write, and one of them a charity sermon. But now, I have taken my pen, and trust to your indulgence. When I give you my assurance, that I have the greatest pleasure as I have always had, in our correspondence, and shall make many sacrifices, before I shall resign the entertainment and benefit I derive from it. Your mind is of too penetrating a cast to rest satisfied with the pail [sic] disguises which the happiness of ordinary life has thrown on to hide its nakedness, and I do never augur that your nature is to be satisfied with its sympathies—indeed I am convinced that were you now translated into the most elegant & informed circle of the City, you would find it please only by its novelty, and perhaps refresh by its variety, but you would be constrained to seek the solid employment, and the lasting gratification of your mind elsewhere. The truth is life is a thing formed for the average of men. And it is only those parts of our nature which are of average possession that it can gratify. The higher parts of our nature find their entertainment in sympathising with the highest efforts of our species, which are & will continue confined to the closet of the sage, and can never find their station in the drawing rooms of the talking world. Indeed, I will go higher and say, that the higher parts of our nature will never have their proper food, till they turn to contemplate the excellencies of our creator, and not only contemplate but to imitate them. Therefore it is, my Dear Carlyle, that I exhort you to call in the finer parts of your mind, and to try to present the society about you, with those more ordinary displays they can enjoy—the indifference with which they receive them, and the ignorance with which they hear them, operate upon the mind like gall and wormwood. I would entreat you to be comforted in the possession of your treasures, and to study more the times and persons to which you bring them forth. When I say your treasures I mean not your information so much, which they will bear the display of for the reward & value of it—but of your feelings and affections which being of finer tone than theirs, and consequently seeking a keener expression, they are apt to mistake for a rebuke of their own lameness or for intolerance of ordinary things—and too many of them[,] I fear, for asperity of mind.

There is just another *panacea* for your griefs which are not imaginary but for which I see a real ground in the too—penetrating & at times perhaps too-severe turn of your mind, but though I judge it better and more worthy than reserve, it is perhaps more difficult of practice—I mean, the habit of many of using our superiority for the information & improvement of others. This, I reckon both the most dignified, and the most kindly course that one can take—founded upon the great principle of human improvement, mutual communication—and founded upon which I am wont, or at least would wish to make my pattern—the example of the Saviour of men, who endured in his errand of salvation, the contradiction of men. But I confess on the other hand, one meets with so few that are apt disciples, or willing to allow superiority, that will be constantly fighting with you upon the threshold, that it is very heartless and forces one to reserve. And besides, one is so apt to fancy a superiority where there is none, that it is very apt to produce over much self-complacency. But I see I am beginning to prose, and therefore shall change the subject, with only another remark, that your tone of mind reminds me more than any thing of my own when under the sense of great religious imperfection, and anxiously pursuing after higher Christian attainments.

I have read your letter again, and, at the risk of further prosing, I shall have another hit at its contents. You talk of renouncing the Law, and you speak mysteriously of Hope springing up from another quarter. I pray that it may soon be turned into enjoyment—but I would not have you to renounce the Law, unless you coolly think that this new view contains those fields of happiness from the want of which the prospect of Law has become so dreary. You know it best, and I would like very well to know it, and shall I doubt not in your next; but still Law has within it scope ample enough for any mind. The reformation which it needs, and which with so much humour & feeling you describe, is the very evidence of what I say. Did Adam Smith find the Commercial System less encumbered; I know he did not find it more—and see what order the mind of our man has made there. Such a reformation must be brought in Law, and the spirit of the age is manifestly bending that way. I know none who from his capacity of remembering and dygesting [sic] facts—and of arranging them into general results is so well filled as yourself. And, with regard to health, calculate upon many years to come—this ought to be a Postulation which every man that purposes any thing should make of nature.

With regard to my own affairs, I am becoming too much of a man of business and too little a man of contemplation. I meet with few minds to excite me, many to drain me off, and by the habit of discharging and receiving nothing in return, I am run off to the very *lee*; as you may easily discern. I have a German Master and a class in College—I have seen neither for a week[,] such is my state of engagement. Engagement with I know not what—with preaching in St Johns once a week a hasty production, and employing the rest of the week in visiting objects from which I can learn nothing unless I were collecting for a new series of the Tales of my Landlord,[64] which should range among Radicals and Smugglers—or preparing a new Edition of the Cottagers of Glenburnie[65] for the Meridian of the callow of Glasgow. Dr Chalmers, though a most entire original himself, is surrounded with very prosaical sort of persons—who please

64. Scott, *Tales of My Landlord*.
65. Hamilton, *The Cottagers of Glenburnie*.

me something by their zeal to carry into effect his philosophical schemes, and vex me much by their idolatry of him. My comforts are in hearing the distress of the people, and doing my mite to alleviate them. They are not in the higher walks (I mean as to wealth) in which I am permitted to move, nor yet in the greater publicity and notoriety I enjoy (every minister in Glasgow is an oracle to a certain number of Devotees)—for I would not give one day in solitude—or in meditation with a friend, as I have enjoyed it oft along the sands of Kirkcaldy[,] for ages in this way. But there is a higher object in life than to be amused, and perhaps there is as high a one as to improve oneself—I mean to impart improvement to others—this is what I am engaged with at the present. I do not think I have any chance for the new church in Glasgow—I want standing—and *friends* and I believe *worth*—but I am little ambitious of it, having enough of occupation with the half of St Johns how should I do with the whole of St James. Tell Dixon to read Shakespeare before he venture to the Bermoothas [sic][66]

I should have written Brown by this time, you may say I will write soon but do not, I pray you, punish me by delay—let me know your new prospect; I am very anxious out of a worthier motive, I trust, than curiosity.

Yours most truly,
Edwd Irving
My kindest regards to Mrs. Duff.

Addressed to: Mr. Thomas Carlyle,
Mrs. Duff,
35 Bristo St.,
Edinburgh.

~

Edward Irving to THOMAS CARLYLE

Glasgow, 34 Kent St., 15th April 1820[67]

My Dear Carlyle,

Right happy shall I be to have your company and conversation for even so short a time, and the longer the better and if you could continue to make your visit so that the beginning of the week should be the time of your departure I would bear you company on your road a day's journey. I have just finished my Sermon (Saturday 6 o'clock) at which I have sitten without interruption since ten—but I resolved you should have my letter to-morrow—that nothing might prevent your promised visit—to which I

---

66. Irving's allusion is to Shakespeare, *The Tempest*, 1. 2. 229: 'the still-vexed Bermoothes.' Frank Dickson was to spend a year in Bermuda as a Scottish Chaplain.

67. NLS, MS 1764: fol. 175.

hold you now altogether bound. It is very dangerous to speak one's mind here about the state of the Country. I reckon however, the Radicals have in a manner expatriated themselves from the political co-operation of the better classes—and, at the same time I believe there was sympathy enough in the middle and well-informed people to have carried a milioration [sic] of our political evils had they taken time and legal measures. I am very sorry for the poor, they are losing their religion, their domestic comfort, their pride of independence, their every thing; and if timeous[68] remedies come not soon they will sink, I fear, into the degradation of the Irish peasantry, and if that class goes down, then along with it sinks the morality of every other class. They are at a complete standfirm. A sort of military glow has taken all ranks; they can see the houses of the poor ransacked for arms, without uttering the poor tribute of an interjection of grief over the fallen greatness of those who brought us our reformation & our civil liberty. And they will hardly suffer any sympathising from any one.

Doctor Chalmers takes a safe course in all these difficulties—the truth is he does not side with any—he has a few political notions so peculiar that they serve to detach his ideal mind from both Whigs and Tories and radicals—that Britain would have been as flourishing and full of capital though there had been surrounding this land a brazen wall a thousand cubits high—that the national debt does us neither good nor ill amounting to nothing more or less than a mortgage upon property & debts. The Whigs dare not speak, the philanthropists are so much taken up each with his own locality as to take little charge of the general concern—and so the Tories have room to rage and talk by about armaments, and pikes and battles. They had Loudon Hill fortified yesterday by the Radicals—and so forth.

Now it will be like the unimprisoning of a bird, to come and let me have free talk—not that I have any thing to say in favour of radicalism; for it is the very distilation [sic] of philosophy & religion & political Economy—but that we may lose ourselves so delightfully in reveries upon the Emendations of the state to which in fact you & I can bring as little help as we could have done against the late inundation of the Vallais [sic].

I like much better the tone of your last letter—for remember I read your very tone and gestures at this distance of place through your letter though it be not the most diaphanous of bodies—I have no more fear of your future success than Noah had of the deluge ceasing[69]—and though the first dove returned as you say you are to return to your father's shelter without even a leaf—yet the next time believe me you shall return with a leaf. And yet another time and you shall take a flight who knows whither.

But of this and other things I delay further parley. Pray write me what day you will arrive on.

My kind love to Mrs. Duff,

Yours affectionately,

68. Timely.
69. See Gen 18:6–12.

Edwd Irving

Addressed to: Mr. Thomas Carlyle,
Duffs Lodgings,
35 Bristo St.,
Edinburgh.

~

Edward Irving to THOMAS CARLYLE

Glasgow, 10th July 1820[70]

My Dear Carlyle,

This is only a put off till you hear from me *at length* from Dublin, where I am to be for residence some weeks—to set off in one or two short and busy hours. I feel how patient and good natured you are, it is what I would be likewise with you. The truth is these 4 weeks I have been little at home but on Sundays—I had verily the most delectable week[,] nearly two weeks[,] I ever spent, with what maiden do you think[?] One whose name will thrill you as it does me, one of whom I am very proud & with whom I am well nigh in love 'Sed Pacae adversae velant'[71]—Margaret Gordon.[72] With great gallantry she committed herself to [be] my escort through the highlands by Inverary & Loch Lomond, Mr. Fergusson of Annan was my friend & Mrs. and Miss Maxton of Alloa hers—but such another scene of heart—content I never shall pass again—the brief time of it lays in my mind like a hallowed sanctuary in a desert or like a piece of enchanted ground in a wilderness. Truly it never strikes me to mingle it with the times which went before or the times which have come after—it would seem a sort of sacrilege to the powers which breathed over it such delight.

---

70. NLS, MS 1764: fol. 179.

71. But adverse fates interpose. He is referring to his engagement to Isabella Martin.

72. In 1818, while still teaching at Kirkcaldy, Carlyle had been introduced to Irving's former pupil, the 'fair complexioned, softly elegant, softly grave, witty and comely' Margaret Gordon, 'who,' Carlyle goes on in the *Reminiscences,* 'continued for perhaps some three years a figure hanging more or less in my fancy, on the usual romantic, or latterly quite elegiac and silent terms': *Reminiscences*, 239. They had met in the autumn of 1818. See Archibald, *Carlyle's First Love*, 2:65.

There are two letters which Margaret Gordon wrote to Thomas Carlyle published in *Carlyle's First Love*. In the first, dated 4 June 1820, she writes 'To *possess* your *friendship*, I have often said, was a constant source of delight to me; to *lose* it, you may believe, was proportionally painful': *ibid.*, 72. She goes on to say she is leaving Scotland for London where she intends to remain for a year.

Edward Irving's delight in Margaret Gordon is terminated when he visits her on his first visit to London. He reports to Thomas Carlyle that after the reception he received 'I am indisposed to go back again.' Edward Irving to Thomas Carlyle, 26 December 1821, p. 122.

Part II: The Letters

Yet in all this there was no love, but there was most delightful sympathy in some of the sublimest scenes of nature, and also in some of the most distressing feelings of the heart—but most of all there was such a hearty wish to give and to receive gratification, which when felt by one so capable of giving it as the first mentioned lady who was my chief companion, produced an effect to which I know of no pen able to do justice except that of Boccaccio.[73] And nothing indeed realised to me the value of some of his sketches of happy companies retired from the world amidst bowers and gardens and music & refined sentiment, so much as what I was enabled to feel upon that occasion. Margaret is now gone to London. I saw her to the track [tow] boat on Tuesday with a heavy heart I can assure you—and she often declared she went back to the gayeties [*sic*] of the City, as a bird to its cage.

I have been likewise in Edin and preached for Andw Thompson, but not at the assembly where there seems to have passed something worth listening to—and in Fife likewise where I spent a few happy days—And now I am on the wing for Dublin where I am to officiate for Mr. Carlisle of Paisley[74] & he for me three or four Sundays—thereafter I cross to Liverpool, and shall have perhaps a week at Annan when I will see you assuredly—if it did not distract you from your plans—it would afford me much pleasure to fall in with you at Liverpool & saunter thro' the Lakes with you—but more of this when I write you from Dublin.

My Dear Carlyle let not the dreams of your head by day or by night distress you. Do your utmost to possess your soul in peace—if I was a prophet I know to whom I would predict many days of honour & influence & all else earthly which goes to combine a happy condition—I regret not that you have to come at it thro' tribulation provided God gives you grace to bear it—because of all hateful things in our men of letters the most hateful is their supercilious looking down upon every thing which was wont to characterise the lot of literary men upon every thing but fortune and éclat which heretofore were wont to be yielded to the Mercantile & Military Casts. There is little enthusiasm among them for self denial, or patient endurance of suffering, or noble superiority to the humble elements of one's destiny, or quiet meditation upon the destinies of man. It is all either Practical Politics, or Scientific Facts. Now if those great powers you are gifted with, shall receive the mellowing influence of solitary and solemn thought, and the sweetening influence of meditation upon nature & the God of nature—and moreover, if you will try and guard them from any embittering influence from wanting the communion of spirits like your own. Then I shall hail as eminently conducive to your future character that when others of your age were figuring in routes & assemblies and coteries you were busy in the solitude of Mainhill.

73. Giovanni Boccaccio (1313–75), Italian writer and humanist.

74. James Carlisle (1784–1854) who had been licensed by the Presbytery of Paisley and who in 1813 became minister of the Scots Church, Mary's Abbey, Dublin. He was a leading evangelical activist in the city.

I have sent Alfieri, and pray you to accept in token of my affection & esteem my old copy of Locke's Essay[75] a work which I know you to value—the man I cannot wish you better than wish you to imitate. My kind regards to your family. Dixon is at Bellcal hill[76]

Yours faithfully,

Edwd Irving

Addressed to: Mr. Thomas Carlyle,
Mainhill by Ecclefechan.

~

Edward Irving to THOMAS CARLYLE

Dublin, 97 Grafton St., 24th July 1820[77]

Dear Carlisle [sic],

I thought by this time to have been in full communication with you upon the memorabilia of Dublin, and upon what I contemplate with still more interest the prospect of meeting you perhaps in Liverpool, and traveling through the scenery of Westmoreland. But perhaps you will be better employed at home, for after all I believe this love of variety in the scenes of life and the scenes of nature has gone in me the length of a disease. It is too much to ask it for any gratification to myself, but at the same time I remember to have heard you often speak of visiting Liverpool, and if it should happen that we were there together it would add to the pleasure, I dare say, of both. For I find that one of the principal draw-backs of my present enjoyment is the want of some one to stimulate me to speech and thought. The sum of the whole is that I would be highly delighted to have more talk, and we would have both more space, and greater variety. However, do not by any means put a stop to any engagements of greater importance for whether or not in Liverpool I shall certainly see you in Annandale, where I hope to spend at least a week & if possible a fortnight. I mean to leave here on Monday by the Liverpool packet so that I shall be there on Tuesday—and in passing to Annan I mean to spend the remainder of that week.

With regard to this city and its inhabitants I am not much in love with either. The public buildings have all been erected by Government grants, and manifest an excess generosity of ornament, and a profusion of outlay to which we are altogether strangers in Scotland. In every thing about the place you are struck with the display. But above

---

75. Locke, *Essay concerning Human Understanding*.
76. Belkathill at Dryfe in Dumfriesshire.
77. NLS, MS 1764: fols. 183–84.

Part II: The Letters

all things by the quantity of two wheeled vehicles. The roads especially along the bay you would liken to nothing but one immense 'merry go round' such as they exhibit in fairs. Irish Politeness I do not like. There is in it far more of *blarney* than I have seen elsewhere. *They seem* rather acting the part than intending your comfort. And the part being acted, there is not matter whether you seem to be comfortable or not. I feel infinitely more relish for Glasgow Society commercial as it is. Throughout their talk there is a constant laying off for [suit ?] of every name, and really their humour so much talked of is rather the stile [*sic*] of talking they are trained in from infancy, than any effort or inspiration of the moment.

This is the first letter but two[,] one to George Little[78] in the North, and one to my brother in Law[79] for Introductions to Liverpool that I have written since I came. So blame me not on particular but on general grounds. There seems no literature floating in the general conversation of this place farther than what finds food in Blackwood & the Edin Review—little religion further than the activity of the Public Societies, and the hatred of Catholics, and the adherents of one or two independent orators so that on the whole I have seldom been in a more looped state—and I shall have merely to say that I have seen Dublin without having benefited any thing from the sight. I am to go to the County of Wicklow to-morrow famed for the beautiful scenery—and to return on Thursday. I am not sure whether a letter will have time to reach me here as they are not given out on Sunday, and I may be off before Post-time on Monday. So direct to me to be left at the Post Office Liverpool—if indeed I do not find yourself instead which were infinitely better. Excuse this—it is written in the recruit inspecting room of Dr Brown, Adam Hope's brother, amidst the conversations & examinations of naked men.

Yours truly,
Edwd Irving

Addressed Care of Revd. Dr Stewart,
Liverpool.
Addressed to: Mr. Thomas Carlyle,
Mainhill by Ecclefechan, Scotland.

---

78. 'Dr George Little, whose nickname was "Parliament" was a surgeon of Ecclefechan whose father George Little, a farmer, lived in Parliament Close, Ecclefechan': See CL, 1:305 n.

79. Irving was not yet married to Isabella Martin, so the brother in law he refers to must be the husband of one of his sisters: Elizabeth, married to William Kennedy, a merchant in Manchester; Margaret married to John Lowther Fergusson a doctor; or Janet, married to Robert Dickson, another merchant who was to be Provost of Annan from 1821–23.

The Letters: 1814–1821

Edward Irving to THOMAS CHALMERS

Liverpool, 3rd August 1820
Written in another hand: 1819 & 20[80]

Dear Sir,

Though not strictly from Dublin according to promise, this is the first act of a writing kind I have done since I left Dublin which was yesterday at 3 o'clock; and had it not been for a very stormy night on the water this should have been dated Irish Channel with all the bearings & distances proper to fix the locality of naval dispatch.

There is a Sunday still to run of my engagement in Dublin, which Mr. Honer, Mr. Carlisle's[81] Colleague kindly undertook, in lieu of double duty which I did two Sundays, and would have been happy to do all the three, so good a hearted man is he. I should have left Dublin on Monday morning which would have given me three days ahead—but by various conversations which I took occasion to hold with the Sabbath school masters in Dublin, there was excited amongst them a general wish I should remain till the meeting of their union on Tuesday—in order to set forth to them *en masse* what of your Local Ideas[82] I had expounded to them individually. This I did not think it right for me to refuse and so I remained, and spent three hours in a most engaging conversation, and so pleasant was the subject to them, they declared they had not had a more agreeable meeting since the union of their body. The result was to chalk off from the map of Dublin a square portion to be surveyed after a schedule they have made answering as near as possible to that of your parish. The two young gentlemen who have undertaken the survey are the two leaders[,] one reckoned their founder, (not a more respectable merchant in Dublin)—the other their secretary who is so taken with it as to have got his place as a Teacher of the union supplied, that he may be *expeditus ad opus incipiendum*,[83] he also a respectable man in the city. So the thing has at least got a beginning. I exhorted them to draw forth in the form of queries any difficulties they might entertain, both that I may possess something to give you insight into their views and that they might have all information necessary to the success of their enterprise.

I have not forgotten my promise of making a survey—but spent one whole day upon it, and have the document for your information.

Moreover, finding Dublin Education for the lower classes to be either gratuitous or insufferably dreary I have unfolded to several private individuals & to the members of Mary's Abbey (where I preached) and still more to the Union Sabbath School

---

80. NCL, MSS CHA 4 15.47.

81. Mr. Carlisle of Paisley—see letter Irving to Thomas Carlyle, 10 July 1820: NLS, MS 1764: fol. 179.

82. As well as asserting that the material needs of the poor could be met from the proceeds of the church collection plate, Chalmers argued that a parish could be divided into 'localities' each under the care of an elder and a deacon, who would look after the spiritual and temporal aspects respectively of the welfare of the poor: Grass, *The Lord's Watchman*, 30.

83. Ready for beginning the work.

Part II: The Letters

Society—the propriety of living off a convenient Locality, and by raising a subscription and endowing a salary, and pervading the district with agency & influence, endeavouring to present to the population the conditions of parochial Education; hoping thereby not only to set on foot something parochial for Dublin, but likewise, if they would choose this district the same with that for Local Sab[bath] Sch[ool], they might be able to detach the technical parts of learning gone through on Sunday from the religious part; and to overcome the only objections which Protestants have still a hold of against Sab Sch Education. To this scheme I found all most hearty.

My materials of a business nature are finished, except one thing, which after your indulgence I know not how to ask; but if it be inconvenient I need only to be informed. By delaying in Dublin till the Sab Sch meeting, I am here in Dr Stewart's my first night, Thursday, and they will not let me away till after Sunday. I have to go to York, Huddersfield, Preston where I am engaged to be[,] having kinsmen there, sons of my Father's brother[84] whom I have never visited. This will take the greater part of next week which it was my aim to have spent in Annan, so I shall be able to reach Annan only that evening I should have been at Glasgow. At Annan or its neighbourhood for what purpose I know not but for some I am certain, my aunt Miss Johnston has a strong desire to hear me another time—but on that day I should be in Glasgow. Now I use the liberty of asking in these circumstances for the indulgence of another Sabbath, and I trust my performance of duty after will shew me not unworthy of it.[85] Perhaps, if this be agreeable, my friends Mr. Thompson or Mr.- (the young gentleman once your Sabb Sch master whom I once got to preach for you—he lives in Salt Market), or Mr. Marshall for whom I have been a liker & shall always wish to be more serviceable, or Mr. Carlyle himself, who, I understand, is not be at home that day, or some other out of kindness might be found to officiate—but if not agreeable, please without any delicacy say so, and address by return of post a letter to my father, he will know to address it to me, and depend upon it if Glasgow can be reached by any conveyance from the place I heartily shall not be or a-wanting.

I should now proceed to detail my Ideas on Dublin and Ireland, but my paper is done and my eyes sealing & so I defer to *viva voce* conversation anything further.

From,
Dear Sir,
Yours most respectfully
& affectionately,
Edwd Irving

---

84. George Irving, Edward's uncle, died March, 1822.

85. Edward Irving had hoped to be in Annan on 5th August but because of his change in itinerary he missed Thomas Carlyle. On that day, Carlyle wrote a letter to John Fergusson reporting the absence of Irving on that day and briefly discussing his friend: Thomas Carlyle to John Fergusson, Mainhill, 5 August 1820: CL, 1:269–70.

Liverpool—Rupert Street,
Aug 3, 1820
To be forwarded immediately.
Rev Dr Chalmers,
Glasgow.
Hand by Jas Stevenson Esq.

~

Edward Irving to THOMAS CARLYLE

15th August 1820, Annan[86]

My Dear Sir,

I am now arrived, after having my heart at once delighted with the kindness and torn with the parting of my friends. This is one of the greatest evils under the sun, and to me the chief source of a longing after immortality—that no sooner have you made a worthy attachment than it must be weakened by separation & distance, or broken by forgetfulness or death.

I could write in a register the account of my days and hours, and no man who has the same views of travelling with me would refuse to acquit me of indolence, or misimprovement. This is a great and perhaps a vain compliment, but it means nothing more than that I looked at much, talked about more, thought what I could, and wrote nothing.

It grieves me for the sake of all my relatives & friends that I am now so limited of time having my seat bespoke, and paid for on Saturday night to Glasgow. And for my own sake it grieves me that I shall be able to have so little of your conversation & intercourse.

But, I understand you are to be down at the ordination to-morrow, it will give me the greatest pleasure to find you there, and not to part with you again till I part with Annandale. This maybe asking too much, for I am aware, after your kind visit to me which I shall not soon forget, it behooved me to have returned the favour at your father's house and so verily I would but that I find it will be impossible to tear myself away on any account. And my friend Warrand Carlyle [sic] I fear I have offended beyond reparation, but again I trust to his forgiveness as I have trusted to yours. Him you will also meet with if you have not already. My Love to the family.

Your very affectionate friend,
Edw Irving

---

86. NLS, MS 1764: fols. 185-86.

Part II: The Letters

This come with a message to Mr. Graham[87] on the same subject from my brother in law, you will make good company. EI

~

Edward Irving to THOMAS CARLYLE

[Letter annotated by hand 'August 1820?'][88]

My Dear Carlyle,

Warrand,[89] your namesake, is making a sooner return to Annandale than you would be looking for, I hope it will be as propitious as you wish him, and so to his care I consign this letter and the books. I would have sent the *Inferno*, but I purpose reading it myself now I am finished with visiting the Parish—indeed, I have the greatest pleasure in my calling, but I fear I do not communicate so much in return, yet I confess I have as high a pleasure in my Excursions and during my last long and varied one, I avow to you without flattery, that neither intercourse with new characters nor the observation of new manners & celebrated scenes, nor yet the domestic affection of relatives by whom I am beloved better than I deserve, afforded me more or even so much delight, as the intellectual feast which I never miss in your company, and hardly find any where else—the more grateful now that we have come to understand each other, and respect each other when we disagree, although I do not despair when we have more leisure to examine the subject, and more experience to understand it, we shall yet be at one.[90]

For your sake, were it for nothing else, I mean for the respect I entertain for your poetical taste, I shall make an attempt upon the Maid of Orleans,[91] little doubting that I shall relish the Idea of her conceived by the German, much more than the Idea by her countryman in whom we have a noble example of how little high power when divorced from moral worth can do for the good of man. The more I think the more I am persuaded that, a virtuous life, nay a sublimely virtuous life, or a puritanical as they

---

87. William Graham, of Burnswark, Annandale, who Carlyle had met through Irving. 'A lumpish heavy but stirring figure; had got something lamish about one of the knees or ancles [*sic*], which gave a certain rocking motion to his gait; firm jocund affectionate face, rather reddish with good cheer, eyes big blue and laughing, nose defaced with snuff, fine bald broad-browed head ditto almost always with an ugly brown scratch wig.' *Reminiscences*, 253.

In 1820 William Graham's family business had been on the verge of collapse. See letter Thomas Carlyle to Edward Irving, 3 June 1820 n: CL, 1: 253–56.

88. NLS, MS 1764: fols. 187–88.

89. Warrand Carlyle (1796–1881), who was to marry Edward Irving's sister Agnes, known as Nancy, on 23 October 1820. After Irving died, their son Gavin was to edit Irving's collected writings.

90. On a visit to Irving in Glasgow during April 1820, Carlyle had confessed to his friend that he had moved away from orthodox Christian belief.

91. Schiller, *The Maid of Orleans*.

would phrase it, is as necessary to great literary performances, as a fine understanding, and much acquired wisdom. Witness for example Newton, who it is said, never knew women, Milton whose romance of character if I may so name it, is to me as astonishing as his loftiness of conception & Locke in whose familiar letters I discover as sedate & severe a mind, as in his philosophy—in so much that of all men that have lived he seems to me to have been more & most habitually above prejudice. Do not you think that this is a just idea and I think it admits of a Philosophical explanation with which, however, I shall not trouble you.

Whether rightly or not I have certainly attempted to perform what you call a *sacred duty* to Margaret Gordon[92] but I confess I did not go into it as a duty—nor yet as a recreation, but in some other sense which I cannot well name—and now you suggest the idea of duty, and I try to recollect my letter[93]—I find that had I it to write it over again I would have written in a very different strain, but this will be my apology for another. One thing, however, I inserted in it which I hope you will approve, that, having heard your good opinion of each other's mind and general character, it seemed to me you were likely to profit by a correspondence. Whether my suggestion will please both or either I do not know.

I commend your resolution of giving your main effort to writing for the Magazine & the Encyclopedia[94] because bread is what you need, and what you have wherewithal, by God's blessing to purchase. And because, it is the only way by which your powers and attainments will come to be known, and also because it will give accuracy to many departments of your knowledge. At the same time, I say from my heart & with manly freedom, that your talents were given you for a higher purpose than to make a livelihood, and that secretly, you should be meditating upon some scheme for doing your best in some way or other to promote the progress of knowledge. Both are compatible at the same time, then one shall give you comfort; the other shall give you dignity in your own eyes. I mean to write a general letter to my sisters upon the bringing up of their children—if you could spare a corner in any of your letters, I would like your Ideas, briefly upon that subject. I shall see & attend to Dixon's request tomorrow, and get the return to go by Warrand who sets out on Wednesday. My kind respects to your family.

Yours affectionately,
Edwd Irving

Addressed to: Mr. Thomas Carlyle,
Mainhill by Ecclefechan.

92. See letter E. Irving to Thomas Carlyle, 10th July, 1820, page 85.

93. *Ibid.*

94. I.e., *Blackwood's Magazine* and the *Edinburgh Encyclopaedia*. The encyclopaedia was published by William Blackwood and edited by the scientist Sir David Brewster.

Part II: The Letters

Edward Irving to THOMAS CARLYLE

34 Kent Street, Glasgow, 21st September 1820[95]

My Dear Carlyle,

I am happy in the prospect of soon seeing you again to renew some of those interesting conversations, which though seasoned with melancholy are amongst the most pleasant recreations of my life. My sister Nancy, you may perhaps know, is to be married to our friend Warrand Carlyle [sic] on Tuesday the 24th and my attendance is needed as Bryde [sic]—grooms man. I will be in the country the Sunday following, and by that means shall have the better part of a fortnight to spend, where my time always passes the most pleasantly—for certainly my mind is most susceptible on the side of domestic affection, which of itself independent of all circumstances of taste or refinement is enough at any time to make me a captive.

I had a letter from our dear friend Margaret Gordon, in answer to that of which I told you something in my last.[96] She is happily delivered into a condition of much thankfulness and affection to her mother & her father & her family; and that mystery which neither you nor I were able to penetrate nor herself indeed, has now opened itself, it would seem, before the explanations which have come out in London, and she appears not to have found reason to take her indignation where her affection was formerly: but I have no explanations, and even this much is given me under a strong discharge never more to mention his name, or make allusions to him, and even under injunction to burn the letter in which she feels enough of confidence in me to have divulged this. Of course I would not, even to you, have mentioned so much, had it not been rendered necessary by what is to follow. I introduced the subject of a correspondence betwixt you and Margaret, for your mutual entertainment, and she has given what I considered rather an encouraging answer. I shall give it in her own words, and thereby give you another [ink blot] entire confidence. 'What a noble character is Mr. Carlyle. Nature has endorsed [ink blot] gift which by properly using will I trust raise him above his present position [ink blot] in saying the correspondence of one with a mind so richly gifted would be [ink blot] and improving to me but it would be unfair. I may write Mr. Irving because no evil can result from the interchange of friendship, he being under an engagement,[97] and I in no danger of falling in love with *any one* least of all with my quondam teacher.'

Now, my friend, I could be jocular and perhaps witty upon this paragraph, but that I would esteem unfaithful to the confidence in which it was written, and untrue to the emotions which it awakens in my mind. I shall rather take upon me the office of a director, if you'll permit me, and point out what conduct it should lead to read it

---

95. NLS, MS 1764: fols. 189–90.

96. See Edward Irving to Thomas Carlyle August 1820.

97. The 'engagement' to which Margaret Gordon refers to in this letter is that of Edward Irving to Isabella. Clearly Carlyle knew of this attachment, which would explain Irving's reticence in confiding to his friend his love for Jane Welsh.

over again and you will see Margaret is alive both to the gain and to the risk of corresponding with you. She has an esteem of your mind & character, but she shrinks from too close an acquaintance of them. What can be the reason of this I dare say she has never defined to herself, but I have no difficulty in defining it. It arises from that strong sympathy which she feels towards mental graces and accomplishments—towards the sublime of sentiment, and the sublime of character—and which she dreads to have awaked lest she might not be able to restrain it within reasonable bounds. For her to hesitate is therefore to doubt of herself, while it is to flatter you. (See what an omen!! my ink bottle has overset and lodged its contents in one globular drop upon the very commencement of my quotation, and while with slow and cautious hand, I endeavoured to pour it back by the top it set in one immense stream away through the very heart of my quotation, and but for my extraordinary undauntedness of mind would have put an eternal stop to all further proceeding in this delicate affair). Now what is to be done, I think there is authority enough for you to write to her, and you may introduce the correspondence by mentioning that in a letter to you I had mentioned, that I had reason to know it would not give mortal offence. I would not presume to suggest any thing farther, but that you should abstain from all allusion to her attachment, or to its suspension, on which I shall never take the liberty of once more making a hint. I am not ignorant of the very strong attachment you have to Margaret Gordon, and I am not surprised at it, neither am I ignorant of the pain which there is I see you evince upon all occasions under the contention of your circumstances with your wishes—and perhaps, while I am in hope of adding a new pleasure to the few which you enjoy, the correspondence of a noble-minded female, I may be leading the way to some new scene of trouble and vexation—I am in doubt, but I mean you well—and I pray the director of all to bring forth to you from it nothing but enjoyment, that you may have new reason to rejoice in your life, and to draw near to him with the voice of thankfulness. It would perhaps have been more prudent in me to have awaited a personal interview, but I know you have need of variety to sweeten the round of your studies & self denial, and therefore I have not lost a day in offering you what refreshment it is in my power to give. Before writing to London, pray answer this and await my reply which shall not tarry. And in the mean time I will write Margaret again.

For myself, I have made little use of Schiller[98] and only read two scenes, having upon me the entire duties of the parish till Dr Chalmers' return. My mind is experiencing a strong set towards the state of religion as it is compared with what it is in the Scriptures, and if I am spared I shall devote some of my leisure time to this subject. Of Literature & Science I am becoming quite forgetful, and yet I would not say but, by them, I may have to live, for the longer I practice my profession I love it the more, while I love the more conceit of almost all my fellow practioners, and feel the more reluctance to any method of acquiring Church Patronage save by the exhibition of my preaching & my conduct. And on the other hand I am so pressed with a lavish generosity, and so

---

98. See Carlyle to Edward Irving, 3 June 1820 n: CL, 1: 253–56.

Part II: The Letters

encountered by scenes & objects of distress, that I almost fear being brought to poverty—while I have neither the will nor the art to take advantage of the celebrity which it were possible to gather from both preaching and practice. My rule is to improve well the present, and trust in God for the future, and if I can only follow it, I have nothing to dread which I have not means to meet.

Write me as soon as you have leisure, and be full upon that subject which this letter chiefly concerns—and take no step till you hear from me again—and if I seem cautious and formal, give me the credit to believe it is from the strong desire I have to see you happy. My kind regards to your Father's family. And to your Mother my bonds of love in our common Saviour.

Yours very affectionately,
Edwd Irving

Addressed to: Mr. Thomas Carlyle,
Mr. James Carlyle's,[99]
Mainhill, Ecclefechan.

~

Edward Irving to THOMAS CARLYLE

34 Kent Street, Glasgow, 26th Sept 1820[100]

My Dear Carlyle,

The very high favour which you made for yourself at Grange, and the very marked improvement in the stile [*sic*] of your intercourse with far inferior personages when I was last at Annan, convince me that the taint of severity which your character had taken from the trials it has passed though is destined to be only temporary, and to give place to the refined enjoyment which your superior endowments of mind should make sure to you. And this pleasing prophecy which I make of your future experience of life, contains within it the grounds of my recommendation to take the offer which Providence has made to you. Did I not think that you were able to bring yourself to associate with the honest but ignorant *statesmen* of Yorkshire, and that you had self-denial enough to take upon you in earnest the charge of a poor unhealthy lad,[101] I would not advise you to it though the emolument were to be changed from hundreds

---

99. James Carlyle (1758–1831), Thomas Carlyle's father.

100. NLS, MS 1764, fol. 191–92.

101. Mr. Hutton of Sobergate. 'Clearly [Matthew] Allen had written Carlyle some details concerning the possibility of his tutoring a mentally subnormal (thought later by Carlyle to be an Idiot) younger brother of John Hutton of Sobergate in the township of Newby Wiske.' CL 1: TC to Matthew Allen, 271 fn. Carlyle did not take the position.

to thousands. But I am satisfied of both, and there I advise you. They will not be able to give you credit for your large acquirements, nay you will often have to hide them under a bushel, but this is no more than you are constrained to at present—nay you are constrained to more, for with the greater part of your associates you have not only hitherto derived no credit for your acquirements, but you have sustained a great deal of envious & secret persecution[,] I mean the persecution of unfair constructions, and unkind representations. I recommend it to you therefore, because I think you can accommodate yourself to its duties; and likewise because it will increase your power of accommodation. You live far too much in an ideal world, and you are likely to be punished for it, by an unfitness for practical life, it is not your fault, but the misfortune of your circumstances, as it has been in a less degree of my own. This situation will be more a remedy for that, than if you were to go back to Edin where I have no doubt of your ultimately finding your way to a congenial circle, but not perhaps till it be too late for enjoying it. Try your hand, therefore, with the respectable though illiterate men of middle life, as I am doing at present, and perhaps in their honesty and hearty kindness you may be taught to forget and perhaps to undervalue the splendour and envies & competitions of men of Literature. I think you have within you the ability to rear the pillar of your own immortality & what is more of your own happiness from the basis of any level in life. And I would always have any man destined to influence the interests of men, to have read these interests as they are disclosed in the mass of men, and not in the few, who are lifted upon the eminences of life, and when these too often forget the man, to ape the ruler or the monarch. All that is valuable of the *literary caste* you have in their writings which will follow you everywhere—their conversations, I am told, are full of jealousy & reserve, or perhaps[,] to cover that reserve[,] of trifling.

Perhaps what I have said, bears too much the stamp of my speculation, barren generality—and it may be necessary to look the condition offered you more closely in the face. This boy's character one would be the better of[f] knowing but if like the rest of his Countrymen he will be good-natured & shrewd. If he be the former, I do not fear for the issue, if the latter so much the better. But if he should turn out a little shrewish—why you must just master him by a little address and for the brother & the sister I calculate much upon the fame of a Scotsman for your introduction, and if once introduced there is no fear of you. But remember you are to put away every scrap of the Philosopher & the recluse, and to be a plain conversable man. You are not to take the footing of the tutor, doling out instruction by the hour, but of the friend and companion & domesticated man. As Cowper did, for example, with the Unwins[102]—or Locke[103] with Lord & Lady [Masham.] You will obtain, I doubt not £150, and certainly

102. William Cowper (1731–1800), poet, lived with the family of the Revd Morley Unwin at Huntingdon and upon whose death he and Dr Morley's widow Mary moved to Olney ministered by the hymn writer, the Rev John Newton, with whom he collaborated and where he remained until his death. See *OCEL*.

103. John Locke (1632–1704): his last years were spent in Essex in the home of Sir Francis and Lady Masham. See *OCEL*.

you may state you think your attainments & employments in Scotland entitle you to so much, I dismiss this subject—for I want to finish before the post.

Now, for the other. Write to Margaret,[104] and all speed go with you but tell her from me, that if she write you one more letter than she does to me, I will discard her altogether. I got over the prayers—so [ink blot] in her letter for daring to hint in mine that she might perhaps not have loved so deeply as she thought, that I pray you for your comfort to express no dubitation upon that subject[;] I thought to have written her again by this time but this letter has taken precedence. Let the example of poor Allen[105] warn you against venturing too far upon the subject of Love I think it as well you confine yourself to the Platonic.

I had a vast deal of other matters to write about, but my time is run up, and I must close. Please to write as soon as you can conveniently—and excuse the abruptness with which I conclude.

Yours affectionately,
Edwd Irving

Addressed to: Mr. Thomas Carlyle,
Mr. James Carlyle,
Mainhill, Ecclefechan.

Edward Irving to THOMAS CARLYLE

Glasgow, 34 Kent St., December 1820
[Postmarked 14th December 1820[106]]

My Dear Carlyle,

Yours is a correspondence which yields me so much intellectual entertainment and affords me opportunities of such elevated sympathy, that I would be cruel to myself to put any obstacle in its way. Had I known your address in Edin[107] you had certainly heard from me a week ago, but, as it is, the only comfort I have for being anticipated is one I did not deserve, to see how entirely your correspondence is relieved from all shackles of ceremony, which gall me in some others which I maintain. You make me too proud of myself when you connect me so much with your happiness. Would that I

---

104. Margaret Gordon

105. Two of Matthew Allen's three wives were dead by this time, and it was perhaps to these sad experiences Irving was referring. See Edward Irving to TC, 4 June 1819.

106. NLS, MS 1764: fol. 195.

107. Thomas Carlyle had arrived in Edinburgh on Wednesday, 22 November 1820. See letter from Carlyle to Alexander Carlyle, 23 November 1820: CL, 1:287.

could contribute to it as I most fondly wish, and one of the richest and most powerful minds I know should not now be struggling with obscurity and a thousand obstacles and yet if I had the power I do not see by what means I should cause it to be known. Your mind, unfortunately for its present peace, has taken in so wide a range of study, as to be almost incapable of professional wield—and it has nourished so uncommon & so unyielding a character as first unfits you, and thus disgusts you with any accommodations which for so cultivated & so fertile a mind would easily procure favour & patrons. The race you have run, these last years, pains me even to think upon, and if it should be continued a little longer I pray God to give you strength to endure it. But, while I speak thus, remember you are listening to one of a most unsanguine temperament, though of a most enduring character—little familiar with the shapes of future good or ill which imagination bodes forth, yet armed cap-a-pie[108] to encounter whatever falls out from the cup of providence. My Dear Carlyle, our characters, for the present should be exchanged, and I were willing for a while to fight your battles of imagination, could I but render you my dull obstinacy to meet your battles of reality.

But, this is not language sufficiently cordial, to express my feeling of your present case. If the Review[109] come to nothing & Translation be unsalable, and Brewster's[110] 'Geographical Articles'—be like the bricks of Goshen[111]—then there remaineth nothing but an independent effort on your own account. You must challenge the world in one shape or another. Edinburgh is not the scene where you are distressed; Mainhill is not the scene when you are sequestered. London, my Dear friend, you must by no means as yet, adventure on. But this Western home will answer well. We calculate upon seeing you at Christmass [sic], and till then you can think of what I now propose. That instead of wearying yourself with endless vexations which are more than you can bear, you will consent to spend not a few weeks, but a few months here under my roof, where enjoying at least wholesome conversation & the sight of real friends, you may employ yourself upon some literary employment which may present you in a fairer aspect to the public than any you have hitherto taken before them. Now, I know, it is quite Scottish for you to refuse this upon the score of troubling me, but trouble to me it is none, and if it were a thousand times more would I not esteem it well bestowed upon you, and most highly rewarded by your company and conversation; and perhaps

---

108. Head to foot.

109. There is an unpublished letter from Brewster (see below) to Carlyle. Dated 28 October 1820, it reads in part: 'I have been maturing along with several other Gentlemen a scheme of a permanent nature in which I proposed that you [Thomas Carlyle] should have an active share. This Scheme if it succeeds will be both creditable and Lucrative to you. I cannot say more of it till I see you personally, that that it relates to the establishment of a new Review in Edinburgh, which is at present a profound secret': CL, 1:289 n. The project did not become a reality.

110. Dr. David Brewster, editor of the *Edinburgh Magazine* (Jan. 1785–Dec.1803), and its successors the *Edinburgh Philosophical Journal* and the *Edinburgh Journal of Science*.

111. The Israelites enslaved in the region of Goshen were required by the pharaoh to famously make bricks without the straw they needed. See Exod 1:8–14; 5:6–9.

I might even be persuaded to take a lesson of German from you, and to give a lesson of Italian in return. Now do not let squeamishness hinder this—I should esteem it an honour that your first sally in arms went forth from my habitation.[112]

Your friend Graham, and my much esteemed friend also, was almost overcome to weeping, when he perused the paragraph of your letter in which he was mentioned. Not that I shew your letters, but that I permitted him to read that which I had not words to express so well. He has now had a meeting of his Glasgow Creditors, highly honourable both to him & them appointing Trustees & thus saving from a public Bankruptcy—but he is still anxious whether his English Creditors will agree, which it seems is necessary, and which there is some reason to fear. Meanwhile, he has removed into lodgings, and feels himself much more comfortable. He anticipates your arrival here at Xmas with great delight as do we all. So if it be barely possible to make the passage which after all is not very unkind, you may rest assured to find your old friends all unchanged. The Grange family are expected shortly. David Hope[113] who has been in Edin, settling two cousins from N[ew] South Wales at the boarding schools regretted not knowing you were in Edin. Warrand and Nancy very happy to appearances are comfortably planted in their own house,[114] where, I *guess* they would be right happy to see their kinsman.

You would have had this letter three days ago but for close visitations in the parish. Accept my kindest affection. Write that we are to look for you at Xmas.

Yours always,

Edwd Irving

Addressed to: Mr. Thomas Carlyle,
Robertson's Lodgings,
15 Carnegie Street, Edinburgh.

~

Edward Irving to THOMAS CARLYLE

34 Kent Street, [Glasgow], 7th February 1821[115]

112. Thomas Carlyle to James Carlyle senior, Edinburgh, 18 December 1820; 'Irving &c send for me warmly to Glasgow during Christmas, I [trust] I shall go. They are most kind people': CL, 1:297. Thomas Carlyle to Alexander Carlyle Edinburgh, 23 December 1820. 'I am going away to Glasgow tomorrow morning very early': *ibid*.

113. David Hope, Merchant in Glasgow (d.1857). A nephew of Adam Hope, and a close friend of Graham and Irving. 'Old David Hope, that was his name, lived on a little farm close by Solway Shore, a mile or two east of Annan': Carlyle, *Reminiscences*, 206.

114. Warrand and Nancy Carlile's house was in Paisley. See Carlyle, *Reminiscences*, 259.

115. NLS, MS 1764: fol. 197-98.

My Dear Carlyle,

I greet you well, in the hope of seeing you on Monday next; and such is my state of engagement I feared I would not have got you informed. Even at the expense of seeing what is defiled, and feeling what is sorrowful, I would give a week of such a life as mine for a day of such a life as yours, and I know not with whom I would make the exchange but yourself, for I think you would not make hesitation. Upon my honest word, I have no thoughts of any virtue or purpose—hurrying from engagement to a little literary trifling which after all becomes a kind of toil from the eagerness with which it is snatched. From morning to night I meet with no one who can excite me into keen sensibility and I have not like you, the faculty of exciting myself. And when a villainous trait of character comes accross [sic] me, or a low rascally sentiment passes my ear, I must just compose myself under my insignificance, and smother my emotion. And even if I have scope for its utterance, I cannot clothe it in any but abrupt and broken language—I can give it no ornament no poetry—I can feel but I either cannot take time, or do not think it worth while to express, depend upon it this is a great distinction between men who can stay upon their sensations and give them distinct utterance and feel relieved by doing so, and sometimes I confess feel embittered and men who are struck somewhat deeper and can come forth in no way but by deep imprecation or desperate resolutions—and seem so entirely engulphed by their power of feeling that their power of utterance has in a manner departed. You are of the first class, and so is Shakespeare and all the old Dramatists of his day. Alfieri is of the latter class and some more of his countrymen, and I think I hold of them by the remotest consanguinity & lowest rank. The former commit them to their sensations because they can drain off their violence by utterance, the latter dare not commit themselves, and so they forget to feel, and either lose their power as I am doing, or if the events of their life have kept it in play, become desperadoes and outcasts & madmen, and very devils incarnate.

Now you are coming to your right mind—and shall soon take your proper level. The life of Locke would not take up your whole mind. It is a work of criticism, and I would rather see you take to a work of creation. There is little scope for wit or fancy or the rich poetry you are master of. But for the enthusiasm of feeling and the estimation of character, and the calm dignified repose of the sage which if you have it not in perfection, you should strive to come at—I know no theme more suitable.

The Schlegels[116] are good critics in Poetry, but in Philosophy they are mystics or rather bablers [sic]. A Schlegel in Philosophy were a new person. Stewart,[117] though he should be spoken of with reverence has no title to this character, and has no deep place in the public sympathies. He is rather a culler of beauties, and a drawer of char-

---

116. August Wilhelm von Schlegel (1767-1845), translator of Shakespeare into German and his brother
Friedrich von Schlegel (1772-1829), theorist of Romanticism. See *OCEL*.

117. Dugald Stewart (1753-1828) professor of moral philosophy at Edinburgh during Irving's student years. See *OCEL*.

acteristics, than a surveyor of the Philosophic Community & philosophic world, and an allotter of its various departments.

I crave your forgiveness for the nonsense of this scrawl. When I write to you I should be master of my time & myself—and this day I have more engagements to go about than I can fulfil. Graham & the Johnstones are well.

Yours most affectionately,
Edward Irving

P.S. Yet I cannot close without an expression of my sorrow that your schemes should have been thwarted—if I should not rather rejoice, for depend upon it, my friend, that your nature neither intends you for a Translator nor a compiler. And perhaps there may be a providence in all this to free you out of the narrow creeks & seas into the open ocean and great concerns of literature—where you may yet do much for your own & the common weal.

Still, while I speak so I am alive to all the difficulties, but if I could see from your hand something on the spirit of the Literature and Science of the day, or, say, of your intellectual city, sparing none, and mistreating none, but giving free latitude to your knowledge of other and better states of it—and to your conceptions of higher states than any you do know—it would make an impression. Edward Irving

Addressed to: Mr. Thomas Carlyle,
16 Carnegie St.,
Edinburgh.

∼

Edward Irving to THOMAS CHALMERS

[Postmark: Glasgow!] 15th Febr 1821
Duffs Lodgings, 35 Bristo Street, [Edinburgh][118]

Dear Sir,

I have heard Wilson[119] lecture and seen Haydon's[120] picture—and in neither case with the satisfaction I could have wished. I am not able to comprehend the picture

---

118. NCL, MSS CHA 4.16.2.

119. John Wilson 'Christopher North' (1785–1854), Professor of Moral Philosophy at Edinburgh from 1820. He lacked the ability to compose competent lectures and a friend for many years wrote them for him. See *OCEL*. See also *Reminiscences*, 410–26.

120. Benjamin Robert Haydon (1786–1846), English painter. The picture that Irving saw was *Christ's Triumphant Entry into Jerusalem*, 1814–20. See George, *The Life and Death of Benjamin Robert Haydon*, 129–34.

The picture shows Christ on a donkey, surrounded by a crowd. Christ points to Wordsworth, Newton and Voltaire standing on his right and perhaps their inclusion in an ostensibly religious picture

sufficiently, but for Wilson I hardly reckon it worth while to comprehend him. There is no scientific conception of his subject, and consequently no distinction in delineating it. There is no metaphysical acumen whatever, nor is there much relief in the delineations of the shadowy things with which he is conversant. But above all his stile [sic] is to my mind rude & even the poetry of it very ungraceful. He seems mystified among the terms in use, and sets himself rather to the description of these, than to the analysing the various parts of our nature whereof these names are only the popular & not the philosophical nomenclature. His mode of delivery is quite vulgar, and would be thought so by any dissenting congregation in Scotland. But I fear I may prejudice you. You will soon be able to judge for yourself.

What makes me write you at present is the request of a relative of mine—a wine merchant in the city, Mr. Robertson whom you have met with at Mr. Walter Woods—I breakfasted there this morning, and found him like the other serious people of the city, full of the idea of locality. He is one of the localising committee whose meeting I am going to attend on Friday. I expressed how happy you would have been to be present, and to understand their method of procedure—he said he would have been still more so but that he would ask Major McGregor and one or two more of the leading patrons of the system to dinner on Tuesday & I thought you would be willing to meet them. Not a formal party, but one for making you acquainted with all that has been done, and hearing further from you what might still be done. I said I would take it upon me in such a case to write you, and present his most respectful compliments, and request you to honour him with your company—without at the same time taking upon me in any respect to give him hopes that you would be able to be present.

Present my kind love to Mrs. Chalmers & the children—and to your neighbours the Woods who will give you further information about Mr. Robertson.

I am Dr Sir,
Yours,
Most respectfully,
Edwd Irving

Addressed to: Rev Dr Chalmers,
Glasgow.

---

caused Irving to find it incomprehensible.

Part II: The Letters

Edward Irving to THOMAS CARLYE

34 Kent St., [Glasgow], 15th March 1821[121]

My Dear Carlile, [*sic*]

I hope this will be in time to reach you before you go back to your Fathers.' It was to have been written on Sunday night but for two English Tutors who have come to overload me with the concerns of another Society and have busied me ever since with their concerns. And if it had been written then it would have been better written for I was in such a serious mood, as seems to me best when I converse with one of so deep thought and so wounded a heart as you. But to your other troubles too hard to bear, at least with the strong representation of your conception and gloomy colouring of your feelings, and with no relief of friendship and not much of hope, I pray you never to doubt of my unbroken attachment, which I think myself honoured rather than you benefited by my retaining. My reason for leaving Edin on Friday was that I might have the Saturday for study which in your town I was altogether unfit for. I should have signified this by letter and done much more, but present engagements press upon me and over me like the waves of the sea, and I long to be at rest from them in some quarter where I could enjoy my own thoughts, and please myself with my own pursuits instead of being hunted as I am incessantly and over-burdened with profitless engagement.

There is not any rest in life—though our condition were all assorted to our minds to day—our minds tomorrow would discord with it—I have given over looking for any and I betake myself to the anticipation of another state where the most weary shall be at rest and I feel that as I translate affection after affection from present being, I enjoy what is good more reasonably, and meet what is evil more firmly.

Oh that I could possess you with some of the quietness which I am enabled to dispense at times to the afflicted body and disquiet spirit of sufferers whom I visit—and which I myself feel at times, or rather hope to feel, or rather see by conviction that I am competent to feel—then would I have you possessed of a resource that would never fail. Nothing would give me greater delight (so little do your deep felt and not affected vexations chagrin me as you unjustly think), than to bear you company homewards, and do my best to entertain and restore you—I see you have much to bear, and perhaps it may be a time before you clear yourself of that sickness of the heart which afflicts you, but strongly I feel assured it will not master you—that you will rise strongly above it, and reach the place your genius destines you to. Most falsely do you judge yourself when you seek such degrading similitudes to represent what you call your whining—and I pray you may not again talk of your distresses in so desperate & to me so disagreeable a manner. My Dear Sir, is it to be doubted that you are suffering grievously the want of spiritual communion, the bread and water of the soul[,] and why then do you as it were, mock at your calamity or treat it jestingly. I declare this is a sore offence. You altogether mistake at least my feeling if you think I feel any thing but the kindliest

---

121. NLS, MS 1764: fols. 199–200.

sympathy in your case, in which sympathy I am sure there is nothing degrading either to you to or to me, else were I degraded every time I visit a sick bed in endeavouring to draw forth the case of a sufferer from his own life that I may, if possible, administer some spiritual consolation. But oh I would be angry or rather I would feel a shudder of unnatural feeling if the sick man were to make a mockery to me of his case—or to decide himself on making it known to any physician of body or of mind.

Excuse my freedom, Carlile [sic]; I do this in justification of my own state of mind towards your distress. I feel for your condition as a brother would feel, and to see you silent upon it were the greatest access of painful emotion which you could cause me. I hope soon to look back with you over this scene of trials, as the soldier does over a hard campaign, or the restored captives do over their days of imprisonment. Meanwhile take with you to your Father's my best prayers for your recovery and reckon upon my more regular correspondence, if such hasty and imperfect a thing can yield you any comfort. Your friends here are well. Commend me to your parents & family and believe me
Yours always,
Edwd Irving

Addressed to: Mr. Thomas Carlile, [sic]
16 Carnegie Street,
Edinburgh.

~

Edward Irving to DR THOMAS CHALMERS

6th April 1821[122]

Dear Sir,
I reckon it singularly opportune that I came down to my fathers': for though my sister[123] is fast recovering from her disorder, and her understanding & recollection quite returned, I find her conscience in considerable disquietude and longing for the peace of the Gospel. In the present state of this parish,[124] it was not possible she could have been enlightened in the knowledge of Christ, and so her trouble might in its most serious aspect have remained uncomposed, and the opportunity been lost which the Almighty has offered. I never saw any instance more striking of the recomposing effects of Evangelical truth, shewing me in another sense that Christ is the physician of

---

122. NCL, MSS CHA 4. 18.4.

123. Elizabeth (b. 1797), Irving's sister, on 24 April 1815 had married William Kennedy who was later to become a merchant in Manchester.

124. William Moncrieff minister at Annan 1784–1824, whom Carlyle recalled as having been over-fond of drink: Carlyle, *Reminiscences*, 207n, Grass, *The Lord's Watchman*, 4, 33.

the body as well as of the soul. The conversations I have held with her have had more effect, I believe in enabling her to struggle with and overcome the nervous influence than all the medicines that have been prescribed to her.

I enjoy myself very much among the simple and heartfelt affections of my father's family[.] I wonder that philosophers and poets have busied themselves so much with the delineation of political and friendly relations to the neglect as I think of the more homely and more fruitful enjoyments of relationship, and which I believe are far more powerful over the heart. Far more are affected by the history of Joseph's filial & paternal virtues than of David's friendship. The habits of the people too afford a great variety; it would have been a great treat to you to have seen yesterday the whole population of the Burgh pound out to elevated points and bridges & embankments to witness the highest tide that has been seen since the terrible flood of '96—and to have marked the timorous and bustling anxiety, and all the sea craft in the river put into requisition to convey families out of flooded houses. And the rapidity with which the tidings of the great bank having given way flew from mouth to mouth. The sight itself was sublime—the whole fields and roads on both sides of the water flooded. Houses & hedge rows and ricks standing here and there amongst expanses of stormy waters. And the people looking out from all the elevations—and the sloops riding with difficulty. My sister that is poorly does not reside here but she is on a visit—her husband is with us and means to return to his duties in the course of next week. I shall take advantage of your kind indulgence and preach to them next Sabbath, and return along with him. His residence is in Ayrshire so that our roads are nearly the same way. I hope to make up for my absence by

[Three line missing]

so far recovered as to place Mrs. Chalmers & you out of anxiety as I am now almost about my sister.

I had almost forgot—the women Maggie Cowan whose brother died in Newfoundland went down for further intelligence from a Captain who wrote to her through her former maid in Paisley. She was to have called upon me on Monday and [Rest missing.]

Addressed to: Rev Dr Chalmers,
Windsor Place,
Glasgow.

~

Edward Irving to THOMAS CARLYLE

Glasgow, 26th April 1821[125]

My Dear Carlyle,

I received your last epistle with great relish, while ministering to the sickness or rather delighting in the recovery of my sister Elizabeth at Annan, whither I had hastened on the first intelligence of her illness—it was so gloomy. But now she is well & with her husband in Galston, her recovery having been rapid beyond all precedent. Her complaint was a fever brought on by bile & nursing which flew to her head for a few days, and gradually subsided leaving her mind as it found it, save that it made her more thoughtful of death & eternity—which thoughts it was my happy office to allay by making known to her the revelation of mercy. Since that I have heard from her, and find her coming from behind a cloud of apprehension which had long lain upon her spirit, and coming into the enjoyment of a serene peace to which she has hitherto been a stranger, and as usual with those that understand religion consulting how she may make her life more serviceable to her family and the world. Your brother[126] spent an afternoon with us, and delighted me above measure with the good sense and solidity of his conversation. I urged the propriety of his coming out to Edin in the winter and as it depends with you, I now urge it again. He is a shrewd boy, and wants only opportunity to become a scholar—that he neither has nor can have in Annan, he will have it in Edin however—to an extent that with his age & your direction will make his progress, I pledge me, most extraordinary. His capacity of taking the rubs of life is far above either yours or mine, and his mathematics, if properly laid out, will obtain him a livelihood until his Education is complete. His ambition, however high it may be, is sober, and by no means restive, and from three hours various & close conversation, I thought I never saw a young man whom it would be more sinful to cramp. My promises you may think have no body in them—but I promise & shall be happier to fulfil, to introduce him to three of the most popular clergymen in Edin, Mr. Thompson,[127] Dr Fleming,[128] & Mr. Gordon[129] as a competent mathematician, and an anxious youth—provided my footing with these gentlemen continue as it is. And, upon a recent occasion I had reason to know that I had some influence with the two former, and for the latter I can pledge him to any thing which is sincere & generous. I would not heed about your brother's present attainments in Latin—it is the field I wish to open up to him, it is not his prowess I wish him, as yet at least, to make shew of.

---

125. NLS, MS 1764: fols. 201–2.
126. Very likely James Carlyle (b. 12 November 1805), who would have been fifteen at the time.
127. See Edward Irving to Thomas Carlyle, 25 September 1819, p 78.
128. Thomas Fleming (1754–1824), minister of Lady Yester's Church in Edinburgh from 1806–24. See Scott, *Fasti*, 1.83. He lived at 26 George Square: See CL, 2:24 n.
129. Robert Gordon, minister of Buccleuch, Edinburgh. Scott, *Fasti*, 1:22.

Part II: The Letters

For myself, were I not most indifferent to almost every other form of earthly good, save the sympathy of a few generous minds, and the affection of my relatives, I were ready to feel disappointed & chagrined, by the unfavourable turn which every effort takes that is made to serve me[.] Dr C and Mr. Gordon have been equally unsuccessful. Kinfauns[130] went to one better backed, and Hamilton went to one earlier promised, and I am here as formerly not once having devoted a thought to either disappointment. I can neither make a jest nor a satyre [sic] nor yet a homily to myself upon succeeding or not succeeding in that which is paramount in the breast of every preacher I meet with. It costs me nothing. Meanwhile my active youth is wearing on during which I could, by this time, if properly circumstanced[,] have made myself been heard and felt in the church & perhaps farther—but it matters not. Life has higher aims than to meliorate any body, or infuse vigour into any councils but here again I am out, for I make no progress in the new man which after God is created in righteousness and true holiness;[131] which in purest faith believe me, is the only ambition I have in life. If I could reach that eminence I would till in a manner that I picture not in my own imagination, least from being heavenly-minded I should become ambitious.

For you I am beginning to see the dawn of that day when you shall be plucked by the literary world, as my friend Gordon has now been by the religious, from my solitary and therefore most dear admiration, and when from an almost monopoly I shall have nothing but a mere shred of your praise. They will unearth you. And for your sake I will rejoice though for my own I may regret but I shall always have the pleasant superiority that I was your friend and admirer through good & through bad report Wd I continue so, I hope, unto the end. Yet our honest Demosthenes or shall I call him Chrysostom,[132] Boanerges[133] would fit him better, seems to have caught some glimpse of your inner man, though he had few opportunities I ween, for he never ceases to be enquiring after you. Waugh[134] is a heavy pompous man of words, I have not seen your paper, well I anticipate it will be unworthy of its company so loyal, so phrasing and so inoffensive. You will soon shift your quarters, though for the present I think your Motto should be 'Better a wee bush than nae field.' If you are going to revert to teaching again[,] which I heartily deprecate, I know nothing better than Swan's conception[135]—although success in it depend mainly upon affect and address and the

---

130. Kinfauns and Hamilton were Church of Scotland parishes.

131. Eph 4:24.

132. St. John Chrysostom (c.349), Bishop of Constantinople and 'Doctor of the Church,' was known for his forthright preaching; his name means 'silver-tongued.' See *ODCC*.

133. 'Son of Thunder,' a reference to the impetuosity of the disciples James and John (Mark 3:17).

134. John Bailie Waugh, Edinburgh bookseller and co-publisher of the short lived *New Edinburgh Review*.

135. William Swan, (d.1833) was three times provost of Kirkcaldy whose eldest son Patrick was a pupil of both Edward Irving and Thomas Carlyle. See CL, 1: 143 n.

Swan had recommended Carlyle to rend a sizeable house and give wealthy borders private tuition to see them through College or High School. See Thomas Carlyle to Alexander Carlyle, 24 March

studying of humour, which, though it be a good enough way of its kind is not the way to which I think you should condescend. In the mean time however you may have it in your eyes and if others offer from any quarter, commence when you think the firm strong enough. I never found any comfort in it—my conscience and the fashion of it could not agree and I never met an employer's face but with a secret shrink.

David Hope is going out to London. He has great things on the anvil. Miss Reily[136] is not to go out with her Mother & Sister, I say no more, and perhaps have said too much. A word to the wise.

Graham and I were at Paisley, Friday last, have not seen him since but am now going out to call on him. Mr. and Mrs. Johnstone are gone down. I would like to make a jaunt with you this summer if our finances will stand it. Mine are the lowest, and sacredly I will not borrow. My sister and brother-in-law are coming north to see the Carlyle's [sic][,] they are going some where. Don't count this letter off by the number of days for I have been jolted about since ever yours was in my possession till this moment. Do write me soon and fully.

E. Irving

Addressed to: Mr. Thomas Carlyle,
16 Carnegie Street,
Edinburgh.

~

Edward Irving to JANE WELSH

34 Kent Street, Glasgow, 5th June 1821[137]

My Dear Jane,
 . . . I may speak out the sense I feel of your Mother's treatment of my Friend[138] and myself; it was so kind and so far from the restraints and affectations of ordinary intercourse. I wish both of us were of that rank and consideration in the world, which could make our acquaintance as creditable before the world as we have found without any of these vulgar recommendations it was welcome in your eyes. But the time perhaps is coming in the good dispensations of Providence when we shall get an establishment

---

1821: CL, 1:348 and 352.

136. David Hope's courtship of this lady was terminated by her reluctance to leave her native home. See CL l: 366n.

137. Carlyle, *Love Letters* 2:412–13.

138. Thomas Carlyle. Irving had taken Thomas Carlyle to Haddington to meet Jane where he made a poor impression. Irving himself had been in love with Jane but by this time his sense of honour may have decided him not to marry her. See Grass, *The Lord's Watchman*, 38.

among the good comfortable conditions as well as the vain and empty opinions of men. Meanwhile I daresay you must be content with the old commonplace returns of gratitude for the present and protestations for the future … You see I will be speaking with the large license of a Tutor, or with the grave ceremony of a Clerical Gallant. The truth is I am not skilled, as I have not been accustomed, to read myself to a lady; and so you see I blunder now upon the one side and now upon the other. And I know your eye is as quick to discern, as your heart is set to abhor the poor wight who has recourse to sentiment, the only recourse which he has in cases of such exceeding nicety.

This (new) page, my accomplished pupil, shall be devoted to a more serious strain … I pray you, my dear friend, not to put religion away from you with that unconcern or slight consideration which the multitude do … Study it with half the intensity you have studied Literature, practice it with half the diligence, and if there flow not in upon your spirit a gust of new nature, and come not forth an efflorescence of new fruitfulness, then do I consent that you shall give it up forever … My warmest affection I offer to your Mother, and my services to the last of my ability. Again I say, if I were a man of might, I would feel more liberty in offering them; but as I am, with my Maker's natural gifts and with the desire to possess my Redeemer's graces, I offer myself to you both, as a most esteeming friend and most zealous to make up by counsel and otherwise that noble-minded Guardian[139] whom it hath pleased our Heavenly Father to remove from you. With the tear of memory in my eye and with the glow of ancient affection in my heart, I am, my dear Jane,

Your affectionate friend and instructor,
Edw[d] Irving

Edward Irving to THOMAS CARLYLE

Glasgow, 24 Kent St., 12th June 1821[140]

My Dear Carlyle,

I think I never left Edin with more sadness than when I parted with you in Princes Street. I endeavoured to banish it (for I cannot like you digest my melancholy into strong mental food) by the reading of those theological manuscripts of our worthy Elder, but what I read I know not, only in the course of five miles they were at an end and I was again without resource. There was the most rueful company of us you can well conceive, a lady who gave no proof of her capacity for speech till long after we had past the Kirk of Shotts, two Gentlemen of taste much about the condition of our solid

---

139. Jane Welsh's father had died suddenly on 19 September 1819.

140. NLS, MS 1764: fols. 203–4. There is a heavily edited version of this letter in Carlyle, *Love Letters*, 1: 413–14.

guard, who dilated with considerable grace upon Turnpike roads & Coaches & Coach proprietors, and the perfect certainty that the opposition horses would never stand it when the 'heavy weather' set in. A dandy in front who wished to wheedle an old steeve Irish-man out of his berth besides the Coachman, which with a solitary word upon seeing some Harriers constituted the whole symptoms of a soul he gave during our journey. A man whom I take for a Journeyman wright but he said not a word. And the Lady to whom I resigned my seat whose cheerfulness made me the only amends that was left.

She had the most delightful thing of a Port-Fol. containing all sorts of extracts in Poetry, of a sentimental & erotic cast, some small man from the inventive heads of conundrum-makers and certain engravings from My Lord Byron's works most tastefully fastened to the leaves of the book, and embroidered around the edges with elegant devices cut in paper. My sober spirit rose[,] what a vanity thought I, filled with the only kind of writing & workmanship which is positively useless. And this is the companion which is to console this lady's journey, and comfort her in the absence of her friends, and form the future mother of a family.

By the way, between ourselves, there is too much of that furniture about the elegant drawing room of Jane Welsh[141] our friend. I could like to see her surrounded with a more sober set of companions than Rousseau, your friend, & Byron and such like, they will never make different characters than they were themselves, so deeply are they the prototypes of their own conceptions of human characters. And I don't think it will much mend the matter when you get her introduced to von Schiller & von Goethe and your other nobles of the German literature. And I fear Jane has already dipped too deep into that spring already—so that unless some more solid food be afforded I fear she will escape altogether out of the region of my sympathies and the sympathies of honest home-bred men. In these feelings I know you will join me, and in giving to her character and speculation a useful and elegant turn I know you will aid me as you have opportunity.

I have been analysing, as I could, the origin of my esteem and affection for you which made me so loath to part with you and shall make me so happy to renew our wanderings. You are no more a general favourite than I am, and in the strong pockets of character we are not alike, nor yet alike in the turn of our general thoughts. And we

---

141. Thomas Carlyle did not know Irving had been in love with Jane Welsh, whom Irving had tutored as a child in Haddington (East Lothian) and had met her again in Edinburgh when she was seventeen. See Oliphant, *Life*, 1:135. We know that he had asked her to marry him, and there is a brief allusion in another letter he wrote from Annan just after his ordination. See Edward Irving to the Elders and Congregation of the Caledonian Church, 20 June 1822: Edward Irving L, MS 23.

Irving had introduced a reluctant Carlyle to Jane on a visit to her at Haddington in 1821 but Carlyle had been immediately smitten; and it was Carlyle that she eventually married.

However, when she became engaged to Carlyle she was encouraged by her friend Mrs Montague to confess to him that her declaration of indifference to Irving was not true. She wrote to Carlyle telling him in fact she had once loved Irving deeply and gave Carlyle the opportunity of terminating the relationship but in the event he forgave her. See CL, 3:356–59 and 356n.

are both too intrepid to seek in each other pity or consolation, and too independent to let any thing sinister or selfish enter into our attachments. How comes it to pass then that we have so much pleasant communion. I'll tell you one thing[,] High literature is exiled from my sphere and simple principle is very much exiled from yours. There we feel a blank on both sides which is supplied in some measure when we meet. I'll tell you another thing—severed from the ordinary stays of men, influence[,] place[,] fortune, each in his place has been obliged to turn, to delight his solitude and hang his hopes upon something higher, and though we have not chosen the same thing, in both cases it is pure and unearthly and next to his own, the thing which the other admires most. I can easily see that in the progress of our thoughts and characters there will be ample room for toleration and charity, which will form the touch—stone of our esteem. I wish the thing you admire had more of body in it, your heart were then more at ease. Reserve your noble parts for better fortune, and let go any thing you hold cheap now that you are only afloat among the denser regions & have not reached the pure elements of your destiny.

There is a clever and well-informed article in Blackwoods last number 'on the Vulgar Prejudices against Literature'[142] which I thought somewhat in your vein. Tell me what you think of it. Did you write to Jane Welsh. I can say nothing yet about our Tour. They are beginning to grumble when I am absent. Yet I think it will come about. But I shall write you so soon as I know any thing positive. I have written Jane Welsh but have not heard from her again. Graham is to dine with me to-morrow I wish you were here also.

Yours most faithfully,

Edwd Irving

Addressed to: Mr. Thomas Carlyle,
16 Carnegie St.,
Edinburgh.

Edward Irving to JANE WELSH

Glasgow, 9th July 1821[143]

---

142. 'On Vulgar Prejudices against Literature,' *Blackwood's Magazine*, May 1821, vol. 9 no. 50. The author was David Macbeth Moir (1798–1851), a Scots novelist.

143. Carlyle, *Love Letters* 2:414–15. Note that this letter is reproduced by Carlyle. He did not print it as a separate item so it has no salutation.

It is wonderfully clear of affectation; and though it might be rendered richer by the study of some of our more ancient models (Hooker, Jeremy Taylor, Milton, &c[144]), it would not gain either in accuracy or propriety. [He confesses, however, that[145]]; In criticism I have no gift; to me it were positively a greater treat to find the tenderness of Christian sentiment and the workings of Christian affection than to see the refinement of Collier or the depth of (de) Staël.[146] My soul is divorcing itself from the world and its tastes, and longing to be wedded to purity and wisdom and effulgence of love which are in God, and which are revealed in Christ. It is not that I despise human ornaments, whereof never having had many, I should have no credit in despising them. I see them to be the purest extract of terrestrial existences, the poetry of what is seen; but I see likewise that the most accomplished may be the most envious and evil-doing and unhappy. And therefore I long for something which, while it graces and becomes my spirit, shall bless it with liberality and love, and set it at rest from quaking fears and restless dispeace. This is my wish, my dear pupil, for myself and for those whom I love.

. . . If ever I be blessed with a daughter of your accomplishments, and have her placed at a distance, in a guileful and heartless world, and if she were weeping the woe of some not distant calamity, I think my feeling towards that daughter were akin to this my feeling towards you.

[The Letter concludes thus:] Present to your mother my kind love, and my sense of the obligation in being permitted to fill up this solemn hour[147] in writing to her daughter, an obligation which I would not have had otherwise than by her full permission, and which, till I am forbidden, I shall not fail often and often to come under. –

I am, my dear Jane,

Your affect. instructor and friend,

Edwd Irving

P.S. I had last night a Letter from Carlyle, about a German Grammar, requesting me to send mine, as one he ordered for you has not come to hand. This I think exceeding preposterous, considering the distance, and that my Grammar is one of the rudest commonest sort. He encourages you to wade onward through the entanglements which grow along the edge that you may swim together down the Ethereal stream of German Poetry, against the Winter. I am happy on account of the interest he conceives in your progress in study. He is very generous and his spirit has been too long land-locked by

---

144. Richard Hooker (1554–1600), theologian of Anglicism, Jeremy Taylor (1613–67), devotional writer, John Milton (1608–74). In 1824 Irving was to give a generous tribute to these three writers who inspired his writing. "I have been accused of affecting the antiquated manner of ages and times now forgotton. The writers of those times are too much forgotten, I lament, and their style of writing hath fallen much out of use.' Irving, *For the Oracles of God*.

145. This insertion is Carlyle's bridge to the next portion of the letter.

146. Mme de Staël, (1766–1817), French writer. First to use the word *romanticism* in French. See *OCEL*.

147. 'Midnight': Carlyle, *Love Letters*, 1:417.

adverse currents, so that when an opportunity occurs of his getting out into the ocean of feeling where he was made to move, it gives me pleasure on his own account. E.I.

~

Edward Irving to THOMAS CARLYLE

Glasgow, 24th July 1821[148]

My Dear Carlyle,

I fear I shall have to deny myself the pleasure of travelling southward with you this autumn, though it is not unlikely I may have it in my power to meet you, and perhaps to return along with you. My mother is to be in Paisley on Saturday first, and will remain perhaps two months at least during which, if other things permitted, it would not be seemly in me to remove. But, in fact, Dr Chalmbers [sic] has said nothing to me upon the subject, and unless he frankly make me the offer I have no inducement sufficiently strong to ask. It may perhaps turn out as well, for had we travelled homeward in company our different periods of rustication would not have permitted us to return together—which may be practicable if I get leave of absence at all. And I have some hope this may be the case as I have not been a day absent from my charge but one since my Sister's illness. Were it not my duty both to my office, and to my worthy mother, I should have felt the disappointment the more keenly, as I had gone the length of casting about for introductions to the various parts of Galloway which it was worth our while to visit. If you still think of taking that route, I shall be happy to put you in possession of these & what others I can procure. And shall expect some time of you as you pass.

I did not follow your injunctions of transmitting to our fair acquaintance my German Grammar & Dictionary—her own being as much to her purpose—but I did not fail to inform her of the cause of your failure, and to instruct her to make a progress through the preliminaries to a sweet and easy perusal of the German poets. I am not competent to judge of their value towards the development of thought or character[;] you are and therefore I should be silent. But if they should tend to cut our young friend off from any of the wholesome intercourse of those amongst whom she is cast, without being able to raise her to a better, I should be very sorry, as it seems to me she is already unhinged from many of the enjoyments her condition might afford her. She contemplates the inferiority of others rather from the point of ridicule and contempt than from that of commiseration & relief—and by so doing, she not only leaves objects in distress, and loses the luxury of doing good, but she contracts in her own mind a degree of coldness and bitterness which suits ill with my conceptions of female character, and

---

148. NLS, MS 1764: fols. 207-8.

a female's station in Society. But I am speaking perhaps away from the truth; the books may not be what they are reported of. At the same time I am daily becoming more convinced, that in all that literature of our own which it is said holds of the German school there is something most poisonous to all that in this country has been named virtue, and still more to the distinctions of conduct which religion makes. It seems to me there is a jumble or confusion of former distinctions as if they were preparing for some new ones. They have the language of the highest purity, even of the most sacred religion in communion with the blackest crimes, and the presence of the former is thought some how or other to compensate for the latter. There is an attempt too I think at two standards of moral judgments[,] one for the man of genius and literature, the other for the vulgar. But I dare say these are rather the extravagances of imitators, than the errors of the masters.

I am making no progress in any studies—one book I read lately 'Caliph vathek'[149] whether a translation or imitation I do not know, but certainly the cleverest, coldest book I have read. It is most amazing to note the union of the warm sensual poetry of the Eastern stile [sic] with the cold sceptical ridicule of the French School. It is altogether very funny and often very grand. I would have you to take an afternoon in reading it, as you like an original. I have undertaken with Cabanis[150]—but I know not what to make of him. The creature has such a pretence to an accurate analysis of the subject, and yet is so insufferably loose in his language and deductions. And comes from his last with so very big an air—that I am ready to spurn him away as a conceited coxcomb. And yet in there a great mass of what is to me original matter & so I shall persevere. Write me soon

    Yours,
    E. Irving

Addressed to: Mr. Thomas Carlyle,
16 Carnegie Street,
Edinburgh.

---

149. Beckford, *The History of Caliph Vathek*.

150. 'Pierre Jean George Cabanis (1757–1808), whose *Rapports du physique et du moral de l'homme* (1802); 'Relations of the Physical and the Moral in Man.' which explained all of reality, including the psychic, mental, and moral aspects of man, in terms of a mechanistic Materialism.' www.britannica.com, 26 July 2010.

Part II: The Letters

Edward Irving to WILLIAM DINWIDDIE

Glasgow, 34 Kent St., 6th November 1821[151]

Sir,

I was spoken to, this morning, by Mr. Laurie[152] about the Ministry of the Caledonian chapel, and for the sake of good understanding I take it upon me with your indulgence, and Mr. Laurie's approval, to explain my self at once & directly to you and the managers for the Institution.

I wish for my part, the time would return when, like Paul, we might minister the Gospel of Christ, supporting ourselves with our own hands, and even ministering to the necessities of others. Such a condition would please me better than the See of Canterbury. But, as it is required by the spirit of the age that they who minister at the altar should live by the altar, I feel justified to my conscience and to him whom I wish to serve, in making stipulations for my temporal support. In Glasgow I have £150 a year, my expenses have been at the rate of £200, and yet my appearance either in respect of lodging or clothing or charity has been no ways above my station if equal to it. To sit down in London with less would be to expose myself to the hazzard [sic] of contracting debt, which I have hitherto conscientiously avoided as one of the sorest bondages of this present life. I had the means when I came here of supplementing my stated income,[153] this I have no longer, and therefore even though disengaged from all occupation in Scotland I would rather take the chance of providence in this country, than adventure to London with a smaller security than £200.

From what Mr. Laurie stated to me, I fear this is more than you can offer—and perhaps the negotiation may stop here. But if you should find it convenient to agree to this, then the next thing I have to mention is that, to come up to London and offer myself as a Candidate among many others, is more than I could think of doing[,] engaged as I at present am—but if upon correspondence with the clergymen I shall refer to below, and enquiries made at them[,] you should be disposed to call me to the ministry of the chapel upon trial being had of me, and upon my having had trial of

---

151. EIL, MS 01. William Dinwiddie (d. 18 December 1830), was Father of the Kirk Session of the National Scotch Church, and faithful associate of Edward Irving. See Hair, *Regent Square*, 98–99.

152. Mr. James Laurie, an elder and a partner of William Hamilton's. 'One of the Regent Square elders, and an Asylum director, as well as an active and zealous supporter of all the Scottish institutions in London.' See Hair, *Regent Square*, 160.

'Well do I remember the morning when, as I sat in my lonely apartment, meditating the uncertainties of a preacher's calling, and revolving in my mind purposes of missionary work, this stranger stepped in upon my musing, and opened to me the commission with which he had been charged': Irving, *The Last Days*, xxxiv. The 'stranger' was Mr. Laurie.

William Hamilton was honorary secretary of the Caledonian Chapel's Building Committee and had supported Irving's appointment as minister. He became Irving's brother-in-law when he married Isabella's sister Elizabeth in 1828. See Hair, *Regent Square*, 48.

153. Edward Irving had received a legacy of £100. See Oliphant, *Life*, 114.

it—then shall I be most happy to come up to London, and make myself known to you in word and doctrine [letter torn] the various duties of the ministerial office.

I thank you for the honour you have done me for thinking me fit for your pastor, and offering to bear my expenses, and am sorry that I have found it necessary to enter upon the above negociation [sic] & not accept at once the invitation you sent me by Mr. Laurie.

I am,

Sir,

Yours most respectfully,

Edwd Irving

PS. I believe I am permitted to name Dr Chalmers—Rev. Andw Thompson, Edin—Dr Fleming Edin, Revd. Rob Gordon Edin—& I am known to Mr. Grey, Sir Henry Moncrieff & Mr. David Dukron

P.S. Upon submitting the above to Mr. Laurie's perusal, he has suggested to me that it is not sufficiently explicit upon the connection between the seat rents & the emolument. In this I meant it to be as you stated it to him, that the seat rents were to be mine, after making the allowance to the hospital, £100 being made certain. Now what I wish is that £200 should be made certain for the reasons mentioned above. E.I.

Addressed to: William Dinwiddie Esq.,
44 Burton Crescent,
London.

~

Edward Irving to WILLIAM DINWIDDIE

Paisley, 16th November 1821[154]

Dear Sir,

I feel very much obliged by your kind and satisfactory letter to which I would have replied in course of post, but that I wished to shew it to Dr Chalmers, with whom I have communicated all along in this matter. The stipend of £150 with half the seat rents, is to me altogether as desirable as the understanding which your friend Mr. Laurie gave me of it. Had I known indeed that so much as £150 was secured, I should not have stipulated for the security of £200, but as you anticipate no objection to it, we shall let it stand. My meaning about the call is altogether understood by you. It was not to get a pledge before hearing me, which were both unreasonable and unscriptural, but to deliver myself from the unpleasant circumstances which are now to attend

154. EIL, MS 04.

candidateship especially when at such a distance, as also to shew to Dr. Chalmers's congregation, I would not leave them but with the purpose of becoming the pastor of a congregation, if my gifts were found to suit it.

So that, you see, there is no respect in which we are not agreed and if, upon bringing it before the managers, you receive their sanction I am ready to come up to London, to preach and reside amongst you for a few weeks, that you may have a full opportunity of ascertaining my fitness for the charge.

It is not that I have a desire to remove from a flock which have given me the right hand of fellowship as if I were their pastor and not his assistant—and from a place in which though an unknown stranger two years ago the Almighty has raised me up many friends—but that I have made up my mind to preach the Gospel wherever I am called by my Master. Thus your invitation has come without any endeavour on my part, and therefore I hail it with more pleasure, than if through influence I had been presented to the best living in my native country. Feeling it to be from Providence upon which I have cast myself, I shall follow it up with more promptitude, than if it were from any hand seen, however noble. So I need only your instructions to proceed. At the same time I am in no hurry and cannot though it should be some time, being full of employment where I am.

For yourself, Dear Sir, I am truly much obliged by your kind expressions—which I trust I shall not live to disappoint. But you must not anticipate too much. Report speaks oftener false than true—and London is a different field from Glasgow[,] which it will take a time for me to study. Not but that Gospel of our blessed Saviour is the same everywhere but that men's habits and opinions are in a different state of preparation. If God be with me, whose presence is not got by talents but by prayers, all will be well—and prosperous.

To you and to your Managers, and to all the congregation I now begin to entertain a warm interest, which, I trust, will yet ripen into mutual esteem and hearty union.

I am,
Dear Sir,
Yours truly,

Edwd Irving

P.S. This is written from my Brother-in-Law; where I am to day. My own address is 34 Kent St Glasgow Edward Irving

Addressed to: Mr. Dinwiddie Esq.,
4 Grocer's Hall Court, Poultry,
London

Edward Irving to WILLIAM DINWIDDIE

Glasgow, 34 Kent St., 12th December 1821[155]

Dear Sir,

I received your letter last night in which is announced your public meeting on the 19th—I had made all my arrangements here and along the road where I meant to stop with friends, for setting out on Monday. But conceiving it to be of importance, and wishing to gratify as much as in me lay Gentlemen who have acted by me so handsomely—I have set myself by all methods to expedite things & countermand my arrangements and now I have all things prepared for starting so as to be in London on Tuesday night—I spend the Sabbath at York, and start from York by the first coach on Monday. It gives me great pleasure to announce this and I hope our meeting will be attended with many happy friends. I pray it may.

I am,
Dear Sir,
Yours faithfully,
Edwd Irving

Addressed to: William Dinwiddie Esq.,
4 Grocers Hall Court,
Poultry, London.

Edward Irving to DR THOMAS CHALMERS

London, 23 Everett St., Russell Square.
24th December 1821[156]

Dear Sir,

This is my first letter dated from London and to you who are my most distinguished friend, and I might almost say my most disinterested, and certainly from what I know you to have done my most zealous, I feel that my first letter is due.

My preaching yesterday, so far as I gather, was very acceptable and my congregation larger than was expected. It consisted mostly of young men, in the proportion I should think to all the rest of two or three to one, so that here you will observe there is agency enough if it could be excited to godly and benevolent ends.[157] The Scotsmen in

---

155. EIL, MS 07.
156. NCL, MSS CHA 4.18.6.
157. A Pastoral Letter by the Scotch Presbytery in London was printed and circulated. There is a reference in it to the young people 'left at large to folly, and in the end engulfed by the wickedness

Part II: The Letters

London, having nothing after business to engage them, and no choice of Society, and being themselves detached from all family society at home, are a prey to amusements and dissipations, to which they are the more inclined that they burst upon them with the freshness of novelty, and the more incited by the vigorous health and constitution which they grow up with in the temperate region of morals from which they come. I know who could give impulse to this mass of unemployed activity, and guide it to ends which would make Scotsmen as much the blessing of London as they are said to be of foreign parts. For me to hope such a commission is presumptuous. The precarious life which I have lived, scorning the habits of my fellows, and not deigning to the helps which a less able man could easily have seized, always ready for the worst chance, and never caring for the best. This has wrought in me a changed character which unfits me for that social converse to which my heart and all its desires draw me so strongly. This is against me, there is a good deal in my favour also of which it is not seemly that I should condescend.

This morning I have spent at the London Missionary Society-house[158] closeted with their Examining Committee, all clergymen, and all save Dr Waugh of the Independent body.[159] Most certainly I am struck, much struck, with the inelegant tone of manners & intercourse which characterises them. There is no polish of a high intellect, or a refined Society—nor is there that which is better than both[,] the over mastering sanctity of Evangelical Counselors—excepting, however, Burder,[160] who has in him what I should like to be acquainted with. This I say to you, not to my good friend your sister, for though I say it, it does not affect either their pastoral nor their personal holiness but only their complexion of character, and their fitness to move this enlightened & polished age.

They have advertised my continuance here for a month, and they contemplate an importance in the additional Sabbath for this reason, that on the third I am to preach a Charity Sermon to which certain leading men will be invited[161] whose disposition to return they would like to try by the opportunity of another Sabbath. I am under no promise[;] I have given them no encouragement. I am your servant, your humble & willing servant, and wait your command. However, I have written to Mr. Collins[162]

---

around them': Cameron, *The Scots Kirk*, 108.

158. Although the London Missionary Society had been founded in 1795 on an inter-denominational basis, it gradually became identified with Congregationalism. "Independent" = Congregationalism.

159 Alexander Waugh (1754-1827) was the minister of the Secession Church in London, and trained the selection committee of the London Missionary Society. See *ODNB*, 57: 748.

160. George Burder (1752-1832) was at this time secretary of the London Missionary Society and pastor of Fetter Lane Chapel in London. He was also the author of eight volumes of wide-read *Village Sermons*, editor of the *Evangelical Magazine*, founder of the Religious Tract Society, and a prime mover in the establishment of the British and Foreign Bible Society. See *ODNB* 8: 735.

161. Leading men included the Duke of York, President of the Asylum. See Edward Irving to Thomas Carlyle 26 December 1821: p 122.

162. See Edward Irving to Thomas Carlyle, 25 September 1819 n.

by this same opportunity, that if agreeable to you no time may be lost in finding the additional supply, which with his known generosity he offered to undertake for me.

My love to your Lady, and my affections to your children. I saw a coach that would have fitted Elsa to a *tee*—drawn by four dogs—but we were hurrying on so fast in the High Flyer coach that I could not stay to make a bargain.

Yours most truly,
Edwd Irving

Addressed to: Rev Dr Chalmers, Glasgow.
With Mr. Laurie's[163] most respectful compl[imen]ts.

~

Edward Irving to THOMAS CARLYLE

London, 23 Everett St., Russell Square.
26th December 1821[164]

My Dear Carlyle,

It is vain for me to think of conveying to you any idea of London. This time, one's wits are lost in the magnitude of the objects, which solicit one on every hand. You can get no help to understand its concerns as a whole[,] every one being content to acquaint himself only with what concerns him. Yet every thing is striking[,] so well managed and so complete in its style that you cannot resist the enquiry how it comes to surpass whatever of the kind you have seen elsewhere. So that between anxiety to know, and difficulty to find out[,] I feel myself rent in twain. This morning[,] to give you a specimen of a day's employment, I strolled out after breakfast to deliver letters in the West-End—resolving to take Dyall St, the winter quarters of the gypsies[,] upon my route. There is no shabbyness [*sic*] outside even in Dyall St., St. Giles.' The houses of substantial brick, three stories well set out with doors & windows. Being the morn after Christmas I found the economy of the Asiatics not a little disheveled. They were strolling about in groups of threes and fours—in much the same atire [*sic*] as you have seen them often, with the same dark complexion, jet eyes, and suspicious look. They seemed struck with me as a phenomenon in their habitations, the women accosted me, the men drew up as I passed, and I was not a little staggered upon the perfect safety of my position—Cuddyasses,[165] without drivers were strolling from side to side of the street, as if in quest of their wonted mouthful. Fortunately I made my retreat good and

---

163. See Edward Irving to William Dinwiddie, p. 116.
164. NLS, MS 1764, fol. 211–12.
165. Cuddy: chiefly Scottish, meaning a donkey.

having threaded their street found myself at once opposite St.Giles' in the Field & at the end of Oxford St the finest and longest street of shops & business I have ever seen. So very near are these winter settlers to the best abodes of the West-End—I strolled into St.Giles' church yard remembering that Milton's honoured ashes lay there, though his tomb long after found its eyot[166] in Westminster Abbey. With difficulty I found the place where he had been laid—by the South wall of the Church, at his head by the wall a short column not much above the height and dimensions of a mile stone with a small pretension to finish, a rough entablature about the top, and three panelled places upon three exposed sides—the stone of poor materials and altogether defaced. Yet I declare before this blank and unlettered piece of stone I felt more devotion from the neighbourhood of his ashes whom I regard among the greatest of men, that I ever felt before or expect to do when I shall visit the Poet's Corner. From thence I made all haste to Berkeley Square, and found our friend Margaret Gordon at home. I cannot help fancying that for the first half hour or so she takes advantage of her fashionable style to teach me my clownishness—but afterwards it goes off, and she becomes nearly as we knew her. I had the honour of being introduced to her sisters—of whom her full sister seems a gay fashionable light-hearted girl—the youngest a great deal of a humorist. They live in stile [sic] if I may judge from what I saw. I have not seen her parents. Still I am not satisfied, and yet I know not why. She is good natured enough. I feel I am not master of the *haut-ton*[167] of intercourse. I feel out not a little which I think she should contrive to prevent. Some how or other I am indisposed to go back again. She has not Jane Welsh's heart.

I have preached, but shall not repeat to you the Compliments which burst upon me. It is so new a thing for me to be praised in my preaching. I know not how to look. At Glasgow I have but toleration from the Westland Whigs—when praised it is with reservation often with cold and unprofitable admonition. And Dr C sometimes in his retailing of the public opinion makes me feel all black in my prospects. Here I have been hailed with the warmest reception. They anticipate great things. Talk of having the Duke of York the President of the Asylum present at a Charity Sermon Sunday week and much more which it is needless to repeat. One thing would have made your heart feel; my audience was almost entirely young Scotsmen—no father[,] no mother[,] no sisters. Seat-fulls of youths—and how grave[,] how attentive. To labour among such is labour to save them from the pollutions of this city which receives them so strict and moral, and contaminates them so sorely. This were an office exactly to my taste. I write Jane Baillie Welsh, my beloved pupil, to-morrow, meanwhile present to her and to her mother my love. And accept the renewed assurances of my highest esteem and affection. Pray write me in a day or two.

Dear Carlyle,

Yours always,

166. A small isle, especially in a river.
167. French: high tone.

Edwd Irving

Say to the Littles and to my friend Mr. Dobbie that Mr. Little is to set off for Scotland the End of this week—by Annan Glasgow & Edin.

Addressed to: Mr. Thomas Carlyle,
Cusines Lodgings,
5 College St., Edinburgh.

Editor's Epilogue

The next two years are concerned with Irving establishing himself in London in the Caledonian Chapel; we read of his negotiations with the stalwart Mr Dinwiddie, and his satisfaction with their outcome. His surprise and delight with the substantial increase in his income to an unprecedented £500, was expressed in his offer to his friend Thomas Carlyle, 'I trust being able to entertain you yet in London as every honest hearted fellow should be entertained.'[168] Thus settled financially he was able to direct his wishes not only to entertaining his friend, but also to considering the serious step of marriage.

---

168. Edward Irving to Thomas Carlyle, 29 April 1822. NLS, MS 1764, fol. 227-28.

3

Letters: 1822–1824

Editor's Introduction

Edward Irving was ordained at Annan on 19th June 1822, and preached his first sermon as minister in London on 14th July. That January he was writing to Thomas Carlyle, 'I have not forgotten my charming Jane Welsh. She shall hear from me before I leave London';[1] and indeed she did. He wrote to her on the 9th February 1822, acquainting her of his new turn of fortune. The fact was that now his circumstances allowed him to contemplate setting up house with a wife, and it was to Jane his thoughts had turned. The child of ten he had tutored as a youth in Haddington had turned into an attractive and intelligent young woman. However, it was not be Jane that he would marry but Isabella Martin, to whom he had become engaged during his time in Haddington.

The year 1823 saw a huge expansion of his congregation, allegedly caused by the chance remark made in Parliament by the then Foreign Secretary, George Canning.[2] The gentry and nobility crowded into the small Caledonian Chapel, and this influx confirmed the plan to build a larger and nobler church.

∼

---

1. See letter Edward Irving to Thomas Carlyle, 3 January, 1822.

2. 'Canning told the House that . . . he himself had lately heard a Scotch minister . . . preach the most eloquent sermon that he had ever listened to.' Oliphant, *Life*, 1.159. George Canning (1770–27), twice Foreign Secretary. First between 1807 and 1809 then from 1822 to 1827.

Edward Irving to THOMAS CARLYLE

3rd January 1822[3]

My Dear Carlyle,

I have something worth the writing about and therefore lose not the moment I have before the Post. A lady, Mrs. Buller[,][4] whose husband now recovering held one of the highest situations in India, whose sister's husband at this time is judge of all appeals in India, and whose sister is connected with the peerage, took so much fancy to my last Sundays preaching that she thought me proper to give advice about the Education of her two boys, 13 and 15 years old now at Harrow and about to proceed to a Scottish University. After a long conversation, and many plans talked of—this was finally agreed on, that to you of whom I spoke to her, this offer should be made—that if you would be their Tutor, and live in their house free of all expense, they would give you handsome terms—I mentioned £200. She said it would be given—that they had been thinking of £250 for an Oxford tutor so that my own opinion is £250 would not be refused if you should think the other too little.[5]

The Lady is accomplished, highly interesting and likely to appreciate your character and attainments—the Gentleman being confined I did not see—but I understand as much of him also. They are immensely wealthy and most highly connected. The boys are of taste and talent, and likely to be moved by admiration of your attainments, and by no means likely to require coercion.—I think you perfectly able to steer your way amidst them all, and most likely to be very happy—at least I should so hope for myself if so circumstanced.—

The family cannot remove to town for three months—the boys would require to be put in training forth-with. To this you would have no objections I dare say—seeing they cannot well be bestowed otherwise.—In that case you would require to take apartments, three bed rooms and a sitting room, and the expenses of your *keep* would be defrayed.

This is to my taste far better than making your bread with the sweat I may say of your heart. You would have as much disposable time for high & intellectual studies. I have prepared the lady[,] a most engaging person, to expect in you nothing but what she will find.—I have even stated that you have not yet had large opportunity of mingling with men, and have acted as a very independent man.—Also that in regard

---

3. NLS, MS 1764, fol. 213–14.

4. Isabella, wife of a retired judge, Charles Buller (1774–1848). See CL, 2:4. Mrs. Buller was described by Thomas Carlyle as a faded beauty, witty and 'ingenuously intelligent': Carlyle, *Reminiscences*, 269.

5. Thomas Carlyle wrote to Jane Welsh saying that 'Irving is speaking about a kind of Tutorship in some great family: and if I accept it, my excursions must be greatly circumscribed. The people offer £250 a-year, the chance of travelling, a number of hours per day to myself and many other advantages, which ought perhaps to induce me. Let me see you before I decide: it may not be so easy afterwards: I have a million things to say and ask': Thomas Carlyle to Jane Welsh, 14 January 1822: CL, 2:15.

to literature, I had no doubt you like almost all Scotch scholars would have to get up your Greek. She said she hoped you were not fixed to Edin for by and bye she might wish the lads to travel. I declare it makes my heart glad that I have not come to London in vain for my friend's sake even though it should be in vain for my own.—But I hope they will succeed in all their arrangements and I shall be their pastor. Their attentions to me are unbounded—and I seem to have made a strong impression. I am in great haste.—Write you coolly and so that if necessary I could shew your letter to their father. I have not forgotten my charming Jane Welsh.—She shall hear from me before I leave London. Write by return of post.

 Yours most truly,

    Edwd Irving

 Addressed to: Mr. Thomas Carlyle,
 Cusines Lodgings,
 5 College St.,
 Edinburgh.

~

Edward Irving to THOMAS CARLYLE

23 Everett St., Russell Square. 4th January 1822[6]

My Dear Carlyle,

I am happy this letter will be delivered to you along with that I wrote by the last post, for the matter I wrote on has assumed a somewhat different Phase. Mrs. Buller upon my seeing her this morning, thinks upon the whole that till they themselves arrive in Edin, it would be better to have the youths[7] under the roof & guardianship of some Family, & she has commissioned me to write Dr Fleming to that effect. So that what I conceive the most weighty and disagreeable part of the charge[,] the domestic one will be taken off your shoulders. Still they wish you to attend them there in quality of Tutor, with the view that if you mutually like each other you should go into the family and be in the whole charge and with the conditions or rather scale of conditions, mentioned in my last.—There is you perceive an uncertainty in the issue—but such an uncertainty as you will like—arising out of the trial which you will have of each other.—Now my opinion is that in the mother you meet a most pleasant elegant and sensible woman—in the eldest boy whom I have conversed with, you meet a rather

---

 6. NLS, MS 1764, fol. 215-16.

 7. 'The youths' were Charles Buller (1806-48) and Arthur Buller (1808-69). They were boarded with Dr. Fleming in George Square, and were tutored by Carlyle and Carlyle's salary was at the much lower rate of £200 a year. See Carlyle, *Reminiscences*, 270.

difficult subject, clever and acute and not ill informed for his age—but his tastes all to boxiana,[8] Bond street, and pleasure—gathered out of the speculation & ambitions of Harrow school—but, while he argued for that stile [sic] of life against his mother & me, he displays a soul far above it, and sporting with it, and easily to be dislodged from it.—And he confessed when his mother was gone that he could apply himself with great good will for several years to study, and would delight to travel. I told him & his Mother I should like myself to be his tutor, and I spoke *bona fide*, for nothing I perceive is wanting but a superior mind to give him higher tastes and to breed admiration of excellence. You could soon master him, and easily direct him, though at the outset it might be a trial of your patience.—But I think you ought not to refuse to submit to such a trial, you would be no worse of it, you labour upon a good subject, for a most accomplished[,] quite a gallant & noble woman. And generous withal, and willing to recompense your labours.

Could you then undertake the tuition of the youths if they were to go into Dr Fleming's say four hours a day, more-or-less, as might be needed, and according to the scale of remuneration mentioned in my former letter—I am almost sure it would be permanent, that is if you could come to give your energies—I do not mean of teaching but of influencing to the lad, and would not fly off from interest in him, upon perceiving his follies and affectations which are not few I confess but of which the better half disappeared from my eye in an hour's conversation. Conversation to argue down his present modes of admired excellence, and to raise up new ones[,] would truly be the better part of your office for a while.

Pray write me, and write me confidentially for I will shew no more of your letter than I judge for the common weal—and let it be by return of post—for I must leave London on Monday week. Believe me greatly attached to your success in life, as I admire much your gifts and attainments, and love your noble spirit, and the overflowing of your good affections and feel honoured and obliged by the regard which you shew and express for,

 Dear Carlyle,
    Your affectionate friend,
    Edward Irving

Addressed to: Mr. Thomas Carlyle,
Cusine's Lodgings,
5 College St.,
Edinburgh.

---

8 7 An allusion to Egan, *Boxiana*.

Part II: The Letters

Edward Irving to THOMAS CARLYLE

Glasgow, 34 Kent St. 22nd January 1822[9]

My Dear Carlyle,

Your letter which I put into the hands of Mrs. Buller with the desire to give her the sight of you even in your most unbosomed moments was by her taken in the best part, and at her brothers Mr. Strachey's she spoke most complimentarily, and engaged to let me hear further before I left London, or if not to write you. Only one day had to intervene and that a Sabbath busy perhaps to us both—and so I did not hear.

But this day I have a letter from Dr Fleming which alters a little the state of the Case, yet naturally enough. The boys are to be in Edin on Thursday—they go to Dr Fleming's family and Mr. Buller feeling the additional expense thereby incurred for the present on that account, finds it necessary to hesitate during their temporary residence upon the Terms formerly mentioned between his Lady and me, and made known to you. He is not the less anxious that you should superintend the education of the young men, and so far as I can gather from Dr F's letter contemplates the former condition of things when the family comes to be reunited. Meantime he commits it to Dr F and me to settle 'what should be the proper amount fixed for Mr. Carlyle's services,' adding at the same time 'I should hope the amount will not much exceed what I should otherwise have to pay.' Dr Fleming will give you further explanations upon the subject of this Letter, and perhaps shew you that part of it which concerns you.

Now, here is the substance of my answer to Dr Fleming which I have requested him to shew to you upon your shewing him this at your first interview[,] which I hope will be very soon[,] that I had it in my view to serve Mrs. Buller not you, and introduced you to her acquaintance not as a Scotch Tutor much less an Edin private Teacher, but as a literary man who might by a proper consideration be induced to undertake the office and if he did would answer, if he did not incline to it I could not find another that would answer.—That I would not for a moment negociate [*sic*] in the matter upon a lower understanding—but that I would advise you, if Mr. Buller had it in view, soon to adopt the former arrangement, to give him a proof of your kindness by consenting in the mean time to suspend your many literary engagements and take charge of his sons upon a smaller consideration say from £100 to £150.—But this not without pledge given that if you harmonised well & were wished to continue your services, it should be upon the conditions formerly mentioned of £200 per annum and an inmate of their family.

This is the purpose of my answer to my most respected friend Dr Fleming, and now to yourself I express myself sorry that any such interruption should have taken place[,] though I foresee in the end the adjustment of it after the first plan.—My regard for the mother will not allow me to see these boys put into the hands of any but an accomplished scholar, and a warm admirer of literature[,] without first informing

---

9. NLS, MS 1764, fol. 219-20.

her of the result[,] which is likely to be fatal to the eldest whom I know.—The whole matter is before you, you need no advice, you have my views fully, and so I leave you & Dr Fleming to converse over the subject, and I hope to hear from you & from him also the result—that I may discharge my duty to that most admirable lady whose heart is bound up in the prosperity of her boys.

I cannot speak with sufficient gratitude of the kindness and frank commendations poured upon me from all quarters in London.—My mind is recovering, is still able to recover the desperate condition of hardihood & resolution into which it was fast cooling in the mould it has been long in, I feel elastic, hopeful, desirous of excellence & usefulness. The pulpit I am now beginning to study as a means of power, formerly I arose no higher than to contemplate it as a means of livelihood, or rather[,] for I never was mercenary, as a prison house of fruitless exertion—I pray you to reserve yourself for a similar brighter dawn. God prosper and guide you through your manifold trials.

The directors have met since I left London[,] voted me thanks unanimous & spoke of me with affection and applause—resolved to get the Gaelic impediment done away forthwith,[10] and if aught unexpected should start up to hinder, they have talked of getting me a chapel on purpose. So may God prosper his faithful servant as me his most unworthy servant he hath prospered.

Yours most affectionately,

Edwd Irving

Addressed to: Mr. Thomas Carlyle,
3 Moray Street, Wilkies Lodgings, Leith-walk.

Edward Irving to WILLIAM DINWIDDIE

Glasgow, 34 Kent St. 26th January 1822[11]

Dear Sir,

Your narrative of things so flattering to me, and so hopeful for my union with your congregation, could not fail to be most acceptable, and it was rendered still more so by the kind interest which in all your communications breathes for the welfare of those over whom you & my worthy friend Mr. Simpson[12] are the spiritual overseers.

10. This was the requirement that the minister conduct regular services in Gaelic. This required the passage of an Act of Parliament before it could be lifted. In the meantime the office bearers of the congregation, who were not the same body as the directors of the asylum to which it was linked, were authorized to ask the directors to allow the congregation to hire the chapel, or to look for an alternate place of worship: Grass, *The Lord's Watchman*, 40, 43.

11. EIL, MS 10.

12. Robert Simpson, elder of the church, elected during the Ministry of James Boyd, 1818-19.

Through you I return my thanks to the congregation of the Caledonian Chapel for the splendid & most honourable token[13] of their regard with which they have acknowledged my unworthy services; and which by so many ties I shall feel bound to preserve, and hand down in my family. To the Court of Directors whose vote of thanks has been conveyed to me by their Secretary I shall lose no time to present my acknowledgements in due form.

For the Sermon, it does not appear to me to convey any new views of Christian and moral truth, that it should be deemed worthy of publication—and, therefore, though for your request & the request of my other friends I have the very highest respect, I feel a reluctance to appear before the public until I have something of moment to communicate, and if it give no offence I shall decline for the present. But if this cannot be done without disobliging those who have obliged me so highly, pray with me, and I shall give it another thought.

With regard to the measures which are pursuing for clearing the way to our pastoral union, may God grant them success! But if nothing else will do, than that I should preach occasionally in the Gaelic, then indolence shall not hinder me from becoming your pastor. I will study Gaelic, having before me the example of the venerable Bishop of Lyons[14] in the second century of the church who[,] to fit himself for utility among the natives, chose to renounce the polished language of Greek, and study the language of that part [of] Gaul, the very same language I believe which I would have to master.—At the same time, beset as I am here with a thousand engagements I would not find time to overtake it now, but I should give my pledge to the Directors to set about it in London before any thing else—and would not doubt to succeed in a much shorter period than that during which Mr. Boyd did never preach in Gaelic at all. You will observe however that this I consider as a Sacrifice only to be called for in case it cannot be avoided. For having many languages and much literature to study besides the arduous duties of my office I would not willingly turn aside from them except to meet a sacred duty. And yet I feel such a love for my native country, its noble aboriginal population, and its antient language linking us to remotest antiquity that I would have a pleasure as well as a duty in undertaking it.—This you are at liberty to make what use of you please. I think my friend Dr Fleming[,] the first Gaelic scholar in the church would condescend to be my Tutor; with him I would ground myself, to become perfect in London. Upon this subject I have nothing further to say than that you would understand me as actuated by a desire for your spiritual not for my temporal welfare, in making this tender if it should be needed.

This closes the business part of my dispatch.—Allow me now to you, your venerable brother Mr. Simpson, your vigilant Coadjutor and my dear friend Mr.

He donated five pounds to the subscription fund to hire Edward Irving and build a new church. See Report, 22 February 1822: EIL, MS 12.

13. The Bible, which was used by the Duke of York at the service.

14. Irenaeus (c.130–c.200).

Robertson—and my no less dear friend Mr. Hamilton, and to all others whose ample hospitality, and free-hearted kindness I did partake in London[,] to you all too numerous to be named[,] allow me to express my attachment[,] my sense of favours received, and my wish to have an opportunity to shew my gratitude.—You made London feel to me like the house of a kinsman or a brother—you aided my enquiries—you served me with your assistance—you accepted my ministry. And now you are engaged labouring for my return. May God reward such brotherly kindness—and preserve me to be the instrument of your eternal welfare—for which end I pray the more firmly he may keep me by his grace till in his good time he shall bring me on my way to minister to you the Gospel of his blessed Son.

My journey was most agreeable—at Mr. Richmond's I found a most hearty welcome, at my Fathers a happy family rendered more happy by my return, and here in Glasgow the heartiest welcome from my distinguished master and his congregation. I shall feel my parting hence more trying than I expected. They load me with their kindness and their congratulations.—I have been living with Dr Chalmers mostly since my return and am come from my Brother in Law's in Paisley this Evening.

To Mrs. Dinwiddie, so often my kind hostess and your accomplished family, I beg to be remembered with the affection which I feel for you all.—May God long smile upon your household, and give you future as he hath given you so large a share of *present* happiness.

I am,
Dear Sir,
Yours most sincerely,
Edwd Irving

P.S. I shall answer Mr. Simpson's kind favour, so soon as he does me the promised favour of introducing me to his friend. E.I.

Addressed to: Mr. Dinwiddie

Edward Irving to THOMAS CARLYLE

Glasgow, 34 Kent St. 9th February 1822[15]
[Annotated:] Encloses a letter to Miss Welsh

My Dear Carlyle,

I snatch a moment from my preparations for to-morrow to acknowledge the pleasure you give me in your letter. You speak in terms too warm of my small services,

---

15. NLS, MS 1764, fol. 221-22.

but not too warm for what I feel towards you in return, and would wish to do if opportunity were offered.

I am greatly delighted with the cordiality between you and my worthy friend and patron Dr Fleming. Your candour to Mr. Buller will not be lost, and is highly to be commended.—A change of subject is what my friend Charles needs as well as a change of method. His mind you see had outgrown the former & was becoming[,] for want of guidance, wild and fantastical. If you have not already written to his Father, I think it equally incumbent, that you advise as well as confess.[16] And for the boy's sake, take a *coup-d'oeil*[17] of the course of study best to be pursued. There is no fear I augur from so open and honest a beginning, that at the end of the trial you be sought after rather than have to seek—and if not, there is as you say no harm.—You are not to be advised—you need no supplement of another's council to win the hearts of the lads, and that being gained all is secure, and it is secured by that which is dutiful and feeling pleasant in the mean time. The Almighty prosper your union to the happiness and benefit of both. Most certainly when I wrote first I had no idea of any narrowness of means, and was given to understand the very opposite—And still I am sure it is only in as much as concerns the Education of the boys, of the allowance for which so much is swallowed up by the board[,] no less I believe than 200 Gs[18] each per annum. Mrs. Buller did certainly talk to me of foreign travel[,] which does not bespoke any straitness upon that score.

I have indeed taken new wing by my visit to London—I see my way distinctly—my intellect is putting forth new powers, at least I fancy so—and if God endow me with his grace I foresee service to his Church. My ambition (a sanctified one I trust) is taking another direction no less than to endeavour to bring the spirit and power of antient eloquence into the pulpit, which appears to me the only place in modern manners for its revival. I would like to have your thoughts upon this subject, both as to the correctness of the idea, and its proper execution. It is for an audience chiefly I am so fond of London—perhaps as much for a school to learn in by conversation & observation[,] for which I think nature has fitted me more than by Books. I have a wonderful aptitude to sympathise with men—their manner of feeling and of thinking

---

16. In a letter to his brother John, Thomas Carlyle wrote, 'The boys arrived about a week ago, and are to continue some six months at board in the house of one Dr Fleming, a clergyman, till their parents arrive. I have entered upon duty, but in a desultory way, and expecting farther advice from London. I have offered to take the matter upon a trial for a month or two at any rate; and then, if it answer, to commence business regularly, and with the regular salary—£200, and an allowance in the interim instead of board. Mr. Buller, the father, wished some abatement in this period of uncertainty. I proffered leaving the payment at his own discretion, *for the two months*, and having *no* farther uncertainty at all. The "Memorandum" in which I stated this together with some other considerations necessary to be impressed upon the man, is now in his possession. It was written with as much emphasis as I could contrive to unite with respectfulness; Irving also has spoken magnificently of me: so that if I enter the family at all, I need expect no supercilious or uncomfortable treatment there: and I still consider the office as lying at my own option, that is, depending on the character of the young men themselves and my suitableness to it': Thomas Carlyle to John A. Carlyle, 20 January 1822: CL, 2:24–25.

17. Glance.

18. Gs: guineas which were worth £1.05p

also is clear to me and even when false[,] interesting from a desire to set them right. Jane Welsh accuses me of intolerance, but I think she is wrong, altho' I fear I have some little skirmishes for approbation but this is not deep, and will yield according as I receive the share which is my due.

And so will yours, My Dear Carlyle, you have within you powers of good the world are not alive to, and which shall yet shine out to the confusion of many who discredit them. Your natural power of devotion will yet have utterance, and your deep-seated reverence of religion[,] the largest expansion & highest attainment of the soul, which makes your Mother so superior to those around her, will yet make her son superior among the rich and literary men that are hereafter to company with him.

My worthy Father, for this remark takes me home, has been near awhile of his grave by a most dangerous fall from the Hay loft which with fracture of the bones brought on obstructions in the bowels that resisted long all remedies. Providence has been kind, and saving most excruciating pain and constant lying on his back, of which he is as patient as a Lamb, [he?] is in a way delightful to us all after such fearful apprehensions.

I enclose a letter to Jane Welsh, hurried like this which I pray you to send to her, I do not know where she is.

Tell my young friend Charles Buller I hope for a fair share of his Scottish friendship—I mean to visit you all soon. Meanwhile may you speed well in your studies. To Dr Fleming I am about to write if I am [not?] hindered from a speedy visit—James Johnstone I shall not forget if any thing is in my power.

Yours affectionately,
Edwd Irving

Addressed to: Mr. Thomas Carlyle,
3 Murray St.,
Leith-walk,
Edinburgh.

~

Edward Irving to JANE WELSH

Glasgow, 34 Kent Street. 9th February, 1822.[19]

My Dear and Lovely Pupil,

When I am my own master, delivered from the necessity of attending to engagements, ever soliciting me upon the spot where I am, and exhausting me to very lassitude

---

19. Oliphant, *Life* 1:134–36.

before the evening, when my friendly correspondence should commence, then, and not till then, shall I be able, I fear, to discharge my heart of the obligations which it feels to those at a distance. Do excuse me, I pray you, by the memory of our old acquaintance, and anything else which it is pleasant to remember, for my neglect to you in London, and not to you alone, I am sorry to say, but to every one whom I was not officially bound to write to, even my worthy father. Forget and forgive it; and let us be established in our former correspondence as if no such sin against it had ever taken place. I could say some things on my own behalf; but till you go to London, which I hope will not be till I am there to be a brother to you, you could not at all sympathise with them.

And know now, though late, that my head is almost turned with the approbation I received—certainly my head is turned; for from being a poor desolate creature, melancholy of success, yet steel against misfortune, I have become all at once full of hope and activity. My hours of study have doubled themselves—my intellect, long unused to expand itself, is now awakening again, and truth is revealing itself to my mind. And perhaps the dreams and longings of my fair correspondent may yet be realised. I have been solicited to publish a discourse which I delivered before his Royal Highness the Duke of York; but have refused till my apprehensions of truth be larger, and my treatment of it more according to the models of modern and ancient times. The thanks of all the directors I have received formally—the gift of all the congregation of the Bible used by his Royal Highness. The elders paid my expenses in a most princely style. My countrymen of the first celebrity, especially in art, welcomed me to their society, and the first artist in the city drew a most admirable half-length miniature of me in action.[20] And so, you see, I have reason to be vain.

Edward Irving, Andrew Robertson, 1823

20. A portrait of Irving preaching, drawn by the artist Andrew Robertson (1777–1845).

But these things, my dear Jane, delight me not, save as vouchsafements of my Maker's bounty, the greater because the more undeserved. Were I established in the love and obedience of Him, I should rise towering aloft into the regions of a very noble and sublime character, and so would my highly-gifted pupil, to retain whose friendship shall be a consolation to my life: to have her fellowship in divine ambitions would make her my dear companion through eternity.

To your affectionate mother, whose indulgence gives me this pleasant communication with her daughter, I have to express my attachment in every letter. May you live worthy of each other, mutual stays through life, doubly endeared, because alone together; and therefore doubly dutiful to Him who is the husband of the widow, and the Father of the fatherless. I have sent this under cover to my friend T.C.,[21] not knowing well where you are at present. If in Edinburgh, offer my benedictions upon your uncle's new alliance. I hope to be in Edinburgh soon, where I will not be without seeing you.

I am, my dear pupil,
Your affectionate friend,
Edward Irving

~

Edward Irving to THE ELDERS OF THE CALEDONIAN CHAPEL

Glasgow. 21st February 1822[22]

To My Honoured friends Mr. Dinwiddie, Mr. Simpson, Mr. Robertson, Mr. Hamilton and others connected with the Caledonian chapel to whom I have the pleasure of being known, and who take an interest in my coming to London.

Gentlemen,

My friend Mr. Laurie, has called to report to me the result of the last meeting of the Directors of the Asylum, and as Mr. Hamilton requested him to make it known to me, I feel myself called upon to do my endeavour to make you comfortable under and also if possible to extricate you from the embarrassment in which you may feel yourselves.

First let my interest be as nothing. The Lord will provide for me—and since I left you, his providence has presented me with the offer of a Chapel of Ease in Dundee, with the probable reversion of the first vacant living in the place. This of course I refused. The people of N[ew] York are enquiring for me to succeed the great Dr Mason[23]—at

---

21. Thomas Carlyle.
22. EIL, MS 11.
23. John Mitchell Mason (1770–1829), pastor at the Scotch Presbyterian Church in New York. He was provost of Columbia University from 1811 to 1816 from which he resigned in 1821 to become

least are writing letters to that effect. This I do not think will come to any head, because I am not worthy of the honour. But I mention both to shew you in what good hands my fortune is when it is left to God alone.

Secondly. But if for the interest of your own souls and religion in general & the Scotch Church in particular, you do still desire my services amongst you—then I am ready at any call, and almost on any conditions for my own spirit is bent to preach the Gospel in London.

Thirdly. If the Gentlemen of the Asylum would not mistake for importuning and seeking of a place, what I offer from a desire to mediate peace, and benefit the best interests of my countrymen—I pledge myself to study Gaelic—and if I cannot write and preach it in six months I give them my missive to be burdensome to them no longer.—There was a time when the consciousness of my own powers would have made it seem a meanness so to condescend—but now the heaviness of condescension for Christ's sake I feel to be the height of honour.

Fourthly. But if not, and you are meditating as Mr. Hamilton says to obtain another place of worship, to which to call me, then be assured I shall not be difficult to persuade to come among you—and I shall not distress your means but content with little[,] minister[,] in humble dependence upon God, the free grace of the Gospel.

Finally[,] Gentlemen—Should I never see your faces any more, my heart is towards you, and my prayers are for you, and the blessing of the Lord God shall be upon us all if we seek his face—and we shall dwell together in that New Jerusalem where there is no temple and no need of any pastor—but the Lamb doth lead them and feed them by rivers of living water and wipe away all tears from their eyes.[24]

Commend me to your families in love and brotherhood and do you all regard me as

Your obliged and affectionate friend,
Edwd Irving

Glasgow, 34 Kent Street.
21 Febr 1822
Addressed to: William Dinwiddie Esq.
4 Grocers Court,
Poultry, London.

---

president of Dickinson College, Carlisle, Pennsylvania. See CL: 2:35 and n.
24. Rev 21:2–4, 22; 21:1.

Edward Irving to THE REV ROBERT GORDON

Glasgow 34 Kent St, 19th Feby 1822[25]
[In brackets:] (Copy)[26]

My Dear Sir,

When I think of you my memory reverts always to the lovely green & picturesque beauty of Kinfauns. I can never bring myself to Buccleuch Place in Edinburgh. This is not sentiment but truth—and it is always in the simplicity of country life that I conceive of you & Mrs. Gordon. And even your pastoral character will not take on the station & dignity of a city cure. I fancy it surrounded with the true dignities of the parochial charge. Walking abroad over the open face of nature, and holding communion with God in the stillness of His own works—& ministering the grace of His Gospel to the real & artificial wants of men. Conceive me then in your parlour at Kinfauns, or if you please upon the green before the door, by the side of your hygrometer & rain gauge.

I am coming to your quarter to spend a Sabbath, & as I did when I first visited you, offer my services half the day (Sabbath after next) having offered the other half to Mr. Andrew Thompson. I have a motive for this besides friendship, & it is this, to leave Scotland, which I have the prospect of doing, with an unblemished name, so far as I am able. Not that I have suffered any stigma or care much though I had, but that there is an *equivoque*[27] about me in some places, which truly suits worse with the open nature of my character than a positive blemish. I shall feed your people with that with which I feed the flock of St. John's, no better & no worse so that whilst I do all to pluck my good name from the mystery of doubt I do nothing to cast over it an artificial cleanness, I should like it were the afternoon at the chapel that I might spend the evening with your family, upon which occasion I would take the liberty of bringing with me my travelling companion, Mr. Graham of Burnswark a Merchant in our city—a countryman of ours, and a most excellent man.

In London, where you did all you could to find me welcome, I met it most heartily, & the whole spring of my mind has taken wonderful vigour. My devotion to study three times as intense, my desire of excellence quite consuming, & my hopes of it beginning to dawn, such power hath approbation over my mind. I shall not forget that very very early I received it from the Minister of Kinfauns.

This confession, which I make I hold to be creditable to myself, the acknowledgment without doubt is creditable to you, for in Scotland there is not a face of disposition so rare as the firing of approbation with a welcome heart & a judicious tongue.

---

25. NLS: MS 23204.

26. The letter is not in Irving's handwriting. The person who copied it out added the word "(Copy)" for clarification.

27. *Equivoque*, i.e. equivocal, ambiguous.

My mind has lately been much enriched by the careful perusal of the Psalms. They came upon a mind fatigued with the controversy of doctrine, like oil upon the troubled waters. What a pity our countrymen were so exclusively intellectual—if they added comprehensiveness of judgment & capacity of permitting & expressing feeling—they would be the Masters of Mankind, & the Models of Manhood & of Christian character.

I offer my love to Mrs. Gordon, & your children, whom I long to dandle on my knee.

I am,
Dear Sir,
Yours most affectionately,
Edwd Irving

Addressed to: Revd. Robert Gordon of the Chapel of Ease, Edinburgh.

~

Edward Irving to ANDREW ROBERTSON

Extract of a Letter from Mr. Irving to Mr. Robertson dated 26th Feby 1822[28]
[Written in pencil:] Reproducedon p. 32 of John Hair's *Regent Square*.[29]

Now here is what I have to propose. That if the Directors do wish me & wld wait for me till by dint of all my powers I can acquire Gaelic, I shall forthwith remove myself to Glenfillass [Glenfinlas] near the Trossachs where I am well known and domesticate myself amongst the hospitable Stewarts there and apply to the Celtic Tongue. Meanwhile forgoing for this interest the desire of visiting my home town quickened by a severe illness of my Venerable Father (from which the Almighty is now delivering him). I shall also come upon trials for ordination before the Presbytery of that county so that the least delay possible will intervene, perhaps four months at the furthest from the date of your order.[30]

~

---

28. EIL, MS 13.
29. In the book the letter is dated 22 February 1822.
30. This final sentence was not published.

Edward Irving to JANE WELSH[31]

Edinburgh, 3 Moray Street, Leith Walk. Wednesday,
[deduced by Alexander Carlyle to be 6th March 1822]

My well-beloved friend and pupil,

When I think of you my mind is overspread with the most affectionate and tender regard which I neither know how to name nor how to describe. One thing I know it would long ago have taken the form of the most devoted attachment, but for one intervening circumstance, and have shewed itself and pleaded itself before your heart by a thousand actions from which I must now restrain myself. Heaven grant me its grace to restrain myself, and forgetting my own enjoyment, may I be enabled to combine unto your single self all that duty and plighted faith leave at my disposal. When I am in your company my whole soul would rush to serve you, and my tongue trembles to speak my heart's fullness—but I am enabled to forbear, and have to find other avenues than the natural ones for the overflowing of an affection which would hardly have been able to confine itself within the avenues of nature if they had all be opened.

But I feel within me the power to prevail and at once to satisfy duty to another and affection to you. I stand, truly, upon ground which seems to shake and give way beneath me, but my help is in heaven.

Bear with this much, my early charge and my present friend, from one who lives to help and defend you, who would die rather than wrong you or see you wronged. Say that I shall speak no more of the painful struggle I am undergoing, and I shall be silent—if you allow me to speak then I shall reveal to you the features of a virtuous contention to be crowned, I repay and trust, with a Christian triumph.

It is very extraordinary that this weak nature of mine cannot bear two affections both of so intense a kind; and yet I feel it can. It shall feed the one with faith and duty, and chaste affection, the other with paternal, fraternal and friendly love no less pure no less assiduous no less constant. In return seeking nothing but permission and indulgence.

I was little comforted by Rousseau's letters[32] though holding out a most admirable moral; but much, much comforted and confirmed, by the few words which your noble heart dictated the moment before I left you. Oh persevere, my admirable pupil, in the noble admirations you have taken up. Let affectionateness and manly firmness be the qualities to which you yield your love, and your life shall be honourable; advance your admirations somewhat higher and it shall be everlastingly happy.

Oh do not forbid me from rising in my communications with one so capable of the loftiest conceptions, forbid me not to draw you upwards to the love and study of

---

31. Carlyle, *Love Letters*, 419

32. Jean-Jacques Rousseau, *Lettres sur les spectacles* (1758); Rousseau, *Eloisa, A Series of Original Letters*.

Part II: The Letters

your Creator which is the beginning of wisdom. I have sent you Erskine's book[33] which though nothing equal to the subject is well worth your study. I have returned Rousseau.—Carlyle is not so aggrieved as I could have figured. Such a parting from you would have gone far to kill me. But this will never happen. Mr. Graham has met with an accident, having been fairly lifted by the wind from his feet and dashed through a window; but he is recovering.

My most affectionate regards to your mother. The time is coming when I shall have an opportunity to testify my sense of attentions from such a mother and such a daughter in a way becoming their worth and station. Count forever, my dear Jane, upon the last efforts to minister to your happiness present and everlasting.

From your faithful friend and servant,
Edwd Irving

Edward Irving to THE ELDERS OF THE CALEDONIAN CHAPEL

Glasgow, 34 Kent St. 12th March 1822[34]

To the Elders of the Caledonian Chapel and my other friends in London therewith connected

Gentlemen

I feel again called on to address you in a body from the new aspect which our affairs have taken. There is a providence in these things above human research, to which first our prayers and then our acknowledgments should be addressed—and if our union be now nearer than before let us give thanks to the Lord, and continue constant in our prayers for its completion.

This letter was meant to have been the vehicle of intelligence painful for me to communicate, and not a little disconcerting to your plans.—And when I came to the intelligence of your new condition I could only clasp my hands in devout astonishment and be thankful that I was delivered from my painful necessity.—In Edinburgh where I spent the last fortnight, I learned from Dr Fleming and others versant in the matter, that to become capable of translating with ease from the Gaelic, was not a work of months but of years, even in circumstances the most favourable—that to acquire ease in it so as to be listened to with pleasure, was barely possible, if indeed possible to one of my years. Dr Fleming said that though the language of his infancy, it required him when presented to a charge in the Highlands where nothing but Gaelic was spoken, not less than three years to be able to do his duty comfortably in the language. Now

---

33. Thomas Erskine of Linlathlen (1788–1870), quite possibly *Remarks on the Internal Evidence for the Truth of Revealed Religion* (1820).

34. EIL, MS 14. Incomplete letter.

the same motive of ministering the Gospel, which made me inflexible to undertake the task while in ignorance of its tediousness, would have made me inflexible in refusing it, when so assured. Not for any language nor all the languages which are spoken would I suspend ministerial labours in the midst of which I am busy for such a space of time. The same motive of responsibility to Heaven would have completely debarred me from resigning my present office unless absolutely secured of election when certified to be fully prepared. So that every thing seemed hostile to that union to which every thing now seems favourable.

It was not needful for me to have made these allusions to a condition of our affair, whereof the fear is in a good degree passed away. But it may yet be necessary at the general Court or elsewhere, and I desire it to be distinctly understood, that I can on no account undertake what would cost such an expense of time with such small prospect of advantage. For the rest, let all things stand as they are written in my former letter—It is indifferent [The rest of the letter is lost]

Addressed to: William Dinwiddie Esq.,
4 Grocer's Hall Court,
Poultry, London.

Extract of a Letter from Edward Irving to ANDREW ROBERTSON

March/April 1822[35]

I could not ask from Dr. Chalmers the liberty of a second visit, because I do not myself see the fitness of it. It would be an act in the face of all my better sentiments, which truly are my whole wealth, and which, therefore, I am the less disposed to trifle with. If I were to come to London a second time, then indeed I were seeking and hunting after a settlement, and that by the stepping-stone of notoriety, the least evangelical of all approaches to the ministry. You all know what I am. I am making great improvement in my own opinion and in the opinion of others, which I date from the hearty reception of my London friends, under God. I have shown you to what lengths my compliance will go, the cause being worthy ... These are the elements of my character, and if they are not sufficient to move decision, then I shall not certainly add to them the paltry element of my being able to excite a popular interest.

---

35. Hair, *Regent Square*, 46. In the book it is explained that this letter was a reply to a letter written to Irving by Robertson about the 27th March 1822.

Part II: The Letters

Edward Irving to ANDREW ROBERTSON

15th April 1822[36]

Upon returning on Saturday evening, with a heavy heart, to my solitary apartments, I found you two communications. They revived me again with the prospect, which had begun to fade from my hope, of yet standing forth in a high place for the defense of Zion.

Edward Irving to THE ELDERS AND CONGREGATION OF THE CALEDONIAN CHURCH

17th April 1822[37]

To the Elders and Congregation of the Caledonian Church Cross Street, Hatton Garden, who have subscribed a Call for me to be their Pastor.

Christian Brethren,

I am not worthy of the honour you have done me in inviting me to be your Pastor—but, trusting to the grace and strength which is perfected in weakness, I do most cordially accept of your Call, and, when God doth join us shall employ the gift given unto me for your Spiritual edification; and for the interests of our redeeming Church.

I shall take steps to be ordained forthwith by my native Presbytery of Annan over whose motions I have through personal acquaintance some influence that I shall employ for expediting the matter. Yet with all dispatch I fear that to deliver myself honourably from my present charge and to go through the forms of the Church will require at the least what remains of this month, and the whole of the next. But not a moments delay shall be allowed to take place.

I wish you the guardianship of the great Shepherd of the Sheep[38]—and longing to meet you all in the bonds of love and peace and pastoral union,

I am,
Christian Brethren,
Your affectionate friend,
Edwd Irving

Glasgow
April 17th 1822

---

36. Hair, *Regent Square*, 34, 35. This is not a complete letter but rather lines from the letter as reproduced in Hair's book.

37. EIL, MS 18.

38. Heb 13:20.

Edward Irving to WILLIAM HAMILTON

Paisley 24th April 1822[39]

My dear Sir,

Though I received so many and so kind attentions from you in London, the great diversity of my occupations, and my frequent visits of late to different parts of the country, in the prospect of removal, have hindered me from ever presenting my acknowledgments, not the less felt, be assured, on that account. The confidence and frequency of our intercourse makes me assured, when I come to London, that we shall find in each other steady friends; and it is delightful in the prospect opening up, that I have such friends to come to. The bearer is my brother-in-law, Mr. Warrand Carlyle [sic], a young man of most admirable character, both moral and religious. He is in London on business, and will be able to inform you in all my affairs. I am doing my utmost to get the Presbytery to consent to my ordination without a bond, and I hope to succeed.[40] But if they will not, I come in June, ordination or no ordination; and if they are not content with the security I am content with, then I shall be content to do without their ordination and seek it elsewhere, or apply for it after. But I augur better . . . Mr. Dinwiddie must not consider me wanting in affection that it is so long since I wrote to him personally; assure him and all his family, I pray, of my gratitude and high regards, which many years, I trust, will enable me to testify . . . May all good be with you, and my other acquaintances; and may I be enabled, when I come among you, to do more than fulfil all your expectations,—till which happy junction may we be preserved in the grace of the Lord.

Yours most affectionately,
Edward Irving

Paisley, 24th April 1822.

Edward Irving to THOMAS CARLYLE

Glasgow. 29th April 1822[41]

My Dear Carlyle,

The enclosed must come a fragment, or altogether hinder me from writing you, for here it lies upbraiding my conscience, and still it upbraids but still I am without time to

---

39. Oliphant, *Life*, 1:139–40.

40. At this time, it was a requirement for ordination in the Church of Scotland that a bond be signed guaranteeing that the congregation would pay an adequate stipend.

41. NLS, MS 1764, fol. 227–28.

finish it, being so engaged with correspondence connected with my departure, and with the arrears of my business, and with the ceremony and the pain of taking farewell.

For it is now at length determined that I go to London, and that *quamprimum*,[42] I have received the call most respectably signed, and what with subscriptions and the first of the seat-rents, the security of £500 a year, so that I trust being able to entertain you yet in London as every honest hearted fellow should be entertained.[43]—I go down to Annan this day (Monday) three weeks, where I am to abide during the month of June, and obtain ordination. Then to London I fear without seeing the metropolis—and yet I would like to see you. Could you come through at the time of the Sacraments, and live among us a few days. Graham is down in Annandale, but by that time he will be returned—do this if you can—for I fear I will not see Edin like I see London, and when after I never fancy to myself.

By the bye, Graham has some chance of getting forward into another line of doing very congenial to himself, upon which I am not at liberty to enter—though I doubt not he will inform you himself—only the knowledge of such a prospect I thought it cruel to withhold.

Many things oppress my spirit at the present moment[,] nothing more than parting with these most worthy and kind-hearted people.—Some other things also that I cannot even render into language unto my own mind. There is an independence about my character a want of resemblance with others, especially with others of my profession, that will cause me to be apprehended ill of. Yet I hope to come through honestly and creditably. God grant it.

I am vexed at Brown.[44] I had occasion to write to him for some papers which I had to use at the Presbytery—in which I prayed him to cast away suspicion, and entertain me like an old & worthy friend. He sent the papers by the Coach, did not deign me an answer of any kind. This was not becoming in one who has had proof of my friendship worth a thousand letters & shall have yet. It hurt me, grieved me much—but perhaps I deserve it all.—Then the Almighty enable me to bear it.

I desire to be remembered always by you with the purest affection.

Yours most truly,
Edwd Irving

P.S. Would you be kind enough to forward the parcel enclosed by the first Haddington Coach, and see it booked. Yours EI

Addressed to: Mr. Thomas Carlyle
Mrs. Wallace's, Moray St., Edinburgh.

---

42. To the highest degree possible.
43. Thomas Carlyle, writing to James Johnstone on 30 April 1822. See CL, 2:106–7.
44. James Brown. See Diary entry for Monday 23 August 1810.

Edward Irving to THOMAS CARLYLE

[Annotated:] Enclosed with the Letter dated 29th April 1822?[45]

My Dear Carlyle,

You have indeed set me a task which I am neither willing nor able to perform, not willing because you are one whom I have been accustomed to defend, and how to judge or condemn you I find not, not able because your mind is dissimilar to my own, and rises, I think, into an altitude where it is not congenial for mine to live. But yet at your earnest request and from regard to your future prosperity in that sphere, more congenial to me, of actual life out of which you must drink your happiness or misery I undertake and shall faithfully perform.

And for the sake of breadth as well as distinctness, I shall take the following order—the habits of your understanding, of your feelings and of your conduct. Your intellect has always appeared to me too accute [sic], whether it be its nature or the impulse of your feelings I know not; but it has an impatience, and quick decision that seems to me against the accuracy of its results, and much against the pleasant communication of them. In writing it is not so, there is much wisdom there, and much truth. It must be the presence of another that excites it to such promptitude—and the perception of his weakness or his prejudice. Now this ought to have the opposite effect, for we have there not only the hurt but the *raiment* of the truth to consult for. Not only the pleasing of ourselves but the not offending of our neighbour.—You bear most impetuously to a point, and have got to an issue, before our minds have addressed themselves to the question, and hence we are obliged to be silent, contented to listen, or we have to arm ourselves with seeming indifference that we may not appear to be outrun, or we have to lose temper and flatly contradict your Conclusion, and shew dislike of the discussion. Guard yourself here well. If I might be bold to hazard a stricture upon the *make* of your understanding it does not proceed methodically enough. You are so full of matter, that you would require double skill and endeavour after distribution. Your argument is too full of particulars, all telling, but the individual or aggregate weight not seemingly told even to yourself. Hence you drop towards your conclusion into a falling key—maintain a running doubt with yourself and at length come perhaps to the conclusion that it is the other way. But this perhaps may be my own defect of particulars justifying itself. It is unfortunate you have not yet joined yourself to any cause in which men are deeply concerned, for then the interests of that cause you prized would to your hand have distributed your knowledge, and given weight and decision to your judgments. You understand rather like a thinking than an acting man. This however is perhaps the necessary consequence of your circumstances. These three things combined, your penetration to perceive the remote bearings of the question, and your impatience to balance and judge the whole, with no call of occupation or authority of any kind to drive you to settled issues, have produced that habit to which

---

45. NLS, MS 1764, fol. 229-30.

none is more alive than yourself of doubting of things certain rather than ascertaining things doubtful. This makes your knowledge yield you so little happiness, and it has not yet yielded you any power, but ministered strength to your ideal existence which was originally strong enough of itself. Now, though I see truth in what I have said I know not how it is to be mended. There are things which you reverence, religion, liberty, domestic ties, trusty friendship, female love, and above all the independence of the soul. Could you not cherish these loves and make them fruitful. Bringing your wonderful knowledge and invention to decorate & strengthen them both within yourself, and for the world's sake find what you love & understand for that, and act for it, and unite friendships upon finding men with similar sympathies. Now, really, this is important, your mind might minister a pillar of strength, and a wreath of beauty to whatsoever is worthy—and at the present moment it is corroding itself. Cast it forth speedily, and oh! let it be upon something worthy of a man, something which you truly love. Your wit, your sarcasm, your contempt, your hatred at this moment threaten to devour your benevolence, your admiration and your tender affection. Permit it not for the Love you bear Heaven[,] Earth and yourself. Not that you should extinguish these sensibilities not less noble nor less bountifully given, because in general harmfully used—but that you should draw them in as helps-meet [helpmeets] for the other kindlier & better sensibilities, for the purpose of withering up whatever opposes them. In that review of Faust,[46] which for all you say against it, it would have been worthy of your great mind to have philosophised the character which Goethe has poetised, and not only so, but to have instructed mankind how to guard against the evil of the tree of knowledge. Carlyle, this is in you, and it will be your salvation, the salvation of many future sons of genius to arise, it is in you to meditate, and map out these obliquities in the path of knowledge, and to trace how it may be made the true path of wisdom and happiness. For surely I cannot be mistaken that to know well this our sphere, is to possess it well, or rather is before possessing it well. And though it will not carry back its limitations, it will teach us full liberty within them. In doing this, which you are so qualified for by having sounded so many of its bitter waters, which others dare not to approach, you serve your species, and our common Father, and in the next sphere of our being, are more worthy of honour for having endeavoured to purify and brighten this. In all that I have said, I do not except revealed religion of which you know the necessity, and feel some of the strongest applications.

Now of your feelings I shall speak first as they bear upon yourself, then as they bear upon others. Your opinion of yourself wants decision, or seems to want it. My opinion of you is made up & need not here be repeated, but for yourself, to hear you speak, one would take you for the most aimless indifferent mortal upon earth, whereas you are one of the clearest-sighted, and acutely-suffering. Now what is the use of this? First you are lost to many who seek for a sufficient tone in a sufficient mind. Thus you lay others off their guard who come on to crush a moth, and find it sting their foot &

---

46. Carlyle's review *Faustus*, which appeared in the *Edinburgh Review* of April, 1822.

escape their tread. Learn to esteem yourself up to your proper dimensions and to act accordingly. In the discourse take tone, take place, they listen to you often as a curiosity of knowledge, not as a man of knowledge. They dread you as a cap-a-pee-armed[47] champion, rather than shelter beside you as a guardian of what is good & peaceful. Give men the right view of you and they will both wonder & respect, for I know no vice in practice or opinion with which you are chargeable. Again I crave your attention to this.—Give men time to know you, and take time to know them. It is this incongruity between what you are, and what you seem to be, which mars their judgment. Not that I ask you to court men's favours, but that I would save you from unhappy encounters from misapprehension and misrepresentation, and smooth the way to honour and to life. Now with regard to your opinion of men you go far too much upon intellect, I mean in the literary world—I do not mean bear [sic] intellect, but you look for something which may be the fruit of much intellect wedded to the other parts of their nature. Now in this Scotland there is a subtlety but no largeness of intellect, there is a caution which is timorous, and an economy which is rigorous. There is a thirst and parchedness in things, which I could long to see removed. But not being able I learn to respect though I love not and practice not their prudences and I wish you were the same. Again I say look for the little good there is in them, though only the grain of corn in the bushel of chaff, look it out, talk of it and respect it, and respect him who has it.

Edward Irving to THE ELDERS OF THE CALEDONIAN CHURCH

Glasgow. 3rd May 1822[48]

To my honoured & Dear Friends,
The Elders of the Caledonian Church London.

Gentlemen,
Ye know how I devoted myself to your interest from the very first, and how little I have been willing at any time, to interpose matters of personal convenience. But there are duties which I have to discharge in Scotland, of which no obligations elsewhere can acquit me. One of these is to live a short while with my parents of whom my Father is just recovered from the jaws of death. To accomplish this, I have foregone my visit to the General Assembly, and in accomplishing it I shall not occupy a day longer than is

---

47. *Cap á pie*, i.e., from head to toe.
48. EIL, MS 20.

necessary for getting ordination. So that while I discharge this obligation of nature I do not postpone my arrival in London a single day.

Since my last letter I have come to know that there can be no meeting of Presbytery during the Assembly and that there is never any in the month of May at all except for extraordinary purposes such as to expedite business for the Assembly. The Assembly rises on the 28th May, and I have got the Presbytery of Annan to consent taking me on trials the 5th June—the trials for ordination are numerous and generally occupy three meetings of Presbytery, but they have at my urgent request consented to take them but twice, and for the same reason, far contrary to their usual rule, to hold the second Presbytery also in June; so that let me do my utmost I cannot leave Scotland till the end of June—and even then I sacrifice many farewell visits to which I stood positively pledged.[49]

You may depend on it I have not lost one hour since I received the Call, and even while things were in doubt I had prepared all things for the speediest arrangement, and they are going to be arranged speedy beyond all precedent.—But really I could not consent to come up to London without ordination, after having put the Presbytery to such a world of trouble—and got them to consent without a bond—at least I hope so, but should it turn out otherwise, then for your sake I will come up unordained.

I am sorry at the postponement of our meeting till the end of June, you seem to set so much store upon being up in May. You do not mention the cause of such urgency, and I am not able to conjecture it; yet upon no shewing but your bare request, I would have made the utmost dispatch, and come off post haste, had I not been involved with the Presbytery as I have stated above.

I hope you will not take this amiss, for truly I cannot help it—my documents were laid on the Presbytery table, last Wednesday, and to retire them now, would be worse than foolishness, discreditable to me, and so not creditable to the congregation over which I am to be placed.

You may rest in my honour, and in my affections which are gone before me to London, and in my Christian longing after the flock and in every other principle which it becomes a Christian pastor to entertain, that I will make all speed consistent with the same principles, to take on me my high office.

I am Gentleman,
Your most affectionate friend,
Edwd Irving

Addressed to: William Dinwiddie Esq.,
4 Grocer's Hall Court,
Poultry, London.

---

49. Irving's trials for ordination took place on 5th and 19th June; his ordination following on the latter day: Grass, *The Lord's Watchman*, 45.

Edward Irving to DAVID HOPE

Annan. 28th May 1822[50]

I am snugly seated in this Temple of Indolence, and very loath to be invaded by any of the distractions of the busy city. I would fain devote myself to the enjoyment of our home and family, and to meditate from a distance the busy scene I have left, and the more busy scene to which I am bound. My mind seems formed for inactivity. I can saunter the whole day from field to field, riding on impressions and the transient thoughts they awaken, with no companion of books or men, saving, perhaps, a little nephew or niece in my hand.

You may from this conceive how little disposed I am to take any task in hand of any kind; and I had almost resolved to refuse flatly the flattering requests of my friends to publish that poor discourse;[51] but yesterday there came such a letter from Mr. Collins, full of argument and the kindest encouragement, that I have resolved to comply, and shall signify my resolution to him by this post.

For the other matter, it gives me the most exquisite delight to think my friends remember me with attachment. That they are about to show it by some testimonial I should perhaps not have known till I received it. It is not my part to make a choice; but if I were to think of anything, it would be that very thing which you mention.[52] But of this say nothing as coming from me.

Edward Irving to THOMAS CHALMERS

Annan. 14th June 1822[53]

Dear Sir,

I dare not take it on me to delay my setting out for another week, however much on every account I would wish to assist at your Parish Sacrament. But though I cannot take it on myself I shall forthwith write to London for their permission which

---

50. Oliphant, *Life* 1:146.

51. Irving, *Farewell Discourse*.

52. 'The matter here referred to was a present which some members of St. John's church were desirous of making him. It was decided that it should be a watch; and I have been told, without, however, being able to vouch for the entire authenticity of the story, that when the matter was entirely decided upon, and the money in hand, Irving was consulted to know whether he had any particular fancy or liking in the matter. He had one, and that was characteristic. He requested that it should be provided by a certain watchmaker, whose distinguishing quality was not that he was skillful in his trade, but that he was an Annandale man. The good Glasgow donors yielded to this recommendation; and Irving had the double delight of receiving a very substantial proof of his friends' attachment, and of throwing a valuable piece of work in the way of his countryman': Oliphant, *Life*, 1:146–47.

53. NCL, MSS CHA 4 21.3.

if I obtain, then with all my heart I shall do what inclination and obligation equally prompt me to. In this letter which to tell the truth is the only one I have written since their pressing invitation that you should honour them at my induction, I shall put a negative upon that hope, for, though I heard a floating rumour that you were going up, I could never persuade myself to indulge a hope so high and honourable lest I might be proportionally cast down by disappointment.

However this may be I shall certainly take away all expectation from them—and from myself also, as I know you cannot move without drawing upon your shoulders a host of burdensome engagements, and of attentions which I know to be almost as burdensome to your retired habits.

I desire my kindest affections to be offered to Mrs. Chalmers. To Miss Ann I never expect to be cordially reconciled until she fall deep in love with my person or my fame which may be calculated on, you may tell her, some eight or nine years after this. For Eliza, my little nephew the young Lord Mayor of the Burgh will grace her well, as she will him. Mr. Crosbie[54] has been with me a week, we were at merry Carlyle[55] yesterday where I spent the day with your friend Mr. Laurie who gave me a letter in charge to your *raverence* as our worthy Irish parishioners call you. My friends here who know you[,] as well as those who do not[,] desire me to signify their highest esteem & best wishes

Yours most affectionately,
Edwd Irving

Addressed to: Revd. Chalmers,
Glasgow.
P.S. The moment I hear from London I will write although I would not have you depend[,] but depend on me for the afternoon of Sunday week. I will come in by the evening mail of Saturday & be with you to breakfast Sunday morning.

~

Edward Irving to THE ELDERS OF THE CALEDONIAN CHURCH

Annan. 14th June 1822[56]

To the Elders of the Caledonian Church.
My worthy friends,

---

54. For Crosbie see Carlyle, *Reminiscences*, 249 and 253.
55. Thomas Carlyle's family at Ecclefechan.
56. EIL, MS 21.

Though I have been remiss in writing, it was because I had nothing to communicate, which, though not a sufficient reason to Gentlemen of business habits, will be taken as sufficient from one who has been so overlaboured with affairs as I have been of late.

My ordination[57] will take place on Wednesday first[,] that is the 19th Inst—the two following days are devoted to the performance of religious duties in the families of my sisters to the baptising of their children, which cannot be done according to the customs of this place without a meeting of their relatives, who afterwards pass the evening together, on Saturday I set out for Glasgow on purpose to preach my first sermon as a minister for my friend Dr Chalmers to whom of all men it is best due. Then I intended after a day or two spent in taking leave of my friends there whom I left such was my occupation without the formality of any calls, to proceed forthwith to London and make good my promise of being there by the end of June. This was my plan, and is still if you refuse the following request I have to-day from Dr C. His sacrament is on Sunday the 30th. He wishes me to assist him but I have told him I cannot take so much upon me as to pass a single day here without necessity or your permission—but that I would write you. And though I now do so, take me as perfectly indifferent, for I am now neutralised from any new obligations by those waiting me in London.

Your request to Dr C I did not neglect to prefer, but as he has been from home I could not answer positively, and I truly did hope at one time to have communicated the pleasing intelligence that he had complied. All hope I fear is now gone. But if I can work upon him I will for your sakes do my endeavour, for myself I am indifferent, being no otherwise minded than to put my trust in the most High—I would like a letter by return of post that I may put him out of suspense.

My love to all my friends,
Dear Gentlemen,
Yours most truly,
Edwd Irving

Addressed to: William Dinwiddie Esq.,
4 Grocer's Hall Court,
Poultry, London.

---

57. See letter Edward Irving to the Elders and the Congregation of the Caledonian Church, 20 June 1822: p. 152.

Part II: The Letters

Edward Irving to THE ELDERS AND THE CONGREGATION OF THE CALEDONIAN CHURCH

Annan. 20th June 1822[58]

Christian Brethren,

To you who have called me to be your pastor and are soon to be my flock, I feel it my duty to communicate first of all the intelligence that I am now ordained to the ministry of the Gospel of Christ.

Yesterday the solemn service was performed in the Church of Annan in which I was baptised by the Moderator of the Presbytery of Annan,[59] and for your satisfaction I have requested & obtained the enclosed minute of the proceeding.

For proceeding forthwith to London I am now at liberty—and that liberty would have embraced without consultation of any interest or my convenience. But my friend Dr Chalmers has requested, has honoured me by requesting that I would discharge for him on Sunday the 30th Inst the solemn service of the communion, for which indisposition hath unfitted him. This gives me, as your pastor soon to be, a certain name and respectability in the ministry to which I was yesterday admitted, that I could not think of refusing and I have consented. Till then I go into retirement to meditate the solemn duty that is before me.

My friends the Congregation of Glasgow have honoured me with a splendid token of their affection[60]—to receive this and to return my farewell salutations to so many whom I love will take me another day or two. Then I have in the East Country a matter of the utmost importance to one leaving his native country to adjust[61]—so that if the first week of July should be consumed in these various offices of Christian love, and personal obligation, you will please to forgive and not take amiss what I cannot as a man of principle and honour avoid. In the second Sabbath of July if God prosper my journey, which may the Lord Jesus make fruitful of blessing to us both.

I am,
Beloved Brethren,
Your affectionate friend,
Edwd Irving

Addressed to: William Dinwiddie Esq.,
4 Grocer's Hall Court,
Poultry, London.

---

58. EIL, MS 23.

59. William Hardie Moncrieff (1761–1824).

60. A watch. See Edward Irving to David Hope, 28 May 1822.

61. This was a visit to Jane and her mother at Haddington: CL, 2:145, Thomas Carlyle to John Carlyle, 5 July 1822; Grass, *The Lord's Watchman*, 46 n.25. According to Froude it was to tell Jane that the Martins would not release him from his engagement to Isabella. Froude, *Carlyle*, 3:29.

Edward Irving to WILLIAM DINWIDDIE

Edinburgh. 8th July 1822[62]

Dear Sir,

I have now got all my arrangements made to set out from here on Wednesday by the James Watt Steam-boat—I could not though my life had been depending on it have got sooner, without indeed doing violence to every sentiment of gratitude friendship and duty. When I do arrive, which, God prospering will be on Friday I hope to yield to no minister in assiduity at my post—I am preparing an inaugural discourse, of which the better part will have to be written at sea.

Dr Chalmers has been taken unwell, and could give me no assistance on the 30th. He is now a good deal better, but from his bad health finds things so backward, that he will not be able to remove any-where this summer—at least so he intends at present—I believe that had it not been this visitation of bad health, he would have been prevailed on, which may give us the more hope against another time.

For my own part I am indifferent, it would have brought me all at once into the eye of the public which I do not like, being desirous to discharge the cure of the Caledonian Church first of all, before taking any part of the public business or public interest. But as it is a form in our church to have an Induction sermon preached by some Brother, I would take it kind if you would ask that favour of Mr. Marshall[63] in the furnoon [sic]—to whom I would have written myself if I had not forgotten his address. Failing him I would beg the same favour of my friend Mr. Crombie.[64] Dr Manuel[65] I understand is in Scotland though I have not seen him. But if it cannot be brought about then I am content to introduce myself.

My love to the brethren of the Session—to your family and to all the Congregation who take an interest in me

I am,
Dear Sir,
Yours most truly,
Edwd Irving

Addressed to: William Dinwiddie Esq.,
4 Grocer's Hall Court,
Poultry, London.

---

62. EIL, MS 25.
63. There is a mention in Hair, *Regent Square*, 21, of Mr. Marshall, minister of the Church of Scotland, congregation Swallow Street, London.
64. Rev John Crombie was minister of St. Andrew's in Shadwell: Cameron, *Scots Kirk*, 39.
65. Dr Manuel of London Wall, at this point also Moderator of the Presbytery of London.

Part II: The Letters

Edward Irving to MRS CHALMERS

London 15th July 1822[66]

My dear Madam,

It is well my part, now that I can do it without offending the modesty of your ear, to make my acknowledgments for the maternal kindness with which for many years you treated me, and which grew in strength to the very last. The happy days which I have spent under your roof, and the enjoyment which I never failed to derive from your enlivening presence, are as sweet in my remembrance, as the favour and confidence of your distinguished husband are honorable. Both of you have bound me in obligations, which I shall carry with me to my grave, yet hanging on me with much sweetness, and bringing to me such pleasant remembrances, that I do not wish to be acquitted from them. Yet if it should ever please providence to order it so that I might be serviceable to you or your family, or any of your friends, then I shall be glad and thankful to serve them to the uttermost. The formality of these sentences seems strange to me when addressed to one who in giving and bestowing uses no form, and could never hear to an end the formality of an acknowledgement. Yet I feel there is something sacred in what I am now endeavoring to express. And that it would be cruel to my feelings not to use the solemn and measured language in which sacred things are wont to express themselves. May your heart be always as generous, your house always as hospitable, and ever find worthier objects than I am.

Our voyage was very pleasant, indeed it rather resembled a party of pleasure than a voyage of business or a journey of inconvenience. In the morning we met and saluted upon a deck as clean as the boards of Mr. Woods drawing room, the gentlemen paying their respects to the ladies and attending them with a grace and assiduity which would not have disgraced the Assembly room of Glasgow. No word of business, none of news, all of kindly solicitude in each other, and tender enquiries after each others good condition. Then from almost a hundred couches we assembled fresh as the sea-breeze which moved us incessantly to a saloon for which I find no similitude in any apartment with which we are mutually acquainted. They soon got to know me for a parson, and most glad were they when I offered my services as chaplain. Such a breakfast. Land and water yielded up their choicest[,] the East and the West sent us the fruit of their herbs, and the finest of the wheat was our morning portion. Then shall I speak of the flowing wit and humour, the compliments passing from Gentlemen to ladies, the *noms de guerre* which we were obliged to give and take in ignorance of our Christian names? All combining a scene over which David Duffle of the Grass Market might have strung many a fustian sentence. Our forenoon spent over the choicest books—our dinner partaken upon the most plentiful and substantial fare. And our evenings spent in talk and tales at which last I was clearly dubbed the Apollo of the Assembly, until they declared if I preached as I told stories I would have no equal in the South

66. NCL: CHA 7.1.23.

We arrived on Friday night late, and after storming fury amongst bargemen porters and coachmen I got safe to the London Coffee-house, where I have abided ever since, and shall continue till I get lodgings. Yesterday I inducted myself from a text Acts X verse—[29.] Therefore I came without gainsaying, read it & tell me if there is such a one in the whole bible—I forget the verse. I am received with great acceptancy, and if I can preserve humility and receive that monthly dispatch my friend Mr. Wood promised I despair nothing of success.

To Mr. & Mrs. Wood give my kindest love. Setting all levity aside it would give me infinite pleasure to hear from either of them. I think ere long when I am in a happy mood I shall [letter torn] with him with a letter. My love to Mrs. Paul, whose affection always 'come over my heart most like that of a sister,' I hope to 'Harry' in town this week.

For 'the Doctor' I shall write to him so soon as I am settled, and for the children tell them to be like their mother. 'Auntie Helen' I hope to escort from London to Gloucestershire ere all be done. And Aunt Ann's heart will be delighted when she hears of a Scotch Kirk in London to rival St. Paul's itself, with her old friend at the head of it.

>Ever remember me,
>My Dear Mrs. Chalmers,
>As your most affectionate friend
>Edwd Irving

Addressed to: Mrs. Chalmers,
Rev Dr Chalmers, . . . Place, Glasgow.

~

Edward Irving to DR THOMAS CHALMERS

20th July 1822[67]

Dear Sir,

The bearer of this is Mr. Hamilton, partner of Mr. Laurie's House here, from whom I thought you would be able to get information both in respect to our affairs, and also in respect to your researches on pauperism, in which respect he has been assisting to Mr. Collins.

Mr. Collins seems to have enjoyed his journey much and to have thriven on it. He is in the clouds or rather above them about Foster[,] 'the great man'[,] that is his *nom de guerre* with the worthy father of your Session.

---

67. NCL, MSS CHA 4 21.5.

My reception has been in much affection and my labours are likely to be blessed, if the Lord strengthen me in his good work. For much expectation hath awaited my arrival, and much interest is beginning to be excited.

Nothing astonishes me more than the classification of men in the religious world—the smallest shade of opinion suffices to join a union so that between our two Scottish distinctions of Moderate and High, there are here no less than five distinct stages. I suppose single men feel so solitary that to preserve their individuality they are fain to club together, be the rallying-word what it may.

For myself I am resolved to thrust my head into none of their Cabals, but to join myself to my people, and walk straight forward in the path of honesty and truth. And if I jostle any man to let him look to himself as I do to myself, and if any like my way he may join it. This you will say is very presumptuous in a hare-brained upstart youth; but it is the only course which preserving the simplicity of the truth I can steer. For in all this city I find not one body whose maxims I could heartily go into.

This is a mere letter of gossip—suggested by the [gap in text] of my much esteemed friend Mr. Hamilton, yet I cannot conclude it without dearest remembrances to lady & household and to your neighbours at the head of the row.

London, 20th July 1822
19 Gloucester St., Queens Sq., Bloomsbury

Addressed to: Revd. Dr Chalmers,
Windsor Place,
Glasgow.

∼

Edward Irving to WILLIAM GRAHAM

London, 19 Gloucester Street, Queen Square, Bloomsbury.
5th August, 1822[68]

My very dear Friend,

I have not forgot you, and if I wished to forget you I could not, sealed as you are in the midst of my affections, and associated with so many recollections of worth and of enjoyment. You always undervalued yourself, and often made me angry by your remarks upon the nature of our friendship, counting me to gain nothing; whereas I seemed always in your company to be delivered into those happy and healthy states of mind which are in themselves an exquisite reward. To say nothing of your bounty,

---

68. Oliphant, *Life*, 1:152–54. Alexander Carlyle quotes from this letter in *Love Letters*, 1:421.

which shone through all the cloud of misfortune; to say nothing of your tender interest in my future, my friends, my thoughts; and your sleepless endeavour to promote and serve them—I hold your own manly, benignant, and delicate mind to be a sufficient recommendation of you to men of a character and a genius I have no pretensions to. So in our future correspondence be it known to you that we feel and express ourselves as equals, and bring forth our thoughts with the same liberty in which we were wont to express them—which is the soul of all pleasant correspondence.

You cannot conceive how happy I am here in the possession of my own thoughts, in the liberty of my own conduct, and in the favour of the Lord. The people have received me with open arms; the church is already regularly filled; my preaching, though of the average of an hour and a quarter, listened to with the most serious attention. My mind plentifully endowed with thought and feeling—my life ordered, as God enable me after his holy Word—my store supplied out of His abundant liberality. These are the elements of my happiness, for which I am bound to render unmeasured thanks. Would all my friends were as mercifully dealt with, and mine enemies too.

You have much reason for thankfulness that God, in the time of your sore trials, sustained your honour and your trust in Himself; nay, rather made you trust in Him the more He smote you. His time of delivery will come at length, when you shall taste as formerly His goodness, and enjoy it with a chastened joy, which you had not known if you had never been afflicted: persevere, my dear friend, in the ways of godliness and of duty, until the grace of God, which grows in you, come to a full and perfect stature.

For my thoughts, in which you were wont to take such interest, they have of late turned almost entirely inward upon myself; and I am beginning dimly to discover what a mighty change I have yet to undergo before I be satisfied with myself. I see how much of my mind's very limited powers have been wasted upon thoughts of vanity and pride; how little devoted to the study of truth and excellency upon their own account. As I advance in this self-examination, I see farther, until, in short, this life seems already consumed in endeavours after excellence, and nothing attained; and I long after the world where we shall know as we are known, and be free to follow the course we approve, with an unimpeded foot. At the same time I see a life full of usefulness, and from my fellow-creatures, full of glory, which I regard not; and of all places this is the place for one of my spirit to dwell in. Here there are no limitations to my mind's highest powers; here, whatever schemes are worthy may have audience and examination; here, self-denial may have her perfect work in midst of pleasures, follies, and thriftless employments of one's time and energies. Oh, that God would keep me, refine me, and make me an example to this generation of what His grace can produce upon one of the worst of His children!

I have got three very good, rather elegant apartments,—a sitting room, a bedroom, and dressing-room: and when George comes up, I have one of the attics for his sleeping apartment. My landlady, as usual, a very worthy woman, and likely to be well content with her lodger. George comes up when the classes sit down, and in the meantime is busy in Dr. Irving's shop. This part of the town is very airy and healthy, close to Russell Square, and not far from the church, and in the midst of my friends. My studies begin after breakfast, and continue without interruption till dinner; and the product, as might be expected, is of a far superior order to what you were pleased to admire in St. John's.

Edward Irving to THOMAS CHALMERS

London, 19 Gloucester St., Queen Sq., Bloomsbury.
9th Sept 1822[69]

My Dear and Honoured friend,

I have this moment received a letter from my Brother Ferguson to inform me that you had called on your way to Gloucester, and requested him to send you my address as I have done above.—

I had been led to anticipate this from a clause in a letter I had lately from Mr. Collins—and also that you would visit London, and perhaps preach for me. This is what is in unison with your former acts of kindness but what I will not ask of you if you have resolved not to preach in your absence from home. I know too well your need of rest, and am too well assured of your interest in me, either to impinge upon the former, or to doubt of the latter.

But if you can preach, though it were but [letter torn] diet, you would fill the heart of my congregation and of their pastor with high delight.—If you propose so to honour us, I should like to hear from you on which day, also on which day you are to be in London that I might be in waiting to receive you.—Indeed to me it would be an exquisite gratification, if not to you an encumbrance[,] to come down to Gloucester & travel to town with you, if I were assured of being at liberty from the preparation of a Sermon. On these accounts a single line would gratify me much.—Meanwhile accept the assurances of my affection & esteem & gratitude.

I am,
Dear Sir,
Yours Most [corner of letter torn away]

Addressed to: Revd. Dr Chalmers,
Care of Re Mr. Hunter, Gloucester.

---

69. NCL, MSS CHA 4.21.7.

Edward Irving to JANE WELSH

London: September 9 1822.[70]

My dearest Friend,

I said in the last walk which we enjoyed together on a Sabbath evening—when by the solemn stillness of the scene, no less than the pathetic character of our discourse, my mind was in that solemn frame which is my delight—that in future I was to take upon me in my letters the subject of your moral and religious improvement, leaving to other correspondents matters of literature, taste, and entertainment. But I have not forgot that you discharged me from preaching to you in my letters, and I fear what you humorously call preaching is the very thing which I shall have to do if I fulfil my resolution. Now I can chat, though somewhat awkwardly I confess; and ten year agone I had a little humour which has now nearly deceased from neglect. My mind was then light and airy, and loved to utter its conceptions, and to look at them and laugh at them when uttered. Then I could have written letters trippingly, and poured out whatever was uppermost in my mind; but I can do that no longer. I am aiming from morning till night to be a serious and wise man, though God knows how little I succeed. The shortness of life is evermore in my eye, the wasting of it before my conscience; the responsibility of it overwhelms me, and the vanity of it ashames me. I cannot make a mock heroic of these things, or laugh them away. I was never so far lost to good sense and good feelings as to try. So they hang over me, and I must either sink down into a melancholy forlorn creature, weeping and sighing and talking over difficulties of living well, or I must rise up in the strength of Him who made me, and endeavour to work my passage through the best and surest way I can. This last I have chosen, like the wise men who have gone before me, and by God's help I will fulfil it.

Now, my dear, dear friend, bear with me if I violate the law of letter writing you imposed upon me by daring to be serious, and to speak to you whom I love of those things and that strain which most I love. The fine promise of your mind has been to me the theme of much conversation and of far more delightful thought. It is not part of my character to withhold my admiration from others, or even from those I admire, and you yourself have often charged me with exaggerating your gifts. Your industry to get knowledge, and to accomplish your mind with elegant learning, no one can exaggerate. Your enthusiasm towards the excellent and rare specimens of human genius is beyond that of any other I know; and your desire to be distinguished by achievements of mind is equaled only by your contempt of all other distinctions. Now there is in these qualities of character not only promise but assurance of the highest excellence, if God give time for all to ripen, and you give ear to his directions for bringing the human character to perfection. Now does it give me great hope that God will yet be pleased to open your mind to the highest of all knowledge, the knowledge of his Blessed Son, and give therewith the highest of all delights, of being like his Son in character and in

---

70. Froude, *Thomas Carlyle, the first forty years*, 1:157–60.

destiny when I see you not alienated from men of genius by their being men of religion, but attracted to them I think rather the more.

I could wish, indeed—and forgive me when I make free to suggest it—that your mind were less anxious for the distinction of being enrolled amidst those whom this world hath crowned with their admiration, than among those whom God hath crowned with his approval. There are two things to be kept in view in judging of the worth of men—first what powers they had, and the what uses they turned them to. You and I agree always when we meet with a person of power, but you do not go as far as I from exacting from them a good use for it. I do not wish it turned to arts of cruelty, which satire and ridicule and scorn are. I can endure this no more than I can endure the tyranny of a despot or the willfulness of a man of power. They prey upon the physical rights and comforts of their underlings; the others prey upon the feelings, by far the tenderer and nobler part. I do not wish it turned to the aggrandizement and adulation of its possessor; for he does not possess it by virtue of himself, but by his Maker and his Preserver. Keep away these two things, the cruel treatment of another, and the deification of one's self, and I will not be offended with the exercises of mental power; but to satisfy me I seek for much besides: I must leave it husbanded and not wasted in indolence, for that was bad almost as the indulgence of superiority. Then I must have it turned to the discovery of truth, and to the undeceiving of men, then to lead them into the way of their well-being. Then finally, which should have been first, or rather which should be the moving principle of the whole, to do honour unto God who has made us masters of our powers. Find people of this kind from the annals of the world; admire them, love them, be like them and God enroll you among them. Oh, how few I find, my dear Jane, hardly have I found a single one, who can stand the intoxication of high talents, or resist presuming to lord it over others. They cry out against kings for their arbitrary tempers. I think men of talents are more so. Nothing can overcome it but the power and wisdom of God, which is in the gospel of his dear Son, your Saviour and mine, and the Saviour of all who believe; who though the brightness of his Father's glory and the express image of his person,[71] and speaking as no man spoke, took upon him the form of a servant, and submitted with to the death of the cross. Therefore God highly exalted Him, and hath given Him a name above every name.[72] So also will He exalt all others who like Him use those their high gifts and appointments to the service of God and their fellows.

Enough of this, for I have much more to speak of. Of my own condition I can speak with great satisfaction, in as far as favour and friendship are concerned, and the outward prosperity of my calling. I have no evidence to judge by farther than that my Chapel is filled, and that their patient hearing of discourses, each an hour and a quarter long, testifies they are not dissatisfied with the stuff they are made of. In another respect I have reasons to be thankful that God has revealed to me of late the largeness

71. Heb 1:3,
72. Phil 2:7, 8, 9.

of my own vanity and the worthlessness of my own service, which, if He follows up with further light upon the best way for me to act in future, and with strength to act as He teaches me, then I have no doubt of a great increase both of happiness and fruit.

I have made no acquaintance in London any literary eminence, but I shall, I doubt not, in good time. I derive little advantage from my acquaintances, my course is so different from theirs. The next moment I have unemployed I devote to my friend Carlyle, to whom I have not yet found time to write. Oh that God would give rest to his mind and instruct him in his truth. I meditate a work upon the alienation of clever men from their Maker. But this shall not hinder me from taking up the life of St. Paul, which deserves certainly the highest strain of poetry, but I am utterly unable for such a task.

My love to your mother. Oh, how I would like to see you both, to live with you in the quietness which I have so often[73] –

The next time I come to live with you I hope I shall be more worthy of your kindness, being more satisfied with myself, and standing firmer in the favour of God, whom that my dear Jane may always set before her is the first and last prayer of her most true and faithful friend,

Edward Irving.

Edward Irving to THOMAS CHALMERS

London, 19 Gloucester St., Queen Sq., Bloomsbury.
10th Sept 1822[74]

Dear Sir,

The bearer, Mr. John Elliot is a preacher of the Gospel and my early friend—He is living in Mr. Hamilton's of Cockney-house as Tutor, and not much acquainted with any of the members of the Presb. I am sure he would be happy to assist you at any time, and would take any attention you may shew him in the best part. He has lived a good deal in the best families of England and is very well informed.

I am,
Dear Sir,
Yours Most truly,
Edwd Irving

---

73. 'Word omitted.' Froude, *Thomas Carlyle*, 1:163.
74. NCL, MSS CHA 4.21.9.

Part II: The Letters

Edward Irving to THOMAS CARLYLE

London, 19 Gloucester Pl Queen Sq. Bloomsbury.
23rd September 1822[75]

My Dear Carlyle,

You gave me time, and I have been forced to take more than I wished, living for the last month at least in a constant battle with my engagements, for a little leisure to write to my friends. My business has grown upon my hands into the double of what I had calculated on. Each week I have to produce two discourses, and whether it is that my mind has taken more important views of the questions I handle, or that the young and thoughtful audience before me, makes me more careful that my argument be more complete and my whole discourse more cogent, certain it is they extend under my hands to at least an hour's length[,] never less[,] generally more. Here then every week I have to write in the best stile [sic] to which I am equal, as much as would make three or four ordinary discourses, and to refresh my mind with reading, and meet the various calls upon my time and thought, which together have occupied me to an extent I have not yet known. But, thank God, I find myself equal to it all, and prospering in the good opinion of the people beyond which I had any reason to expect; and, which gives me greater satisfaction, I feel that I am rising in my own good opinion, since I have become master of my own affairs. The relations of truth do occupy my thoughts a good deal more, and the interests of truth are more consulted for in my time, and industry. Since I have arrived at a comfortable settlement in life my own deservings and my own interests are less frequently and less intensely before me—and being more in repose upon this most disquieting of all subjects, I feel more disengaged for the great truths which it is my office to hold forth to the people. The proof of my success is in this; that the church is now filled though I have adopted no popular acts, but brought forth my thoughts most ingeniously, and with all my power upon every subject—and the people listen without the least symptom of impatience to discourses which reach often to an hour & a half in length.

My mind & character must have something in them very leaden and immovable, otherwise I must have been overflowing with a world of new feelings to communicate to you. There is nothing I am more impressed with than the want of high & commanding minds in any direction—there is no profound thinking or cool investigation upon any hand. Every effort of mind has a popular & ephemeral cast—from the writers whom Carlyle the Atheist[76] patronises, up the highest walks of intellect. And yet there seems to me no want of the gifts out of which great efforts proceed, but a prodigious want of the patience to mature them, and of the industry to supply them with materials. I wish you to give yourself to philosophy, and to bring forward the properties of human nature which seem to me in danger of being underrated to the properties of a triangle or of a plant, or a mineral specimen. I conceive that a great deal may be done

---

75. NLS, MS 1764; fol. 233-34.
76. Richard Carlyle (1780-1834), radical publisher and atheist propagandist.

to cast light upon the philosophy of law and policy and morals, or upon the principles in our constitution which give birth to these departments of knowledge. Our Scotch Philosophers, I am more & more persuaded have done nothing. And Locke for all he did was modestly conscious that he had done little. His great work he projected upon [letter torn] never came to light. My own notion is that your [letter torn] possesses the knowledge, the acuteness to discover its revelations, the system to put it together, the poetry and the skil [sic] to make it interesting. For myself, my province is well defined and by God's blessing I hope yet to do something in it worthy of the labour.

I heard of your engagement in Annandale with Graham that worthiest of men, and most intelligent of merchants—and entered into it all. For in truth I think one of the chief blessings of this confined and plodding life is to prepare one for tasting with greater zest the pleasures of retired and simple society. And most clear proof to me it is of a pedant, who has not the enjoyment of them. Will you write me soon, and let me know both of your outward & inward employments.—Also let me know of Mr. Johnstone, whom I should have written to, but finding that Collins of Glasgow had done it already I did not feel called on so much. How is your Brother. If I can be of any service to him now or afterwards, freely use me.

Most kindly give my remembrances to your pupils, and to their parents—to the worthy Dr Fleming & his family & to all my friends

& believe me,

Yours Most truly,

Edwd Irving

How is Dixon? I wrote to him inviting him to visit me but he did not answer me.

Addressed to: Mr. Thomas Carlyle,
Care of Rev Dr Fleming,
George Square,
Edinburgh,
at Mr Fowler 10 India Street.

Edward Irving to THOMAS CHALMERS

1st October 1822[77]

Dear Sir,

I hope you will receive this at Laurie's—to all the good family there I beg to be most affectionately remembered.

---

77. NCL, MSS CHA 4.21.10.

Part II: The Letters

I know your mind does not bear to wade through preparatory matter, therefore I advise you to begin with the beginning of the work itself and if it do not [sieze?] you with admiration I am ignorant of your genius.—When old Isaac begins to be very instructive upon angling,[78] and all its art and your eye begins to glance over the pages, I pray you to beware and keep a good look out for in the midst of these technical instructions there is the sweetest relief imaginable of eloquence and poetry, and genuine heart.

I wish I could find another man like yourself—and that you were always yourself not harassed as you are with more than one mind can overtake, then I would be happy, and you would be happy. It is this which makes it painful for me to part with you, that I lose the most instructive and genuine of friends—and that I fancy to myself that friend I love so much makes his way to work that is over much & and not all-congenial to his mind.

I hope to be worthy of uttering these sentiments to one of your name and character—for I feel that at present it is not a little presumptuous.

Soon may you return amongst us—again to load us with your favours, and to receive every tribute of our esteem & gratitude.

The Almighty convey you safe to your worthy and delightful fire side.

My blessings & affections go with you.

Your most affectionate,

Edwd Irving

London
19 Gloucester St Queen Sq
1st Oct 1822

~

Edward Irving to DAVID HOPE

19 Gloucester Street, Queen Square, [London.]
5th November, 1822[79]

My dear Friend,

You have too good reason to complain of me, and a thousand more of my Scottish friends; but be not to severe; you shall yet find me in London the same true-hearted fellow you knew me in Glasgow... But I had another reason for delaying; I wished, when I did write, to be able to recount to you an exact account of my success. Thank God, it now seems beyond a doubt. The church overflows every day, and they already begin to

---

78. Isaak Walton (1593–1683), *The Compleat Angler*, first published in 1653.

79. Oliphant, *Life*, 1:157–58.

talk of a right good Kirk, worthy of our mother and our native country. But into these vain speculations I have little time to enter, being engrossed with things strictly professional. You are not more regular at the counting-house, nor, I am sure, sooner (*Anglicè* earlier), neither do you labour more industriously, till four chaps from the Ram's Horn Kirk,[80] than I sit in to this my study, and occupy my mind for the benefit of my flock. The evening brings more engagements with it than I can overtake, and so am I kept incessantly active. My engagements have been increased, of late, by looking out for a house to dwell in. I am resolved to be this Ishmaelite no longer, and to have a station of my own upon the face of the earth.[81] So a new year will see me fixed in my own habitation, where there will be ever be welcome entertainment for him who was to me for a brother at the time of my sojourning in Glasgow. When I look back upon those happy years, I could almost wish to live them over again, in order to have anew the instances I then received of true brotherly kindness from you and so many of your townsmen.

You would be overjoyed to hear the delight of our Scottish youth, which they express to me, at being once more gathered together into one, and the glow with which they speak of their recovered habits. This is the beginning, I trust, of good amongst them. So may the Lord grant in His mercy and loving-kindness.

Now I wish to know about yourself—how all your affairs prosper . . . I could speculate much upon the excellent fruit season, and the wretched oil season; but you would laugh at my ignorance. And there is something more valuable to be speculated upon. I do hope you prosper in the one thing needful, under your most valuable pastor; and also my dear friend Graham. Give my love to him, and say I have not found time to answer his letter; but if this thing of settlement were off my mind, I should get into regular ways. Do not punish me, but write me with all our news; and believe me, my dear David,

Your most affectionate friend,
Edward Irving

～

Edward Irving to MRS WELSH

London, 19 Gloucester St., Queen Square.
6th December 1822[82]

---

80. 'One of the Glasgow churches, popularly so called': Oliphant, *Life*, 1:157.

81. Ishmael lived a nomadic existence with his mother, Hagar after Sarah had them evicted from Abraham's household (Gen. 21:1–21). One wonders whether Irving also had in mind the prophecy regarding Ishmael that his hand would be against everyone, and everyone's hand would be against him (Gen. 16:12).

82. NLS, MS 1764, fol. 237–38.

Part II: The Letters

My Dear & Well-beloved friend,

It is past midnight, my candles are burnt to the socket and I have put one out, to give me greater hope of finishing this before I sleep. For I feel one of those strong movements to write you which whence they are I know not, but they are to me like monitions of higher spirit.

Right beneath my window I have at this early hour in concert the most melodious of the softest[,] most melancholy music. They have performed as if by direction my greatest favourite 'Erin go Braugh'[83]—they have performed another dear to me by friendship 'Caler Herring' [*sic*].[84] And now they are gone and have left me to the silence of my own thoughts. Now it comes again more sweet from distance, and I can do nothing but throw myself upon the sofa and listen to it. It is 'Lochaber no more.'[85] There again 'Auld Lang Syne.' And between every tune a man calls out in a loud voice something to 'All ladies & gentlemen' but what it is I cannot make out.

All now is silence and I hope even such divine interruption shall no longer hinder me from the great delight I have in expressing how dear to my memory, how ever dear shall be the recollection of your home, and of the happiest days of my life which have past [*sic*] beneath its roof. I know not how it happened but I always felt when with you and my Dear pupil, as in a sanctuary—nowhere did thoughts of piety and virtue come to me so little sought, nowhere was I more mindful of all the office of piety or feel so much disposed for all the duties of benevolence. My mind had a Sabbath-rest which it seldom tasted elsewhere, and which it would most gladly renew.

My condition here, which you will desire to hear of, is far more honourable in every respect than was to be looked for. Already my church overflows, & many are the testimonies which are brought to me of happy effects from my preaching. I have dispensed the sacrament to more communicants than have ever before sat down in the place. And there are already £3000 subscribed to build a new church which will be finished in less than a year to contain 2000 people and cost toward £10,000.[86] But that above all which gives me happiness, is the liberty I enjoy of testifying without any restraint my full conception of that blessed Gospel of which I am the unworthy minister. My study is my daily business. My thoughts are my gains—that were enough but my people cease not to express their gratification & improvement. I hope soon to be in my own house by the middle of next month—so that I will be soon settled and fixed—no longer the wandering uncertain creature which for 13 years you have known me.

---

83. 'Ireland forever.'

84. *Caller Herring* by Carolina Oliphant (Lady Nairne) is one of a song collection (anonymous until after her death) including *Charlie is my darling*, published as *The Lays from Strathearn* in 1846. See *OCEL*.

85. The poet Allan Ramsay (1686–1757). See Miles, *Our National Songs Collection*.

86. See Grass, *The Lord's Watchman*, 55.

Since I came to London I have preached in the Evening Lectures on St Luke, and the people are longing to have them published.[87]—And so I have devoted the profits of a first edition to the new Church, and as I intend introducing the volume with a discourse on the preparation for reading the scriptures, and concluding it with a discourse on the advantage of obeying them, I use the liberty of requesting from you the copy which I gave you of the four sermons—I shall take care to return it safe and along with it a copy of the new volume.[88] You can make a Coach-parcel of it the sooner the better, as the winter is advancing.

How does my Dear Jane? I think she is in my debt, for truly I account it a debt of which I would not willingly lose the repayment. But I must stop—my candle goes down—to-morrow I will finish. Three days have passed such is my state of engagement, and I take up my pen to finish this illegible scrawl. A person who only signed his initials wrote me the other week a most intelligent letter enclosing a poem 'Vision of Judgment' extorted from him by the irreligious and unworthy treatment given to that solemn subject by Byron & Southey.[89] He visited me afterwards and I found that he was an engraver without learning, with no reading and little acquaintance with nature or with life—I transcribe the two first verses, and pray you and your fair daughter to send me an answer to the lad's question 'Is it poetry'?

> I saw in vision the great Judgment day!
> It was the hour when morn should break, the night
> Was spent, but darkness made a long delay
> As striving to defraud the world of light
> The charist of the Sun was stayed, by might
> Superior to his own great strength, & earth
> And sky lay sickly to the palled light
> The stars were hid nor was there grief or mirth
> But silence reigned around, as at an Earthquake's birth
>
> And men were dead or dumb or sleeping—still
> Was all creation, as the slumbering deep
> Beneath a moonlight sky, & earth was chill
> As if twere nursed in Death's cold lap to sleep
> All look'd as dreary, as with Simoom[90] sweep
> Life had been blasted & the world were dead
> And naught was stirring save that worms did creep
> Most lazily mid graves where they were bred
> Or round the unburied course whereon they sweetly fed.

87. These lectures appear to have continued at least until 1829, see Grass, *The Lord's Watchman*, 69.

88. Introductory and concluding sermons appeared in his *Orations*: Grass, *Irving*, 69.

89. For Irving's critique of these works, see his *Orations*, 325–26, cf Grass, *Irving*, 71.

90. Simoon: a violent hot sand-laden wind on the deserts of Arabia and North Africa

Part II: The Letters

Now you have deciphered it. What do you think of it? The first reminds me of Spenser though the lad has never read Spenser. The next is equal to the best stanza of Jane's favourite Byron. I encouraged him, and gave him Books. I can never close any letter to you or to my dear pupil without praying the Lord to be gracious to you both, and to put His Holy Spirit within your hearts. I have read this morning part of the life of Thos Scott[91] the Commentator on the Bible which lies in your drawing room. He was a *man*. He was a *Christian*. If it come in your way I recommend it to your perusal. I also recommend Newton's *Cardiphonia*[,][92] a series of letters. May I have an interest in your prayers and be often remembered in your conversations together. For surely you are dear to my heart and often in my thoughts. My love to your friends who happen to be mine. Farewell! May God give to you all I wish for myself. And assemble us with the worthy of this earth in heaven. So prays

Your warmly attached friend & Servant,

Edwd Irving

The bookseller is at me already for the introductory discourse.

Addressed to: Mrs Welsh,
Haddington,
N[orth] B[ritain].

The Rev Edward Irving, Richard Dighton, 1823

---

91. Thomas Scott (1747–1821), biblical commentator and rector of Aston Sandford, Bucks. See *ODCC*. His biography which Irving refers to is *The Force of Truth* (London: Keith & Johnson, 1789).

92. John Newton. See Edward Irving to Thomas Carlyle, 20 September 1820 n.

Edward Irving to THOMAS CHALMERS

19 Gloucester Street, Queens Sq. [London][93]
21st January 1822 [1823]

Dear Sir,

This is a Letter of business—I am about to publish a book to consist of three distinct and separate parts.—Perhaps at some future period I may divide it into three separate Books. The first part is Four orations for the oracles of God—the second of Judgment to come an Argument in five parts.[94]—the third is The Incarnation of Christ[,] in 6 or 7 Lectures. These I mean to dedicate to three of my Dearest and most honoured friends, setting forth in each dedication something concerning the necessity of new *forms* of Theological Literature, of which these three are instances—with some expressions of my affection and esteem, but nothing to offend the delicacy or privacy of my friends. To you I mean the first—to Mr. Gordon the second, to Mr. Martin the third to be dedicated.

I should take it kind to be indulged in this suggestion of my friendship and esteem and I hope you will indulge me.—But if you have any weighty objections against it, you need only to let me know, for in doing a gratification to myself, I should never risk to do it at my friend's expense.

I can give you information which will both please your good and benevolent heart, and encourage your many liberal devices for the well fare [sic] of men.—Yesterday, at the desire of a young Lady[,] a friend of mine resident in Richmond, I went up and had the pleasure of expounding to a large assembly the nature of your schemes for the amelioration of the lower classes, and left them resolved to commence something upon the local system immediately. Last night I had a letter from your worthy Elder and my esteemed friend Mr. James Thompson, to which please say to him I will pay every attention that is practicable, and write when I obtain anything for communication.—Does it infringe upon your time or is it taking liberties with your dignity to ask you to request Mr. Collins to send us another supply of Psalm books not quite so *ornate* as the last, and invoices both of the purchase and sale price.—And say to him that soon I will redeem my promise to him on the other subject.[95]—Perhaps you may forget this; my dear 'mamma' Mrs Chalmers will take it in hand.

---

93. NCL, MSS CHA 4. 21.1.

94. Irving's first book *For the Oracles of God*. 'When published a copy of the Book was sent to Miss Welsh and her Mother, with this inscription: "To Jane Welsh, my beloved Pupil and most dear Friend, and to her Mother whom I love no less—to whose smiles upon his labours the Author is indebted for much—very much of his present ardour"': Carlyle, *Love Letters*, 2:422n. See letter to Jane Welsh, 23 February 1823.

95. Collins would later have cause to rue Irving's slowness to fulfill promises to write for him, in one case keeping him waiting for at least two years: Collins to Chalmers, 29 March 1825, NCL MSS CHA 4 42.42.

Part II: The Letters

I have had no advances made to me by any Clergymen under this London Regime except to ask favours which I have not time to grant.—They consider me a kind of comet that may trouble some of their spheres—or an exotic that they cannot well class.

My connection with you reflects the only credit or honour upon me which I have not to work for.—Steep, steep is the hill I have to climb[,] for my soul cannot rest amidst these abominations—and to make a testimony with effect is an enormous undertaking.

I send this by Mr. Hugh Tennant, who showed [his] face in the Caledonian last Sabbath *Admodum Miror!*[96] *Heu* tempora, *heu* mores![97] there is a pun I perceive as well as a lamentation over a worthy outer-kirk man coming to hear such a renegado[98] as me.

The little infantry, poor things! how are they? I wish I had gained more of their affection, it would have been better for my recollections. Elisa jolly lass! I will go and see her when ever she comes to London.—And Grace that *ettercap*,[99] I have a little nephew at Annan a perfect Madcap, more than ginger Alick Tom Dickson, who will do to tame her should she grow shrewish.—It would be ineffably sweet to me to bundle up and pass another month with you at sea bathing quarters.—I hope yet to see your Lady yet riding in my Carriage to behold the vicinity of London. Farewell for I do but talk nonsense to a grave & serious-minded man. Yet though nonsense affectionate nonsense and therefore I indulge in it.

Addressed to: Revd Dr Chalmers, Glasgow.
Hand by Hugh Tennant Esq.

~

Edward Irving to THOMAS CARLYLE

London, 19 Gloucester St., Queen Sq.
14th February 1823[100]

My Dear Carlyle,
Did I not know both the good sense and toleration of your mind, and the ample allowance which you can make for my circumstances, I would begin this letter with fear & trembling for the reception it might meet. But I feel that I am the loser by this interrupted correspondence, for much to the happiness of receiving the approbation of those to whom I devote the labours of my life, to receive the approbation[,] and

96. What a great surprise.
97. Alas the time, alas the customs.
98. A renegade.
99. Fiery person.
100. NLS, 1764; fols 243–44.

affection of minds like yours is my highest delight. I declare that the thing which has supported me hitherto through life; and given me the silent consciousness that I might yet bless my day & generation with my exertions, has been not public approbation of which I have not till late had any, nor the countenance of men already in elevated & settled stations, but the warmth of private friendship, and its frequent testimony to the integrity of my character, and the soundness of my mind. From you I have had more of these, and these more frankly uttered, not to say beautifully & powerfully, than from any other man, and when I look back upon the unkind return I have made, I do truly feel ashamed, and pray you to forgive me for it all consists with the utmost esteem and affection for your person, and the utmost admiration of your powers.

I take my place here slowly but I think securely. My people love me, and they are a host. Those that need my services court me. Those that do not dread me. They circulate strange accounts of me which come to my ear such as 'that there is a new method of preaching the Gospel found out.' 'That I have come to preach only to Scotchmen.' 'That I pit myself against the Evangelicals'[.] 'That I keep myself apart & want nothing to do with *them*' and much more which I would not trouble you with but that you commanded me in your last letter to let you know all about it. Meanwhile I sit here alone from breakfast to dinner employed in study from Tuesday till Sunday for I have two discourses to preach each Sunday. Monday I devote to enjoyment either in the country or about philanthropy in the city. The evenings I am frequently out and this will continue till I have completed the acquaintance of my flock and the religious people who know me. You have not, you cannot have an idea of the new liberty of thought I enjoy in this City of free men, and of the effect it is working upon both my character & my mind, especially the latter, which though reckoned free I find had been dreadfully confined by the shackles of the North[.] I do feel like a man floating in a sea of thought. I see before me immense tracts to be reclaimed—I am happy that God hath cast my mind towards religion for it both needs expansion and can bear it, and doth not wear out like the literary minds which you men of letters work in.

I have met with no minds like your own to teach me humility and that may account for the extravagance of the feeling mentioned above. In this respect I am unfortunate, but perhaps by and bye the temptation may be removed, for surely there are very great men to be found in such a congregation as are here assembled. My Company is altogether miscellaneous, mostly with my people and their friends; and I must confess to you it is far the most profitable whether taken as the stimulus to thought or the cultivation of good feeling. For though I endeavour to defend myself as much as may be when in company with literary men or men of my own profession from all feelings of rivalry, it is apt to steal in upon the one side or the other & to produce both an unpleasant atmosphere to think in or to feel in. There is something so overawing in a great mind to me, that my thoughts do not come away freely. For example you are the only man to whom I cannot write an amusing or an entertaining Letter. Perhaps in making you acquainted with my new acquaintances I should mention Allan Cunningham the poet, a good-natured intelligent man with a genius that much might have been made of.[101] There is another also a poet who solicited my acquaintance by submitting a poem to me; and who, though untutored and unacquainted with the varieties of human life, promises in my opinion to be a first rate man.—I am making no advances in learning or book-knowledge, but some I fancy in the knowledge of men, and ordinary things. I am a student perhaps as severe as any in London so far as writing is concerned but in reading I am one of the least so.

Now this will do about myself—the most important of the three persons and now for thyself the next in importance. I could find no information about that Professorship[,] all I could do—but I am not wishing to see you so employed. You will take your place in another field of Service less occupied, and which calls for more immediate culture, I mean philosophical thinking upon the nature of man. You are better fitted than any man I know to draw full from the storehouse of history and feeling, the various shapes & colours, shades and deformities, also virtues and powers which his nature is capable of putting on. Then I shall come in your train and shew how I have in my field, a shield for the weak, a hiding-place for the shameful, a comfort for the afflicted, as well as an armour of might for the noble and great. And thus between us we shall do some good. But you must go first, and I will follow. But I am about to publish, without waiting for you, that which I fear will not do me much credit, and yet I will put forth my strength. Of the orations you know something—of the argument for Judgment to come, you can have no Idea, but I am resolved to hold the ring against all the Poets and Sentimentalists and Jurisconsults and prove that I have an instrument or organ for the amelioration of men far better than any they possess. The third part of the volume, if indeed there be room for it, is more a [think?] of imagination & of feeling.—Oh what a criticism I shall meet with if they deign to notice it at all. If I did not hate to see you among that ignoble throng I would be almost sueing the defence of your mighty arm. But I do so utterly despise both the Canons and the practice of Criticism that I would sooner see you a member of the Holy college of Jesus than of that brotherhood.

My brother George demeans himself here with great approbation of all his friends & is yet I think to turn out a respectable if not a distinguished man. His application is so constant, his character so excellent, and his progress, I think so good, that I hope yet to see him practicing in this Country with credit to himself and his friends. I do not doubt I shall receive the same account from you of Brother John to whom I pray to be remembered with every good & kind affection, as also to the rest of your family. I know not whether I shall visit Scotland this year or not, nor can I say when I shall be settled in my own house to ask a visit of you—but the sooner the better, for it is both most uncomfortable, and most expensive, living in apartments.

I pray you to give my dearest affection to my beloved pupil Jane Welsh if you are in correspondence with her. I shall never cease to love her like a Brother.—Now that I have shaken off the lethargy of winter, I shall write to her. If you have half the

---

101. Allan Cunningham (1784-1842) from Kier, near Thornhill, Dumfriesshire, poet. See *OCEL*.

enjoyment and improvement from the family you are engaged with, which I have for the sister's family here Mrs Strachey,[102] I congratulate you for in her I think I have found the best of women & in her husband one of the most honest & intelligent of men. Present my most respectful compliments to all the family. Do, I pray you write me soon—remember my banishment from literature & literary men. If I do not receive a letter within a fortnight, this shall be followed by another perhaps overtaken if this storm abate not.

I am,
My Dear Carlyle,
Yours most truly,
Edw Irving

Addressed to: Mr. Thomas Carlyle,
3 Moray Street,
Leith Walk,
Edinburgh.

~

Edward Irving to JANE WELSH

[London], 23rd February 1823[103]

Surely when I write this Poem I am projecting upon the Pleasures of Affection, one niche in the temple, and that among the most honoured, shall be devoted to a mother and an only daughter entertaining a young man of feeling and sentiment with the kindness of their affections and the hospitality of their home. It is what the world does not understand, and ever fails to mistake for some other and more common and intelligible relation. And truly, I myself hardly understand or trouble myself to enquire more but that I was exquisitely happy.... I was forcibly reminded of my neglect to you, for when I wrote you last I have forgotten, it is so long (ago) ...

I have such a treat every day[;] I pass a window in which there is a beautiful head of Miss Kelly,[104] the exquisitive [sic] performer of *Juliet*; it has the very cast of your eye in one of its most piercing moods, which I can never stand to meet, and the roundness of your forehead, and somewhat of the archness of one of your smiles. I must positively

---

102 99 Julia (aka Kitty) Strachey, sister to Isabella Buller, whose sons Carlyle tutored. See letter Edward Irving to Thomas Carlyle, 3 January 1822: NLS, MS 1764: fol. 213-14. Thomas Carlyle gives an affectionate description of her in *Reminiscences*, 283.

103. Carlyle, *Love Letters*, 1:421-22.

104. Francis Maria Kelly, known as Fanny Kelly (1790-1882). Famous actress and singer to whom Charles Lamb proposed, but she refused him.

have it brought and send it when I send the copy of my volume. That is to be a curious book, a kind of defiance rather than defence. I know only one thing; they will call me the most impudent fellow in his Majesty's dominions. . . . The whole will be a *rudis indigestaque moles*[105] of materials that an abler less burdened man might have made a noble monument to himself out of . . . With my love to our mother, adieu for the present, and expect to hear from me soon.

Yours most truly,
Edwd Irving

~

Edward Irving to THOMAS CARLYLE

19 Gloucester St., Queen St., London
23rd February 1823[106]

My Dear Carlyle,

You are a very worthy man, and your will shall be done. This same post shall carry a letter to poor Robert Kemp for whom I am truly more distressed than I can utter, the more as I had never heard a word of his calamities, but I can now figure all. His health has failed under his labours and his pittance of money has worn down, and he finds himself without means and without strength in a place almost of strangers. For Johnstone[107] I have already had to do in his case, and have incurred, I doubt it not a deal of odium from his employers because to their importunate Letters to interfere I would make no reply but that I considered them exceedingly impertinent, and so far as I could judge at this distance exceedingly foolish.

The truth of the matter is this. I am encumbered with a heart of too large sympathies both for the dimensions of my head, and the power of my hand and also for the measurements of time; my wish to be useful to every one I meet, my desire not to disoblige them, or rather to benefit them, brings upon me such a tide of present occupation, that I am driven to trust to the generosity of my friends at a distance. But if they fancy that they are less in my mind's presence, and my heart's love, they mistake, for my affections are as constant as they are warm, and though they be warm to every

---

105. A Rude and undigested mass.
106. NLS, MS 665, fol. 28–29.
107. 'James Johnston is gone to Broughty-ferry (Dundee) some weeks ago. He seems to aim at being a Scottish Teacher for life . . . He has got planted among a very melancholy race of people—Psalm-singing Captains, devout old women, Tabernacle shoemakers &c &c, who wish him to engage in exposition of the Scripture, and various other plans, for the spread not of grammar and accounts, but of the doctrines of Theosophy and Thaumaturgy.': Thomas Carlyle to Robert Mitchell, 23 December 1822: CL, 2:243.

living creature as becomes my office, and my principles, they soon cool to those who are not worthy, and those which remain, remain stable and firm.

But I had intended to write to you on a different subject which I now desire your attention to. The other night at Allan Cunningham's I met with Taylor the Editor of the London Magazine[108] which Scott formerly conducted, and took that occasion of introducing to him the poem of the young Gentleman of genius I mentioned in my former Letter. A day or two after I called along with him at Taylor's Converzatione [sic] place, and fell into conversation with him at large. I think of him very highly, of his magazine, though doubtless the most respectable of that genus I think not much, but still it is a book which means well if it could but perform, and it has the advantage that one may publish there in detail what they afterwards mean to publish in whole. Now this is my scheme that both to obtain that ear of the public, which you must have, and which you cannot get like me by preaching, and in order to have a fund of money lying here in London for the expenses of your jaunt when you come to see me, and finally in order to open up the berths & places in this world—you do forthwith, set about these portraitures of men of genius and character, and month after month present them to the public through that magazine.[109] I shall take care to secure the very highest terms that Taylor gives, and perhaps by way of foil shall put forth a portraiture of a religious noble along side your literary noble—*comprenez vous*, do you hear me—well do if you please ruminate the matter. Taylor's a good fellow and has got around him men—that you & I would despise, I told Taylor that I would be at dagger's drawing with one half of them in a week—so he had better keep us apart—yet men the literary world exaggerates Barry Cornwall,[110] Carey[sic] the translator of Danté,[111] Hazlitt[112] & many more such. But the book might be made an organ of much noble & much good sentiment—and therefore is no objection but rather an inducement to all the personal advantages to yourself mentioned above.

Now if you say no to this I am not a wise man & what is more Thomas Carlyle is not a wise man—unless indeed you should chance to be over occupied with matters of higher account.

---

108. The *London Magazine* (1820-29). The editor was John Taylor (1781-1864). John Scott the previous editor was killed in a duel in 1821. See *OCEL*.

109. 'That magazine' is *The London Magazine*. Taylor did publish Carlyle's translation of the life of Schiller in 1823-24. See *OCEL*.

110. Barry Cornwall, pseudonym of Brian Waller Procter (1787-1874) husband of Mrs. Basil Montagu's daughter Ann (b.1799) by her first husband Thomas Skepper. She was a friend of Edward Irving and lived with her husband at 25 Bedford Square. See Carlyle, *Reminiscences*, 285-86.

111. Henry Francis Cary (1772-1844) published his translation of *Divina Commedia* in 1814 at his own expense. Coleridge praised it in the *Edinburgh Review* and when lecturing to the Royal Institution: and it became the standard edition.

112 109 William Hazlitt (1778-1830). His *The Spirit of the Age* (1825) contains a study of Edward Irving.

My Book! my book! will have stuff in it—both thinking and writing this age of the church is not accustomed to. It is not all orations, only four of these. The avant-courier of the main body which is 'An Argument for Judgment to come' Addressed to: such heads as yours, and I do aim a blow at many things among your tribe which will make them wince—I want to invite the *stolida quies*[113] of the literary and scientific men, and bring them forth from their fancied fastnesses to try conclusions. The notoriety I have will sell the first Edition which is devoted to Charity and in the next I shall make three separate books out of it. The last part is Messiah arrived—a series of I know not what to call them religious meditations upon the wonderful events in the first chapter of Luke.

Remember London is your destination yet, I see the literary world at your feet not in the north but here. For here things are open, with you they are shut. Therefore I tell you send us some pioneers to open the way—Scotland breeds men, but England rears them. Wait though till I have got my house rigged up, and my wife and so forth. Then I can back you, and will too which is better. And as I used to tell you we will yet shake hands across the Strand, and it will be said that two fellows of unknown lineage from one unknown valley, took the precedence of the literary and religious hosts of Old England. If you repeat what I have written to another year [ear] I will trounce you at meeting.

Never think of me but with confidence, for with all my faults I fancy myself worthy of it and surely you have mine. Tell Jack[114] that he too must become a great man, that George has taken a long step in advance, and begins to develop understanding or rather to perceive what is before him to be accomplished, which is the first symptom of accomplishing it. I could say much more but I hurry for the post.

Yours most affectionately,
Edwd Irving

Addressed to: Mr. Thomas Carlyle,
3 Moray St.,
Leith Walk, Edinburgh.

Edward Irving to THOMAS CARLYLE

London, 19 Gloucester St., Queens Sq.

---

113. Dull repose.
114. Carlyle's brother John.

Letters: 1822–1824

8th March 1823[115]

My Dear Carlyle,

I have been to Taylor, and explained to him your project and the nature of its execution so far as I could prophesy. And I find him still most desirous to see the thing fulfilled. The highest terms he gives is *sixteen Guineas* a sheet, and in case of separate publication there is this condition attached, that if his house be the publisher you have *one third* of the profits, they taking the risk, if you wish to become proprietor of the work yourself, you purchase back the copy-right by paying them one half of what they originally allowed viz 8 *Guineas* a sheet. So that you can draw 16 Guineas in the mean time, and afterwards by paying 8 Guineas have back your writing, to do with them what you please. Of course you will regard the above not as contracted for, but as the thing which will be contracted for when Taylor sees the first specimen and is satisfied with it and the inducement for you to begin. When I receive from you the first Article, and you need not wait till the whole life is completed, for if it pass the bounds of an ordinary magazine-article it will have to be divided, send it up and if you could contrive to get it in some book-sellers parcel it would save expense, to my address and after I have read it I will come to terms with Taylor, and cause him to exchange missives regularly, and draw your money and buy 3 p[er]cent Stocks or do any thing with it you may please to commission.

I have not one word of advice to give you about the execution of the project, so much confidence do I repose in your own judgment. I know that all which is exalted in sentiment, and manly in conduct will receive your countenances and all silly affectations will meet your exposure—I also know that the thing which I revere above all things will always meet with the reverent handling which its sacred nature deserves even from those that esteem it not, among which number I know that you are *not* one; for however much you may be in darkness about the grounds of our belief, you never see the sincerity of it, or hear the heroism of it, without yielding to it the full heart of your admiration. I do most highly regard the sublime character of Schiller, which I understand his works exhibit under many forms, and I anticipate strong and striking lights of contrast between it and the satirical un-enthusiastic character of Voltaire. Whatever is sacred do touch with a serious & sacred hand, then will you be yourself, and you will be happy in yourself—whatever is cold-hearted, or unsound at heart expose with your most powerful weapons, I would do the same, though with weapons perhaps of a different make. But it becomes me not to seem even to advise you prospectively.—Surely I will give you my opinion honestly afterwards. And though the whole world were to call you weak and misguided in your writings and sentiments, it would not shake for an instant the entire esteem which I have for your mind, and for your *character also* when it is not girt about with these fears which have hindered its true form from venturing abroad—I do think you are too timid and mistrustful a man till you are roused to a pitch, then you are terrible.

115. NLS, MS 665, fol. 30.

Part II: The Letters

Allen[116] is come to town to day, and is to be with me soon, he is to me an unpleasant man, I know not why? One thing is his desire of self-accommodation, and yet withal he is kind—but still the glow is not pure and salutary; he seems to care for you only as you bring credit upon himself. He is only to be with me a day or two. There is nothing which is to cost me in life so much as my easy access and general good-will. But nature will put on a self-defence against manifold intrusions, and the steadfast parts of character will arise—and perhaps even London may thus be instrumental in forming my character as well as my mind. It is a place of terrible labour & industry. You get wedged and wrought into your place, like a soldier in the battle—and miserable is he who has not his hand-full. And miserable also are they who have too much to do, which seems to me a far more fertile source of misery than the other extreme.

I did that night send of [*sic*] the Certificate to Johnstone[117] I will have [letter torn] to do with any men in the shape of an Evangelical. They do [letter torn] work by human nature, and you cannot work with them if you do [letter torn] undervalue worldly principles of honour & honesty instead of making them [letter torn] and enlarged. All which I mean to set forth in this book of mine. I hope both he and I will be delivered honestly & honourably out of their hands, for had I not been a firm man they would already have involved me also head & ears against poor Johnstone whose defence I ought rather to be.

Last night was to me a sorrowful night, the news having reached Annan that my brother John was dead—this is a joyful day for it turns out to be false. Regard this as a Letter of business—written at the end of the week, of which I spent the three first days in cheering the heads of four Missionaries with their wives who were detained at Gravesend, for the sailing of the vessel when we launched from the shore in our boat, to reach the ship, they lifted up a hymn of joy and trust, which makes my very blood thrill at this moment. So sublime it was, and the gusts of the gale came and bore it off, as it were and fell amongst the dashing of the surly waters, and the whistling of the gusty wind. The seamen came to the bow of the ship, and as the solemn sounds were borne down upon their ears trained to other sounds, they were silent, and seemed amazed. Afterwards to the men & women assembled in their little cabin, I recounted the providence of God over the wanderings of his people, Abraham Joseph Daniel Jesus & Paul, and concluded with telling them the story of Mungo Park and the little flower blooming in the sandy desert,[118] which seems to me the best interpretation & sublimest use of our Saviour's famous instruction 'Take no thought for to-morrow- Consider the lilies of the field.'[119]

---

116. See letter Edward Irving to Thomas Carlyle, 4 June 1819: p. 70.

117. *ibid*.

118. Mungo Park (1771–1806), West African explorer. On one occasion, far from European assistance, he came across a small clump of moss in the wilderness; at a time when his spirits were failing, he took heart from concluding that the God who watched over that plant would watch over him also.

119. Matt 6:24–28.

It is very extraordinary that you should be almost the only correspondent to whom I could expatiate on such a scene, the religious are so unsentimental, unpoetical rhapsodists of a few things they understand not—I am convinced under God, you are destined for good which if you humbly trust in him he will bring to pass in his own good time. My love to your Brother.

Yours Most affectionately,
Edwd Irving
Alas! Alas! the accounts of my Brother's death[120] are too true!

Addressed to: Mr. Thomas Carlyle,
3 Moray Street,
Leith Walk,
Edinburgh.

~

Edward Irving to THOMAS CHALMERS

19 Gloucester St., Queen Sq., London.
10th March 1823[121]

My dear & Honoured friend,

If you had recommended me to this congregation of London as a minister of the Gospel known to you and approved for fidelity and wisdom; and this congregation had not found me suit their London notions of preaching, albeit I was found faithful in all the duties for which you commended me—and they should write to you at Glasgow setting forth in a general way my unsuitableness to meet their peculiar views, I ask my friend Dr Chalmers if he would have involved himself in the dispute at the distance of Glasgow his residence, or if he would have reflected upon himself that in choosing a worthy judicious man, he had not hit the fancy of a people he knew not. Is there aught in Johnstone's[122] duties unfulfilled[,] aught in his character blameworthy, aught in his history out of keeping with his vocation. Is he wanting in piety[,] in principle[,] in learning & diligence. He does not suit the notions of people whose notions I believe I would as little suit, and therefore neither will my sense of justice, nor any hope of

---

120. John Lowther Irving (1790-1822). 'The eldest, whom old friends speak of as "one of the handsomest young men of his day," and whom his father imagined the genius of the family, died obscurely in India on Edward's birthday, the 4th of August, in the prime of his manhood, a medical officer in the East India Company. But henceforward the day, made thus doubly memorable, was consecrated by Edward as a solemn fast-day, and spent in the deepest seclusion': Oliphant, *Life*, 1:4.

121. NCL, MSS CHA 4.26.59.

122. See letters Edward Irving to Thomas Carlyle, 4 June 1819, 23 February 1823, and 8 March 1823.

good that I can see, permit me to interfere. Let them find an umpire of their quarrels upon the spot. I neither can nor will have any thing to do with them. I never yet knew religion promoted by an invasion of sacred justice. It is too much the fashion of the time. You suffer from it & I suffer from it, and every honest man suffers from it; but it is a principle essentially Jesuitical and I can do nothing but abhor it as ungodly & unchristian.

I shall do your commission to Mr. Crosbie the first moment I see him, and every other commission you can lay upon me which does not like the above run counter to my sentiments of justice.

I do approve most heartily of your going to St. Andrews[123] because it will renew your youth, and give your mind a new field to expatiate over. I labour to convince all I meet upon the subject. The other night I attempted it to Sir Thos Baring[124] & Wilberforce at a dinner of the *religiosi* but they are essentially stupid people, blighted with a loss of faculties, and an overgrowth of prosing. Wilberforce sees a little further; he confessed to me the constraint of preaching and talked with some sense about Calvinism. But depend upon it this *Regime* cannot last. It makes converts, but it knows not what to make of the converts when they are made. Oh such prosing! Such idle prosing! May the Lord refresh the waste places of his church, and send us men of some English understanding & English character.

My dear Brother in the Indies is gone—I think I could have died in his stead. He was so endeared to myself and our family—so gallant, so generous & so good. But God hath otherwise appointed & I must labour on in the midst of an uncongenial generation. I would not give the memory of what I have conversed with yourself & Gordon[125] for all the vain realities of religious talk they indulge in here.

Only one thing gladdens my heart, I have a congregation that loves me & whom I love in return. I have a head full of unexpressed thought and a heart full of friendship for men, and I hope not without tender affection to my God & his Church. Which declaration my prudent countrymen would call vain-glory, to cure which my Aunt of Dumfries[126] is going to send me a book on humility—but I call it just acknowledgment to my God for his manifold mercies to his sinful creature.

My love to your household & those of your friends that are also mine
Your affectionate friend,
Edw[d] Irving

Addressed to: Revd Dr Chalmers, Glasgow.

---

123. Chalmers became Professor of Moral Philosophy at St Andrews University in 1823.

124. Sir Thomas Baring (1772–1848), banker, MP, and supporter of evangelical causes: BDEB.

125. See Edward Irving to Thomas Carlyle, 26 April 1821; p. 107.

126. Mrs. George Irving, widow of Edward Irving's uncle George, who lived at Bogside, Dumfriesshire. See CL, 1:166.

Edward Irving to THOMAS CARLYLE

London, 7 Middleton [sic] Terrace, Pentonville.[127]
16th August 1823

My Dear Carlyle,

You are of more understanding than to take up against me the vulgar accusation of forgetting former friends, and yet I seem to myself to have given you too great occasion, but I will bear my reproaches no longer, and write though it should be but a line to tell you how I retain for you as well as my other Scottish friends all my wonted regard. It is very extraordinary this lethargy of my nature, for I am now willing to confess and allow it, for it consists with the utmost attention to any thing I have in my power for the sake of my friends. For believe me I gave myself no rest till I had read your paper and finding it what I expected, though not all that I expect I handed it to Taylor,[128] who seems not less impressed with it than I was myself. But he thinks it does not suit to divide and cut down so valuable a thing into a magazine form and recommends that you should publish it separately, and offers to become the publisher upon the conditions which I made with my publisher *viz* to run all the risk and share the profits of the first Edition, and have things open for a second should it be called for. I recommended him to write to you a business letter and negotiate the matter, but this I confess was no apology for my neglect of friendship, which I know however you will excuse. Now for my part, if you are to publish in that form this life apart, I think you cannot do better than accept Taylor's offer, but if you propose thereto to add any other lives, it is for you to consider whether they might not be better printed together than separately. I am to be in Scotland next month, when we shall contrive to meet, and talk over all these things. I shall soon be in a condition to reform some of my private and personal negligences and this of my correspondence is to receive my first attention so give me a little grace.

I have had to pull against the whole stream of the religious, and half the stream of the irreligious. My every motive is watched, my every sentiment waited on; I am like our Saviour among Pharisees, these vile panderers of the Ecclesiastical & political state would glory to cut me down. If I can keep the field a little longer I shall establish the greatest influence over the public mind, which any person in my station has had for an age. And perhaps may be able to serve my friends, when I shall shew that petty negligences in friendship as in manner & dress may consist with the utmost rectitude and firmness of principle. If you can write without scolding me, write so soon as you have a

---

127. NLS, MS, fol. 32–33.
128. See Edward Irving to Thomas Carlyle, 23 February 1823.

Part II: The Letters

moment's time, but if you are to scold, put it in the Postscript, for it is like a rock at the mouth of the harbour for me to be scolded at the beginning of a letter. I cannot bear ever the distant look of a friend. But I wish to convene an arrangement for meeting in Scotland. I come down in September on an errand somewhat important to a man.[129] And I think I shall remain for four or five weeks if I can find a substitute so long. In the midst of a thousand cares believe me to retain the same sentiments of esteem for you as I have ever done & to remain

Dear Carlyle,
Yours most truly,
Edwd Irving

Addressed to: Mr. Thomas Carlyle,
– Buller Esq.,
Kinnaird House,
Dunkeld, N.B.

~

Edward Irving to MRS MARTIN

[Post mark: Huntingdon, 23rd September 1823][130]

My Dear Madam,

Whom I hope soon to call by a dearer name, when all the anxieties of this probationary state of mine shall have been brought to a close, and I shall have been united to your daughter whom God appointed to be the companion and comforter of my pilgrimage. For sure I am when I review this wayward and most extraordinary history of mine I should have been several times shipwrecked but for the guardianship I have had from her tender spirit, and sure moreover that without her future consolation I shall not be half so useful to this world or to myself. In which declarations, I make no compliments to a kindhearted mother, but express the most sober convictions of my own mind better acquainted with itself than heretofore. Most sorry I am that I should ever for one moment have had trial cast over me, which did shake me but not my integrity.[131] All this is past and with affections doubled, nay with more affection, with a devotion as it were to my preserver, I look forward to the happy day which is to bring me nearer to her affections and her consolation. I shall give her an unconditional heart, and a hand which will lose its cunning sooner than desert her sustenance and defence.

129. To make arrangements for his marriage to Isabella.
130. ML, MS 101a, b, c, d, e.
131. This would appear to be a reference to his contemplation of marriage to Jane Welsh.

And I think Providence whose peculiar child I seem to be, will yet put it in my power to prove not an unworthy son of your family.

My old and reverend Father has promised to accompany, and one or other of my Brothers–in–law. I wish Samuel[132] to be my bridegroom's man, that we who are to be joined in profession and in brotherhood may be likewise united by attachments of gallant service done for me. I have done many for him. I leave Isabella to fix the day, and if I be at Annan over Sabbath I shall be proclaimed there three times on one day—I shall write Isabella the next rest.

Now where do you think this is written from, the place in all England where most of your affections are. I mean not myself for I consider myself only a prodigal boy, but your dear sister Mrs Clark in whose parlour I now sit. We came (the Montagues[133] and I) to Alconbury Hill last night late, and Charles and I have walked over to breakfast. They are all well and desire their kindest love. We set off again immediately. Say to Isabella if she is at home, I shall be ready to proceed for Annan in three weeks but I leave the day to her fixing and shall appear with [letter torn] joy, and more than poet hath ever described [letter torn] priest ever desired for the holiness of such a union.

    Farewell The Lord bless you all.
    Your most affectionate friend.
    Edwd Irving

Addressed to: Mrs Martin
Manse, Kirkcaldy, NB

Edward Irving to THE BRETHREN [OF] THE CONGREGATION OF THE CHAPEL, HATTON GARDEN

Bolton Abbey, Yorkshire
[September 1823][134]
[Annotated in pencil: 28th September]

Dearly Beloved Brethren,

---

132. Samuel Martin (1802–54) was Isabella's brother. He was ordained at Kirkcaldy in 1825. He joined the Free Church and became minister of Bathgate in 1843: see Grass, *The Lord's Watchman*, 80, 120, 194.

133 131 Basil Montagu was a chancery barrister and Mrs. Montagu was his second wife who Edward Irving named the 'Noble Lady.' See Carlyle, *Reminiscences*, 285–87. It was Mrs. Montagu who advised Jane Welsh to be frank with Thomas Carlyle about her relationship with Edward Irving. See Edward Irving to Thomas Carlyle, 12 June 1821; p. 111fn.

134. EIL, MS 26.

Part II: The Letters

  Having spent the greater part of so many Sabbaths in your instruction, it has now grown into a taste and a pleasure, and I feel that during the weeks of my absence I should feel unhappy were I not both to think of you and do something which might testify the regard in which I hold you, therefore permit me to indulge myself on the first day of the week to set down on paper something which may be pleasant for me to write, and by the grace of God not unprofitable for you to hear; and let me consign it monthly to the hand of our worthy and reverend Elder to be read by him at the monthly meeting of the church.

  I thank God that he hath given me so many immortal spirits to watch over, and I pray the great Shepherd of the sheep for grace to fulfil the duties of a pastor faithfully amongst you. And not only by word to instruct but by example of righteousness to edify you in our most holy faith. For I never allow myself to forget with what evils you are compassed around and beset in the midst of the populous & busy city. And these three last days I have spent in the stillness and solitude of this sequestered place, I could have wished that you had all been with me to taste the refreshment of communing with God through the works of his hands. The more need have ye therefore to betake yourselves to the word of his grace which is able to build you up and give you a place amongst all them that are sanctified.

  You know brethren how necessary to every good work is mutual help and encouragement, therefore I pray you to join yourselves together, and exhort each other to whatever is good, and to make the edification of your souls this great object for which you *meet* and converse and join friendships. Let your intercourse with each other be after a godly sort, not to gratify humour or indulge merely social feeling, but therewith to mingle pious and devout breathings unto God the giver of all good, and to Christ who hath laid down his life a ransom for your sins. So it shall come to pass that you shall grow in grace, and the brethren walking in love and unity shall be edified. Let not any Brother, in whose soul the spirit worketh strongly, be silent but speak to the rest words of zeal and comfort, and testify by the words of his mouth no less than the good works of his life, the praise of him who hath brought him out of darkness into his marvellous light. And especially in his family and his family circle let him adopt such a walk and conversation as may silently rebuke the evil-doers, and recall the backsliding and encourage the righteous and do good unto all. Thus we shall be interwoven and intermixed with the spirit of holiness. Every one will be a monitor to every other one, and all of you an admonition to me; and our prayers arising to God continually, and our good conversation before him being manifest shall draw down copious blessings upon the head of all the congregation.

  I have reason to thank God continually for the great fruit which he hath already given to my unworthy ministry in the midst of you, and here in sweet and quiet solitude it is the constant theme of my discourse & the constant burden of my thoughts and prayers, how I may in future prevail more mightily against the powers of the wicked one. In this I rest, and for this I labour, and for this I pray that by means of me or some one more worthy the Almighty would raise up in the land a spirit of zeal and of resolution to contend against the high places and strong holds of vanity and error and false philosophy in which Satan hath entrenched himself. I shall do my endeavour to return furnished with new knowledge & strength, and I trust also with more abundant grace for this great and glorious object.

In this land to which I sojourn it is my intention to converse with all the worthy servants of Christ upon the same subject, and to stir in them a spirit of strife and of contention against those barriers which hinder the progress of pure & undefiled religion. And for that end, as well as for the sake of rest to my wearied mind I have resolved to abide by my resolution of not preaching publicly but confining myself as Paul did when he went up to Jerusalem to those who are of reputation,[135] and with them only in private discourse. For I am wary of being run after and being a bone of contention in the midst of the people. And therefore I refuse every solicitation with which I am met, conceiving it little better than a public exhibition of the Gospel of Christ. But the time is coming when, upon a second visit to my native country I shall preach unto them that same Gospel which ye have heard with so much acceptance.

But with whatever treatment I may be treated I shall return to your bosom as to a home, and in the Caledonian Church shall abide while it continues to desire my ministry, and if the time should ever arrive, when you would rather have the ministry of another, I shall be content with the dispensation of God who findeth me present occupation in this holy office whereof I am altogether unworthy.

And now, brethren, being assembled in important affairs of the church I recommend to you mutual kindness and love, and pray that the same spirit of unity may continue to prevail amongst you as hitherto. The object has cost you much trouble and is still involved with difficulty. But it is a great object, and magnifies upon our hand, and being conducted to a happy issue may be greatly serviceable to the interest of religion in the metropolis. Waiving public considerations altogether, it will stand a monument of the blessing with which God blesseth the union of people & pastor when it is joined upon the principles of the Gospel, without any direct or indirect mixture of selfishness and worldliness.

But I must bring this letter to a close. My next embracing the thoughts of your Sabbath evenings will be more full of general instructions than this which is but a breathing of affection, and an expression of confidence to my beloved flock. I have spent a most tranquil and untroubled Sabbath in a portion of this Abbey now dedicated to the service of the Protestant religion, and occupied by a most pious and most pastoral clergyman of the Church of England,[136] who is to me an example of what a pastor should be. May mercy and peace be with you all I pray.

Your affectionate pastor,

135. Gal 2:1–2.

136. Jacob Costobadie, Rector of Wensley, under the Patronage of Lord and Lady Bolton. www.archives.northyorks.go.uk. Accessed: 10 July 2010.

Part II: The Letters

Edwd Irving

Bolton Abbey 28th Sept

～

Edward Irving to WILLIAM DINWIDDIE

29th September 1823[137]

My Dear Honoured friend,

I commit to your hands the enclosed letter of affection to my people, which I pray you to read at the general meeting, and by no means to allow to be copied, for it is as purely a letter of private affection as this which I now write to you.

Much do I regret that I have not your company in the quiet walks which I take around the environs of this old abbey so full of meditation and so instructive of our mortality and the morality of all things. It is here that I could suggest such thoughts as might harmonize with the present state of your soul, and enable it to derive the good fruits of the better dispensation which it hath pleased God to send unto your house. But God is present in the populous city no less than in these solitudes and his comforting Spirit is ever in the bosom of his people, and to you who are wont to regard him always in the light of a good Father, it will come more easily to receive this Fatherly chastisement at his hand. His own only begotten son suffered on our own account, he spared him not, but gave him up to the death for us all.[138] And it is by the fellowship of his sufferings that we are to reach the fellowship of his resurrection.[139] Now if we are to forsake Father & Mother and Brother & Sister & our own life in order to become his disciples,[140] then being his disciples, we should be content with the privileges & honour of that high rank, though all worldly objects of affection be removed out of our sight. And we know that nothing can separate us from the love of God in Christ.[141] Therefore let us not be cast down, but endeavour to improve the temptations which work in us patience and experience, & hope[142] and every good gift of the Spirit of God.

I am enjoying the rest and deriving the refreshment which I so much needed. The family in whose bosom I am happily domesticated are a source of constant consolation & happiness to me. I shall yet remain a few days for I find it conducive to the most useful ends. Then I shall proceed to Scotland from whence you shall hear from me.

137. EIL, MS 27.
138. Rom 8:32.
139. Phil 3:10.
140. Compare Matt 19:28 with Luke 14:26.
141. Rom 8:39.
142. Rom 5:3–5.

I desire my love and consolations to Mrs Dinwiddie and the family, and pray to be remembered in all your hearts, and to have an interest in all your prayers. And with pastoral regards to all my people who enquire after me I am,

My Dear friend,
Your most affectionate pastor,
Edw Irving

Bolton Abbey, 29th September 1823

Edward Irving to WILLIAM HAMILTON

[Bolton Abbey,] 29th September 1823[143]

My Dear and valuable Friend,

I write you thus early by my brother, merely to inform you of my health and happiness; for as yet I have had no time to do anything but walk abroad, among the most beautiful and sequestered scenes with which I am surrounded; and which never fail to produce upon my spirit the most pleasing and profitable effects. When I shall have rested I will write you and my other personal friends at length, and let you know all my plans and purposes during my absence... I shall not write you till I get at my journey's end, and have, perhaps, completed its chief object. But, late though it is, I cannot help telling you how happy I am, and how tranquil and holy a Sabbath I spent yesterday, and how every day I engross into my mind new thoughts, and ruminate upon new designs connected with the ministry of Christ in that great city where I labour. The Lord strengthen me, and raise up others more holy and more devoted for His holy service. I foresee infinite battles and contentions, not with the persons of men, but with their opinions. My rock of defence is my people. They are also my rock of refuge and consolation. We have joined hands together, and I feel that we will make common cause. I hope the Lord will be pleased to give me their souls and their fervent prayers, and then, indeed, we shall be mighty gainst all opposition.

Will you be so good as to give my brother[144] an order upon my account for whatever cash he may need to enter himself to the hospitals with, or, if it more orderly, to give it him yourself, and consider this as your voucher should anything happen to me before we meet? I should be happy to hear from you that all things are going on well.

Yours most affectionately,
Edward Irving

---

143. Oliphant *Life*, 1:176–77.
144. George Irving.

Part II: The Letters

Edward Irving to DAVID HOPE

[End of September 1823][145]

I have been unwell, and living in the country, and not able to attend to your request, but I propose that we should erect a monument, when I will myself compose elegies in the various tongues our dear and venerable preceptor taught,—all which I shall concoct with you when I come to Scotland. Tell Graham, and all my friends, if they knew what a battle I am fighting for the cause, and what a single-handed contest I have to maintain, they would forgive my apparent neglect. Every day is to me a day of severe occupation—I have no idleness. All my leisure is refreshment for new labour. Yet am I happy, and now, thank God, well—and this moment I snatch in the midst of study.

Edward Irving, unknown artist, c. 1823

---

145. Oliphant, *Life*, 1:183.

Edward Irving to THOMAS CARLYLE

Scotts Hotel Princes St Edinburgh.
7th Oct 1823[146]

My Dear Carlyle,

I am just arrived from Annandale on my way to be married. But though in Annandale I have been in Scotland but five days and had time only to see my Father's family. I heard however of your friends that they were all well. I am to be married on Tuesday that is the 14th Oct, and after that shall proceed in the first place by Dundee to Perth. We shall be at Perth I think on the 16th that is Thursday perhaps on Wednesday. Once I thought of visiting Dunkeld, but when I take the measurements of my time, and what I have to do in it, it is barely possible, if indeed it be possible. But should my wife wish it, I will make it convenient. Now I go over to Fife on Saturday, and after making the arrangements with her I shall write you, and if possible come to Dunkeld and pass a day or two at the Inn away from the bustle of the world, where I might enjoy conversation with you and my wife at liberty from intrusion.[147] For I have a plan in my head of your visiting London, and passing the summer with us, if we get into a house of our own in the Spring as I expect. But of this more when we meet, and concerning our meeting more when I write from Fife.

I am much obliged to Mrs Buller for her very kind invitation but I fear it may not be in my power to visit Kinnaird-house, having so many friends and relatives in Scotland to whom I stand indebted and who would not forgive me if I neglected them. If however I come so near as Dunkeld I shall be strongly tempted to take the very great enjoyment of conversing with her, which is to me a treat that I meet with seldom. You need not write till you hear from me again only you may hold yourself in readiness and your hearty pony for an excursion in the end of the next week.

Yours most truly,
Edward Irving

Addressed to: Mr. Thomas Carlyle,
Kinnaird House by Dunkeld.

---

146. NLS, MS 1764, fol. 263–64.

147. In fact Thomas Carlyle did stay with Edward and Isabella Irving at Dunkeld from Thursday 16 October to Saturday, 18 October 1823. See CL 9:387n

Part II: The Letters

Edward Irving to THOMAS CARLYLE

Kirkcaldy. 11th October 1823[148]

Dear Carlyle,

I am here, my Father and two brothers-in-law, and I expect my two brothers from the west so we shall be jolly company—here in the room where in days of old we have handled so many questions with the gudsire of Kirkcaldy.[149] And among other notables of the place I have been showing my worthy Father the place where Thomas Carlyle lived,[150] and where would be found ghosts of more departed good sense than in any other place in this Kingdom. For there his hopeful son and the wittiest of men were wont to discourse of all things written & unwritten, thought of and unthought of. These our happy communings I propose to revoke from oblivion if you be as willing as I am and as able as you are wont to be. For I purpose, having gained my wife's most willing consent to be at Dunkeld on Thursday, I think to breakfast or soon after it, and to pass the time with you till the Monday following.[151] But further than an exchange of visits perhaps, to Mrs Buller, I propose nothing, being resolved to devote myself for these days to the best friend I have in these parts. I think we may lay many plans useful to us both, and if I can get you to consent to a Summer visit to us in London, I doubt nothing of your speedily finding your way to the level in the Society to which your genius drives you in spite of yourself, and which I hope to see it long adorn. Be it understood therefore that, if you can accomplish it, we pass the greater part of Thursday Friday & Saturday and Sabbath together—and after if you will join us and complete our tour by Paisley to Annan, you cannot conceive what a blessing we would account it, and I take it, it would be a blessing to yourself.

My Dear Carlyle I did not know how much you esteemed me, until I witnessed how for my sake, you subdued your natural feelings when I put them to such a test by my seeming neglect last summer but truly my excessive occupation. Nor did I now how much I loved you till I came to Edn and found you my former companion, and friend absent, and no one who had any power to move or to console my mind. I feel assured that nothing shall divide us till death, and that we may help each other most mightily in our passage to what is high & honourable, as surely you have helped me already.

There arise before me in dim perspective many visions of happiness to us both and to some others in whom we are dearly interested, but I dare not cast these into shape much more give them utterance. You cannot be more happy to meet me than I am to meet you. And we shall not be the less delighted that Isabella whom I love and you highly regard should be our only audience. The Annandale men delight at your very name.

---

148. CL, 9: 385–87: Addr: Kinnaird/by Dunkeld. PM Kirkcaldy. MS: NLS Acc. 6181.

149. The 'gudsire' was Irving's future father-in-law, the Rev John Martin (1769–1837). Edward Irving and Thomas Carlyle had been frequent visitors at the Manse.

150. Mrs. Skene's, Kirk Wynd (now demolished).

151. The eve of Irving's marriage.

There is one sentiment over all their rude minds that you are formed for strange and wonderful things tho they consider a fellow that will not heed to any thing, but drive on some hope to greatness and goodness, most prone to misery and ruin. Nevertheless my faith standeth sure. And I know in whom I have believed. And never of my destinies did I feel more secure than at this moment when I write. Our purpose is to be at Perth on Wednesday by the Steamboat. If you thought of riding to meet us—how acceptable it would be. But in all this consult duty more than feeling. And believe me

Your most true-hearted friend,

Edwd Irving

Isabella and Edward Irving to JOHN MARTIN & FAMILY

Many happy happys [sic]
16th of November 1823[152]

My dear Father,

Your very welcomed letter & the parcel from my dear Mother containing Sisters letters all came safely to my hand though not till Monday last as Sister Agnes always kept the parcel in hopes I would again visit Paisley.

Edward received your letter too since we came here forwarded from Glasgow which place we left at 6 o'clock on Wednesday morning accompanied by Father Irving & Mr. Brown. We were a considerable time at Moffat & at Dumfries we tead[153] with Aunt Johnston of a house I think very highly. She received us most kindly & good lady, though she is now much better, was still far from well. Every friend here I find kinder than another but nature, my dear dear Parents is nature & sometimes I feel as if my heart would burst & the suppressing of these feelings is most difficult. This is the last Sabbath God willing for many months I shall spend in my own patrie & though we are far far removed from each others House your prayers go with us. We have a slight cold but I hope before Tuesday or Wednesday we leave this [place] I hope we will both be quite well. On that day we only go to Carlisle & on Wednesday go so far as Bolton. Thursday Edward intends we should spend with a Glasgow lady who is married near Bolton & Friday & Saturday's journey will bring us to London. Edward had an extremely kind letter from Mrs Montague asking us to spend some time with her on our arrival. I have however declined her invitation for the present. We arrived here about 9 o'clock Wednesday where sisters & brothers were awaiting us. Next day they all dined here. Friday we were at Sister Janet's with whom I am highly pleased. Saturday at Sister

---

152. ML, MS 08a, b, c, d, e.
153. Had tea.

Margaret's and our Dearest Charles Montague, who is still here, rode to Ruthwell on horseback. I am very much taken with Mrs Duncan. Mr. D is from home & I hope Charles will feel himself most comfortable.

Say to my dear sister how much, very much I am delighted with their kind letters. Every letter now will be doubly precious. I beg Anne to accept of my Leghorn Hat which I will send by the carrier from this [place] and a pair of boots also I send. They are so clumsy that I hardly dare to ask Janet to accept of them but perhaps she may. They have been on the top of Beneraird [Ayrshire] & many other noted places.

My kind kind love to everyone, particularly my dear Mother, Sisters & Brothers all. I hope Janet will be happy at Dundee if she go. Say to father I received his letter from him but I have no time to say anything in answer at present. There strikes the post hours. We have heard nothing of the bad roads you have been urged about—fear not. Commit us to our Heavenly Father.

Edward sends his love & thanks for your criticisms but at present he cannot write you.

Many are the remembrances & wishes to see you here & see you all.

    Ever my dearest Parents,
    Your affectionate Daughter,
    Isabella Irving

Excuse my poor reading [sorry?]

I must remain your debtor in kindness and affection and every thing until the Almighty grant me more leisure from the pressure of affection at hand. EI

Edward Irving to MRS JOHN MARTIN

London 24th December 1823[154]

Honoured Madam and Mother of my wife,

I have little, indeed no time, for enjoying any one affection of my heart, and must for a while suspend the gratification to myself, and bear from those not acquainted with my circumstances many hard judgments. I fear none from you or your family, though I must for a while seem an unworthy member of it. But in time I hope to be recognised as not unworthy, if so the Lord prosper me in the way that is right. It is impossible for men to judge of another, so as to give him advice, but my wife and I who are interested so deeply in one we so dearly love as a Common Father, both judge it our duty to recommend to Mr. Martin for the happiness of his ministry, and for the enjoyment of your tender affections therein, and for the ease and health of his declining life,

---

154. ML, MS 06d.

to take[,] if it be honourably within his power, the Church of Methuen. I think I would do so myself if I were Minister of Kirkcaldy because I could better in the one place than the other do the work of an evangelist. But he is the best judge. My condition here is one of restless labour, a post of extreme difficulty and trial and God only knows how long I may be equal to the discharge of this and I now undertake it, but while if it is his will I will continue to spend & to be spent, and when he pleases to remember me, I can remove with submission and thankfulness. I may say with Paul, that I have none minded as I am, nor with whom I can have any fellowship of the Spirit except my flock and my dear wife[,] whom may the Lord long preserve for consolations upon the earth.

My love to you all. E.I

Caricature of Edward Irving, Isaac Robert Cruikshank, 1824

Edward Irving to WILLIAM COLLINS

7 Middleton Terrace,[155] [London],
24th February, 1824[156]

My dear Mr. Collins,

---

155 164 The Irving's only lived at 7 Myddleton Terrace (Mrs. Oliphant misspells the address) until March 1824 when they moved two doors down to number 4. The name of Myddleton Terrace was changed to Claremont Square in 1825–26.

156. Oliphant, *Life*, 1:194.

I pray you not for a moment to imagine that I have any other intention, so long as God gives me the strength, than to fulfil my promise faithfully. I am at present worked beyond my strength, and you know that is not inconsiderable. My head! my head! I may say with the Shunamite's child.[157] If I care not for it, the world will soon cease to care for me, and I for the world. If you saw me many a night unable to pray with my wife, and forced to have recourse to forms of prayer, you would at once discover what hath caused my delay. I have no resource if I throw myself up, and a thousand enemies wait for my stumbling and fall.

I am now better, and this week had set to rise at six o'clock and finish it,[158] but I have not been able. Next week I shall make the attempt again and again, till I succeed; for upon no account, and for no sake, will I touch or undertake aught until I have fulfilled my promise in respect to Gilpin. But one thing I will say, that I must not be content with the preface of a sermon or patches of a sermon. The subject is too important—too many eyes are upon me—and the interests of religion are too much inwarped in certain places with my character and writing, that I should not do my best.

The Lord bless you and all his true servants.
Your faithful friend,
Edward Irving

Edward Irving and Isabella Irving to MRS MARTIN

Post Mark: 11th March 1824[159]

My dear mother,

Isabella takes such a time, and we are at present in such a hurry, that I have snatched the pen out of her hand to say what is to be said briefly.

1. If it is possible to get a servant who will commit herself to our honour and care, she shall have for wage £10.10 with the prospect of its being increased if she give satisfaction, but let her be assured that I will be to her for a parent if she behave herself well.

2. Let the furniture Isabella has at home be sent up (*not the grate* but the fire irons) as soon as convenient to you. Be assured all my Dear relatives that I hold towards you the greatest affection though I have so few opportunities of manifesting it in writing— I am barely able to make head against my engagements, hardly able indeed. My head is like to fail under it.

---

157. 2 Kgs 4:19.

158. Edward Irving had been asked to write an introductory essay to a life of Bernard Gilpin (1517–84), known as the 'Apostle of the North' and the result was published in 1824. Edward Irving, 'Introductory Essay,' in Gilpin, *The Life of Bernard Gilpin*: See Grass, *The Lord's Watchman*, 117 and n.

159. ML, MS 070a, b, c, d.

We enter to our house next month, and shall be most happy in being able to welcome our Scottish friends & to entertain them with the best in our power.

Your most affectionate son,

Edwd Irving

Edward Irving to WILLIAM DINWIDDIE

[London], 20th April 1824[160]

My Dear and worthy friend,

I have enclosed a letter[161] which I have left open for your perusal, and commit to your care.

There is one thing I have not mentioned in it, which I reckon of high importance, that the vaults should not be used as an expedient for raising money, which were to found our church in filthy lucre, but as a sacred and holy means for comforting the hearts of the people and joining us together as a Christian Church. Let us beware, being most of us mercantile men, lest we introduce the spirit of mammon with the spirit of Christ. They cannot, they will not unite together.

I know well the purity and the high honour of all your intentions, that I have no doubt you will endeavour to keep all things as much after the true ecclesiastical spirit as possible.

The Lord bless us all and wisely direct us all. This is the first and last prayer of your faithful friend and Pastor.

Edwd Irving

Addressed to: William Dinwiddie Esq.,
4 Grocer's Hall Court,
Poultry, London.

Edward Irving to JANE WELSH

London. 10th May 1824[162]

---

160. EIL, MS 29
161. Letter not found.
162. Carlyle, *Love Letters*, 1:423–24.

Part II: The Letters

I promised to write to you when I had got settled in London in my own home in a condition to receive you under my own roof ... But I am still unsettled and still without a home, and still unable to press the visit ... The cause of my unsettled condition at present is chiefly my occupation which is the cause of all things peculiar in me at this moment. My head with difficulty sustaineth my labours, and these moments I now steal from the midst of hours devoted to the Lord. But now I think I shall be settled in a fortnight, and I would now ask the favour of your visit but that for these reasons I shall request you to postpone it a season: I have no money, and my house will be furnished piecemeal, and will hardly be ready for the habitation of a lady till the end of Summer. My Wife's Mother indeed comes up to wait upon her some time during the next month and to remain with us for some weeks. My Father-in-law and Sister-in-law are coming up in the end of July to remain a while; and about the time of their removal should come the time of my annual rest, if indeed this year I am to have any rest. These things are rendered necessary by my dear wife's present state, and you will see how on every account it will be more convenient and pleasant for us to have your company next Spring.

One thing more, my dear Jane, into your own ear. My dear Isabella has succeeded in healing the wounds of my heart by her unexampled affection and tenderness; but I am hardly yet in a condition to expose them. My former calmness and piety are returning. I feel growing in grace and in holiness; and before another year I shall be worthy in the eye of my own conscience to receive you into my house and under my care, which till then I should hardly be.

... Be assured, my dear Jane, whom I may still, I trust, without offence call the child of my intellect,—be assured of the same sincerity of affection from me as ever, and as I have said, purer and more pure.

Thomas Carlyle is to be with me this month; and it is an inexpressible delight to me

I am, my dear Jane,
Your most affectionate friend,
Edwd Irving

Edward Irving to JAMES GILLILAND SIMPSON[163]

Sydenhame [sic], near London. 2nd June 1824[164]

Dear Sirs,

It has[,] for a long time, been the anxious desire & prayer, & the subject of frequent conversation to Mr Dinwiddie and me, that the Lord would direct us in the selection of men from amongst the congregation to fill the office of Elders. And, for a good while our minds have been directed upon five of the Brethren for their piety, integrity, soundness in the faith & good report in the Church. These are Mr Horn, Mr Whytt, Mr Hamilton, Mr Blyth & yourself.

And now my dear Brother, I write to lay this matter before you, that you may cast it in your mind & may make it the subject of devout meditation & prayer until Wednesday Evening which, I propose, if convenient, to spend with you, at your own house, & hear your judgment in this matter.

That you may be rightly informed of the nature of the Office, I refer you to Titus I v 6[,] I Timothy V 17[,] Acts XX vs 7–end. And that you may further know the power with which the founders of our Church have invested this office I extract the following passage from the Second Book of Discipline drawn up & adopted by the General Assembly in the year of our Lord 1590.[165] Book Second Chapt VI 'What manner of persons (*viz* Elders) ought to be we refer it to the express word, & mainly to the Cannons written by the Apostle Paul.'

'Their office is, as well severally as conjunctly to watch over the flock committed to their charge, both publicly & privately that no corruption of religion or manners enter therein.'

'As the Pastors & Doctors should be diligent in sowing the seed of the Word; so the Elders should be careful in looking after the fruit of the same in the people.'

'It appertains to them to assist the Pastor in examination of those that come to the Lord's Table. Item in visiting the sick.'

'They should cause the acts of Assemblies as in all particulars as general to be put in execution carefully.'

'They should be diligent in admonishing all men of their duty, according to the rules of the Evangel.'

'Things they cannot correct by private admonition they should bring to the Eldership.'

---

163. James Gilliland Simpson (1781–1840), a dealer in animal hides, settled with his wife Jane at the Caledonian Chapel. He declined the invitation to become an elder, and was a steady though not uncritical supporter of Irving for some years, until they fell out after Irving refused to acknowledge Jane's prophetic gift as from God.

164. NLS, Acc. 12489/15.

165. It first appeared in 1578.

'Their principal office is to hold Assemblies with the Pastors & Doctors, who are also of their number, for establishing of good order, & execution of discipline. Unto the which Assemblies all persons are subject that remain within their bounds.'

And now, my dear & worthy Brother, we pray of you to join with us & help us in the duty for which we are of ourselves unequal, of administering rightly the spiritual affairs of the congregation. No one feels himself to be able for the duties of a Christian, much less of the Overseer of Christians and you may feel unwilling to engage in that for which you may think yourself unworthy—But we pray of you to trust in the Lord who giveth grace according to our desire of it, & perfecteth his strength in our weakness.

If you refuse, we know not which way to look; for, as the Lord knows, we have fixed upon you & the other four because you seemed to us the most worthy. I, as your Pastor, will do my utmost endeavour, to instruct you in the duties of the Eldership; I will be ready at every Spiritual call to go & minister along with you, and by the grace of God, having no private ends known to me but the single end of God's glory & the edification of the people, we, who are at present of the Session will join with you hand in hand in every good & gracious work. If you refuse I say again, we know not which way to look for help & even now we are suffering no small loss for want of Spiritual council & direction to guide our affairs, & Spiritual help to administer the ordinances & Sacraments of Religion.

If you feel a good will to the work, a wish to prosper & make progress in your holy calling, and a desire after the edification of the Church the gift will be given you & the graces will not be withheld.—Therefore if it can be consistently with your conscience & judgment, we pray & entreat you to accept of this our solicitation, & to allow yourself to be constrained by the needs & importunity of the Church to be named for this Holy Office.

On Wednesday, I shall come & spend the Evening at your house & converse with you on this matter. Meanwhile accept of my heartfelt wishes for your spiritual welfare & let us rejoice together in the work which the Lord is working in the midst of us.

I know you will not take it amiss for I have used the hand of my Wife in the copying of this letter [the rest in Edward Irving's writing] who is well worthy of the task though I cannot get her either to think or wish so.

    I am,
    My Dear Brother,
    Your most affectionate Pastor and Friend,
    Edwd Irving

Revd Edward Irving
2nd June 1824 on the Duties of an Elder.[166]
Mr James Simpson,

166. Annotated: Edward Irving, June 1824 introducing me to the Eldership.

2 Bush Lane,
Cannon St.[167]

Edward Irving to REV WALTER TAIT[168]

[Undated. Annotated: 1829][169]
Monday

Dear Sir,

A long while ago I promised that if any case of great poverty and necessity should occur I would make it known to you. This is one into which I have particularly enquired. He and his wife & three children have come from Scotland very foolishly thinking to find occupation and here they are encompassed with misery and without a friend. He wants to return and with a few shillings would set out. I have done for him the little which I can, but I am almost always in a state of exhaustion by the demands which are made upon me. And the only resource I have that the people may not starve is to mention them to my friends.

Our relations are gone, I sought to get them to come out to Sydenham, but they had so much to do in town, and were always so uncertain of their movements that the time passed away, and it was not accomplished.

I hope Mrs Tate and the children are well. Poor Caroline Houram I fear from the accounts I hear will not be able to return soon as she will be wanted.

My wife joins me in kindest love to you all.

Your affectionate friend,
Edwd Irving

Edward Irving to JOHN MARTIN

Pentonville. 22nd July 1824[170]

---

167. Irving wrote a similar letter to William Hamilton. See Oliphant, *Life*, 1:208–9.

168. Walter Tait (1771–1841) was minister of Trinity College in Edinburgh. Deposed on 22 October 1833 for allowing members of the congregation to speak in tongues and prophesy during services, he became the first Angel of what became the Catholic Apostolic congregation in Edinburgh. See Scott, *Fasti*, 1:128.

169. NLS, MS 967, fol. 204.

170. Oliphant, *Life*, 1:211.

Part II: The Letters

My dear Father,

Isabella was safely delivered of a boy[171] (whom may the Lord bless), at half-past eleven this forenoon, and is, with her child, doing well; and the grandmother, aunt, and father newly constituted, with the mother, are rejoicing in the grace and goodness of God.

Mrs. Martin and Margaret are both well, and salute you grandfather, wishing with all our hearts that you may never lay down the name, but enjoy it while you live.

I am well, and I think the pleasure of the Lord is prospering in my hand. A wide door and effectual is opened to me, and the Lord is opening my own eyes to the knowledge of the truth. Your arrival and our great-grandfather's (whom, with all the grand-aunts, salute in our name—I know not what they owe us for such accumulated honours) is expected with much anxiety. I feel I shall be much strengthened by your presence.

Your dutiful Son,
Edward Irving

Edward Irving to THOMAS CARLYLE

London. 22nd July [1824][172]

My Dear Carlyle,

I am now the Father of a little boy who with his Mother is doing very well. You must now exalt me a little in your reverence. And defer to my patriarchal saws, and family instances. And when I talk with you I should now & then say my child instead of my friend you must not take it amiss.

You are already recherché in this Capital. The Editor of the Europa Review in which men of science and literature all over Europe, & Goethe among the number, are to write has been inquiring after you by one of his gang Mudie whose address I give you. I take it he is the Mudie of Dundee celebrity.[173] However I undeceived him in one respect by telling him you were not come seeking employment which some blundering blockhead in Edin seems to have conveyed to them, but that you were seeking health, enjoyment, and the knowledge of new things and good men. But said he, such are those we want, men of character & condition. And what we wish Mr. C for is to translate our papers out of the German as they come over. He seemed to say you might make from £150 to £200 a year by it at odd & idle hours. Be that as it may I have a strong

171. Edward born 22 July 1824, and died of whooping cough 11 October 1825.

172. NLS, MS 1765, fol. 10-11.

173. Probably Robert Mudie (1777–1842), a schoolmaster and journalist who moved from Dundee to London around 1820.

notion Mudie is a *whiffler*[174] and that the whole must be taken not *cum grano sed cum multo salis*.[175] His address is Mr. Mudie[,] 2 Westbourne Terrace[,] Bayswater, London. I think you may safely say you will translate Goethe's first article. The Review is to be published at one time in the principal languages of Europe. Take your own judgment in the matter, and the counsel of your *medical man* as they would call Badomer [Badams].[176] I call him your guardian Angel, and my dear & valued friend to whom [he] be kindness from all who know him for to all he is kind.

There is Goethe's other novel the Lehrjahre[177] with a note for Robinson[178] & a letter I know not whence. We all present you with our love & shall rejoice at your return, and in your recovery. I may see you or not in Birmingham. I know not.

Yours most truly,
Edwd Irving

Addressed to: Mr. Thomas Carlyle,
J Badomer Esq.,
Birmingham.

Edward Irving to THOMAS CHALMERS

Mydelton [sic] Terrace Pentonville
21st September 1824[179]

My Dear Sir,

I was not unmindful of your letter, but replied to it immediately, and in order to save you the trouble of a communication with Mr Parker I replied directly. And the purport of my letter is that for his sake and yours I would take James[180] into my house at the rate of £200 in the year—and that for his own sake, if our house and establishment did not suit him and his parents' views I would do all that I would do [for] a Brother in the way of introducing him to my friends and being to him a friend. So that

---

174. Variable or evasive.
175. Not with a pinch but with a lot of salt.
176. John Badams. Carlyle's doctor in 1824. See CL, 3: 112 and Carlyle, *Reminiscences*, 291.
177. Edward Irving is referring to *Wilhelm Meisters Lehrjahe*.
178. Probably Henry Crabb Robinson (1775–1867), diarist. Carlyle had been taken to meet him by Edward Irving at Charles Lamb's on 5 July 1824. Irving had described Carlyle to Robinson as 'a friend of mine who has translated Wilhelm Meister': See Wilson, *Carlyle*, 1:399.
179. NCL, MSS CHA 4 34.54.
180. James Parker, a law student who boarded with Irving. See CL, 3:195.

it was a matter of small consequence whether he was in my house or not that is with reference to the service I would like to be of to him.

Now I am truly sorry that this scheme of church communication intended to save you trouble has caused you trouble, but having done it out of such an intention you will excuse my not having written to you[,] occupied as I am with so many things, as I had intended to write you with a young friend of mine coming to your university, which I will yet do. His name is Montague and his bent is to the Church, and the wish of his Father[,] a barrister in town[,] is that he should apply [himself] to his studies according to the ordinary course of the University. My object in making him known to you is that he may not be cooled out of his piety by the cold communication of Moderate professors and preachers[181]—be frozen alive in the Iceberg of a University, but kept in health and life by the blessing of God upon the conversation & example which he will see in you, for the profit of his soul and the use of his future ministry. And now after saying so much of him to you I think I will change my mind and write to my Glasgow mother your dear wife and commend him to her tenderness.

And now business being aside—I tell you that I begin to understand this mystery of mysteries the Gospel of Christ, and to feel my way towards the peace of it beyond all understanding. I had upon coming to England to double or treble the length of my sounding line, but now it seems to me as if there were no depth which could reach the bottom of these thoughts with which my mind is filled. Moreover I am able to stand for my Master, and to keep the field with dispassionate truth against this behemoth of a city, and to contend for the faith. And if the Lord prosper me I hope yet that the fire ship which alarmed the Scottish Coast may return laden with treasures to her shores. But I wait the growth of faith which is in me as a grain of Mustard-seed.[182]

I do enquire in your doings and sufferings for the good Cause. The Lord has advanced you as a chosen one. Be on your guard against the fear of your fellow-men. And let not the desire of approbation from those you love withdraw you from your own course. Let thine eye be single & thy whole body shall be full of light.[183] When shall I receive councils from you fain would I converse with you in a lovely isle. But the time cometh.

My wife joins me in love to Mrs Chalmers, and the children. Tell Elisa I have a little boy for her husband his name Edw Irving.

Yours most truly,
Edwd Irving

Addressed to: The Revd Dr Chalmers,
Professor of Moral Philosophy,
University St Andrews.

181. The anti-Evangelical party.
182. Matt 13:31.
183 181 Luke 11:34.

Edward Irving to JANE WELSH

Dover.[184]
12th October 1824[185]

My dear friend and pupil,

I am very sorry, my dear Jane, that anything should have occurred to interrupt for a moment the sweet relationship which we stood in to one another when we parted in Scotland, and you sent the pledge of your regard to my wife by her husband's hand. I was in fault apparently but not inwardly in fault. You should have given me large credit, and there I think you were in fault. But we must amend our faults . . . Let us forget all the past occurrences of the last two years, except to reap from them wholesome lessons of self-knowledge and self-improvement; also let us return to the unsuspecting and unfearing intimacy in which we stood to one another before. My wife desires her affectionate regards to you and your dear mother; and my boy (who is Edward after all, John being objected to by the higher power), my dear smiling sensible boy, would kiss you and smile on you till he made your heart glad, if you were here to nurse him on your knee.

Farewell my dear friend,
Yours most affectionately,
Edwd Irving

Edward Irving to WILLIAM DINWIDDIE

Dover. 20th October 1824[186]

My Dear and Valued friend,

Your care over the flock in my absence, and the occasional communication you make to me of your arrangements, are very pleasing to my spirit, and have my true and heart-felt thanks. The three weeks that I have been here have been industriously and conscientiously occupied with study so far as is compatible with the recovery of my health which for the common welfare I am called on to attend to. And this has

---

184. From Dover, Carlyle joined a party that went to France, which did not include Irving. See CL, 3:178–83.
185. Carlyle, *Love Letters* 2:424–25.
186. EIL, MS 30.

hindered me from answering to your letters to which indeed I had nothing to say but that I was fully satisfied.

I am truly happy for his own sake, and the sake of the Church of Christ, that Mr. Anderson proves himself so good and able a preacher of the Gospel, and I think that if he could be got to undertake to edify the church again, it would be profitable and well, but if not then we must have recourse to such as the Lord hath put within our power. And let us constantly remember that it is he who giveth the increase though a Paul should plant and an Apollos should water.[187] I was pleased as I always am with your zeal for the welfare of the branches of the Church of Scotland established in England and I am sorry Dr Chalmers has not been able to come to Birmingham but though he had been able I confess to you I would not have besought him to come to London, because I think it is setting too much store by the human instrument, and may withdraw our trust from the great rock of our strength. Indeed I feel that this is one of the greatest temptations to which my church is liable, that they should look to me, who alas! am but a broken reed that bruiseth the hand of him that leaneth to it.

I have studiously refrained from preaching here, or engaging with any duties but those of my own study and church, being desirous to follow out such reflections & meditations, and form such plans and resolutions as might be profitable to my flock who kindly permit me the relaxation for my many labours. My wife and little child are in good health, and I feel myself much revived, I bathe every morning before breakfast, and generally walk forth by the shore of the sea once or twice each day, but I employ in my study three or four hours each day. Mrs Strachey is to me a great spiritual consolation, for in her I find a true child of God & disciple of the Lord Jesus. Upon the whole you would be well pleased with our whole condition, it is so simple and private, for I have diligently refrained from making any acquaintance with the people; and we are truly as much alone as [if] we were planted upon the most desert coast. I have no desire to go to France,[188] for my soul has no kindred there. And I do not think that I shall be persuaded to go.

I have written my brotherly feelings towards you and the Elders in the enclosed sheet which I pray you to communicate. They are simple but sincere. Our strength is from above, and the earthly manifestation of it is in unity. I look to you with reverence, and thank God for having joined me to one so faithful in his vocation. I pray God to reward unto your own bosom and to your family, manifold of that care which you bestow upon his church. I pray him also to direct your zeal unto the best and truest channels, and long to spare you in the midst of us.

---

187. 1 Cor 3:6.

188. The Irving family had gone to Dover for a holiday on 25 September 1824, to be followed by Carlyle two days later: See CL, 3:160. From Dover, Carlyle joined a party that went to France, which did not include Irving. In a letter to Jane Welsh of 28 October 1824, Carlyle gives an account of the visit. CL, 3:178–83.

My wife & Mr Carlyle join me in affectionate regards to you Mr. Dinwiddie & your family

Your affectionate friend & Pastor,

Edw Irving

Addressed to: Wm Dinwiddie Esq.,
4 Grocers Hall Court,
Poultry, London.

Edward Irving to THE ELDERS OF THE CALEDONIAN CHURCH

[In pencil: Undated]
[Possibly the enclosure for above letter.][189]

My Dear Friends and Brethren,

I use the interval of public worship of this Holy day to express to you some of my thoughts and feelings concerning the charge over which the Lord hath made us overseers in common.

There is nothing of which my spirit accuses itself more in the review which I take of my past ministry, than the want of travail of soul concerning the flock. I think we who are appointed Elders over the heritage of God ought to be full of a divine concern, not only that the flock be fed with the bread of life, but that they thrive and grow under the ministration of it. And this concern, like every other care of the Spirit, ought to express itself in prayers to God, frequent and fervent prayers that the soul of the people may be enlarged with all spiritual understanding & feeling of the truth. Now I do feel a lacking of this grace with which Paul and the other honoured ministers of the Gospel seem to have been so abundantly supplied. And, being conscious that until this grow in our hearts largely, we are not good stewards of the household[,] I entreat you to continue constant in prayer for me and for one another as I also, by the grace of God[,] will do for you, so that our hearts may be enlarged, and the pleasure of the Lord may prosper in our hands.

I pray you also to take into your thoughts what can be done by us in Session most likely to promote amongst us the grace of the Gospel of Christ, and to make it known to me at our meeting, that while we are all constant in prayer for one another we may not be slothful or inactive in our Spiritual business. Regard me in all things as no more than your fellow-labourer, of slender years and small experience, yet sincere, as God

189. EIL, MS 30a.

knoweth, in the work; and without any hesitation make known to me your mind for the edification of the body of Christ, since we are brethren in this holy ministry let us be brethren in the oneness of our spirit, and in the freedom of our communications.

I am resolved by the grace of God to give myself with more zeal and spiritual industry than hitherto in the work of watching over the souls of the flock, and by your help I hope to be much strengthened both in counsel and in action.

It gives me pleasure to hear that several have applied to sit down with the church around the table of the body and blood of Christ. Let us encourage such, and wisely direct and instruct them, setting them in all things examples of the love and piety of that holy brotherhood to which they are about to be joined. It is well said in the book of discipline, that the office of the Pastor is to sow the seed of the word, the office of the Elder to look for the fruit of the same amongst the people. And it must be pleasant for you to see the fruit shewing itself in this eagerness to partake of the bread of life. You will do well diligently to enquire into the walk and conversation of these applicants, that when I come to take them upon examination I may have before me all the necessary information. I trust our approaching communion will prove to us all a day of the Lord which we tasted that he was Good, and felt that he was with us of a truth.

Be not discouraged my beloved brethren, by the difficulties of the work, but seek supplies of grace according to your need or help. It is a great work to lay the foundation of a church upon the Apostles & the Prophets, Jesus Christ being the chief corner stone[;][190] it is an honour & high preferment to labour therein with all faithfulness, for therein we shall both save others and save our own souls also. Yet let us never forget that we are but instruments in the hand of God, that our salvation is not in us but from the Lord Jesus Christ. That we are poor lost sinners redeemed by his blood. Stand fast in his righteousness. Rejoice in his salvation and the God of grace keep your souls and the souls of all the people for which we watch and pray.

My antient & formerly my only help-mate in this work Mr. Dinwiddie will let you know concerning my health and condition and present occupations, to whose hands I commit these words of spritual friendship, which I thought it good to write to you.

Your affectionate Pastor and Brother Elder in the Church of Christ,
Edwd Irving

~

Edward Irving to WILLIAM DINWIDDIE

[October 1824?][191]

190. Eph 2:20.
191. EIL, MS 30c.

My Dear and Worthy friend,

I thank you for your dispatch to which I have made answer with equal dispatch, and would have enclosed the letter but that I wished it to proceed by this night's Post. These oppositions will try the cause not ruin it, they will separate the chaff from the wheat and open to Mr. Crosbie the trustworthy part of his friends, and disclose the unworthy[.] I have counseled him to be of good cheer. I thank Mr. Murray for his information & shall not fail to call upon Mr. Rose as often as my other duties will allow me, and [at] the first opportunity I shall call upon Mr. Young. I would have seen you yesterday if I had had a moment of time. We shall converse at large upon the subject when we meet.

Yours most truly,
Edward Irving

Edward Irving to ISABELLA IRVING

Birmingham. 29th or rather 30th November, 1824[192]

My dearest Wife,

I am arrived safe, notwithstanding your evil auguries, or rather suggestions, of doubt and unbelief, which the faith of God's providence can alone dissipate, and the assurance that I am about our Father's business; and I have found a home here at the house of Dr. J-, my father's adjoining neighbour, and my very warm friend, into whose heart I pray the Lord I may sow some spiritual seed in return for his temporal benefits, for, as yet, he is in the darkness of Unitarianism. Nevertheless, they have family prayers at which I this night presided, and while I sought I could not find to avoid in my prayers the matters in dispute between us but was constrained, as it were, by superior power to make cordial testimony to our risen and reigning Lord, our Saviour and our God.

I have seen the Committee, and find all things looking prosperously ... Mr. L- has had so much distress in his family that he was content I should come here, and not to him; but I go to-morrow afternoon to weep with him and his motherless children. Mrs L- loved you to the end with a strange and strong love, and it was her greatest earthly desire to have seen you. There is something so uncommon in this that it seems to me to point the way that you should love her children, and do for their sakes what she longed to do for your mother's child. Therefore, my dear Isabella, do write Miss L-, and strengthen her, and invite her when she can be spared to come and spend some time with us ... Be careful of yourself and the little boy—the dear, dear little boy, my

192. Oliphant, *Life*, 1:216–17.

greatest earthly hope and joy—for you are not another, but myself—my better and dearer half. I pray the Lord to bless you, and be instead of a friend and husband and father to you in my absence. Let not your backwardness hinder you from family prayers night and morning.

I hope I shall find time to write to Margaret, our beloved sister, to whom I have much that is affectionate to communicate, and something that may be instructive … Forget me not to Mary,[193] over whom I take more than a master's authority, feeling for her all the guardianship of a parent, which she may be pleased to permit me in … My brotherly and pastoral love to the elders of the flock … Say to Thomas,[194] the moralist, that I love him at a distance as much as at hand—I think sometimes *full better,* as they say in Annandale. To my Isabella I say all in one word, that I desire and seek to love her as Christ loved the Church.

Your most affectionate husband,
Edward Irving

Editor's Epilogue

When this last letter was written to his wife, she was already pregnant with their first child, Edward who was born on the 23rd July, 1824. He doted on his baby son. Nothing had prepared him for the great love and delight that this boy was to bring into his life. All the greater then was his profound sorrow at the child's death, only fourteen months later. Mrs. Oliphant declared that he never recovered from this tragedy, which he now had to strive to reconcile with his faith and his mission.[195]

---

193. 'One of his servants': Oliphant, *Life*, 1:217.

194. Thomas Carlyle.

195. But as Mrs. Oliphant noted, 'so far as I can perceive, no other event of his life penetrated so profoundly the depths of his spirit': Oliphant, *Life*, 1:247–48.

4

Letters: 1825–1826

Editor's Introduction

During this year a deputation approached Edward Irving from St. Cuthbert's in Edinburgh with an invitation to become their minister at Hope Place chapel, which he refused. It was understandable. By this time the family were settled in a house in Myddelton Terrace and Irving had met the three men who were to influence his theology: Samuel Taylor Coleridge,[1] Henry Drummond,[2] and Hatley Frere.[3] He also felt a strong sense of loyalty to his flock.

Later in 1825 the family had travelled to Isabella's family home in Kirkcaldy for the birth of their second child. It was there that little Edward died on October 11,

---

1. Samuel Taylor Coleridge (1772–1834), poet, critic and philosopher of Romanticism. Basil Montague introduced Edward Irving to Coleridge in 1823 where he was living in Highgate fighting his long addiction to opium.

2. Henry Drummond (1786–1860). Henry Drummond was a son of a Scottish banking family, an MP, independently wealthy and interested in apocalyptic prophecy. In 1825 he asked Edward Irving to preach at the anniversary of the Continental Society which he chaired and which he had founded together with Sir Thomas Baring and Robert Haldane. He had been living in Geneva but in 1819 Drummond returned to England and bought Albury Park in Surrey, which he commissioned Pugin to remodel. At Advent in 1826 there the first conference to study unfulfilled prophecy took place, and as it was prophecy that Irving had preached on to the Continental Society, he too was invited. Henry Drummond also financed *The Morning Watch* (March 1829–33), a publication that the group used as a mouthpiece. See Bolitho, *The Drummonds of Charing Cross*. Thomas Carlyle, when taken by Irving to dine with Drummond, was struck by his 'enormous conceit.' See Carlyle, *Reminiscences*, 334. He was called as an Angel in 1832, and as a Prophet in 1833. See letter EI to Henry Drummond, 13 October 1833: DFP: C/9/25.

3. Hatley Frere (1779–1856). A man of evangelical persuasion who, whilst a Lieutenant in the Artillery, had suffered a spiritual crisis and a nervous breakdown. He resigned his commission with the idea of becoming a minister, but family prejudice regarding his religious convictions and his delicate health caused him to join the Army Pay Office as a clerk and he relinquished the idea of entering the ministry. However, this did not deter him from pursuing his study of biblical prophecy. See Grass, *The Lord's Watchman*, lo.9–10.10.

Part II: The Letters

1825, aged only fourteen months. Irving left his wife there with their newborn daughter Margaret. After visiting his family in Annan he travelled to London, and after his arrival there his letters take the form of a journal for her.

⁓

Edward Irving to JAMES BRIDGES[4]

4 Myddelton Terrace, Pentonville.
24th March 1825[5]

Sir,

I have read this circular concerning the conference and like its objects well, though I fear it is to degenerate into a Counter-working of the ruling power in the General assembly, and to be only another *expedient* for doing that which never was done, and cannot otherwise be done than by the preaching of those mighty doctrines which are the power & wisdom of God. I fear, I say, that it will turn out another Company-formation upon the religious exchange, without the real capital of sound doctrine & spiritual mindedness, of which there is a famine at present in the land, and whereof the clearest proof in the number of expedients to do without it. I admonish you not to make it such, to have none but men of God appertaining to it, spiritual men, men imbued with the antient spirit of the Church of Scotland if you can find such, for in my paths they are exceeding scanty. But if ye take in men because they have a title, or are Whigs, or are upon the left hand of the Moderator it will come to naught.

Assuredly it is the answer of many prayers (I know that many have been offered) that such a device hath come into your hearts. But the lean years, the lean years have eaten up the fatness of the Land, and are grown in the end to skeletons. Yet let me not limit the mighty power of God, nor deny him the glorious things which he hath wrought by a small band, even a handful. Be strong, and courageous. Put expediencies and *lawyer-like* prudences from the midst of you. Be spiritual men and fear none evil. That leanest and baldest and weakest of all God's opposers, I mean moderation[6] must come to an end, but I fear it hath done its work in propagating a progeny of lean, bald & weak skepticism, yet sufficient to keep in ground in the present philosophical biggotry [*sic*] of Scotland, but which would not stand a breath-full of true philosophy, and will not stand the blowing of the horn of true Theology.

---

4. When Edward Irving visited Edinburgh in 1828 'he was to live in the house of Mr. Bridges, now a friend of some years standing, who lived in Great King Street, one of those doleful lines of handsome houses which weigh down the cheerful hill-side under tons of monotonous stone.' Oliphant, *Life*, 2:17.

5. NLS, MS 5139, fol. 117.

6. I.e., Moderatism.

I feel obliged to you for your two communications and shall pray for their success, and contribute (though I should like to see you independent of that broken reed) whatever money I have to spare, certainly enough (and send more if needed), to constitute me a member of the Conference which I do now bless in the name of the Lord, as I bless you and all who love the Lord Jesus in sincerity & in truth,

I am,

Your brother in the Gospel of Christ,

Edwd Irving

I have no paper money fast me, but I shall send a Guinea by Henry Paul who is at present in London.

Addressed to:
James Bridges, 60 Great King St., Edinburgh W.S.[7]

~

Edward Irving to JOHN MARTIN

[London], June 3rd 1825[8]

My Dear Father,

I have not been without the deepest sympathy with your sufferings and earnest prayers for a blessing upon them and you and all your family and flock; and I now commend you in whatever state this may find you to the good grace and tender mercy of the Lord. We have reason to thank God for the good estate of body and I trust also of Spirit in which we are all found. Samuel[9] is a great consolation & enjoyment to us all. We delight to find in him so many evidences of a Gospel minister and trust that he will not be diminished in aught by his residence amongst us. Margaret is full of life and activity, and I hope not without admonitions of God's good spirit in which I pray earnestly that she make daily progress. Isabella's spiritual state, if I judge aught[,] has never been more prosperous since I knew her. For myself though with many thorns in flesh and mind, and messengers of Satan to buffet me, I do yet rejoice in the good and sufficient grace of God, and am daily enlarged in the revelations of his word. I am about to publish another discourse whose object is to fix down the point where we at present stand in the prophetic history, and sketch out that which the church is speedily to expect.[10] I wonder at the supineness of the Church of Scotland in things pertaining to spiritual doctrine, and if I might be instrumental I have caused that discourse to be

---

7. I.e., Scottish equivalent of a solicitor.
8. Letters source: WCL, MS 4.
9. Edward Irving's brother-in-law.
10. Edward Irving, *Babylon and Infidelity Foredoomed of God*.

published in Glasgow by our true friend Collins, that it may have a chance of circulation in the north. I have been solicited to publish another discourse which I preached lately before the Society for propagating Xian [Christian] knowledge upon the insufficiency & illiberality of all Education that did not include religion, but I think I shall refrain.[11] I have desired Collins to send a copy of Horner on the Psalms to my dear Mother upon which I pray you write my name with my dutiful love.

Your affec Son,
Edwd Irving

Addressed to: The Revd. John Martin,
Kirkcaldy.
Annotated: Letters from Ed & Is Irving & Margt Martin. [Isabella Irving's letter is missing.]

Edward Irving to THE MEMBERS OF THE CALEDONIAN CHURCH

Kirkcaldy 14th July 1825[12]

My Dear Friends and Brethren,

I have a few minutes before the departure of my young friend Mr. Thompson Preacher of the Gospel, and I embrace the opportunity of writing to you however shortly, because I know it will give you pleasure to hear of my welfare and prosperity.

I have nothing to communicate, (having not yet removed from this place) beyond my own personal condition and that of my wife and child, which I thank God is good both temporally and spiritually, and I trust the Lord is equally gracious to you his servants and to your families and the members of our church. While the season of our prosperity endures let us be diligent to improve all our gifts and graces that when he seeth it good to try us with affliction, we may remember his loving-kindness in the time that is past. You will find this to have been the frequent resource of his servant David and the most experienced of his saints.

Since my arrival here I have continued night and day constant in remembering you all in my prayers, being mindful of the love which has grown and increased amongst us; and the ready ear with which you have listened to the doctrines of the Gospel from my

---

11. In fact, Irving's sermon, preached on 17 May, on behalf of the Society in Scotland for Propagating Christian Knowledge, was reported: *The Pulpit*, 23 June 1825, 385–94. He included it in *Sermons, Lectures, and Occasional Discourses*, 3:781–844.

12. EIL, MS 3 1.

mouth in which I pray you to continue faithful yourselves and watching over the flock that they may abide therein to the saving of their souls.

I have been occupied all the day with the finishing of a work upon those prophecies which have respect to the papacy and to infidelity,[13] which I trust the Lord will bless to the stirring up of the church to expect speedily the Coming of the Lord. My views upon this subject I have not yet fully explained to our flock but this will form, if God spares us[,] a part of the occupation of the next year. My own soul shall be much built up in faith and patience by the study of those Prophecies which are truly the rich inheritance of the Church.

My wife and little son by the Mercy of God are both doing well and we soon expect an increase to our family on which occasion I often pray the Lord to be gracious to us. And I request, dearly beloved brethren, in this as in all other things the fellowship of your prayers. We pray our kind salutations to your wives & families.

Be of good cheer, and hope unto the end, and encourage the faithful to trust in the salvation of Christ. To all the flock I pray my dearest love. Time forbids me to say any thing particularly. The young man Mr. Thompson has been licensed to preach these four or five months, and will be glad to be of service in any way among the churches. I expect much from him.—The Lord conduct him in safety to his Father's house.

I am Dearly beloved Brethren,
Your fellow Elder and Pastor in Christ,
Edwd Irving

Addressed to: Wm Dinwiddie Esq.
The Members of the Kirk Session of the Caledonian Church.
Favd by Rev Mr. Thompson.

~

Edward Irving to THE ELDERS OF ST.CUTHBERT'S, EDINBURGH

London 16th July 1825[14]

My Beloved Brethren in the Gospel of Christ and the Eldership of his Church.

I rejoice to have received by your hands and from your lips the assurance that such a grave and spiritual body of Christians as the Eldership of St Cuthbert's Edinburgh have judged me a fit person to be presented to the people of Hope-place Chapel, as one worthy to exercise the ministry of word and sacrament over them, if they should see

---

13. Irving, *Babylon and Infidelity Foredoomed*.
14. NLS, MS 1002, fol. 283.

it good and profitable to call me. The more when I consider the character and gifts of my dear friend and Brother in the ministry who has been called from amongst them to labour elsewhere. You know and can bear witness to your brethren, how deeply I have considered the matter, and how much I have listened to your representations and weighty reasonings and what pains I have taken to weigh all things in the balance of spiritual judgment. Also how anxious that you should confer with the Session of my church, that we might find out that which was most profitable to the common church of our Saviour.

All that has been said on both sides has sunk deep into my mind, and I have sought grace to enable me to come to a true and righteous determination; and after much thought and anxiety I have expressed the state of my feelings towards both sides in a letter to my Session and people of which there is enclosed an exact copy.[15]

You will perceive from that letter by what strong and enduring ties I am drawn towards my native country and my beloved church; and by what present stronger though not so enduring ties I am held here. I have no doubt the time is coming when the Spirit will press me to declare in the bosom of the Church of Scotland, that truth which I am bound at present to declare here until I shall have finished the burden of it. When that time comes you will find me in the midst of you, or if any emergency should occur before that time to hasten my resolution, it is I think to my own Country and to the chief city of it that I will present myself.

You have been faithful to your trust, and are worthy to be the messengers of such a spiritual body. The Lord conduct you on you way to your home, and bring you in peace to your office in his church. And be assured of the Communion and fellowship of

Your Brother in the Gospel and [in the] Eldership,
Edwd Irving

Addressed to: Messrs.' Paul and Howden,
Elders of the Session of St. Cuthbert's,
Edinburgh.

~

Edward Irving to THE CONGREGATION, DEAR BELOVED MEMBERS, AND OFFICE BEARERS OF THE CALEDONIAN CHURCH

London, 16 July 1825[16]

---

15. I.e., the following letter.
16. Fife Council Museums: Kirkcaldy Museum and Art Gallery, MS 49/2: fol. 1950–52.

Dear Men & Brethren, Dear beloved members, and honoured office bearers in the Caledonian Church.

The invitation to minister the Gospel in my native country came recommended to my mind by many grave and weighty considerations of which these are the chief.

First my desire to embrace all the Ministers and members of Christ in the Church of Scotland, who love the Lord Jesus and are under the Holy Spirit, with the aim of communion, and to make manifest unto them the Spirit and doctrine which I am of and whereof very few of them are at present assured.

Secondly to warn the worldly part of my countrymen as I have warned this worldly part of this city, concerning their scoffings and their false opinions, and their unsanctified learning, and the power, and the various forms of their infidelity & opposition to the Lord and Saviour Jesus Christ, in which if they continue they shall assuredly perish.

Thirdly to have a corner of the vineyard laid off by the church to my pastoral watchfulness, with which I might go up and down, in the spirit of faithfulness, and come in and go out in the spirit of love, and find a home and abode for my labours, which here be more scattered abroad, than we can overtake.

And the expression which you have conveyed to me to continue my Ministry in the midst of you, is recommended to my mind by other grave & weighty considerations of which these are the chief.

First. The assurance you give me of your love and of your purpose to aid to the utmost of your powers in the work of my office, which I understand to imply a desire to hear my instructions at all times, and to give ear to them as God opens your heart, and to confirm to the good discipline of the Church, and to do whatever lies in your power for the outward welfare and comfort of the people.

Secondly. The conviction of my own mind that I have not yet declared all my message for the salvation of your souls, having only of late begun to enter into the interior sanctuary of sound doctrine and spiritual perfection, to the riches of which I must introduce you before my soul will entertain any overtures of going elsewhere.

Thirdly. The conviction that the members of the Scottish church who or whose Fathers have been baptised into her faith, are in the very lowest spiritual condition of any people in the metropolis; and must underlay the heavy judgments of God for the instruction & education in the faith which they have hardened their hearts against: and though I have little hope of seeing them roused to the sense of their hardened condition, I deem it not yet the time to cease crying aloud in their ears.

Fourthly. Your daily and great love to me and my family and my ministrations which continues unabated even til this present hour and which must make it heartbreaking for me when God shall refer [?] me elsewhere.

Now, my Dearly beloved brethren, I have resolved after much prayer and consultation of wise and spiritual men to refuse the invitation of my Countrymen and deny my heart's longings after my church, and to accept the expression of your desire to minister amongst you, until I have established you, by the grace of God, in the communion of a Christian Church, and can find one who may be fitted to watch over the flock in my absence. But it is manifest unto my own Soul, and therefore I make it manifest unto you, that when the time shall come that I think my commission to this city fulfilled and my doctrine fully expounded to my people, I must listen to the calls of other parts to preach the Gospel there also, and to my own Countrymen first of all. For I am convinced in my own mind that the spirit of the Christian Church needs to be roused to the knowledge of many things, and to the pursuit of many things concerning which she seemeth to be dropping asleep. But if God in the mean time should raise up another there to do the work, I shall be satisfied; if he should call me I dare not disobey. Therefore I do intreat [sic] you, my beloved brethren, to use well the time which is present in giving ear to the doctrines which I set forth, and joining yourselves in the communion of the Church, and doing what other things seem to you most likely to be profitable to the stability and well-being of the flock in the midst of which I will labour with increased diligence, knowing not when my spirit may call me elsewhere which, believe me, will not be for fame nor for lucre nor for ease, nor I trust for any other cause but the advancement of the glory of God and of his Church.

I have sent this to my beloved flock through the hands of my Brother in the Eldership, my Father in much affection, and the constant and most persevering friend of the church Willm Dinwiddie. The grace of the Lord Jesus Christ be with you all, and establish you in the unity of the faith and the love of the brethren, so that you may be spoken of in all the churches, and be honoured of God and blessed with a succession of faithful pastors.

Your loving Pastor who desires to be found faithful to the Lord.

Edwd Irving

Edward Irving to ISABELLA IRVING

25 Bedford Square, 19th July 1825[17]

My Dearest Wife,

On Sunday I desired a meeting of the church and congregation at six o'clock last night, and then laid before them both my resolution to remain amongst them, and the grounds of it; and I now haste, having completed my morning's study, to lay before you what I laid before them, that I may have your approbation, which is all that now remains to the full contentment of my own mind.[18]

---

17. Oliphant, *Life*, 1: 237–39.

18. 'I attended a meeting at Caledonian Chapel on the subject of a call Mr. Irving had received to a chapel in Edinburgh. The meeting were unanimous in their expression of attachment to him and

The invitation, I said, had three chief reasons to recommend it, and by which it still remains on my mind weightily recommended: First. That so well advocated in your letter, which sunk deep into my thoughts, that it might be the call of Providence to do for Edinburgh what I had been called upon to do for London, and what no one of the ministers of God had done before I came. Secondly. The desire I had to be restored to the communion of the true ministers of Christ and servants of God in the Church of Scotland, who heretofore, with a very few exceptions, have estranged me from their confidence. Thirdly. The love which I had to a manageable pastoral charge. On the other hand, three more weighty reasons prevailed with me to remain: First. Their desire of my ministry, and assurance of co-operation in my official duties, which, going elsewhere, was all to work for. Secondly. The consciousness that I had not yet told half my message out of the Gospel, and but partially fulfilled my ministry. Thirdly. The desire I had that my countrymen should yet have a little longer trial, and the opportunity which a new church would afford them of returning to the bosom of the Church. Lastly. The strong love which I bore my people, and which made me shrink from any call to depart but such a one as was very imperious and strong. But while I consented to stay in my present ministry for these weighty reasons, I gave them, at the same time, distinctly to understand, that such a call might be given me as would be able to call me elsewhere; and that, without a call, if the Spirit moved me, I would certainly go to the world's end. Having said this much I left the desk, and the people remained to consider what was best to be done, and I have but heard imperfectly from Mr. Paul and Mr Howden, who breakfasted with us this morning, that it was conducted in a good spirit.

I trust that my dear Isabella will approve of what I have done, which I have certainly done by much patient deliberation, yet with a strong resolution, and at the same time a high sense and feeling of all the considerations of the other side. The thing has done much good already, and will do much more, chiefly as it has brought out the declaration and understanding on all hands that I may be called away, which the people here had little thought of. Also, that I will stand justified before incredulous Edinburgh by two other witnesses. For I am not to seek as to the true sentiment that is still entertained by the religious part of men there concerning me, and would gladly see it wiped away.

Last Sabbath I preached in the morning on the subject of the Trinity, showing that the revelation of the Word consisted of three parts—Law, Gospel, and Obedience—which were severally the forms of the Father, the Son, and the Holy Ghost; so that a trinity was everywhere in the Word of God; I intend to continue the same subject next Sabbath, and on the following one to show that there are three constant states by which the soul expresses her homage to the Father, Son, and Holy Ghost:— First, prayer; secondly faith; and thirdly, activity, which are a trinity in unity with the

---

thought it quite impossible Mr. Irving could think of leaving his present congregation and deputed the elders to convey the sense of the meeting to Mr. Irving.' J. G. Simpson, *The Story of the Simpsons*, 156. NLS: Acc 12489 No 14.

new man. In the evening I lectured on John sending his disciples to inquire at Christ of his Messiahship,[19] showing thence how his mind, partaking of the vulgar error, had lost the impression of the outward signs shown at his baptism,[20] and then arguing the total insufficiency of that manner of demonstration and proof to which the last century hath given such exaggerated importance. I showed that Christ's action before the messengers, and his message to the Baptist, was a fulfilment of the prophecy in the 61st of Isaiah, which led me to explain the great point, that miracles were nothing but the incarnation or visible representation of the Holy Ghost, as Jesus of Nazareth was the Word of God; and that, as His work was the will of the Father, so were His works the acts of the Spirit dwelling in Him, and about to proceed from Him.

We were at Allan Cunningham's last night, where I met with Wilkie.[21] They all desired their love to you and Margaret. Everybody inquires after you, and rejoices in your welfare. You must keep yourself quiet. Let not ceremony or any other cause take hold of your kind heart, and disturb you from necessary quiet. I trust little Edward continues to thrive. Cease not to pray for him and me as for yourself. I see not why we may not pray in the plural number, as if we were present together. I shall keep by eight in the morning and ten at night for my hours of prayer. Oh, Isabella, pray much for me! I need it much. These are high things after which I strive, and I oft fear lest Satan should make them a snare to my soul . . . The Lord protect you all, and save you!

Your affectionate husband,
Edward Irving.

~

Edward Irving to ISABELLA IRVING

London, 25 Bedford Square, 2nd, 1825[22]
4th August: *Dies natalis atque fatalis incidit.*
The day of birth and of death draweth nigh.[23]

My Dearest Wife,

. . . I have not altered my mind upon the course of my journey, which I will direct forthwith to Kirkcaldy by the steamboat, without passing at the present through the towns in England, which, if all be well ordered, I can take upon my return . . . I greatly

19. Luke 7:13–23.
20. Luke 3:21–22.
21. Sir David Wilkie (1785–1841), Scottish painter who moved to London in 1805 and was celebrated for painting scenes of everyday life. See *ODA*.
22. Oliphant, *Life*, 1: 239–41.
23. Irving is referring to the fact that the 4th August is both his birthday and day his brother John died in 1822.

rejoice that you are enjoying the quiet and repose whereof you stand so much in need, and that little Edward is thriving daily. The Lord give health and strength to his soul! I pray you, my dear Isabella, to bear in mind that he has been consecrated to God by the Sacrament of Baptism, where Christ did assure to our faith the death of his body of sin, and the life of his spirit of righteousness; and that he is to be brought up in the full faith and assurance of the fulfilment of this greatest promise and blessing, which our dear Lord hath bestowed upon our faith; wherefore adopt not the base notion, into which many parents fall, of waiting for a future conversion and a new birth, but regard that as fully promised to us from the beginning, and let all your prayers, desires, words, and thoughts towards the child proceed accordingly. For I think that we are all grown virtually adult Baptists, whatever we be professedly, in that we take no comfort or encouragement out of the Sacrament. Let it not be so with you, whom God hath set to be a mother in Israel.[24]

Since I wrote, I have passed a Sabbath, when I had much of the Lord's presence in all the exercises of public worship, and was able to declare the truth with much liberty; preaching in the morning from Rom. viii. 3, 4, and opening the sentence of death which there was in the law, and the reprieve of life which there was in the work and gospel of Christ,—a subject which I mean to follow up by showing that the reprieve is for the end of our fulfilling the law, which, as an antecedent to the Gospel, is the form of our death, as the consequent of the Gospel is the form of our life, to be perfected and completed in the state of complete restitution, when Christ shall present His Church without spot to His Father, and shall then resign the mediatorial kingdom. This all deduces itself from the doctrine of the Trinity: the Father is not beloved nor obeyed without the Son; but the Son sends forth his Spirit, that we may be enabled to come and obey the Father. So that, unless the law be kept in our continual view, the Spirit hath no end nor operation. In the evening I lectured upon Luke vii. 29, 36, setting forth the three forms of the Pharisees: First,—The Pharisee of the intellect or reason (of whom Edinburgh is the chief city), who contemn faith and form equally. Second,—the Pharisee of form, who cannot away with spiritual regeneration. Third,—The Spiritual Pharisee, or religious world, who take up notions, and language, and preachers upon second hand from spiritual people, instead of waiting for them directly from the Spirit by the working of faith upon the divine Word. I pray the Lord to bless these discourses.

I have agreed with Collins about the publication of the *Original Standards of the Church*, concerning which I pray you to say nothing.[25] I shall write my essay on the

---

24. 'Mother in Israel' was the description of Deborah (Judg 5:7), who won renown as prophetess and judge. The phrase came to be used by Evangelicals of any women (particularly a minister's wife), whose pastoral wisdom, practical assistance, and spiritual advice were recognized by the congregation to which she belonged—hence Irving's application of the phrase to Isabella.

25. The collection of the Kirk's oldest doctrinal standards were to be published in 1831 (but not by Collins, with whom Irving would fall out), as *The Confessions of Faith and the Books of Discipline of the Church of Scotland, of date anterior to the Westminster Confession*: Grass, *The Lord's Watchman*, 229–30.

salt sea where Knox first matured his idea of the Scottish Reformation[26] ... My dear Isabella, guard against the formalities which abound on every side of you. Let me find you grounded and strengthened in the spirit of godliness. For the other book,[27] it is nearly finished. I have just brought to a close the destruction of Babylon. And I have a part to write upon the things which follow till the revelation of our blessed Redeemer in the clouds of heaven. Pray God that my pen may be guided to truth, and that much profit may flow into the Church from what I write! ... I pray the Lord to bless you and Edward continually; write me, when you can do it without wearying yourself or injuring your health ... Say to the patriarch that I have got a noble New Testament, in Greek, with all the Glosses and Scholiæ of the Fathers, with which I delight myself. The Lord bless you all! Forget not to give my kind regards to Mary, and to encourage her to walk steadfastly in the faith.

Yours in one body and soul,
Edward Irving.

~

Edward Irving to THE ELDERS OF THE CALEDONIAN CHURCH

Edinburgh, 3rd October 1825[28]

To the Elders of the Caledonian Church.

My Dear Brethren,

I have waited and delayed my communication with you in the expectation that I should have been able to convey to you information with respect to the family concern which chiefly drew me to Scotland. But though I was afraid I should not have been here in time to afford the consolation of my presence to my wife in her trial, it has happened otherwise, and to this hour[,] though every day looked for, it pleases God still to exercise us all with patience. And now as a fortnight only remains to me of the time which I had set to myself for this and other duties, I feel it my duty to delay no longer but to

---

26. John Knox (c1513–72) was educated at Haddington School, though it is thought his birthplace might have been Morham. He attended Glasgow University. In a deed of 27 March 1543 he is styling himself as 'John Knox minister of the sacred alter of the diocese of St. Andrews, notary by Apolstolic authority.' By 1546 he was preaching Protestant doctrines, and soon after in 1551 he was chaplain to Edward VI. He arrived in Geneva in 1554 and there fell under the influence of Calvin. He was pastor of the English congregation at Frankfurt am Min until 1555 and lived in Geneva from 1556-58. From there he wrote epistles to his brother clerics in England and Scotland persecuted under the Catholic rule of Mary Tudor in England, and the regency of Mary of Lorraine in Scotland. His circumstances in Geneva resulted in the publication of his *First Blast of the Trumpet against the Monstrous Regiment of Women* (1558). See *OCEL*.

27. *Babylon and Infidelity Foredoomed.*

28. EIL, MS 33.

write to you how I now stand conditioned in respect of time. The daily expectation in which my wife was kept of her confinement, and the strengthening which my presence gave to her, made me continue at Kirkcaldy to this day, except a rapid journey of three days which I made to my Brother's ordination at Bathgate[29] and to my sister who had been confined in Paisley,[30] so that I have not yet seen my dear old Father whose age and infirmities call much for my affectionate support; and there remaining but ten days until I must be upon my journey to London, I feel that I must either leave my wife to the discomposing of her spirits, or leave my Father unvisited which would be a sore trial to him and the rest of my dear friends dwelling in my native place. For if it should please God to be merciful to us in giving us a living child, it would not be proper that I should leave the country without having it admitted a member of the visible church,[31] or that I could with any comfort to my own mind withdraw from my wife till I saw her state of health for a day or two after her confinement. Yet if there was any imperious call of the church I would set all these personal and domestic feelings at naught, and haste to fulfill my vocation. But seeing that I have laboured diligently in word & doctrine, and here do labour in another way, by continual meditation and writing[,] for the behoof of the Christian Church, and for the behoof of our English churches particularly, I have thought it better to provide for the public service of the Sabbath following the next, as I scarcely forsee [sic] the possibility of my accomplishing the end of my journey within the time, seeing it has been ordered of God otherwise than I had expected. Now I dare say Dr Blyth[32] would, if not prevented by other duty[,] undertake for me, or perhaps Mr. Woodrow,[33] or Mr. Thompson with whom I sent my former letter to you. I would thank you to make the application to them, and if it can be brought about well, if not, the time of opening the church must stand over as a delay which could not be forseen [sic] nor provided against.

Yesterday (Sabbath) was the first day I have spent in Edinburgh and I now haste over again to Kirkcaldy. I am stopping with Dr Gordon whose opinion I took in this matter and he urges it upon me as a point of duty to make this provision for the Sabbath following the next whatever may happen. As I have now desired that you would do for me. On Saturday I saw Mr. Blyth's worthy father who with his family is well. I have not yet seen Miss Hope not having had time to be any-where in the anxiety and expectation in which we are. That we cast our cares upon him who cared for us. I pray

---

29. It was, in fact, Irving's brother-in-law, Samuel Martin. See letter EI to Mrs Martin, 28th September 1823.

30. Margaret.

31. I.e., through baptism

32. John Blythe (1767–1829), Minister at Woolwich from 1795 until his death. See Scott, *Fasti*, 7:501

33. Mentioned in Edward Irving's journal in an entry for Friday, 25 November (1825): 'Mr. Woodrow and I came away at eight o'clock, and I bore him company through Russell Square. I think he is likely to be elected* [*As minister of one of the Scotch churches in London] but it is by no means certain yet': Oliphant, *Life*, 1:359.

the Lord to bless you and your families and the flock over which the Holy Ghost hath made me overseer. I long to return to you all, and nothing would have delayed me beyond my [proper?] time but the things which I have stated above over which I had no control. I hope all the Brethren prosper, and continually pray unto the Lord on behalf of you all. The Lord be with you all.

From your Affectionate Pastor,
Edwd Irving

Addressed to: Wm Dinwiddie,
4 Grocer's Hall Court,
Poultry, London.

~

Edward Irving to WILLIAM DINWIDDIE

Kirkcaldy, 7th October 1825[34]

My Dear and Worthy friend,

When I was writing you and your Brethren of the Session on Monday last from Dr Gordon's house, my wife had been safely brought to bed of a little daughter the day preceding at 1/2 past 7 o'clock as I learned upon landing here on Monday afternoon. And for a living mother and a living child I desire to give thanks to God, and request all my friends to give thanks along with me. They both continue well by the great mercy of our God. But dear Edward continues still to be tried with the whooping cough, which these East winds have brought back upon him. In so much that we propose taking him to the milder air of Annan which I will do on Monday, the day after his little sister's baptism. I shall remain over the Sabbath with my dear Parents and Brothers families, and on Monday I propose at present setting out and taking Manchester and Birmingham on my way. I must for the present decline the Northern Presbyteries not being able to take up the three in one week. I mark what you say about Mr. Crosbie[35] and shall do my utmost to ascertain the wants of his people and prepare things for the Presbytery. In Manchester I shall see how things are, and if the Lord open a door I shall not be wanting to enter in.

It gives me much pain to be absent from my flock and ministerial duties, but as it could not be otherwise without either neglecting my duty to my wife or my parents I rest contented. I have been continually occupied since I left you in meditation and writing, or in discourse with the minister of the Gospel; and I am pleased to think that

---

34. EIL, MS 34.
35. See letter Edward Irving to Thomas Chalmers, 14 June 1822: NCL, CHA 4: fol. 21.3.

there is an outpouring of the Spirit upon our Church, and desire to be thankful for the remnant which is still left of the antient spirit in which she heretofore flourished. I desire my love to you and your family, and to all the Brethren of the Session and of the Church. I am very sorry to hear of poor Hall's affliction.[36] The Lord comfort and restore him. Say to Mr. Hamilton[37] that I shall write him perhaps from Annan when I shall be able to give you further account of all [letter torn] do. I thank the Lord that he doth not forsake my soul, however unworthy, but teacheth me in his statutes. So be it with you and with all his faithful servants. We were much refreshed by your two letters, and desire our warmest thanks. The Lord bless your grey hairs, and your undiminished activity in the service of his Church.

Your affectionate Pastor & Brother Elder,
Edwd Irving

Addressed to: Wm Dinwiddie,
4 Grocer's Hall Court,
Poultry, London.

~

Edward Irving to JANE WELSH

8th October 1825, Kirkcaldy[38]

My dear Jane,

... I thought by this time to have seen you in Dumfriesshire, where it was my purpose to have passed about a fortnight of my time, and I had schemed it to have ridden up Nithsdale with Thomas Carlyle, for I had many things to say both to you and him.

It relieved my mind greatly to hear of your kind visit to my Father's house;[39] for it made me hope you had relented of the hard things you had thought of me and the hard things you had said of me,[40] which I never resented, nor will ever resent, but with words of affection and much love. And if the Lord hear my prayer, the time is coming when communion shall be established between us through the bond of the spirit of

---

36. Hall was the husband of the housekeeper of Edward Irving's family. See Oliphant, *Life*, 1: 262.
37. See letter EI to the Elders of the Caledonian Chapel, 21 February 1822: EIL, MS 11.
38. Carlyle, *Love Letters* 2: 425–26.
39. 'During her visit at Hoddam Hall, Miss Welsh and Carlyle called on Irving's father at Annan': Carlyle, *Love Letters* 2:425 n.
40. 'The "hard things" thought and said of Irving by Miss Welsh were no doubt reported to him by Mrs Montagu, with whom Miss Welsh was corresponding, and in whose house Irving had been living while his wife was gone to Kirkcaldy with her invalid child': Carlyle, *Love Letters* 2:425 n.

Christ,—which may the Lord hasten in his good time. . . . The Lord bless you and all your friends, to whom I desire to be remembered with affection.

Your affectionate friend,
Edwd Irving

⁓

Edward Irving to WILLIAM HAMILTON

Kirkcaldy, 11th, 1825[41]

Our dearly-beloved Friend,

The hand of the Lord hath touched my wife and me, and taken from us our well-beloved child, sweet Edward, who was dear to you also, as he was to all who knew him. But before taking him, He gave unto us good comfort of the Holy Ghost, as He doth to all His faithful servants; and we are comforted, verily we are comforted. Let the Lord be praised, who hath visited the lowly, and raised them up!

If you had been here yesterday and this day when our little babe was taken, you would have seen the stroke of death subdued by faith, and the strength of the grave overcome; for the Lord hath made His grace to be known unto us in the inward part. I feel that the Lord hath well done in that He hath afflicted me, and that by His grace I shall be a more faithful minister unto you and unto all the flock committed to my charge. Now is my heart broken—now is it hardness melted; and my pride is humbled, and my strength is renewed. The good name of the Lord be praised!

Our dear little Edward, dear friend, is gone the way of all the earth; and his mother and I[42] are sustained by the Prince and Saviour who hath abolished death and brought life and immortality to light.[43] The affection which you bear to us, or did bear towards the dear child who is departed, we desire that you will not spend it in unavailing sorrow, but elevate it unto him who hath sustained our souls, even the Lord our Saviour Jesus Christ; and if you feel grief and trouble, oh, turn the edge of it against sin and Satan to destroy their works, for it is they who have made us to drink of this bitter cup.

Communicate this to all our friends in the congregation and church, as much as may be, by the perusal of this letter, that they may know the grace of God manifested unto us; and oh, William Hamilton, remember thyself, and tell them all that they are dust, and that their children are as the flowers of the field.

---

41. Oliphant, *Life*, 1:245–46.

42. Edward Irving (22 July 1824 to 11 October 1825). Mrs. Oliphant observed, 'So far as I can perceive, no other event of his life penetrated so profoundly the depths of his spirit.' See Oliphant, *Life*, 1:247–48.

43. 2 Tim 1:10.

Nevertheless, God granting me a safe journey, I will preach at the Caledonian church on Sabbath the 23rd, though I am cut off from my purpose of visiting the churches by the way. The Lord be with you, and your brethren of the eldership, and all the church and congregation.

Your affectionate friend,
Edward Irving
My wife joining with me

~

Edward Irving to MARGARET MARTIN

12th November 1825[44]

My dear Sister Margaret,

You have been very much in my mind since we parted with so many painful emotions, after a season of such sorrowful trial,[45] out of which I have ever sought the Lord that much profit might come to all whom it touched, and to those whom it wounded very sore, of which number you are one. And now on this day of the month when the dear spirit departed from the midst of us and at this hour, when we sat side by side endeavoring to stay its departure, I sit down to write unto you what is sweet and dear to my own soul, that you may be a partaker of my faith and joy.

There is no blessedness my dear sister in the natural man, however accomplished with all graces & endowed with all gifts and gratified in all its desires; nay the more it obtains of its own pleasure, the more it is separated from the communion which can bring to it peace. And the pursuit of our own will is therefore nothing so painful from the vexations & resistances which we encountered as for the possessions which we gain. The road is full of harassments and the place to which it brings us is full of misery. This I know by my own experience, having from my youth despised the world, but not despised myself; and I have tasted the bitterness of the draught from which I would warn my beloved sister, of having too much communion and fellowship with the natural forms of our own spirit. The fear of the Lord is the beginning of peace, and it is the beginning of wonder, whose ways are pleasantness & whose paths are peace.[46] Submit yourself unto the Lord, and do his will with an implicit obedience, which that you may be strengthened in, place your trust in the Lord Jesus and he will supply you with his Holy Spirit. Then every thing in you will be brought to act lovingly and willingly, and your progress in every grace and gift will be amazing even to yourself. And

---

44. NCL, Box 9.2.3.
45. Irving's first son Edward had died on 11 October 1825.
46. Prov 3:17.

remember, my dear, that as Christ's disciples we are bound to crucify ourselves, and cannot otherwise enter into a glorious resurrection. But you know as I also do, that this is not our work upon ourselves, but God's work in us, wherefore let us be in intent in prayer, full of prayer for one another. Oh! When shall I see my dear Margaret brought into the meekness and loveliness of temper which is proof to us of our holy profession. The Lord haste her deliverance from her enemies.

I am full of gratitude to you, my Dear Margaret, for all your loving-kindness to us and our little darling, and I have no other testimony of it to offer but this anxiety for your soul, which I shall not cast away, while I continue to be anxious for my own. With respect to the family at Annan, its chief recommendation is that they are orphans, and need all assistance. But I fear you would be much limited. There is a great-aunt a great economist and very managing lady and an aunt of whose good temper they do not speak very highly. And there is about the family a pride which has nothing much to build upon, so that they stand between the simplicity of native townspeople, and the second rate autocracy of the county without holding of either. And I fear the salary which they would be able to offer is not near what you would consider a fair remuneration, when I said £70 at the least, they seemed to think it being the most which they can give. But if the plan seems likely to afford you a sweet and agreeable occupation, and to bring you amongst pious and affectionate people, I would set less store by the matter of salary. But I think the best thing you could do, would be to pay a visit to my Father and Sister and pass the hard several months of the year away from these cold eastern winds. And then you would be able to judge for yourself; but I have written above the bad account I can give you of it. The children give the impression of having been spoiled. But the Great Aunt who is a good disciplinant of children would cure that.

James Parker is come, and seems to like his house well in very truth. Hall and his wife make all things very comfortable to us. And I trust that my present widowhood is not without its advantage to my soul. My mind would oft despond and be cast down, had I not a continual desire of commune with that spirit which is joy and peace, to which I invite you and all our dear Sisters and Brothers And I pray you not to take amiss what I have said in this letter but when you write to me, to discern your inward trials & struggles, that I may feel over you a Ministerial watchfulness as well as a Brotherly love. If this should reach you in Edinburgh, say to Andrew that I have already put things in a train, and shall write him when I know the result of our enquiries about the mercantile house. Also to your Uncle and Aunt offer my affectionate regards, and my sympathies with him in his present affliction, with my prayers that it may be blessed to the Salvation of his Soul. Be assured of my love and desire to profit you according to my ability.

Your affectionate Brother,

Edwd Irving

4 Claremont Sq. 12 Nov 1825.

Addressed to: Miss Margaret Martin, Manse of Kirkcaldy, N.B.

~

Edward Irving to REV JOHN MARTIN

[London], 21st January 1826[47]

My dear Father,

I have heard from Elizabeth of the loss[48] in which you have been involved by wicked and worldly men, which is nothing new in the history of God's faithful servants, and ought not to trouble you. He that hath the stars in his right hand may say to you, as to the angel of the Church of Philadelphia, 'I know thy poverty (but thou art rich).'[49] Remember we are but promised to lie by the altar, and the rest is so much burdensome stewardry, to which we submit in accommodation to the weakness of our people ... Therefore, be not cast down, nor let my dear mother be cast down. Though the worst should come to the worst, what mattereth it? The kingdom of Heaven is still ours, unto which all things shall be added. And unto the new Jerusalem, the city of our habitation, the kings do bring the riches of the earth.[50]

But we must provide things honest in the sight of all men,[51] that the name of Christ and his Gospel be not blasphemed, and that I may be partaker of your trial, and partaker also of your joy in rising above it, we, Isabella and I, must be allowed to contribute our part ... I shall now also see to a fourth edition of the *Orations*, the third having been nearly sold off some months ago ... Isabella and I feel much for you and our dear mother, but we are not amazed or confounded as if some strange thing had befallen you[52] ...

~

---

47. Oliphant, *Life*, 1:398–99.

48. Mrs. Oliphant writes: 'The minister of Kirkcaldy had been the unfortunate possessor of shares in the Fife Bank—a local joint-stock banking company—which had fallen into sudden ruin by the misconduct of some of its managers; such an occurrence as unhappily has been familiar enough to us all in more recent days': Oliphant, *Life*, 1:398.

49. Rev 2:9.

50. Rev 21:24.

51. Rom 12:17.

52. 1 Pet 4:12.

Part II: The Letters

Edward Irving to WILLIAM HAMILTON

Annotated: 1830[53] [1826][54]

My Dear Brother,

Upon conversing with my wife, I find that it was the notice about the insurance of the furniture she referred to. The other notice she never remembers to have received, and I am sure if I were before a magistrate I would swear I never received it. Nor do I think it ever reached this house. I perceive this present notification is Addressed to: 4 Claremont Square; perhaps the other being so addressed may have lost its way. Certain it is we have never received it and I think it is hard to be called to pay a fine without having had the notice.

I would thank you to signify this to the conductor of the Institute.

Yours faithfully,

Edwd Irving

Addressed to: Wm Hamilton Esq.,
137 Cheapside.

~

Edward Irving to HENRY DRUMMOND

London, 4th September 1826[55]

My Dear Sir,

I think very highly of this proposal,[56] and pray for its success. But the time you have fixed is too early for gathering the sense of those who might wish to take a share in it. I should propose the first week of Advent. It were a fit way of spending the festival of Xmas. Besides[,] so many are out of town in Sept to whom it would be inconvenient to return and separate themselves from their families. I hear that Dr Gordon of Edinburgh is beginning to preach upon the great subject so dear to us all. I believe the Lord's hand to be in the vocation of such men. They are his servants sent forth the second and last time to tell the bidden of the visible Church that the Supper is ready.

---

53. Irving notes in his letter that it had been addressed to: 4 Claremont Square, which was the new name for Myddleton Terrace. The place name had been changed in 1825/6, and in 1830 the family were living in Judd Street. Clearly the date of this letter is c.1826

54. ML, MSS O71a, b, c.

55. NLS, MS 1810, fol. 93.

56. Members of the newly formed Society for the Investigation of Prophecy had decided that a residential conference would enable them to get away from the distractions of London and Drummond had offered to host it at Albury Park

I mentioned this to Mr. Strutt[57] and he agreed with me as to the fitness of the time. Farewell—The Lord preserve us against the day of his coming

Your affectionate friend,
Edwd Irving

Addressed to: Henry Drummond Esq.,
Banker,
Charing Cross,
London.

~

Edward Irving to THE HON. J. J. STRUTT

Caledonian Church, London 12th Sept 1826[58]

My dear Brother in the Lord,

I send you herewith the first part of a work which I am translating out of the Spanish that I may make it accessible to the Church of Christ in these lands.[59]

It was published some twelve years ago in Spain being written by a Jesuit of the name of Lacunza and is a work well worthy of your most careful study. I shall continue to send it you until it is completed, unless you should signify to the contrary. And if it should seem good to you to help me in this labour of love by sending me any remarks which might make it more profitable to the body of Christ I shall take them into consideration & if they seem appropriate insert them amongst the Notes; since my only object is that it may build up the true Church of Christ of all Communions & warn the World to flee from the wrath to come.

The work is now printing at the Expense of a pious Lady after reimbursing whom the profits of this Edition at least are to go to the Spanish Emigrants.

Farewell! God grant unto them to increase and abound in the riches of the knowledge of our Lord & Saviour Jesus Christ. Amen.

Your dear Brother in the faith of the Gospels.
Edwd Irving.

Written by the hand of my wife in my entire occupation with the work itself.

A token of my love to you, and a help to your diligent studies of the Kingdom to come.[60]

---

57. The Hon. John James Strutt (1796–1873), Anglican, later Member of Parliament, subsequently Lord Rayleigh in 1836. Shown as attending the first Albury Conference.

58. Strutt, MS 3a and 3b.

59. Lacunza y Diaz, *The Coming of Messiah*.

60. The token was presumably the book itself.

Part II: The Letters

Addressed to: The Honbl J. J. Strutt, Care of Rt H Pelham Esq, Witham.

∽

Edward Irving to DR THOMAS CHALMERS

Caledonian Church London.
12th September 1826[61]

My dear Brother in the Lord,

I send you herewith the first part of a book I am translating from the Spanish that it may be accessible to the Church in this land. It was written by a learned Jesuit (by birth a Jew) named Lacunza & published in Spain about twelve years ago & is well worthy of your most careful study. I shall continue to send it to you until it is finished unless you signify to the contrary. If it should seem good to you to assist in this labour of love by sending me any remarks that may make it more profitable to the body of Christians—if they seem appropriate, I will insert them among the Notes,[62] my desire being that it may bind up the true Church of Christ of all communicants & warn the Brethren from the wrath to come.

The work (of two vols 8vo[63]) is now printing at the expense of a pious lady. After reimbursing her the profits of this Edition, at least, are to go to the Spanish Emigrants.

Save this will God grant unto them to increase & abound in the riches of the knowledge of our Lord and Saviour Jesus Christ. Amen. I am your affectionate Brother in the Church of the Gospel.

Edwd Irving

Written by my wife's hand in my extreme occupation with the work itself.

Remember, my honoured friend, the Kingdom of this world and all their speculations 'let the dead bury the dead!' and give yourself to the speculation, the faith and the illustration of the Kingdom to come. E.

Editor's Epilogue

The correspondence available for 1826 is sparse. It was in this year that he attended the first of Henry Drummond's Albury Conferences, and translated a book written by a Chilean Jesuit, Manuel Lacunza *The Coming of Christ in Glory and Majesty*, learning

---

61. NCL, MS CHA 4 57.29.

62. Chalmers did not supply notes but Coleridge did.

63. 8vo: the size of a book whose pages are made by folding a sheet of paper three times to form eight leaves—eightvo, octavo.

Spanish for that purpose. By now he is embarking on his mission of proclaiming the Second Advent.

The following year 1827 was to see the triumphant opening of the National Scotch Church at Regent Square. It was also confirm his belief and commitment to announcing the Second Coming of Christ.

5

Letters: 1827–1828

Editor's Introduction

The National Scotch Church, Regent Square, its twin towers resembling those of York Minster was triumphantly opened on 11th May 1827 with a ceremony attended by the nobility and gentry, and an inaugural sermon given by Dr Chalmers. However, although no longer drawing attendances of 1400, there was still a respectable congregation of 1000 or so. The novelty, which had attracted the *bon ton* to Cross Street, had worn off quite quickly and the fashionable society had passed on to other amusements.

Edward Irving was still in touch with his great friend Thomas Carlyle who clearly valued his friend's help and advice on his future. During Edward's yearly August holiday, he writes to Carlyle from his brother-in-law William Hamilton's house in Norwood, giving support to his project to secure a professorial chair at the new London University.

However, the first signs of the storm that was to eventually engulf Irving had were already becoming apparent. In July 1827 he preached in London at the anniversary meeting of the Gospel Tract Society, in which he made reference to the Incarnation, stating that when the Word became man, He 'took upon himself a body like ours.' He also alluded to the coming of the Son 'under accursed conditions.'[1] A Church of England clergyman, the Rev Mr Cole of Clare College, Cambridge, was so incensed by hearing this perceived heresy in a sermon at Regent Square that October, that he published a pamphlet criticizing this view. The publication aroused suspicion as to Irving's orthodoxy, and the controversy grew.

As at the time of little Edward's birth, in May 1828 the family journeyed to Kirkcaldy for Isabella's fourth confinement, and the birth of another short-lived child, Samuel. Edward Irving while there embarked on a successful twelve day tour, preaching on the Book of Revelation. But there was an undercurrent of public disapproval

---

1. Reported in *The Pulpit*, 2 August 1827, 417–25, 432.

of his Christology. The church in Kirckcaldy was packed with people to hear Irving speak, when the balcony collapsed, killing over thirty and injuring a hundred of the congregation, and some blamed Irving. They saw the accident as a sign of God's displeasure at his mistaken theology.

Edward Irving to THOMAS CHALMERS

4 Claremont Square, 3rd January 1827[2]

My beloved friend and Brother in Christ,

The Revd. J Wolff[3] is desirous to have an introduction to you & I am also desirous of commending him to my brethren in Scotland that they may assist him & strengthen him by their counsels & above all by their prayers. He has been hitherto enabled to stand against numberless trials & difficulties & now that man shews him favour & honour may he by the grace of God be enabled to maintain his profession. I had faith unto the end but you well know that it requires more grace to resist the world than to die a Martyr at the stake.

I trust you will persevere in your study of the prophecies. In so doing you will have a rich reward & your letter was to my spirit a great refreshment indeed—like the dew on the thirsty ground for my Soul does hunger & thirst after my native land & I mourn over the Church in it as a Son mourneth for a beloved Mother & I hail the first dawning of light in your mind as a token of good not to your own Soul only but to the Church of which we are the members & Oh my friend hide no talent under a bushel bring them all into the Lord's house & sanctify them to his use.

That every day & every year may find you & your dear Wife & family increased & blessed in knowledge & love of God is the sincere prayer of my wife & of your affectionate Brother in the Lord.

Edw[d] Irving

[This letter was dictated by Edward Irving to his wife and only signed by him.]

---

2. NCL, MSS CHA 4 77.6.
3. Joseph Wolff (1795–1862) was a Jewish convert, linguist, and missionary.

Part II: The Letters

Edward Irving to AN UNKNOWN RECIPIENT

February, 1827

For myself, I feel the burden of sin so heavily, and the unprofitableness of this vexed life, that I long to be delivered from it, and would gladly depart when the Lord may please; yet, while He pleaseth, I am glad to remain for His Church's sake. What I feel for myself, I feel for my dear wife, whom I love as myself. And at present my rejoicing is, that she is able to praise Him in the furnace of trial and the fire of affliction.[4]

∽

The Session and Edward Irving to THE REV THOMAS CHALMERS [written by Isabella Irving]

London, 26th February 1827[5]

Reverend & Dear Sir,

It has long been a subject of deep regret among the friends of the Scottish Church in London that amid the many noble edifices which have been erected in this metropolis for the service of God there should not have been one in any degree worthy of our Nation or of our venerable Mother Church. The Congregation of the Caledonian Church feeling this stain upon their piety & patriotism, and experiencing great inconvenience from the want of a suitable place of worship proceeded to take measures for erecting a building which might do honour to our Mother Church, and at the same time be the means by the blessing of God of contributing to the spiritual welfare of many of our Countrymen who come to reside here. Every Scotsman whose mind is impressed with a just sense of Divine truth has deplored that so many of his Countrymen on arriving here cease to reverence the ordinances of God and become a prey to the innumerable temptations which surround them on every side.—There exists also among our countrymen in the City an unfortunate feeling towards the Scottish Presbytery as if they were not a true representation of the Church of Scotland.—This has arisen in a great degree from the lax discipline and easy accommodation to the forms of the Dissenters, and interchange of pulpits which existed formerly amongst the ministers of the Presbytery and which has been not a little promoted and kept alive by the frequent Custom of the Brethren from Scotland preaching indiscriminately, and even more frequently for the dissenters than for the Presbytery.[6] This we propose to remedy by all the means in our power, and of these one which has seemed to us most

---

4. Irving's first son, Edward, born on 22 July 1826, had died in October 1826.
5. NCL, MSS CHA 4 77.12.
6. On the uncertain legal status of the Presbytery of London, see Cameron, *Scots Kirk*, and Appendix D.

reasonable to begin with is to have our new Church opened by a Scottish Clergyman of good report & approved by God in the ministry of his Word, and thus our first application is made to you because we know not any other who stands so high in the estimation of the Church of Christ in these or in any other parts. You cannot conceive the indifference of a large proportion of our Nobility and Gentlemen here resident to religion in every form. It is indeed a thing to be deplored for Scotland's Sake that the Patrons of her Churches should be so indifferent to her religious Ordinances.—We would not become sanguine but it is not too much to hope that your assistance in the opening of the Church with Dr Gordon preaching during the month of May and the continual labours of our beloved Pastor might under God be instrumental in turning this evil tide which is against the work of the Lord. You have laboured much & honourably in behalf of Missionary Societies and preached & travelled for their sake but there is no mission which seems to us so imperative in its calls as that of 120,000 Scotchmen or their descendants here in London of whom not 1,200 that is not one in a hundred are found in communion with all the churches. It is not one sheep that is astray & out of the fold[7] but ninety & nine that are astray and only one in the fold. It is ours to lay open to you the exact & true state of the case & the urgency of the call—to a minister & servant of God for whom we have such honour & esteem it were unbecoming to say more.—You are a better judge of it than we are and you only know the other Calls of duty which may be present to you; therefore we conclude with simply declaring our great affection for your person, and thankfulness to God for the gift of you unto the Church of Scotland, whereof we are members.

We expect the Church will be ready for opening by the middle of April about which time we trust you will be able conveniently to leave home. But should that period be too early we shall, notwithstanding our anxiety to open the church, be most happy to delay it for a week or two or even longer, if we can only thereby obtain your much desired & valuable assistance.

        With much affection and esteem,
        We remain,
        Reverend and Dear Sir,
        Your Brethren in Christ,
        Edw[d] Irving Mod of Session.

        Wm Dinwiddie
        Archd Horn
        Dav Blyth
        Wm Hamilton
        J A Nisbet
        Andw Panton
        Duncan Mackenzie

---

7. Cf. Luke 15:4.

My Dear Sir,[8]

I know not that I can add anything to this excellent letter of my Session: there are many reasons of a more private kind for which I could desire to see you and converse with you at length. I have many views and convictions to impart concerning the present aspect of things both political and religious. If the Lord will, it will come pass; if not I must continue to communicate with you in prayer as heretofore. My wife has brought me another daughter[9] and is doing well. My love to your wife and children. The Lord bless and long preserve you, my dear & worthy friend.

Yours affectionately,
Edwd Irving

Addressed to: Revd. Dr. Chalmers,
St Andrew's,
N.B.

Edward Irving and William Hamilton to THOMAS CHALMERS

London, 8th March 1827[10]

Rev & Dear Sir,

The Session of the Caledonian Church have instructed us to express their deep sense of the kindness which you have shewn in giving so favourable an ear to their

---

8. In Irving's hand.
9. Mary, born 23 February 1827, died 14 December 1827.
10. NCL, MSS CHA 4.77.14.

request: and they have further instructed us to lay before you the exact account of our circumstances with respect to time.

We must leave this present Church on the 30th of April, when possession is to be given to the purchaser or renter of the premises: and therefore the last Sabbath of April or the first Sabbath of May, would be to us the best time for opening the Church; or rather we should say of preaching in it on the Sabbath; for it is our purpose that it should be opened on a week-day, which will serve many purposes of advantage that we need not enter into. If the Friday before the last Sabbath of April or the Friday before the first Sabbath of May would answer you to open it with one Service; and to preach the Sabbath following, all our desire would be accomplished; and there would remain for us nothing but the greatest thankfulness to God and to you his servant for having honoured and helped us so abundantly. This would afford you plenty of time to be at the General Assembly even after spending a week or fortnight in London if your affairs should require you; for our part we have nothing further to ask, and would do our endeavour as men most true to hasten your return or to welcome your stay amongst us, as might seem to you best.

We are,
Revd. & Dear Sir,
Your Faithful friends,
Edwd Irving
Wm Hamilton

London, 8th March 1827

Edward Irving to THOMAS CHALMERS

4 Claremont Sq., Pentonville. 26th March 1827[11]

Revd. and Dear Sir,

It is impossible for me to express the sense which the Session in common with myself entertain of your kind attention to our request, for which we trust the Lord will make a way, if so it seemeth to Him good. The Committee who administer the affairs of the New Church and the whole Session, find that it is impossible without great loss to postpone the opening of the church beyond Friday the 13th [11th] May. Into the particulars of this I am not able to enter, but it is some way connected with the time of letting the seats, and would occasion the loss of a quarters rent which would be several hundred pounds. And this is more than they can bear with the great expense they have

---

11. NCL, MSS CHA 4:77.7.

been at, and [the] engagements they are under. If the Lord should clear the way for your coming, we will, therefore, look for your help on that day. There will be only one service in the forenoon, after which the committee and Session propose entertaining the higher classes of our countrymen here, and endeavouring, by the blessing of God, to endeavour if possible to rally the feeling of Scotchmen around the church. Your presence, and the presence of Dr Gordon who is then to be in town[,] and the presence of the Presbytery will[,] it is concluded[,] give a religious and certainly an Ecclesiastical tone to the meeting. On Sabbath the 15th [13th] you will be relieved of half the duty by Dr Gordon if you so wish, for by an extraordinary combination of Providence he has engaged long ago to preach for us on that day. If it should so come to pass in the good pleasure of the Lord, I should look on in silent wonder to behold his goodness to me, and his honour to the work we are engaged in, that after five years of perilous and laborious service (yet after all a most unprofitable service) he should so signally acknowledge me in the sight of the Church, as that two of her most famous and honoured servants should open the house in which I am to minister the Gospel; and which I may say was undertaken and through long difficulties hath been completed with a view to my ministry in the first instance. If you see it good to receive Dr Gordon's help for the afternoon service on the Sabbath, the Session would be most happy that on the Wednesday night when we have public worship you should preach to us a Sermon for our Spiritual edification, when we can assemble without any of the extraordinary excitement of the first Sabbath. And this is all which I have to request; I feel it to be a very great deal: but if you knew the moment at which it is made, and the ends under God's blessing which it is likely to serve to his Church and to the Scottish people in particular, and to my ministry which the guiles of Satan cannot prevail against though he assaileth it in every possible way;[12] you would see reason for a far greater anxiety for the success of this request, than I have expressed to you, or than I have permitted myself to feel. In I remember the word of the Apostle 'be careful for nothing'[13] and of our Lord. 'Take no thought for the morrow.'[14] My Dear Brother if you knew as I do, the endeavours systematically made here against the Gospel of our dear Lord, the traducing and dishonouring of his name in one place, and of his Church in another; if you knew, moreover, the sapping and mining liberality amongst the dissenters, and the timorous expediency amongst the Evangelical body, and the legality of the High Church as I do; and if you felt convinced as I am of the issues which are overhanging men and kingdoms, and the near coming of the Lord to a house in such wild disorder & confusion, you would indeed pity the burden with which my Spirit is oppressed daily, and gladly help me: and the help which two such sound-minded men as you & Dr Gordon would bring to that Gospel of the Kingdom which I preach, and which even now is beginning to break, and force the barriers of the public mind, is not to

12. Matt 16:18.
13. Phil 4:6.
14. Matt 6:34.

be reckoned upon. It is not by concurrence of opinion that I mean, for you have not had time nor opportunity to study these things as I have; but it is by the esteem of my character & the testimony to my uprightness and worthiness and to the respect in which I am held by the most notable and worthy ministers of the Church of Scotland. My greatest enemies have been the dissenters whose only principle of communion I can see is the demolition of all Established Churches. I have found the Evangelical people but a broken reed 'Ichabod! Dear Brother, Ichabod!'[15] the glory of the reformed churches are gone.[16] The revival of the last 50 years is the dying out of the Spirit, his last effort to enliven the rotten and corrupt Gentility which is soon to end. But more of this when we meet. I say it now, however, to assure you that, let the Dissenters speak to you as they please & entreat you as they please[,] with one or two exceptions there is only a most inveterate & deadly hatred to all Established Churches. They are being to the established churches what the radicals are to the established government. And if you were to give the weight of your character and preaching, while in London[,] to the Scottish Presbytery[,] as I believe Dr Gordon is resolved to do, you would violate the Brotherly Covenant to none, and keep it with those who both do love & honour you as a Father in the Church. These things which I wish, I wish in the spirit of truth and also of love to the Catholic Church of Christ and the Communion of Saints. But rejoice with me in this, that since the days of the Reformation, there never perhaps was a man more blessed in the fruitfulness of his Ministry, or in the Godly communion of his flock, than I have been: because I have not been ashamed of the testimony of the Lord.

I have forgot to invite you to my own house, where Dr Gordon will also reside. We can make you as private as you please. And we will make you welcome and most dear. My wife is well recovered and I have now two daughters, praised be the Lord. I forget again what I have been told to remember a hundred times, that all your expenses will be gladly borne. My love to Mrs. Chalmers and all the Children.

Your affectionate and dutiful friend,
Edwd Irving

Addressed to: Revd. Dr Chalmers,
Professor of Moral Philosophy in the University of St. Andrews.

---

15. 'The glory has departed.' Cf. 1 Sam 4:21–22.
16 [typesetter: there is a line break here that I cannot remove]

Part II: The Letters

Edward Irving to THOMAS CHALMERS

4 Claremont Square, 27th April 1827[17]

My Dear & Honoured Friend,

I write this letter not to trouble you, but to fulfill two requests made to me by two of my dear brethren of the Presbytery; the former[,] Mr. Crosbie[,][18] an alumnus of your university and a most faithful and able minister of the Gospel, that on any of the days when you are in London disengaged, you would preach for him, or in the Sabbath afternoon or evening. He has been a most labourious and disinterested minister, and by his services has formed a church and congregation: he has also I may say by his unwearied diligence got a Church built in which he has contributed himself with the utmost liberality, stinting himself of everything but daily bread (this in confidence) in order that he may present unto his countrymen a church disencumbered of all debts. No man can possibly be more honourable to prefer, nor more easy to advocate, but my time, and the ear to which I speak render it unnecessary. The second in order is from our friend Mr. Woodrow your agent, whose case has its claim upon support not so much in that way, as in another; he has been most unworthily persecuted by a discontented member of the Congregation, who was disatisfied [sic] with the proceedings of the Elders, and being radically inclined and well backed out by a radical news-paper Editor over a Scottish School master and worthy friend of mine, has vexed them with a law-suit in Chancery, so that poor Woodrow[19] needs heartening. You can consider these two petitions, and do what you can to answer them. It goes rife here that you are to be Professor of Moral Philosophy in the new University, I can give you much insight into that University, having been one of the original conferents thereupon, but soon a solitary seceder. Isabella requests you to bring your sheets of Lacunza with you, that the set may be made up, and her Fathers which you will get at your Brothers in Kirkcaldy, and like Dr Gordon to do also. Farewell. The Lord bless you your wife and gentle daughters.

Your affectionate friend,
Edw[d] Irving

The whole world is alive to hear you. You will have a braw opportunity of teaching any lesson, or subverting any errors. The Lord be your strength.

---

17. NCL, CHA 4 77.9.

18. See letter Edward Irving to the Elders of the Caledonian Church, 14 June 1822: EIL, MSS 21.

19. It was alleged that Woodrow's election as minister of Swallow Street was irregular, but the ensuing legal case ended with it being confirmed: Cameron, *Scots Kirk*, 44–45.

Edward Irving to THOMAS CARLYLE

31st May 1827[20]

My Dear Carlyle,

Mrs. Montague's[21] frank gives me the opportunity and awakens in me the duty of writing to you in a few lines, that I retain towards you and your excellent wife, the same sentiments of esteem for the integrity & simplicity of your character, and admiration of your great gifts, which I always entertained. As my faith deepens, I grow perhaps what some would think more bigotted [sic], but assuredly not less affectionate towards those who have reverence for what I believe, for the great name and power of my God, though they have not yet attained to the same light of knowledge & conviction of faith.

I was very much gratified by your remembrance of me in sending me those volumes of romances which I have read, all but the fourth. If I mistake not I discern a theme in one or two of them[,] another land as dear to my memory as that of 'my old friend Thomas Carlyle.' The translation is infinitely felicitous—I know of no other way to express my judgment of it. Your biographies and strictures evidence a pliableness of thought which passes my comprehension. But that is a small though very rare endowment, compared with the much wisdom which you have thrown out and scattered about.

But my friend why do you not gather up these fragments of wisdom and construct some standing pile. These seeds of thought need only the brooding of meditation and the Spirit of God to bring out the most noble plants and plentiful fruits. I pray God to grant you leisure and composure of soul to occupy the ten talents which you have. Oh! What you know. And what it is given you to feel. Steer clear of solitariness, my Dear Friend, I mean of mind and spirit. Cultivate the Catholic, and by prayer and grace the Lord may bring you through your sad and sore trials to minister unto his own glory. I have translated a book out of the Spanish, I send it to you and to my dear friend your wife. She shall not cast me off and I know you will not. The book is theological but it is the finest specimen of Logic you ever read. And it restores that side of Christianity which has been hidden from this age, and hitherto by being hidden from it the age has drifted into infidelity. Dear Thomas! I desire nothing more than to see you and your

---

20. NLS, MSS 3823, fol. 226.

21. Anna Dorothea Benson Montague, named by Edward Irving as 'the Noble Lady' and the Mrs. Basil Montague of 25 Bedford Square. She had been a friend of Irving's since 1823, and had been introduced to Thomas Carlyle, and also corresponded with Jane Welsh. She was also acquainted with Coleridge and Wordsworth. It was she who in a letter to Jane Welsh on 20th July 1825, before her marriage to Thomas Carlyle, warned her that 'There must be no Bluebeard's closet in which the skeleton may one day be discovered.' Four days later Jane wrote to Carlyle confessing that she had 'loved him [Edward Irving]—must I say it—*once* passionately loved him': CL, 3:356-57. She goes on to say that she had persuaded Irving to marry Isabella Martin to whom he was engaged, and save him from scandal.

Carlyle observes that Irving 'Spoke much about Mrs. Basil Montague, elderly, sage, lofty, yet humane, whom we got to know afterwards': *Reminiscences*, 276. And he also observed in a letter that 'She loves and admires the orator (their name for Edward Irving) beyond all others': Thomas Carlyle to Jane Welsh, 23 June 1824: CL, 3:84.

wife happy. Believe this I am whatever you know me. I hope not worse sometimes I think better by the Lord's grace.

Farewell My Dear Friend,
The Lord be with you for ever.
Edwd Irving
31st May 1827
I send the book to your bookseller by the first parcel.

~

Edward Irving to JOHN MARTIN

8th June, 1827[22]

My dear Father,

We have all great reason of thankfulness to the Giver of all gifts, and the Fountain of all strength, for the recovery of Isabella and the children, whose health is now so far re-established, as that Dr. Darling recommends her going to the country in a few days. I am now fairly entered upon my duties in the new church, and, by the grace of God, have begun with a more severe self-devotion to secret study and meditation. In the morning I propose to expound the whole Epistle to the Ephesians, in order to clear out anew some of the wells of salvation which have been choked up, at least in these parts, and to see if there be not even deeper springs than the Reformers reached. In the evening I am to discourse upon the sixth vial,[23] which I propose as a sequel to my discourses upon *Babylon and Infidelity Foredoomed*, and which I intend to print in the fall of the year. I thank that, by God's blessing, I can throw a new and steady light upon the present face of Christendom and the world. Besides this, I have a little tribute of friendship to pay to Basil Montague . . . and an aphoristic history of the Church of Scotland, from the primitive times to this time, for an introduction to a work containing the republication of our authorised books at the Reformation.[24] It is for man to design but God to permit and to enable; yet, if He spare me, I hope to do His Church some service. I ask your prayers, and entreat solicitously for them; although I know that we must have the spirit of prayer in ourselves and for ourselves. Farewell; may the Lord make the going down of your age more brilliant than the beginning of it, and enrich you all with His divine grace, and enlighten you with His countenances. Amen.

Your affectionate son,
Edward Irving

22. Oliphant, *Life*, 1:415–16.

23. Rev 16:12–16; for three sermons on this passage, see Irving, *Sermons*, 3:847–92, 964–1024, 1094–1198.

24. Irving's *Historical View of the Church of Scotland* was prefixed to his *Confessions of Faith*, and reprinted in *CW*, 1:543–96.

Edward Irving to THOMAS CARLYLE

Norwood,[25] Surrey.
27th August 1827 Monday[26]

My Dear Friend,
It delights me now, as it hath ever done[,] to be deemed worthy of being consulted by you and if I can any way guide or help you towards a good issue of your present projection I shall be very glad indeed. Your idea of the University is exactly my own: and I had good opportunities of judging, being, as it was so ordered, brought into the confidence of the whole scheme from the very first both on the side of the religious & the political people; until I left them under a solemn protest against the unholy and unwise precipitancy with which they were casting and the most momentous considerations. And since that time I have refused to make or to meddle in the matter though oft invited. Nevertheless I am not averse but rather favourable to your purpose, or rather projection, of presenting yourself for some one of the chairs: First, because, I am afraid that you will not suffer yourself to be carried by the stream-tide of infidelity, which you have already suffered too much from, and are now seeking means of resisting in yourself and in others: therefore I do not fear the temptation to you as my very dear friend in whose present and eternal welfare I do feel a tender interest. Secondly, because I am afraid that on the other hand you will both in your private carriage & conversation, but especially in your public offices, resist the evil-tendency of the times to the merely useful and profitable view of every thing: and become a helper in your plan to the few enlightened men who understand the grounds of human wellbeing and are seeking to make them good against an Evil. Thirdly, because I believe you to be an honest and true-hearted man, and daily inheriting more and more of your Father and Mother's prayers; and such are wanted sadly in this outward and hypocritical age; and in that infidel university.

I make no mention of private considerations, which are very strong: for I can never forget, neither my wife (for we oft speak together of) the sweet and high discourse which we were wont to hold together: and which I would gladly renew, if God in his Providence should see it good. And I would like to have you and your wife sitting under my ministry, that I might continually pray for you both, and open to you whatever the Lord is pleased to give me for the edification & enlargement of his Church.

---

25. Where William Hamilton had a house. 'The following week we are to be at Norwood at Mr. Hamilton's a most elegant minded man': Isabella Irving to her mother, 26 March 1824. Letter from a private source.

26. NLS, MSS 665, fol. 40–41.

Part II: The Letters

When I first knew them, it used to be a dream of mine, that I would like to preach to her Father and Mother and be helpful to their faith and consolation. Perhaps the Lord may fulfil this to their daughter.

You mention two classes, the one symbolising with Morals, the other with Taste, for I know not the nomenclature of the Lord Ruler of Glasgow College & Chief Editor of Colburn's magazine.[27] Let me tell you a word in confidence, but of which be altogether assured though you speak of it no further than the ear of your wife; that Dr Chalmers has been solicited on all hands to undertake the former, and, I have little doubt, is not disinclined to accept it, if he should not in the meantime be called to Edinburgh or some more congenial sphere than he occupies at present. Now observe he would be the scape-goat both of the Infidel politicians, and the compromising dissenters, who would immediately chain themselves upon his head. And be assured beyond all doubt that no living man but Dugald Stewart who is all but dead, would stand the competition with him[,] standing as the above parties do in rather a bad odour with the solid-minded people of England. You ought, therefore, not to hesitate a moment in giving the preference to the latter subject which though not so dignified in itself, would in your hands stand forth most sufficiently and to which your mind draws you more, and for which you are completely ripe[,] which you are not for the other. Pardon my liberty; I speak to my friend.

Now if you take this direction, which believe me is the only hopeful one[,] I will be serviceable to you to the utmost that one honest and honourable man can be to another, it matters not how closely they be united together, friend or brother. I will give you my own testimonials if you value it aught; and if you come up to solicit your own cause; you shall have my help wherever it can be of service to you; and I think you have other friends who can help you here, Basil Montague for one and Willie Hamilton for another, whose interest reach two different classes of the council. Write me, what your purpose is, when you have resolved, and I will answer you promptly. Your letter would have been answered in course of post, but that I was very sick the beginning of last week, and had to begin on Friday in my week's preparation with a sore pained & weakened body.

The Lord blesses us exceedingly, praised be his name! because we endeavour to serve him faithfully. My faith strengthens, and my knowledge increases and my peace grows, blessed be the Lord! My wife and children are in the way of being restored to health and my church and congregation are full of thanksgivings unto the Lord. I fear not my enemies, [letter torn] that the favour of the Lord is with us, and that his strength is on our side. And so, my [letter torn] friends, be assured the Lord will bless you in like manner, after he has tried you for a while. Love one another with pure hearts fervently: and let the love of Lord Jesus into his Church, and the love of his Church under him be your example: for that is the mystery of wedded love.

27. Henry Colburn, (d.1855), a very successful publisher who founded the *New Monthly Magazine* in 1814 and the *Literary Gazette* in 1817. See *OCEL*.

You will find the book directed to you and sent by Bridges Esq. N.S, Great King St, Elder of the West-Kirk. He was to have sent it down to you. There is one there for my Father[:] would you send it down by the Carrier, and there is along with it a parcel of the preliminary discourse to be also sent amongst my kindred: and Addressed to: them with my own hand.[28] I am sorry you should have this trouble; but I never had time to visit to George. I have not seen Mrs. Strachey for a long time, nor heard of the Bullers. Present my most respectful compliments to your wife, and upon whom and upon yourself I pray God to shower his blessings & to make you exceeding fruitful—also good.

Farewell,
Your affectionate friend of a long time,
Edwd Irving

Addressed to: Mr. Thomas Carlyle, Esq.,
21 Comely Bank Row,
Edinburgh.

~

Edward Irving to THOMAS CARLYLE

Norwood, Surrey, 6 Brown's Buildings.[29]
21st September 1827

My Dear Carlyle,

After a good deal of time consumed in the enquiry pursued under the disadvantage of my residing 7 miles out of town, I have ascertained that Mr. Brougham is not in town nor likely to be here till about the beginning of Novbr so that it would be an unnecessary and I fear a fruitless thing for you to come up to town now all-empty as it is. I have not positively ascertained that Mr. Brougham is at Brougham Hall (by Penrith) but almost positively so; nor how long he is to be there, for then we gain no account of their days here during the vacation season: being seldom or never enquired after. Only the circuit is concluded some weeks ago & I think it exceedingly probable he will rest at Brougham Hall. His wife indeed is at Ramsgate I have discovered, but the great men are not so attracted to the orbit of their wives, as plain men like you and me, nor have they such good reason to be so.

For the rest, I am clearly and decidedly of opinion that if you find the Moral Philosophy chair free from Dr Chalmers pursuit, you should never hesitate for any

---

28. Irving's *Preliminary Discourse to the Work of Ben Ezra*, newly published. See Lacunza y Diaz, *The Coming of the Messiah in Glory and Majesty*.

29. NLS, MSS 1765: fol. 75–76.

other man in Great Britain. And I know you too well to think that the interests and principles of true morality would suffer in your hands: for the blood of your honest Father is too true in you to be corrupted though it may sometimes be a little troubled by these assertions of men who club themselves into Schools because without many they cannot make one man complete. If you give me permission I shall both write to Dr Chalmers to ascertain the best of his inclination and if I can to interest him for you.

You should proceed thus; make Mr. Jeffrey[30] the confidant of all your measures, obtain from him an introduction to Brougham, find out from him of enquiries made in the county how long B is to be at B Hall: and certainly wait upon him yourself. I fear my name would be against you at the first, but in the end after you had made good your being no biggot [sic] it might perhaps weigh with the politician; for Dear Carlyle, believe me you will find him no more. If I hear of B coming to town I will inform you, and then come and welcome as usual to the share of all I have. But no time is to be lost. Write me by return of post, that I may take the measures you judge best with respect to Dr Chalmers. Farewell. The Lord bless you and your wife & and all your household.

Your affectionate friend,
Edwd Irving

George is with us and desires his respects to you and Mrs. C. This is written in great haste in town.

Addressed to: Mr. Thomas Carlyle Esq.,
21 Comely Bank,
Edinburgh.

∼

Edward Irving to DR THOMAS CHALMERS

6 Brown's Buildings, Norwood by London.[31]
[*This was probably written in the Summer of 1827.*]

My Dear and Honoured Friend,

I have caused a copy of Ben-Ezra with the Preliminary Discourse to be forwarded to you along with the Pamphlets in the same Parcel with a Bible which the Session of our Church is sending for your acceptance. And for the sheets do you take some of them and transmit them to me by any opportunity, and I shall get the Volumes completed. The Lord resolve you aright in this great matter.

---

30. Lord Francis Jeffrey (1773–1850), Scottish judge and critic, M.P for Malton and, after 1832, for Edinburgh. He was one of the founders and, in 1820, editor of the *Edinburgh Review*. Carlyle wrote of him in his *Reminiscences*.

31. NCL, MSS CHA 4 77.10.

The thing which occasions my writing at present is as follows: my friend Thomas Carlyle, whom the world now knows as the author of several works connected with literature wrote me concerning a purpose which he had of applying either for the Moral Philosophy or Rhetoric Chair in the London University. In reply to which I wrote to him mentioning in confidence how you had been entreated to accept the former, and explaining to him how vain it was for any other man living to enter into any competition with you, set as the Directors were upon you, and all interested in your acceptance of it. But nothing of this kind was necessary to [deter?] him—for the moment he heard of your name being before the Directors, he resigned the thoughts of presenting his: and began to prosecute enquiries by the help of his friend Mr. Jeffrey concerning the Chair of Rhetoric: in the pursuit of which certain things came to his knowledge which led him to believe that you had given a formal refusal to their application, and at the same time he found this sphere of the Rhetoric Chair so narrowed & circumscribed in the idea of the directors, as to lead him greatly to prefer the other, if it was open to his pursuit. But being unwilling to take any measure whatever until he shall have ascertained exactly the ground which you occupy at present, he has requested me to write to you, which I also was willing and indeed offered to do, in order to have from yourself the information direct. Would you be kind enough to let me know by return of Post: for it would seem that in the Month of November the Professorships are all to be appointed to. Be assured that I will make no improper use of the information which you are pleased to communicate to me.

My feelings towards Thomas Carlyle are exactly such as your feelings are towards Mr. Jeffrey with whom he takes counsel in this matter. I trust and pray that the Lord would open his eyes to the beauty and all-sufficiency which is in the face of our Lord and Saviour Jesus Christ. And I hope the Lord is leading him in that way. He has a very deep-feeling of 'what is true and honest and pure and lovely and of good report';[32] and I think he has a right idea of 'Wisdom': but it has not yet pleased the Lord to bring him to that condition of 'the bete' to whom it his will that the things of Christ should be revealed.[33] What a mystery, Dear Doctor, that is of the great Counsel of Eternity, to bereave the glory of the human understanding by the foolishness of preaching that no flesh should glory in his presence.[34] And how needful for an intellect like yours to bear it in even mind. For myself I ever pray to be enabled 'so to receive that I may be worthy to understand', 'so to believe that understanding may come as the reward of my faith.' My Dear friend Carlyle is making approaches to this ground but hath not yet been permitted to stand firmly upon it. And being conscious with myself that he is an enemy of all unrighteousness, and of all those who profane the holy name of our Lord Jesus Christ, and set at naught his Holy Gospel, I feel that he is of that class 'who

32. Phil. 4:8.
33. '... because thou hast hid these things from the wise and prudent, and hast revealed them unto babes': Matt 11:25.
34. 1 Cor 1:29.

are not against us, and therefore for us.'[35] Sir if I thought that he was to oppose in any thing the name of Christ I durst not upon the fealty to my Sovereign Lord give him any encouragement in any way, remembering the word of the blessed Apostle 'that we should not bid such God-speed.'[36] But feeling on the other hand convinced that he is a proper person to reclaim the rage of those disputers of this world who would cast off the bonds of our God and his Church, and to lead man into views of truth. I feel very desirous that he might succeed in this object, and should augur better for his success than that of any other moralist of the School of Stewart[37] and Reid[38] or even Locke.[39] And I can find no one except 'our old Coleridge' who goes higher. You know my feeling with respect to yourself. I stated them fully and have seen no reason to change them. That unless you were in some way to add to the discipline of a Professor's claims the trumpet-voice of the Preacher, you shall never be able to give a right amount of your gift. I never disapproved of your going to St Andrews[,] it was God's presentation of rest to his wearied servant. But if God spare you, you must again disentangle yourself from all systems of Church's polity except *the Church* which is our true polity; for this is the reason we become *statists* and politicians that we have ceased to know what it is to be *a churchman*. The Church is the parent of all *bodies-political*. It is the idea of the perfect aspiration, which hath heard full this multitudinous praying. Become this and be a churchman and you will find all your political speculations sanctified. And to this add the preaching of *the truth*, into which you had a glorious introduction, yet only the porch of the Temple towards which God is conducting you I have the feeling that it were more to the glory of God and the good of the Church that you should be delivered from the fear of men, and the cause of your own reputation, and preach the fullness of the Gospel of Christ, than that you should be Professor of Theology in Edinburgh. But the work of the world be done. May he direct you into his own ways by his own burden. I always fulfill my offer of a friend in writing to you, and perhaps I sometimes forget my office of a junior brother in the ministry. But when you have my idea fully & faithfully stated, I leave it to your own better judgment to adopt it or reject it.

We are living in the Country and you will address our Letter according to the superscript of this. My wife is well again thank God, so are my two children.[40] And we prosper in the Church by God's great mercy. Farewell, my beloved Broth[er], the Lord's

---

35. 'He that is not with me is against me: and he that gathereth not with me scattereth abroad': Matt 12:20.

36. 'If there come any unto you, and bring not this doctrine, receive him not into *your* house, neither bid him God speed': 2 John 1:10.

37. See Edward Irving to Thomas Carlyle, 27 August 1827: NLS, MSS 665: fol. 40–41.

38. Thomas Reid (1710–96), an accomplished mathematician and scientist as well as a philosopher. See *OCEL*.

39. John Locke (1632–1704), philosopher.

40. Margaret (born: 2 October 1815; died: 25 November 1853) and Mary (Born: June 1826; died: December 1827). From a private source.

Counsel be around our path. We commend your dear wife and children unto the Lord with the fondest affection of my wife and myself. Again Farewell

Your affectionate Friend and Brother,

Edwd Irving

The Rev Dr Chalmers,
Professor of Moral Philosophy in the University of St Andrews.

～

Edward Irving to THOMAS CARLYLE

Post marked 9th October 1827[41]

Dear Carlyle,

I have just received the enclosed which I think it best to transmit to you as the Doctor gives me the power to do so. It gives you the fullest encouragement to pursue your object which now I think you should do without delay. I understand Leonard Horner[42] came to London last week with his family to settle. If my negotiation with him can be any service use it with all freedom After seeing Brougham which I think you may, and ought now to do in the quietness of Brougham Hall; if you receive no discouragement, you ought then to come up to London and be your own solicitor. But if you think otherwise, use me for that or any other righteous & honourable end. But it is yourself, yourself with all your peculiarities about you, that must accomplish it if is to be accomplished. Your clear understanding, your sincere honesty and your wisdom & [letter torn] united in a form so unpretending, must sway them into [letter torn] and the formalities will follow. My house in town is at your service. Isabella was regretting that in its present dismantled state it was not worthy to offer to your wife also if she should think of accompanying you. It is undergoing a repair in several parts to make it habitable for the winter; but for hardy men like you and me, accustomed to [unreadable word!] entertainment it does well enough. The Lord prosper you in all grace and righteousness and peace. Farewell.

I am Dear Carlyle,
Your affectionate friend,
Edwd Irving

The letter came only this morning & I hasten to answer it by the Post; for that is the interval we have in these outlandish parts.

41. NLS, MSS 1765, fol. 77.

42. 'Leonard Horner (1785–1864) was a geologist, educator, and first warden (1827–31) of London University. In 1833 he was made one of the commissioners of the inquiry into the employment of children in factories, and until 1856 was a chief inspector under the Factories Act': CL, 4:259 n.

Part II: The Letters

Addressed to: Thomas Carlyle Esq.,
Comely Bank,
Edinburgh.

∼

Edward Irving to THE ELDERS AND DEACONS OF THE NATIONAL SCOTCH CHURCH, LONDON

London, National Scotch Church, 9th of January 1828[43]

My Dearly Beloved Brethren,

When it pleased the Presbytery of London to appoint a day fasting and humiliation for the children of our people in these parts, I greatly rejoiced in the Lord to see with what cordial satisfaction you received the intelligence, and with how much good heart you addressed yourselves to the work; and being noting loth to it myself, I cast about for some deeply concerning and tenderly touching subject, which might strike the chord of our common grief: for well I knew, dear brethren, it was no formality with any one of us, who had oft together taken painful counsel concerning the desperate condition of our prodigal brethren. And when the Lord directed me to the difficult and dangerous tract which I have pursued, I may say that every step was taken in fear and trembling, lest I might pass the bounds of your convictions, and pain your affection for the mother church, lest I might wound some natural feeling of the heart, or otherwise beak the harmony of sorrow which we desired should that day ascend from every grieved spirit. But God was with us of a truth, from the beginning to the ending of that long service. It was a season of true heart-searching affections, a day of tears to be remembered by all the congregation. Bt what amazed me the most was that you should, without a moment's hesitation, or apparent deliberation, as it were by one instant act of the common spirit, request with one voice that the sermon might be printed. When I hesitated for a moment, in the view of combining it with some other manuscript into a general discourse upon the state of religion in Scotland, to be printed in the third part of the volumes which I am now publishing, the repeated affectionate request of thirteen men, who I love so tenderly, and value so highly, prevailed over all my views of expediency: the more so as, in my unworthy fears, I had anticipated the very reverse of such a cordial approbation of the substance and spirit of a discourse which I had thought too high strung for almost any one but myself, who have meditated and mused so much upon the declensions over which I lament. But the Holy Ghost wonderfully

---

43. Irving, *A Sermon preached on the Occasion of a Fast*, Dedication.

convinceth of truth; whose presence I believe we had on that day, in a most remarkable manner: for which let us be ever most thankful.

Remember, dear brethren, therefore, that its publication is our common work, and that we must follow, or rather prevent, it with our common faith and prayers. The Lord may do with it as seemeth to him good. It is a small stone from the brook which may do execution to the battle, if he pleaseth to bless it. We offer it to Thee, in faith, O thou Head of the church! Praying thee that it may turn unto us for a testimony, and to our brethren of the mother church for a word of instruction and profit. Amen.

Your affectionate Minister and Pastor,
Edward Irving

Edward Irving to THOMAS CARLYLE

23rd January 1828[44]

My Dear Carlyle,

I am sorry to put you to the postage of two sheets, for what is not worthy of the postage of one. I am totally unacquainted with what a Certificate[45] ought to be. But you have it according to the first Idea and also the first execution. In I am very busy, and very much overborne with work. But always at leisure for you and ever ready to do my utmost to bring you to that position which your creator expects you to occupy, and for which you will be responsible in the great day, of speaking out the [letter torn] you have of the Infidel and Sceptical Spirit of the times. This is your present talent. Use it well, and God is [letter torn] to your humble requests to grant you the knowledge of the light of his own countenance, and the secret of the wisdom of his Eternal purpose. Which is what I pray for you and for your wife and for all whom I love. I am busy with many things and had at one time four different writings in the Press, of which I will send you specimens when they are finished. I have not seen that last review. You are in bad company with Brougham. Dear Carlyle I pray you guard against the cant of natural religion which that man is adding to cant of natural science in order to mystify people to his own ambition.

Jeffrey is another kind of man, kind, affable, vain foolish and worldly he may be a helm to you in the Mediterranean sea of prudence and worldly wisdom: but in the ocean of heavenly wonder, no one can steer you but he that made you, unto whose

---

44. NLS, MSS 1765, fol. 86.

45 49 'Meanwhile I am as diligent as possible storming the battlements of St. Andrews University for *the* Professorship in which I have actually, eight days ago, declared myself formally a candidate! . . . and this morning, came a decent testificatory letter from Buller, and a most majestic certificate in three pages from Edward Irving': Thomas Carlyle to Margaret A. Carlyle, 27 January 1828: CL, 4:310.

Part II: The Letters

tender mercies in the Lord Jesus Christ I commend you and your wife in which my wife joins me. I do intend if I can get a pulpit to come down to Scotland at the assembly and preach every night for a fortnight's continuance, opening the Scriptures upon some point, concerning which the Church & the world are alike asleep or deceived.

Your affectionate friend,
Edwd Irving

Addressed to: Thomas Carlyle Esq.,
Comely bank,
Edinburgh.

~

Isabella Irving to HON. J. J. STRUTT

6 Euston Grove, Euston Square. 13th Feby, 1828.[46]

My dear Sir,

I daresay you deem it very strange that you have received no answer to your letters Addressed to my husband. The truth is I have been unable to write & on my pen he generally depends for his correspondence. There is also another reason which has prevented me writing you there from days past, since my health was a little improved, which is this that we have been in the daily expectation of having a reply from Dr. A. Thomson of Edinbr to whom a request has been made that he should take Mr Irving's duty in the month of May & Mr Irving thought that if he gave a favourable answer that he would be a very suitable person to preach for the Continental Society this year. Although we have not heard from him Mr Irving thinks, that, if the Society approve of him he is as fit a person as any you can apply to. Dr Chalmers intended being up this Spring; but since his appointment to the Theological Chair in the University of Edinburgh, he declined coming. Dr. Goodson we also know does not wish to visit London this year & I have understood that Dr Thomson rather does—He is to be requested that some of his later papers, which originated in the Apocryphal Question have been so personal &, I fear, I may add abusive although I think he has had much provocation.

Were Mr Irving at all able to attend the Com[mittee] of the Continental Society he would do so with much pleasure but most of his energies are occupied in some public way, so for instance he preached last night is preaching tonight & does so tomorrow again –

With much esteem,
I am yours truly & obligedly,

---

46. Strutt, MSS 14.

Isabella Irving

Addressed to: The Honbl J. J. Strutt, Terling, Witham, Essex.

~

Edward Irving to THE ELDERS THE NATIONAL SCOTCH CHURCH

Postmarked 12th May 1828[47]
For the Session also.

My Dear Brothers in the Eldership and our Common Father,

I felt that I was strong yesterday being strengthened by your common prayer and this day also. We did but arrive an hour before public worship but I was in time to exhort several tables[48] for Dr Gordon and Dr Thompson. And I am now done preaching to a very numerous people; and I trust the Lord was with me. I hope you will all abide in prayer for me as I also shall for you.

I go to-morrow to see my wife and child and on Wednesday I travel by the Mail to my Father's after which being a rest I will write you and the Brethren at large. Dr Thompson prefers to live at some Hotel in the neighbourhood of the Parliament House where he may go in and come out at his pleasure without causing trouble to any one. Where also he might be without much cost. I told him we would look to that. Perhaps the true way would be for you and the Brethren of the Session to look out for some plain thereabouts. He prefers a public to a private house being desirous to attend the Parliament which is often late.

I pray God to bless and keep you all & all the flock unto his Kingdom and Glory. Give my love to them individually and collectively.

Farewell. The Lord bless you aye and reward your labours for the church by giving you faith and assurance in the blessed Gospel

Your affectionate friend
Edwd Irving

Edin. Monday

Dr Thompson comes by the Coach and intends going to into retirement for three days at Mr Alex Haldanes before engaging with the city.

Addressed to: Wm Dinwiddie,
4 Grocer's Hall Court,
Poultry, London.

---

47. EIL, MSS 35.
48. The meaning is unclear.

Part II: The Letters

~

Edward Irving to [an unknown recipient]

Annan, 18th May 1828[49]

My Dear Friend,

I have just a moment amongst much most acceptable and profitable labour, to introduce to you, my very dear friend, Mr. David Hope,[50] a Glasgow merchant, who come up to consult A London Physician. I have great countenance from the Lord in my many labours. I have preached every day when I have not been travelling: twice to day and in the open to more than two thousand people.[51] God bless you & your wife. Amen

Farewell, my beloved friend

Your affectionate Pastor

Edwd Irving

~

Edward Irving for MR JAMES BRODIE

Kirkcaldy, 1st July 1828[52]

I do hereby certify that Mr. James Brodie Preacher of the Gospel well known to me both by personal intercourse and by the report of faithful and godly Ministers, is a young man of a blameless life & a holy conversation, who appears ever to live under the influence of the Holy Ghost. The bent of his mind and the inclination of his heart is wholly to the sacred office of the ministry, and at all times that I have been with him, our discourse has been constantly directed to divine subjects, upon which I have found

---

49. WCL, MSS 6.

50. David Hope was a cousin of Adam Hope, and Edward Irving and Thomas Carlyle's old schoolmaster. See footnote to a letter from Edward Irving to Thomas Carlyle, 24 July 1820 re: Adam Hope. 'David Hope (Cousin of old Adam's but much younger, an excellent guileless man and merchant) was warmly intimate and attached': Carlyle, *Reminiscences*, 248.

The letter could not have been addressed to Thomas Carlyle who was also a friend of David Hope but it was possible that it was to William Hamilton.

51. 'In May, Mrs. Irving, whose health was still delicate, went to Scotland to her father's house, and about the same time Irving himself left London to travel by the slower route of Annan and his native district, preaching as he went, to Edinburgh and Kirkcaldy. His object in this journey was not relaxation or pleasure. He went, counting himself "most favoured of the Lord," to proclaim in Scotland, as he had already done in London, the coming, of his Master': Oliphant, *Life*, 2:13.

52. NCL Box 9.22.

him both well informed & very inquisitive after more information. Theology is with him a desire and delight; and his views are orthodox and spiritual of his own accord he hath without money and without price,[53] while staying with his Grandfather, the Revd. Dr Martin of Monmail, given himself in labour in the parish both as a preacher, a Sabbath School teacher, the visitor of the sick, and in every other way proper to an unordained man; which shews that his heart is in the pastoral and ministerial work: and that he only waits the call of a flock & the ordination of the Presbytery, to approve himself a faithful labourer in the vineyard. In all these offices he has been very acceptable to the people. I have one thing further to testify what I conceive to be of great importance, that he has great spiritual discernment, and distinctly perceives both the Apostasy of the Roman Superstition, and the progress of infidelity amongst ourselves, under the disguise of intellectual preaching, and works of natural benevolence. His eye is single and his body will become full of light.

Finally, though I give these things with a clear conscience and an faltering hand, I hope no one will choose a clergyman by my recommendation or the recommendation of men, but upon their conscience & by the guidance of the Holy Spirit.

Edwd Irving A.M
Min of the Nat. Scotch Church, London.

~

Joseph Wolff to EDWARD IRVING

18th July 1827?[54]
Wednesday

My very dear Irving,

The discussion with the Jews is a very serious thing and I wish therefore to come to you this night at ten o'clock and spend with you till three o'clock in the morning in consulting with such a dear brother as you are.[55] In case that you are willing send to me an answer immediately, if the bearer of this letter finds you at home, if not send this evening an answer to 65 Newman Street, Oxford Street at Miss Dornford so here I shall dine to day—be so kind and do me this favor,[sic] and recommend me to the prayers of your Congregation.

Your brother,
Joseph Wolff

53. Isa 55:1.
54. ML, MSS 109a, b.
55 54 Joseph Wolff kept extraordinary hours. See Palmer, *Joseph Wolff*, 83. Alas, there is no record of Edward Irving's response to this proposal.

Part II: The Letters

~

Edward Irving to HENRY DRUMMOND

Postmark: 15th November 1828, Saturday.[56]

My Dear friend,

We have a meeting of the Presbytery, which I must attend on Tuesday, so that I cannot come down on Monday, which would have gratified me exceedingly. I feel very much indebted to Lady Harriet[57] and yourself, and hope to approve myself sensible of it. I do not look for Mr. Vaughan[58] at Albury, in a letter I had from him, and in a meeting I had with him at Northampton he told me he did not think he could arrange for Albury. I doubt whether you know his doctrines sufficiently, certainly I have not found any reason but to rejoice in having known him. I pray God to give us a profitable meeting. Farewell. The Lord keep all your house unto himself for ever.

Your affectionate friend,
Edward Irving

P.S. I have just learned from Mr. Tudor that you wish Mr. Borthwick's[59] address. He does not live in the college but he is student in Jesus College, and this address will I think find him. I gave him a letter to the kind Mr. Skinner, Fellow of that College; and I dare say he will have delivered it; so that if you please you may add that to the direction. Again I desire to express myself sensible of the honour you do me, and the grace you do the Church in inviting me and others to this conference. For I fear our narrow feelings sometimes hinders us from feeling these things aught and from expressing them as we aught. This I can truly say is not the case with myself. But you and your honorable Lady look for your reward where you shall certainly receive it, if you hold fast the beginning of your confidence steadfast unto the end. Continue patient in so doing for in due time you shall reap if you faint not. I have just learned from Miss Tessa that Cunninghame has co-equalled you in your readiness in writing a reply to Hamilton's book. Farewell my beloved friend. E.I.

Addressed to: Henry Drummond Esq.,
Albury Park,
Guildford.

56. DFP: C/9/1.

57. Lady Harriet Drummond, Henry Drummond's wife and cousin. Born Henrietta Hay-Drummond. They were married in 1807. See Bolitho and Peel, *The Drummonds of Charing Cross*, 136.

58. Rev E. T. Vaughan (Anglican), Vicar of St Mary's, Leicester. Listed as attending at the first conference at Albury in 1826.

59. Mr. T. Borthwick. Listed as attending the first Albury Conference. He later became an M.P. See Drummond, *Narrative*.

Edward Irving to HENRY DRUMMOND

13 Judd Place, Euston New Road.
1st December 1828[60]

My Dear Friend,

I am once more sitting in my own house after experiencing so much of the love and hospitality of yourself and others, for which I desire to love you and all the holy brethren. Having nothing prepared for preaching I cast myself upon the Lord, and was enabled to preach two Advent-sermons from the concluding verses of the IXth Chapter of the Hebrews. That same Mr. Brown for whom you shewed much kindness was present and I think between your pamphlet and my sermons we have fixed an arrow in his heart which will dilute his peace if he will not turn unto the Lord in this matter. He acknowledges deep obligation to your pamphlet. I am about to write two sermons for next Sabbath upon the signs of the times; to which you shall be welcome if they will afford you any assistance towards the last number of the Dialogues of the new series. I hope you will go on with that work, and put into it a still more solemn and severe Spirit. Only guard yourself against the Spirit of ridicule, and seek the Spirit of solemn earnestness. There are two or three passages in your last Pamphlet,[61] which convince me that in this council I am but echoing the conviction of your own mind.

And now I hardly know how to thank you & Lady Harriet for the great grace which you have done me these three times in permitting me to form one of that company whom you assemble at your house. It becometh you well to take the station of assembling Gods people around you and endeavouring to promote the gospel of his Kingdom. I feel daily more and more the necessity of present and constant readiness to depart and be with the Lord.

I forgot when I was with you to speak about that poor orphan destitute boy Knox whom I am endeavouring to get into the Caledonian Asylum. I wrote asking for your Proxy. If it be not promised to another, may I hope to receive it for him, as he is very destitute & his poor mother just about to be put to bed of another child. The Father had been a soldier during the wars and an honest industrious man since until his death in August last. The voting is on Thursday next. If your polling paper be at Charing Cross I shall take all the trouble about this if only I have your permission. I pray God to bless your wife and children and all your house in which I have enjoyed so much of God's favour and of your kindness.

I am,

60. DFP: C/9/2.
61. Drummond, *Observations on Matthew xxiv.*

Part II: The Letters

My Dear friend,
Yours most affectionately,
Edwd Irving

P.S. Since writing the above I have been in the City and had some conversation with Mr. Henderson the Printer. The Church Committee are the proprietors of the book, and ought to be responsible of course for paying the expense of its printing; so that the amount should be sent to them and not to you. At the same time I have learned that they have very large payments to make about this time when the Church is completed; and if it were convenient for you to be the responsible person, I should take care that the first part of all the proceeds were paid into your hand. This I suggest without any authority to do it; but I feel that it might be an encumbrance for them to have to pay the amount when they have so much to pay.—It does indeed lay the burden upon you: if it be inconvenient for you to bear it, let me know, and I will take order that it be properly met some way or other. Mr. H. was suggesting that the time was come for undertaking a Magazine[62] in order to expound the prophetic views, but I like magazines ill and I fear there is little hope of making them better. E I

Addressed to: Henry Drummond Esq.,
Albury Park,
Guildford.

Editor's Epilogue

During the two years that have passed since the beginning of this chapter, Edward Irving had lost another child, Mary, born in February 1827 and living only until December. In all he was to have eight children of whom only three survived to adulthood.

Over the next three years Irving's beliefs and ministry were perceived as increasingly unorthodox and exposed differences between him and the Presbyterian church authorities which eventually became irreconcilable.

---

62. The first quarterly edition of *The Morning Watch* was published by James Nisbet of Berners Street, London, in March 1829.

6

Letters: 1829–1831

Editor's Introduction

In May 1829 Edward Irving returned to Edinburgh to deliver another series of lectures. He found that facilities for these were not so easy to obtain and nor was the interest in them quite so keen.

In 1830 his London Presbytery tried to condemn him for his heretical views *in absentia,* but his loyal congregation supported him. The London Presbytery had no authority over him because he had been ordained in Scotland, and Irving dealt with any further attempts to discipline him by withdrawing his membership from the London Presbytery, which he did on 19th October 1830.

Further he had to endure more grief and loss over the death of two more of his children; Samuel died in 1830 and Gavin had been born in 1829 but lived only a few hours,[1] although Martin who did enjoy a long life was born on 21st February 1831.

Two of the signs of the Second Advent are miracles and the visitation of the Holy Ghost, and in 1830 these were believed to have manifested themselves.

In April 1830, the Macdonald family of Port Glasgow reported receiving the Spirit's gift of tongues and healing. The party that investigated these phenomena included the Cardale family, who were to become members of Irving's congregation and eventually prominent members of the church.

~

---

1. In her letter to Jane of 22 October 1829 Mrs. Montagu had written, 'Mrs. Irving has lost her last born Child which only lived a few hours.' CL, 5:24 n.

Part II: The Letters

Edward Irving to THOMAS CARLYLE

Edinburgh, 60 Gt. King St. 30th May 1829[2]

My Dear Carlyle,

Since I wrote to you from Annan I have had reason to alter my plan a little, and shall not be at Craigen-puttock[3] till after the Sabbath I preach in Dumfries. That night I intend to sleep at Holywood manse, and next day sometime I will be with you God willing. It is a rule of mine to which I know you will not object that in whatever parish I sleep a night, I should offer to the minister to preach to his people. This I have done to Mr. Bryden[4] and have received his invitation. Whether it be on the Monday or Tuesday night I do not yet well know: but which ever it be nothing will give me more pleasure than to have my Host and Hostess to be of my congregation. I must preach in Glasgow on the Thursday night, and in Paisley on the Friday night following and at Helensburgh on the Sabbath. Thence I proceed to Liverpool to preach there on Wednesday & Thursday. I mention these engagements to shew you that it is nothing but the urgent claims elsewhere which shortens my visit to you and your excellent wife.

Since coming here I have preached every day and shall continue to do so while I remain; which is till Friday night when I take the Mail. The General Assembly has rejected my commission, but with Circumstances of great consideration and even honour to myself.

Your mother, worthy woman, was my hearer at Annan and sought me out in a crowd of 10,000. Till I see you farewell, & may the Lord's blessing rest upon you & your wife

Your affectionate & true friend,
Edwd Irving

~

Edward Irving to JOHN FERGUSON[5]

[undated, 1820]

Francis Jeffrey[6] said you have not enough of worldly wisdom[;] at Mr. I's there is a wisdom of a higher and better kind which cometh from above. Oh yes but not for worldly purposes. Certainly not but I love my friend and hope to see his affections set

---

2. NLS, MS 1765, fol. 127.

3. The marital home of Thomas and Jane Carlyle.

4. Rev Robert Bryden, minister of Dunscore Church. See letter Edward Irving to Isabella Irving, 12 June 1829 n: Oliphant, *Life*, 2:84–85.

5. John Fergusson was Irving's brother-in-law.

6. Francis Jeffrey (1773–1850), was a friend of the Carlyles.' See CL 1: 68n.

upon the things above. This short dialogue took place in the Advocate's[7] reading room between him & your humble servant. E.I.

~

Edward Irving to UNKNOWN RECIPIENT

15th June 1828, Kirkcaldy, Sabbath Evening[8]

My Dear Sir

We have had an aweful [sic] visitation here of God's providence this night in the falling in of a Gallery of the Church[9] by which it is reckoned that about 17 persons have lost their lives. I have a moment before the Post leaves thus to inform you that we are all safe by the good care of God, but deeply distressed with our sorrowing brethren. May the Lord keep you & all the brethren and all the people from the Calamity of sudden death.

With Affectionate love from Mr. Hamilton who is here, I remain as always
    Your affectionate Pastor,
    Edw[d] Irving

It took place a few minutes before divine worship began. I was not in the Church, but on my way E.I

Let Alex Hamilton know that Millie is safe and well.

~

Edward Irving to HENRY DRUMMOND

London, 13 Judd Place East.[10]
7th July 1829

My Dear & Honoured friend,

I am about to travel out of my vocation and to do a thing which I have never done before and which I did not expect that I should ever have had to do, and indeed had laid down a resolution never to do on any account whatever. Whether the extraordinary call and occasion will justify it or not, you will judge. But first I have to request

---

7. 'In 1829 he [Francis Jeffrey] was unanimously elected Dean of the Faculty of Advocates and retired from being directly involved with the *Review*': *Reminiscences*, 349.

8. EIL 36.

9. An event which some saw as a punishment from God owing to the presence there of Edward Irving.

10. DFP: C/9/3.

that after considering it you will feel yourself in the most perfect and entire liberty, and rather forgive me for my boldness than feel a moments scruple to decide the one way or the other: and next that you would not mention what I am now to communicate, for it is very delicate and pains me not a little to mention it even to you whose generous kindness & noble friendship I have so much proved, and shall do all things to merit and nothing to abuse; God helping me.

I am the second son of a large and much respected family. My Father and Mother are two of the most worthy and true-hearted people you have ever known: my four sisters are patterns of wives and Mothers in their several neighbourhoods and the youngest of us, my only surviving brother you have seen & been kind to. The eldest son of my Father's family a young man the pride & honour of our town, went out to India as a surgeon,[11] and died there in an act of care and consolation to the widow and the fatherless. It was the maxim of my Father ever from our childhood to give to all his children the very best Education the County could afford both to boys and girls, and he was wont to teach us that this was all our portion and truly so it was; but my portionless Sisters were selected for wives by the most worthy young men of our neighbourhood and live in comfort and happiness with their husbands & their children: for God hath blessed them with numerous families, and there never has been a death amongst them. These trials were reserved for me a man to be subdued only by rough handling. Notwithstanding this expense of giving to his sons an Education at the University and his daughters at the best schools in the County my Father and Mother by the blessing of God upon their industry were able to secure of property as much as when their old age came enabled them to live with rigid economy in decent and comely wise as they had ever done: and so I found them a month ago when I visited them able to receive their children and their grand children about them as they were brought in God's providence to bless their aged eyes. They are now near to 70 dwelling alone, their children loving and honouring them, as also all their neighbours and acquaintances. For they were always good & charitable and hospitable. Pardon me this minuteness. It is necessary to represent the feeling under which I am now to write.

When my Eldest brother John Lowther Irving, now no more, had taken his diploma as a surgeon, and was ready to undertake the business of life, my Eldest Maternal Uncle, the laird to a good estate, and himself a man of good estate which he had realised by Merchandise, being also a very generous man, but of a most untowardly temper and fearful in his revenge, and a bachelor withal, took for my brother a very great liking and evil or wrong would have him to go out to India, for which the outfit and expense was more then than it is now, indeed so much that my excellent and honest father would never have dreamt of endeavouring to meet it. But the obstacle and uncontrolled benevolence of my Uncle overbore the good nature of my Father, when he frankly offered and pressed upon him to accept all that was necessary to John's outfit. It was accepted & my brother went in the year 1810. The expense was about £500. For

---

11. See letter from Edward Irving to Thomas Carlyle, 8 March 1823: NLS, MS 665: fol. 30.

this my Uncle asked no acknowledgement whatever, other than that which gratitude gives and benevolence is more than contented to receive. In the course of events, through causes which it were tedious and troublesome to recount to you, it came to pass that by degrees this generous but most testy old Uncle became alienated from my Mother's family though not to the extent of any outbreaking: but as it grew he asked my Father to give him some acknowledgment in writing for that which he had advanced on my Brother's account. This my Father consented to do: the more as my Mother's portion of £500 at her Father's death of which she was life-renter lay in his hand a part of the burden upon the Paternal estate to which he had now succeeded. Having obtained this acknowledgment he afterwards required another acknowledgment for the Interest due upon it, which he likewise held in his hand; these together amount to £858. And he continued to retain in his own hand the Interest which my Mother should have received as the life-renter of her Father's legacy to her. But this they did not mind as there still remained from their own property enough with strict economy to support their old-age. I foresaw the blow that was impending and did all I could to ward it off: but in vain. Yesterday I received the enclosed letter which I pray you to read. My Uncle has given these vouchers into the hand of a man of business to obtain the payment of them. My Father is willing having obtained consent of his children to surrender the £500 and I am sure there will not be an objection to it on the part of all his family. There still remains £358 from which my Uncle is willing to take security upon my Father's small property which is barely sufficient to support his and my Mother's old age. And if a better cannot be made of it; this must be done. But I am very loathe indeed that they should be at the mercy of such a Merciless Man, and am labouring hard to deliver them out of his hand. My Father's property is already burdened with some debts but still it yielded about £60 clear on which with frugality they supported themselves comfortably. There was always elegance a plenty in my mothers house as every friend of mine that has been in it knows. For she was kind to the poor, and I think God blessed their litel [sic] share for it. My only aim beyond supporting my own wife & children was to redeem my Fathers inheritance, that he and my Mother might enjoy it unencumbered while they lived, and my wife & children when I should be gone to a better country. The profits of my books I intended to devote to that end: for I hold it to be a principle that what comes from the Church should not be laid up or diverted to other uses, but go to the expenses of the Minister's house, to hospitality and to charity. And on this primitive principle of a Bishop I will act till the day of my death! The printing of my three volumes will I expect be cleared off by the sales, this month which is Midsummer. And all the sales upon them, and upon the book which I am now publishing on church & state after Miss Farmer is paid in her expense in printing it, and any new editions of my other works which may be called for (except the Last Days which is the Church's after you are reimbursed) and my book upon the Lord's Supper which I have about ready, and my Lectures on the Apocalypse—which the Edinburgh people are pledged to have from me, and my popular Theological Tracts

Part II: The Letters

which I am about to put forth for the people all these I will freely make over to you until you are reimbursed, if you will advance for me that £358.2.4,[12] perhaps to keep my Father's person from restraint. I will not touch a farthing of all the profits of them till you are fully paid. If it is not convenient for you, for your generosity is sorely drawn upon, and I never thought I should have had to draw upon it; never mind. Think no worse of me for troubling you in such an emergency, and I will think nothing of being refused. I would have come down with Lady Olivia[13] but I could not speak so much about myself and my family. I desire my Love to Lady Harriet and the lovely children. Farewell.

May Gods grace ever [letter torn] you,
Your faithful friend,
Edwd Irving
Addressed to: Henry Drummond Esq.,
Albury Park,
Guildford, Surrey.

~

Edward Irving to HENRY DRUMMOND

9th July 1829[14]

My Dear & Honoured Friend,

I trust your bounty will abound in many thanks givings unto God and will be returned in additional blessings upon yourself and your children.

I do hereby acknowledge myself your Debtor for the amount of Three Hundred and Sixty Pounds earning Interest from this date and for the payment of it I hereby bind myself to give over to you all the Profits from the sales of my books from this time forth until it is paid, and all the Profits of any books which I may publish till that time of full repayment. And if God should remove you or me before that time, this Letter will be binding upon my heirs as upon myself and will be security to your heirs as to yourself. And this I do without being asked to do it by you, because it is honest and right to do it. It being understood that my present accounts due for printing my Books

---

12. Three hundred and fifty eight pounds, two shillings, and five pence.

13. Lady Olivia Sparrow (1776–1863) of Brampton Park, Hertfordshire. Lord Manderville, later to be the Duke of Manchester, was her son-in-law.

14. DFP: C/9/4.

be first paid off, and the amounts to be incurred by printing new books: but nothing more whatever than that and the other necessary charges for publication.

The above, well beloved and most kind Sir, is but the act of justice; but how shall I requite the act of grace?

By being gracious unto others, and acknowledging the grace of God—for his servant. I desire you to believe that I am very thankful, and will do every thing to acknowledge and requite your goodness.

It is my purpose to come down on Monday by the first Coach and to remain with you that week; I am much beholden to you for this early opportunity of pledging my acknowledgements in person to you and Lady Harriet & your family, and to see my favourite Albury in its Summer dress. I desire my love to your family and to the friends which are now within your gates. Lady Olivia was a little unwell, she is gone to our Scottish Aesculapius[15] and will be with you to-morrow. Indeed, all joking to a side, Whitelaw has wrought a wonder in her Ladyship. Farewell May God bestow upon you abundantly of all good things.

Your affectionate & faithful friend,
Edwd Irving

3 Judd Place East.
9th July 1829
Addressed to: H. Drummond Esq.
Albury Park,
Guildford, Surrey.

Edward Irving to WILLIAM HAMILTON

London, 18th November 1829[16]

My Dear Sir,

I hereby give you full power to settle my accounts with Mr. Panton Bookseller, and shall thank you to do it with as much expedition as possible: also to obtain his consent to my taking the risk of the Confession of faith etc wholly upon myself, as it is not yet completely finished off. And to bring our transactions in the way of business to a fair and honourable termination. As you are better acquainted with business transactions I ask this as a favour and shall abide by your doings in it.

Your affectionate friend & Brother,

---

15. Aesculapius: personification of medicine or healing arts and its ideals.
16. MS: ML 072a.

Part II: The Letters

Edwd Irving

Addressed to: Wm Hamilton Esq.,
127 Cheapside, [London.]

~

Edward Irving to DR CHALMERS

London, 1830[17]

My dear and honoured friend,

I hope this will find you well. I wish to introduce and certify Mr. James Scott[18] who has been here during the Summer. He is truly a man of God who has forsaken all to devote himself to Christ. Orthodox in the faith and zealous in every good works. The Lord strengthen you in the ways of all truth and righteousness.

Your faithful friend,
Edwd Irving

London 1830

~

Edward Irving to REV MARCUS DODS

London, 13 Judd Place East[19]
8th March 1830

My Dear Brother,

It is reported to me (and indeed without any signification of doubt a friend who wrote me the other day a Letter from Edinburgh approving what you have written, speaks of it without even an allusion to uncertainty) that you are the author of two critiques in the Christian Instructor upon some of my writings. I do not ask you whether you are or not; indeed I would rather not know by whom they are written, for I am told they are very severe in their language and unkind in their Spirit, though I can only speak from report of others; not being myself in the habit of reading that work. The object for which I write is to ask the favour of your setting down in a brief form what

---

17. NCL, CHA 4 140.57.
18. Perhaps a relation of Irving's assistant, Rev Alexander Scott.
19. NLS: MS 1002, 121.

is the doctrine you hold on this subject, that I may leisurely consider it in my own mind; for I am afraid you would not write on such high subjects without having well considered them—and I will set down for your perusal the sum of the doctrine which I hold, of which, let me say, till within these two years. I never knew that there were two opinions in any orthodox creed and true church I believe, then,

1st That all things with man as their Lord were created holy and sinless.

2nd That since the fall they have all with man as their head become altogether sinful without the power of redeeming themselves.

3rd That the eternal Son of God, very God of very God, by Incarnation unto death and resurrection—out of death redeemed man then died & man's inheritance.

4th That flesh in human nature was created all good, then it became all evil, then in Christ it became all holy, and by the resurrection it became all glory.

5th That by generation our nature is all sinful as Adam's was after the fall, that by regeneration it is strengthened of Christ the regenerator, the second Adam, to overcome all sin, and that by resurrection is changed into Christ's glory.

6th That Sin in the regenerate ariseth not from the weakness of the Spirit of Christ in them, but form their own moral weakness, which they give place to, and so contract guilt, which needs a continual atonement or forgiveness whereof we are assured in the great work of God's having rendered himself to our nature and sanctified it.

7th With respect to the experience of the Son of God in our nature I am content to say that he was tempted in all points like as we are, and yet never sinned. When I want to have this truth expounded I study the Psalms and the Prophets which testify of him.

Now, Dear Sir and fellow labourer in the Ministry of truth, I shall take it very kind if you will set down in a form somewhat similar to this, the views which you hold upon these subjects, that I may consider them at my leisure. For, God knows who knoweth all things, that I have no desire upon this earth but to know his truth and to declare it. I would rather that you exhibited your views in a summary form, than that you extend into criticism upon mine, although I should take it very kind if you should notice any thing wrong that you would mention it. If you lived nearer me, I should think nothing of coming of to converse with you at length upon these great points of our Christian faith. It is not the first nor the second time that I have travelled 100 miles to converse with men who were making the deep things of God their meditation.

Though certainly that having heard that these Articles so severe on my writings as I am informed, were written by you, was the occasion of this letter I beg there may be no reference whatever to that subject, for which I do not know I do not need to think about, and I did know that you had said or written or deem the severest things to me; which is that but a call for me to forbear, and endeavour either to know your truth or to make you know mine. If you say why not read the articles? My reason is that for many years I have walked by the rule, of not reading any thing personally addressed to me, unless the name of the person who writes it be subscribed. And this I do as the only way of honouring our Lord's rule given in the XVIIIth chapter of Matthew for the redress of all personal offences, requiring that the persons should know one another. Let, therefore, every thing connected with that subject be as far from your mind when you answer, as it is from mine, while I write this letter. Let us just regard each other as in truth we are two brethren, two fellow-labourers in the vineyard of our Lord. I write this without the knowledge of any one my wife who is [letter torn] meekly lying asleep upon the sofa beside me, and my porridge cooling before me. If ever you come to London, we shall talk this matter over at large; you shall be welcome to my house, as every brother is. Farewell. May God bless you and bless your labours, and lead us into all truth. This is the prayer

of your Faithful Brother and Fellow-labourer,
Edwd Irving
Minr of the Nat. Scotch Church

Addressed to: Revd. Marcus Dods, Belford, Northumberland.

Edward Irving to HENRY DRUMMOND

13 Judd Place East, 7th July 1830[20]

N.B. 'Mr. Magus need not come away before the end. Miss Ferrar has not got a church as yet'

My Dear friend and honoured host,

I was so much stunned by the unexpected blow which it pleased the Father to give to what I had thought was my faith in him, so staggered and at my wits end, that I could not present myself before the brethren with any proper words, but felt it my duty to retire into my own heart and seek there for the Lord's instruction before I opened my mouth to instruct others. Till this time half past one o/clock in the day I have been in great perplexity and trouble of Spirit; not from the loss of my child,[21] of my four children taken from me one by one:[22] for here both my wife's spirit and my own are at perfect rest. Our faith hath taught us that death is indeed deliverance, and we can thank God in very truth for having taken them to himself. The thing which

---

20. DFP: C/9/5.
21. Irving's son Samuel who had died the day before.
22. Edward, Mary, Gavin, and Samuel.

hung over my mind with dark perplexity was this, that God's word seemed to have failed; for that many of God's people had been agreed to ask this matter of him I had no doubt, and that I firmly believed his promise I seemed to myself to have no doubt. And yet behold He hath not done it. I cannot, and I would not if I could, describe the temptations which have been presented to my mind, of either disbelieving God's word as it is written & admitting the glosses of man's understanding & power, or of disbelieving that there is a Church upon the Earth any longer, to whose prayer God is attentive. Now I seem to myself to have obtained deliverance, and I conceive it of so much importance, as to ask you to communicate it and if you please the whole of this Letter to the Assembled brethren.

Upon consulting the instance of resurrection for the dead performed in the Acts I find that the brethren (Acts IX v 30) sent for Peter, and did not undertake either by prayer or otherwise the work themselves. If the case of Eutychus (Acts xx [vs. 9–13]) be also a case of resurrection, it was in like manner performed by an Apostle. It is however to the case of Tabitha[23] that I would turn your attention; from which it clearly appears that the Spirit moved the brethren not to take the offer of raising the dead upon themselves, but to send for one in whom the gift of miracles resided. That Peter was famous for this gift is clear from Acts V v 15. Now upon consulting I Cor XII v 10,28 we find that the gift of miracles was connected with certain persons in the Church who were not Apostles but distinct from them. This proves that this gift and the office for which it was the qualification were not limited to the persons of the Apostles nor to the Apostles times, but belonged to the Church as much as pastors and teachers and governments do. The whole of that XIIth chapter breathes a constant and not a temporary meaning. It is the manner of the organisation of that Church whose duration on the Earth and authority and privileges are thereby set full by our Lord (Mat XVIII v 15–21)[24]. Be it so then that for each work or gift of the Holy Ghost then was an appropriate Ministry (I Cor XII v 9, 10 with v 28) and that the Holy Spirit did work the work of healing or miracles or instruction through the person whom he had set for that end in the body and not by another person who was there set for some other end; and what is the conclusion, but that we have not now the answer of our faith and prayers on behalf of the sick the disabled & because we have not the office bearers, the persons through whom that gift comes to the body of Christ. What makes the Church so careful of ordination? What but the conviction that only through ministers thus carefully and orderly set apart with the blessing of spiritual instruction and the grace of life in the Sacraments be conveyed. And why this of prophesying only? Why not of 'miracles, gifts of healing, tongues' also? Surely no sufficient reason can be found for taking a part out of that chapter of gifts and miracles to the exclusion of the rest. If so, then see the conclusion which we come to, that though the prayers of the Church may be most faithful & fervent for healings and miracles and other works of the Holy Ghost which

23. Acts 9:39–41.
24. Irving may also to have meant to refer to Matt 16:15–21.

testify to the power of Christ and his presence in his Church, the answer in such cases cannot be obtained because there are no persons who are set apart to minister the gift which the church has besought & which God waiteth to bestow. 'We have no prophets nor any one who knows how long? We see not our signs.'[25] Think you not that if there was a person gifted of the H-Ghost with the power of miracles & whom I could send as the brethren sent to Peter, that my child might not now by his hand be raised up. For my part I dare not to doubt it, without doubting God and Christ, John XIV v 12. I feel therefore that of all members of the Church and especially of those who prove as I have done the inefficacy of prayer to bring these extraordinary blessings, it is the duty to pray without disguise and with all earnestness that God would again set in his church persons for these several offices which now are closed. I do not think that there is any power on Earth which may appoint such ministers, but that the same Holy Spirit who loves to testify of Christ's fullness, and who so constituted the primitive church, will to our faith and prayers grant therewith every thing which is needful for the full manifestation of our Redeemer. I believe there is such a power with God always to revivify the withered branches of the vine, or rather, to use our dear Chevalier's language, that there is a law in the church ever assuring to body forth[26] her own completeness. We did not need an Apostle's presence to bring the abomination of the Mass back to the simplicity of the Lord's Supper, nor to restore the pure Episcopal succession oft-times as it has been interrupted. Such interruptions and alterations & abridgments are not good, but when they occur through our wickedness there is a power which God reserveth with himself and yieldeth to the faith and prayer of the church to reproduce all her last ordinances and offices in their original purity. I believe, for example, that when MacDonald called upon his sister in the name of Christ to arise, and she arose, when he wrote to Mary Campbell and she arose, God pointed him out as one whom he endowed in his Church with the gift of healing, and to whom therefore the ministry thereof should be entrusted. If that person had been near me, I would have sent for him to lay hands upon my child, as it is I wish to ask their prayers. So much for this subject. The use is that as ministers and members of Christ, the brethren should strive to understand the mind of God in respect of those offices and gifts which have ceased in the Church, and if they come to these convictions not to hide them, lest God bring them into the straits out of which their views have delivered us.

The above is written in great infirmity of mind but with clear persuasion of the Spirit and I commend it much to the consideration of the brethren, and entreat them not to put it away because of the weak and uncomely form in which it is given forth. My mind is weakened with much weeping and sore distress, not so much sorrow as perplexity. Yet by the grace of God I will preach to-morrow night.

My wife desired her thanks to Lady Harriet, and entreats her prayer. She cannot at this moment give any answer to my Dear Lady's kind invitation—God bless her and

---

25. Ps 74:9.
26. *MSND*, Act 5, Sc. 1, Theseus, line 14.

her children. Your son[27] fell the sacrifice in the first Albury meeting, my daughter[28] was stricken that night I returned from the second, then Mr. McNeil's son, and now my Samuel. This prophecy is bitter in the belly, how sweet so soon it be in the mouth. Is this like Ezekiels loss of his wife.[29]

I think it would be good before you part to go swiftly over the XII XIII, XIV chapters of 1st Corinthians. David Brown[30] is coming[;] God be praised for him. May the Lord abide amongst you in all wisdom & understanding and love & truth.

Your faithful brother and servant,

Edwd Irving

Addressed to: Henry Drummond Esq.,
Albury Park,
Guildford, Surrey.

Edward Irving to SAMUEL MARTIN

[Undated] [31]

Isabella grows much in the Lord, and has upon he whole enjoyed very good health through faith and prayer, EI

My Dear Samuel,

I pray the Lord to enrich you with all grace and goodness and to grant you with all boldness to preach the truth for the witness of which our names have been cast out as evil. My soul has been much exercised and is still as to the light in which these ministers who deny the three great essential truths of the Godhead. The Father's love to every man his sins notwithstanding, the Sons atonement for the sin of every man in our flesh by contending with and overcoming the sinfulness and mortality thereof, the Holy Spirit's work of assuring the soul of is salvation & working in it till the love power and holiness joy and gladness and other forms of life which are in Christ Jesus

---

27. Henry Drummond (1811–22).
28. Mary 1826–27.
29. Ezek 25:15–27.
30. David Brown (1803–97). His mother was one of the Chalmers family. He studied divinity at Aberdeen and Edinburgh, and was licensed as a preacher in 1826. For a year and half (1830–32) he was assistant to Edward Irving at Regent Square, London. See *The Scotsman*, 5 July 1897.
31. UEL: DC.4.103. Undated but Irving speaks of David Brown helping him and this would suggest a date c.1830. See letter Edward Irving to Henry Drummond, 7 July 1830 n.

our risen and glorified head. Such men as deny these truths are Antichrist beyond all question. I mean, as in the heart and will the lips deny them (for I am not ignorant how good men are bamboozled & terrified by the words *sinful flesh [revival?] pardon and assurance of Salvation*) and if they be ministers of Antichrist, I know that it is as much as your life and mine are worth to call them brother yea not to denounce them as false prophets ravenous wolves in sheep's clothing. Be fully persuaded in your own mind; but for myself I would sooner part with my right hand, than give it to such men as Patrick Macfarlane, and lose my tongue than wish him God speed. I feel also pretty well convinced that it is our duty to open our pulpits to these ejected men come what will; and that it is the duty of the people not to hear these ministers who bring these damnable doctrines, but rather to abide apart in prayer and supplication till God send them ministers according to his own mind. At all rates, however you may think in these matters, and I confess they are difficult, it is your duty who know the truth, to make men know what side you are on, I do not mean Campbell's or mine but Christ's against that diabolical assembly. If you do keep any temperisings, and speak not out, be afraid God will and shake you; for now is the time of witness-bearing.

For myself I can only say I have never had so much power in the Holy Ghost as since the last assembly. And my flock are feeling it. And God is stretching out his hand to heal, and he is bestowing his gifts upon divers of my flock, and preparing the hearts of many people. The Congregation is more numerous than I remember to have seen it. The young men are stirred up to gather the people together in the courts and alleys and speak to them concerning the things of their fears. David Brown & I have preached in the fields to the people strolling there. A good spirit of prayer is found out amongst the people, and we are preserved in much peace. For all which I thank the Lord daily.

Remember us in your prayers. Believe me to be a true Brother in Christ, a sufferer not for my own folly but for his truth's sake. Put away the spirit of such criticism and tell the heavenly truth, the round and full orbed truth to your heart. Stand fast and be faithful & wear the martyr's crown.

Your faithful Brother,
Edwd Irving.

Edward Irving to REV MARCUS DODS

13 Judd Place East, August 5th 1830[32]

My Dear Sir,

---

32. WCL: MS 8.

If you will examine the Letter which I wrote to you, you will find, so far as my memory serves me for I kept no copy of it, that my object in it was to find out from you, what other doctrine was held upon the subject of the Lord's nature than that which I had maintained; in order that I might reflect upon it in my own mind, and, if I should find it more accordant with the truth than my own, adopt it. Your kind answer offering to open a correspondence with me upon the subject, I would long ago have acknowledged in the way you wished by entering upon the consideration of the view you unfolded, but that I have ever since been plunged in deep domestic distress of one kind and another;[33] which prevented me from being able to consider your views so as fairly to improve wherein I thought them wrong and wherein I thought them right. I have written nothing to any person upon the subject since save those letters to which you refer, of which I do not now remember the contents at all, except that they were written to prevent the horrible tenet from being imputed to me of maintaining Christ to be a sinner either as to his flesh or as to his mind. But, well believing what you write, that I did there charge the Christian Instructor with misrepresentation, you will observe that there is nothing personal to you in this because I opened my Letter with you upon the express condition that you should not be confounded with the writer in the Christian Instructor of whom I knew and wanted to know nothing. And this condition you observed in your answer. You and I therefore are known to each other as brother ministers communicating with one another concerning the common faith; and not as reviewer and reviewed. I think, my Brother, we had better continue on that footing. This I should consider a sufficient answer to your Letter; but I must not be on ceremony with one whom I name my brother and therefore I further explain.

That the Christian Instructor I did not censure from hearsay, but from meeting its words and sentences in quotations everywhere. For I have those, I know not whether to call them friends or enemies who are very careful to send me tracts and papers where I am reviled; and also in the defenses which have been made of me. I have seen the pages of that book quoted. One page in particular afflicted me, where, a passage which I had written to shew that the devil was always [beaten?] out of and kept full of the flesh of Christ, being overcome by him in the Spirit; is from an ambiguously but not ungrammatically placed comma made to speak the very contrary, and I am represented as holding that Christ's flesh was devil possessed. This being easily remembered has been written of me and circulated all over the world to the entire contradiction of the truth, and to the utter destruction of my good name. And the accidental (for it was but such) alteration of the comma point in the tract is brought against me as a concealed retraction of the false doctrine. Read that passage over again and tell me if the intention of the writer of it was not to shew that at all times Christ's flesh was delivered out of the hands of temptation and that 'Satan had nothing in him' in one word that He was holy, though liable to all our infirmities & temptations. My Brother if over all Christendom you were represented as saying the very contrary of what you had said,

---

33. His son, Samuel, had died on the 6th July.

and that in so awefully [sic] vital a point, would you consider it an evil thing for you to write to your personal friends that you had been misrepresented. Oh! let me entreat you not to be carried away by any nice sense of right to wound the vitals of Charity which seeketh not her own. I have been too much abused already on every hand to care about this fresh communication which you say you meditate. I count it all joy that I am counted worthy to suffer for my Lord's sake. But oh! do not by unnecessary publication of our personal intercourse with one another prevent it from growing into the bond of perfectness. This is all which I have to say. Fare well. May the Lord have you in his holy keeping.

Your faithful Brother,
Edw[d] Irving.

Addressed to: Revd. Marcus Dods,
Belford,
Northumberland.

Edward Irving to WILLIAM GRAHAM

[Undated[34]]

Sufferings and trials, my dear friend, are the good of faith, they work patience and patience is the way to perfection. I have a fiery conflict; my enemies have now become those of my own household, the members of the Church of Scotland; but I am only the more confirmed in my faith of a present Saviour and of a future reward. Oh, my dear William Graham, let your disappointments and trials in this world wear you into the fold of the grace of God, our Blessed Lord and Saviour!

Edward Irving to THE ELDERS AND DEACONS OF THE NATIONAL SCOTCH CHURCH

c. September 1830[35]

---

34. Oliphant, *Life*, 2:116.

35. EIL, MS 27a. This prayer, to be included in the preparatory fast day before communion, was found among the archives at Regent Square Church. Although undated, a clue to its time of composition can be found in the opening lines. 'O god! Who hath quickened us together . . . and united us into a believing and confessing church, who hath also made to endure much evil report for Christ

Oh God! Who hath quickened us together, according to the good pleasure of Thy goodness, and united us into a believing and confessing church, who hath also made to endure much evil report for Christ our Saviour's sake, and for the testimony of His eternal unity, do Thee, mindful of the many enemies inward and outward who are conspired against our prosperity, be pleased in Thy great mercy to forgive us all our sins and shortcomings, both as individual persons and as a Church and Congregation, and to grant to our prayers and confessions Thy convincing Spirit on the day set apart by the Rulers of the Church for fasting and humiliation; that being brought to the knowledge of our great unworthiness in Thy sight, being washed in the blood of Christ, and visited with the refreshings of Thy most comfortable Spirit, we may all together, and with one accord, draw near unto the mystery of the Holy Supper, and with faith beholding, handling, receiving, and eating, the very body and blood of the Lord Jesus, may be greatly delighted, yea, and ravished with His enjoyment, and filled with great strength and holiness, to our personal edification in Thy most holy truth to the growth of our Church in all faith, hope, and charity, to the refreshment of the whole body of Christ, and to Thine own glory, from which all good floweth, and in which it bideth earn the glory of the Father, and the Son, and the Holy Ghost. Oh Lord! our God and Father; hear this prayer of Thy Church, for Christ Jesus, His sake; and to Thy most holy name shall be all the praise. Amen and Amen

To the Elders and Deacons of the National Scotch Church.

My Dear Brethren,
I have written out the above, and caused a very confidential friend of mine to make a copy of it, and send it by Hall to each one of the Session, in order that our prayers being united together at the throne of grace, for the same good and gracious end, we may obtain the blessing of God upon the congregation.
Your affectionate Pastor,
Edwd Irving

Addressed to: Mr. William Dinwiddie.

---

our Saviour's sake, and for the testimony of this eternal unity, do Thee, mindful of the many enemies inward and outward who are conspired against our prosperity, be pleased in Thy great mercy to forgive us all our sins and shortcomings, both as individual persons and as a Church and Congregation.' The congregation at this time were clearly still supporting him to the extent that they were to make the *Declaration on the Divinity of Christ* in December 1830, endorsing Edward Irving's preaching on universal redemption. (See EIL 38, 18 December 1830)

Part II: The Letters

Edward Irving to REV PROFESSOR HENSLOW

Judd Place East, 20th October 1830[36]

My dear friend,

The same post which brought me these two letters from you and Mr. Smith, brought me accounts of my wife being ill at Brampton Park, which makes me feel it my duty to go down today, and will prevent me from coming to Cambridge on Monday. Will you please communicate with Mr. Smith and inform [him] that for the present we shall hold it suspended, and when I come I will choose a more serviceable time and endeavour to make a longer stay. Thank him for his kind letter and appraise him of my fervent love; I will ever remember your simplicity and loving-kindness towards me, and feel kindest affection towards you. Oh my Brother our occupation ought to be in sighing and crying for the Lord's appearance.

Farewell,
Your faithful & affectionate friend,
Edwd Irving

Addressed to: Rev Professor Henslow,[37]
Cambridge.

~

DECLARATION on the DIVINITY of CHRIST

[This was published in *The Times*, Saturday Dec 18, 1830]
London, 18th December 1830[38]

We, the Minister, Missionary, Elders and Deacons of the National Scotch Church, Regent Square, feel it a duty we owe to ourselves, to the Congregation to which we belong, to the Church of Christ and to all honest men no longer to remain silent under the heavy charges that are brought against us, whether from ignorance misapprehension, or wilful perversion of the truth, and therefore we Solemnly declare:

That we utterly detest and abhor any doctrine that would charge with Sin, original or actual, our Blessed Lord and Saviour Jesus Christ, whom we worship and adore as 'the very and Eternal God, of one Substance, and equal with the Father: who, when the fullness of the time was come, did take upon him man's nature with all the essential properties and common infirmities thereof, yet without Sin' 'very God and very Man,

---

36. BL: MS 29960 fol. 14.

37. John Stevens Henslow (1796–1861), Professor of Botany, Cambridge; friend and tutor of Darwin. He co-founded the Cambridge Philosophical Society.

38. EIL, MS 38.

yet one Christ, the only Mediator between God and Man': who in the days of flesh was 'holy, harmless, undefiled and full of grace and truth'; who through the Eternal Spirit offered himself without spot to God: 'the Lamb of God that taketh away the Sin of the World,' 'a Lamb without blemish and without Spot': in which offering of himself 'he made a proper, real, and full satisfaction to his Father's justice in our behalf.' And we further declare that all our peace of conscience, progress in Sanctification, and hope of Eternal blessedness, resteth upon the sinlessness of that Sacrifice, and the completeness of that atonement, which he hath made for us as our substitute.

And finally we do solemnly declare that these are the doctrines which are constantly taught in this Church, agreeably to the standards of the Church of Scotland, and the Word of God

Edwd Irving Minister
David Brown Miss[ionar]y

Archibald Horn
David Blyth   Elders
Wm Hamilton
James Nisbet[39]

Charles Vertue
Alex Gillespie Jnr
John Thomson   Deacons
J Henderson
Thos Carswell
David Ker

Edward Irving to MR MACDONALD

December 1830[40]

I desire very much, if possible, to come to Edinburgh for one fortnight, to preach a series of discourses upon the nature and acts of the Incarnation. I wish it to be during the sitting of the college, and in the evenings, or evenings and mornings, when the divinity students might attend. Ask Mr. Tait if he would risk his pulpit, or could you get another?

---

39. Of James Nisbet & Co., 21 Berners Street, London, who were publishers.
40. Oliphant, *Life* 2; 157.

Part II: The Letters

Edward Irving to MESSRS BALDWIN & CRADDOCK

Thursday, 27th Jany 1831[41]

My Dear Sir,

As my Printer's bills become due, I, being a poor man, am obliged to trouble you by requesting that you would make over to Messrs Ellister and Henderson what of the proceeds of my lectures & the tract on the Humanity are due at the time. I am about to publish the fellow of it, which I consign to your care.

I should mention to you, that while the General Assembly was last year and this great question was at front I wrote in all haste through the post a small tract upon the same subject, and had it published in Edinburgh but there was not time to have it Published here so as to serve the end. It was without my name and I am now about to acknowledge it. I mention this lest you should think it odd that I should not have mentioned it to my Publishers here. And also that if you can you may promote its sale; it is called 'The Opinions circulating concerning the human return of our Lord held by the Westminster Confession of faith' and was published by Lindsay without his knowing the author of it.

I thank you for all your endeavours to promote the sale of my books & hope that we are fellow labourers therein to the glory of God.

Yours faithfully,
Edwd Irving

Edward Irving to JAMES HARGRAVE MANN ESQ

London, 7th Feby 1831[42]

Dear Sir,

At the last meeting of the Session I caused your Letter to be read in their hearing, and it was our common mind to return you thanks for the pains which you had taken to investigate the subject, as also for the feeling which moved you to lay the result of your investigations before them. Several of us disagree with your conclusions, but that did not prevent us from honouring the pains and intention manifested in your communication.

I must add for myself, that the reason why it was not laid sooner before them, was simply this, that till the last meeting they were engaged upon the subject till far more than the time of our sederunt [sitting] was exhausted, and I did not think it right to lay your paper before them in an exhausted state.

41. Archives of the New Apostolic Church, Hamburg, folder 'Irving'.
42. MSS: ML 105a, b, c, d.

My mind gathers strength daily in the conviction that the Lord hath again visited his Church with the supernatural operations or rather outward manifestation of the Holy Spirit:[43] and I pray continually that he would incline your heart and the hearts of all to come and share of the benefit. Never since the commencement of my Ministry did I feel his Spirit so much with me in the manifold duties of my office; never was the church so numerously attended; never were the instances of conversion that come to my knowledge so many; never were there so many works of Charity and labours of love proceeding full from it upon this City. I beseech you, my Dear friend, to pause and consider well before you be in any way instrumental to stop the glorious work which the Lord is carrying on. I love you and therefore I beseech you to give weight to the manifest hand of the Lord with us. I desire my respectful love to Mrs. Mann and your family.

Your faithful friend,
Edwd Irving

Addressed to: Mann Esq.,[44]
Great Queen St., [London.]

~

Edward Irving to HENRY DRUMMOND

16th May 1831[45]

My Dear friend,

I thank you for your mindfulness of the poor distressed family. The lad's name is Ebenezer Whytt, his age eighteen last Nov. and his mother's present address at Mrs. Gordon's 12 Barnsbury Place or Street Islington.

We have with us Mr. & Mrs. Caird (Miss Mary Campbell)[46] two children of God, to whom I should like to introduce you; if you would come to breakfast on Wednesday Morning at half past 8 or on Friday at the same hour. Come in the love of the Lord, and it may please the Lord to give you such a gracious manifestation of speaking with a

---

43. In April 1830, the Macdonald family of Port Glasgow reported receiving the Spirit's gift of tongues and healing. A necessary manifestation for the Second Advent See Waddington, *The Rev. Edward Irving and the Catholic Apostolic Church in Camden and Beyond*, 31–33.

44. J. H. Mann, a trustee of Regent Square church, was to lead the prosecution against Edward Irving when he was summoned before the London Presbytery in May 1833. Subsequently Irving and his congregation found they were shut out from the church on the morning of 7th May 1833. See Oliphant, *Life*, 2:262 et al. James Mann had also been Chairman of the church's Building Committee. See Hair, *Regent Square*, 48.

45. DFP: C/9/6.

46. See letter Edward Irving to Dr Chalmers, June 2 1830 n.

tongue and prophesying as we had on Saturday last: concerning which I shall only say, that it removed not doubts (for I thank God I did not doubt) but cleared difficulties from my mind, and much edified us all.

The Presbytery of Paisley have unanimously pronounced my 'Printed book and pamphlets blasphemous' and overturned the Assembly to call me before them, and if I own the same, to cast me out instanter,[47] and take order that all persons circulating or according with them may be proceeded against. I think it not unlikely, such is the rashness & headiness of the times, that I may stand at their bar within a week and not impossible but that within another I may be ejected without indictment hearing or trial. But breathe this fear only to our God.

We have established a prayer meeting in our church at half past six every morning to continue till eight; there were more than one hundred persons present this morning. It was a scene of great refreshment. Droppings of the gift of tongues are beginning to be experienced by a dear friend of mine here; for whom I ask your prayers. My dear dear brother, let us wait upon our God, with all clearness of the mind and of the spirit, and he will soon draw near to us also. Let me encourage you to begin along with me a nearer & a closer walk with God in our inward heart and mind; and a holier life to utter his truth. Please also with my love make these thoughts known to my honoured friend Lady Harriet, whom with her dear children I commend to the Lord

Farewell, my Dear friend,
Your faithful friend & brother,
Edwd Irving

London, 16th 1831
Private: Addressed to: Henry Drummond Esq.,
Charing Cross, [London.]

P.S. My wife begs your votes for this orphan one of six if they are not engaged. The clergyman of the parish thought so much of their helpless case that he preached and published a sermon for the family. His brother for whom you gave your votes, was not successful at the last election. E.I.

~

Cope of a Letter from Rev John Martin to MR HAMILTON

London, June 1831[48]

---

47. Without delay.
48. WCL, MS 11.

My dear Sir,

I cannot but express to you how much I am grieved at the proceedings of the General Assembly in Mr. McLean's and Mr. Irving's cases—and especially at the very harsh & uncharitable spirit which was exhibited by some of the speakers. I am not prepared to justify the expressions which have been used by either of our Friends, but as they are known to be men of piety and great zeal for the truth and of singular devotedness to the service of our Lord and Master I did hope that they would have been treated with more brotherly kindness. Edward in particular had strong claims on the consideration of his Brethren. With all his faults, I wish from the bottom of my heart there were more like him. His labours are unceasing, and, blessed by God, they have also been wonderfully successful. He has been instrumental in bringing many to the knowledge of the truth, and notwithstanding all that has occurred I trust will be spared for much further usefulness. Our congregation happily continues very much united and though the Assembly's resolution may shake a few wavering individuals I hope it will not cause dissension amongst us. God has hitherto most wonderfully protected us and provided for our wants, and I have a good confidence that He will still be a present help to us in the hour of need.

Manse—June 1831

As to the sentence pronounced against Mr. Irving—I cannot say as much as of that pronounced against Mr. McLean. I think, and I have told him over and over, that his language, if not his meaning is heterodox; and gives abundant occasion for all that has been said and done against him. I am not the only one of his Friends who has said and written this to him; and really if he would not retract, or at least give up that language it could not in my opinion be any cause of surprise whatever source of grief it be, that such proceedings as have taken place should be adopted.

Annotated: Copy of a letter to Mr. Hamilton

∽

Edward Irving to Dr C. E. H. ORPEN

London 21st July 1831[49]

My dear friend,

I write this by the hand of a young man, a converted Jew for whom I stood witness in his Baptism. His name is Joseph Irving Herschell, he has learned the trade of a

---

49. Lambeth Palace Library: MS 1812, fol 70.

shoe-maker and is proceeding on his way to the Revd Mr Cleaver of Dalgany. Having no acquaintances in Dublin, I thought I might take the liberty of introducing him to you, that you might guide him on his way. He is accompanied by another Converted Jew of the name of Freidenthal for whom my wife stood witness.

But I more particularly write to inform you of the work of the Lord proceeding amongst us. The gift of tongues is communicated to several in this place. And the raising up of the sick, and the restoring of those who have been long lame are now occurring more frequently amongst us. Further the last fortnight two as wonderful *healing* [letter torn] are recorded in the New Testament have occurred amongst us within my own personal observation, not indeed through the instrumentality of any gifted person but in answer to the faith of the persons themselves, after they had been instructed in their [liberty?] to look unto Jesus as a healer.

Moreover, and this concerns you still more as one who has laboured much for the sake of the insane, a clergyman of the Church of Scotland the Revd David Dow of Irongray by Dumfries went to visit an incurable Lunatick, [*sic*] and being filled with the Spirit, said 'In the name of the Lord Jesus come out of him,' and after a slight convulsion over his whole body the man returned to his right mind, and continues so to this hour. Think of these [letter torn] and stir yourself and your friends up to believe. I write this on the morning of a day of fasting and humiliation which we have appointed for the sin of this nation. The Lord be with you & your wife & household. Commend me to all the Brethren whom I used to meet with you.

      Your faithful & obliged friend,
      Edwd Irving

 Addressed to: Dr Orpen,
 North Great Georges Street,
 Dublin.
 Favd by J. Herschell.
 [The letter was further inscribed:]
This autograph letter from Edward Irving written to Dr Orpen, first incumbent of Colesberg, S. Africa, was given by his son (a member of the Cape Parliament) to the Rev Dr Wirgman Rector of St. Mary's Collegiate Church, Port Elizabeth, & by him presented to the Lambeth Palace Library.
 June 9th 1893.

Letters: 1829–1831

Edward Irving to MR RICHARDSON

Bayswater, [London,] 8th August 1831[50]

Dear Sir,

I thank you for your careful attendance upon the vaccination of my babe[51] and I enclose you a sovereign as some recompense for your trouble

I am
Dear Sir,
Yours faithfully
Edwd Irving

Addressed to: Mr. Richardson,
Surgeon,
Bayswater, [London.]

~

Edward Irving to JAMES NISBET

[Annotated: 07 Sept 1831[52]]
Tuesday one o'clock

My Dear Friend & Brother Elder,

I had intended, when I found your card upon my table last night to call upon you this forenoon but that Mr. Brown told me you purposed to call on me, and explained to me in part the object of it with great kindness to us both. I have remained at home till one, and being now for the whole day engaged with Pastoral duty I sit down to express my love and carefulness towards you in a few words.

I have great tenderness for the scruples of a brother on the subject of the manifestations, and while I as a responsible man and a Minister of the Lord Jesus Christ, do plainly and honestly express & maintain my own opinion, I will never thereby involve any Elder or member of my flock in the consequences of my opinion and faith though I may long & labour to bring them to the same because I believe it both to be true and important. Therefore I beseech you not peremptorily to take any measure on this account, nor hastily to decide the one way or the other upon the gifts, but to be open to larger & fuller manifestations.

With respect to my preface to the Church Documents on which I have heard you have difficulties, I have to say that every word was written with great deliberation and

---

50. WCL, MS 7.
51. The 'babe' was Martin Howy Irving—born on 21 February 1831.
52. UEL D.4.103.

firm conviction as under the eye of my Master and messenger that there is no unnecessary much less intended offence to any one. I am responsible for the sentiments therein expressed, and I think them conformable both to the Word of God and the Standards of our Church. There is always a certain latitude allowed to men by every church to comment upon her Constitution, to point out deficiencies is to suggest improvements according to the mind & word of God. This I have very sparingly done, but never irreverently or rashly as my conscience bears me witness. I entreat you not to be disturbed on this subject, for it is my book and I am responsible for it.

The proper time for an Elder to entertain the thought of laying down his Eldership, is when he sees the discipline of the Church conducted contrary to the word of the great Head of the Church, or the teaching & preaching disagreeing with the oracles of truth. What I as a Preacher commissioned to every creature under heaven,[53] and an Instructor of the Church in general may put forth or do beyond the bounds of that jurisdiction concerneth him not so much, unless it should affect the integrity of my character as Pastor of the flock and Head of the Eldership.

My very dear Brother, every one knows how open I am to hear any grievance and to listen to any counsel. Therefore I beseech you to be confident towards me, and when you see an infirmity to bear and forebear with me, as I know also you do. For great is your love towards me. I add but one word more[,] that I believe the Kingdom of heaven suffereth violence and the violent take it by force.[54] 'Add to your faith valour' 'Be not afraid at this time but be bold for God, and full of that wisdom which is first pure then peaceable gentle'[55] and easy to be entreated full of mercy and good fruits without partiality & without hypocrisy. Wait at all events till after I have furnished my expositions on the gifts, which I begin after the Sacrament on Wednesday evening.

Your faithful & loving Pastor,
Edwd Irving

Addressed to: James Nisbet Esq., Berners Street, [London.]
[Annotated in pencil: Mr. Hamilton, Dr Chalmers]

~

Edward Irving to LADY OLIVIA SPARROW

27th October 1831[56]

My Dear Lady Olivia,

53. Cf. Eccl 1:23.
54. Matt 11:12.
55. Jas 3:17.
56. BL, Letters of Lady Olivia Sparrow 1803–54, MS EG 1966 fol 18–19.

I feel bound in Spirit to declare to you with all love and faithfulness, that I believe Mr. Caird to be a man of God, sound in the faith and devoted with all his heart to the work of teaching the Gospel of Salvation to the people and that I believe Mrs. Caird to be a prophetess of the Lord gifted with the gift of tongues & prophecy, and as such a precious gift to the Church of God. And being so convinced I cannot look forward to your separating them from your service without much painful apprehension for the effect upon your own Soul; because I feel assured that they are benefit to any family or people to whom the Lord may send them, whose benefit we may not rashly refuse or having received lightly esteem.

If you had the same convictions of his soundness in the faith, you would feel just as I feel. I was at pains to ascertain which were his views as to the Imputation of our Lord's righteousness, and our practical Holiness and found them to be the truth; and as the Lord so ordered that Lord Mandeville should come into my house, I was at pains to bring them to speak together upon the subject. My dear friend and honoured Lady, you must always make large allowances for a Teacher, who is not judging concerning opinions, but addressing the Truth to the wants of the people. His discourses are often after the nature of medicines very bad for a healthy person but quite necessary for a diseased person.

The thing which I think best to be done, is, that you should make no change till Mr. Maclean come, which I understand is not till Christmas, and when he comes, take Counsel with him whether with confidence you might entreat/extract your Essex people to their tuition. But while Mr. Caird is with you, I beseech you give no hint as if you disapproved or mistrusted his teaching. Oh my dear Lady it is sore sifting time and blessed are they who still abide the proof. My days are full of trouble for the Church, because his day of judgment is come. The Lord greatly confides and edifies me; though I stand girt about with thousands of enemies.

Much I wish is moved by my love for your Ladyship's prosperity that you may do nothing displeasing to our Master: but for the Cairds my house is ready to receive them, and I doubt not the Lord will call them and use them for his glory. Your kindness to them has been very great. They write me the largest acknowledgments. I beseech you to be in your guard against nice and critical judgments, and to be enlarged unto charity and hope. God have you in his holy keeping, and preserve you therein unto the end. This is the prayer of

Your ever loving & faithful friend,
Edward Irving

Addressed to: the Right Honbl The Lady Olivia Sparrow,
Brampton Park, Hants.

Part II: The Letters

Edward Irving to THE REV. EDWARD PROBYN

13 Judd Place East, 10th Nov. 1831[57]

My Dear friend and Brother,

I rejoice in the power and holiness; in the nearness and faithfulness of our God. This morning after breakfast I gathered the gifted brethren together with half a dozen of the most judicious of the brethren and read your letters in their hearing. Before the second letter was half read, one of them was made to speak in great power calling to try the Spirits, whereupon I rose in the middle of her utterance and put the question, 'Oh Spirit believest thou that Christ is come in the flesh.' She continued to prophesy in the most glorious and powerful manner confessing and adoring and lauding the humiliation of Christ and his glory, one joined and another, like they all as it were in a divine chorus went on testifying to the whole truth. Then singly one and another took up the burden of their Redeemer's work and did so magnify and celebrate the Lord as that I never heard the like. So that we were all lost in admiration of the Unity of the Spirit, and the superabundant evidence which he gave us of his being the Holy Ghost. We were all constrained to cry out for some song of praise to our most gracious God, and we joined in the XXIIIrd Psalm. The Spirit having thus entirely satisfied us of his oneness with Jesus Christ, we proceeded after a second prayer to deliberate concerning you and your dear children. I had just opened my mouth intending to shew my mind which was that you must not be content with categorical answers, but observe whether it be the habit and delight of the Spirit to testify unto the personal work of Jesus in the flesh his present glory and work in the Spirit, when Mr. Taplin was made to speak with great power these words first in a tongue and then in our own language. 'Tell him to hear no Spirit that testifies of *himself*, but that testified of *Jesus*, that he was crucified in the flesh, in the flesh, in our fallen flesh, and that he reigneth in the heavens, and that he will be glorified in his members who shall reign with him on the Earth for ever and ever.' Then Miss E. Cardale was made to speak much and powerfully 'Why is there not discernment of Spirits? Is it not written to another the discernment of Spirits?[58] Cry for that. Oh for the discernment of Spirits. Think you not that you need it? It is the eye of God in you. He it is that can discern the Spirits. O Cry for it. Ask and ye shall receive it. He knoweth our need. He knoweth the power of the enemy. He careth for the sheep. Make your wants known to him. He is very pitiful. He will hear you. He will answer you.' Much more was spoken to the same effect by others amounting to this that there was no safety or protection against the Evil Spirits but by abiding in Jesus, and watching our most secret thoughts.

We then proceeded to deliberate and were all of one mind that the Spirit was an evil spirit, and that its answering *yes* or *no* to the test was no proof, and that this is not the thing intended by *confessing*, but a thorough impenetration of their utterance

---

57. Strutt, MS 42 a, b, and c.
58. 1 Cor 12:10.

Letters: 1829–1831

with the Spirit of that truth, and that you *must seek to be filled with the Spirit in order to discern this*. It was observed by one that Hermes in his shepherd gives it as a test of the Evil Spirits that they desired to be consulted like the oracles, but the Holy Ghost speaks full of his own will. I never knew such a thing in any of the gifted persons among us, or in Scotland, and nothing approaching to it here save in one person whose gift I have doubted of, and prevented her from exercising it in my congregation, to which she does no longer belong. Furthermore I had been convinced by [letter torn] Miss Banke's Spirit was a very questionable spirit if not a false one; and no doubt the spirits in your children are of that family; and it was thought by one that you and Mr. Wolff should go and prove that Spirit in her. I have no doubt it is an evil spirit from its having testified that Jesus is come to the Earth already & that Elias is come; and also from its leading her into such extravagancies, severities etc and condescending upon such trifles, and domineering with its messages over Gods ministers; which is not the way of Christ as you see by his epistles to the Angels of the Churches.[59]

We prayed much for you, and I believe we prevailed with God. Now then give the Spirit no rest till you dislodge him by prayer and fasting. And give God no rest until like Mary Magdalen he fill these daily with the Holy Ghost. This is all that I remember and the Post now being come I conclude with my own & wife's tender sympathies and fervent prayer, also with thanks for your letters and a earnest wish to show all particulars which may occur. Be of good courage. The work of the Lord will proceed and cannot be let. May God have you all in his holy keeping.

Your faithful brother in the Holy Ministry,
Edwd Irving

Addressed to the Revd. Edwd Probyn, Longhope Vicarage, nr Gloster.[*sic*]

~

Edward Irving to THE TRUSTEES OF REGENT SQUARE CHURCH

November 22nd 1831[60]

My dear Friends,

I think it to be my duty to inform you exactly concerning the order which I have established in the public worship of the church, for taking in the ordinance of prophesying, which it hath pleased the Lord in answer to our prayers to bestow upon us. The Apostle Paul, in the XIVth chapter of the first Epistle to the Corinthians hath ordered

---

59. Rev 2 and 3.
60. MS: ML 18a, b, c, d, e, f.

in the name and by the commandment (v 37) of the Lord Jesus, that the Prophets shall speak 'when the whole Church is gathered together into one place' (v 23) 'two or three' and hath permitted that 'all the prophets may prophesy one by one, that all may learn and all may be comforted' (verses 29, 31): and he hath given instructions concerning the comely manner in which women shall prophesy in chap XI of the same Epistle. Walking by this rule I have appointed for the present that immediately after the reading and exposition of the Scriptures by the minister, there shall be a short pause for the witness of the Holy Ghost by the mouth of these to whom He hath been given (Acts V v. 32); and the same have I appointed to be done after the sermon. And this I intend shall have place at all the public congregations of the church; because I believe it to be according to the commandment of the blessed Lord by the mouth of the Apostle, and according to the practice of the Church so long as she had prophets speaking by the Holy Ghost in the midst of her.

The Church of Scotland, at the time of the Reformation, turned her attention reverently to this standing order of the Church of Christ, and appointed a weekly exercise for Prophesying or Interpreting of the Scriptures' (First Book of Discipline, chapter xii.) expressly founded on and ordered by the XIVth chapter of First Corinthians, 'to the end that the Kirk may judge whether they be able to serve to God's glory and to the profit of the Kirk in the vocation of the ministry or not.' At that time they had adopted the prevalent but erroneous notion that 'the office of the Apostle, of the Evangelist, and of the Prophet, are not perpetual and now have ceased in the Kirk of God; except when it pleased God extraordinarily for a time to stir some of them up again' (Second Book of Discipline, chapter ii). God hath now proved that he both can and will raise up these offices again, having anointed many, both amongst us and elsewhere with the gift of prophesying after the manner foretold in Isaiah XXVIII v 11, fulfilled on the day of Pentecost, and particularly ordered in 1 Cor XI and XIV. These persons having been fully proved at our daily morning exercise, and found to speak by the Spirit of God, I have in obedience to the Apostle, and in the spirit of the Church of Scotland, permitted to exercise their gift in the congregation, according to the order laid down above.

Now, my Dear Brethren, it is well known to you that by the Word of God, and by the rules of all well-ordered churches, and by the Trust-deed of our church in particular, it lies with the angel or minister of the church to order in all things connected with the public worship and service of God. For this duty I am responsible to the Great Head of the Church, and have felt the burden of it upon my conscience for many weeks past: but consulting for the feelings of others, I have held back from doing that which I felt to be my duty, and most profitable for the great edification of the Church of Christ over which the Lord hath set me. I desire to humble myself in His sight for having too long lingered to walk in the way of His express commandment, and having at last obeyed Him to whom we must all answer at the great day, I beseech you, dearly beloved, to strengthen my hands, and uphold them, as in time past ye have always been

Letters: 1829–1831

forward to do. But if ye cannot see your way clearly to do this, I entreat you not to let or withstand, lest haply ye be found fighting against God. And the more as it is expressly written in the only place where the method of prophesying in another tongue is mentioned, that it should be for a rest & refreshment to some, for a snare and stumbling unto many (Isaiah XXVIII v 12, 13).

For the rest, dear brethren, I need only add, that if you should see it your duty to take any step towards the prohibition of this (as I have heard that some are minded to do, which may God, for their own sake prevent and for the sake of all concerned), I pray that nothing may be done till after a friendly conference between the Trustees on the one hand, and myself, your minister with some friends to assist me on the other. For as we have hitherto had good Christian fellowship together, we will do our part by all means to preserve it to the end, without compromising our truth and duty.

I have done myself the satisfaction of sending to each one of you, dear brethren, a copy of the first part of a treatise on the subject of the Baptism with the Holy Ghost;[61] for your further information on this subject, which I beg you will accept as a small token of the esteem and gratitude of

Your faithful and affectionate friend and minister,

Edwd Irving

Finally may the Lord guide you in upright judgment, and preserve you blameless unto the day of His appearing & then receive you into His glory. Amen, and Amen!

[Annotated: This letter received the 22nd Novr: 1831 and entered on the Minutes of the Meeting of that date, of the Trustees of the National Scotch Church.

Charles Vertue,

Interim Secretary

Received in evidence before the Presbytery of London April 26th 1832. J. Miller.]

Isabella Irving to THE HON. MR J. J. STRUTT

25th Novr 1831[62]

My dear friends,

Be assured that although I have not written to you, you have not been the less upon our minds or the less frequently remembered before the Lord.—And we do trust to hear from you that as the Lord, no doubt for wise ends has suffered you to be much tried He has poured into your hearts abundant consolation.—We feel now satisfied,

---

61. Irving, *The Day of Pentecost*.
62. Strutt, MS 28.

indeed both the Miss Banks have themselves been brought to acknowledge that they have been under an evil influence—Their Father has separated them. I have not seen them but Mr Irving has very frequently as has several of the members of our Church & on Sunday eveng Mrs Caird & Miss E. Cardale to (*sic*) gifted persons were with Miss Banks for some time—Oh draw close to Jesus for yourselves & for your dear, dear Children. There & there only are we safe. The g.p. [gifted persons] has been for very many months so peculiarly precious to me.—Mr Irving wrote Mr Probyn what had been the result of the trial of the Sprits here. He also caused a friend to write to Port Glasgow. Our friends letter was read aloud in the meeting of the gifted persons there and the result has been most satisfactory. Should you desire it I shall send you a copy of part of a letter from Port Glasgow containing an account of the meeting.

You will be glad to hear that Elizabeth Hall[63] has also been delivered from the power of the Enemy . . . Dear, dear friends the Lord doth not lay on his people more than they are able to bear & He knows how to sustain & comfort under any trial. Mr Irving has at present a great fight of affliction to endure—Many of the members of the Church have taken offence at the voice of the Spirit being heard in the public assemblies of the church & have therefore left his Ministry—Almost all the Elders and Deacons have left it and the Trustees of the building have met & are again to meet in order to examine if their power as Trustees does not enable them to put this down by law.—Meanwhile Mr Irving enjoys perfect peace & comfort of Soul giving himself entirely up to the Lord in this as in any other matter. Pray for him especially in this that he may do that which is according to the mind of God.

You will be glad to hear that Mr Dodsworth has resolved to have a Meeting for prayer in his house every Thursday Evening. I have just been to see him and Mrs Dodsworth. Though I cannot say that he fully recognises the manifestations as the work of the Spirit yet I feel assured he will soon be enabled to do so. He is waiting upon God concerning the matter. I think dear Mr Strutts last visit to him was much blessed to him.

Your dear Children were specially remembered by us at our family prayers that Morning & Mr Strutt told us afterwards it was their birthday.—The Lord grant unto them the blessings asked for them & the comfort & joy besought for you & your dear husband.

I feel my dear Sister & Brother in Christ as if what had occurred in your family may deter you from seeking the Lord for His own Spirit—Oh let not this be. I *know* how you will have to guard against this temptation of Satan—I think saying read our blessed Lords last discourse in John's gospel is the best counsel I can give on this subject. It is brought to my own mind just now with great conviction.

Mr Irving has ordered the Services in public assemblies of the Church thus—that after the reading & exposition of the Chapt (what you call the lesson) and also after

---

63. It was a Miss Hall who had been the first person to burst out with the gift of tongues at Regent Square on the 16th October 1831.

the Sermon there should be a pause for a minute or two that if the Lord by the mouth of any of the gifted persons should see meet to speak it might be then.—On Sunday forenoon after the Chapt Miss Cardale was made to speak and in the Afternoon she & Mrs Cardale both spoke out after the Chapt the other after the Sermon.

A friend has come in to whom I wish to talk so I must conclude with asking you to write me soon enclosed to J. Percival Esq, 6 York Street, St. James's.

With our affectionate regards & kind love,
Your sincere friend,
Isabella Irving

~

Edward Irving to MR JAMES FRASER

National Scotch Church, Dec. 24, 1831[64]

My dear Friend,

Your urgent request that I would permit you to publish, through your Magazine, some authentic account from my own pen of the work of the Spirit in my church and elsewhere in order to stay, if possible, the torrent of blasphemy which is sweeping through the land, and give reasonable and religious people the means of making up a judgment upon so important a matter, has at length prevailed with me; and I sit down faithfully to narrate which hath come under my own eye, or been brought to my knowledge from the most certain and authentic sources; For, while it is a great point of duty not to cast pearls before swine, nor to give that which is holy unto the dogs, it is so also to sow beside all waters, and especially to make known the work of the Lord among other classes, now that the religious world are violently rejecting it. These two duties I shall endeavour to unite in this narrative, by presenting the subject in an historical form, with only so much of doctrine intermingled as is necessary for right exposition of the matter. Referring you and your readers, for the mysteries of the subject, to my public ministrations, to the papers in the *Morning Watch, or the Baptism with the Holy Ghost,* I shall merely set down in order the particulars of this work, as they are most certainly known by me to have taken place.

Your faithful Friend and Pastor,
Edward Irving

---

64. Irving, *Facts connected with Recent Manifestations of Spiritual Gifts.*

Part II: The Letters

Editor's Epilogue

At the end of 1831 Irving was again causing a public stir with the manifestation of 'tongues' in Regent Square Church; among those giving utterance were two members of the Cardale family. Despite the doubts expressed at the veracity of both the 'gifted persons' and their outpourings, Edward Irving refused to harbour any doubts, or curtail their activities, for which in 1832 he was to pay a very high price.

7

Letters: 1832–1833

Editor's Introduction

By this time Edward Irving was deeply committed to his proclaiming the Second Advent, from which even the earnest entreaties of his friend Thomas Carlyle, among others, could not divert him. A solicitor, Robert Baxter of Doncaster, who was later to renounce his prophecies, had joined the 'gifted persons.' Meanwhile the London Presbytery were becoming dismayed by the disruption to the church services and good order and on 6th May 1832 when Irving and his followers arrived for their 6.30 am service, they found the church locked against them. Temporary accommodation was found and subsequently they acquired more permanent premises in Benjamin West's picture gallery in Newman Street; the Irving family also moved there to live. The final blow to Irving came on 13th May 1833 when he was deposed by the Annan Presbytery on the grounds of his 'unlawful' doctrines on Christ's human nature. There was a further controversy also between a Mr. and Mrs. Simpson and the Cardales regarding Mrs. Simpson's visitation of 'tongues,' which resulted in the Simpsons leaving the newly formed church. And as if this was not enough, shortly before his trial Edward Irving's brother George and his baby son Ebenezer both died.

~

Edward Irving to REV DR MARTIN

January 1830[1]

---

1. Oliphant, *Life*, 2:232.

Part II: The Letters

I desire to give thanks to God that He has spared us all to another year and I pray that it may be very fruitful in you and in us unto all good works. We have daily reason to praise the Lord. He gives us new demonstrations of His presence amongst us daily. There is not any church almost with which He hath dealt so graciously. May the Lord revive and restore His work in the midst of you all! I would there were in every congregation a morning prayer-meeting for the gifts of the Spirit.

~

Edward Irving to ROBERT BAXTER

Postmarked 2nd March 1832[2]

Dearly beloved brother in our common Lord, To you and your wife and your children and your house and all the saints of God to whom you minister the word of life, I wish peace and prosperity in the divine life from God the Father, the Son and the Holy Ghost. The comfort and edification which the Lord ministered to you by you fills my heart with praise and thanksgiving to our God upon every remembrance of it. You have communicated to us in the word an unspeakable gift, you have been used by our Shepherd to direct us more steadfastly in our faith towards himself. We greatly long after you in the bowels of love, and much desire your reappearing in the midst of us with the full power of an apostle to minister the Spirit unto us by the laying on of hands. The Lord lifteth us up with [letter torn].

This morning another mouth was opened in the Church speaking in tongues and prophesying, and I heard of two others whom there is reason to believe have been visited privately, as also one in whom there seems to be the movements of the Spirit of discernment with the casting out of Spirits. Oh my Brother be strengthened in the Lord, be of a good courage & of a strong heart and do you Oh Sister whom the Lord hath appointed to be a help meet for your husband in this matter. But the post is come.

Farewell,

Your faithful Brother in [letter torn]

Edwd Irving

Alas! It hath been spoken by the prophets that Foley has spoken by Satan, I have communed with him & he is humbled. E.I.

Addressed to: Robert Baxter Esq. Doncaster

~

2. BT, MS 2.

Edward Irving to ROBERT BAXTER

7 Gloucester Terrace Regent's Park.[3]
3rd March 1832

My Dear Brother,

This moment the Lord hath sent me a very wonderful and wonderfully gracious message by our dear sister Miss Emily Cardale concerning the time which you have been made so often to put forth—rebuking me for having repeated it, and counseling me not to do it any more—declaring the word to be a true word but containing a mystery—declaring that the day is not known, and commanding me to write to you, to say that you must not repeat this in the flesh, but suffer the Spirit to say it how & when he pleaseth.

Here I leave it without any comment whatever. I am not equal to the work of commenting upon these words of the Lord. I am contented to walk in the darkness. The same message which said that the word you spake was true said also that the day is not known, and that it is a mystery, and that you as well as myself had erred in repeating in the flesh this matter of the time. The Lord lead us aught.

I was cut short in my message to your dear wife. Tell her she must look to her husband in the Lord, as the Lord's ordinance for her instruction and guidance; and thus doing she will be a defence unto her husband should he be overseen or snared in any matter. But if she look away from him or look to him not in the Lord but in himself she will prove to him a heaviness and not a comfort. This is my message to your dear wife. Let her lay it to heart.

Now Dear Brother let thy hands be strong, and thy tongue be willing to speak the word of the Lord. The work will not stand still. Thou art called to bear the chief burden in it at this present time. But the Lord will soon bring the helpers. We bear thee upon our hearts before the Lord. Fare thee well.

Your affectionate and faithful Brother,
Edwd Irving

Addressed to: Robert Baxter Esq.,
Solicitor,
Doncaster.

---

3. BT, MS 3.

Part II: The Letters

Edward Irving to THE TRUSTEES and BUILDING COMMITTEE and to THE ELDERS and DEACONS of the NATIONAL SCOTCH CHURCH, this NIGHT the 17th DAY of MARCH 1832, to CONVENE in the SESSION HOUSE of the SAID CHURCH.[4]

Men and Brethren,

As a man and the Head of a Family bound to provide for himself and those of his own house, I am enabled of God to be perfectly indifferent to the issue of your deliberations this night, though it should go to deprive me of all my income and cast me after ten years of hard service upon the wide world with my wife and my children, forth from a house which was built almost entirely upon the credit of my name, and primarily for my life enjoyment, where also the ashes of my children repose.

As a minister of the Lord Jesus Christ, who hath been Honoured of Him to bring forth from obscurity a whole system of precious truth, and especially to proclaim to this land the glad and glorious tidings of his speedy coming, and strengthened of Him to stand for the great bulwark of the faith oft times almost single and alone, I am still left indifferent to the issue of this night's deliberations, which can bring little addition to the burden of one groaning under the reproach of ten thousand tongues in ten thousand ways put forth against his good and honourable name. For I am well assured that my God whom I serve and for whom I suffer reproach, will support and richly reward me—even though ye also should turn against me, whom the Lord set to be a defense and a protection round about me.

As the Pastor also of a flock consisting of several hundreds of precious souls; and the minister of the Word unto thousands weekly, yea daily congregating into our beautiful house though it hath cost me many a pang, I am also entirely resigned to his will, and can cast them all upon his rich and bountiful Providence who is the good shepherd of the sheep, and doth carry the Lambs in his bosom and gently lead those who are great with young. On no account therefore be ye assured, personal to myself, as a man, as a minister of Christ, or as a Pastor of his people do I intrude myself upon your meeting this night with this communication; but for your sakes I do it, even for yours who are every one of you dear to my heart. Bear with me then the more patiently, seeing it is for your sakes I take up my pen to write.

I do you solemnly to wit, men and Brethren, before Almighty God the Heart-searcher that whosoever lifteth a finger against the work which is proceeding in the Church of Christ under my Pastoral care, is rising up against the Holy Ghost; and I warn him even with tears to beware and stand back for he will assuredly bring upon himself the wrath and indignation of the God of Heaven and Earth if he dare to go forward. Many months of most painstaking and searching observation, the most varied proofs of every kind taken with all the skill and circumspection which the Lord hath bestowed upon me; the substance of the doctrine, the character of the Spirit

---

4. ML: 106a, b, c, d.

and the form and circumstances of the utterances tried by the Holy Scriptures, and whatever remains most venerable in the traditions of the Church, the present power and penetration of the word spoken over the souls of the most holy persons, with the abiding effects of edification upon hundreds who have come under my own personal knowledge; the nature of the opposition which from a hundred quarters, most of them unholy, indifferent, infidel and atheistical hath arisen against it, together with the effects which the opposition hath had upon the minds of honest and good persons who have stumbled at it, their haste and headiness, their unrest and trouble of mind; the attempts of Satan by mimicry of the work and thrusting in upon it of seduction and devil-possessed persons to mar it, and the jealous holiness with which God hath detected all these attempts and watched over his own work to keep it from intermixture and pollution; and above all the testimony of the Holy Ghost in my own conscience as a man serving God with my house, the discernment of the same Holy Ghost in me as a minister over his truth and watchman over his people:—all these and many other things, which I am not careful to set out in order or at large, seeing the time for argument is gone bye [sic] and the time for delivering a man's soul is come, do leave not a shadow of doubt upon my mind that the work which shall begin under the roof of our sanctuary and which many of you are taking steps to prevent from proceeding there, is the *Work of God*, is verily the *Mighty Work of God*, the most sacred work of the Holy Ghost, which to blaspheme is to blaspheme the Holy Ghost, which to act against is to act against the Holy Ghost. This is the *guilt* of the action you are proceeding in, whether there be sufficient cause for bringing down such a load upon your heads, dearly beloved brethren, judge ye. For my part I would rather, were I a Trustee, lose all my property ten times told than move a finger in hindrance of this great work of God, which God calleth upon you to further, by all means in your power, and to abide the consequences of a prosecution, yea all consequences between life and death, rather than hinder; 'for what is a man profited if he gain the whole world and lose his own soul, or what should a man give in exchange for his soul.'[5]

You have determined to lodge a complaint against me to the London Presbytery for no immorality of conduct, for no error of doctrine, for no neglect of duty, for no breach of good faith, for no change of ordinance proper to the Church of Christ, for no departure from the constitution of the Church of Scotland, for no cause in point of fact which was, or could have been contemplated in the formation of the Trust-deed; but simply and solely because God in his great love & mercy hath restored the gift of Prophesy to the Church under my care, and I the responsible Minister under Christ being convinced thereof have taken upon me to order it according to the mind and will of Christ the only Head and Potentate of his church as the same is expressed in the Holy Scriptures. I ask you before God and as ye shall answer at the great day, if the Trust deed could have been intended to prevent the spiritual gifts from ever being exercised within the building, or from being ordered according to the word of God.

5. Matt 16:26.

Nay I go further and ask whether the constitutions of the Church of Scotland or any church could be intended to keep the voice of Jesus from being heard, as heretofore it was wont to be, within the assembly of his people. Oh! beloved brethren how can you find in your heart to complain against one who hath been so faithful amongst you to declare the whole counsel of God, and to do every thing by night and by day for the good of the flock & of all men, merely because he hath been faithful to his Lord, as well as to the people of his Lord, and would not by a mountain of opposition be daunted from acknowledging the work and walking by the counsel of his God. I beseech you to search your hearts and examine how much of this complaint ariseth from a desire to do your duty as Trustees, how much from dislike and opposition to the work from the influence of the popular stream and the fear of the popular odium, from your own pride of heart and unwillingness to examine any thing new, from the love of being at ease in Zion, and from other evil causes over which I have a constant jealousy in myself, and in my flock whom I should love better than myself. I do not judge any one in this matter, but I would be blind indeed if I did not discern the working of these and the like motives of the flesh in many of you, and I would be unfaithful if I did not mention them. I fear lest I may have been unfaithful in times past; if so God forgive me, and do ye forgive me, and take this as the last and complete expression of my love to all of you.

Oh! my Brethren take time and think which tenant may be expected to come and take up his abode in that house from which the Holy Ghost hath been cast forth? It will never prosper or come to any good until it hath been cleansed from this abomination by sore and sorrowful repentance. How can you make a fashion of calling it a House of praise or prayer any longer after having banished forth of it the voice of Jesus lifted up in the midst of the Church of his Saints which is the temple of the Holy Ghost. Surely disappointment and defeat will rest upon it for ever. God will not bless it. The servants of God will flee away from it. It will stand a monument of folly and infatuation. Nay so much hath the Lord made me to perceive the iniquity of this thing, that I believe it will bring down judgment upon all who take part in it, upon their houses, upon the city itself in which the National Scotch Church hath been a lamp, yea and a light unto the whole land and to the distant parts of the earth. Oh my Brethren, retrace your steps, leave this work in the hand of the Lord, come forward and confess your sin in having thought or spoken evil against it, come to the help of God against the mighty. I beseech you to hear my words. They have been written with prayer and fasting, and when I read them over about an hour ago in the hearing of one gifted with the spirit, that the Lord, if he saw good might express his mind; the consequences which He denounced upon the doing of the act were fearful to hear. I had little thought of mentioning this to any one, but it seemeth to be not right to hide it in my own heart.

If you desire, dear brethren, any personal communication with me upon this awful subject, I beseech you to send for me, and I will be at your call; for I could stand to be tortured from head to foot rather than any one of you should go forward in such an undertaking as to prevent the voice of God from being heard in any House over which you have any jurisdiction. May the Lord preserve you from all evil and lead you into the way of His own blessed will. Amen and Amen.

Your faithful & loving Pastor and Friend,
Edwd Irving

13 Judd Place East.
17th March 1832

~

Edward Irving to J. G. SIMPSON[6]

[Undated[7]]

My Dear Sir,
Your note has come too late to prevent the meeting of the gifted persons to-morrow at 4 o'clock, when Mrs Caird has written me that she will be present. I desire it as the Pastor of the Church, because it is written 'Let the prophets speak two or three and let the rest discern.'[8] I desire that the rest should be present in order to discern what the mind of the Lord in his utterances is. I also ask Mrs Simpson's presence in the matter of Mr Taplin also, because I believe him to be a spiritual person, one who 'hath been used of the Lord,' and I think it is meet that you as her husband should be present also.

Now, dear Sir, my sole object in all these things is to serve the Chief Shepherd, and to preserve his flock from the snares and wiles of Satan, which are around all especially the spiritual. And I trust you will not stand in the way of them but further them. Still I must fulfil my duty to the great Head of the Church in waiting on his flock.

My heart has been much drawn to Mrs Simpson to see her delivered out of every snare, for that Satan hath been drawing snares around her I have no doubt, and that we will deliver her through humility and watchfulness.

Farewell,
Your affectionate Pastor,
Edwd Irving

Thursday 3 o'clock.

~

6. See letter J. G. Simpson to Edward Irving, 2 June 1824, NLS, MS Simpson, Diary 104.

7. According to the entry in NLS, MS Simpson, Narrative 102, this letter was written on Thursday 19th April 1832: NLS, MS Acc 12489/15.

8. 1 Cor 13:29.

Part II: The Letters

Edward Irving to ROBERT BAXTER

London 13 Judd Place East, 21st [March] 1832[9]

My Dear Brother—Read this Letter with your eye on God.

We have great need, especially the spiritual amongst us to walk humbly with the Lord. Your first Letter containing the utterance of the Spirit without any expression of his intention in sending it to me, led me very deeply to ponder the subject of our Lord's flesh and to examine myself before the Lord, and to cry upon the Lord to examine me and to the same exercise of soul had I been drawn by the utterance of the spirit and the experiences of the spiritual of my flock in these days past. These things put me into a fit condition for receiving the full impression of your last Letter, which arrived last night after I had preached a sermon on the Holy generation of the flesh of Christ. This I had done in order to express anew before my people with all Caution and Consideration what I firmly believe to be the truth; and to guard them against the effect of any rash and unguarded expressions which I might at any time have used. All night long my soul & waking was exercised upon the subject of your last Letter;[10] and it being wonderfully ordered in God's providence that Mrs. Caird should be in town for a day or two, and that Miss E. Cardale though desirous to go home before breakfast was so burdened as not to be able to go; these two prophetesses of the Lord who have been his mouth of wisdom & of warning to me & my church in all perplexities I called along with my wife who had read your Letter & read it to me, and having spread the whole matter before the Lord, and twice besought his presence, we proceeded to read your Letters in order; upon the first Letter there was no utterance of the Spirit nor expression of any kind amongst us but that of assent. When we had read the two first pages of the second, wherein you reason upon the words of the Spirit 'he has erred, he has erred' given to you upon two sentences in my book,[11] and bring forward your views of our Lord's flesh, and of the believer's holiness in contradistinction from mine, we paused, and seeing there was so manifest a discrepancy between us, I solemnly besought the Lord that he would speak his own mind in the matter. Instantly the Spirit came upon Miss E. Cardale, and after speaking in a very grieved tone & spirit in a tongue she was made to declare many words which I will not take upon me to attempt to repeat seeing the Spirit hath discountenanced such attempts, but the substance was most precisely this; that you had been snared, by departing from the word & the testimony; that I had maintained the truth, and that the Lord was well pleased with me for it; that I must not flinch now but be more bold for it than heretofore; that he had honoured me for it, and that I must not draw back; that in some words I had erred, and that the word of the Spirit by you was therefore true and that if I waited upon the Lord he would

---

9. BT, MS 4.

10. 'The letter I had written in power, setting forth that the carnal mind was not in Christ': Baxter, *Narrative of Facts*, 103 n.

11. *ibid*.

shew me them by his Spirit, but that he had forgiven it because knew my heart was right towards him; that I had maintained the truth, and must not draw back from maintaining it. Thereupon we knelt down and having confessed my sin & thanked him for his mercy, I proceeded to entreat him for you that you might be delivered from the snare in which you were taken concerning the flesh of Christ and the holiness of the believer. This done I sought to recover and recount the substance of the utterances as above given that by their help I might report it to you exactly. My wife was mentioning a doubt as to whether it should not be simply left to the Lord, and not dealt with in the understanding at all, seeing that in your Letter you had gone astray by commenting in your understanding upon the words of the Spirit 'He hath erred' as applicable to two sentences of my book and applied them to my whole doctrine which the Spirit held just declared to be 'the truth' that 'must be maintained': when Mrs. Caird was made to speak in a tongue with great authority and strength, and immediately after in English to the effect, that you had stumbled greatly by bringing your own carnal understanding to spiritual things, that truth in the inward parts, the law of God in the heart wrought in us the fulfillment of the righteousness of the law in all our members, and that union with Jesus brought into us the holiness of Jesus in body Soul and Spirit, that the Lord would have a church upon the Earth holy as he is holy, the light of the world as he is the light of the world, that some had sought to bring this about in the flesh, that you had been snared in the opposite extreme of denying it altogether and making a distinction between Christ's holiness and that of his Church, that you must be informed of it, because this it was which was preventing the work of the Lord. There was a third utterance through Miss E. Cardale to teach me that Satan sought to overthrow my confidence in the truth and to bring me into a snare, but that I was called upon to maintain it now more firmly than ever.

There were no more utterances but when we came to that part of your Letter where you say 'Concerning the vessels by whom he speaks you have fearfully provoked Him and they are ready to burst under your hands' there was great indignation felt by both the vessels of the Lord present, and great sense of injustice felt by myself, for oh! Dear brother, I have done all things to know and follow the mind of the Lord in respect of them. It was indeed said I think in the Spirit, that this in you was the same spirit of 'the accuser of the Brethren'[12] which hath manifested itself lately amongst us in one of the gifted persons who spoke evil of me in the midst of the congregation,[13] but the Lord hath shewed him that though it was with power, the power was not from God but from Satan to whom by hard and unjust thoughts of me he had opened the door. Ah! dear Brother you have surely been much overseen in some way or other. Search it out.

12. Rev 12.10, i.e., Satan.

13. 'In the case of Mr T[aplin] alluded to in Mr Irving's letter, he, who was, and I believe is still, received as a prophet, had, in the midst of the congregation, with tongues and in English, spoken evil of Mr Irving': Baxter, *Narrative of Facts*, 119.

Part II: The Letters

The thing you spoke of Foley and Miss Hall[14] was not of God. I fear and am persuaded in my own mind, that you have not discriminated duly what is of the Lord and what is not of him; and that sin in this matter undiscerned and unconfessed hath brought on greater falls as we have seen amongst ourselves; and that now you are brought to oppose that doctrine which alone can bring the Church to be meet for her bridegroom that as he was holy in the flesh so are we through the grace of regeneration brought to be holy, planted in a holy standing the flesh dead to sin, as his flesh was dead to sin, and that by the Baptism of the Holy Ghost we are brought into the fellowship of his power and fullness to do the works which he also did and greater works[15] than this. When we came to that passage of your Letter where you censure as 'fearfully erroneous' a passage in Day of Pentecost, we were all made to feel that you were forgetting what you yourself had been made to utter so abundantly concerning the Baptism with fire and the spiritual ministry [letter torn] read this to my wife Mrs. Caird and Miss E. Cardale, and they say—it is a full and exact account. Now upon the whole my well-beloved Brother, and Prophet of the Lord, I give you counsel to search and prove what it is that sits so heavy upon your conscience, for the Lord will surely reveal it. Concerning the flesh of Christ we will discourse when we meet. I believe it to have been no better than other flesh as to its passive qualities or properties as a creature thing, but that the person of the Son of God as Son of Man in it believing in the Father did for his obedience to become son of man receive such a measure of the Holy Ghost as sufficeth to resist its own proclivity to the world and to Satan, and to make it obedient unto God in all things; which measure of the Spirit he received in his generation and so had holy flesh, and by exercise of the same faith he kept his vineyard holy and presented it holy to the great husbandman. Regeneration through faith sealed in Baptism doth [letter torn] the same measure of the Spirit to do the same work of making our flesh the holy thing, the temple of the Holy Ghost, body, soul and spirit holy, whereupon we have the name 'saints' or 'holy ones,' 'sons of God' as he received those names in virtue of his generation of the Holy Ghost. If we were to meet I think we would not find much difference of mind as to the flesh of Christ; but as to your view of holiness it is the very deepest and

---

14. 'Disturbance at the National Scotch Church—On Sunday the Rev. E. Irving delivered two sermons on the extraordinary gifts of the Spirit, on each of which occasions the congregation were disturbed by individuals pretending to the miraculous gift of tongues. During the sermon in the morning, a lady (a Miss Hall), thus singularly endowed, was compelled to retire to the vestry, where she was unable (as she herself says) to restrain herself, and spoke for some time in the unknown tongue, to the great surprise of the congregation, who did not seem prepared for the exhibition. The rev. Gentleman resumed the subject in the evening, by discoursing from (or rather expounding) the 12th chapter of the 1st Corinthians. Towards the conclusion of the exposition, he took occasion to allude to the circumstances of the morning, and expressed his doubts whether he had done right in restraining the exercise of the gift in the church itself, and compelling the lady to retire to the vestry. At this moment a gentleman in the gallery (a Mr. Taplin, who keeps an academy in Castle-street, Holborn) rose from his seat, and commenced a violent harangue in the unknown tongue': *The Times*, 19 October 1831. Miss Hall was a governess (in the Perceval household). See letter Isabella Irving to Robert Baxter, 26 August 1831 n: BT, MS 1.

15. John 14:12.

darkest & subtlest snare of the enemy. If you understood thoroughly the one subject you would understand thoroughly the other. I say not that Christ had the motions of the flesh, but that the law of the flesh was there all present, but whereas in us it is set on fire by an evil life, in him it was by a holy life put down, and his flesh brought to be a holy altar whereon the sacrifices and offerings for the sin of the world, and the whole burnt offerings of sorrow and confession and penitence for others might ever be offered up and thus ought we to be, and shall be when the flesh becometh the sackcloth covering. Oh brother I have had many trials, but the Lord hath sustained me, and I dwell before him in peace of soul, though in much sorrow because of the condition of his Church. I shall be glad when we meet, but oh! I beseech you lay to heart the words which have been spoken by the Spirit, and doubt any words which may be spoken to you contrary thereto; & though an angel from heaven should come to me testifying to your views of holiness I would not receive him, Do you hold correspondence with any one of my Church that you should speak so positively yet so unjustly concerning my treatment of the spiritual persons, or is there some meaning couched under it which I do not understand. Did the Spirit say so in you? If so, Doubt that spirit, for certainly it is not true, they themselves being witnesses. Fare you well. May the Lord have you in his holy keeping. Amen.

Your faithful Brother,
Edwd Irving

Addressed to: Robert Baxter, Solicitor, Doncaster

PROTEST to THE PRESBYTERY OF LONDON[16]

26th April 1832[17]

I protest in the presence of Almighty God and the Lord Jesus Christ the only Head of his Church, that I was not permitted in questioning the Witnesses to refer to the word of God, which is the only appeal in all questions, that my judgment was therein taken away and that I will put no further questions.

Edwd Irving

[Annotated:] The above is the protest written by Edward Irving and thrown down on the Presbytery Table as he left the room and the Church of Scotland after entering a copy of the above in the Minute Book it was taken home by my late father the Revd. James Millar Minister the Bethlehem Scotch Church London who was Moderator of

---

16. See *A Word of Testimony; or, a corrected account of the evidence adduced by the Trustees of the National Scotch Church in support of their charges against the Rev Edward Irving*, 1832, 9–10.

17. NLS, MS 1030, fol. 55.

the presbytery I do not know the date but it can be found I think in Mrs. Oliphant's Life of Irving. Signed Emma Margaret Millar, Aug 24th.

Jane Simpson to EDWARD IRVING

London, May 1832[18]
[Annotated: 8th]

My dear Sir,
The burden which has been upon my Mind for the last month has been the subject of much prayer and I believe the Lord has since given me discernment respecting it and I pray that the Lord may enable me faithfully to shew you the light which He has given to me respecting myself. Fear is of the Flesh, and I know myself to be liable to it from my earliest days I have had to contend against it, at School it brought a snare, and in the Exercise of any Accomplishments such as music, singing etc in Company fear brought a Snare[;] for the last few years I felt it had been overcome, until the Gift of the Spirit began to manifest itself in Utterance, when I was soon made to feel that the Enemy was assailing me on this weak point and bringing me under the bondage of fear in the exercise of the Gift in the presence of any person, even in the presence of my Husband at first, for when the power of the Spirit came upon me, the Tempter came to me, and through the fear of those who might be present, tempted me to resist & quench the Spirit. In private the Lord enabled me to overcome this Temptation & I was made a willing instrument in the hand of the Lord. I felt myself quite passive in his Hand, willing to utter his word when he gave it, and willing to be silent. But when I was called to Exercise my Gift in Church, it was a greater trial to the flesh than I am able to describe. However I felt it my Duty to bring it into the Church, the Lord had spoken by Mrs Caird and said it was for the Church, and you the Angel of the Church had called upon me to come forward among the other Gifted Persons and Prophecy [sic], and it was my own earnest desire to use it for the *Glory of Him* who had given it. Therefore I laid the matter before the Lord and Pray'd very earnestly that he would enable me to overcome the tempter, and give me power to Exercise my Gift in His Church for His Glory, and I did receive courage to come forward and utter in the meetings of the Church. However I never was delivered from the temptation of the Enemy, who contrived to Assail me as above described. Often when I felt the movement of the Spirit I was tempted with fear lest it should not be the Mind of the Lord that I should utter, and thus I was made to restrain the movement of the Spirit, & I would Pray the Lord to send his Message thro' other Prophets that the Church might be edified. On these occasions I had assurance

---

18. NLS, MS Simpson, Diary 16–23.

that it was truly the movement of the Spirit of God which I had resisted, because the thing revealed to me, was afterwards invariably given to the Church either by you or through some other, again when I have been pressed to utter, I have repented of having grieved the Spirit and when the power was decreasing I have uttered, again I may have uttered when the Spirit was moving me to utter before I got the Commission from the Lord, in order to resist the Tempter, who was ever tempting me to quench the Spirit. In this way, it may be, that Miss Cardale had not Sympathy with me in *my* utterances, therefore it was a grieved Spirit in the assembly; of the Saints, I am quite Assured of that, but it was through quenching, through restraining and not yielding to the Spirit, Satan Tempting the flesh to desire to govern the Spirit, whereas the flesh should have been passive, the willing servant of the Spirit. The Lord used the utterance by Mrs Caird to cast light on this matter. However[,] from some remarks which you made, I put this application of the utterance away from me, and tried to discern some other snare. Until the Lord has clearly shown me that the *Enemy did not tempt me with power*, and now the utterance has been aply'd [applied] to my own experience and both are found to harmonise. It was said (in Mrs Cairds Utterance) He said he had his Arms arround [sic] you, he had his Arms arround [sic] you, he hath been faithful to you, when you leaned upon him, but there has been times & seasons when ye let go part of your Armour and the Enemy got an advantage through the flesh, for faith is the shield by which we are enabled to quench the fiery darts of the Enemy.—And in knowing that it was from want of faith in the presence of the People, that prevented me from lying [sic] passive in the hand of the Lord, for in private there was always a full yielding to the Spirit and then it was remarked that my Utterance was always full rich and it had just been brought to my mind that when I have been alone with God and led out in prayer by the Spirit, that the Spirit has cried for liberty, that he might not be restrained by the Flesh. Even that Morning on which you and Miss Cardale came to Cross Street, I had been made to Pray in the Spirit that the Lord would break all the Snares which restrained the Spirit from full liberty, and on the Sabbath after, being the following day. Although I began to pray under a very different impression, namely that the movement of power which I had for some time had been from the Enemy. However[,] the Spirit came speedily upon me and carried me out in a Tongue in which I was made to chant for a length of time having great Joy and communion with God, and after this while in the Spirit I was made to cry that the Lord would give the Spirit full liberty.

I will now give my reasons for believing that the Enemy did not tempt me by giving power to the Flesh. First because I did not desire power when I was lead [sic] earnestly to pray for the Gift of the Spirit. I desired it that I might worship God in the Spirit and in truth that I might love God and be one with Jesus. It is now about 12 months since I was conscious of receiving the indwelling of the Spirit and there is a remarkable coincidence betwixt my case and that of the Disciples, the Lord delivered to them the promise of the Father, he told them they were Clean through the Word which had been spoken to them but they were to abide at Jerusalem until they received the Promise of the Father and they did abide with Prayer and supplication 10 days when they received the Promise. The Lord spoke by Mrs Caird to me. She was made to say I was washed and clean, and made to call upon me to be filled with the Spirit, then I firmly believed that I had received the Promise of the Father, that it was his will to fill me. On coming Home from your House, I opened the Bible at that part in the Acts where the Lord commanded the Disciples to abide in Prayer & supplication until they received it. It was applied to me, I felt my self placed in precisely the same condition in which they were and I did abide in prayer and supplication for the Promise just about 10 days and while I was praying on Sabbath afternoon alone, I was conscious of receiving the Gift—from that time I have been in the enjoyment of the presence of God, the Love, the peace and Joy of God and the power follow'd without being desired, and during the period of the Exercise of my Gift in Church my Supplications have always been for closer union with Jesus, for a deeper entrance into his Mind and to be filled with the Love of God, my earnest desires have been to have the Life of Christ to be perfected in me, and since the first warning was given regarding the Snares which the Enemy was laying for me. (I believe the Snares would be those of giving power to the flesh), and I continued to pray very earnestly that the enemy might not be permitted either to give the word or the power, and that the Lord would consume the flesh in me that it might not rise to seek its own Glory. Now I have strong confidence in God as the hearer and answerer of Prayer, the Lord hath been very gracious to me in this way. I can truly say that whatsoever I have ask'd of Him I have received. The 3rd Reason I shall mention is that during the last Month, when I entertained the Idia [sic] that the Snare into which I had fallen was that of receiving power from the Enemy, the movements which I believed to be movements of the Spirit were the movements of the Enemies [sic] power, then it has been that the Lord hid his face from me, then have I been shrouded in Darkness and the Enemy has come to me in all his power saying where is your confidence now ye trusted in Him but ye have been deceived, ye believed ye were abiding in the Love of God, ye believed that the Lord was present with you especially in Church Revealing his Mind to you etc. But it has been all a delusion for that power which gave you Joy was from the enemy and not from God. He then tried me by shewing me that if I had been so deceived in the communications between God and my own Soul in Church & in the Joy which I had drawn from the movements of that which I had believed to be the Holy Spirit, then indeed I had been in a delusion from the beginning, and it must be all a delusion. However[,] I praise the Lord, that I was not permitted to yield to these Temptations, the Lord sustained me by drawing to confidence in Himself by Assuring me that the Love of God which I had experienced in my Soul was truly the Love of God, for having tasted the sweetness of Him no one should be permitted to persuade me that it is bitter, that the movements of power both in Church and out of it which gave me so much Joy, and drew me into such close communion with God were truly the Movements of the Spirit of God. Thus being established again in the firm belief that the communications which I had experienced betwixt God and my own Soul were real and not delusive that the power which I had was the power of God and not of the enemy, then again did the face of my heavenly father shine upon me, the Love, the peace & Joy of God were restored to me & faith & confidence & Power & Utterance. Now my dear sir I have faithfully stated to you the working of my own Mind, and God's dealing with me respecting this deep matter, will you lay it before the Lord and he will enable you to discern it. I only desire his Glory in it[;] I have been Taught an important Lesson through these temptations which Assailed me. When I had yielded up the communications between God and my own Soul and called on the Word uttered by the Prophet, I aught to have maintained a firm and unshaken confidence in God, I aught to have rested Assurred [sic] that I had not been deceived in my Experience regarding the Communications between God and my Soul, and waited for the Lord to aply [sic] the Word. That no word Uttered by a Prophet should separate between God & the Soul, that the Word of the Prophet should be left with the Lord to aply [sic] it to the conscience.

Since the Lord has restored me to confidence in Himself, by shewing me that my Experience of his goodness was real and not delusive, I have Pray'd to him in faith for light regarding the true burden of the Spirit regarding me, and have desired most sincerely to know the thing in which I have grieved the Spirit, and that which it contained in the first part of this Letter has been clearly revealed to me, so that there was a true burden of the Spirit. Nevertheless the communications between God and my Soul, I now see distinctly the Love of God in calling upon me to Exercise my Gift in your presence, that I might be strengthened in faith and confidence, and be enabled to cast my self freely upon the Lord. However in this discernment of the Utterance the Enemy laid a snare both for Miss Cardale and my self, for a few days I ask'd Miss C if she knew in what way the Enemy was laying snares for me. She said she had no Utterance regarding it, but the Enemy gave great power to the flesh if we were seeking our Own Glory. Now it appears to me that from that period, having no intercourse with me that her Mind was impressed with the Idea that giving power to the flesh was the Snare,—I believe, if I was correct in the discernment of that Utterance by Miss Cardale in yr presence at Cross Street—it convey'd the Idea that through the desire of self Exaltation I had received Power from the Enemy, though I desired the Lord to aply [sic] the Word she uttered God gave no witness to it during the Utterance, I felt myself leaning upon the Lord all the time she spoke, & at that part of it regarding self Exaltation, these words were presented to me—'he will not break the bruised reed nor quench the smoking flax';[19] and these words sustained me. Nevertheless I did not assay the word by Miss Cardale. However the Utterance has not been aplied [sic] to my conscience, though the burden of the Spirit has been aply'd [sic] as described above. I have only to Add that I am still Assurred [sic] the Lord spoke by me to you that mor[nin]g. I have considered what you stated regarding Self Justification and have laid it before the Lord but have discerned no Self Justification in it, I observe in it great Jealousy over the faithfulness of God, as the hear[er] and Answerer of Prayer, and

---

19. Paraphrasing Matt 12.20 and Isa 42:3.

I was made to feel this very deeply during the Utterance. Now My dear Sir If you will just reflect on the ground on which you stood at the Moment, you was [sic] in the belief that my case was precisely the same as Miss Hall's, that I had received power in the flesh from the Enemy that the Spirit did not dwell in me, was it then wonderful that the Holy Ghost dwelling in his Temple should undeceive you and warn you, against entertaining this opinion and call upon you to Sift the matter & search because it was a deep & Solemn matter. Now my Dear Sir were these not words of truth, and after sifting it, have you not found that it was a case quite different from Miss Hall's; yea I feel assured that if you lay this case before the Lord, you will be made to see that it has not been a Work of Satan in the flesh either at one period or another, but Satan tempting the flesh to the unwilling Servant of the Spirit and so grieve the Spirit by restraining it and not yielding to it even in the Utterance. Now my Dear Sir after having sifted this case had you found, that given first impressions regarding it were correct then it would have been a lying spirit which had spoken. But as you have discovered that the impression on your Mind at the Time, when I was made to speak were erroneous that then you did not believe that I had received the Gift of the Holy Spirit and that afterwards you were brought to believe that I had, surely it has been a Spirit of Truth which spoke to you. I am assured it was not the flesh from the State of depression in which I was at the moment, when the power and utterance Rushed upon me I was ready to fall from my seat. Now my dear Sir I have communicated all my impressions regarding this matter to you, with the freedom and confidence of a child to a Parent, I have not premed[it]ated any thing I have stated, but have sought the Lord that He would guide my Pen, and enable me to be faithful, it is my sincere desire to Serve the Lord with my Gift. I have no object but his glory who gave it but I feel myself under a stronger bondage of fear in the Congregation than I ever did. But this I may be delivered from through confidential intercourse with you and the other Gifted Persons. I desire to be delivered from this fear that the Lord may use me for His Glory, I therefore cast my self upon your care, and will in all things be guided by your council. If you had an opportunity [sic] of hearing the Exercise of the Gift in Private, I might be strengthened to use it in the Congregation.

Jane Simpson to EDWARD IRVING

London, 31 May 1832[20]

My Dear Sir,

Having been lately much ingaged [sic] in pleading with the Lord that he would heal all the breaches in our Church, and cement us in Love and build us up in Strength

---

20. NLS, MS Simpson, Diary 25–27.

and Show us the cause of our present weakness, the Enemy having come in like a flood and nearly swept away the standard of the Spirit—It was revealed to me that our breaches could not be healed until we received the Gift of Discernment of Spirits, that in weakness in the Spirit has altogether proceeded from the want of this Gift in the Church that wherever Spiritual Gifts were given to a Church the Gift of Discernment was an ordinance of God, therefore it would be given if ask'd in faith, that the Enemy had got an advantage over us through the want of it and had brought us into weakness and confusion and desired to keep us in this state, by shewing us that the Prophets were to Discern each other's Spirits, and that all the church were to Discern and Judge the Utterances, in this way the Enemy would soon put down the work of the Lord. It being manifest from the 11 Chpt of Corin[thian]s[21] that the Gifts may be professed without Love, therefore if the Prophets were to try each others Spirits the Enemy would Snare them by giving them power to Rebuke each other; and in this way bring in strife and division, and a House divided against itself cannot stand,[22] and likewise the People being at liberty to try the Spirits, would open a wide door for the Enemy to introduce suspicions and doubts, and might cause the Word of the Lord often to be rejected.—It was presented clearly to me to be the Mind of the Lord concerning His Church was as follows.—Let the Prophets speak two or three and let the Church consisting of Prophets and Spiritual persons Discern the Mind of the Spirit in the Utterances,[23] that all may learn and all may be identified, that the Discernment of the Spirit which speaks shall be trusted with the Person or Persons in whom the Gift of Discernment rest according to the Will and appointment of God, and that he will use the Person who hath the Gift of Discernment to Rebuke the false Spirits or the flesh—if the Prophets were capable of Discerning each other's Spirits there would be no necessity of an Especial Gift of Discernment of Spirits, and as the distinct Gift of interpretation of Tongues, shews us that the Tongues spoken by the Spirit were not understood in the Church so the appointment of a distinct Gift of Discernment of Spirits shews us that neither the Prophets nor Spiritual persons could discern the Spirits or was intended to discern the Spirits; and as it would bring a Snare to Seek interpretation out of the way of God's appointment, so it has brought a snare, and well still bring a Snare seek[in]g Discernment out of the way of God's appointment.

I believe that is the Mind of the Lord, that the Angel of the Church should try the Spirit by the report[?][24] of the Prophets, the Lord is not the author of confusion, but of order & of Peace.

The body is one having many members, but God has set any Member in the Body as it has pleased him,[25] and one Member must not take the Place of another Member

21. Actually 1 Cor 13:2.
22. Matt 12:25.
23. 1 Cor 14:26–33.
24. This [?] is in the *Simpson Story*. It may reflect uncertainty regarding the word 'report.'
25. 1 Cor 12:12.

otherwise the Body becomes disorganised and weakness and Disolution [sic] follows, and it is Expressly said to One he hath given the Gift of Prophesy, to another discerning of Spirits Distinct Gifts.[26] Therefore According to the Ordinance of God the One must not mingle with the other. The Lord is Jealous of His ordinances, and will not suffer them to be trod[d]en[?][27] down, the Prophets must not take the place of the discerner of Spirits. If he does the Enemy will Snare him and give him discernment and use him to Rebuke his fellow Prophets. However I say not that a Prophet may receive from God the Gift of Discernment, but without having received the Gift He must not seek to discern or rebuke, otherwise the Enemy will use him, because it would be a violation of the ordnance of God, just as who Prophecyeth [sic] must not attempt to work Miricles [sic] without having received the Gift, otherwise the Enemy would deceive him. Therefore[,] in order to keep Every Member in his place in the Body, the Apostle say let him that Prophecyeth, prophecy according [to] the proportion of faith let him that Exhorteth wait upon Exhortation and faith and so on.

Now My Dear Sir, I believe most firmly that the Work of the Lord will not prosper in the midst of us until we receive this precious Gift of Discernment of Spirits so that the Prophets may be kept in their place, that the Spirits appearing [sic] in the Church may be tried according to the Ordinance of God, and not by each other, which opens a door for the entrance of the Enemy to catch the Prophets in his snares, and that all things being put in order the People may receive the Word of God through the Prophets without suspicion and *that a Spirit of Judging may be put down.*

[Annotated:] This letter has been Published by The Revd Dr. Bonar in the *Journal of Prophesy* as a letter from a Lady to Mr Irving. July No.1871.

J. G. Simpson to EDWARD IRVING

Monday, 10th June 1832[28]

My Dear Sir,

While in direct communion with God regarding the Awfull [sic] Scene which was transacted in your House on Saturday last.—The Lord directed me to wait upon you and intreat [sic] of you to call your Session along with other grave and Spiritual Members of the Church to Judge and give council in the important matter which the Lord has laid before you, by the Mouth and Pen of One of his Prophets, for it is a Solemn matter and the Lord will not allow it to lye [sic] Over unattended to.

26. 1 Cor 12:10.
27. The [?] is in the *Simpson Story*, perhaps reflecting uncertainty about the original letter.
28. NLS, MS Simpson, Diary 35.

I remain my Dear friend, your Friend,
J. G. Simpson

~

J. G. Simpson to EDWARD IRVING

Cross Street, Islington. 16 June 1832[29]

My Dear Sir,
On my return from the City this afternoon my dear wife read to me the enclosed Letter,[30] in the contents of which I feel concern, and now permit to say that if you considered that I used too strong language at any of our Meetings anent[31] the very important subject in which we dissagree, [sic] I Pray you not to impute the same, or my great Earnestness to any want of respect for your high office, or want of Love for your self, but rather to the true cause, namely that I felt that I was setting the very truth of God on a matter of greater importance than Life or Death. If it is your wish that we separate from your Church, we are ready to obey, although in Separating our Selves from one we much Love and Vallue [sic] pangs of Sorrow must be felt. But as I have not the least doubt of my dear Wife having received and still holding pure, a great & gracious Gift from her Heavenly Father for the Right and faithful use of which he holds her responsible, and which she was not, yea dare not, quench or resist. Although all on Earth were to Testify against her, I say knowing that Mrs S. has the testimony of God in her own Soul in that it is the Spirit of God which speaketh by her, & Having the witness of God to my Soul that it is the Holy Spirit which speaketh by her, and having before my Eyes the good fruit which has arisen from the gracious witness to the truth of God by her lips, who am I having such a Witness, that I dare question this great work of the Lord. Yea indeed I should truly prove my self unworthy were I to allow a day to pass in which, I did not cause thanks givings to flow from my lips to my Bountiful Heavenly Father who has so honoured and blessed my House, etc and now may the Lord bless you in your own Soul and in all your engagements etc.

I remain,
My D Sir,
Yours truly,
J. G. Simpson

~

---

29. NLS, MS Simpson, Diary 41–42.
30. Jane Simpson to Edward Irving, NLS MS Simpson, Diary 42–44
31. concerning.

Part II: The Letters

Jane Simpson to EDWARD IRVING

14 Cross Street, 16 June 1832[32]

Revd Irving & Very Dear Sir,

I take up my pen to request of you most sincerely that you would forgive me and my dear Husband for any apparent want of Reverence or Respect for your office at our last meeting or at any of our Meetings. I beg to assure you *most solemnly that all that I said* flowed from the distress of my heart neither to Justify my self nor the Gift but dear, dear Sir, so to have inlightened [sic] your Mind that you might have looked into my very Soul in order to discern the Spirit for I felt it to be such a deep and solemn matter, not between two Individuals but between man and the Spirit of God having Assurrance [sic] in my conscience that it was no other Spirit but the Holy Spirit that spoke by me, and that assurance proceed not from confidence in myself but in God. I know I have been continually waiting upon my Father, for the Holy Spirit, and desiring that Jesus's living word by me would open his written word; and I believe firmly, that when I ask bread my Father would not give me a stone, and when I ask'd a fish my father would not give me a Serpent, and that when I ask'd an Egg my father would not give me a Scorpion,[33] in one word that my Heavenly father who is the hearer and answerer of prayer would give me nothing but the thing I asked from him and would not permit a child who was trusting in him to be deceived or Answered by any other Spirit. And my conscience bears Witness to me, that my father has kept me standing in the blood of Jesus and in communication with himself, therefore I solemnly believe that it would be a grievous departure from God to give up the inward Testimony of God to the conscience. I believe that there never will be any other Seal given to a Man but the witness of the Spirit to the conscience. Our Fathers suffered and bled for the liberty of conscience, and this liberty dear Father in the Lord I now desire, I dare not Resist the Spirit of God.—Should the Power come upon me in Church I will leave the Meeting or Pray to my Father to restrain it there. But in opening the Scriptures at Home my conscience tells me I mustn't restrain the Spirit, but if you object to this have the kindness to inform me, and I believe the Lord will Send me to another City. The Lord gives no Gift in vain but to be used for his Glory. May the God of Peace be with you may he fill you with His Spirit and bless you abundantly with Heavenly blessings is the Sincere Prayer of your

Very Sincere and Affect.,
Jane Simpson

Excuse me D. Sir for adding a P.S.

Did I understand you right when I believed you to say, that the reason the Evil Spirit in me was not silenced at your House on Saturday was because you did not Rebuke it. Very dear Sir will you excuse me for stating the correction which the Lord

---

32 28 NLS, MS Simpson, Diary 42–44.

33. Luke 11:11–12.

has given to me, if it had been the cry of the Holy Ghost, that ascended to the father to rebuke the Spirit, the Father instantly would have answered by closing my lips, he might have used you or might not have used you, but of this I am assured if Satan had been Singing by me and the Holy Ghost detected it and cried to the father to Rebuke Satan & put him down the father would instantly have answered the Spirit just as Ananias & Sapphira[34] were discerned by the Holy Ghost and struck Dead instantly, so would Satan in me have been Rebuked, but it is from the Communion which I had with God, that I am assured that I was Singing by the Spirit of God, forgive me for Stating these things to you, I do it that you Lay them before the Lord in Prayer. I know your Sincerity in all things and desire to glorify the Lord, and may the Lord grant you his own Eye of Discernment and by his Spirit may you be lead [sic] into all truth—

~

J. G. Simpson to EDWARD IRVING

London, 4 Cross St., Islington. 19 June 1832[35]

My Dear Sir,

My Dear Wife has read to me the inclosed [sic] and I am assured that its contents are truths of God. In faithfulness to my God, to you, and to my own Conscience I must Address a few words in reply to your letter. I am Assured that in great Love and Sincerity you give your advice that Mrs Simpson aught to refrain from using her Gift for some time. I believe you give this advice under an impression that the Power which Mrs Simpson has is not from God, and while you hold this belief you must in faithfulness testify against its being Exercised. But believing as I do that it is of God, I am constrained to hold quite an opposite view, and my wife and self are quite agreed on this point, you being aware that Mrs S although pressed by you to Utter in the Church, has refrained from doing so, ever since Jealousy was declared by certain Individuals against her. You may Rest satisfied she will not *now* Utter in the Church in opposition to your injunction, and *while* the original cause still remains. But every where out of the Church and your House I have advised her to yield to the Spirit of the Lord, for conscience sake, and for the edification, and comfort of all who may be present, you desire Mrs S to give you that which she may be made to Utter, this I think she aught to do, *not* to Satisfy doubts resting on our Mind *but* because you, the Angel of the Church require her so to do. I conclude by Praying that Love and Unity may abound more, & more, among us, in proportion as these are weak so does the Evil One gain an Advantage over us.

34. Acts 5:1–10.
35. NLS, MS Simpson, Diary 45–46.

Part II: The Letters

On Tuesday 25 June Doctor Thomson called at Cross St and left the two pre-ceeding [sic] letters from Mr Irving, neither Mrs Simpson or myself being at Home, on Wednesday we saw Dr T and appointed Thursday at three o'clock to meet at Mr Irving's House, but we sent him, Mr Irving, the two following letters previous to the Meeting—

∼

Jane Simpson to EDWARD IRVING

14 Cross St. 27 June 1832[36]

Revd and my dear Sir,

I have received both your letters and although very pained nevertheless I am quite assured of your sincerity and faithfulness according to your conviction. On one or two points matters between God and my own Soul I desire in great Love to put you right. The first is concerning the Prophets, that I have judged them without Love to me and therefore, I have not received the word through them, dear dear Sir I Solemnly declare in the presence of my Heavenly father that in this matter I have not Judged, I have always declared to you, and I believe that Mrs Caird is dwelling in Love. I always had great communion of Spirit with her, and the Lord has given me great Love for her. I have ever felt my Spirit drawn to her in a very peculiar way, for thro her the Lord has blessed me abundantly, by her lips hath he spoken to me again & again, twice was she made to Answer the Prayers which I had presented to my Heavenly father shortly after they had been offered, the first before I recd the Gift, calling upon me to be filled with the Spirit, the second after I rec'd the Gift. I have also Ever discerned much Love & kindness in Mrs Caird, again I am drawn to State that in yr Library in faithfulness to you as my Pastor, and one whom I Ever Loved, & recd as a father in the Lord, I was led to State out a circumstantial account of facts regarding Miss E. Cardale with drawing from me, and Refusing to come and Pray with me at different times, and Especial about the time, dear Sir when you desired me and entreated me to Utter in the Church, at that time I recd much power in Church which I believed to be in answer to yr Prayers. But I did not dare to yield, until Miss E. C. and I had Pray'd together concerning it, and I Earnestly desired that she might come that we might commune together and Pray to our Father, but could not prevail. These things grieved me very deeply, for I was so fearful of the stumbling of the flock through me. Nevertheless this remained a matter betwixt God and my own Soul. Until my Husband observed it and spoke of it to you, which grieved me exceedingly, then in yr Library in faithfulness to you and feeling myself in the presence of [the] Host, I was made to confess (tell out)

---

36. NLS, MS Simpson, Diary 46–49.

the whole. But no Judgment was past [sic] only Facts were stated. Again I told Miss E Cardale the same in *your* presence in yr Library, and in Mrs. Cardale's presence, and Miss Cardale Stated she did not feel want of Love, and I stated I believed her word, only I believed the Enemy had kept us separate. As I now believe for had Communion flowed I am assured these differences would not have taken place, without passing Judgment who is right or who is wrong, of this I am assured free and easy fellowship and communion is the only way to prevent the Enemy taking us in his Snare, for it is the desire of the Enemy to bring in division, this he can do more effectual by Separating those whom he wishes to Snare, only one thing my conscience accuses me of in this matter, that is, mentioning the above to Doct Thompson, and I have besought the Lord's forgiveness. Now my Dear Sir, I assure you most solemnly this is not the Root of the word not Entering. The Word which you call upon me to obey, I understand to be those Utterances in your library. Now my dear Sir you know on Friday eveng you requested me to meet Miss E Cardale in yr House for the sake of love. All the following morning I was engaged in Prayer that my Father in heaven would fill me with his own Love, and that he would be present with us, and that I might be kept leaning upon Jesus & that love might flow among us. I came from my own Room filled with more of the presence of God that usual. His presence continued with me, the Utterance by Mrs Cardale ended *thus*, 'Yield to His Love' & at these words I was full of the Love of Jesus & the Spirit breathing with Love, & Joy sought to Express itself & burst forth in a Song of Praise to Jesus, & you know what was Uttered by Miss E. C. desiring it, but the words did not Separate me from Jesus. Now my Dr & Rev Sir I believe solemnly that it was the Lord that would not allow me to Bow down to this word. Oh my Dr Father in the Lord if ever I Uttered in the power & Spirit of the Lord it was on that occasion, from the communion I engaged with the Lord, it was a Song of praise and Love to Jesus. Again the Word Uttered by Mrs Cardale 'Ye Rebeled [sic] against the Word.' The Spirit burst forth from me before I was aware. 'No, no, no Rebelion, [sic] the Moment the Voice burst forth from me the Voice in Mrs Cardale was silenced. Now Dr Sir I declare to you that my conscience bears Testimony to the Word which I was made to Utter, the Lord knoweth there has been no Rebelion [sic] in me, that is in my Flesh against any word. If you will refer to the first letter, which I wrote you, after lying [laying] before the Lord a Month in Prayer & Humiliation immediately after Miss E. C.'s Utterance [here two unreadable words] wherein is set out a faithful Account of the workings of the Mind, you must discern from that the opening of God's dealing with me that I was most Earnest with the Lord that He would Apply the Word. Now regarding dear Mrs Cairds Utterance, regarding my Utterances. Upon discernment etc. I do feel that a Snare was laid before her, for I do believe that it was the Truth that was Uttered by me, and you have clearly made the Distinction in your last Letter which I made to you sometime ago in Utterance, in y[ou]r former communication with me you did not make this distinction. I read my Utterances to Dr Thompson and he read me a paper which he had written some time ago & he stated that this paper contained all that was in my Utterances, and I Discerned the same. [H]e is also about to Publish this Paper when you will be able to judge more correctly.—Now My Dear Sir, Although I had Assurance from the Lord, that morning in your Library that my Dear Sisters in the Spirit were in a Snare respecting me I did not the less believe that they encountered Prophets of the Lord, for I believe if one Prophet can be taken in a Snare all are liable, none are infalable, [sic], and the Richer the Gifts are Used the more vulnerable they are, the more assiduously will the Enemy desire to use them. He will Especially desire to use them in Accusing the Brethren.—Oh Excuse [me] for what I have written I feel it is deep & solemn Matter, that I dare not keep back any feelings or light I have recd. Now my Dr Sir you think the Enemy answered when I desired power to be used without the understanding.—Dear Sir consider the Nature of my petition and I am assured you will see that my Father would not thus give me up, most Earnestly did I desire that my Father would keep me from all Snares of the Enemy, that he would be as a Wall of Fire around me, that he would take and use me for his Glory that there might be no mixture of the flesh at all, that He would Even use me without my Understanding, this was not from the desire of knowledge but just casting my self wholy [sic] into the Hands of my Father, this was the Character of all my Prayers, therefore have I confidence in him. I know the Gift and Calling of God are without Repentance therefore I feel I would be dishonouring God, to seek that which I believe he has not taken from me. I feel that in every movement of the Spirit I am drawn to Jesus. It is a Spirit which draws me [unreadable word] Father's Throne. It is a Spirit which Loves Jesus, and continually testifies of Jesus therefore my Dear & Respected Sir, rather, yea much sooner, would I lay down my Life at this moment than seek to be separated from this Spirit, which binds me to Jesus. I know my walk with God has been closer during the last 3 months than it ever has been, therefore I believe as God is faithful. I have the same Spirit now as some Months ago, therefore Dear & Honoured Sir Loving you as a father, I cannot refrain from beseeching you to Pause and beware Denouncing the Spirit which speaks by me,

     I remain,
     Yours –
     J. Simpson

J. G. Simpson to EDWARD IRVING

14 Cross Street, 27th June 1832[37]

My Dear Sir,

---

37. NLS, MS Simpson, Diary 49–50.

Your letter Addressed to: my D. Wife is before me in which you say, the Root of all 'Is your believing that you are dwelling in Love and that the other Prophets are not, this is at the bottom of both you and Mrs Simpson's present act of feeling.' I beseech you my D Sir to recolect [sic] the History of this Distressing Case, and you will discern your error in the above assertion. [W]hen you and Miss E Cardale Visited us about 3 months ago you may recollect that she made an Utterance, which I declared to your self before you left my House I could not receive from the Lord, and I stated then and have often done so since the reasons why I rejected the Word Uttered. Namely, Because I knew some things asserted were not true, and that the rash and unmeasured Terms of Reproach used, were not like the voice of my gracious Heavenly father, to a child who had been waiting upon Him in much prayer and fasting for weeks before, that He would lead and guide her into the ways of truth and Holiness, the want of Love in Miss E Cardale was neither mentioned nor held as a ground of rejecting the words by her. If you will refer to Mrs S statement to you (which was forced from her), regarding the want of all manifestations of Love on the part of Miss E. Cardale you will find it does not allude to any want of Love on the part of Miss C until a date long after my rejecting the Utterance referred to on other side. Endeed [sic] the facts stated regarding Miss C want of all Manifestations of Love, were brought forward not to convince my self that the Utterance aluded [sic] to were not from the Lord, but with the View of convincing others who believed the Word to be from the Lord—And I beg to remind you that at all our Meetings I ever intreated [sic] that all Persons should be loss'd [sic] sight of. And as the subject we had before us concerned the good Estate of the Church of Christ it became us to avoid personalities, these few remarks I write for the sake of truth, and I trust you will not be offended at my bringing them to your recollection circumstances which may have escaped you.

    I am,
    Yr,
    J G Simpson

Edward Irving to REV JOHN MARTIN and FAMILY

September 1832[38]

The Lord prospers us otherwise very much. He hath provided us with a house and church under one roof, where I believe the Lord will work blessings manifold, not only to this city and nation, but to the whole world; because He is gracious, and the

---

38. Oliphant, *Life*, 2: 318–19.

time to visit His Church is come, and we were the most despised among the thousands of Israel.

~

Edward Irving to REV JAMES MONILAWS[39]

London 1st Sept 1832[40]

Revd. & Dear Sir,

I received the very important communication from the Presbytery of Annan only a fortnight ago; and on a matter of so much importance I desire to take the full time permitted by the forms of the church, to the end I may not rashly involve within the Presbytery on myself in the consequences which must necessarily flow from my answer. Many are the feelings and many also are the questions which are connected with my answer of these several interrogations, and I am sure the presbytery will not attribute it to want of respect to them but quite the contrary that I postpone my reply to your letter. I could have compassed the subject within the fortnight but that I have had for the consideration of it, but that I have been occupied with the examination and instruction of nearly 70 communicants who are tomorrow to sit down with my church for the first time. This together with the constant duties of my ministry has entirely engrossed me and not permitted me the leisure to consider all the questions connected with the jurisdiction which the assembly have taken over me. But you may depend upon an answer within the sixty days, God willing.[41] I desire my love to all the brethren of the Presbytery, and my personal acknowledgments to them for their respects paid to the memory of my worthy Father. Farewell, may the Lord have you in his holy keeping.

Your brother in the Ministry of Christ,
Edward Irving

P.S. Your letter dated the 10th August came to my hand by twopenny post on the 17th that is yesterday fortnight. EI.

~

---

39. James Monilaws (1787–1871).

40. NCL, MS Box 9 13.15.

41. See letter Edward Irving to Members and Elders of the Presbytery of Annan, 13 October 1832 NLC, MS Box 9.2.19.

Edward Irving to HENRY DRUMMOND

Postmarked: 8th September 1832[42]

My Dear friend & Brother,

My advice to Mr. Paul is not to go out at this time, but to exercise himself in his present retirement with works of piety and secret communion with God. If the providence of God had any member of my flock any where I exhort them to speak to the people what they themselves have surely believed but I feel as if it were stretching beyond my measure to send any one forth from the flock without a direct instruction of the Lord to do so. In his walks about Albury, and wherever you may take him along with you or where he may be carried in the occasions of life, or in his return to town, or in accompanying Mr. Caird, or any other the like providential goings out and comings in, he would I think do well to speak as often as his soul is drawn to it, but to go forth on an express errand of preaching through the villages. I do not see my way to advise but rather the contrary.

In respect of Elders, we do not deliberate nor will we do any thing, without the presence and guidance of the Spirit of the Lord. If the Lord should declare any thing by you, let me know; otherwise I should judge it wiser for you having the keeping of God's word, to think not much about it, lest you might take up opinions in the understanding what might prove stumbling blocks in the way of God's free and sovereign spirit.

Mr. Taplin was made to say in our presence last Monday night words signifying God's wish for Elders and our liberty to chose them out and set them before him for his approbation. Miss E. Cardale to rebuke us sharply and to express God's great jealousy lest any thing should be done in the flesh. The Port Glasgow brethren have given no testimony as to the spirit which speaketh in Mrs. Simpson when she speaketh in [tongues?] for she was not made to utter in their hearing, and without utterance the Prophet hath no discernment, 'Let them speak & the others discern.'[43] Nor had they any revelation. There it rests, till the Lord shall call upon me to act again as a Pastor; for I am set not for speculation but for action.

Your faithful friend & Pastor,
Edwd Irving

9th Sept 1832
Addressed to: Henry Drummond,
Albury Park,
Guildford.

---

42. DFP: C/9/7.
43. Cf. 1 Cor 14:29.

Part II: The Letters

Edward Irving to HENRY DRUMMOND

London, 14th September 1832[44]

My Dear friend and Brother,

The Lord spake twice upon our entering in to Mr. Perceval and receiving from him the tidings of your condition. The first word was a warning of snares which the enemy was laying for you, and out of which you should only escape by great watchfulness and tenderness. It was born in upon my mind, that it was something of the same kind with which the Portglasgow [sic] brethren have been taken, seeing these were so many gifted persons without a head. And I expressed this to Mr. Perceval, and sought his discernment & that of the elect.—While we were yet speaking, the Lord spake the second time, and signified that it was jealousy over his ordinance of a Pastor that moved him, that you were all lacking in your estimate of this ordinance as the representatives of Jesus in the Church, that you were not enough grieved over the want of it, and that if the Lord's word was not heeded, he would ever place stumbling blocks in your way to make it be learned. I confessed our common sin in this respect (for the Lord added that the word was to many more besides you) and my own in particular, whose part it was both to know and to head my own office more perfectly) and I had very full discernment of the truth of this matter in consequence of which I had been writing in the afternoon beside my wife (who is well and graciously delivered of a dear boy) touching the relation which I as a Pastor bear to the Annan Presbytery who are seeking jurisdiction over me. I saw that the offices of Apostles and Prophets are *unto* the right settling the Church with Pastors, (Timothy had his gift from the Apostle's hand and also by Prophesy), the Eldership over the Church *unto* the receiving of the Pastor endowed of the Apostle designated to his charge & sent out by the Prophet: so that Christ downwards acteth by Apostles & Prophets unto the appointment of a representative over the flock; the flock acteth upwards by its Eldership (the laying on of the hands of the Presbytery) unto the receiving and grateful accepting of them of Christ. And so the union being rightly and duly accomplished, he standeth there as Christ's representative to feed the flock with truth and rule in righteousness. I could not have entered into the word of the Lord so jealous of the Pastor's function and office had I not been led into this truth during my meditations & writings in the morning.

But however you may be able to discern my receiving which I have not time nor space to unfold, and which doth not derogate from the Apostle and Prophet, of whom the former is the power the latter the word of God, I beseech you & all the brethren to be on your guard here where the Lord hath warned you, and to account it a very great privilege to be under the daily feeding of a faithful pastor, a very great trial to be without it. And I commend this instruction to you also and to none more than my dear Mrs. Caird where temptation lieth on that side, as indeed doth that of Scotchmen in

---

44. DFP: C/9/8.

general. For we are a very stiff-necked and rebellious race: yet mightily for God, when well guided of his word & spirit.

I did not think I should so soon have had to notice an instance when you have been overseen in this matter. Mr. Paul I have counseled *not* to come and settle at Albury but to abide in the Church at the work whereto he hath set his hand, *not* to seek after the unequal yoke of his wife from which God so wonderfully delivered him unto liberty until God shall incline her heart unto him. And she knows well that his heart is inclined to her, *not* to obey her Father whose rule over him is ceased in matters where the orders of God lie upon him; for he was one of these to whom the Lord said 'Go forth two & two' and whom God hath much guided counselled reproved & otherwise dealt with in this matter. Your counsel to her was a practical illustration of our forgetting the sacred importance of a Pastor, in which I have been alas as guilty as any of my people, perhaps the most so. The Lord enable me to stand as the representative of the good shepherd. I desire my true love & Pastoral blessing to you all. Farewell

Your Brother in the Common faith,
Edwd Irving

Addressed to: Henry Drummond Esq.

⁓

Edward Irving to HENRY DRUMMOND

London, 17th September 1832[45]

My Dear friend & brother,

It is through the love which suffereth long and is kind, that our Lord is to be glorified in the union of his members. Mr. Paul has shewed me your Letter, and I have undertaken to set one or two things right which you have taken up wrong. While his wife was with him I counselled him to act in the Spirit of 1 Cor VII v 12, 13, 14; and when she left him in the Spirit of v. 15 which I pray you to consult. When she had forsaken him and committed the sin Matt V v 32 against her husband, I felt that she should have had this her sin held up before her in his after dealings with her, and I think that he made too little of his own honour and of her offence in the great assiduity & kindness with which he sought her back, without shewing her the sin of leaving him. But when to this desertion of her husband was added the guilt of stealing away his children, I saw that to seek and to enforce union with such an one in her present state of heart was to tempt the providence of God, and to abandon all sense of what is due unto a husband's sacred place. And my counsel was and still is, do nothing further

45. DFP: C/9/9.

in this matter till God open the door, but abide in prayer for her and the children, that she may be brought to see her sin and come back with repentance, and be you ever ready to receive her. Now reflect upon this and you will see that it is wholesome and holy advice. At that time I was given to understand that the children were by law under the power of the wife till they arrive at the age of seven; and could not till then be recovered without also enforcing the return of the wife which I could not advise without confession of sin. This day for the first time I have come to know that he may recover the children without enforcing the return of his wife, which changes the case in respect to them but not in respect to her. What is his duty in respect to the children of whom the eldest is but two years and a half old I have not reflected, acting all along upon the false information I had received as to the law.

In respect of his preaching I also for the first time learn by your Letter that his doctrine is not sound; and of this I shall take care satisfy myself. Mr. Armstrong[46] this afternoon bore testimony that having preached along with him, there was not one word which he could object to. In all my intercourse with him I have not ever had reason to suspect any other doctrine to be held by him or any of the young men, but that which I preach myself; and he himself declares that he is not conscious of any difference. Into this matter I shall examine, for surely there ought to be good cause for the very strong expression which you mention that Mr. & Mrs. Caird & Mr. Smith have used, I wonder that Mr. & Mrs. Caird did not take an opportunity of telling Mr. Paul; I know their love and faithfulness, it must have been lack of opportunity.

You seem to think that Mr. Paul came like Balaam[47] seeking counsel of me a second time and that he received different counsel from that which I gave him through you when he was at Albury. But it is not so. If you will consult my letter you will find that my counsel had not respect to preaching there where he happens to be in the providence of God, but to going forth through the towns & villages of Surrey Sussex & Hampshire. My mind was that he should lift up his voice, as man to man, wherever he might be, but not go forth as upon a commission, till we should have the word of the Lord to that effect. And so when he returned to the city he took up his former work as a thing of course, unless some cause should have occurred to prevent it. In respect to going to Saffron Walden, I heard [letter torn] it was by special invitation but rather incline to his abiding where he is. My wish is that both he and the rest of us should seclude ourselves more to prayer and meditation than we do.

Now, my Dear Brother, count not this Letter as written for self-justification still less for a trouble to you; but for the sake of the truth and to prevent mistakes. Nor do I intend to say any thing more, but to commend my Pastoral love and blessing to all my

---

46. Rev Nicholas Armstrong (1801–79), Anglican priest called as an apostle in 1834. He was made the angel of the Salem Chapel, Southwark, London (one of the Seven Churches), but only for a very short time. He was allocated the 'tribe' of Zebulun responsible for Ireland and Greece; he also briefly visited the United States. See Shaw, *The Catholic Apostolic Church*, 82.

47   Num 22:38.

flock assembled with you, and to beseech you by the love of the Lord, and the misery of his poor body, that ye would be well guarded against the snares which the good Spirit of God warned you of as about to assail you through a too low estimate, or unguarded oversight of the office of the Pastor, whereof for the present ye are deprived. I pray the Lord to bless you with all conformity to his holy will. Amen.

Your affectionate and dutiful Pastor,

Edwd Irving

P.S. The Letter written above was finished last night before I went to bed. I have perused your Letter to myself, and have simply to say upon it, first, that in respect of your doctrine concerning relationships natural and ecclesiastical I agree that the latter are for the sustenance of the former, and may never supersede but ought to instruct and comfort them & see them fulfilled. And be assured in respect of myself, that I have never at any time done otherwise. I have always refused solicitations to intermeddle, or to receive into my hands a responsibility which belongeth not to me. Mine is to teach, theirs to obey the teaching of the will of God. Be comforted on this head and judge me not for I am guiltless in this as God knoweth. Secondly In respect to Mr. Paul, my counsel having been so constantly of love to his wife, and his word to me having always been so, I never did suspect any thing but that she was the offender & the only offender; and truly I feel grieved beyond expression to be thought to have interfered between man and wife in the way supposed in both these Letters. Except my love and patience were strengthened of God, I do assure you the very suspicion of having done such a thing as is presumed upon in these letters would go far coming from you, to oppress my sore burdened spirit. If I might say so, it is in these suspicions and speculations as if I had done such a thing that my Pastoral honour and purity is wounded. I say this for your sake not for mine. Truly, Dear Brother, I have behaved myself in this honestly and uprightly. But if I find that, contrary to the appearance, Mr. Paul should have essentially sinned against his wife & caused her to leave him, which till this hour I had not even a suspicion of, nor now believe, I will urge him to make reparation. In respect to the preaching I do not believe that the young men have been preaching error over the law. I do not believe it: and I beseech you by no means to say such a thing again lest you offend God and his people, I have heard them whenever I had an opportunity, I have heard from them & of them nothing but good. And the Lord's testimony concerning the work I have much heard, and [two words unreadable] said that he is well pleased with them who serve him well [words unreadable] things. I call upon every one of you to rejoice in the work which the Lord is doing amongst us, by these very young men. I beseech you not to suspect evil, nor to speculate about it. The Spirit speaking about it said 'That not I but he would teach them,' they are most dutiful to me, every one of them and if there be any one to blame it is I. Yet am I aware of the snares around us, and thank you for your counsel, it is Spiritual Witnesses the Lord wanteth, and to this I do daily direct my prayers & pastoral admonitions. You know not what the Lord is doing in this city by these poor vessels, who I believe am filling themselves by filling others, enriching by scattering. The Lord hath opened three, or four more mouths within the last fortnight, one a great opposer. Truly it hath been fulfilled 'I will make them come & worship before thy feet & to know that I have loved thee. Give god glory & rejoice before him.' I do beseech, I do entreat you all to beware of the spirit of a conclave. It is not literal opinions, but spiritual wickednesses we have to contend against. Take care for yourself that in remembering a wife's privileges you forget not a husband's dignity and prerogative. E.I

Addressed to: Henry Drummond Esq.,
Albury Park,
Guildford.

~

Edward Irving to THE MEMBERS and ELDERS of the PRESBYTERY of ANNAN

London 13th October 1832[48]

Men and Brethren,

I avow myself to be the author of the three Tracts[49] whose titles are recounted in the General Assembly's injunction to you and in your Letter to me, whereof the first named was written to set forth the foundation of the Christian verity[,] *viz* Christ's oneness with us in the flesh[;] the second the glorious headstone of the same[,] *viz* our oneness with Christ in the Spirit; and the last to denounce the General Assembly of the Church of Scotland as one of the most *wicked of all Gods enemies upon the face of the Earth for having denied and fought against all the foundations of the truth as it is in Jesus* and cast out his servants for preaching the same. With that wicked assembly now three times tried of God and three times found wanting and with all who adhere to or in any way aid and abet its evil deeds, I can maintain no relationship but that of avowed and open enmity 'Do not I hate them O Lord, that hate thee? and am not I grieved with those that rise up against thee? I hate them with perfect hatred: I count them mine enemies.'[50]

I am grieved at my heart that you should yield obedience to the desires of that *synagogue of Satan* and thereby make yourselves partakers of is evil deeds and I beseech as many of you as are of the Lords people to come out of that *Babylon, which* she ruleth over that yea be not partaker with her of her plagues which are ready to come upon

---

48. NCL: MS Box 9.3.19

49. Irving, *The Orthodox and Catholic Doctrine*; Irving, *The Day of Pentecost*; and Irving, *A Judgment*.

50. Ps 139: 21 and 22.

her. The Lord would have healed her but she would not be healed; therefore flee ye out of her. Every spirit that confesseth not that Christ is come in the flesh is of Antichrist and every man who divideth between Christ and his members by denying our oneness with him both in the flesh and the Spirit is a heretic. They have denied yea mocked and derided both, and the honour of that Lord whose minister I am, they have trampled under foot; and it is my duty and will be my labour to fight against them and to spare no arrows till they have repented of their evil deeds, and turned unto Him from whom they have deeply revolted. I entreat every one of you to save his own soul by coming out of her and fighting manfully against her. Farewell. May the Lord deliver you out of the snares in which your feet are taken. In love & in blessing I do pray that you may be delivered, as I and the flock over which I am the Pastor have been delivered. Again I say farewell. May the Lord deliver you from that *wicked assembly*. Amen

Your humble & faithful servant in the Lord,
Edw[d] Irving

~

Edward Irving to JANE SIMPSON

London, 13 Judd Place East.
6th December 1832[51]

My dear Madam,

You have grievously offended against the Lord Jesus Christ the Chief Shepherd, who hath called me in his grace to watch over your Soul, in that you have set at naught all my counsels and would [have] none of my reproof; and arise in direct rebellion against my authority, and the Church of which I am the Angel under the Lord Jesus Christ. I require and command you, as you value your precious soul for which He died; and which is His, that you would lay down the weapons of your rebellion and humble yourself in the sight of the Lord and confess your sin before his Church, and be absolved from it, and delivered out of the hands of the Enemy, who hath you now and if you repent not will have you for ever.

You have not resisted man but you have resisted the Holy Ghost, and do resist Him; and He declareth of you that if you repent not, Jesus will come and cut you altogether out of his vine, wherein you have been grafted, and should bear fruit unto the Father's glory.

Oh let me have joy of thee who hast caused me so much sorrow. Thou hast troubled Christ's Church, beware lest He trouble thee. I beseech thee by the mercies

---

51. NLS, MS 1676, fol. 232-33.

of God, that thou obey the word which he speaketh unto thee through his Minister & through his Prophets.

Meanwhile I have seen it to be my duty to set your Husband and you on the outside of the fold by resuming your Tokens,[52] and I do call upon you to return again into the bosom of it by humbling yourself in the dust, and repenting, and confessing your sins. Then shall my heart rejoice which now grieveth over you.

I am,
Your faithful Pastor,
Edw[d] Irving

Addressed to: Mrs. Simpson,
At Mrs. Horsburghs, Peebles, N.B.

Edward Irving to REV SAMUEL MARTIN and a REPLY from WILLIAM HAMILTON to SAMUEL MARTIN

London, 13 Judd Place East.
7th December 1832[53]

My Dear Brother,

The whole of my transaction with Mr. Dodds [sic] and Mr. Lockheart are as follows. I write this because I see you are distressed for my honour, and give you leave to do with the narration as may best suit you.

About the time the first review of my work on the Incarnation appeared in the *Christian Instructor* our friend Mr. Petrie[54] ([Church] of Leith) wrote me a letter in which among other things, he said that I might learn from the review though the Spirit of it might displease me. And he named Mr. Dodds as the author of it. Of old I had taken a resolution to seek for nothing written against me or even about me which had not the name of the author subscribed to it, being unable to apply the Lords remedy given in Mat XVII. To be at a loss to know what other faith could be held by any sound-minded man than that which I held and had put forth in my publications. I wrote a letter to Mr. Dodds to ask him what he held that I might consider it and lay it to heart. And in the same letter I gave him in three or four short propositions the sum total of what I maintained I would stand by. To this I received an answer very promptly giving me, but not in any set form of propositions an account of what he

---

52. These were the tokens for the Simpsons to be admitted as participants to Communion.
53. WCL, MS 12.
54. Peter Petrie, M.A; St. John's, North Leith, (1828–31): Scott, *Fasti*, 1:158.

maintained, which being incomplete he proposed to continue the correspondence. But having no purpose of doing this, I did not answer the letter though I had a desire if my occupations had permitted to endeavor to lead him into the faith. Meanwhile month after month brought me through many channels of friends and newspapers and letters accounts of the way in which I was traduced and held up to scorn and derision in the Christian Instructor, all by the hand of the same Mr. Dodd's. But still I withheld from reading one word of that publication, save what came to my eye and ear in the way mentioned above. For I have also laid it down as a rule that while I would not seek to know what was written anonymously against or about me I would not shun whatever was sent or brought to me in the course of God's providence and the Lord hath said. 'Go not after them that bring false doctrines,' and he hath also told us not to be afraid of them. So whenever any thing came to me in the Providence of God, I made a point of reading it and so I came by a pretty correct notion as to the Spirit and tenor and substance of these reviews; but I never read one of them. At length when I heard how they had leavened Scotland and were working much against the truth and likely to prejudice the case of Mr. MacLean[55] and others I felt my duty was to do what I could to disabuse the judgments of men, actually asked our brother William Hamilton for the Nos containing the articles in question, and had proposed a series of letters, in reply to these, but when I came to look into them I was utterly disgusted and could never read a paragraph as it ought to be read. So that they lay beside me all unread and to this hour I know not the doctrine which they contain so as to be able to state it in propositions to any reply. But this I saw at once that it was written in a Spirit half and half between the speech of a blackguard and a sharper, the sharper to steal your honest and good meaning away, the blackguard to heap opprobrious words on you after it was done. Still however I kept the odium of all this as much as I could from Mr. Dodds because I had no certainty that he was the author, and in my letter to him had mentioned that the paper or the author of it should never be spoken of between us. And accordingly when I received another letter from him complaining of not continuing the correspondence and of certain strictures I had made upon the Christian Instructor in a private Letter by friends in Edinburgh, and threatening me with some thing which he was about to publish, I contented myself with simply explaining to him wherefore I had done so, and advising him not to violate Charity any more. It must be at least two or three years since I wrote this Letter and have my correspondence terminated with him; not out of any anger and retaliation of any kind but simply because I had more important matters to mind, and never intended more than the exchange of one letter or at most two to arrive at his doctrine & give him mine, that we might be mutually profitable to one another.

As to Mr. Lockheart, having known him when I was at Glasgow and seen him in London soon after I was settled here, seeing him in my Church some time in the Summer before last I asked him to breakfast with me and among other conversation he

---

55. See letter Edward Irving to Rev Marcus Dods, 5 August 1830: WCL, MS 8.

charged the Morning Watch with willful misquotation of the Fathers, which I rejected with scorn with knowing the author of the article. He gave a kind of challenge to meet him and examine the author, which I heard as if I heard not for I was so ashamed of his behaviour and sentiments expressed at my table, that I was resolved never again to ask him to my house, and I think I refrained also from giving him my hand at parting and since I have neither seen nor heard of him.

Now, my dear Samuel you have the simple facts to do with them what you like. I had not ever heard they were abusing me in the Instructor like you mentioned it in your Letter to our brother. I am sorry that Ministers of the Gospel should not have other things to do and grieved that the creatures which God made should turn to destroy one another. If I have given any cause of offence to the wickedest of men out of scorn or slight, I humble myself for it before God in whose images they are made, but if I have hated them because they rise up against Christ, I have pleased God and shall not lose my reward. But it is the hatred of God with which I hate them, Answereth with both blessing and praising them. My brother go not in the way of the wicked, sit not in the seat of the scorner. We are all wicked & the Lord forbeareth greatly with such unworthy creatures, and aboundeth all love to us for Christ's sake.

Your faithful and loving brother,
Edwd Irving

William Hamilton to SAMUEL MARTIN

Written crosswise on EI's letter.[56]

My Dear Brother,

Edward's letter will shew that your favor of the 20th ult[57] reached me and that I delivered your message to him. I hope his statement will enable you to put an end to Dodd's abominable misrepresentations. His conduct would disgrace a man of the world much more a Christian Minister. I am truly glad that the £100 enabled you to make a satisfactory arrangement with the Banks.

The acknowledgement you have sent is amply sufficient for every purpose. Elizbt[58] tells me that you and Mr. King take the Scottish Guardian between you. It is an able paper and contains in perusal much interesting information on matters connected with religion. If you and he are willing to part with it within a reasonable time after its publication I shall be glad to take it from you—at one third of the expense.

I have heard little of Edward's Church lately but I believe it is well attended. Edwd says that the office of the Apostle and of the Evangelist has been restored amongst

---

56. Presumably Samuel Martin had sent Edward Irving's letter to William Hamilton for his information, and William had returned it with his reply.

57. Short for Latin *ultimus* (last).

58. Elizabeth Hamilton, William's wife and sister of Isabella Irving.

Letters: 1832–1833

them—the former was the person of Mr. Cardale and the latter in Mr. Drummond. I apprehend but am not quite sure. I agree with you in believing that Edwd & his congregation have the truth amongst them but mingled with some errors. It is a pity they are not more sober and judicious in their views and proceedings. I was much pleased with the decisions of the Synod in Mr. Grey's case and with the appearance your worthy Father made. I hope it will be confirmed by the Assembly. We are still thinly attended at the National and it is not likely we shall be otherwise until we get a Minister. Mr. Thomson from Shields has been preaching for 3 Sabbaths and finishes tomorrow. We don't yet know who we shall get next but shall learn on Monday. Mr. Begg of Paisley is to be with us on the 3rd Sabbath of next month for four Sabbaths and Mr. Lewis of Leith is to succeed him for four more Sabbaths. Mr. Patterson of Leith has been named to us as a very able and Godly man. Do you think he would suit the church and be likely to come in the event of his getting call? At a meeting of the Session and Committee a few nights ago nine members who were present subscribed ab[ou]t £1000 for the relief of the church. If the congregation all should be equally liberal and our worthy Countrymen here assists us as they ought the church will be well kept-up with plenty God's blessing.

Elizabeth had a fall and hurt her shoulder the other night, but not seriously. In other respects she is well—she unites with me in love to you and I ever am

My dear Samuel,
Your aff Brother,
Wm Hamilton

Is Andrews, poor fellow, likely soon to get his affairs [settled?]

Edward Irving to HENRY DRUMMOND

London, 14th January 1833[59]

My Dear Brother and Fellow Labourer in the care of Christ's flock,

I rejoice in the work of the Lord begun in the midst of you, and pray always, that ye may be confirmed in his love and perfected for his holy service. He hath shewn his grace in the midst of us by stretching out his hand and ordaining our dearly beloved Collnigs Carré[60] to the ministry of an Evangelist, and hath sent him forth by the authority of this Church in me represented to labour in Brighton for the gathering in of souls, till such time as the Lord shall ordain his servant whom he hath called there to be an Elder, after which he is to return hither and give an account of his ministry to

---

59. DFP: C/9/10.
60. Collinge Manger Carré, Angel, Paris.

the Church. And forasmuch as the Lord hath specially laid Brighton as a charge upon you and your Church I send him to Albury that he may receive your blessing before proceeding in his work and be furthered by your prayers on his way. You will therefore, Dear Brother receive him as an Evangelist duly ordained by the Apostle of the Lord, and sent forth from this Church; and encourage him in his labour of love.

The Lord hath taught me in this Act of His. That the laying on of my hands and the hands of my Eldership is not proper to such a case inasmuch as he is one not called to labour in my Church but to go forth from my Church. But that it is proper he should not go forth without my sending of him, and that he should return after the work on which he is sent forth is accomplished. This answereth to the doctrine which I had taught in the last No of the Morning Watch, concerning the laying on of the hands of the Eldership, that it is the ordinance for conveying power and authority over the flock. Comparing this with the separation of Paul and Barnabas (Act XIII & XIV v 26) I am led to infer that those prophets and Teachers who laid hands on them were not the statutory Elders of the Church but spiritual office-bearers (Eph IV v 11), who were there abiding for the nursing up of the Church. Moreover I am taught that the Eldership with the Angel at their head, are to the spiritual persons who speak in the message of the Lord, which the Crowned Elders around the throne are to the Cherubim within the throne. Nevertheless I feel that every Angel of a Church aught in the fullness of his office to speak in the Message of the Lord, and be apt unto the heavenly as well as the Earthly things. I beseech you to stir up the spiritual gift in you and our people. And to beware how the ordinance of power overrule the Spirit; and pray for me that the Lord would give me to speak not only in the wisdom of a man but also in the power of the Holy Ghost. This very day I was served by the men of business here with the notice of a libel from the Presbytery of Annan concluding for my deposition from the Holy Ministry did the Lord stretch out his hand to ordain and commissioned me to send forth an Evangelist into the bosom of Babylon. The Lord hath taught me that Babylon is the manifestation of 8 y[ear]s on the earth, and the church therein contained is Christ in the prison, and the bringing up of the Church thence is the manifestation of that most mighty power which led the Captivity Captive. And many other precious mysteries of his word openeth here daily unto me in the ministry & confirmeth in the Spirit. For he is gracious and his mercy endureth for ever.

Say to Mr. Taplin to wait on his gift & keep it by [letter torn] Ghost, and to his wife to strengthen his hands, to Mr. Orr to seek the Lord's [letter torn] to beware of using Providence as a walk by Light. My love to dear Mrs. Caird and tell her that she knoweth not yet how much the Lord hath honoured her and that she will discern it by being more and more abased in his sight. Say to Lady Harriet to leave her children with the Lord both for things spiritual and temporal and to worship and obey her Lord in you her husband. And doubt not through much patience that the Lord will perfect you to every good word & work. The peace of God be with you all. Farewell.

Your affectionate brother in the Lord,

Edwd Irving

Addressed to: Henry Drummond Esq.,
Albury.
By the hands of Mr. Collinge Carré:
Irving for Mr. Carré
14th Jany 1833

~

Edward Irving to HENRY DRUMMOND

London, 14 Newman St.
22nd January 1833[61]

My Dear Brother,
Having never entertained the purpose of taking any jurisdiction over Mr. Carré the Evangelist from my Church, while at Brighton, I should not have thought it necessary to answer your letter, save for the end of comforting you and strengthening our mutual love one towards another. It were indeed a terrible snare of Satan should he be able to introduce jealousies into the bosom of the Churches wherein the one Spirit of God speaketh and ordereth all things. The Lord who hath cleansed my heart from it will keep my head clean from it; yet do I thank Him for your letter though proceeding on a misunderstanding.

I desire to be on my guard against judging in the understanding, and I warn you against it as one of the temptations which must easily beset you. Certainty cometh by the gradual breaking in and springing up of light within the soul. All my conclusions concerning all things have thus come, especially in what concerneth jurisdiction. Now the truth in respect of Mr. Carré is this. He abideth, my [dear] Sir, in the Gospel, one nursed up in my Church unto the stature of an Evangelist and mine it is to counsel him as a Father, the Church as a pillar to hold him up at all times and in all places; Christ's it is to feed Him with oil, and to shew his Father's face through him: and thine it is to have him in thy house and to bring him in thither with thy blessing & to use him for the good thereof according to thy Charge therein under Christ our common head. And his it is to obey thee to obey me, and to obey Christ, and it is a want of love to suppose that our orders should not be one, and to provide for their not being one is a breach of love. My brother the natural understanding divideth and shareth things, the spirit of Christ uniteth the divided things into one. Now love thou me and I will love thee, and we will not dream of any division. Do thy duty to dear Carré and I will

---

61. DFP: C/9/11.

Part II: The Letters

do mine and out of the mouths of two witnesses it will be confirmed. But truly I have nothing to say to him but 'serve the Lord Christ, and let me hear from thee whenever I can help thee.'

I have a letter from him this morning which comforted me not a little. May the Lord abundantly bless thee and thy Church. I am well pleased with thy diligence in rule, though not without a jealousy lest the sharpness of thy wit and the promptness of thy decisions should at any time bring thee into trouble. Farewell, dearest brother.

Edwd Irving

Addressed to: Henry Drummond Esq.,
Albury Park,
Guildford.
[Annotated: Irving on Carré.
22 Jany 1833]

～

Edward Irving to HENRY DRUMMOND

London, 3rd February 1833[62]

My dear Brother,

Let patience have her perfect work, that we may be completed in all things wanting nothing. Have no doubt that it is the Lord's mind *you* should use unleavened bread in the communion, for you have been told to do so in the message of the Lord. You neither wait for Apostle nor counsel of any man to obey the word of the Lord; obey and be blessed of Him. And I have no doubt that *we* should use leavened bread as we have done hitherto; until the Lord by his own voice shall put it away from us, and then I trust I also shall be ready to obey; and till that time that the Lord saith do it, I will not do it, I will not sacrifice without Samuel the Prophet. This I saw to be right in my own discernment, and I have received the same in the message of the Lord, when your last letter was read over by me in the hearing of one of the vessels through whom the Lord speaketh. The word to me was to seek counsel only of the Lord, and that he would lead me and my flock, if I would unreservedly resign myself to Him and let him do His own will in His own way in His house.

In meditating upon the way of the Lord by you and by us, and resolving to obey I have received light and I think full discernment of the Lord's purpose in it. You are set for the testimony and example of the new thing which the Lord is about to do in all the earth: therefore before he called you to the Angel's trust, he made you to speak in

---

62. DFP 3/9/12.

the spirit, and in that way gives you to minister and order his Church, to bless and to choose out your office bearers. And for this reason He shall put away the leaven from your bread, because he would put away the flesh from your services, and all mixtures of hypocrites from your communion as also He did by sending forth one through the clarity of his word, that woman of whom you spake to me. And thus you are as it were our pilot-boat, and the little company through whom he will make us to understand his way some time before he doth require us to follow it. To this effect also hath he put the Church in your own house, and as it were wholly under your own hand; growing as it were out of yourself that you may be the more able to follow his instructions whatever they be. When the Lord therefore requires of you to do any thing, do it, waiting for no one, and only taking counsel to the end you may better understand what the mind of the Lord is in the word spoken in the midst of you. And have steadfast faith that the Lord will not lead you along.

His purpose in us is different, *viz*, to shew forth his way of bringing a clean thing out of an unclean, the spiritual out of the fleshly ministration. He will save all that are faithful to him in these few things, and give them greater things. He will not cast away, but gather up the body of the corruptible seed into the glorious place of renown that springeth out of it. He will not offend one of His little ones. He will prune the branch that beareth fruit that it may bring forth more fruit. Yours is a spiritual plantation, ours is a transmutation from the carnal to the spiritual form of the heavenly life. However much I may grieve therefore over our unprepared state, I will do nothing until the time of the Lord be come for doing it amongst us, and he give full the word to do it. You blamed me for running before the Lord both in the matter of sending forth the young men into the streets and of the Elders, but in both cases I did but shew a readiness to do the work of the Lord, and a far-off discernment of his way, and waited & watched still for his word. On Saturday morning he declared that we should choose deacons, we straightway did so, and presented them before the Lord and he accepted them all but one, saying that he must wait. All the remaining seven with a ready mind accepted the vocation of the Lord, and yesterday I presented them before the people, who also with a willing mind received them. They are Frederick Ingles, Christopher Heath, Charles Stevenson, Charles Wallis, John Carlile, Frances Woodhouse[63] and Archibald Barclay. But the Lord answering you named John Frost by his Spirit. And he said to me that He humbly would set these Deacons apart, but when I know not. He also by an express utterence said that it belonged to *us* to choose them; *you* was the word but I discerned that it was not *myself* alone, but myself with the Elders and the Deacons in Council. And so it was done in His presence, and as I said when I submitted the eight one by one, he said of one of them let him wait. If this letter satisfy the matter on which you want to speak with me, well; if not; I would rather you came up because I cannot get away this week, and I shall say *Thursday*. Nevertheless I intend visiting you and

---

63. Francis Valentine Woodhouse (1805-1901). A barrister and son of the Dean of Lichfield. The youngest and longest lived apostle. He died at Albury.

spending some Monday & Tuesday with you & your dear household before going to Scotland, whither I stand summoned for the 13th March. Farewell. The Apostle sees with me in respect of him doing nothing without the Word of the Lord expressly for ourselves to do it. As to the rest I have not spoken of it to them, for I saw it but yesterday. The Word of the Lord to us is of wonderful things which he is preparing to do in the midst of us.

Farewell my Dear Brother,
Edwd Irving

Please read this to Mr. Taplin, and if he need any further communication I will write to him personally.

Addressed to: Henry Drummond,
Albury Park,
Guildford.
[Annotated: Irving: Unleavened Bread 5th Feb 1833]

Edward Irving to HENRY DRUMMOND

London, 15th February 1833[64]

My Dear Brother,

I do intend, God willing, to come down to Albury on Monday by the first Coach, and to make the best of my way either from Guildford or from Clandon or from Ripley. If I can get a coach coming through Clandon I will walk over the hill, if not I will alight at the nearest point on the Ripley road and walk along the hill: so as to get to you the soonest possible. And I will remain till Wednesday in time to be home to the evening service. And do you pray that my coming may be for our mutual profit, and for the good of Christ's Church.

As concerning the Deacons, I beseech you to think no more about it lest you fall into temptation and a snare. Your care is over your flock and mine is over mine, and though we do well to take counsel together, we must be careful of intermeddling the one with the other. I feel always that your conclusions are sharper than need be, and that it is rash to say that but for one precept any chapter may be expunged from the bible. Bear with me, Dear Brother, in love. I am not jealous over my own things but jealous for you lest the enemy should get any advantage over you. For he much desireth it. I rejoice that the Lord hath given you another Deacon; and I pray that he may bless you a thousand fold.

64. DFP: C/9/13.

Mr. Carré speaks much of the edification which there is in Mr. Bayford's[65] preaching. They are in good heart. Farewell.

Love to all the Brethren,

Edwd Irving

Addressed to: Henry Drummond Esq.,
Albury Park,
Guildford, Surrey.
[Annotated: Irving 15 Feby 1833
Objecting to my opinion of 7 deacons.]

～

Edward Irving to HENRY DRUMMOND

London, 23rd February 1833[66]

My Dear Brother,

You have done well and as becometh the servant of the Lord in writing this Letter; and I will give the greatest heed to it, and correct every disorder in my habits & behaviour, which I discern to be such. In respect to Chaunting [*sic*] in my prayers, I believe that to restrain it would be to restrain the joy and the enlargement of heart out of which it procedeth. Nevertheless I will take this matter to more close and diligent observation, and to the Lord in prayer. It was the way of my Father and of all the pious old ministers & men of my youth; and long before the Spirit was manifested, it was occasionally my way, and is proper to all right and unrestrained speaking as is shewn even by the Heathen orators of Greece and Rome, who pitched their voices by the help of a pipe. I believe that both you and Lady Harriet are a little restrained of your spiritual liberty, by the thorough good-breeding which you have received in your youth. Wherein I desire to take a lesson from you, but by no means to give in to it. So much do I desire to please the Lord in little things as in great ones, that I committed in charge to that holy matron Mrs. John Cardale, to tell me, if in any thing I did grieve the spirit within her. Therefore doubt not at no time to go as far in counselling and entreating me, as the Lord sheweth to you, that you ought to go. I owe you much love. The Lord who is the fountain of love requite you through me. Of that dear servant of the Lord, Mrs. Caird, think and speak always as of one of God's dear saints upon whose soul he layeth many things.

---

65. See letter Edward Irving to Isabella Irving, 2 July 1830 n: Oliphant, *Life*, 2:145–46.
66. DFP: C/9/14.

Part II: The Letters

I enclose you, because you can afford to pay the postage, and it is worth ten times as much, a letter from Mr. Dow entreating me help them when I go down. But I must first read it to the Church and then I will send it.

Fare you all well,

      Your faithful & loving brother,
      Edwd Irving

Addressed to: Henry Drummond Esq.,
Albury Park,
Guildford.
[Annotated: Irving 23rd Feby 1833
His reasons for Chanting.]

~

Edward Irving to HENRY DRUMMOND

27th March 1833[67]

My wife desires me to say that these Letters were in the hands of Mr. Barclay & she could not get them till my return else they would have been sent sooner.

My Dear Brother and Fellow-servant of our Lord & Master Jesus Christ,

You do well in taking no step without the voice of the comforter who is to us what the Angel of the Covenant was to the children of Israel whose office and dignity and sanctity will profit you to meditate and to open to your people Ex XXIII v 20–24 as I have been doing to mine. For I am more and more convinced that the voice which we have in the church is not to be ranked in the order of the gifts, but as the voice in the wilderness preparing the steps of our King, and setting in therein Ps LXXXV; through the guidance of which we shall come forward together, and grow up into the capacity of receiving and occupying the gifts and the ministries of the Lord. Since my offence in the matter of doing what I did in Scotland without the word of the Lord, I have been much humbled and taught of the Lord herein; and I see it as one of the blessed fruits of our godly sorrow for that offence. How needful and how instant is the voice of the Holy Ghost, and how supreme above all ordinances Apostolical or Pastoral, see in Acts XVI v 6,7. Therefore teach your people to be ware and be thyself ware of ranking the voice we have merely as prophesying for the Children. It is that, my brother because we are and which we are children; but it is the voice which hath opened the mysteries of

---

67. DFP: C/9/15.

God's purpose and which will seal the witnesses. I do admire and adore the patience of the Lord with me and my people.

The Lord hath laid much affliction upon me and my children of whom the youngest[,] dear Ebenezer[,] is dangerously ill[;][68] we have cast them entirely upon the Lord, believing that he knows best what is good for them and for us; not despising medicines but content to be afflicted which we are afflicted; and seeking to return unto the Lord from all our backslidings.

In respect of the baptism of Mr. Taplin's child I give my full consent to this being by you administered and if the Lord should shew you any thing of his mind in respect of Baptism please shew it to me. Dear Perceval[69] has been called to be an Elder in my church with promise of something far beyond. My love to Lady Harriet and the children and the two guests[70] once in my house always in my heart.

Your faithful brother,

Edwd Irving

27th March 1833
Addressed to: Henry Drummond Esq.,
Albury Park.
Favd by Mr. Taplin
[Annotated: Irving
The voice of the Spirit now not one of the gifts.]

Edward Irving to D. DOW

London, April 1833[71]

My dear Brother,

I sit down to record, for your praise and thanks—giving and that of your church, the doings of the Lord in the midst of us during these days past.

On the Lord's-day before the last, when as usual during the forenoon service, I proceeded to receive into the church the child of one of the members, who had been baptized at home during sickness, and had desired the father to stand forth, the Lord by the mouth of His apostle arrested my hand, saying that we must tarry for a while. Though I wist not wherefore this was done, I obeyed, and desired the parent to postpone it. Then the Lord further signified it was His will we should know, and the whole

68. Ebenezer Irving (born: June 1832; died: 23 April, 1833).
69. He was called as an apostle in 1833. See letter 14 September 1832: DFP:C/9/8.
70. Presumably Mr and Mrs Caird.
71. Drummond, *Narrative of the Circumstances*, 34–53.

church feel, that we were without ordinances, to the end we might altogether feel our destitute condition, and cry to Him for the ordinances from heaven. Then I discerned, that He had indeed acknowledged the act of the fleshly church, taking away the fleshly thing; and that He was minded, in His grace, to take us under His own heavenly care, and constitute us into a church directly in the hands of the Great Shepherd and Bishop of our souls; for He commanded us to rejoice, and confirmed our souls with words of prophecy, assuring us that He would build the house, saying unto Jerusalem, 'Thou shalt be built,' and to the Temple, 'Thy foundation shall be laid.' We did accordingly take heart and sing, 'When Israel out of Egypt went,' &c. (Ps. Cxiv.)

The night before this, at our church meeting, the Lord, in he midst of many precious words spoken by the mouth of His apostle, had said, 'Sanctify yourselves; call a solemn assembly:' which words some of my brethren the elders thought did require the setting apart of a particular day; but it rather bore to me, that we were to abide in a sanctified state, washed and cleansed—ourselves, our little ones, and our houses—and to continue instant in prayer and supplication before the Lord, until He should fulfil all the words of grace and love which He had spoken over us. Accordingly I took order that, beside the meeting of the church for prayer every morning, there should be a meeting of as many of the flock as could assemble, that we might not cease praying to our God to restore His ordinances to us, and deal with us in all things according to His own mind; for I felt that it was our part to inquire of Him for this, and leave every thing in His own hand. He whom the Lord has most frequently used among us to bring words of authority, and whom He hath since ordained prophet by the laying on of hands, had been absent for some time at Albury; but the Lord, having a work to do by him, brought him back on the Wednesday, and he was in the church on the Thursday morning; when I asked him, after I had finished my part, to conduct the worship. After singing, he read the first chapter of Jeremiah, and being come to these words, 'I see a rod of an almond-tree,' he was made in the Spirit to speak much upon it, and to apply it to the spiritual ministry, which even now was beginning to bud; and in the midst of it be brought a message, or rather delivered a command, to the apostle to ordain me Angel over the church on the morrow evening, and to charge me and the flock with such words as the Lord should then give him. For this holy action I sought to prepare myself and my flock with all diligence; and being assembled on the Friday forenoon, which is a constant service in the church, after the service I spoke to them all very solemn words concerning the work which the Lord had set to be done in the evening. And the Lord opened the mouth of the apostle to charge the people with words of the most severe holiness, and the most terrible majesty. The Lord had forbidden the profane from being assembled with the church, and that the church alone should be assembled, and I charged the deacons accordingly.

After the service of the Friday forenoon, the apostle, whose seat is behind mine, sought my liberty to go away the next day to Albury, being pressed in the Spirit that he had something to do for the church there. But having learned through experience, that it is through word the Lord confirmeth and determineth every thing, I felt that I might not give my permission without the word of the Lord, especially at a time so momentous to the church, when the Lord seemed to have a work to accomplish in the midst of us by his hand; and I took him, with the servant who is now ordained prophet, and the two handmaidens whom the Lord hath chiefly used in bringing water of life to the people, into another place; and having told them, or being in the act of telling them wherefore, the Lord opened the mouth of His prophetical servant, and commanded the apostle to go; defining also the errand to be, to ordain the Elder of Albury Church, who has been named, and for the last three months been labouring at Brighton. This done, the Spirit of the Lord came upon one of the handmaidens of the Lord; and she was made to speak unto the prophet words more flesh-crucifying, exhorting him to be broken with Jesus, and to prove the blessedness thereof: upon which he knelt down to utter his heart's fulness to the Lord; and being ended, ere yet he was risen from his knees, the Spirit of the Lord came upon the apostle, and he was made to go to him, and lay his right hand upon him, and ordain him prophet of the Lord to the church, with a short charge to faithfulness, and to require him to 'rise up, calling on the name of the Lord.'

We assembled in the evening, and while reading the Scriptures, as my custom is, for one quarter of an hour before the service begins, that the people may come in and sit down under the sound of the word, it came in course to read the fiftieth chapter of Isaiah; and being come to these words, 'The Lord God hath opened mine ear,' The Spirit of the Lord spoke to me through the ordained prophet words of great assurance, to the effect that the Lord would give me the opened ear to bring instruction to His own people; and His own eye, to discern in the darkness as in the light; and he added words to the flock, which were mostly in an unknown tongue, concluding with these words: 'He giveth you the sign of unbelief'—namely, the unknown tongue. We humbled ourselves, and gave thanks to the Lord, and then I finished the chapter, when it was time for the service to begin.

We always begin with prayer, coming to the Lord through the Blood by confession of our sin and supplication for His mercy. This ended, the Spirit of the Lord, by the apostle, said, 'Sing the fortieth Psalm;' to which we addressed ourselves with strength of heart, for it did relate our experience as a church. Being well nigh ended, while we were singing the 11th verse, the Spirit of the Lord spoke through the ordained prophet words to the ordering of God's house, saying, that God purposed giving us the mystery of the candlestick in the holy place, with his shaft and his branches, his almonds, his knops, and his flowers. Then he placed the elders, who from time to time had been named heretofore, but none of them, save the two who had come out with me, had been permitted to occupy the places of office, which are three hairs upon the one side and three upon the other side of my chair; which the architect, guided in this, as in many other things, by the Lord (for he is a deacon of the church), had caused to be placed there. He set His servant Horne upon my right hand; His servant took it, and began to speak to the congregation, all in the Holy Ghost, that the church had rejected the voice of God, in order to give ear unto the wisdom of man: that at length the Lord, wearied out, had withdrawn His voice from midst of her; that the thing which we had seen in these days was but the shewing forth of what had been done in the church of old; that we had been guilty as the rest in all these sins, and that it was not for any thing in us, but for His purpose, and for His name's sake; that He had returned unto us, and that we must know this, that He had judged the churches: His word was gone forth against them, *but their entire destruction should not be seen till Solomon; the Man of Peace, should come.* He then began to charge both me and the people, saying to me, that by faith I stood, faith in the work of the Lord; from which if I fell away, for as high as God had lifted me up, I should be cast down with sudden destruction;—that the sword of discipline belonged to me, to chase all evil-doers from the congregation of the Lord, and to keep away the unclean;—that the people must obey me, and give heed to my words, which if they failed to do, it would be visited of the Lord, for it should be different with us from times past. Then commanded he, with very awful words, all unclean and unbelieving persons to depart, yet the Lord would rather they should abide, being cleansed in the blood of Jesus, which he even then preached to them; Jesus their Redeemer, Jesus their Sanctifier; and all who know Him as such besought he to take part in the solemn work which the Lord was doing. Then he came from the place of testimony on my right hand, and knelt beside me on my left hand and prayed in the Holy Ghost over the flock and me, joining us together in the presence of our God; and then he arose, and, laying both his hands upon me he ordained me angel over the church, bidding me be filled with the Spirit of grace, and of wisdom, and understanding, and the fear of the Lord; to be filled with the gift of the Holy Ghost for the office wherein I was now set. This done he gave out the xxxiid Psalm, and all the congregation arose to sing it with one heart. When we were well nigh finished with it, the Holy Ghost came upon him to say, 'And shall not the Lord seal up His covenant with His servant in the sacrament of His body and blood? Let the deacons go forth, and let them bring in bread and wine; let them find unleavened bread, bread without any leaven.' And the deacons went forth accordingly.

He then said, 'The Lord would have read in your hearing the epistles to the churches, and take you bound in your angel to keep all His charge, the promises and the threatenings therein contained: what is spoken to the angel is spoken to the churches in the angel, and what is spoken to the churches is spoken to the angels over the churches; for these times are they written, for churches having angels they are written.' And again he charged the profane and the unbelieving to go forth from the congregation. Therefore he again took the place of testimony, and read in the power of the Spirit the second the third chapters of Revelations, laying an emphasis on certain parts which gave them a significance that I undertake not to convey; only he said in plain language that Satan's seat was in this city, and that Antipas is he who resisteth man's authority in the church.

Before he had finished this part of the action, the deacons had returned, bringing wine in one of the silver cups, and unleavened cake, which with their own hands they had prepared, on one of the silver plates of the church; and two of them were standing ready to minister to him; but he bade them tarry, and gave out the 25th Paraphrase 'Twas on that night when doom'd to know;' which having sung with one accord, he asked me if I would engage to keep these charges of Christ to the churches, which I engaged in the hearing of all the people to do. He then passed to the deacons, and took a piece of the cake, and, lifting it up between his hands, he broke it, and said, 'The body of Christ broken for you,' and, having required me to kneel, he gave it to me; so also he took the cup, and having lifted it up, he said 'The blood of Christ shed for you,' and gave it in like manner to me; and then said, 'Do thou give it to the elders and other officers of the church, and any of the congregation;' which also I did, giving it to him among the rest.

He had returned to his seat; and when the cup was given to him, he rose up to receive it, and partook standing. Some sat, some knelt, and some stood while they received it; and there was no word concerning this save in my own case, which I understood to be a token of my receiving the seal of the covenant from the hand of Christ in the person of His apostle. While the cup was passing among the brethren who received it, there came from the Holy Ghost these words: 'You refused to take bread and wine with His enemies; and now He giveth you the wine of the kingdom to drink;' and with this ended his part of the service: to which I added words to explain and improve unto my flock that which had been done amongst us of the Lord, as the same was brought to my own mind by the teaching of the Lord. Then I prayed, and we sang the xxxiiid Psalm, and parted with the Doxology and Benediction, as usual. The whole service occupied a little more than three hours.

Such is the simple and true account of that great act of the Spirit through the apostle of the Lord. I have sought much to enter into it since: and so far as I have been taught it amounts to this: 1st, A casting off, so far as London is concerned (for the Lord hath repeatedly said, that the burden of the whole city is laid on us) of the old ordinances, which they have polluted, and a giving of them anew from His own hand from heaven. 2dly, A purging out of the old leaven of the flesh, and the requirement of a purely spiritual service, which we must grow up into from childhood into manhood, beginning from that day, by the forgetting of the former things, and the never bringing them into mind. 3dly, A constituting of the church in the angel, by the taking of him bound in all the words spoken by the Lord to the churches, that we might henceforth cease altogether from the canons and laws of man.

The next night, the Lord by the mouth of his prophet, in a glorious song, partly in tongues and partly in English, called out John Tudor, a man of much learning and wisdom, the Editor of the Morning Watch, who has for the last year been waiting on the Lord to be employed in the ministry: him he called to be an elder, which completed the number: and at the meeting of the session that morning, the Lord, by his apostle, had made choice of three of the deacons to be helps; so that there were now six elders and five helps named of the Lord, with the promise that He would speedily make another help. At the same meeting the Lord shut the mouths of all the members of the church who had heretofore gone forth into the streets, commanding that none should go but such as were sent. This shut me up to cry earnestly to the Lord for evangelists, especially on the afternoon of the Lord's day, which is not a meeting of the church, but for preaching the Gospel to all who come. This prayer the Lord heard; and at the evening service of the church, when the congregation was in the act of departing, the Spirit by the mouth of the prophet called John Francis, a young gentleman who for more than a year has given himself to the Lord, enduring all things for His name's sake in the streets with great quietness and charity. Him also the Holy Ghost charged before all the people to summon the people out of Babylon, and to carry them the glad tidings of salvation.—From all that has been spoken to the evangelists, it seems that it is not preaching the Gospel to the heathen, but preaching deliverance and life to the captives of Babylon.

Nothing further was done of the Lord till Thursday morning. When the apostle, being arrived, was in the meeting for prayer, and while I was speaking to him after the service, the Spirit of the Lord came upon him to go up to two of the brethren, one a help and the other a deacon, and to name them evangelists, the hands of the church for bringing in her children. They were by name Archibald Barclay and Charles Wallis, who had also abounded in labour and sufferings for the Gospel's sake in the streets. These, together with one who had been ordained some months ago to go and labour at Brighton with the elder there, made four, of whom three waited for ordination, and were commanded not to go forth without it. This made them cry much for ordination. Next night, which is an open meeting of the church, I felt constrained in spirit to rise, in order to call the church together next night, specially to inquire of the Lord concerning the ordination of the evangelists and the elders; for as yet I had no clear light concerning the helps, what was their present standing, and whether they would be ordained or not. But while I was yet speaking, nor had yet delivered myself of the burden of what I had to say, the mouth of the prophet was opened to declare that on the morrow evening the Lord would ordain the evangelists by the laying on of the hands of the apostle, and on the Lord's day forenoon He would do likewise by the elders, after which the Lord's Supper should be administered to the flock; and that the flock only should assemble, and of them only such as had faith; for many of them had been defiled by coming without faith on the former day of my ordination.

Being assembled on Saturday night in faith of the Lord's word, after which we had offered to Him our worship, we inquired of Him concerning the ordination of the evangelists by prayer. After which I gave out to sing part of the lxiid Psalm; during which, when we had come to the 18th verse, I found the Apostle standing at my hand, called in the Spirit to do his office; but previously, while I was reading the verses to be sung, the Holy Ghost by the prophet had called out His servants, whom the Lord had named evangelists, to come forth and kneel at the altar; and they did so at my bidding, and then kneeling there, when the Apostle was brought to do his high calling: he began by pronouncing 'woe' many times, and judgments nigh at hand: he charged the flock that they must go forth with the evangelists in faith and prayer continually; and the evangelists, that they must pronounce the judgments against Babylon, and the woes which were at hand: that their words must drop as the dew, and as the honey from the honey-comb, and pour forth the water of life; preach the Gospel of peace, and the love of God; and many precious words were spoken by the Holy Ghost. Then over each of them the Spirit spake according to His knowledge of their case, and laid hands on them. After which the Evangelist already ordained was called to come forth and kneel beside the rest; and I was required to lay hands on them and send them forth. I stood ready to perform this; for the Lord had shewn me in the light of His truth, that while it was the prophet's part to call by name, and the apostle's to endow with the gift, it was mine, as the constituted angel of the church, and head of authority in this city, to give them of my authority to go forth within that bound, and fulfil the ministry which they had received of the Lord. I was also required to give them a charge, which I did, after one of the elders had read the xth chapter of Matthew, and the last chapter of Second Timothy. To my charge, the Lord added another by the mouth of His prophet, commanding them to go to the lost sheep of Israel; to heal the sick of Christ's flock, whom the pastors had afflicted by trampling down the pastures and fouling the waters; to raise the dead in trespasses and sins; to cleanse the lepers, which are the Infidels; to do these things in the spirit, and they should soon do them also in the letter. Having been thus graciously dealt with of the Lord, we departed much rejoiced in heart for the great gift which He had bestowed on this city in these four evangelists.

Next morning the church assembled, as usual on the Lord's-day, at ten o'clock, to receive from the Lord ordained elders, and afterwards to eat the Lord's Supper with unleavened bread. It was appointed of the Lord to be only the members of the church; and when one, at the meeting of the church on Saturday morning asked of me concerning their servants who were not members, I was answering that they were covered by their masters, when the Lord interrupted me with strong confirmation, that the believing master sanctified his servants, the believing husband his wife and children. These I permitted to be present, but desired to sit apart lest they should eat the Lord's Supper along with the flock, and so be defiled. And, indeed, the Lord hath shewed us that it is His mind the flock should sit apart, and that a bound should be set about them, for they have been sanctified to him by covenant. I had a discernment of this when we came to our present habitation, and even before; but the Lord hindered then, until it should have been separated by the act of the angel's ordination, and the covenant of Christ's statutes, and the sacrament of unleavened bread then given to us.

Being thus assembled on the forenoon of the Lord's day, after the exhortation and the confession, the Holy Ghost by the mouth of the prophet, in an utterance partly in tongues, partly in English, called 'His servant Gambier' a captain in the navy, who has laboured much in His service, to be a help; thus filling the vacant place—six elders and six helps—and His servant Thomas Evill (he who wrote the 'Cry from the Desert' and other little works concerning the Advent) to be a deacon: whom having called forth before me in the sight of the people, and inquired of them their willingness to obey the word of the Lord and serve in these offices, I charged them with it till they should receive ordination, and required them to take their seats with the brethren. Then we proceeded with our offering of worship, which was the xxiid Psalm, in order; and having offered it first in prayer, reading it, and then sung it in praise, as our manner is, we knelt down to offer our morning prayer; and being ended, I recounted to them the Lord's goodness in having promised ordination to the elders this day, and called upon them to sing with a steady faith the cxxviith Psalm, after which, if the Lord permitted me, I proposed specially to enquire of Him by prayer, for the accomplishment of His promise. But the act of faith by the people was enough; and when we had done singing the Psalm the Spirit of the Lord came upon the apostle, and he began to utter in a strain of grief over the church which had polluted the ordinances of the Lord, 'leavening the bread and mixing the wine with water;' therefore the Lord had rejected them, and gave us 'a new thing; and yet not a new thing, but the old thing which we had had from the beginning.' Then He charged upon the congregation its great sin in having restrained the work of the Lord, whereby souls were perishing through our unmeetness for the Lord's use; after which, in a most soul-searching prayer, which dissolved the whole flock in tears of contrition, he confessed our sins unto God, and in the end pronounced an absolution. Then he required the elders to kneel, and helps also—for the helps were elders; for none but elders, could be helps to the elders, yet in subjection to the elders, and under silence in their presence. Then went he in the power of the Holy Ghost from one to another; and, with words of surpassing grace and nicest appropriation, he laid his hands upon the elders after the order in which they had been named on the night of my ordination; and then upon the helps, after an order in which the Spirit seemed to move him from one to another. Over some of them he uttered prophecies of a higher vocation, as also he did over some of the evangelists. Only the help called that morning ordained he not, but bade him serve for a while in the power of the word which had been spoken to him. This done, he returned to his own seat; and, the elders and the helps still kneeling, I was beginning to speak, and to take my part—for the Lord had shewed me His order in my own mind, and also in the word of prophesying, the Friday night before—when the Holy Ghost also, in the hearing of all the people, charged me to lay hands on the elders, and then, with the elders, to lay hands on the helping elders; which also I did, giving them power and authority to minister the word and sacraments within the bounds of this city, and sharing with them of the gift which the Lord had given to me. Then I called the helps one by one, and, with the elders, we laid upon them the hands of the presbytery, and gave the same power under our hands. Then I called the helps one by one, and, with the elders, we laid upon them the hands of the presbytery, and gave them the same power under our hands. Then I read the last chapter of John's Gospel and the last chapter of Peter's First Epistle, with words of charge and instruction to them, whereof the Holy Ghost sealed some by his own word; especially that they must be husbands of one wife, when I was charging them not to meddle with things or churches beyond our bounds, save in the communion of the saints: also not to remove them from their charge until the Lord should remove them. This done, we undertook to glorify God in singing certain verses of the xlvith Psalm; rejoicing in one another as husband and wife, and altogether in the Lord Jesus as our common Husband.

Meanwhile I asked the deacons to go and bring bread and wine, and set it before me; for it was shewn me in the message of the Lord that this pertained to the deacons, as having the charge of the goods of the house, until the elements became consecrated, after which they become the charge of the pastors or elders. The jealousy of the Lord over the order of His house was here very remarkably shewn. Our free-will precentor is one of the helps, who had been called from among the deacons; and, standing beside me, he asked me if he should go, and Charles Buchan take his place. Not remembering for a moment, I permitted it; but before we had sung a line, I remembered that he had been ordained a helping elder, and I immediately dispatched one of the helps to recall him; which seemed as if two helps had gone with the deacons, but they had both been deacons before. When they were done with singing the first verse, the Spirit of the Lord came upon the prophet and he cried out with tongues that the help must not be mingled with the deacons; and added, that the Lord's order was to set seven deacons in His house. By this time the helps had both returned, according to my instructions; and here the Lord gave, in sight of all the people, a proof of the simultaneous oil whereby He putteth the same thing in the heart of the angel and the mouth of the prophet of the church. Surely this is the mystery of the angel to be the ruler and discerner of whatever is said and done in the flock by pastor, evangelist, prophet, or apostle.

When we had sung the Psalm, I proceeded to administer the ordinance after our customary form, expounding the word of the institution, and fencing the table at the same time, confirmed at times by the Spirit: then singing some verses, to permit those who were consciously unclean to remove to the end of the gallery of the church. After I had given the bread to the elders and the helps one by one, and was proceeding to desire them to carry it to the people, the Holy Ghost, by the mouth of the prophet, directed me to give it also to the deacons: after which the elders and their helps carried it round to the people, and so also of the cup; and then was a wonderful presence of our God in the midst of us, which also He testified by many precious streams of living waters. Perceiving, from what had taken place at my own ordination, that it was the mind of the Lord that all the bread and wine should be consumed by the church, and there being not a little left, I desired it to be carried round; and the Lord confirmed it by His own word, saying it was the eating of the offering in the holy place, the leaving nothing of the sacrifice till the morning. I felt a special presence of the Lord with us in this part of the action, as it were breaking up the formality of one bite and one sip, and giving the true feeling of eating the Lord's Supper.

The Supper being ended, it was shewed me, in the light of God with me, that I ought to make one of the elders read the words of the covenant, in which I had become bound for the church—namely, the iid and iiid chapters of the Apocalypse;—and having called Mr Perceval to do this, the Lord shewed His well-pleasedness, by requiring the people to stand; which also they did with great solemnity: then we offered our acknowledgments to the Lord in solemn prayer, and sung a Doxology, and I gave the Blessing; but the Lord suffered us not to depart without a glorious ascription of praise in a song from the Holy Ghost. It was a day much, much to be remembered, and ye may well praise the Lord with us.

In the afternoon it hath bee my custom to preach to an indiscriminate assembly, but still to offer something like the worship of a church; but as the Lord has been separating and defining His offices more clearly, I have felt that it was sowing two kinds of seed in the same field, and ploughing with an ox and an ass. Also, since the Lord called me to be an angel of His church I have felt my gift of preacher or evangelist failing, as it were, not for want of will, but for want of warrant. At the meeting of the session the day before, we were speaking of some things the Lord had ordered at Albury, concerning the evangelist's not holding forth the word of life where the pastor fed the flock; when the Lord said by is prophet, that He had put a difference between me and His servants there, for I was set both as an evangelist and as an angel of His church. Nevertheless, the Lord forbade me to go forth, like the rest, but to abide where he had set me. I take this as a very great grace of my God, that He hath put this precious name upon me, and I shall indeed labour, with His help, to fulfil it. It is two-fold: one, to explain to the people the Babylon wherein they are held captive; the other, to proclaim sweet strains of Gospel, preaching liberty to the captives.—Wrestle ye much with our God, that when His church here hath been built up sufficiently to do without my presence, He would spare me to come to Scotland, in the full commission of an evangelist; for His word hath passed upon me to that effect, and I long much to serve Him there. This afternoon I did therefore drop what is proper to the service of the church, and addressed myself to the work of an Evangelist, first out of the Prophets, then out of the Gospels; with short prayers and singing appropriate thereto, but chiefly discoursing.

In the evening it fell out that there should be two baptisms, which could not well be overtaken in the morning. My custom is, that one of the deacons should hold the water and the towel, while I charge the parents and instruct the people; but sometimes I had omitted it, and the water was standing on the ground at our feet. The Lord by his apostle noticed it, in the message of the Lord to the elder who sits at my right had, who came and told me that it was the mind of the Lord that one of the deacons should hold the water; and it was accordingly done so, and so the custom was sanctioned. When speaking of this, I may mention a thing which occurred some time ago. After having baptised a child according to the precise form used in the Church of Scotland, the father had taken the child down the steps which lead up from the body of the church to where the rulers of the church sit, and, behind them, those who speak in the message of the Lord. I had also knelt down and rendered thanks unto the Lord; and we were risen up again, when the apostle, who had been moved immediately after baptism to do it, but had refrained out of fear and reverence, was constrained to call back the child; which the father brought upon my bidding him; and he apostle took it into his arms, and received it into the church, and blessed it. During the remainder of the service the Lord shewed me that this was done for my sake, to shew me the completeness of His ordinance; and that it pertained not to the apostle, but to me. As we walked home together (for at that time I lived away from the church), upon my asking him concerning the act, he said he felt while he did it that he should never have to do it again; and I said, 'I felt the Lord made you do it, that I might see what was lacking in the form of our service.' Ever since I have, after baptizing the little one in the arms of the father, received it into mine, or rather into Jesus's, and blessed it with its Father's blessing.

Besides what I have written, I remember nothing more, save one thing, which I ought not to omit. At one of the meetings of the church I presented a special note of thanksgiving for your brother being called to be Angel, and for the permission you had received to partake of the Lord's Supper, and the comfort you had enjoyed therein. The Lord spoke by the apostle concerning you, that, while the Lord had permitted it, it was not His order, for He would have His holy sacraments ministered by ordained pastors; that we might return thanks, but still he was grieved in it; that you had prayed for apostles, but not understood your prayer. I discerned from this, that if you sought the Lord, He would either raise up an apostle, or send him whom He hath here raised up, to give ordination in the Spirit, as He hath given us; as also I sorely rebuked myself of not having recalled this to my remembrance when I met with you to inquire about your eating the Lord's Supper; but found I had forgotten what concerned myself, and I was therefore not permitted to be profitable to you. Lay this to heart, my brother; for thou art a son whom the Father loveth, and will not spare to chastise; and so is your brother. You have been sons of consolation unto me.

Edward Irving to HENRY DRUMMOND

7th April [1833?][72]

My Dear friend,

---

72. DFP: C/9/45.

Part II: The Letters

Will you do me the favour to be present in my Library on Monday at a precognition (as we call it in Scotland) upon that matter of Henschell's.[73] Mr. D Farrer and Mr. Tudor are to be present. I am perfectly amazed at the amounts of heat and violence which I hear from Edinburgh. The hour fixed is 3 o'clock.

Your faithful friend

Edwd Irving

If you should like it, I could go afterwards with you and spend the evening with you and Lady Harriet.

∼

Edward Irving to D. DOW of SUMMERHILL

London, 14 Newman Street,
April 25, 1833[74]

My dearly beloved brother,

In my former letter[75] having given you a narrative, according to the best of my remembrance, aided by my friends beside me, of God's way and work in respect of the ordination of the angel of the church, the elders, the prophet, and the evangelists, I do now, by the grace of God, undertake to do the same in respect of the seven deacons, who are now set over the congregation. When we were cast out of our beautiful house into the streets, for adhering to the work of the Spirit, and refusing to suppress His voice in the great congregation, two of the deacons, by name James Henderson and David Ker, had grace given to them to go out with us, and to cleave to the Lord. These, with the two elders, Archibald Horn and Duncan M'Kenzie, who also followed Naomi, were wont from time to time to convene with me in my own library, for taking counsel together concerning the church over which we were the overseers; and we saw it our duty, from the time of our casting out of Egypt, to require the attendance of those who spake by the Holy Ghost, both men and women, that we might neither counsel nor act in any thing but under the correction of the voice of the Spirit, for which we had been witnesses. The very first time we were thus assembled, we were led to consult for the filling up our numbers, which were originally seven elders and seven deacons; of whom one elder had been removed by death; another, being lifted up, had fallen into the condemnation of the devil; another, a deacon, being removed in the providence of God to distant colony; and the rest—namely, three elders and four deacons—had remained behind in the house of bondage, for lack of spiritual discern-

---

73. Ridley Henschell (1807–64)

74. See Drummond, *Narrative of Circumstances*, 53–63.

75. *ibid.*, 34–53.

ment. While we five, the remnant of fifteen, were thus taking counsel in my library concerning adding to our numbers, we deemed it dutiful to Jesus, our great Head, to pray for the guidance of His better wisdom; and we were answered in the message of the Lord to cry for life, for living stones, which the great Builder Himself would place in His house. In obedience to this word, we resolved to meet weekly, and call upon the Lord. At one of these meetings being led again to this subject- for the flock was very numerous, not fewer than five or six hundred—the Lord answered, and said, Choose out men full of zeal for the house of God, and set them before the Lord, who are of a willing mind to serve the Lord. Which we forthwith addressed ourselves to obey; but had not finished our selection until the Lord checked us, with words expressive of His grief over the unpreparedness, the deadness, that there was amongst us; rebuking us also very sharply for the dishonour which we had brought upon His name, and again calling upon us to humble ourselves, and cry to Him for the quickening of life in the midst of the flock,—insomuch that we desisted, and resolved to go no further without the express word of the Lord. I remember that I was greatly distressed in spirit after this meeting, by the apparent encouragement and discouragement at one and the same time; but I soon came to see that this is the way of the Lord,—to call us to a duty, and then to stay us until we have obtained from Him the charges for performing the duty. It is also worthy of remark, that every name which at that meeting was proposed amongst us, hath been since accepted of the Lord, without one single exception that I can think of: one for apostleship, one for the angel of another church, the others for elders or deacons; which shews that the Lord rebuke proceeded not from our unfaithfulness in counsel, but from the Holy Ghost's office to reprove all men of sin, of righteousness, and of judgment to come; also because the times and seasons are in the Father's hand, and we must wait His pleasure, nor presume to do His work in our own time, any more than in our own way. From this time forth I took no steps, save that I reported to the people these things, and asked such of them as desired to serve the Lord in these offices to mention it to me privately: one of the flock did so, and be hath been since chosen by the word of prophecy in the midst of the great congregation; another I was told was constrained in his private prayers to cry out that he might serve the Lord as a deacon, and he also hath been accepted of the Lord with words of singular grace. But, abiding by my purpose, we were content to watch over the church the best way we could; to commit it to the good Shepherd, and to cry to Him for living men, whom he might set in the charges of His house. Yet was I sore pressed in spirit by the insufficient oversight of the flock; and perceiving two men of the flock to be of a very excellent spirit, and disengaged from other duties, I ventured to propose them to my two elders as proper persons for helping them in their labours. All being agreed that they were worthy, and they also being willing, I required them to attend at our weekly meetings; and while I was propounding the matter in order, the Lord broke in with His word, and said that He set them as helps, and gave them a charge to feed the flock, in subjection to the elders. Until this moment I had never formed an idea of what the ministry of 'helps' did mean, which the Lord hath since constituted a standing order in His house; one of the three bowls in the branches of the candlestick. But the Lord would not suffer these helps to assist at the communion till after they had been ordained; and one day, when they were seated in the seats of office, to the exclusion of one of the deacons, the Lord by is own voice rebuked it, before all the people, saying 'Let not the unordained take the place of the ordained, but let them wait.' An in many other ways did the Lord manifest His jealousy concerning ordination, both preserving the things that remained and encouraging us to look forward to better things about to be given. Also from time to time the Lord called one to be an elder; and another He called, ordained, and sent forth, as an evangelist; but nothing was said or done in the matter of deacons for seven or eight months; during which time the whole burden lay upon the shoulders of David Ker, whom the Lord hath since set to be the head of the deacons; for Mr Henderson was in poor health, and barely able to wait on public worship. The way the Lord took to revive the matter of the deacons was very remarkable and instructive.

There was a society in the church of charitable and godly women, who yearly, about the setting in of the winter, were wont to combine their charity and their labour together, providing clothes and other comforts for the poor; and the time drew nigh for the re-commencement of their labours. I had always felt a doubt as to the propriety of this in a church; and felt that, so far as the poor of the flock went, it should be done by deacons, or deaconesses, as in the primitive church; and with respect to those without, I perceived their charity did little good, in proportion to the means expended. But yet I would not stop nor discountenance it, but left this, as every thing else, in the hand of the Lord. At this time I was sore troubled in spirit for the poor of my flock, who came to me, and I was not able to visit or help them; insomuch that I was constrained as in an agony to cry out for deacons, and to engage myself to live on bread and water, and share all with the deacons, if the Lord would only grant me them for the poor of His house. A few days after this came meeting of the ladies to provide the poor for the coming winter. They were to meet at the house of a lady who took a great charge of it, and my wife was to go to preside; but not being able, I asked a matron, to whom the Lord hath given the word of the Spirit, to take her place; and she waited, with another of the gifted sisters, in my parlour, while I went to my study to write a letter to the ladies. Moved by the Spirit, they came to me there, and the elder of them was made with sign of tongues to declare to me that the Lord loved not these confederacies; that He would not only bring forth the gift for His church; but also give persons to minister the gift. This comforted me very much; and when I was explaining what had been said in my letter, still intending to send it through their hands, the Lord shewed me farther, by his other handmaiden, that it belonged to me to minister His word, and added much encouragement; whence I gathered that it was His mind I should communicate to the ladies the words which He had spoke. So I postponed the meeting till I could preside myself; and early brought it about that this way of administering charity should be given up amongst us; and we were again shut up to the necessity of crying for deacons or deaconesses; and meanwhile we made the best use we could of what had been prepared.

Shortly after this, at our weekly meeting of the session, the Lord spake by the mouth of His servant the apostle, saying, it is the pleasure of the Lord that ye choose deacons: the Lord Himself will name the elders, but it belongs to the elders to choose the deacons. When we had prayed for unity of mind with the Lord Jesus and with one another, we proceeded about the work whereto we had been called by the Holy Ghost; and we speedily found ourselves to be of one mind in respect to eight men; whom having named over, one by one, the Lord said, 'It is the mind of the Lord that Mr Trimer wait a while,' which we received as an acceptance of the other seven. I then recounted, in the hearing of the brethren, the custom of the church to present their names before the people, and require any who might object to them to lodge their objections before the elders; but the Lord signified with a strong hand, that it belonged to us to choose them; and I did accordingly set them next day before the people, as men chosen of us and accepted of the Lord, for they were all willing to use the office; and I asked the people to signify their acceptance of them by rising up, which they also very readily and thankfully did. Nevertheless I heard that the orders of the Lord in this matter were a stumbling block to one of the flock and it was not without a certain trouble to myself, when I considered the order taken by the Apostles in the church of Jerusalem; but, having the fullest confidence in the word and wisdom of the Lord, and perceiving also that it was given into the hands of Titus to ordain elders, and much more deacons, in every city; and considering the changed circumstances of the church; I was contented, yea, and glad, to obey the directions of the Lord, perceiving ever the holiness and goodness of His own mind in every word which He spoke. There were now nine deacons, and, as it appears in the sequel, there ought only to be seven; but the Lord had His own uses for the men, and opened His mind as we were able to bear it. As the time drew nigh for the ordination of elders, I think it was the very morning after my ordination to be angel of the church, when we were assembled together, the Lord moved His servant the apostle to go up to one and another and another of the deacons, saying to them, The Lord calleth thee to be an help, which left but six deacons; indeed, there were but five, for one of them, Mr Henderson, had been called to the eldership on the night of my ordination. On the morning of the ordination of elders, before the service began, the Lord by prophecy called a help and a deacon from the midst of the congregation. But there still lacked one of the number which the Lord had taught us by an express utterance was the proper number. So being assembled in session on Saturday the 20th of this month, after we had gone over the names of those who during the week had applied for communion, the Holy Ghost said, It is the mind of the Lord ye should choose a Deacon: 'wherefore I gave forth the name of him whom the Lord had desired to wait; unto whom all the elders heartily consenting; and having with prayer presented him to the Lord, the Lord said that He accepted the service of His servant, who was also willing to serve his God. This was by the mouth of the apostle: then there came forth a word from the mouth of the prophet, that the Lord would have them ordained this night by the laying on of my hands and the hands of the six elders; after which I should give them a charge, and then bring them to the apostle, that they might receive his blessing; On a former occasion by the mouth of the apostle it had been said. The order of the Lord in the ordination of the elders is, that the hands of the apostle be laid upon them; then the hands of the angel of the church; then that the angel of the church with his elders do lay hands on the deacons, and bring them to the apostle that he may lay his hands on them. So far as my part and mine elders in the action was concerned, it was precisely the same in both utterances; and whether the apostle's blessing would be conveyed by the imposition of hands I could not say, but left it with the Lord. When the evening was come, and the people assembled; after we had offered our usual worship, I began to open to them what had been done in the morning; and having called Mr Trimer, and asked him of his willingness, and found him heartily assenting, proceeded to the ordination, by singing the xvth Psalm, then reading the ivth chapter of Nehemiah and the vith of Acts; during which I required the seven men to kneel on either hand of me before the elders, at the top of the steps, in the face of all the people, Then, after solemn prayer for the presence and power of the great Head of the church, I called them, one by one, to keel on the little elevated platform on which the desk or altar stands; around which stood the elders; and by the laying on of our hands we gave them power and authority to fill the office of a deacon, with charges and a benediction. Then they descended the steps and stood before me; and I charged them, from the words of Paul, 1 Tim. iii.14, opening each grace and duty in order. And this done, I called them one by one up the steps, to receive the blessing of the apostle, who stepped forth before the elders to receive them as they came. They stood in the same order in which they had been ordained, wherein I was guided chiefly by the period of their connection with the church. I felt, while I was taking this principle, that it was not the true one, and that I ought to have left myself in the hands of the Spirit; but of one thing I felt no doubt, that David Ker, who had served so laboriously, should have the first place. He did accordingly come up first to receive the benediction of the apostle, who, being in the act of giving it in the power of the Spirit, was carried out suddenly into greater power, and made to set him head over the deacons, and to give him a charge of his brethren. Then, having named the next in order as they had been ordained and stood before me, the word of the Lord came, saying 'It is the mind of the Lord that His servant Inglis come,' who was the fifth in order. He was the same who had been constrained of the Spirit to pray that he might be set a deacon. As he came up the steps the Lord promised him that he should yet be called to a higher ministry, and blessed him with a great blessing. Then He said, It is the mind of the Lord that His servant Wallis come next—(he is one of the evangelists, for I perceive that the evangelists are taken from the angel, the deacons, the helps, and the people indiscriminately)—who, having received His abundant blessing, descended. And now there was a long pause, for He named no other; and I, seeing the Lord took His own order, dared not to meddle, until the apostle said to me, 'I have no more word;' whereupon I called the rest in the order to which they had been ordained. Mr Stevenson, the architect of the house, who was indeed guided in his work of the Lord, after his blessing he was charged to be enlarged. Then came John Carlyle, the cousin of Warrand, my brother-in-law, one who for ten years has been the most diligent unobtrusive lover and helper of the poor, stealing out at all hours, when his work is done, to visit them. The Lord did reward him openly, receiving him thus: The Lord loveth thee, the Lord delighteth in thee; and, dismissing him, Go in peace, thou blessed of the Lord; also promising that the Lord would advance him. Then came Thomas Evill, whom the Lord blessed and charged to be faithful; and, finally, Mr Trimer, who had waited, and had helped Mr Ker much: he had also gone out preaching in the streets, and stood a very patient and faithful witness for the love of God to all, against one who was controversially given. Him the Lord received with great enlargement of love, promising to send him forth as an evangelist; in the mean time requiring him to use the office faithfully, and abide in his calling. These benedictions, like the benedictions or rather the ordination words, of the elders, were very glorious, full of grace and love and goodness, reminding me of nothing so much as the words to the Angels of the church, so full of encouragement and blessing. It hath been observed to me since that the words to each of the elders were characteristic, not only of them as persons, but had in them a certain diversity of gift. To the first on my right, obedience, with rule; to the second, holiness, and an example to the flock; to the third, light; to the first on my left hand, power; to the second, love; to the third, wisdom. To the first of the helps the Lord said, that He had other work for him; to the third, that He had filled his heart with love. And so spake He words of His own most gracious heart to all the servants of His house, which I thus delight to record as they are brought to my remembrance. When the deacons had been ordained, charged, and blessed, and stood again at the foot of the steps, the apostle still standing at the head thereof, he was made in the Spirit to speak words of great light, touching the thing that had been done; declaring that they had not been ordained by the laying on of his hands, and that they were not filled with the heavenly gifts, because there was not yet a church filled with the Spirit to choose deacons; that this should yet be; that the whole church should be filled with the Spirit, and should choose deacons; and that the deacons should then be ordained, and be filled with all the gifts of the Spirit. Meanwhile the Lord's mind was to prepare the people for receiving the Spirit by the teaching of the elders whom He had ordained, and through whom He would surely minister His word unto them; that the deacons were, as it were, the hands of the congregation to receive the word of God from the mouth of the eldership, and to convey it to the people in their goings out and in amongst them. The idea conveyed to my mind was as if the deacons were the vessels put forth from the congregation to receive the heavenly gifts conveyed by God through the eldership; as it were, the hands of the needy people stretched out to receive the treasures of goodness which the Lord, through the stewards of His mysteries, was minded to give the congregation. Into this matter I do not enter further than as it was expressed; which having ministered and applied unto the people, we praised the Lord, and gave Him thanks; and having commended all the people to His keeping, we blessed them. And parted.

And thus have you a true narrative of God's way of ordaining His house with an angel, elders, helps, deacons, prophet, and evangelists; all which may the Lord enable you to receive with faith and love, and to render thanks for His wonderful doings in the midst of us.

Nevertheless we are a most unprofitable people, as I now go on to relate, in the removal of my dear babe Ebenezer, who now lies in the adjoining room laid out for his burial. Oh, he is such a monument of our unbelief! The Lord hath, indeed, shewn us the nakedness of the church, and brought us to the dust. We offered him to the Lord the very night we took possession of this church, into which we were brought by the word of prophecy; and we named him our Ebenezer. Our stone of help; and the very night the elders first ministered to the people in their places, last Sabbath, they came up with one accord to pray for him, nor departed until the Lord had taken him, and refused to give him back to our prayers. He was a child filled with the beauty of God from his mother's womb; peace, patience and joy, and boundless love, were in all his way, until about the time I was cast out of the church; when he was smitten with a gradual fading away, and never smiled again. After I returned he never smiled; and before he never but smiled; and now he lieth in peace, like one whose spirit is in the arms of Jesus. And yet I can see the Lord's goodness to me and the elders, and the church—for we are one—in taking the child, rather than healing or returning him. We cannot bear it, brother. We must be humbled far lower yet, before we can receive power from on high. I would not have otherwise; save that I might be exercised, and my flock as the Lord would have us to be. O, brother, pray for us, for we have a direful conflict before us. The humblest shall fare the best in the fiery fight.

Edward Irving to HENRY DRUMMOND

London, 14 Newman St.
26th April 1833[76]

My Dear Brother,

We thank you very much for your tender sympathy and kindness to us under our sore bereavement;[77] but my wife is not disposed at this time to leave our home, nor doth she need it through the sustaining grace of our God. The end of the dispensation

---

76. DFP: C/9/16.
77. The death of Ebenezer. He died on 23 April 1833.

is to make us partakers of his holiness by acquainting us with his indignation and wrath against our sin; first against my own sin and the sin of my house, then against my sin and the sin of my Church in me represented. And that which becometh us all is to humble our selves under the mighty hand of God.

In respect of the gifts of healing & the other things connected therewith in your Letter, I have been led to see very much as you have written, but not so definitely to firm my thoughts into judgments, lest I should prejudge and prevent the work of the Lord. When I would discourse to the people of James V v16 & I was constrained to go back to Matt XVIII v 18 for the foundation. But I see no reason whatever for limiting the visitation of the Elders & the unction of oil to cases of judicial infliction. The Church hath always see it as a universal ordinance for the visitation of the sick of the Church. Nevertheless every instance of sickness in the Church ought to be confessed as a judicial visitation for sin and treated accordingly.

My Brother, I am again afraid lest the enemy should gain any advantage over thee. There are two words that I would have thee bear in mind the first that charity hopeth all things. This is suggested by the judgment expressed in these words of your letter 'There is a universal skepticism concerning the work of the Spirit *in those who most profess to believe in it.*' If this thought arise whisper it unto thy God, and hold them up in hope and love. For I feel that unless there was one—yea and many so holding me up, I should utterly fall. That one is Jesus; these many are his loving people. My second word is that the office of Angel so vastly encompasseth that of Prophet, that the devil is spoken to in the seven Epistles. Now beware lest the word in thee as a Prophet from its striking character match itself with the word of Edification in thee as the Angel. The Prophet is the Eye, but the Angel is the hand of the Church, the prophet the watchman, the Angel the Father of the house. May Jesus lead thee to the Father, that thou be filled with the Father's love. Fare thee well. The Lord make thee to abound in all grace & thy house & thy church.

Your affectionate and faithful brother,

Edwd Irving

Addressed to: Henry Drummond Esq.,
Albury Park,
Guildford.

[Annotated: Irving (office of Angel encompassed that of Prophet) 26th April 1833]

Part II: The Letters

Edward Irving to HENRY DRUMMOND

London, 14 Newman St.
1st May 1833[78]

My Dear Brother,

May the peace of God rest upon you and your house and the flock of God given into your hand. I have been much exercised in my spirit lately concerning the mystery of iniquity about to be revealed in the fifth trumpet.[79] Believing the word spoken through Baxter concerning the Trumpets, that they are now fulfilling in this land in a Spiritual way apprehensible only by the spiritual; and that he himself is the star wormwood in the third trumpet and that the new ordination and sacraments is the smiting of the old system of Christian power and rule and authority of the fourth trumpet, I am looking for a spiritual unfolding of the fifth; and I discern that the star is a spiritual person, and that the key of the bottomless pit, is the key of interpretation with which to open the infinite errors and delusions with which the Church was deluged in the times of Gnosticism and Manichaeism, chiefly it is believed through the spiritual covetousness of Simon Magus[,] a fallen star.[80] You can have no idea of the power of ingenuity and craftiness, and the infinite boundless speculations and subtleties, and cunning analogies, and coincidences of number and other things which poor Smith poured forth to me in letters, which no eye ever saw but my own. My conviction is that such a thing will be realised in the midst of the church which is now separated by the Spirit, that some one of these who have received gifts of interpretation or are to receive them, will be carried away of the enemy from the root and ground of love, through envy and covetousness and that the gift remaining to him will come to be exercised in infinite discoveries of curious and crafty things, whereby Satan will lead many astray, and cause the true work of God to be evil spoke of. I have given both the apostle and the prophet notice of this, and warned them much to abide in the love of the body[,] and to keep themselves in the love of the Lord Jesus, and see not that the evil one touch them not. And though I have no key-gift for opening the deep things of God, but only for using them when opened for the edification of the people, I have been much exercised before God that he would keep me from this snare, and now I write to you that you may also be on your guard.

When I lately was led as it seemed to me by the providence of God and a desire of unity in the Church, and brotherly love, to deliver Mr. Miller[81] and His flock out of the state of separateness in which they have stood from the Apostle of the Lord & the Church where the Lord had raised up such a gift, the Lord reproved me from

---

78. DFP: C/9/17.

79. See Rev 8.

80. Acts 8:18–23.

81. Rev. J. L. Miller, and one of the angels of the Seven Churches; his was Bishopsgate, (formerly the congregation of the Old French Chapel).

meddling in other people's matters and bade me wait till they should come seeking help and counsel of me; and he required him to submit to the ordinance of the Apostle by receiving the laying on of hands and it should be well with him, even unto the raising of him to be an Angel in his Church; but I felt that they were nothing profited, and I apprehend much evil there unless the Lord interfere to prevent. I mention this for your instruction, that you may not in any seeming good intentions at any time stretch yourself or be tempted beyond the line of your border.

There was another thing of which I had intended to write you, but it is gone from me; and the Lord is over my memory as well as other things.

My brother sinks fast,[82] I ask the prayers of you and your church for him. Mr. Taplin has been forbidden to read in the church, and we were prevented from reading together in private, and he has been forbidden to write unless he be commanded so to do; but simply to open his mouth in the Congregation, when the Lord is pleased to open it, and we have been commanded to pray much that it may be opened in great power. And so it hath been, and will be more and more. The Elders have had grace given to them to open their mouths freely, and I trust the Lord is edifying the people much through them. It is evident to my mind, that as a Prophet you ought to wait for the word of the Lord, but as an Angel you ought not, but to speak out of a heart filled with grace and love, and overflowing with rivers of goodness. I am oftimes sore troubled, and much cast down and broken in spirit, but my faith in the Lord abideth & delivereth me. In this I stand, and without Him I sink into my original nothingness. Be of good courage, brother, and strengthen your heart. The Lord will bless you more and more through your love of Him and of His people. I desire my love to Lady Harriet and the dear Children, to Mr. and Mrs. Caird, and all the office-bearers of your Church & to the whole Church. Peace be with you.

Your faithful brother,
Edwd Irving

Addressed to: Henry Drummond Esq. of Albury Park, Guildford.
[Annotated: Irving on Fallen Stars.]

Edward Irving to HENRY DRUMMOND

London, 4th May 1833[83]

---

82. Edward Irving's brother George.
83. DFP: C/9/18.

Part II: The Letters

My Dear Brother,

I meant no more concerning the subordination of the Prophetical gift to the office of the Angel, than what I expressed: and my fears as they concern yourself arise from your strong propensity to wit and argument[84] which siezeth upon the brilliant and striking points of interpretation, and Communicateth them in the clearness and baldness of intellectual truth, rather than in a state of growth and for the ends of edification. For example in your strictures upon the word of the Spirit concerning Mr. Taplin's not writing, there is a sharp decision and I would almost say a wrecklessness [sic] of language which beseemeth not the reverence with which any thing ever alledged [sic] to come from the Holy Ghost should be entertained. It shook my very nerves to read line after line of that Postscript. Now the whole matter proceeds upon a misunderstanding which your own wisdom would in the exercise of quiet reflection have discerned, and, if not, it were far more pleasing to wait and calmly to enquire than to put down strong conclusions grounded upon a hasty presumption. The Lord in the word spoken to him would mark the difference between word *written* and *spoken*, whereof the former pertaineth to the prophet no less than the latter, but only when the Spirit doth so move him or express it by him; at other times to do it, to cast down the dignity of the word written, and bring it into the mere usefulness of the word spoken. For example that word concerning the Candlestick written by Mr. Cardale is evidently for calm consideration and not otherwise to be made out but by the whole submitted to one's mind together; but what Mr. Taplin wrote was the gathering together and the ordering after his own mind of certain lights and utterances which had been given through him. And forasmuch as coming through his hand it would be by many taken for express revelation, it would lead many astray, as it did me a little, notwithstanding that I had discerned Mr. Cardale's form of it to be the truth before any utterance was given through the one or the other. Yet from the due reverence which I have for a revelation, I set my own idea of the three bowls upon the branches to a side and took up Mr. Taplin's, and spoke of it in the Church, but only cursorily and when not many were present. No wonder that the Lord was angry with both of us, and did censure me and rebuke him with a strong hand. But then this hath nothing to do with his reporting to you or to any other man whom for ends of Edification it concerneth to know, what the Lord has been saying or doing in his Church. Because it then pertaineth to his Church, when in his Church it hath been spoke or done. And even tho' God permitteth it not for any other end but that of preaching abroad his wonderful acts and ministering Edification to his little ones. To do it as a curious thing, to send it in its baldness without the forthsetting of the goodness and mercy and grace in the bosom of which it came, is not right; and I think I have seen something of this in your communications. Bear with me, my brother.

---

84. 'A sharp, elastic, haughty kind of man, had considerable ardour, disorderly force of intellect and character, and especially an insatiable love of shining and figuring.' Thomas Carlyle's description of Henry Drummond in *Reminiscences*, 326.

In respect of receiving the members of my Church or any other Church without previous conversation with them, it aught not to be done, because they may have turned aside or slidden back in the mean time, or the angel of another church may have failed in keeping the table of the Lord from profanation. Lane never received a token from me nor sit down with us at the table of the Lord. Poor old Mrs. Bishop; tell her from me, by no means to keep away from the table of the Lord, and on no account to doubt of disbelieve the work of the Spirit, but to open her heart to instruction and submit to the ordinance which the Lord hath given her, yea and to rejoice in them. There is oft much more of the life of God in the heart, than there is word of it on the lips, & it is always better that it should be so; and I have frequent occasion to defend the people from over harsh judgments of themselves. The fiery darts of Satan they mistake for positive unbelief. Also I have never prevented a member of the Church from coming to the Lord's table, because he had not yet attained clearness as to the work of the Spirit, but enjoined upon him reverence and patient waiting upon the Lord; but those who made light of it, I have separated after a first and second admonition and sometimes at once suspended them when I found them contemptuous upon being spoken to. [In faint pencil: Francis Bishop]

Dodsworth,[85] poor dear Dodsworth is a tale-hearer and a tale-bearer, for at my own lips he hath heard nothing of the kind he writes to you, and when I with Dr Thompson[86] waited upon him to set him right, he had nothing to find fault with but the doctrine of being holy because he thought it bore against the article about original sins. Let not such reports of me leave any dregs behind them, for truly the Lord teacheth me daily more and more to know and worship Him as one Father Son and Holy Ghost. He is at present the greatest enemy of the truth in this city, and yet I would not lift my finger to hurt him, for he is the Lord's anointed, & I trust may yet be brought into the way of truth. You do right in not receiving him into your house or wishing him God-speed; Gambier[87] refused to give him the right hand of fellowship. It is more than twelve months since I proposed to Mr. Miller[88] and that more than once, to bring the gifted members of his Church whom he had faith in, and to make proof of the Spirit which had begun to speak in his Church, and I expressed my willingness to sit as his assessor giving to him the principal place. In all that respects him and his flock I feel that I have been faithful to my Lord save that I have forgotten a little His dignity in me represented. I have done every thing I can to make Mr. Taplin comfort-

---

85. Rev W. Dodsworth (Margaret Chapel, London). So listed as an attendee at the first Albury Conference.

86. Dr James Thompson, who was one of the party that went to investigate the manifestations in Scotland in 1830 and a member of Irving's congregation. When the Rev David Dow defected from the apostleship he and Duncan Mackenzie were called. Duncan Mackenzie was chosen but Thompson became Chief of Pastors, second only to 'apostle.' See Shaw, *The Catholic Apostolic Church*, 79.

87. Capt. G. Gambier, lay attender at the first Albury Conference (Anglican, later Admiral). See Flegg, *Gathered Under Apostles*, 37

88. See letter Edward Irving to Henry Drummond, 1 May, 1833 n, DFP: C/9/17.

able in every way, and he hath no need to be in any anxiety, and now I pray the Lord to sustain him, and I feel assured that He will. But be not anxious that the other spiritual persons understand not his gifts. Theirs it is to speak, it belongeth to the Angel to apprehend the thing spoken and to the Elders. For the Lord in rebuking Mr. Taplin privately in my presence for not opening his mouth to speak, said 'The ministries have [letter torn] Whereby I was confirmed in my judgment that his gift is one [letter torn] ours to bring forth the treasure and appropriate it to the Lord's service. Now it [letter torn] me that this very word casteth light upon the subserviency [sic] in yourself of the prophetic word to the Angel's care. It is to choose out the persons and to open the scriptures according to your flock's need, not according to your own appetite. Therefore it is withholden because the flock hath not yet appropriated and digested what was given. I have erred grievously in not ministering the Song of Solomon long ago, as the prophet opened it. But I am a fool, and need chastisement to make me wise in the latter end. The thing which moved me to write so was that I heard you had resolved to be silent unless the word of the Lord came to you. This would be to revive Quakerism. The Port Glasgow brethren are altogether left behind, yet I believe abiding in the Lord. The Dows go forward with steadfast faith; and the brethren in Edinburgh come on. But oh! we are all a sore grief and trial unto the Lord our God, and none I think like him who writes to you. I am sore troubled as I write, my heart is oftimes like to break with the force of natural sorrow, and spiritual affliction. The Lord burdeneth me sore, and giveth me water of a bitter cup to wring out. But I know his hand is about me and over me, and I am daily more and more in his love.

This morning the Lord spake at my breakfast-table to dear Tudor,[89] to the effect that he was a vessel now close of the Lord for his own work, and that he must cease from the work where to the Lord had not called him, and entirely devote himself to the Lord's work; and other words clearly shewing to us all that the Lord's mind was the Morning Watch should no longer be continued. He told me afterwards that there was nearly a debt of £200 upon it, we must raise it for him amongst us. For dear man, through the badness of the times casting two of his homes upon his hands, he told me what I may tell you but not another, that his whole income to live upon was but £35 a year.

I am really glad that the Lord restraineth Prophetic utterance in you. Be assured it is unto the using up of all that you have received in living instruction & consolation to the flock. My love to Lady Harriet & the Children, to Mr. & Mrs. Caird, and the flock. My poor brother at whose house this is written is no better, but rather worse.[90]

Farewell,

Your loving friend & servant,
Edw[d] Irving

89. John Tudor (1784–61), a Welsh artist and writer, and editor of the *Morning Watch*.

90. George Irving's house was at 6 Woburn Buildings, [now Duke's Road] where Isabella Irving was nursing him. He died on the 8th of May 1833.

Addressed to: Henry Drummond Esq. of Albury Park, Guildford.
[Annotated: Irving 4th May 1833
Leave for Taplin to write the expositions given to him.]

Edward Irving to HENRY DRUMMOND

c. 26th May 1833[91]

My Dear Brother,
Be patient and slow of wrath, long suffering and kind, faithful and true, in all thy ways and thy vow shall abide in strength, and thy flock shall grow and flourish.

I was handing the Cup at the communion, the Lord arrested me on the steps as I returned from serving the Deacons; and made a revelation, that he had set us as the moon, and as the sun also. That we must have seven cups each containing four cups, four sevens, twenty eight the number of the moon. That we should have four loaves. That he would in due time give us to be clothed with the sun, and the moon under our feet, when he would give us his royal numbers, and then the man child should be brought full to rule & break the nations. This I discern to the order of Canticles 'Who is this that looketh out as the morning fair as the moon, clear as the sun and terrible as an army with banners.'[92] The Lord shewed me in his own message expounding that the seven larger Cups or flagons are seven churches each containing four cups (which I take to be churches four in one, the four living creatures and four & twenty Elders, the four of the vision in Rev IV, V). The seven large churches being the substance of the first verse of the apocalypse, which you know he made to be read over to me & charged me with the keeping of all the seven. But he charged Mr. Miller only with one, the Church of Thyatira[93] and the Spirit among them ordered them to have only one cup. Also there were words but not fully expressed to the effect that he would have to come up to us for counsel. I take the mind of the Lord in setting the seven flagons with each four cups fully upon our table doth signify the measure or extent of our Church, the bounds of our habitation seven churches each containing four. The four loaves are the fourfold ministries of Christ's body, which he hath now in his grace given amongst us. I think the four churches in one is the same mystery; *viz* that though an Angel be the representative of Christ, he will divide that representative fourfold & give it in fullness

---

91. DFP: C/9/24.
92. Song 6:10.
93. Rev 1:11; 2:18–29.

to no single person, you hath he set a prophesying Angel, me an Evangelising Angel, yet not to the suppression of the other three gifts, but to the revelation & manifestation of only one. This to keep us in our place. And so would the mystery of the 24 Elders also appear. These things are for discerning not for direction of the Lord's way. Dear Brother the Lord wonderfully openeth his way to us. Let us be very humble and reverently follow him. Faith not knowledge is our guide.

He hath also given us the privilege of offering our Eucharist our thanksgiving over his broken body & blood, on the three days the nativity, the resurrection, the Pentecost. So next Lord's day we keep the Lord's supper. May He remember us. Farewell, my Dear brother, be weak with the weakness of thy people & they shall become strong with thy strength.

Peace be with thy house & thy Church,
Thy loving brother,
Edwd Irving

[Annotated: E. Irving, 7 cups & 4 loaves.]

Edward Irving to HENRY DRUMMOND

London, 14 Newman St.
20th June 1833[94]

My Dear Brother,

On Tuesday night when the Church was assembled, the word of the Lord came to us urging haste upon us in our journey to Scotland. It was when I was laying out some things for which I more specially sought to Elders to pray; and the moment that I touched upon our journey the word came reminding us of what had been spoken before concerning haste & the enemy being there before us, and our being sent to pull down what he hath already been building up there. With these repeated admonitions I feel that I may not any longer postpone, and do accordingly set Monday for our going forth, if Mr. Cardale be returned and ready to go on that day. I offer myself to the Lord for this and shall submit it to Him on Saturday morning, and if permitted I think of ordaining a Fast as in the Church of Antioch, and setting out thereafter. I will let you know on Saturday if there be any further light cast upon this matter; and I would not have you to make any arrangements till you hear from me again. I communicated your request in your own words to the assembled Church, and besought the Elders & the people to make mention of your flock and of you continually in all their prayers.

---

94. DFP: C/9/19.

The cause of our dear brother Mr. Cardale's absence along with Mr. Percival at Oxford, is that there hath arisen up in the bosom of Mr. Hinton's Church there a female taking on herself the name and office of an Apostle, approved therein by both Mr. Hinton and Mr. Symes, an Irish free will Evangelist who was there helping Bulteel[95] when he fell, and now helps Mr. Hinton. Mr. Cardale & I were apprised of this a month ago, but having no word nor cause of interference, we said nothing of it, and it was all unknown here till on Tuesday morning I received a letter intending that her Pastor & she were coming up the day following. This letter set out her doings, her healings, orderings in the Church casting out of Spirits, ministerings etc. I discerned that it was not of the Lord and sent it with my observations to the Apostle,[96] desiring him to read it before his wife through whom and my maid we had been mightily warned on Friday & Saturday before. The word of the Lord came to him through her, commanding him to go down and scatter them, that they might not be suffered to come up, and to take another with him. His heart drew him to Mr. Percival, and they went down that night nor are yet returned. Only Mr. Hinton & she came not up last night, and I hope they have prevailed through the good hand of our God upon them. Pray for us, for surely we are sore assaulted.

In respect of my going to Scotland I have no light; and my prayer is for a broken head & with a broken heart; for they are exceeding desolate. Nor know I whereto the Lord calleth upon me. The only measure of the Lord is obedience. There is nothing else that I remember. I desire my love and blessings to Dear Gambier and to all the flock

Your loving brother,

Edwd Irving.

Mrs. Caird's blunder made no difference upon our expectations; all is ready & nothing but the will of the Lord is waited for. Let her come whenever she hath liberty. This is in answer to Lady Harriet's letter of this morning.

To Henry Drummond Esq.,
Albury Park,
Guildford.
[Annotated: Irving June 1833]

---

95. Henry Bellenden Bulteel (1800–1866), Protestant controversialist. He had become curate of St. Ebbe's church in Oxford in 1826. He had been made a Fellow of Exeter College but relinquished this when he married in 1829. In 1831 he was invited to preach a University Sermon when his remarks on the behaviour of the inhabitants of the University were frank to say the least. See Bulteel *A Sermon on I Corinthians II*, 44–45. BL 764.g 22 1–7. Not surprisingly after this outburst and together with his preaching in dissenting chapels, the Bishop of Oxford revoked his licence. He became a parishioner and follower of Edward Irving for a short time in 1832.

96. John Cardale.

Part II: The Letters

Edward Irving to HENRY DRUMMOND

London, 7th August 1833[97]

My Dear Brother in the burden and labour of the Lord,

I write you out of a troubled and heavy heart over all the iniquity which I behold and feel in the Church of God, yet with increasing confidence in the Lord's purpose at this time to bring his people through fire and water into a wealthy place. He hath answered us to the judgment in the midst of us, and is troubling every house which is not ordered according to his mind. For the weakness and sickliness of my children I had purposed they should by this time have been so far upon their way to Brighton along with my wife to partake the hospitality of good Mrs. Sober: but the Lord shewed me that it was a grief and sorrow to him for his people to be so slow and slack of faith to trust him for health, that it is not his way but a going down to Egypt for help.[98] So I desired the Elders to come in after worship and forbore the journey. At prayers I thought good to minister a word of rebuke to my servants for certain manifestations of discontent and rebellion when one of them who has been much cherished & much forgiven burst out before them all into open rebellion, and seeing no repentance this morning I have resolved to put her away. I see the Lord dealing in like manner with my flock to bring all hidden things to light and to put away all iniquity, which while it is for the present very grievous, doth yet comfort me very much as magnifying the holiness and the grace of our God, who is known by his judgments.

It hath been a great dealing in respect to the prophet, unto the magnifying of his office, unto the diminishing of both him and us as triflers therewith. The Lord's end is not yet attained and to the effect of bowing us down the more effectually, he stayed me from baptising by a word from the prophets mouth on Sunday night: 'Knoweth thou not Oh servant of the Lord that the laver stood without the Holy Place,'[99] concerning which when I more particularly enquired before the Elders, the Lord signified that the cloud rested & we could not proceed till the unholy thing was purged (burned) out from the midst of us. So is the Lord's work stayed for the present and we are shut up in the dungeon of our uncleanness. These things trouble me sore but I faint not.

In respect to what you say about the office of the Apostle, I know this that I know nothing as I ought to know it and I doubt not I have grieved the Lord in this as in every other thing. But I cannot charge myself with any willful omission or transgression of that ordinance. I did not refuse the word spoken at Oxford for all the Churches, nor did I refuse the word spoken here for the order of our Service. I believe them both to be from the Lord, and I wait for the ability to carry them both into effect, which in his time he will give. God hath manifestly given us the service of the Holy Place to keep and to shew forth, where was neither altar of sacrifice nor laver of regeneration: and I

---

97. DFP: C/9/20.
98. Isa 31:1
99. Exod 30:17–18

purpose in my heart to keep his charge. And yet I believe that in all the churches, the order of service spoke through the lips of the Apostle will be observed, as was said. Be not rash, brother. Tell what is a Church? The Lord hath set upon our Table his symbol seven churches *each containing four*. What is that *four*? [letter torn] and let the Lord reveal his own mysteries.

I am much exercised in Spirit, whether you do right in permitting Mrs. Caird who with her husband was given to you by the word of the Lord, to come up hither without the word of the Lord. I would not be the gainer if it were not His pleasure. I throw out this for your consideration. Your narrative seemed to me to lack sanction much and I think your judgment in respect of Mr. McNeill[100] [sic] to be hasty, and I hope yet to see him serving the Lord. I apprehend that your scrupulous jealousy of truth-speaking bind you up in the Letter and off-time quenches the Spirit. For the Spirit which is in any work of God is *the truth* of it, not the letter of the veil narrative. I am conscious to myself of coming short here also, as in all other things.

I desire my love to all the brethren, especially to Lady Harriet and the children and dear Mr. Wales. We have made all things ready for Mrs. Caird and Mrs. Campbell, and shall quietly rejoice in their company *Deo volente*. [God willing]. To them as to dear Gambier, who is a great joy to my heart, though a great perplexing at times to my understanding 'he is so crank.'[101] My dear love to you all & my blessing to the Church. Farewell.

Your faithful servant,

Edwd Irving

Addressed to: Henry Drummond Esq.,
Albury Park,
Guildford.
[Annotated: Irving 7 Aug 1833]

Edward Irving to HENRY DRUMMOND

London, 2nd September 1833[102]

My Dear Brother,

---

100. Rev Hugh McNeil rector of Albury and later Dean of Ripon. He had attended the first Albury conference and participated in the others but refuted the 'gifts' on the grounds that the Holy Spirit would have manifested only through the ordained ministry. See Flegg, *Apostles*, 53

101. I.e., difficult to understand.

102. Alnwick Castle, DFP: C/9/21.

Part II: The Letters

There is no doubt that the Angel of the Church is set to rule in the word, for it hath been often expressly said so to me; and there is no doubt that if false doctrine arise the Lord looketh to Him as responsible; for He and the Elders are one in the sight of the Lord; they in him, he in them. And both over him and them the Lord the Chief Shepherd sitteth watching for the safety of the flock, and will, by the Prophets, or the Spirit of prophesying in the body, warn them of the word of Error. And if the people and their rulers together do receive the error through unwatchfulness & disobedience, then it runs it course and brings forth its bitter fruit.

It hath occurred more than once in my flock that an Elder hath by the Spirit of God been admonished and reproved; and when once one Elder complained to me by Letter of another I brought them both into my presence and the presence of the Lord and was then taught expressly that the Lord would keep the mouth of his Elders and reprove what might be spoken amiss. The complaining Elder felt himself reproved and confessed Sin to the Lord. Nevertheless I have seen it good more than once to admonish an Elder and instruct them when I saw partiality in their doctrine. Yea I do daily before the ministry begins convey my mind both to them and the flock in a word of exhortation, bearing myself with all humility therein as the responsible representative of the Lord Jesus. And at the end of the ministry I do minister in such wise as to set in the true light as the Lord giveth me, whatever I perceive to have been set by them in any distorted light. But while I do thus stand watchful, I wonder greatly & do admire the great goodness of the Lord to them and to me and to the flock in the oneness of the doctrine and of the spirit which is made to appear from the mouth of so many men.

Our office herein is one of great delicacy, and responsibility, and I feel that I ought to take counsel with none of my flock, while I have an open ear to their troubles. And least of all with those who speak by the Spirit, lest they should bring a stumbling block before themselves and me. I know not whether I have well answered your letter but this is the way in which the subject presents itself to me and I have the conclusions for action in your own hand.

Your faithful & loving Brother,
Edwd Irving

Addressed to: Henry Drummond Esq.,
Albury Park,
Guildford.
[Annotated: Irving 2nd Septr 1833
Angels responsible for doctrine.]

Edward Irving to HENRY DRUMMOND

London, 16th September 1833[103]

My Dear Brother,

I thank God that I am quite recovered though very much pained all Saturday and all Monday, on Sunday happily free and I am very much comforted by the assurances of your love especially that I see I have not been the occasion, whether innocent or guilty, of any breach of Christian love.

From the first perusal of Mr. Dow's letter I saw that he was either *the* star or one in his train. And also that as Baxter who afterwards embittered the fountains of the Church, had been made most conspicuous in prophesying the coming of the Spiritual ministry, so David Dow who was made to open Leviathan and with Carlyle's ministry to publish it, is indeed, I fear, to be the opener of his den. But withal as the former so trust I the latter is likewise destined to be recovered. God thus magnifying our infirmity and instability out of our own warning mouth and this our grace to these who fell notwithstanding the warnings which they gave to others of the snare. My brother, the only infallible distinction between a work of God and a work of Satan is this: that in the former good and evil are separated, in the latter they are confounded; and he only makes progress Godward who increaseth in his abhorrence of sin. Therefore be thou holy, and teach thy Church to make progress in holiness; so shall you be secured from all the wiles of the Devil.

A Scotchman Dr Tyler by name from the E. Indies who has seen Wolffe is come to England with Letters to you, as I believe he is possessed I believe with a familiar Spirit, mighty in the letter (Cabalastice)[104] [sic] of the Hebrew Scriptures to the confusion of Jews, Brahmins, and Mahammedans [sic] in their own Temples. A great writer on prophesy. I had an interview with him yesterday. He came with a Letter from poor Smith who is now serving Owen by the command of the Evil Spirit in him, and wedding their Infidelity to his Christianity, to this End I have no doubt of ministering to their Satanic power, and bringing himself forth as a head to them, their Prophet as I think. They are to be shunned; save when the Providence of God brings them to us; then they are to be meekly instructed, if per adventure God may give them repentance. He writes to me that the Infidels are the Jews who have crucified Christ in the Spirit, whom he will first bless by gathering them to himself, and so he lectures to them in Charlotte Street at our very door every Sunday morning, and writes papers in their newspaper The Crisis. Oh it is fearful very fearful to see our flesh and blood so possessed & overpowered of Satan without being able to bring help. While the Church is truly exercised in such a way as, I believe, to retain the ordinance of a Prophet, poor Mr. Taplin seems doing every thing to provoke God to supersede him, and to cast him off. He baffles all dealings, and makes void all prayers. I am almost in despair of him.

---

103. DFP: C/9/22.
104. Cabbalistic: Jewish mystical thought.

Part II: The Letters

No one knows how my heart has been broken with that man. The Lord is very very gracious. My love to all your house and Church.

Yours in love & faithfulness,

Edwd Irving

Addressed to: Henry Drummond Esq.,
Albury Park,
Guildford.
[Annotated: Fallen Stars 16th Sept Dow, Smith.]

Edward Irving to HENRY DRUMMOND

London, 14 Newman St.
26th September 1833[105]

My Dear Brother,

I have given glory to God with all my house for the great grace shewn to his Church in giving to me another Apostle in your person;[106] and I do now present to you my hearty congratulations that you should have been deemed of our Lord worthy to stand in this the first of the Ministries of His Church. I rejoice greatly and give thanks to the Lord. Be content to be accounted the off scouring of all things, and to be held up as a spectacle to Angels and to men of suffering patience. For it is through much dishonour that you are to reap the honour and the fruits of your high calling. Be not burdened with care, for the Lord will supply all the charges of your office; but be ever ready to obey his Call.

We also have proved the goodness of the Lord within these few days past. One of the flock who resides at Harlesden Green about 7 miles from town, Christmas by name, has for about two years laboured much by himself and with the help of others for the poor souls there, and when this brought them under the discipline of the parish Authorities, for their bodies also: but fearing to offend, now that the Lord hath ordered his Church, he sought counsel of me, and I brought if before my Council, where the Lord called him through the Apostle to be an Elder, and to feed his people there. Praise the Lord with us for this. I have praised him for the calling of dear Mr. Ballard, as also for the purpose of grace towards America in sending Mr. Holmes.

---

105. DFP: C/9/23.

106. Henry Drummond was called to be an apostle on 25 September 1833. It had been prophesied the evening before that a divine act was imminent and the next morning when prayers were offered for further clarification of this Drummond was at once called, 'protesting his unworthiness and asking for divine strength and counsel to undertake his new responsibilities.' See Flegg, *Apostles* 64–65.

The Prophet continues in strict obedience of the word which I spake to him, but he comes not in to me and I do not feel that does him any good for me to go into him. Barclay has conversed with him and hopes well of him. I am greatly troubled and ashamed for Scotland, for fault-finding Scotland. According to them Sin is their judgment; the fault-finder the accuser of the Brethren is come amongst them, and gets himself a name by blaming men, whereby he paves the way for teaching that Christ was only Jehovah apparent in flesh and not the Son of God become man to make atonement for the Sins of man. He began an utterance through Anderson 'God the Father did not create the world.' The people would bear it no further but howled and yelled against him. Carlyle was preaching at the time in the Church when it took place, and got the people pacified. I have this from Matthew MacDonnald who is in town on business. I have no doubt, the drift of it is to bring in the old heresies that 'the Creator of the World' is a different being from the god when we worship, the Father of Christ. I am glad to say that Mr. MacDonnald does not recognise his own ordination, and is more than doubtful of the whole work there. This I learned when he asked me to pray along with him, and I told him I could not, without telling him fully what I feel about the work and how I must speak of it in the presence of the Lord. I desire my love to Lady Harriet, Mr. & Mrs. Caird, Capt Gambier & all the house and Church.

Farewell,

Yours in love and faithfulness,
Edwd Irving

Addressed to: Henry Drummond Esq.,
[Annotated: Irving 26th Sept.
H D Apostle & Anderson utterance.]

Edward Irving to HENRY DRUMMOND

13th October 1833[107]
[In pencil: after 13th Oct 1833]

Dear Servant of the Lord called to be an Apostle of Jesus Christ,

I do thank you much for your many acts of loving kindness and for the continual ministry of your prayers on behalf of me and of my flock; and I am conscious to myself of having come far short of a loving and bountiful requital of your goodness, and of having judged by the appearance and so of having judged by the appearance and so of having judged unrighteous judgment. For though I bear to you and to all saints a true

---

107. DFP: C/9/25.

and loving heart and am willing to give up all for Christ's sake, I have seen that the enemy hath much in me which I suspected not, but which my God daily revealeth, and pulleth away through the sprinkling of the blood of Jesus upon my conscience. Therefore I desire to be reconciled unto you my brother for all evil thoughts words and deeds which I have been guilty of towards you, although unknown to yourself or to me, and to be forgiven of you and of Christ whose little one you are, so shall I come and lay my gift upon the altar, that it may be accepted of God and made profitable to you, for he alone it is who maketh to profit.

Also I have not loved our dear Sister Caird as I ought, though by God's help I have ministered to her many a blessing as a Teacher of the Truth, and have been much blessed through her in the messages of our God. His name be praised who hath wrought such strength in her, and kept both her and her little one from the [ink blot] of death. Now the Lord's way, be assured, is good, and this baptism of suffering is greatly for her soul's profit. For though as a type it standeth good for Edification of the Church, unto her as a person it is sent first for her own soul's health. It is to help her down into the fellowship of the Church's hard travail, and of the man child's birth out of the very jaws of the dragon who standeth ready to devour his life; to the end she may be a prophetess of sorrow to utter forth the sorrow of God in Christ over his spouse and her children lying under the bondage & captivity of Babylon.

[The letter continues in Isabella Irving's handwriting.]

My dear Sir,

Mr. Irving was here interrupted by many visitors & by the time they were gone he had to set out to keep an engagement with Mr. Armstrong[108] whose soul I am glad to say seems much enlarged & comforted.—Mr. Irving had many things in his heart which he desired to communicate to you & trusts leisure may be given to him in the course of a few days to write to you He longs much to hold converse with you face to face & should the Church be shut up from the congregation during next week by the painting of it & if he is not hindered or sent to some other places he proposes going to you.

The Lord's dealings with our beloved Sister Caird have been very deep & I feel that to you the Lord will give wisdom to understand them & grace & power & teach them to His.

[Here the manuscript ends]

[Annotated: Irving's Confession of Want of Love.]

---

108. To be called as an Apostle in 1834.

Edward Irving to HENRY DRUMMOND

[In pencil: 18th October 1833[109]]

My Dear Brother,

I give you thanks for these Letters of Mr. Caird's. I would have returned the others as soon as read, but that I grudged to put you to the expense of postage; and even now I know not whether I do right in enclosing them both. I am sore grieved to have prevented the work of the Lord from being accomplished in respect of Scotland when he intended and in what way; but I know his hand, and see him in the cloud, and shall cleave closer and closer to him; and fully believe that when he hath marred us enough he will make us vessel for his service. I have been given to see much of my uncleanness, and to confess it unto the Lord; for pride and envy and unfaithfulness. I have been much moved in Spirit to write a tract containing further light upon the manifestation of God in the flesh & in the spirit; particularly as to the sacrifice of Christ, and the holiness of God, and the baptism of the Holy Ghost. We have professed ourselves of this much, *viz* that the Lamb of God was taken from the flock, and that he was without fault fit in all respects for the Sacrifice; and in doing this have learned the practical lesson how we also may and ought to be holy: that all which respecteth the offering of the Sacrifice, its dying, and its laying in order and the descending of the fire upon it to change it into glory, though we have been made always to see and acknowledge it, yet I feel that it that hath not been opened to the Churches. God permitting & favouring me I will undertake this task for the sake of all his Churches. Pray for me that my hand may be kept from including any false or uncertain word. I am much comforted in the Lord by his goodness in the Churches and I am able to rejoice in him; and my faith though weak waxeth stronger and stronger. He only knows what a hindrance I have been to him. Oh! his mercy that I am here to write these things and not dashed to pieces as a potter's vessel.[110] I shall bear upon my heart what you say concerning dear Gambier. My love be with you all. The dear babe![111] Oh! that the Lord might spare him, but be it as the Lord best discerneth. These babes shall be the hosts he cometh with to still the enemy and the avenger. Farewell.

Your loving brother,
Edwd Irving

P.S. Not having your orders I grudge to send the other letters until I have an opportunity.

---

109. DFP: C/9/26.

110. Ps 8:2.

111. Not Irving's child. Ebenezer had already died in April 1833. Nor was it Henry Drummond's. His first son Henry had died in 1822. The other two Malcolm and Arthur died in 1842 and 1843 respectively. It must be the Cairds' baby, which is referred to in the letter Edward Irving to Rev John Martin, 23 October 1833: Oliphant, *Life*, 2:359.

Part II: The Letters

Edward Irving to HENRY DRUMMOND

London, 21st 1833[112]

My Dear Brother,

I give you thanks for your very great mindfulness in sending me these letters from Edin, and rejoice much in the work which the Lord hath already accomplished through Mr. Caird. In my last hasty note, I forgot to ask whether the saying in your letter that the word of the Lord about our going to Edin was 'made void' came from the Authority of what Mr. Taplin was made to utter in the Church one night during the prayers of one of the brethren. If so, I have no doubt, you should not in any way be influenced by it in your prayers or proceedings, for the Lord hath expressly forbidden us to drink from that fountain or to obey that word, although the word is true. This is a strange dealing into the manner or measure or relations of which I am not careful to enquire, but clearly discern that it is righteous and its end is good. It is righteous to prevent in free drinking of a pure flowing stream, which we have long undervalued and soiled with our foolishness; and it is good to humble him by teaching him that the work of prophesy is little better than a curse if it be without a church to hear and use it. We have despised the waters and he hath despised the lip that drinketh and both have despised God in despising one another. And we lie under the interdict of God until this day. That it is not taken off was manifest last night in a way which I will explain to you. But first I will speak of what took place after the forenoon service.

Mr. Gardener, a Gentleman from Southampton came up on Saturday to seek counsel concerning their affairs there, and in such cases my custom hitherto has been to take them to the Apostle as being without my jurisdiction. But having received from him a copy of the word of the Lord spoken through you to him, I felt afraid lest I should have erred in this matter of jurisdiction, or should now err, and after much searching of heart, I saw it best to gather my Council of Elders together with the vessels of the Lord, but without the Deacons or Evangelists. And being assembled after the forenoon service I sought their counsel as to what I should do in cases of the like kind which came from beyond my border. In doing this I made reference to the word which had come to me through you, and with Mr. Cardale's permission I made it known to them as a help to their counselling, for I perceived that it was a matter of jurisdictions. The Lord shewed us through the mouth of Mr. Cardale, that his order concerning bringing matters before the Counsel was this, that the discernment of what things should be brought up thither lay with the Angel, and that if I felt equal to the giving of Counsel in a matter I should do it, if not I should bring it to my Counsel for

---

112. DFP: C/9/27.

their help; also that if the Elders had any matter, they should bring it first to me, and if I saw it good to bring it before the Council, it was for me to bring it and not for them. Having ascertained that we were of one mind concerning the words which had been spoken, I rendered thanks for the guidance of the Lord, and we were ready to depart, when the Spirit of the Lord came upon Miss Emily Cardale, and she was made to call for empty vessels and to reprove us of pride and want of humility in this matter. And being ended, I rise to apply in a few words the utterance to myself and the Elders and the Apostle and all present. When the word was taken out of my mouth by the Spirit in her and addressed to the Apostle individually, who was forbidden to use himself and required to permit the Lord 'to enlarge his burden' and that the Lord would surely do it, and give us a mighty blessing through him. For which we gave thanks unto the Lord, and so parted. Now, Brother, I believe the whole purpose of the Lord is this and the former utterances to the Apostle, is that *qua* [as far as] Apostles, you should neither write nor speak but by the Holy Ghost, and that you should be exceeding jealous of learning from any other source but the word of the Lord and the mouth of the Teacher. The *mind* of the Apostle is no ordinance in the Lord's house: we should all have the mind of Christ. The Apostle may not stretch out his hand, and may not speak in his office but by the Holy Ghost. And when any word comes forth concerning the meter and bounds of offices and ordinances, it pertainneth to the Angel with the Elder both to teach it and see it fulfilled.

I have had a very great jealousy (I believe of God) over both you and Mr. Cardale in this matter, lest you should foreclose or prevent God's teaching in the matter of the Apostolical office. In your letters to me there have been more than once things concerning it, which I felt at the least to be premature, and I have felt the same in respect of some of the conversations which I have had with Mr. Cardale, as if there were a hasting to know, instead of a waiting to believe the word which should come, when God should see good to send it. For myself I have been able to thank God that he hath chosen others for I feel that I could not have born it in addition to the honour which the Lord hath put upon me, and I believe he hath purged my heart of malice, and that I am standing in the light which I look upon you both; and beseech you not to forecast any form, measure, or device concerning your calling, but to do your daily work in faithfulness as you have done, and leave the Lord to lead out the glory.

I thought I might resume my liberty of opening the mysteries of Leviticus and Ezekiel which we are reading as our offering of fine flour, and did so in the morning but in the evening the Lord stayed me through the Prophet referring me to his former commands; I obeyed in silence, resolving to wait upon the Lord in counsel with my Elders. And having done so, he said by Mr. Cardale 'The word of the Prophet is true, but the Lord calleth you not to obey it.' Now the word was a reference to a former command of the Lord given in the matter, which was through Mr. Cardale, that the oil poured upon the fine flour was utterance of the spirit from the prophets & the ministers. But I had not understood this as a command, and had thought that my liberty remained. I rather

Part II: The Letters

rejoice to be curtailed herein, as it shews how the Lord will enrich his service with the true oil, and separate spiritual utterances of the Prophets and Pastors from the mediated matters which the Elders are required to speak in words 'few & well-ordered.' I know that you have been wont to take liberty in reading to expound, nor do I think you should make a change till the Lord sheweth you, but of this you nor I are judges. I wish it chiefly to shew you that the interdict still abideth in Mr. Taplin. Pray much for him. My love to dear Mrs. Caird and my blessings on the babe. I have desired my wife to write to Lady Harriett, nevertheless present to her my love and to the children.

Your faithful friend & brother,

Edwd Irving

The Lord said in the full church while I was praying for the Apostles 'He hath sent none forth yet, he longeth to send them forth—·—he longeth to separate them.' Also a week ago that he would give the Holy Ghost by laying on of the hands of the Apostle. E.

[Annotated: Irving 21st Oct 1833]

∼

Isabella Irving to HENRY DRUMMOND

26 October 1833[113]

My dear Sir,

By my letter of last night you will have learned that poor Mr. Carlyle was with us. My dear Husband felt from the first Mr. Carlyle must not come to the table of the Lord but he felt no hesitation in showing him all hospitality. However this morning as some months ago there had been an especial dealing with one on whom an evil power had been. Mr. I. asked Council . . . They then showed Edward that our poor friend must not be an inmate of them—must not assemble even with the flock etc (From different circumstances I've had to have had a bed for him these two nights in the Hotel but today his room & bed were quite prepared)—After Council Mr. Irving sent for him & kept Mr. Perceval and Dr Thomson with him & communicated the will of the Lord to him. He bowed submissively & dear Edward led him to the door of the Church. After breakfast Edwd assembled the family & asked those of the Brethren to remain who could. Mr. I then communicated the Lord's mind to us—I felt it not a little but I trust I seek *to do* the will of the Lord in this matter. Thrice then did the Lord speak to us—thanking us for not grieving at the dishonour done to Jesus. Telling us Satan had come up into the midst of us & we had not feared that if there had been a preparedness to meet the Enemy would they not have been sent forth. Satan had come disguised &

113. DFP: C/9/29.

they were not able to penetrate the vail [sic]—Then calling upon us to praise Him who had delivered us who had put us in a city fortified.

This hastily have I written to you as I feel that the Spirit in you may have been much grieved by the intelligence of this morning. And now oh my beloved friend hold my Husband up by your prayers as this moment I know Carlyle is with him—I was in the study when he came in. I remained at Edwd's desire a few minutes. Mr. I communicated the utterances of the Spirit as I have noticed it above. Then Mr. C clasped his head groaned heavily & said 'the Lord is recompensing me according to my way. Blessed be His Holy Name'—Oh Lord Jesus be with thy Servant.

The Lord has set Mr. Tudor as Scribe to the Apostle *to record*, with Mr. Barclay for his help & Mr. Miller Scribe in his own Church expressing a desire to have a Scribe in every Church.

Mrs. Campbell & daughters are quiet souls—I long for Cairds return.

I hope you are all well & Mrs. Caird gaining strength –

May the Lord ever keep thee & thy flock.

Oh remember Mr. Irving. Just cry to the Lord for him & for poor Carlyle that he may be delivered.

     I am,
     My dear Sir,
     Your much obliged,
     Isabella Irving

Addressed to: Henry Drummond Esq.,
Albury Park,
Guildford.
[Annotated:] Irving 26 Oct 1833
Directions respecting Carlisle. [Sic]

Edward Irving to HENRY DRUMMOND with a POSTSCRIPT written by ISABELLA IRVING

           London, 29th [Oct] 1833[114]

My Dear Brother,

Carlyle came on Thursday night with a letter from Mr. Tate [115] [sic] requesting me to receive him, as he came at his command; which I did after taking him engaged to

---

114. DFP: C/9/28.

115. The Rev. Walter Tait, formerly of Trinity College Church, Edinburgh. According to the Rev R. Herbert Story in his father's *Memoirs*, the Rev Tait had allowed the manifestation of tongues in

yield to the power neither in secret nor in public. I took counsel with the Elders who were at hand next morning after prayers before the Lord, who warned us as before oftimes of the great subtlety and craftiness of the snare, but gave me no specific guidance as to receiving him into my house or into the Church. Nevertheless I was ill at ease and took further counsel on Saturday morning before them all, when by many utterances through diverse persons, I seemed to discern the mind of the Lord that he should be kept apart from my house and my flock, which I did execute upon him before I went up to eat bread. And it then looked to me as if the Lord's way were to deal with him by discipline, for I cleaved to the thought that he had been brought for deliverance amongst us. Accordingly having separated him to his inn apart from all my flock but myself, and permitted him at times to come to me for the help of his conscience, I thought it dutiful to ask all the brethren present at breakfast to go up to the drawing room, and pray together for his deliverance. The Lord spake many words all tending to rebuke me of rashness and fond affection, and the Elders counseled me much, but I felt no clearness to do anything beyond what I had done without an express word of the Lord. I saw him at 5 o'clock and he passed an hour with me in confession of his spiritual sins. On the Sunday morning the spirit was much burdened in Miss Emily but had no utterance in the midst of my family, but perceiving the Lord had some matter for me, I desired my wife to bring her where we three might be alone, and then with much expression of sorrow over me as one who would have his own way, the Lord plainly said that I should send him back, which I did straight way communicate to him. He worshipped in the Church, and after the service passed two hours with me alone, and without being asked did solemnly renounce the whole work in Scotland from the time of the ordination as not being of God, and gave God glory for his work amongst us but could not say that the spirit of God had never been in power with him. He went away on Monday at Midday. I have no time to do more than write this imperfect narrative. The Lord gave Mr. Cardale Tudor Barclay & Miller on Saturday, renewing in our hearing the word spoken to him through you. Farewell

       Your faithful brother,
       Edwd Irving

 My dear Sir,
 Though you know almost all contained in this letter I send it & add *dear Caird* is arrived in safety by the gracious hand of our Heavenly Father but being late my husband sent to his mother & sisters desirous to see him, he purposes remaining till tomorrow by himself. [Written by Isabella Irving]

 [Annotated:] Irving 29th Oct 1833
 Dealing with Carlisle [*sic*]

---

the church with the result in 1833 he was deprived of his living. However, he became a pastor of the Catholic Apostolic Church: See Story, *Memoir of the Life of The Rev Robert Story*, 226.

Edward Irving to HENRY DRUMMOND

[Dated by Henry Drummond: 18th November 1833][116]

My Dear Brother,

I cannot charge my memory with the words of the utterance of the Holy Spirit which was addressed to you in my presence just before your departure from London, but the substance of it I can safely undertake to deliver. It was that the long utterance through dear Arthur was a work of the Enemy, who had sought and found a lodgment amongst you in that little Lamb of the flock of Jesus; that you had narrowly escaped a former snare, wherein you were all well nigh taken, through the using of the treasure of God in the flesh (or 'permitting the flesh to use the treasure of God'); that you should stand in awe of the power of the enemy who had reached the Lamb in Christ's own bosom; that you were not to lay this burden upon him but to bear it yourself and to know the unity of the body both in the coming in of it and in the being delivered from it. I understood the former snare to have reference to the work in Edinburgh, but as to the using of the treasure in the flesh or the flesh using it, I have no light, and it is not good to write conjectures. There is a point, however, wherein I had discernment *viz* that [letter torn] Mr. and Miss E.Cardale, which were spoken to you in my presence on the Friday [letter torn] the Council room had not been sufficient to expose to your mind the extent of the enemy's devices, and that the Lord would not let you depart without fully acquainting you with it, for the sake of his Church which standeth headed up in you. For he is gracious for his mercy endureth for ever.

Your letter to Capt Gambier he very dutifully submitted to me, and we read it together this morning, and I thank you for your love both to him and to me. Mr. Miller asked me to-day for copies of your narrative to put into the hands of his called helps and Elders. Not having any I said I would make his request known to you. Mrs. Campbell and the Misses Campbells left us on Thursday. We were all sorry to part with them, they were so quiet and peaceful in the midst of us, and so inoffensive, I have truly a great love for them.

With affectionate remembrances to Lady Harriet and the Children, to Mr. and Mrs. Caird and my blessing upon the babe,[117] and my prayers for you all

I am,
My Dear Brother,
Yours in love and faithfulness,
Edwd Irving

116. DFP: C/9/30.
117. See letter Edward Irving to Henry Drummond, 18 October 1833: DFP: C/9/26.

Part II: The Letters

Mr. William Tate [*sic*][118] is with us, and I trust profiting. When he hath got what we have to give him, he will come to be further strengthened & confined amongst you. I welcome my dear Mr. Caird to the office of an Elder. Farewell.

Addressed to: Henry Drummond Esq.,
Albury Park,
By Guildford, Surrey.
[Annotated: Irving containing utterances from Emily C. about Albury.]

Editor's Epilogue

By the end of this year, Irving, now no longer a member of the Presbyterian Church, had been 'ordained' by John Cardale as an Angel of what was eventually to be called the Catholic Apostolic Church. This office was subordinate to the Apostles, Prophets, Evangelists, and Pastors, the ruling authority of the new church. In fact the majority of the hierarchy who now ruled this fledgling tradition were lay. The leading and most powerful member was John Cardale, the solicitor whose wife and sister were two of the 'gifted persons,' whose utterances were instrumental in the running of the nascent establishment.

---

118. William Tait (1793–1864), bookseller, and from 1832 to 1834 editor of *Tait's Edinburgh Magazine*. See CL, 1:240.

8

Letters: 1834–1835

Editor's Introduction

Irving still battled on, his role now much diminished as he was caught up in the internal conflicts and dissensions of his new flock. Understandably, his health was breaking down, but he was resolved to start a branch of the new church in Glasgow, despite the advice of his doctors. He set off from London in September, on what was to be his last journey. Thomas Carlyle had unexpectedly met him in May 1834:

> It was indeed Irving; but how changed in the two years and two months since I had last seen him! In look he was almost friendlier than ever; but he had suddenly become an old man. His head, which I had left raven-black, has grown grey, on the temples almost snow-white; the face was hollow, wrinkly, collapsed; the figure, still perfectly erect, seemed to have lost all its elasticity and strength.[1]

He died in Glasgow on 8th December 1834. He is buried in Glasgow Cathedral, and a commemorative window there depicts Edward Irving as John the Baptist. In addition there is also a statue of him erected in his honour in his native town of Annan.

~

Edward Irving to HENRY DRUMMOND

London, 11th January 1834[2]

My Dear Brother,

---

1. Carlyle, *Reminiscences*, 343.
2. DFP: C/9/31.

Part II: The Letters

I have no distinct recollection of the utterances at your dinner table concerning your administration of the Patronage of Albury, as to its words or even the substance of it; but only as to the impression made upon my views and opinion in respect to such matters. Before that word of the Lord, I had thought it a thing right and dutiful in you to administer in that as in other trusts which were in your hand, and I had spoken to that effect in opposition, if I remember aught to a sentiment or purpose you had expressed to the contrary, but I felt at the time and do still feel that the word of the Lord which came through yourself was unto the discountenancing of that which I had said, and to the support of what you had said. So far as I discerned at the time, I feel clear to say, that it was against you intermeddling with or mingling in the matters of the Church as a patron. I have consulted all the passages where Gilgal is mentioned in the Prophets[3] (for Gilgal was in the utterances) but have been able to make nothing out which I may add of the above.

If I may be permitted to add a word of my own; I think with all my Fathers that patronage of Churches is a very evil thing, and that unless it be an obligation incumbent upon you to present a person, I would rather decline it altogether. But if it be a thing which you *must* do, then I would go about to do it in the best way possible, praying God to bring good out of an evil thing through my ministration of it. But if it be the Church of England as in the Church of Scotland that after six months the patronage falleth into the hand of the Bishop *jure devoluto*;[4] [by devolved right] then would I let it so fall with an intimation to the Bishop that I did it by design and not by neglect; adding, if you see good, the reasons wherefore I did so.

I thank the Lord first, and you his honoured servant and most fruitful son of my church, for the light which your Letter brought me in respect of the help designed for Scotland. I have laid it to heart, and sought to humble myself and my people for our having caused his word to fail. If you have any word of counsel to me in respect of it, I shall receive it most gladly on that as on all subjects. And wherein I have not valued your counsel enough in times past, I ask forgiveness of the Lord & of

Stained glass window in memory of Edward Irving, Cathedral Kirk, Glasgow

---

3. 'And he went from year to year in circuit to Beth-el, and Gĭl-găl, and Mĭz-pēh, and judged Israel in all those places': 1 Sam 7:16. Also mentioned in Deut 11:30; Josh 4:19, 20; 5:1–3, 9–11; 9:5–7; 10:5–10.

4. Provision by which the right and responsibility to make an appointment passes to a church authority if the person or body first entitled to appoint fails to do so within the set time limit.

you; but oh be not sparing of it nor of your rebukes either, for I stand greatly in need of both.

We have all here slid into the thought that Mrs. Caird would surely accompany her husband if there was no word to the contrary, I find from Mrs. Wales that you have slid into the opposite thought; perhaps we are equally in fault to have thought any thing about it, but should have waited till the Lord shewed his mind. There was nothing in the council particular: and my time is run out. I desire my Love to all the brethren.

Yours faithfully,
Edwd Irving

Addressed to: Henry Drummond Esq.,
Albury Park,
Guildford.
[Annotated: Irving 11 Janry 1834
Living of Albury.]

Part of a Letter: Edward Irving to THE REV SAMUEL MARTIN

London, 14 Newman St.
22nd January 1834[5]

My Dear Samuel,

No one can know the Lord who does not follow on to know him; for those who do so his coming is prepared as the Light, for those who do not he cometh as a thief in the night[6] and they shall not know at what hour he cometh[7] upon them. You have not cared to follow on to know the Lord you have hidden under a bushel the light which he gave unto you and that Light is fast hasting to become darkness and then shall thy darkness be greater than the darkness of others. My very dear brother you have suffered every truth which is precious in the sight of Jesus to be persecuted, reviled, and cast out of the Church in the persons of those who were near and dear unto you, most blameless and inoffensive men, yea and blessed benefactors of the Church and of Thine own Soul, and then had kept silence, nor cared to wash thy hands of the sin nor to comfort Christ's little ones, and dost then expect that thou canst be blessed until then

5. WCL, MS 14.
6. 1 Thess 5:2.
7. Rev 3:3.

Part II: The Letters

[Up to here the letter is in Edward Irving's handwriting, the rest is in that of Isabella Irving's.]

speaks much & very mightily by this Holy Spirit & as extraordinary appearances we have had no supernatural appearances among us if it be that you mean. To mention only last night to you two Angels & two Elders & one Evangelist were ordained by Mr. Cardale in the power of the Spirit. They were Mr. Green of Chelsea & Mr. Armstrong & two Elders of the names of Brown & Shepherd to Mr. Green's Church. By the mouth of the ordained Prophet of the Church Mr. Joplin an Evangelist was called to go forth to France but to wait for ordination. A Deacon was also called to Mr. Armstrong's Church—these things my dear Brother are all done in the form of the Holy Ghost. I reason not about it. I am as little for arguing as you do & perhaps I know more of its insufficiency than you do. I am glad your parish is quiet though I would just remind you that fire is more dangerous when it is proceeding unseen—but when there is no note of its advance by crackling noise or blazing flame. But what saith the Lord 'All the earth sitteth still & is at rest—Peace, peace & behold sudden destruction.'[8] I remember of your writing me how the cloud of infidelity was arising was no bigger than a man's hand you said but you seem now to think, if I understand you aright that it is passing away—I believe the contrary & that ere long there will be an awful explosion in this land & that Scotland as it was said of Gideon will have famines pestilence and blood in her streets as truly as that the Lord will be glorified in the midst of her. I think that the Lord will not arise to avenge the blood of His own Elect which hath been spent in our land and to redeem the name of Jesus which hath lately been so fearfully blasphemed. The Spirit of the Devil called the Spirit of Jesus!! The Lord will arise & that speedily & will send forth His own witnesses endowed with power from on high.

We are mercifully all well. The dear Children have measles but neither sick nor unwell from these blessed be the name of the Lord. I had a note from Eliza she is quite well & Edw_d_ & William in the city. He was

[Here the manuscript ends.]

Edward Irving to REV WILLIAM WALES

London, 26th Jan 1834[9]

My Dear friend,

You have kindly permitted your precious mother to communicate to me the burden of your head, and I have endeavored to hope the best. But, clearly perceiving that

---

8. 1 Thess 5:3.
9. UEL 61452.

it was not fit things should continue as they now are, I counselled her to come down to you and strengthen you to do that which is right to be done in your present circumstances. And I now pray there may be a good issue to her journey.

It is I well know my dear friend, a vain thing to write to you upon that which so widely devideth us. The time is coming when we shall see eye to eye, for I believe that you are one of the great company of the priests who will be made obedient to the faith. I beseech you not to speak against that which you understand not, and not to press our mothers conscience but to honour and obey as well as love her as a mother, and let her do likewise to you as a Minister of Christ, and the head of the house. Farewell, my dearly beloved friend.

Yours faithfully,
Edwd Irving

Addressed to: The Revd William Wales, Rector of Northampton.

Extract from a Letter by Edward Irving

Edinburgh, 31st January 1834[10]

The Lord worketh very graciously: He hath made dear Emily's words, (the words of the Comforter spoken to me before I left home), Spirit and life to me here, by enabling me to speak of this sorrow to this people, and so to lead them out of their own into His, and to set them as intercessors for the multitude of His children in this land. I know not that I have ever felt such bedewings[11] of heart in the presence of any people.

The Lord by the mouth of his Prophet hath called Mr. Tait to be the Angel of the Church: Mr. Cannon, (who was called by the Enemy as Evangelist) to be an Elder; Mr. Pitcairn to be an Elder; and hath just pronounced our dear Carlyle such a word of sorrow & forgiveness as hath melted us all. (Mr. Tait's Family). The Lord hath been dealing with dear Macdonald, I believe, unto the deliverance and also with Mr. & Mrs. Dickson who are deeply entangled with David Dow.[12] When we were speaking of dear Duncan, the Lord commanded him to be sent for, because He would have him in the midst of you. Tell the people, & the Ruler of the people that the Lord doth hear & answer their prayer daily. I have no doubt the Lord is working a very great work by us of preparing His way for a still greater ... Oh that we could all learn that the Government is *not* upon our shoulder. But I am not careful; the Lord will sustain him that standeth

---

10. DFP: C/9/32.
11. To bedew: to wet as if with dew.
12. 'Mr. and Mrs. Dixon are brother and sister in law to Mr. Dow.' DFP: C/9/32 n.

in my place, as He hath sustained me. He is the Shield of my flock: His not my deputy, but the Lord's Angel while I am the Lord's Messenger to this people.

~

This is written in great haste. It is very late. I teach twice each day, at 2 & hlf past 6. The Mornings I go about among the flock.

~

Edward Irving to REV HUGH B McLEAN[13]

London, 3 [Judd] Place. 1st February 1834[14]

Brother,

Thou will be convinced as Thomas was convinced, & till then it booteth not to speak with thee. Thou knowest not the spirit thou art of; thou - - anything but thy Father remembereth the former days & spareth thee! But go thou not too far my Brother in blaspheming the name & the work of your God. Go softly & speak not with a stubborn neck. Be assured that into thy house not into thy congregation will I not come while thou settest up thy banner against the Lord. Nor can I say fare thee well, nor can I pray for thy peace. Yet love I thee dearly as a very brother.

Edwd Irving

[H. B. Mclean's answer.]

My heart doth so yearn upon thee, I cannot send this away without a word of help. Look then upon the Jewish people & tell me if the words of the prophets have been fulfilled, look then upon the Christian Church & tell me if the words of the Lord & the apostles have been fulfilled. And yet they believe in the faithfulness, & we believe in the faithfulness of the God whose word hath failed in their hands & in our hands by our unbelief of it. And why do we believe, because our conscience beareth witness to the Spirit of truth that is in His word, & to the unbelief that is preventing the fulfillment of his word. So my brother do we believe & confess that we have caused his word to fail, & we are at his feet for mercy. And we fear the punishment of our sins of which I feel that you ... to be a part with me, until He himself arise & vindicate his own cause. Meanwhile he beareth (?)[15]—in that we are no better than our fathers, to

---

13. There is a Rev Hugh Bailey Maclean, listed as Presbyterian Minister of London Wall, in the list of attendees at one of the Albury Conferences (1826–30). See Flegg, *Apostles*, 37. At the general assembly in 1831 had been deposed from the ministry for heresy. See *ONDB*.

14. NLS, MS 77, fol. 234–35.

15. The (?) was added by the person that copied the letter and could not make out the word after

the end we may not be puffed up by the abundance of his revelation, & he sheweth us our sin to be the same with you who are in Babylon, to the end we may intercede for you and cry to him day & night that you may be delivered through the manifestation of Himself in the Church. Amen.

Addressed to: Rev Hugh B Mclean
21 Warriston Crescent, Edinburgh.
[Annotated: Copy of a faded letter by Edward Irving to Mr. Hugh B.H.]

Edward Irving to AN UNKNOWN RECEPIENT

2nd February 1834[16]

This day has been most blessed to us all. The Church met at ten o'clock, and while I was in doubt what to teach, the Lord, before the service began, opened the mouth of the prophet to encourage the flock to bow under their understandings, and guide me to teach the manner of God's worship, of the holy race, and the altar, which I did forenoon and afternoon, with greater presence and power of teaching than I ever felt ... In the evening the power came upon the prophet to direct me to Ezekiel xxxvii; which I chose of myself, and had power to minister it, marvelous to myself.

Edward Irving to HENRY DRUMMOND

London, 24th Feby 1834[17]

My Dear & well-beloved Brother,

I am in very great darkness concerning many things in this dealing of the Lord; but of this I am convinced in my conscience that I have wronged you, and I sit down to confess and acknowledge it, in the hope that the Lord will shew me more to confess & acknowledge. Though I was not able to discern the justice of the Lord's rebuke, I should not have been offended in him whose painful office it was to bring it: and though I had believed you to be in some snare, I should have dealt both in greater tenderness and

"beareth."

16. Oliphant, *Life*, 2:371.
17. DFP: C/9/33.

Part II: The Letters

wisdom. The Lord hath made manifest before you and the Council the heat of my spirit that you might not look upon me otherwise than as a poor rebellious worm in whom He will be glorified by making manifest all its vileness. I ask your forgiveness, knowing that it is only making reparation to my brother when I have offended that I can find acceptance with the Lord for any offering.

And this which I now do to you personally. I had purposed in my heart to do before the Council on Saturday, whether you might be present or not. May I now request your presence that when I did dishonour you, there I may humble myself before you.

Give my love to Lady Harriet, Mr. Caird and all your house

Your faithful brother,
Edw[d] Irving

Addressed to: Henry Drummond Esq.
Albury Park, Guilford.
[Annotated: Irving 24th Febr 1834
Apology for rebellion to rebuke.]

~

Edward Irving to HENRY DRUMMOND

London, 17th March 1834[18]

My Dear Brother

I had purposed writing you to-day in any case, to let you know how it fared with young Godden, my charge for which I hold myself responsible to you. His faults in one word are indulgence of the flesh; he loves bodily ease and bodily pleasure, he uses the words of the Lord which have been spoken over him as an encouragement to his natural self-love, and his heart hankers about Lymington instead of enlarging itself with the opportunities which Providence affords him. I have given him for his reading Prideaux's Connections[19] and my Homilies on Baptism; and I think he is becoming alive to his true condition and under the blessing of God & through the ministry of our common prayers will grow into a meekness for his calling. This is in confidence between ourselves and except in a remote way should not by you be communicated to him. Leave him in our hands till I see you again, and give yourself to other burdens.

I need not repeat over again what you have doubtless heard of the Lord's doings in the midst of us. And which I have communicated to Mr. Cardale or Dr Thomson. Mr. Dalton who was called to be an Angel of the Lord's church at the Council on

---

18. DFP: C/9/34.
19. Prideaux, *The Old and New Testament connected in the History of the Jews*.

Saturday, was permitted to abide over the Lord's day by Mr. Leighton taking his duty. And this morning when I was presenting him to the Lord in the Church as I do always, and praying that if it seemed good to the Lord you might be brought home by him to impart unto him some blessing, the Lord by the mouth of the ordained prophet spake to the effect that you should come in by him, and that he should call his people together and pray for a blessing though you. The Lord also said that you should come in by Mr. Thurgan (who is at Birmingham) and bid him to be obedient unto Jesus. As the Lord hath shewed us so expressly that the Angel is responsible to see every word obeyed which is spoken in his church, I do communicate these messages to you & Mr. Cardale, with my prayers that you may have grace given you to obey them in Spirit and in truth. The utterances then ascended into a very sublime prayer to the Lord Jesus to rend the Heavens and pour his Spirit down. I have desired this Scribe to give me the record of the words, which I will for your better guidance. And that you may be helped, I will let you know the cases of these two men. Mr. Dalton is a very pure hearted man who believes in the work of the Lord with great simplicity and has attained to no small knowledge of his way. Till within the last two years he laboured at Wolverhampton, and being removed to Bridgnorth by a very strange and remarkable providence, the remains of his flock at W.hampton have been well tried, and are, though few, the strongest in the Lord's work and way. The faithful in Bridgnorth have had no trials to separate them from the [unreadable word] mass of hearers which a pious and popular preacher gathers around him. I have advised him when he goes home to gather into one there to whom he can fully communicate his mind, and to teach them plainly of the Lord's work, and according to their faith to pray with them for the Apostolical blessing. And to prepare his own heart to cleave to the Lord and obey him, and leave him to deliver him.

Mr. Thurgan is a very bad case. He was originally a Baptist minister and one who used to importune me very much in old time to come and preach here & took it very much amiss because I gave not more heed to his importunities. This parted us at that time, but within these few months he came up to look upon the work of the Lord and for a good many days, went in and out with my flock. And I had an opportunity of shewing him much kindness and giving him much information and insight into the doings of the Lord. So that if any thing would have prevailed to knit him to the Church here, our dealings or rather the Lord's dealings with him at that time should have done it. And this the more as before his coming up he was greatly shaken by the Portglasgow brethren, and suspicious of the Lord's work here: but all these suspicions were triumphantly overborne by what he saw and felt and this, with his own mouth he oft times declared. But self-importance, the evil leaven of the Independents,[20] was not overcome; for as soon as spiritual power came into his own church, he suffered it with out any jealousy or watchfulness for Christ, alleging that it was mistrustful of the Father of whom they had sought bread; and this has gone on until by the force of

---

20. I.e., Baptist and Congregational dissenters.

which I believe are evil spirits working upon a Dissenters unreclaimed heart, he has come into the notion of being a distinct church, and will have no communication with the church here. These things I have from Mr. Dalton's mouth, and do not in the least doubt. Nevertheless though I am greatly grieved with him, I have not ceased to bear him before the Lord, and receive this as an answer of many prayers.

I am troubled, much troubled in spirit for the state in which you have found things in Edin,[21] the more, as I fear, I have myself been in no slight degree the occasion of it. The Lord therein led me into crooked paths and not into straight ones in commanding me to return by the spirit when I should not have returned. I suppose I should have acted like Paul who went up to Jerusalem when they said by the spirit he should not go up, but I understand not the way of the Lord and am but a child when for him I should have been a full grown man. Yet have I a strong confidence that the Lord will set up his candlestick in that church and bless his Deacons. I know much their faults; many of them are in myself, and all of them are in the Scotchmen of my flock. But there are no soldiers like them for the onset, though the English know better how to keep rank. Be patient, my Dear Brethren, for the Lord will keep your flocks, your wives and your children, for which I pray continually and have great delight in praying. May the Lord have you in his holy keeping.

Farewell,

Your loving brother & humble Servant,

Edwd Irving.

I find the Scribe has sent the utterances by this Post. I commend them to you & Mr. Cardale for your obedience to the Lord who speak them in my Church.

Addressed to: Henry Drummond Esq.,
Waterloo Hotel, Waterloo Place,
Edinburgh.
[Annotated:] Irving 19th Mar: 1834
about Dalton & Thungan

~

Edward Irving to HENRY DRUMMOND

London, 22nd March 1834[22]

(Oh I commend Oxford to your prayers & pity & of the Lord to your help. E.I)

My Dear Brother,

---

21. See Extract from an Edward Irving Letter, 31 January 1834. DFP: C/9/32.
22. DFP: C/9/35.

I have neither much time nor much occasion for writing, and yet I feel a strong desire just to say how gladly I do welcome the word of the Lord which sets you in London, though I neither well see the beginning nor the ending of it. But leaving that with the Lord I do rejoice in your being brought within the bounds of my habitation. I feel as if it were in preparation for your occupying my room when I am called to Scotland, whether for a time or permanently I have again no light. In that case or in any case, my wife and I think you should come and dwell with us and for your accommodation you shall have the quietest bed-room to sleep in, and the front drawing room to rest in, whenever you desire to be alone—with an express prohibition to all men to enter therein but at your bidding. For I feel that whosoever steps into my room should become acquainted with my people from my own heart where they lie. But be this all as it appears good unto your better knowledge of your own convenience, and judgment of what becomes your various relatives in life of which I know so little, and none of which you should despise, though you should be grieved by none of them. Yet as Abraham did the Angels[23] I constrain thee my very dear Brother.

You & Mr. Cardale will have by this post a painful letter from Mr. Owen.[24] I seem to myself to have seen the occasion of this stumble in a certain spirit of all going on swimmingly, a certain bravura, and very great bonhomie but, oh brethren, the first ingredient in the Anointing is the 500 shekels of myrrh, may it never be wanting in you.

I had not the notion of overseeing obedience to the word of the Lord beyond my habitation, but of delivering it even to the Lord's Apostles with the solemn authority which is due unto every word coming from between the Cherubim, as if it had entered unto their own ears. For such I judge to be my duty.

Please say to Mr. Cardale that Mr. Millar received his letter in a very becoming manner, he shewed it to me after the Council and communed with me about it. He is much to be pitied.

There was nothing at the Counsel of a general import save that the Lord was better pleased that the Elders did not present themselves for Evangelists, signifying that it was in his mind to separate men to their several places; and that he did not approve Mr. Owen's admitting a woman to speak in the Church until she had passed the pillars of the vail [sic] whereupon he thought it was better to wait.

I give great heed to all that you write to me, though I say nothing about it; and trust that I ponder my own ways in the light of God's word. Still many things are above me, on which I can do nothing but hold my peace.

I had hoped that word about the Counsel, which Barclay was given in charge to communicate to the Angels at a distance might have been communicated to them (for he entrusted the knowledge of it to me) but he had no liberty: to the end the Council might sit & deliberate in the light of it. But Barclay is a man of steel, he had no liberty:

---

23. Gen 18:3–5.

24. Rev H. J. Owen, angel of Chelsea (formerly the congregation of Park Chapel), one of the Seven Churches. See Flegg, *Apostles*, 68.

and I did not try to bind him. Perhaps Mr. C. might give liberty to communicate it. But I am perhaps heavily beyond my border. I do rejoice greatly that the Lord findeth room for your hands. Farewell. My wife is still as you left her.

E. Irving

I conclude that Dr Thompson is gone I do rejoice in it. I trust it is the evidence of great good. He hath my blessing and my prayers.

Addressed to: Henry Drummond Esq.,
Waterloo Hotel, Waterloo Place, Edinburgh.
[Annotated: Irving 22nd Mar 1834
Offering his house.]

∼

Edward Irving to HENRY DRUMMOND

London, 14 Newman Street. 2nd April 1834[25]

My Dear Brother,

I do thank you with all my heart for your very great mindfulness of me in giving me the earliest intelligence of the work which the Lord worketh amongst my people. And this I do not from any selfish thirsting for news, but because it gives me opportunity night and morning and all the day long of magnifying the goodness of the Lord, and interceding with him for those who provoke him to anger. I am greatly afflicted by the state of things at Port Glasgow and have cried unto the Lord without hearing from them, and been made oft times in secret to forgive them all their injuries against the Lord in me and in his Church under me, and to cry greatly that they might be forgiven. But I have no assurance and hardly any hope that they will be restored at this time. They have thought to hold the Spirit as persons, which is to usurp Christ's personality whose person is the person of the Son of God. Out of his fulness we all receive and grace for grace,[26] that is after a measure, gifts differing according to the grace given to every one. And we hold it as members of a body and for the body 'the Spirit is given to every man for the common-weal.' The men at Portglasgow acknowledge no body of Christ, and would not come into the real and true communion of the Saints, but stood aloof for a Church to be manifested in Spiritual gifts, and office bearers in Spiritual Ministries, and again and until this should come to pass they held aloof in their hearts, doubted, and were willing ready to symbolise with the rebellion; and so leaped into the snare which the Enemy prepared for them in that wicked woman Jezebel.

25. DFP: C/9/36.
26. John 1:16.

And having no Church in which to see the word of Prophesy realised outwardly, they were constrained or tempted to realise it in their own discernment, which serve them for a while but soon failed them, because they were an *ultima ratio*[27] unto themselves, judges in their own cause, every man his own Church, which is every man usurping to be Head of the Church. So they have made the sure word of Prophesy contemptible by making it an idol, and God hath given them up to blindness of discernment because they counted their discernment the sanction of his most holy word. Oh their way hath been very foolish, it hath been very grievous and they will take counsel from no one, because they are the sufficient reason unto themselves. It is such craft, and master-craft of the Enemy, such a victory, such a triumph, tell it not in Gath.[28] Oh that God's prophets should have risen up against his Church! But every bone must come to his place at length, and God's own order be established, first Apostles, secondarily Prophets. I seem to be more deeply grieved for David Dow than for them. They have gone astray with their eyes open. He hath been blinded by what I discern it, and so brought into the ditch. I fear he hath not kept his manhood but made an idol of the body, lost his personal standing in the Lord, for a Spiritual fellowship in the Church. This is the most fatal snare of the two. You have it in a small scale in Barclay the Elder in Edinburgh. Oh that the Lord might send you to his help and deliver him! The Lord one day in my house bade me cry for them all, and said that Campbell and Erskine[29] were stones whom he would bring out of the rubish. [sic]

My eyes were holden from understanding your position as one of the four pillars of the veil,[30] by not knowing that you were to be removed from your charge at Albury into the bosom of the Church. I knew that the pillars of the veil and every pillar and every board and every piece of the Sanctuary, I am responsible for as an Angel of the Church; not responsible for the Spiritual utterance save to see it obeyed, being satisfied it is from the Lord, but responsible for their persons, and for their ways and for their acts yea, and for their words also, to give God glory and praise in the Church for all the good, to take unto myself the shame and reproach if there should be any evil. This was shewn in the case of the Prophet whose sin I was required to bear, and whose deliverance was given to my prayers, I mean not to me as a person but as the Angel of the Church. Until the Lord shewed us that you were to be placed in London, I saw not how you could stand as the pillar of the veil, and had nothing for it but to suppose that what the Lord spake to me and respect to the fourth. And it seemed to me no more unprofitable that I should be keeper of the doctrine and yet one of the Elders, than that I

---

27. Final authority.

28. 2 Sam 1:20

29. Thomas Erskine, one of the people who went to investigate Mary Campbell's [Mrs Caird] miraculous cure. 'Mr Erskine of Linlathen went upon a mission of personal inquiry, which persuaded his tender Christian soul of the unspeakable comforts of a new revelation': Oliphant, *Life*, 2:290.

30. J. Cardale was the pillar of apostles, Henry Drummond the pillar of angels, Dr J. Thompson the pillar of pastors, and E. O. Taplin the pillar of prophets. See Shaw, *Apolstolic Church*, 175.

should be keeper of the oracle and yet one of the pillars; which in deed and in truth you are at Albury. But the Lord hath given us perfect light in this matter at diverse times lately by which I perceive that you are one of the pillars of the veil, and as such have a seat ordered for you in my Church, with Mr. Cardale & Mr. Taplin and Mr. Hair when his mouth shall be opened in the Spirit, or whenever the Lord requireth it. Last night by the word of prophesying Mr. Cardale was separated from his seat and Mr. Heath set in his room. I know your dignity as pillars of the veil, and as God enables me I will uphold it; but I know also my own responsibility as Angel of the Church, and by his grace I will acquit myself of it. In their office they are no less than the Oracles of God whose words I must obey and not the words, the *The Word* in them in their persons they are the sheep of the flock who must obey me, and not me but Jesus the good shepherd in me. I do not think there is any spiritual difference of judgment between us in this matter; if there be let it rest till God bring us face to face. Meanwhile I do praise the Lord exceedingly both in the Church and in my house, that he hath set you one of the four pillars of the veil in my Church. As to your standing in the Counsel where also you are a pillar of the veil for other Churches. I say nothing, because that jurisdiction pertaineth not to me. I will not break into another man's house willingly, nor wittingly suffer my own to be broken into. I trust it is not the personal jealously of covetousness which bringeth forth these things from me, but the jealousy of the ordnances of the Lord: and yet I know that nothing but the blood of Jesus keepeth me clear from these powers, for I know that the Spirit which is in us leadeth to envy. I am sure your love to me should have melted the rocky heart long ere this for it hath been very great. I have received Mr. Cardale's communication through the Scribe this morning, and I do thank him for adding the words which were spoken in rebuke to me personally, for I desire to have them in my mind. The tender love of woman's tenderness hath been a great snare to me. I know well, and I do believe that this added to the gratitude I feel for Emily's services, and the admiration I have of her character, did give to her word a preponderance which was dishonourable to the Word himself; and I also believe that I was forgetful of the word spoken that the work of the Lord should not in the marchings be ordered by women; also I believe I had suffered personal defects to prejudice the Word in others. Oh! How suspicion and fault-finding is rooted in a Scotchman's character. It is the bane of the land. I am not worthy of the place to which the Lord hath called me. There are many better men serving him than me. Pray for me that I may learn from the past; there is no safety but in being lifted up by the Holy Ghost into the bosom of Jesus. I intended writing to Mr. Cardale by the same post. I have not got it done. Love to the brethren, wherever this finds you.

      Farewell.

      Your loving friend.

Edwd Irving

I am much better in my health.

Addressed to: Henry Drummond Esq.,
Waterloo Hotel,
Waterloo Place,
Edinburgh.
[Annotated: Irving 2nd April 1834
McDonald, Pillars & E. Cardale.]

Edward Irving to HENRY DRUMMOND

Monday, 7th April 1834[31]

My very dear Brother,

The very reason, as it seems to me, why the Lord desires to separate you for a season from your flock (and here remember how the Lord spoke through your mouth when sending Mr. Place to Mr. Armstrong's room, that he would separate all the ordained Angels) is that you may be where his work of building, setting in order, and preparing a refuge and defense for all the Churches is proceeding. It is the same word which came through Mr. Cardale. 'He will have thee in London, fear not to commit thy flock to his servant Brown.' I beseech you not to be careful of this nor to suspect or surmise evil as that the Lord is tempting you, nor to measure the Lords orders this day by his order a year ago; *to be in holy orders*, is to be at the Command of Jesus every day. I do further beseech you not to set one of the four heads of the Cherubim under another. I mean in what respects the utterance and word of the Lord, which though fourfold in form is only one in authority to be obeyed by the council Elders of the Church; not to measure one by another, because they are diverse and incommunicable; the gift of a Prophet is not a function (as they say in Mathematics, and I have no other similitude) of the gift of the Apostle. There is an especial difference of kind, whereby the Apostle heareth the Prophet by faith, the prophet the Apostle etc all to the End of *Word* may be all in all. This I know is the principle of it, and I have seen it also in the manifestation—as to your being for a time under me, see me under Mr. Tait without the advantage of spiritual utterance. As a man you are under me, as a spiritual Minister bringing the word of God I am under you. In one word shall not the Commander in Chief gather all his strength to meet the chief's attack, or to carry the Chief strength of the Enemy. In all this I contemplate not a permanent but a temporary removal of you; but for my own part, I stand ready for a permanent removal from this people, if the Lord please, altho' I have no thought of it, nor of the contrary, for I know nothing

31. DFP: C/9/37.

as I ought to know it. I do beseech you to keep yourself from forecasting evil, lest that come which you forecast.

While I thus write, I am not without the assaults of the same enemy, and receive with great consideration the burden of your spirit. And I will be watchful against evil looking always more and more to the Shepherd and watchman of Israel. I have searched myself and sought much to be searched of the Lord in respect to my spiritual subjection to the ordinance of Apostles; because I do well know that the Lord will not suffer me to fall under temptation save to reveal and to put away spiritual evil. I have also weighed much the word spoken to the Angels concerning the ruling of the Prophets. But note what I now write: it is written[32] first Apostles, secondly Prophets, thirdly Pastors and Teachers[,] and the word was very authoritatively laid upon me when I went to Scotland with the Prophet, and I acted in the light of it. Now what doth this ruling of a Prophet by the Angel mean, more than ruling any other member of the flock, and an Apostle also as such. The word that cometh from the Prophets mouth and the word from the Apostles, and the word (in the Spirit) from an Elder and from an Evangelist, discerning to be the word of the Lord. I am equally and alike bound to obey. For the Angel is the head of the obedience. Besides this I do well know that it pertaineth to an Angel fully accomplished of the Holy Ghost for his office to minister and to rule and to discern in a fourfold measure, Apostolical, Prophetical, Evangelical & Pastoral, whereby he is enabled consciously to apprehend and with discernment to obey every thing spoken by the Lord through this fourfold headship in the house. But to my shame be it spoken and to the shame of the body which is contained in me, we are not so accomplished.

If you have been much tried and burdened about my Church these last three weeks, for which I render you both my hearty thanks and pray God to lay your burdens also upon me and my Church, that we may be helpful to one another, I fear you will be still more burdened with the contents of this day's record, and yet I beseech you not to receive it in a skeptical but believing spirit. I mean as concerneth the going forth of the Evangelists without ordination, which the Lord [letter torn] mouth of the Prophet yesterday required, and which I obeyed, just as I obeyed the word heretofore preventing them from going forth. While I pray that if there by any thing evil in my house, it may be set in order by the Apostles where it is set in order, I do beseech the Apostles to bear upon their hearts also, that the foundation is prophets and apostles; and I reach to Mr. Cardale's mind how the Lord admonished me that I had undervalued the office of a prophet in the filling of the Candlestick with oil. I feel afraid that—both in respect to the governments and the Evangelists & everything else an integral part and that the initiating part of the proceeding belongeth to the Prophet, which the Apostle may not think that he can overlook, comprehend, or other wise receive than by faith; and that another and that the consummating part belongeth to the Apostle. I thank you for your caution as to the governments, it is good and one which I have already

32. 1 Cor 12:28.

admonished concerning, but the order now pronounced by the Prophet, answereth precisely to the constitution of the thing given by the Apostle, that it belongeth to the deacons to know and bring up the cases of the people, to the Elders to go down and bless them with heavenly blessings. As concerneth the Evangelists, it seems to me that God proveth and prepareth them unto ordination when he shall send them forth. That he accepted the former free-will service of the youth, and those who had proved their armour & were fit to use it he ordained and by them, Completed the Evangelical Ministry in the house and the four pillars of the Court gate; and now he taketh witness & maketh preparation for something beyond, which in his own times he will shew. That it proceedeth from no spirit of insubordination to the Apostolical office in the prophet, is to me clear from the word in his mouth having ruled that the Pillars should not minister in the house till they should be ordained, and that I should make no difference as to my mode of admission into the church through the Deacons & the Elders but wait for the Apostles. Nevertheless he is fallible, I am fallible, & you are fallible, and I am the apologist of no man but the servant of the Lord Jesus' Church the only Head of his Church & the life & authority of all the ordinances thereof.

In respect of the revelation touching the Council as being the wall, the defence, the bulwark of the whole city, it is just the prophetical enlargement and precious garnishing of that foundation word which came from Mr. Cardale in our last dispatch concerning the council. The Counsellors the Lord himself will choose as it liketh him, men in their various offices gifted with Counsel, whom he will fetch from all parts of the Church and these their tents abide for them when they come up. How surpassing the will of man is that revelation. My brother it is not the love of the marvelous but of the true, which hath guided my path through these thorny brackens of doctrine we have passed through, the unspeculative love of truth, unabated by the strangeness or marvelousness of the discerning, for marvelous are his ways. Grace be with you, write me whenever you can, for I love you very much

... [*letter torn*] friend Edwd Irving

The bed is ready for Mr. Dundass & the chair and the benches such as they are, and a most hearty welcome. My wife and the babe are most graciously dealt with of the Lord E.I[33]

[Annotated: Irving 7th April 1834
Defence of Taplin.]

~

33. Edward Irving's daughter, Isabella, had been born on 23rd March 1834. In a letter from Elizabeth Hamilton to her mother Mrs Martin, it is clear that soon after her birth baby Isabelle had not been well and 'Dr Darling recommended that she should have a wet nurse': (letter from a private source) but she lived to 1878.

Part II: The Letters

Edward Irving to HENRY DRUMMOND

London, 1st May 1834[34]

My Dear Brother,

I sit down to write to you because you desire that I should do it, as oft as I can conveniently. That which presses most upon my mind is that we beware of undervaluing the office of the prophet because of the many stumblings and offences which have come through them into the work of the Lord. I perceive the relation of the prophet and the apostle to be the same as the relation of the Old Testament, the word of God's purpose, to the New Testament the beginning of the fulfillment of that purpose; it is the relation of the Word to the Church. Jesus was pointed out by a Prophet[35] him who came in the spirit & power of Elias;[36] all the prophets witnessed of Jesus and the Church,[37] of the Church of God, the testimony of Jesus is the spirit of prophesy. When Jesus began to teach he declared that he was not come to destroy the law and the prophets but to fulfil them, and after his resurrection he was at pains to shew them the things which had come to pass out of Moses and the prophets and the psalms.[38] And the Holy Church in the Evangelists and the Acts and the Epistles and the Revelation, followeth the same course of shewing all things that happen and are done, as taking place in the fulfillment of the prophetic word. The Apostles might not be conscious in all their actings of an adherence to and obedience of the words of prophesy; but the Holy Ghost who wrought all their works in them, is ever conscious that He is doing nothing but obeying the Word, taking the things of Jesus and shewing them to the world by & in the Church. Such a relation be assured the Prophet will ever continue to have to the Apostle, and the Apostle to the prophets, and therefore it is God is so jealous that the prophet pass not his border, and that the Apostle build not without the prophet.

Now concerning the border of the Prophet, I have learned by sad experience this much, that however it hath been in time past, and however in peculiar circumstances it may be in time to come, the order of the Lord is through the Prophet to bring the word of what he will do, but the ordering of it to be done, and the setting it into fact, he will perform by his Apostle, and the keeping of it so as in the word of the prophet it hath been said, and by the hand of the Apostle it hath been set, he leaveth with the Angel of the Church, whose it is to defend the institution and constitution of God from all power of man and of devils. To the prophet is revelation, to the Apostle is inspiration by word & by hand, to the Angel of the Church is faithful keeping of the word and traditions of God. The prophet ought to have no fear in bringing the word,

34. DFP: C/9/38.
35. John the Baptist.
36. I.e., Elias. Cf. Luke 1:17; 9:8 and Matt 11:14.
37. Matt 5:17.
38. Luke 24:44.

and leaving it as he hath brought it, to be set in order and obeyed by those whose part it is. If the prophet occupy himself in his heart with the setting in order and the obedience, he layeth a snare for his own feet and for all the church because he is breaking into the house of another and cannot be guiltless in the eyes of the great householder. I nothing doubt that this was the sin of the ordained prophet in these weeks past, and that he hath been the occasion of much grief and shame to the Lord and to his people. My error lay in judging of the future by the past, for every thing which I was required to do by the Prophet, I had been required to do the like of in days past. I am convinced that it was not in the power of man without direct revelation to have gathered the place and purpose of the Council, the way in which the seven churches of this city were to be gathered into one. And I feel that in these things I have been sorely smitten for sin that was not altogether my own. Surely it pertain to Apostles to give the bounds and measures of these things. It was righteous in God to smite me, because I had not sufficiently sustained the Apostles nor honoured them, nor in my spirit been subject to them; but surely one word to me concerning the Authority of the Council would have kept me from offending in returning from Scotland, one word concerning the uniting of the Seven Churches & the Evangelists in the building of the tabernacle would have preserved me and the prophet and the Church; and I feel as if this word should have come through the Apostles. Ofttimes in looking back I think I have been hardly dealt with but I murmur [letter torn] for I am conscious of great disorder in my Spirit needing to be manifested & put away. Some of the words which have come to me through you have been as drawn swords, they have sounded as taunts of me rather than words for godly edifying; which shews what a proud and rebellious spirit I am naturally of, and what need of being humbled to the dust. The Lord bringeth me under law to Christ; he boundeth the almost boundless field in which he permitted me to go like a wild ass alone ere yet he had begun to set his Church in order. So much for the interlays of thought.

In respect of fact, the Lord shewed on Tuesday night in the Council of my church, that the Angel should take a share with the Elders in the subdividing the labour in the flock, as being an Elder with them, and that therefore the Lord had given seven helps: also that the Lord will give more helps when needed; also that Mr. Barclay & Mr. Sturgeon who were set Heads of the Evangelists in Mr. Millar's church and Mr. Owen's should not minister as Evangelists in my church. This makes it unprofitable to obey the prophet's word requiring them to sit and minister with me in my Church, and to instruct the Evangelists along with me. And unless the Lord shall shew me otherwise this night when we meet together, I will discontinue the instructing of the Evangelists, and minister alone from henceforth as an Evangelist till the Lord recover his own word out of the present disorder. I felt it my duty to cleave to the word of the ordained Prophets, till the Apostolic word came not to seek to reconcile what could not be reconciled, then I ceased. But oh! I am sore sore troubled in heart that any word of the ordained prophet should seem to fall to the ground, is a fearful blow to the

Lord's work. But the work is the Lord's. Yet am I not without guilt herein. Yea all of us. And let us be humbled together. While I was praying for you in your perilous work, it arose upon my heart that I should write this letter, which you may read to the Prophet or not just as you see good. My love to [letter torn]

Yours faithfully & lovingly,

Edwd Irving

P.S. I had a strange letter from Smith at Irvine claiming upon me or upon you or upon both for £20 or more which he had incurred in debt at Irvine, while working his way forward. Upon me he held no claim of any sort and I am sure still less on you. I sent him £10 some time ago, and this is thanks to bring me as a debtor for another £10 or even for £20. EI

~

Edward Irving to HENRY DRUMMOND

London, 6th June 1834[39]

My Dear friend and brother,

I am much gratified by your remembrance of me in connection with my native Annandale, which is very dear to me, though it may have little to commend it to the eye of one of such exquisite taste and enlarged knowledge of nature's beauties as yourself. That very Beatock inn and the Beatock road from which it has its name, I used in my day of youthful enthusiasm to connect with the *Legio Boeotia*[40] of which I discovered from inspection of the reliquiae[41] of the Roman encampment at Maryport in Cumberland some cohorts had been detained in those parts.

But I am much more deeply interested with the substance of your letter which concerns one of the most revered of all my friends. If I may judge of others by myself, it was our idolatry of that man which made his downfall for a reason to be an act of mercy, and some sort of necessity: and so also I may say of Carlisle [sic] but how this came to pass in respect of these two persons I know not for I never felt it towards others. To all when the Lord hath called and used in his work I feel brotherly love, and perhaps towards some of them I might feel envy, but to none save David Dow & Thomas Carlyle felt I anything like idolatry. And I perceive the same to have been in the mind of most who knew them, at least the Scotchmen. Perhaps this simple state of the fact may keep you towards the understanding of the Lord's dealing with him.

---

39. DFP: C/9/39.
40. A district of central Greece.
41. Leavings.

In respect of the past I have acted, I am conscious of having acted any thing but a natural part. I should have received David Dow as I did Carlyle into my bosom, into my house, into my church; but after the many marked dealing which the Lord took in the case of Carlyle I dared not to do it. Besides I had it in David Dow's note that he came by the direction of the Spirit in Anderson or in himself, I forget which, neither of which I could in any way recognise after the things which had taken place in Edinburgh, in the faith & testimony of which they still abide. I might have seen him or written to him, but I felt that if I drew near to him in any way or permitted him to draw near to me, I perilled my flock. And so I preserved silence and distance, and denied my Elders, in whose counsel I acted, so to do likewise. God knows that an evil thought or judgment of him I have never indulged, but that I have pitied him and besought God for him more perhaps than for another man, and so tenderly that many thought I dishonoured God by the nature of my pleas. Also I was so rebuked for writing three letters which I wrote to him and others upon my deserving of the work at Edinburgh, which was through my own discernment confirmed by the witness of the Spirit, that I shrunk from having any more dealings with him in the flesh, waiting for the spiritual help which I daily expected & still expect with confident faith to bring to them and to all my countrymen as to any private or underhand dealings with his servant, I utterly abhor and reject such a charge. He sought to disburden his conscience to me, and after warning him to remember his duty to his master, I permitted him to do so. But this was after my declaration to him of the evil work had confirmed & reawakened his own suspicions. One thing I do confess to have been wrong that I permitted him with my approbation to go down to Albury instead of sending him directly home. And this I did, because I feared you might if you saw him not & heard him not, think my judgment rash, and any schism might come in. But I should have left this wholly to the Lord, and dismissed the servant so soon as he was sufficiently refreshed to return. This I confessed to William Dow was wrong & I desired him to confess it for me to his brother. Again I say that it was without malice of any kind, and through no information of any kind but Mr. Dow's own letter, that I judged the work at Edinburgh & Dumfries to be evil. I never have heard any words spoken of D. Dow by the Spirit that I can remember. I know not any thing that I can do for him else I would do it most heartily for if there be a man whom I love on earth I love him. God's word to me was not to meddle with it in the flesh. This word I dare not to disobey. If I should receive liberty in the spirit to do so how gladly would I compass sea and land to comfort him.

I wrote to you Addressed to: Liverpool, to ask you to go to Ashton-under-line, [sic] and seek out Huot and bring him to his post, which he seems to have shamefully deserted for what reason we [letter torn] not, being utterly in the dark. My love & duty to [letter torn]

Farewell,

Yours E.I

Part II: The Letters

PS It is now brought to my mind, that one day when I was praying for him, the Spirit of the Lord spoke mighty earnestly to me to intercede for him. EI

My health is quite restored and my strength growing apace.

Addressed to: Henry Drummond Esq.,
Care of The Revd Walter Tate [sic],
3 Carlton Place,
Edinburgh.
[Annotated: Irving 6 June about D. Dow.]

~

Edward Irving to HENRY DRUMMOND

Bayswater, 28th June 1834[42]

My Dear Brother,

I thank you for this letter, which in every line of it is well worthy of consideration. I have no doubt that the two great lessons of God intended by this trial to be taught us, is, first to put away the superstitions fear and idolatrous reverence of a man speaking of a thing spoken, by a Spirit, which fear and worship the Holy Ghost is not profited by, but every evil spirit findeth in it the open door to his seductions. Secondly, to draw forth the *discernment* of *believing* men, that our faith may issue not in delusion but in light, that we may become men in understanding.

But you err greatly if you think that I took in hand to be the Apologist of these words; when I spake to the doubts and misgivings which were in your mind & Mr. Cardale's, in order to lead you to your acquaintship with God in your vocation as Apostles, whereby alone you could be recovered out of this pit of fear and doubt. Did I not tell you to separate the precious from the vile, and diligently point out to you where the vile lay; and for the sin did not I recommend that we should search into it and confess it? And is there any other way whereby we can either attain unto the hatred of sin past, or escape from its present power, but by these two things, confessing what we see, and casting away as a menstruation cloth that evil root out of which it came. Your eye was already too much riveted [sic] upon the sin. It had petrified you, you were ready to give up all; nay from our conversation the previous day, it seemed to me you *had* given up all. There was no other way of deliverance but that which, not I chose, but God directed into. For truly until the day of the Council I was as much stunned as any man; and it was given me at the time to refuse to Cognize the utterances. But the time

---

42. DFP: C/9/40.

will come to do this, when the messengers return and then I trust to be found faithful to the truth as it is in Christ Jesus.

Now O Jerubbaal[43] be strong, and O Joshua be strong, and be strong O ye remnant of the people and build. My Brother as you value your soul pull away all sharpness of mind and lightness of speech. Why should you seem other than the painful and mortified man which you really are. Yet I fear for thee in this. Do stand in Jesus alone for Jesus alone, my well beloved brother. Would I weaken the weak by having thee to lean upon another. Hate all men, thy very wife thy very self, that thou mayest love Jesus only. The Lord did put that Spirit in the Elders greatly on Wednesday & Thursday. What an error it was to think that we were any of us striking at man, or seeking to oppress our failing brethren. They will need this service from the Apostles another day. Now fare thee well, my best beloved brother in the Lord. I have endeavoured to make Mrs. Caird acquainted with the matter as well as I could. My love and blessings to Lady Harriet and all the children.

Yours faithfully,
Edwd Irving

Addressed to: Henry Drummond Esq.,
Albury Park,
Guildford.
[Annotated: Favd by Mrs. Caird.]

Edward Irving to HENRY DRUMMOND

10th July 1834[44]

My Dear Brother,

I am greatly, greatly comforted by your Letter and should have hastened upon the wings of love & joy to Albury to embrace my brethren honoured of the Lord: but He hath seen it better by bringing this very morning to a crisis a threatened or rather past miscarriage of my wife (I do not speak of this to others as I do to you for there is a modesty in these things which is too often violated). It was brought on three weeks ago by a sad fright we were put into of having lost our precious Margaret in the ocean of London. I feel that the Lord hath sent it to enchain me here against the impetus of my love and joy: for it is far better we should not meet till the Council of the Churches

---

43. Jerubbaal, who is Gideon. Judg 7:1.
44. DFP: C/9/41.

Part II: The Letters

So that except you should be able to have a Council this week, which pertaineth I suppose to you the President to determine, I should say let Mr. Ryerson[45] rest at Albury over Sabbath, for rest he needeth, and come up with you and Mr. Caird to the Council. For it were not good that he should be in my church without the matter being noticed as the Lord hath evidently been preparing things for the next Council. I think all should wait till then.

Now, my Brother dearly beloved in the Lord, be thou steadfast and faithful unto the Lord thy God. Cast me not off from thy wonted confidence but hear me still as a Teacher of truth and verity. Things are much out of joint; the Lord openeth to my meditations, my painful doleful meditations much light which I will not hide in the Congregation of his children. I thank you greatly for your confidence and love. Rest assured that it is in the holy communion of Saints that we must stand to our God faithful true and to Him alone true. Say to our dear Brother Caird & Ryerson, how greatly I rejoice over them in the Lord, and how very dear they are to me for their works sake. Yet my heaviness is oft more than I can bear. I am full of sorrow. But in this all my faith waxeth stronger & stronger.

Poor dear Godden, hath not been greatly in fault. His heaviness brought the question in Miss Cragcroft whether aught had been heard from Mr. Caird, and he gave a hint of the matter to Miss Cragcroft who is such a person, that I think if I had been living closely with her, I should have felt it a duty as well as a relief to have raised it in order to engage her intercession. She is one among ten thousand. I have desired the broken-hearted lad to be comforted & to write to you the circumstances, improving it to him in the mean time, and I plead for him he is a precious son, and will yet be the joy of his Mother. Farewell.

Your loving friend & brother,
Edwd Irving

Addressed to: Henry Drummond Esq.,
Albury Park by Guildford.
[Annotated: Bayswater Thursday, Irving, 10 July.]

Edward Irving to DR MARTIN

July 1834[46]

---

45. George Ryerson (1792–1882), Canadian Methodist. To be the Angel of the Church of Toronto. See Shaw, *Apostolic Church*, 115.

46. Oliphant, *Life*, 2:374–75.

Give thanks with me unto the Lord for the preservation of your daughter and my dear wife from an attack of the cholera. All that night I was greatly afflicted, I felt the hand of the Lord to cast me down to the greatest depths. It was on my heart on Friday night, and it was on hers also, to bring out the elders of the Church which I did on Saturday morning, when, having confessed before them unto the Lord all my sin, and all her sin, and all the sin of my house, without any reserve, according to the commandment of the Lord (James v. 16), I brought them up to her room, when having ministered to her a word to strengthen her faith, they prayed to the Lord, one after the other, and then strengthened her with a word of assurance and blessed her in the name of the Lord. They had not been gone above five minutes when she asked me for something to eat ... While I give the glory to God, I look upon Dr. Darling as having been a blessed instrument in His hand, and am able to see the hand of the Lord in the means, as clearly as in my own case, where there was neither means, nor medicine, nor the appointed ordinance of the Church.

~

Edward Irving to HENRY DRUMMOND

26th July 1834[47]

My Dear Brother,

Upon re-examining myself in the light of the words which came from Albury and Leamington, confirmed indirectly by words which were spoken in my Council here, I am satisfied that I was unfaithful to the discernment which the Lord *did* give me during the utterance of Mr. Godden, and spoke contrary thereto when I said that I hoped & trusted it was of the Lord. In so much that I found myself able to give my sanction and cooperate with Mr. Bayford when he came up by the word of the Lord in his own Council to deal with Mr. Godden and convince him of this thing, that his mouth had *not* been opened of the Lord but of Satan. And yet not till I had taken counsel upon it, and heard the word of the Lord in the Council reproving us, and as I felt it myself personally. Mr. Bayford and I had much dealing with Mr. Godden, and since I have seen him twice, but there is no light of conviction come into him as yet: and I charged him at no rate to yield himself unto any ordinance however high and venerable until he should have the answer of the Spirit within his heart. For otherwise it would nothing avail in the sight of God from one of his free-born children.

In considering within myself wherefore he should be in such darkness, I have been led to perceive in the light of the word which was spoken to him in your Church that he should abide at Albury (which I did not know till now) that you and I have

---

47. DFP: C/9/42.

been going counter to the Lord's mind in keeping him in London since your return; and that he ought to come to his appointed sojourn as soon as possible. (This word was spoken when you were meditating his return to Leamington). I am persuaded therefore that the light will come to him at Albury, when he shall hear himself directly spoken to of the Lord. For I am assured the Lord will give him deliverance & by this dealing prepare him for his work of an Evangelist.

Now, my dear Brother, I will bring him to you at Berners Street Hotel about half past 4 o'clock on Tuesday night if we be spared; that he may hear your mind from your own lips, and that I may surrender my ill kept charge.

I have been overwhelmed with sorrow, beyond any other I have ever endured by the prospect of losing my excellent, my invaluable wife in cholera; but the Lord hath this morning heard the confession & supplication of the Elders and we are much lightened. It hath been a wonderful dealing both with her and me for the subjugation of my intractable Spirit to the Lord's own way. Oh pray much for me I beseech you.

Your faithful & loving brother,

Edwd Irving
London Saturday Evening.

Addressed to: Henry Drummond Esq.,
Albury Park by Guildford.

Edward Irving to ISABELLA IRVING

Blymhill, by Shiffnel, 6th September 1834[48]

Visiting the brethren, strengthening and fitting me for the journey, the Lord deals very tenderly with me, and I think I grow in health and strength. What I could not get in London or Birmingham.

I found lying for me here—the gift of Mr. Cowper, of Bridgenorth, a sort of *trot-cosie* of silk oilcloth, which will take in both hat, and shoulders, and cheeks, and neck, and breast. I saw the hand of Providence in this.

---

48. Oliphant, *Life*, 2:379.

Edward Irving to ISABELLA IRVING

Bridgenorth, 7th September 1834[49]

[Anxious about the health of his son Martin he writes] Ask them to come in after the evening service, when I shall separate myself to the Lord with them. [And he sends a message to Martin to tell him] the horse is brown, with black legs.

[Continued the next day.] I did separate myself, according to my promise, and was much distressed by the heavy and incessant judgments of the Lord, and afterwards I had faith to plead the promise that the prayer of faith should heal the sick.

This Bridgenorth is one of the most beautifully-situated towns I ever saw. But no matter—I feel that I am serving the Lord daily, and I think He daily giveth me more strength to serve Him.

～

Edward Irving to ISABELLA IRVING

Shifnal, Blymhill, 10th September 1834[50]

I am greatly pleased and comforted by all I [hear] about Henry Dalton's two flocks, and have no doubt that the pleasure of the Lord is prospering in his hands; nor am I less pleased here with Mr. Brydgeman, whose labours for the Lord are very abundant.

～

Isabella Irving to HENRY DRUMMOND

Liverpool, 19th October 1834[51]

My dear Sir,

Your & dear Lady Harriet's kindness is indeed wonderful unto us. And did I not know from whence it springeth I would scarcely believeth but it cometh forth from Him who is love & who sheweth forth His love through His ministers—I was just about to depart & I gladly caught Capt Gambier to beg him to express my thanks to you & to your dear Lady but I did not feel that I could accept your kind invitations for our dear children as I did not think it right to let them go from home without their Father's approval & I had made arrangements for Miss J Symes as well as Miss Rook

49. Oliphant, *Life*, 2:379–80.
50. *ibid.*, 2:380.
51. DFP: C/9/43.

Part II: The Letters

being with them in Newman Street. The Lord had put into Mrs. J Cardale's heart also to invite Baby & her Nurse but I had declined her kindness on the same grounds.

But my husband, my Husband, what shall I say of him. He is ill, very ill, and faith alone can support me. It is faith now when all sight is against me & by the good hand of the Lord I am sustained. The left lung is very much oppressed, his breathing is short, his cough troublesome, his sleep very disturbed, though mercifully it has been more regular & quiet since I came to him; for ere I arrived his nights had sometimes been nearly sleepless. I see all this & yet praised the Lord I am not suffered to have a wish but that he should proceed immediately to Glasgow. I have a strong feeling as if the enemy were permitted to try him at present to see if it be possible to shake his faith & get him to mistrust the Lord. Oh uphold him by your faith & prayers.

I am sorely tried & grieved & bowed down although I am sustained in quietness & peace before the Lord. I see that the enemy draws the third part of the stars to the earth. Now I must say I feel as if there were a great drawing down again to the earth in my dear husband being thus oppressed & so held as not to be able by faith of Christ Jesus the Lord to put forth the sickness even as through Him we are brought to be Holy. The gift of faith is not to be confined, as I think it has too often been of late, to faith to be healed; but I see that the promise of the Lord is distinctly I will put none of these diseases upon you. And the threatening is sickness & sore diseases. Ex. XXIII[;] Deut XXVIII 59.60.61. Bear with me my dear Sir, I trust I write of & also feel these things much not from discontentment with my husband's state but because I feel that the Lord is much dishonoured by all the weakness & disease in the midst of His people so manifesting the Sin that cleaveth with us & I fear lest we should sit down in case both with the Sin & the manifestation of Sin.

My dear Husband will add a few words,
Yours most faithfully,
Isabella Irving

~

Edward Irving to ? (dictated to Isabella Irving)

Liverpool, 19th October 1834[52]

My dear Brother,

I was not able to go up to Church yesterday by means of the harshness of the weather but I sent a message of respect & love to Mr. & Mrs. Stewart by the hand of Mr. Jasbet, which brought him in his kindness to see me in the Evening when we had much conversation by this of a kind which I can liken only to the dialogues between

---

52. DFP: C/9/43.

Job & his friends. He, good man, seeking to reprove me with the Sin of having spoken presumptuously & erroneously of the human nature of our Lord whereby an entrance door was made for Satan to work his delusions in the Church. I, rejecting his charges & upholding the truth of what I have taught to the Church of God. He complaining much of the strife and discord that had been kindled & I showing him little of that had proceeded from us, have much come against us.

Mr. Jasbet came in and added his testimony to the character of the doctrine & of the people and pressed Mr. Stewart with the fearfulness of observing these words I follow after Charity & desire Spiritual Gifts but I am sorry to say he did not humble at the word the Lord which I told him was the reason he was not delivered according to Isaiah 66 Chapt. It was altogether the most painful interview I have had. The words were so smooth their edges so sharp but he was like a man constrained of God to tell out all that was in his heart & to hear all that was in mine & in Mr. Jaspet's. Yet he prayed very sweetly & I believe departed in a very profitable mood. This is very much a private matter & therefore I have put it into this private letter entreating you to use it with all discretion.

I desire my love to Lady Harriet & your Children, to Mr. & Mrs. Caird and their Babe. Peace be with you. Amen.

I am,

Your affectionate Brother,

Edwd Irving

~

Edward Irving to THE NEWMAN STREET CONGREGATION

Glasgow, Oct. 25th 1834[53]

My Dearly Beloved Flock,

I do find that no time nor place doth separate you from my heart, that you should not be dearer to me than my own life. It is the Lord who hath joined this bond of love, which death itself shall not divide; for are ye not our crown of rejoicing in the presence of our Lord Jesus Christ at His coming? Dearly beloved, you must not be sore troubled when I tell you that the hand of the Lord to afflict me is heavier upon me than it hath ever been. I am greatly weakened and wasted, and have little strength for anything save to pray unto the Lord. Yet am I nowise cast down in spirit, desiring only the glory of the Lord in whatever way He shall be pleased to reveal it. Yet is it a sore thing that for our sin we should thus be visited at the hand of a gracious God. Let us repent, and humble ourselves more and more, and walk more and more softly and tenderly in the

---

53. Wilks, *Edward Irving*, 285–86.

sight of our God, putting away all vanities and idolatries, if haply our God may have mercy upon us, and remove far away the stroke of His hand.

Much have I sought to find out, and much have I besought the Lord to reveal unto me, the manifold causes of this sad separation and utter weakening of your head; and it is made manifest unto me that we have not been taught by the *Word* of the Lord: we have not been broken by it, neither I; and, therefore, the Lord hath come in with His judgments, and laid his hand upon the head of the offence, and will utterly cut us off except we repent. Our hardness and impenitency of heart, under those streams of love which flowed fresh from the bosom of God, hath at length provoked Him to anger, and He hath arisen in His faithfulness to smite the shepherd of the flock; and I confess that in righteousness He doth afflict, yea, and in mercy, and in loving kindness; and if He Should slay me with the sword of His judgment, I would justify the dealing of His mercy, and put my trust in Him. Oh! I have had many deep exercises of soul in my absence from you, and Satan hath been suffered to buffet me; but the Lord hath stood with me, and brought me up out of the depths, and comforted me with His own free Spirit. My confidence in Him in whom I have believed hath been enlarged, together with the assurance that he hath arisen up to build His Zion and Jerusalem, that the nations and kings may assemble all to praise the Lord. But, oh! My children, we have held this faith with a slack hand, with an unjoyful heart; and, therefore, the Lord hath been provoked to smite. I have sinned, and you have sinned, in not yielding to the voice of the Lord, by reason of the hardness of our hearts, and now the Lord breaketh them with sorrow. Sure I am that this affliction is to the working of tenderness of heart both in you and in me. Moreover, I discern that the Lord will utterly separate my name from the work which He worketh for the blessing of the whole world. Oh! What a grief it hath been to me that my name should be familiarly joined with the work of the Lord. Oftimes in my prayer I have been so ashamed and grieved that there should be any name but the name of Jesus, that I have almost besought the Lord to be taken out of the way, rather than eclipse in any way the name of His honourable Son. And it is, indeed, my chief consolation in being so far apart from you, my children, and our brethren around us, that it will be seen, even by the enemies of the Lord's work, how little I have had to do with it—how little any of us have had to do with it, save to mar and hinder it. Again, I have discerned that the Lord, who had made me strong in the flesh to serve Him, would in me first give before the Church the fulfillment of the word, "All flesh is grass, and the glory of it is as the flower of the grass."[54] The hand of the Lord hath touched me, and I am consumed like the moth: but He sendeth forth his quickening Spirit, and the decayed face of the earth is renewed again. Oh! Cry ye for the outpouring of the Spirit, then shall there be the melody of health and joy in the habitations of the righteous.

Dear beloved in the Lord, give thanks and rejoice together, for the Lord hath heard your prayers and helped His servant. Since the last Lord's-day, when ye partook of the

---

54. 1 Pet 1:24.

sacrament of the Lord's Supper, I have been sensibly revived with a little strength, and have been able to resume the exercise which is recommended, *viz.*, riding on horseback; and I am able to conduct the worship of the family, who have received us under their roof with joy. Oh! Rejoice ye in the blessings of the Church of God; for sad, sad is the condition of many in these parts, who received the Gospel gladly, but have not been builded into a church. It is the great grace of God to this city, and to Greenock, and to Paisley, to have begun to build His people into the unity of the Church. Surely it is the fold whereof the Porter keepeth well the door; but, oh! Give Him the glory of your safety: so in Him shall ye go in and out, and find pasture. Ye ministers of His, let the Word that was with God, that was God, speak through you all; and ye people of the Lord, into the ear of the Holy Ghost, which abideth in you, let the word of God be spoken. So shall you be His witness along with the other Churches of the brethren, the pillar and ground of the truth. Be ye of one heart and of one mind in the Lord. Put away divisions and doubtings, for is not the unchangeable God your trust?

Peace be with you and with all the Israel of God.

From,
Your faithful and loving Pastor,
Edward Irving

Extract of a Letter from Edward Irving to MR CARDALE

Glasgow, Nov. 5th 1834[55]

The hand of the Lord is still upon me as heretofore, under which I desire to be humbled with all the flock, and to wait and learn the purpose of the Lord in such a separation. Oft-times I think that it is the Lord's gentle hand, breaking that bond by degrees between me and my flock, which threatened to grow up into a kind of necessity, and even to pass over into idolatry. O how I love them! How I am thankful to them! How I am laden with their benefits! And I am sure that their love to me is stronger than my love to them, and I do see it is of the great goodness and tenderness of God to take order that such affection should be stayed from passing over into unholiness; and that He that done us a great favour to put us so far asunder, and for such a time, that we might try our hearts and prove ourselves that our mutual love is in the Lord. O how terrible a thing it is in any way to eclipse or defraud that Brother, who purchased every soul with the blood of God! O be thou jealous for Him, my dear son, and jealous for that Church which He hath betrothed unto himself a chaste virgin. O let no minister

---

55. Wilks, *Edward Irving*, 287.

of Jesus seek to win her affections unto himself, for doth he not therein withdraw them from her Husband—from his Lord.

Edward Irving to HENRY DRUMMOND (dictated to Isabella Irving)

Glasgow, 11th November 1834[56]

My dear Friend & Brother,

The hand of the Lord still lieth heavy upon me & yet he beareth me up under it so that my faintness & weakness are comforted and I am not suffered to fret at His doings. If He give me a little strength then He weakeneth me again; and breaketh me of all natural hope into the simple utterance upon the words which have passed upon me. Nevertheless I feel it my duty to take all care of this mortal body which the Lord hath redeemed by His blood. I wish to strengthen my digestion by eating only the most nourishing meats with bread & drinking one or two glasses of my fine East India Madeira & sometimes instead of it a tumbler of excellent ale. Also I make a rule to ride for two or two hours & half every day about midday & after dining at 2 o'clock I rest till 5 without seeing anyone. I am sponged with vinegar and rubbed with a coarse towel every morning before getting out of bed & I have never yet gone out after dinner save to take a short walk with my wife when the weather is fine. The house we live in under the roof of a generous Brother in the Lord is lifted up above the smoke and moisture of Glasgow streets & yet the cold does not affect me but favourably.

The coldest wind of the sea & the coldest wind of the Mountain blowing in my teeth does not raise one cough from me nor one fit of coughing which seems altogether to depend upon inward or outward excitement. On the Lord's day when assembled with the Church I sit & minister some few words of edification to the Brethren but I have refrained as yet at all other times. I have got a chamois jacket & stockings lined with fleecy hosiery & gloves of the same kind & I never go out & ride without being carefully wrapped up from head to foot. I write you these particulars both that you may suggest according to your experience & knowledge anything to me and also that you may see that I neglect no means of comforting & strengthening this feeble frame. At the same time I will not, for any man, take mixtures of foxgloves & prussic acid & other acids as I did at Liverpool without any effect upon my pulse but almost to the slaying of my body utterly. Under the Lord I will abide my own Physician with the Counsel of Charles Buchan unless symptoms of a more unsettlingable kind should arise. Truly I live by faith in the Word of the Lord alone I would feel it a vain thing to struggle against this disease. Indeed I don't struggle against it but suffer this to do what seemeth

---

56. DFP: C/9/44.

to Him good. I am able to pray & sing psalms & read the Holy Scriptures & to receive & answer letters concerning this work & I am content. But it was not to write, my dear Brother, about myself that I asked my wife to take her pen, but to render my grateful thanks to you in the name of the Church in Newman Street for your bounty in remitting the debt of £140, with which Mr. Kerr informs me we were chargeable for the American Mission. The Lord make you to be the man which I scattereth yet increaseth. The Lord bless your basket & your store—Your Wife your Children your household and all that are within your gates.

Since I came here I had three interviews with John Campbell, one in the house during which his spirit of confusion, suspicion & accusation (for it is such I am sorry to say) was borne down by the tide of love which had long been accumulating in my heart towards him & then found its first bent. He was a silent hearer of the longing & yearnings of my soul over [word uneadable] in the truth; but when we came to ride together he would practice upon myself false doctrines concerning ordinances; as if they were instead of, & not in order to, the answer of the conscience in every man. He was forced many times to confess that I had uttered the truth; nothing but the truth but that at other times I had uttered a different thing, and that I was not able to distinguish these. At length he came so far as to say that I was not competent to be a witness of the work of the Lord. Not from any lack of honesty but because I could not apprehend the matter, and he concluded notwithstanding of free will & with good heart that it was not the abuse of a good thing which we had but the mixture of a good thing & evil thing. Truly he sitteth a *despotes*[57] in the house of God—a ruler & a judge over his brethren and I perfectly acquiesce in the justice of your observations upon him in the fourth tract & can find no other similitude for his conversation but the *little foxes* to eat up the tender shoots of the vine.[58] He hath been dandled and fondled, & no man hath dared to stand up & tell him his offences. He is a deep deep offender but the Lord will be gracious unto him & deliver him in Jerusalem.

My love to Lady Harriet your family, & Mr. & Mrs. Caird in which my wife joins. My wife had your letter from Birmingham—glad I hear of the Lord's doings there. Paid your £10 to Buchan to pay Mr. Jackson.

Your most loving & obliged Brother,
Edwd Irving

Addressed to: Henry Drummond Esq.,
Albury Park,
Guildford.

---

57. In the Greek New Testament dictionary *despotes* is a lord, master, or owner (including slave owner) but also simply master of the house.

58. Song 2:15.

Part II: The Letters

Robert Story to EDWARD IRVING[59]

Late 1834[60]

Oh! my beloved brother, what in this whole matter has given me so much pain, is the infallible proof I have received thereby of the backsliding of one[61] whom I so confidently set forth to the Church, as possessed of a like spirit with her departed sister. From the time she conceived that she had become the recipient of supernatural powers, she lost much of what I had witnessed in her, of the mind of Christ. The simplicity was no more, and the love of display, which was natural to her from her childhood, was visibly, but I doubt not unconsciously to herself, an element in all her saying and doings. Upon natural bias does the Tempter erect the most efficient munitions of his warfare; and here he found in poor Mary what was sufficient for his purpose ... My brother, I state to you mere outlines, that might be filled up with particulars, which would show you what a wild and troubled sea of uncertainties my mind must have been doomed to walk upon had I admitted Mary's claims to inspiration. I feel I have greatly sinned in not having publicly given to the Church, for its direction, a faithful narrative of the beginnings of these things. I am peculiarly guilty in not having written to you at the time, but a tenderness towards Mary herself, which ought not to have been, and perhaps the solicitations of Mrs. Story, who had great love for her, aided to prevent me doing what would, in all events, have more thoroughly furnished you with premises for a righteous judgment ... Hers was the *first* of all those cases which, within the last five years, have led so many to think that the Holy Ghost is again with power in the midst of the Church. By most—if not by all—who so believe, her case is considered the most remarkable and conclusive; and to me, who know it better than any other human being, it is an unchangeable stumbling-block, which I could get over only at the cost of all the powers of moral and spiritual discernment by which I can know the things of God at all ... O! my friend, what will you judge of these terrible scenes, when I tell you that when poor Samuel was racked through his whole frame by the shouting and leaping, and singing overhead, he rallied as by a desperate effort of nature, his decaying energies—left his pillow, and ascended the stair—and when he entered the room and entreated them to be silent—(not *Mary*, as was stated in a scurrilous publication) addressed him, the head of their family, 'Get thee behind me, Satan.' You will be tempted to think that I am indulging in a strain of uncharitable details like those that are found in the pamphlets of godless and hostile scorners; but it is not so; and it is remarkable that all the published accounts were so incorrect that I could always, when I met them,

---

59. "In the end of 1834, Irving came down to Scotland ... Mr. Story met him in Glasgow ... It was after this interview that Mr. S. wrote the letter, of which the following is an extract.... Before he could read this letter, Irving was called into that Presence where the mysteries of the spiritual life would be at last unveiled, and where turmoil and uncertainty would no longer vex his soul": Story, *Rev Robert Story*, 228-33.

60. Story, *Rev Robert Story*, 229-32.

61. The 'she' he is referring to is Mary Caird (née Campbell).

deny their truth; while I knew things much worse than the gainsayers every got hold of. A fatal disinclination to expose persons I loved—whom I was unwilling to judge—of whom I yet hoped well, kept me from doing what I ought to have seen to be my part, as a teacher of truth and watchman of souls.... You know what occurred afterwards. She was in the midst of those tumultuous meetings in Helensburgh and Port Glasgow, receiving the homage of all classes of those religionists who were panting after novelties. I attempted from time to time, in vain, to rescue her from such a perilous fellowship, and at last, with much ado, and only after a schism had occurred among the 'gifted' people, I succeeded in prevailing on her to live for some time away from excitement, in the loneliness and quiet of the cottage, at Mamore, where we then resided. Then, when away from those blasphemous scenes, where such gross familiarity was dared with the name of the Eternal, she came to herself, and confessed that she had spoken and prophesied in the name of the Lord God Almighty, when only giving vent to her own fancies.[62] ... It was remarkable enough that while she and Caird (after their marriage) were in the Manse, I received a letter from Prince Edward's Island from a parishioner who had emigrated, and there become a new creature, earnestly calling upon me to sent out to that desolate land preachers of the gospel: 'Here,' said I, 'is an opening at once.' 'No,' said Caird, 'we must first witness to the *Roman* earth.' I saw even then how a Divine counsel or command could be tampered with, if not agreeable to our feelings; it was a simple matter to apply a '*prophetic theory*' in palliation of disobedience to a voice which, if they were sincere, that still believed Divine....

I take for granted that Mr. Drummond received from Mary the notices regarding Isabella[63] and the Johnstons, which his account of the rise of the Church at Albury contains. The halo around Isabella's head is a pure fiction.[64] Mrs. Johnston denies entirely the statements respecting her husband and her sister.

O! my beloved brother, do you not hesitate before you admit such things as possessed of Divine authority. Are there in the Acts of the Apostles, written by Luke, such exaggerations, as in Mr. Drummond's account of transactions which he would represent as not less important. What an awful compromise of truth there must be, and what guilt does it involve, gravely and as by Apostolical authority, to give for infallible statements the false glosses of an excited and imaginative girl.

---

62. 'At an earlier period than that now alluded to, she had written to Mr. Story—"I had, before receiving your letter, come to the resolution to write to you, and to confess my sin and error for calling my own impressions the voice of God. Oh! it is *no* light thing to use that Holy *Name* irreverently, as I have been made to feel"': Story, *Rev Robert Story*, 331–32 n.

63. Isabella Campbell, Mary Caird's sister.

64. 'A halo which, according to Mr. Drummond, shone round her head as she lay dying. Mr. Johnston was a devout man, who died at Port Glasgow': Story, *Rev Robert Story*, 231.

Part II: The Letters

Frances Woodhouse to HENRY DRUMMOND

Thursday, 20th Novbr 1834[65]

Mrs. McAlpin's, 50 North Albion St., Glasgow.

My dear Brother,

I received your letter communicating to me the Word of the Lord spoken by Mr. Bayford, which word by some means had come to my ears before I left London, as also a word spoken through Mrs. J Cardale respecting the powers Satan had over the Angel through the sin of the church, and the need for intercession; both these words I heard in London and they have both been again brought to me here, one by Mr. Irving himself, the other by your letter; and I just wait to see the Lord's way and to act and speak as the Lord shall shew me the time and season.

Mr. Irving is very ill; his own account of his own state, in which he said he found himself a little better, were only the daily variations; but upon the whole there is no doubt he is very ill. It was only two days ago that I happened to go to him in the morning, and he said that if I had not come he must have done what he never did in his life before, *viz*, ask his wife to pray, because he had not, breath to pray, and he is at times so oppressed as to fear the total loss of breath. It seems to me that his restoration must come from the cry of the people of whose common sin he is the sign & manifestation; for though he does not appear to me to be conscious of the reason of the continued chastening of the Lord's hand upon him, nor very desirous at present to enquire concerning it, yet I think he is to this moment unconsciously to himself *patronising* the churches & people which the Lord has gathered (witness his ministering here and his taking the headship in Mr. Taylor's house not without invitation but still as I think not seeing that the Lord is more honoured by every man being priest in his own house (which is *His own* order) than by any order which man can devise). I doubt not the enemy has great hold on him, and I can only pray the Lord for him, and cry that the church in Newman Street may lay it to heart and intercede for him also.

On Tuesday Mr. William Tait and Mr. Wilkinson came over from Greenock in Great Haste by a word through Mrs. Provand commanding them "as Elders in the Church of God to come over speedily, and anoint Mr. Irving with oil in the name of the Lord and to pray over him & that he should be healed" when they delivered their message and had expressed their certain reliance upon the Word though the handmaid and had brought forward many analogies confirmatory of the propriety of their conduct in the matter, and had alluded to your coming to London by a Word through Mrs. Caird to summon the angels and tell them of a snare, and had also mentioned that when you were at Greenock and a blind or deaf & dumb person was present the Word came to Mrs. Provand to command you to lay hands on the person that he might recover, and that though Mrs. Provand did not yield to the Spirit and utter the words, yet that afterwards when she told you of it, you did not tell her such a word would be a

---

65. DFP: C/9/46.

going beyond her border, and many other like cases. Mr. Irving to my great satisfaction told them the oil was lacking; they had not the anointing, and he would be unwilling to proceed in such a solemn matter without further light on the subject, and then he asked me what counsel I should give on the matter; and I endeavoured to show Mr. Tait, that the Angel's duty was, not only to keep the Prophets within their border, but also to keep within his own border; and as the thing he came to do was quite beyond his border; he must see that he had sufficient authority for doing what he purposed to do, and that a word through a woman was not sufficient—and afterwards when they had left Mr. Irving, and had come to my lodging to dinner, as Mr. Tait said he still felt that the Lord would in some way give him more light on the matter if it were a snare, I read to him the Word you had written to me, and sent him back with a warning not to try and cleanse dirty water which he was very anxious to do. By a letter received today he seems to have come to the conclusion that, as the word was "ye elders to go" the prophetess was right, but he took the word to himself, which did not belong to him. Yesterday evening Mr. Campbell was with us (five o Clock being the time we sit to receive & counsel those whom the Lord shall send to us) and he rode out with us today. He is in great darkness; I told him that until he was decided either for or against the work of the Lord; he might hear us set forth the Doctrines which the Lord had taught us, but could not understand one word of them, and in endeavouring to set forth those doctrines, he was only misrepresenting and misstating, and in endeavouring to answer or confute them he was only confuting the lie his own heart had conceived and his own tongue had uttered and I advised him instead of judging another man's servants to make up his mind what he believed himself.

Mr. Irving says he thinks himself set as a sign in this land; I think it too; and when I look at his figure & person & height and stature and his character as a man whose life has been devoted to the Lord's Service, and his reputation as a man of great scientific and literary attainments, and his name known through the world and when I consider my own insignificance in all these things and see myself leading him about at a crawling pace and waiting upon him as a nurse, the sign seems more apposite. Here is the Pride of Scotland moral intellectual and personal brought to naught by the hand of the Lord and a little child leading and turning about the headstrong the stubborn and the haughty "The despised office through which the blessing shall come." This letter is not for the council; but as you wished me to write. I have written.

Yours faithfully in the Lord,
Francis V. Woodhouse
P.S. Mr. Irving has received your letter this evening.

Addressed to: Henry Drummond,
Hotel Berners St.,
Oxford St.,
London.

Edward Irving to REV JOHN MARTIN

Glasgow, 21st November 1834[66]
[dictated to Isabella Irving]

My dear & Reverend Sir,

I am in pretty good health, by the goodness of God, and ride out in the open air from two to three hours every day—Isabella often accompanying me through the kindness of John Campbell, my fellow sufferer at the hands of the Church of Scotland. His pony being always at her service. Now dear Sir, I declare to you that the coldest air of the Mountains never provokes a cough but on the other hand give such pleasure & health to my frame as I cannot describe to you. I have also been overtaken with rain & thoroughly wet without being at all affected, in the seat of my complaint, one way or another. My frame cries out for cold air & not for Madeira or Malta or any such places & here I have got it. We live in a house very nearly on a line with the tops of the Cathedral Church steeple. And now with respect to some work that you have followed the newspapers in believing I am sent to do here—that work is just to *rest* and abide patiently and to give Counsel to those whom the Lord shall bring to me for Counsel and that I may not even be burdened with this the Lord hath sent Frances Woodhouse Esq.,[67] one of the Elders of my Church, and named to be an Apostle, to be joined with me in this office of giving Counsel. None comes to me for Counsel till 6'o'clock in the Evening the former part of the day being all my own for care of the body & the Soul. Now dear Sir I ask you can there be a man out of health surrounded with more blessed Conditions than I am? I wish you would praise God with me instead of murmuring & complaining about me.

Isabella has never failed in her dutifulness to you nor in her dutifulness to me. It was a great sense of dutifulness that made her hesitate to answer that awful letter which you wrote to her. Our bosoms are not made of the adamant [diamond or other hard substance] nor our hearts of the flint stone. Why will you then speak with such inveterate & express Contempt of him whom we believe to be the Holy Ghost. Do it not again on any account in any letter to her or to me as you would not wound two hearts which love & which honour Him as we are bound to do. She was afraid lest if she should answer it she should be answering again to her Father & if she took no notice of the blasphemies against the Holy Ghost she feared to be unfaithful both to

---

66. WCL, MS 15.

67. The youngest apostle. See letter Edward Irving to Henry Drummond, 3 February 1833: DFP: C/9/13.

her Father in Heaven & to her father on earth. This is the true reason why your patient & enduring daughter passed that awful letter unnoticed.

Now as to writing once a week concerning my health, it is not done to any and I would count it a poor substitute for faith. This lack of faith in God the presence that oft times causes us to hasten to see & hear from one another, but truly I am a man not in any peril of life—or with any perilous symptoms yet weakened by the hand of the Lord to be exhibited in this land in weakness & helplessness before He send me fully armed with the armour of God against the battlements of that Babylon of which you are *still* a watchman to shatter them to pieces that Children of the Lord and a good company of the priests who may come out to be baptized of the Holy Ghost & builded together into the true Church the Bride of the Lamb. Oh Sir you have allowed the streams of light & life to flow past you & you have abiden as you were & many walk in your footsteps, taking you for an example. Reckon then that when you hear not from us I am as usual & we will write you if I should take any turn for the worse. I trust to be in Edinh ere long to tarry there some short while & it is our purpose to offer a visit to our Brother Samuel by the way when we have fixed the time for going.

I am glad that your health has not suffered materially from the heavy duties before and the many Services during the Communions.

May the Lord strengthen you more & more unto the end. We are sorry that dear Janet has been weakened by disease but we were also gladdened to hear from Mrs. Alexander she was better—grace be with her.

Our love to dear Mother. May she ever abide in the Lord. When we heard from London last Saturday our dear Infants were quite well and dear Baby got a tooth quite easily, praised be the Lord. Mr. & Mrs. Hamilton are at Dover. Isabella joins me in all love and dutifulness to you and to all the friends in all parts.

Your faithful & dutiful Son,
Edwd Irving

Addressed to: Revd John Martin,
Manse,
Kirkcaldy.
[Annotated: Edward's last' 21st Novr 34]

~

Francis Woodhouse to HENRY DRUMMOND

29th November 1834.

My dear Brother,

Part II: The Letters

Mr. Irving has suffered very much during the last few days, and indeed he has been so tried by pain, that he hardly knows what he does; and last night he sent for me in the middle of the night, and told me to be strong and anoint him, for that unless I would anoint him, he knew not what he should do. He is wounded with a very heavy dealing; his faith has almost left him, and he has looked on me as though I were God, and is only recalled to himself by finding that I can do nothing and I find it a very difficult matter to forget him and myself and speak to him as I ought to speak.

We had purposed to leave this to morrow and still purpose it, but unless he is very much better we cannot move him; and I have told him I should not think of going to Edinburgh while every step of our way would put him to torture. But I trust that Help is not far off. Truly it is a fearful thing to fall into the hands of the living God and if the righteous shall scarcely be saved, alas for the ungodly.

I shewed Mr. Irving your letter two days ago and the next day he said he fully went along with it and acknowledged his sin, and his jealously of the Apostleship and then added that he continued unto this day to feel a fear lest they should take too much upon themselves, and immediately he left the room, and sent for me ten minutes afterwards saying[,] with tears in his eyes[,] that he had been in agony ever since he had left the room; and when I told him that I did not doubt the Lord's controversy with him was on that very account of jealousy & suspicion, he said he believed it was so, and desired the Lord to deliver him from it. Oh! Pray, pray, pray for him[;] O! that those who have been his abettors in this sin would fear and cry to the Lord for him and for themselves.

I received Mr. Cardale's letter, and thank him for the word of encouragement to me, while the word came through you sending me forth I was painfully conscious of my own insufficiency; but the Lord will be the strength of those who call upon his Name

Yours affly in the Lord,
Francis D. Woodhouse

Sunday Night.

Francis Woodhouse to HENRY DRUMMOND

Glasgow, 5th December 1834[68]

My dear Brother,

---

68. DFP: C/9/48.

I am grieved to hear the account you gave of yourself, for truly the Lord hath need of all his servants at this time and there be but few who will come to his Help against the mighty.

When I wrote to you *before* I spoke of his great illness (Mr. Irving's) but *to this moment* his fever has increased, and though his bowels act and the other impediments have been removed yet his fever increases. He is attended by two medical nurses who see him three times a day, and their account this morning is that he was much worse but his recovery *was not impossible*; so much for the Help of man: I will not wonder at being told that his recovery *is impossible* for I have earnestly entreated the Lord so to deal with His servant that *no man* may have the Glory and I trust *the Lord* will accomplish His work and go forth in strength to heal. Mrs. Irving's Mother and Father & Brother are here and have been a comfort to and much help to her, and today Mr. Irving's Mother and Sister come to see him yesterday morning (when every medicine had failed of producing any effect on the bowels, and thee clysters had been applied during the night and had also proved unavailing). I thought the Lord had given us up, not that I doubted his purpose, but that I feared the resistance and feared the more from having found Mr. Irving just as strong to resist the Lord as ever (no doubt through the hold Satan has had on him) and after worship at six o'clock in the morning in his bedroom at which I could only pray for submission to the Lord's will and for willingness to yield up those whom the Lord chose to take. I took Dear Mrs. Irving aside and asked her if she had looked at the possibility of the death of Mr. Irving, and I told her that I had felt it my duty to point out to her the very great danger in which Mr. Irving was. Let the Lord above be exalted! My faith seemed to waver and my heart failed me in waiting for my God. However, in the middle of the day I was again strengthened to entreat the Lord and to plead with him and this day I have found confidence and have been further strengthened by a letter from Mr. William Tait containing the words spoken in his church last evening to the effect that when help from men faileth then the Lord will send help of his holy habitation and further speaking of the resisting and rage of the adversary and the unbelief!

Whilst you were being made to send me hither, I thought it was unwillingness on my part but now I know that the Lord was making me to feel what I was coming to, for it seemed as though I was sinking into the earth under the words and the grief which came over me was truly a foretaste of the shame and grief and sickness of heart which I felt almost ever since my coming proceeding from a consciousness (felt more specially during prayer) of the very great resistance which with many tears I have been made daily to mourn over.

Again my dear Brother I desire to remind you of the need the Lord hath of all, and as you have received a gift for the whole church let not the talent be buried but stir up the Gift and the faith which are both of God; and if the Lord has not yet thoroughly restored you, hinder Him not in doing it.

I have been as one in whose mouth were no reproofs, I have heard in silence the words of those who *know not the Physician nor the Balm*, feeling that silence and shame and confusion of face belong unto us because we have sinned; the Lord accept of it and wherein I have been led into doubt, the Lord forgive and send help unto us.

I purpose to write to Mr. Cardale tonight, but unless some change occur I can only tell him that Mr. Irving *is all but given over*. I hope the Lord has been dealing with the people in Newman Street as with me to make them hope in *His alone Mercy*, and to receive with confession of unworthiness what help He may be pleased to send.

Unless something should occur before night I shall not add any thing to what I have written.

Yours ever affly,
Francis D Woodhouse

P.S. I have received your letter. Mr. Buchan's address is 107 George Street not *West* George Street.

Addressed to: Henry Drummond Esq.,
Albury Park,
Guildford, S. B.

Rev John Martin to WILLIAM HAMILTON

Parson's Street, St Mungo, St., Glasgow.
7th December 1834[69]

My dear Sir,

What our fears anticipated is, to all human appearances nearly consummated. Our beloved Edwd now lies, in a state, so far as one can perceive or judge, altogether incapable of perceiving, aught that is about him. Neither eye nor ear seems susceptible of any impression for some hours past (it is now past 7): and though he continued to speak, his articulation has also become very indistinct: & his efforts to express himself are often interrupted by hiccup; so that is has been very seldom that we have been able to make sense of what he would say. The greatest number of continuous words that I have been able to catch, were pronounced perhaps 3 hours ago 'and if I die—I die to the Lord Amen!' A good many more preceded these; but I could not make them out. His mind has been in a wandering state almost the whole of this day, and I may say, since last night. But it is delightful to observe that, in all its wanderings, it took a direction to spiritual things. He was often praying for the Church—confessing sin—giving praise

---

69. ML, MS 21.

for mercies. Sometimes he was exhorting the church, sometimes giving counsel to individuals, and so forth. Since 5, he began 'Lord pardon all.' He was stopped by hiccup and after attempting several times to finish the sentence, he was still unable to get father than repeating 'all'—'all'—'all.' Again he said something about 'keep unto that day.' But it is seldom we can make out so much as three words together, or connect them so as to discover any meaning. We have seen persons, after severe fever, & the like, fully as weak as he is at this moment, or weaker, who have yet recovered. But it is the opinion of Dr. Laing, who was here about 6, that he will not survive this night. I see no probability of life lasting longer with him. What the Almighty may do, we are not to limit: but unless his disease take a very extraordinary turn, we must be prepared to resign him, I apprehend before another day's light shines upon the earth! The Lord, on whom he has so often called, will receive his Spirit! How thankful might we all be, to share his same blessed reception! Once to-day, observing that he mixed a number of foreign words in his speech, some of which seemed to be Hebrew, I repeated to him the first v of Ps: 23rd, in that language. It seemed instantly to fix his attention: & he replied in (I apprehend) two or three verses in the same tongue. Partly, however, from not being accustomed to hear Hebrew spoken and partly from his mode of pronouncing being different from mine, I did not clearly apprehend what he said.—Dear Isabella is most sorely tried. How she is able to bear up under so much want of rest is astonishing. She has watched him for above a week, day and night: & except a few short sleeps, which she got, when he was a little quieter than usual; & when having her mother beside her, she could trust to being awakened, the moment she was wanted, she has had no repose. Ma, too, has only been in bed about two hours each morning since Wednesday; with sometimes a few minutes intervals on an easy chair in the sick-room, or on a sofa, in the room adjoining. Old Mrs. Irving & Mrs. Dickson arrived on Friday. The latter was very willing to take Mama's place but Edwd being accustomed to Ma, did not chuse [sic] to have any other to assist Isabella; & the latter, perhaps felt herself, from the same cause, more at her freedom with her mother, than with any other person. We have reason to be thankful, Ma has hitherto been strengthened to go through the task. Many are the prayers which have this day been offered, and specially, I doubt not by his own church, for our beloved friend. I trust they will be interested in the peaceful translation of his soul to the world of light; which, to him, will doubtless be far better: though to many, it would seem to have been more expedient that he should have remained in the flesh. But if the Lord be pleased to take his servant home, and in this way to prepare him for it, shall we dare to find fault with what he has done? To ask the petition of which I heard part, as I suppose "Whether we live, may we live in the Lord—and if we die, may we die to the Lord!"[70] and, as my father used to add, when he employed the same text in prayer, "Living and dying, may we be the Lord's!"

---

70. 'For whether we live, we live unto the Lord: and whether we die, we die unto the Lord: whether we live therefore, or die, we are the Lord's.' Rom 14:8.

Part II: The Letters

8th December; 20 mins to 1 am: But 2 or 3 hours have passed since what precedes was written: & it is now nearly ½ an hour since all that was immortal of Edward Irving ceased to belong to this world: the animated countenance, the athletic form, are cold and without life. Isabella is bereaved of her almost idolized husband; her children of their father; his church of their pastor; and many attached friends of the object of their respect and esteem. Alas! I hardly expected my own prediction to be so soon fulfilled; when, finding that he would not comply with my urgent entreaties to leave Scotland, & hasten to a milder air, I said 'It seems, then, to be God's purpose that you never leave Glasgow.' The family, with whom he and Isabella have staid [sic] ever since their arrival here, was one wholly unknown to them. But Mr. Taylor had read Edward's works, & embraced his opinions, and esteemed himself indebted to him for the best of knowledge. And more kind and attentive persons to them and us, could not be. Good Mr. Woodhouse has acquitted himself with the most devoted attention, of the trust committed to him; doing every thing in his power to assist or serve either Edwd or his wife. I shall ever esteem and love him for what I have seen of the unassuming goodness of heart, which he has displayed. I know, my dear Sir, this is most afflicting tidings to you, & Elizabeth both. The Lord spare you to each other! Please communicate this intelligence as soon as you can, & as gently as you can at Newman Street. I wrote Miss Rooke, forewarning her of what would probably soon take place, & requesting her to make Maggie sensible that it was not improbable she would never see her father more—in this world, at least. And you may mention to Miss R, with my best regards, that I would have written to her again at present: but that time forbids, as I have other letters which must be written without delay. O Lord! The father of the fatherless, and the judge of the widow! Remember and pity those, to whom thy Providence hath given a right to call upon thee by that name, by placing them in those conditions! And may the great Teacher teach us all the right improvement of their sore visitation! I am, my dear Sir,

Aff Yours,
John Martin

P.S. Dr. Black of this city, to whose kind attentions we have been much indebted, gives a good report of Mr. Alexander: though he hardly knows him personally.

P.S. Not being accustomed to think of Andw as an inhabitant of London, I find I have not mentioned a request that you would notify this sad event to him. I will perhaps, write him by next post.

Addressed to: William Hamilton Esq.,
127 Cheapside, London.

Rev Samuel Martin to HENRY DRUMMOND

8th December 1834[71]

Dear Sir,

Our beloved friend Edward Irving breathed his last this morning, a very few minutes after twelve. For some days he had been sinking under his extremely feverish pulse, accompanied with crustification. But for his two last days he sunk very fast: his mind wandered, he lay before us truly the wreck both in body and mind of a mighty man. For the last 24 hours he knew nobody, except his wife for about half the time. His words, which were many, indicated very plainly, that there were before his mind nothing but thoughts of his Lord, his Lord's work & church. And without a struggle, he yielded up his "spirit to him," who gave it. May he enter into rest with him.

His bereaved wife is sore crushed under the trial. She hoped against hope: & felt, therefore, the more bitterly the stroke, which fell on her beloved, & which has, as it were, smitten her life down to the dust.—Long watching & want of rest have doubtless, helped to unnerve her.—May the Lord be her stay—

I could not allow myself to send you merely a formal intimation; & yet time allows little more.

I am,
Your obed. servt.
Samuel Martin

Glasgow.
Decr 8th 1834

~

Isabella Irving to MR AND MRS LAURIE

9th December 1834[72]
[Annotated: Thomas Erskine, Linlathen]

My dear friends,

I feel that my pen at this time ought to be first employed in expressing to you in some full sort the gratitude of my heart and yet now when I take it up what thanks can I render you my dear friends for having so nobly and generously offered unto me, a stranger & a sojourner in this place, one of the choicest sepulcher's[73] in the land wherein I might bury the precious remains so very dear to my heart. I find no words

---

71. DFP: C/9/49.
72. ML 041a, b.
73. Edward Irving is buried in Glasgow Cathedral.

whereby to tell out the feeling of my soul & it is in vain to attempt it. What you so freely offered I willingly & heartily accepted. In the Lord I look as He who will reward you and I know He will not fail to do it. He ministreth with a cup of cold water given to one of His disciples and it was as a faithful Servant of the Lord that you ministered unto my husband whilst he lived and when he died you forget not the righteous man's remains. You have in a peculiar manner obeyed the injunctions "let mine outcasts dwell with thee." May the Lord remember you & your family my dear friends in this that you have done, and may His blessing, the blessing that maketh not and addeth no sorrow rest upon your heads now & forever. Amen

      Your attached & much obliged,
      Isabella Irving

Rev John Martin to MR LAURIE

Sir,
 Your company at the funeral of the Rev Edward Irving my son-in-law on Friday 12 Inst at 2 o'clock is requested by
    Sir,
    Your ob Servt,
    John Martin

St Mungo St.
9th Dec 1834
[Written on the same page of the letter above.]

Francis Woodhouse to HENRY DRUMMOND

            Glasgow, 14th December 1834[74]

My dear Brother,
 I have just received your letter and have only to say that the Lord who is wiser than we, has taken away his Servant and has not been pleased to be entreated for him and it becomes not us to mourn as those who are without hope.

---

74. DFP: C/9/50.

I am obliged to you for your suggestion to me to look to the Lord and not to you and Mr. Cardale and it is my intention acting upon that advice to go on Saturday to Edinr to fulfill the Lord's word there unless Friday's post brings me any word of direction different from what is my present purpose.

When I wrote to Mr. Cardale two days ago, it was not settled what Mrs. Irving would do, but now she has resolved on going Home with her Father and Mother to Kirkcaldy for the present, and this she has done in compliance with their earnest solicitation and in conformity to my own advice for I thought *that* her proper place till she was stronger in body and able to return to London. If Mrs. Irving returns to London with me it is most probable our first days journey will be to Barmoor,[75] but if I return alone it is not my intention to stop at any place on my road because the directions given me were quite explicit to go to Glasgow and from thence to Edinr & to return to the Church.

Mr. Tait and all but two of the Elders from Edinr were at the funeral and from what passed afterwards at dinner (for most of them dined with me) I thought this dealing of the Lord would be a means of preparing the Elders & people there to be taught that there was such an office in the Church of Christ as that of Apostle and that the work now doing was indeed something more than man's work and when that truth lays hold on their hearts they will feel the need of Guides upon Holy Ground lest when the blind lead the blind both should fall into the ditch.

I heard that the Lord had declared a short time since that the rebellion to the apostleship had not been subdued yet, but this was before the Lord had taken this last dealing with us. I am sure that the form in which the sin, of which the Lord spoke, presented itself to the minds of the people was just the same as was the case with Mr. Irving, he always spoke of the men as those whom he was to obey, and spoke of the *Apostles* and of his jealously lest *they* should pass their border without any apparent consciousness that Jesus is the Apostle and that the question is between the Lord, (asserting his Lordship in the Church in the *flesh* and in the *spirit*) and those who say who is Lord over us? personified by the Angel resisting in the flesh till be brought death upon his flesh, (for this was literally the case) and the Prophet resisting in the Spirit unto the second death—But oh may the Lord deliver him—I would hope the death of Mr. Irving may awaken him to a sense of his own worse share in this perilous warfare.

When will we all learn; it was the *Name of Jesus* through *faith in that Name* as opposed to our own *power* and *holiness* that Peter declared to be the means by which the lame man's *ancle* [sic] bones received strength and we are all equally and together unwilling to give up *our own* power and holiness that Salvation may be only of the Lord. If a letter to the Prophet could avail I would write but I just tremble lest he should be sealed up & hardened by it.

I am glad to hear you are well again. Mrs. Irving since her Husband's death has been very much strengthened, and I have seemed to feel the truth of my being to her

75. Home of F. Sitwell.

Part II: The Letters

an Elder and having in measure the Shepherd's heart, in the strength and comfort she seems to have received in looking to me in that ordinance.

I am, dear Brother,
Ever truly yours,
Fran V Woodhouse

Addressed to: Henry Drummond Esq.,
Newman Street,
Oxford St.,
London.

∼

John B. Cardale to THE CHURCH of GOD in LONDON with THE ELDERS and THE DEACONS

24th December 1834[76]

Dearly beloved in the Lord,

I present you with a transcript of the last words (contained in two Letters) Addressed to: you by our late beloved and revered Pastor, as the most acceptable legacy from him, from whose lips you will no more in this age hear the words of life; who addressed them to you when separated for the last time from you; and who herein, as in all the words of God uttered by his lips and treasured up in your believing hearts, 'being dead yet speaketh.'[77]

I have added thereto an extract from another Letter subsequently written to myself; and extracts from the Letter of a Brother, containing some particulars respecting his last hours.

Believe me to be, dear Brethren,
Your faithful and affectionate Servant,
John B.Cardale.

24th December, 1834.

Glasgow, Oct. 25, 1834

My dearly beloved Flock,

I do find that no time nor place doth separate you from my heart, that you should not be dearer to me than my own life. It is the Lord who hath joined this bond of love which death itself shall not divide; for are ye not our crown of rejoicing in the presence

---

76. Cardale, *Two Pastoral Letters to the Flock of God*.
77. Heb 11:4.

of our Lord Jesus Christ at His coming? Dearly beloved, you must not be sore troubled when I tell you that the hand of the Lord to afflict me is heavier upon me than it hath ever been. I am greatly weakened and wasted, and have little strength for any thing save to pray unto the Lord. Yet am I no wise cast down in spirit, desiring only the glory of the Lord in whatever way He shall be pleased to reveal it. Yet is it a sore thing that for our sin we should thus be visited at the hand of a gracious God. Let us repent, and humble ourselves more and more, and walk more and more softly and tenderly in the sight of our God, putting away all vanities and idolatries, if haply our God may have mercy upon us, and remove far away the stroke of His hand.

Much have I sought to find out, and much have I besought the Lord to reveal unto me, the manifold causes of this sad separation and utter weakening of your head; and it is made manifest unto me that we have not been taught by the *Word* of the Lord: we have not been broken by it, neither I nor you; and therefore the Lord hath come in with His judgments, and laid his hand upon the head of the offence, and will utterly cut us off except we repent. Our hardness and impenitency of heart, under those streams of love which flowed fresh from the bosom of God, hath at length provoked Him to anger, and He hath arisen in His faithfulness to smite the shepherd of the flock: and I confess that in righteousness He doth afflict, yea, and in mercy, and in loving kindness; and if He should slay me with the sword of His judgment, I would justify the dealing of His mercy, and put my trust in Him. Oh! I have had many deep exercises of soul in my absence from you, and Satan hath been suffered to buffet me; but the Lord hath stood with me, and brought me up out of the depths, and comforted me with His own free Spirit. My confidence in Him in whom I have believed hath been enlarged, together with the assurance that He hath arisen up to build His Zion and Jerusalem, that the nations and kings may assemble all to praise the Lord. But oh, my children, we have held this faith with a slack hand, with an unjoyful heart, and therefore the Lord hath been provoked to smite. I have sinned, and you have sinned, in not yielding to the voice of the Lord, by reason of the hardness of our hearts, and now the Lord breaketh them with sorrow. Sure I am that this affliction is to the working of tenderness of heat both in you and in me. Moreover I discern that the Lord will utterly separate my name from the work which He worketh for the blessing of the whole world. Oh! What a grief it hath been to me that my name should be familiarly joined with the work of the Lord. Ofttimes in my prayer I have been so ashamed and grieved that there should be any name but the name of Jesus, that I have almost besought the Lord to be taken out of the way, rather than eclipse in any way the name of His honourable Son. And it is indeed my chief consolation in being so far apart from you, my children, and our brethren around us, that it will be seen, even by the enemies of the Lord's work, how little I have had to do with it,—how little any of us have had to do with it, save to mar and hinder it. Again, I have discerned that the Lord, who had made me strong in the flesh to serve Him, would in me first give before the Church the fulfillment of that word, 'All flesh is grass, and the glory of it is as the flower of the grass.'[78] The hand of the Lord hath touched me, and I am consumed like the moth: but He sendeth forth his quickening Spirit, and the decayed face of the earth is renewed again. Oh! Cry ye for the outpouring of the Spirit, then shall there be the melody of health and joy in the habitations of the righteous.

Dearly beloved in the Lord, give thanks and rejoice together, for the Lord hath heard your prayers and helped His servant. Since the last Lord's day, when ye partook of the Sacrament of the Lord's Supper, I have been sensibly revived with a little strength, and have been able to resume the exercise which is recommended, viz. riding on horseback; and I am able to conduct the worship of the family, who have received us under their roof with joy. Oh! Rejoice ye in the blessings of the Church of God; for sad, sad is the condition of many in these parts, who received the Gospel gladly, but have not been builded into a church. It is the great grace of God to this city, and to Greenock, and to Paisley, to have begun to build His people into the unity of the Church. Surely it is the fold whereof the Porter keepeth well the door; but, oh! give Him the glory of your safety: so in Him shall ye go in and out, and find pasture. Ye Ministers of His, let the Word that was with God, that was God, speak through you all; and ye people of the Lord, into the ear of the Holy Ghost, which abideth in you, let the word of God be spoken. So shall you be His witness along with the other Churches of the brethren, the pillar and ground of the truth. Be ye of one heart and of one mind in the Lord. Put away divisions and doubtings, for is not the unchangeable God your trust?

Peace be with you and with all the Israel of God. From
    Your faithful and loving Pastor,
    Edward Irving

To the Flock of God, which the Lord Jesus Christ hath given into my hand to keep and to bless them, with the Elders and Deacons.

Dearly beloved Ministers and Members of the Lord Jesus Christ,

It well becometh me, who was the chief instrument of bringing in that sin for which the hand of the Lord hath long lain heavy upon us, to do my utmost part to remove the same, that He may again lift upon us the light of His countenance: and, because no sin can be removed otherwise than by the confession of it, and our confessions are greatly helped by our knowledge, discernment, and hatred of the sin which we would confess, I think that I shall best serve my God, and my flock, and the quiet of my own soul, and the health of my body also, be endeavouring to lead you into the nature and aggravation of that sin of ours, which the Lord nameth and describeth by 'the making of a calf.'

You will understand then, my dearly beloved, that the Lord, in His great grace towards London, the city of our habitation, hath purposed for the good of the whole

78. Isa 40:6.

Church to set therein a complete and perfect pattern of what His Church should be, endowed with a fullness of the Holy Ghost; that is, having no lack of any gift or grace or fruit of the Spirit, to shine with holy beauties not only through this land but unto the whole earth, that the people may come up hither, as heretofore they did to Zion and Jerusalem, in order to learn the way and word of the Lord. This is the great purpose of good, which our God is slowly but surely accomplishing unto the faith and prayers of all His children who call upon His name. Of this purpose we have dared to hinder Him; we have plotted against it to bring another to pass; and it is of His mercy that we have not been dashed to pieces in the kindlings of His wrath. It is true we did it in ignorance: but we should not have been ignorant of the way of or God, having Prophets to reveal it, and Apostles to dispense and to order it, according to the mind of the Holy Spirit, who speaketh by them; and having Pastors to break down the revelations of God in simple and faithful ministrations unto the people; and having, moreover, the Holy Unction of the body of Christ, by which we should be able to know the truth, and to be kept from all seducers. But our fatness of heart, our fullness of bread, and our misuse of the Lord's most blessed gift of His word spoken in the midst of us, brought it to pass that we fell easily into the snare of the devil, by which he thought to mar and thwart the purpose of our God. Oh! I came far short in the office of the good shepherd, not to have been your watchman and your guardian in that day; for which I do now taste the bitterness of sorrow in my heart, and the hand of the Lord upon my flesh—But to return to my purpose of shewing you our sin. Understand, dearly beloved, that such a fullness of the Spirit as our God proposeth to give to His Church in London can only stand under the headship, government, and administration of the Lord Jesus. No Apostle, Prophet, Evangelist, nor Pastor, no Angel of any church, no man, nor creature, hath more than a measure of the Spirit. To Jesus alone pertaineth the fullness, and to the Church over which He ruleth. And seeing He hath given it forth as His purpose to give unto His Church in London a fullness of the Spirit, He Himself must rule over it. He that sitteth between the Cherubim alone ruleth over them. But we were beguiled to think that the full measure of the Tabernacle of the Lord would be given to that Church over which I preside as Angel; which was no less than the exalting of the Angel of the Church into the place of Christ. I tremble when I think of the awfully perilous place into which I was thrust. Now the figure by which the Eldership is known in Scripture is the calf; and this exaltation of the Angel of the Church to sit head over the fullness of the Spirit, was truly the making of the calf to worship it, instead of worshipping Him who sitteth between the Cherubim. I speak not at present of the injury and dishonour done to the other ministries of Christ by this setting up of one. I am contemplating our sin as it beareth upon Christ Himself, upon the person of the Son of God; and I do see it as nothing less than a cunningly contrived plot to take out of His hands the dearest and noblest of all His prerogatives, that of Head of the Church, and giving it to another. In the same light I see the naming of Evangelists by me, which pertains not to any one but to the Second Adam; His it is to give names to every beast and every tree in the spiritual Eden. And of this also I do repent, and call upon the whole flock to repent along with me. In the same light also do I see the sending forth of the Evangelists unordained, which was the slighting of Jesus, the Apostle in His apostles, to whom it appertaineth to send forth. In all these things I grievously sinned against the Lord, and you with me. We were blinded. We were unwatchful. We were covetous. We were contented to be made rich. We thought not upon the poverty of others. We were impatient of the government of Apostles, of the Lord in them. We sought independence as a church; and, but for the grace of God, we had reaped the very independence of Satan.

God saw that it was not in our heart to do these things; He saw that nothing was farther from our hearts; that we had been taken, through our simplicity; by the craft of the devil, and therefore He had mercy upon us, and began to take the veil from off our eyes by the hand of His Apostles, to whom He gave timeous discernment of these things, with utterance of that which they discerned; but I confess for myself that I was very slow, yes, and reluctant to turn back from my evil way: whereto I do trace the heavy chastisement of the love of my God; and the Lord hath declared that there was the same cleaving to the evil thing in the Elders and in the people. Let us now, my dear children, he of one mind to put it away with abhorrence and loathing, that we should have been found in such deceivableness and so fearfully deceived. For I am assured, that though the Lord shewed us at the last Communion such a token for good, it was unto the awakening of us, by his returning love, to consider our past ways, and with haste to turn our feet into the way of His commandments. But if we remain in a state of lethargy, not laying this thing to heart, nor truly repenting of it, I know not with what new and more severe trials He will try both you and me. I have a good hope, however, in my heart, that there will be an awakening to understand the purpose of the Lord, and patiently to wait for it. Yet am I not without fears for some, lest they turn aside from the way of the Lord, and abide from the way of the Lord, and abide in their former ways, which are not good. Oh! Remember, my beloved, that we are not now what we were when the Lord's word did find us: we are called, and chosen, and set apart to a great work, which the Lord seeketh to accomplish in and by us, and for all His Church, yea, for all the world. We may not dwell in our ceiled houses: we may not abide by the sheepcotes: still less may we lie down beside the flesh-pots of Egypt; but we must gird up the loins of our mind, and go forward. We must bear the burden of the Lord: we must remember that His presence is in the midst of us, and take off the shoes from our feet, because the place where we stand is holy ground. It is the word of the Lord which we have received to kept holy, and to obey. And blessed be the Lord that He hath kept the witness of the Spirit in the midst of us, and reproved every one who hath been betrayed into any mingling of His Word. Oh! Reverence the word of the Lord whenever it is spoken amongst you. Ye Elders, reverence it; ye People, reverence it. Cry for the Prophet, for he was a chosen vessel. Hold ye him against his own rebellious heart. Let him not go; and it he will not return, Oh! be ye guiltless of his fall.—For myself, while I am conscious of being led about by the Lord amongst His servants, and of being used by Him in giving them counsel, I am also conscious of his hand abiding upon me to weaken me; nor do I expect to see it removed until we have together thoroughly repented of our sin, and been cleansed from it in our inward parts.—The grace of our Lord Jesus Christ, the love of God the Father, and the fellowship of the Holy Ghost, be with you all. Amen.

       Your faithful and loving Pastor,
       Edward Irving.

F. Sitwell to HENRY DRUMMOND

24th December 1834[79]

Dear & honoured brother,

I desire to thank you for your letter with the answer from the Council to my questions which I recd on my return from Glasgow. I had heard from Mrs. Irving that her husband was so ill, & thought it right to go down & see him but on arriving in Edinburgh recd the unexpected intelligence of his Death. I say unexpected for I had always formed the idea in my own mind that it would be the Lords will to raise him up. However[,] now that Infinite Wisdom & Love has decided otherwise, I see many reasons why it has happened as it has. First I think it has been given me to see that in the present state of the Churches (specially if I may at all judge of them from the state of my own people) that they are not in a fit state for such an event for that if the Lord had vouchsafed to do such a thing straitway [sic], they and him thought themselves *well* & rich in faith because The Lord had thus answered their prayers whereas in fact they are exceedingly low & poor (not in spirit) in faith. They *know* a great deal but that knowledge has not been apprehended in the spirit & thus become *life*. There is a hanging back & shrinking from the close & personal Communion & walk with God to which we are called, therefore I believe in stead of flattering them (which The Lord will never do) into a delusive view of their own state as to real faith by healing him who is gone, it was necessary to shew them their unbelief by the event that has happened. 2ndly If there was rebellion (lurking perhaps but *there*) in our most faithful & honoured brother against the rule of Jesus in His Apostles, which some things mentioned by Mr. Woodhouse gave good reason to suppose, & that also in his own church it existed to a greater extent & an idolizing of him, then it is clear the sin *in himself would* produce chastening, & in *them*, out of love to them made his removal necessary, for The

79. DFP: C/9/51.

Lord will not allow any one however faithful & honoured (& none were more so than he of whom I write) to stand in his way.

Doubtless also he had done his part of the work. As I was given to observe to my people[,] 'It is very striking that Mr. Irving has never been allowed to have any part in the bringing out the form of the Church, nor in setting any one of them in order so as utterly to preclude them being called "Mr. Irving's churches." His standing was that of an Angel of a Church a teacher in Israel an expounder of the Word, an interpreter of Scripture, & beyond this his border he never was allowed to go. I see great mercy & wisdom in that no gift beyond this was ever given to him but that being used in the bringing out & clearing away of the long forgotten, long buried truths of the Doctrines of God. I say having been used as the instrument in this, then The Lord called him to his rest that truly His churches might not be called by the Name of any man which if he had been used in the calling or in the ordaining might have been the case.

It is not for any worm of the dust much less for such as I to scan the reasons of The Lord but to know His will is His reason, & that it is good, but certainly these things do throw some light upon what has happened in the trying occasion. What you mention concerning the spiritual person at Albury occurred also at Greenock when the Spiritual Sister there on receiving the news of Mr. Irving's death the day of that event, said, 'Well I knew there was something going to happen for the good of The Lords church for the Spirit within me has been rejoicing all the day.' The same thing occurred to myself the Evening after Mr. Irving's funeral when I knelt down to pray there was a power came on me which made me feel so happy that I was almost tempted to think is was evil (for which may The Lord forgive me) as I thought it so incongruous with the event.

In regard to the circumstances attending the last hours of Mr. Irving as I observed in a letter to Mr. Cardale there was reason—both to rejoice & be sorrowful. Our brother Woodhouse was much cast down & appeared to think that there was a want of the peace that should attend the end of a righteous man, but let us examine this & it will be seen to be otherwise. I do not wonder that there was a melancholy & unpleasant impression made upon the mind of Mr. Woodhouse, for he had undergone many trials & much sorrow of heart & spirit for some weeks of unwearying attendance on a dying man, that The Lord had laid much upon him the burden of the unbelief of the Church, that his hopes (lingering to the last) of the raising up of his Pastor through his hands had been miserably disappointed & add to this the witnessing of the sufferings in the flesh & the hearing of the moans of him whom he loved & we need not wonder at the cloud overshadowing his view of all that had passed, but it appears to me we must separate the end of the life of the flesh, from the abiding of the endless life in the spirit. From all I could gather from those who witnessed the closing scene of Mr. Irving's life, it manifested the same unshaken faith, the same patience, the same joy & peace in believing, the same glorious hope which had animated his breast, the same looking for & hasting the Coming of the Day of The Lord & the Coming of The

Great God & Our Saviour Jesus Christ, which had always been the object & end of his existence. The last rational words to his wife were to ask her to read the XVIII Psalm & the IV & V Chapters of 1 Thes & then to add 'Peace be with thee.' To his landlord (a member of the church, Mr. Taylor) 'Cleave you to the church stick to the Church' to his father in law 'If I die I die to The Lord' & 'O the depth of the joy & consolation there is in Christ Jesus' & when complaining to Mr. Woodhouse of the terrible night he had spent when he, Mr. W, asked him if it was in his mind he repelled the thought by a 'O no not in mind.' It is most manifest that in his soul his last end was the last end of the righteous with peace. That he suffered much in the body is certain. Worn out & exhausted, the whole organs of nourishment & digestion seem to have refused to act, his bladder & his bowels refusing their office, he sank at last into insensibility & stupor, but even in his wanderings it was the words of life & truth that came from his lips for the last intelligible words he uttered were 'keep that Day' which was supposed to be that verse in 2 Tim 1st chapt 12 verse 'I know in whom I have believed etc.' Why it pleased our Heavenly Father thus to chasten His beloved & faithful Servant in the flesh in this way, who are we that we should presume to scan His reasons, but stand in awe & sin not lest we also through the headness & rashness & hasting of that flesh, should tempt Him to chasten us also, for He is no respecter of Persons & will render unto every man according to his work. This is my view of the case & the light I have upon it that we have reason, *great reason* to rejoice & give thanks for his unshaken faith, his dying testimony to the truth of what he had witnessed for in his life. (Oh how the enemies of the truth watched round that dying bed to catch but a word that might have enabled them to say he wavered in his opinions), while we have also reason to sorrow at the remembrance of his sufferings & of any sin in the rebellion of that flesh that would have deserved & incurred such a chastisement, but what of that now, its work is done its rebellion is finished, The hand of The Mighty Lord hath lain it & it will tempt him no more & his Spirit is with his Lord, The Lord whom he loved & served. He is gone to his rest. 'Blessed are they that die in The Lord.'[80] Yea saith The Spirit for they rest from their labours & their works do follow them." Certainly it was a sorrowful day when we laid his honoured head in the grave. Mr. Woodhouse & I were pallbearers. Woodhouse felt his last hope go when he let go the ribband [sic]. For my part I cannot tell how I felt the emotions were so mingled & contradictory, but somehow I felt I would not part with the honourable place of helping to carry him to his burial to be King of England.

Poor Mrs. Irving. May the Lord be gracious to her. He was so the day of the parting with his flesh. I prayed with her in the morning that she might be restrained & she told me in the evening of that sad day the prayer had been answered. Indeed she was much so. She was so quiet that if it not been for the involuntary rubbing of her hand upon her heart one would hardly suspect of what was fighting within.

I have nothing particular to add. I think the church here has been somewhat stirred up since this event we need it much. May the Lord sustain you in your arduous

---

80. Rev 13:14.

Part II: The Letters

Office & with affectionate & respectful remembrances from Mrs. S & myself to Lady Harriet & your family & yourself

believe me faithfully & affectionately,
Yours in The Lord,
F Sitwell[81]
Barmoor.
Dec 24th 1834

Addressed to: Henry Drummond Esq.
Albury Park,
Surrey.

~

William Hamilton to DR JOHN MARTIN

London, 30th Jany 1835[82]

My Dear Sir,

Your much esteemed letters regarding our lamented friend have remained longer unanswered than I intended, but I have been very much occupied, and I had scarcely anything worth communicating, besides Elizth dispatched a letter to meet you on your return home. Few events have happened in the course of my life, which have given me such deep concern as dear Edward's death. For years he was my bosom friend, and my most intimate and constant companion. The affection we cherished for each other was strong and sincere, and not a few of my happiest days were passed in his society. Tho' much separated during the last two years, yet on neither side was there, I believe, any diminution of real affection. I loved him sincerely, both as my friend, and former Pastor, from whose faithful and powerful ministration I chiefly derived whatever knowledge I have attained to, and alas it is but little, in divine things. To you who know and value him so highly, it is unnecessary that I should say anything as to his sterling worth. With all his peculiarities we shall not, I believe, see his like again. I have met with only one feeling on the occasion that of deep sympathy & regret even from those who latterly differed from & greatly blamed him. He has, I doubt not, made a happy change and I trust we shall yet meet in those blessed regions where many dear to us are celebrating the praises of His love who redeemed them by his blood & made them Kings and

---

81. Frank Sitwell (1797–1864), owner of Barmoor Castle in Northumberland, and brother-in-law to Archbishop Tait of Canterbury. He was called as an apostle in 1835, and his tribe was Zebulon (Spain and Portugal). See Flegg, *Apostles*, 66 and 71.

82. MS: MSS 096b.

Priests unto God. I feel very much for dear Isabella under her sore bereavement, and the disappointment of her fondly cherished belief in his recovery.

I am thankful she is so greatly supported and so resigned to the Will of her Heavenly Father, who hath promised to be the husband of the widow and the father of the fatherless. She has many kind & attached friends here, who will cheerfully endeavour to comfort and encourage her amid all her trials, and, as for dearest Elizth and myself; that nothing we can do to promote her happiness & welfare shall be wanting. I know not what are the intentions of the friends in Newman St regarding the future support of herself & the children. When I saw Mr. Horn a few days ago, nothing had been done, and I therefore ventured *confidentially* to suggest that *instead* of an annual allowance, which would necessarily be uncertain in amount & continuance he should recommend a liberal subscription at once similar to the one made in the case of Mrs. Dr Thompson & that it should be placed into the hands of trustees for the benefit of the widow and children and I further mentioned that another £2000 for which Edwd's life was insured was secured by the members of the *old* Church & that as the present Church in Newman St had paid only two years of the premium on the policy: that sum (the £2000) should not be considered as relieving them in any degree from the duty of making a liberal provision. Mr. Horn agreed with the propriety of these suggestions and promised to act upon them as if they had originated with himself. I have not yet heard the result.

I can do nothing about the £2000 until Isabella arrives. If Edward has not left a will, as I supposed, she will have to administer to his estate. It would have been gratifying to us to have had as many particulars as could be given us of the few last days of his life. He may however have communicated a little to *you*, Mother or Samuel. From Isabella we have not heard since Edwd's death, and are therefore in ignorance as to her future instructions. May she be wisely guided! You would of course hear that Mr. Cardale had been appointed to succeed Edward!! I do not know what other arrangements have been made or intended in Newman St. Maggy was with us all last week, seems quite well, as was also the Baby. We have had moving late accounts of Martin.

Mr. Norbet left us about a fortnight ago, not in very good humour I understand. His preaching which appeared to me to be more shewy [*sic*] than substantial pleased a good many, and they made a movement in his favour, which he very imprudently, in my opinion, did all he could to be Edwd but it failed, in consequence of several of the Session & to me of the most solid and judicious members of the Church, not being satisfied. He is too susceptible to praise & has not discretion or sound judgment enough, for such a charge as ours. I mention frankly to you, and in perfect confidence without however intending to prejudice him in your estimation for he has many good qualities. Mr. Alexander is a substantial good preacher. Mr. McNicolson from Paisley is to succeed him & between the two I trust we shall get a suitable minister. Tell dear Sister Janet with my love that the moreen[83] of which I sent her a pattern was sold

---

83. Moreen: a stout woollen or woollen and cotton material either plain or watered, used for

before I received her reply but that I expect to get three more pieces in time to forward by the smack[84] next week. We have a good deal of political excitement here but no disturbance.[85] It seems to be doubtful if the Ministers will join in sufficient strength to enable them to win. Elizth and Andrew are both well & unite with me in wishing you *all* many happy returns of the season and I ever am

                My Dear Sir,
                Affectionately Yours,
                Wm Hamilton

Addressed to: The Rev Dr Martin.
Manse, Kirkcaldy, Fifeshire.

Editor's Epilogue

We leave his grieving widow Isabella with the three surviving children to face life without their beloved head. To be fair, they were helped and supported by the members of the Catholic Apostolic Church. Martin, (1831–1912) eventually emigrated to Australia where he had a distinguished academic career. He died in Albury on the 23rd January 1912.[86] Margaret Irving (1825–53) died at the age of twenty-nine. Isabella Irving (1834–78) in 1856 married the historian Samuel Rawson Gardiner (1829–1902), by whom she had six children, died aged forty-four.

However, perhaps the last word on the humane, devout, and indefatigable man that was Edward Irving should again go to his life-long friend Thomas Carlyle: "But for Irving, I had never known what the communication of man with man means. He was the freest, brotherliest, bravest human soul mine ever came in contact with."[87]

---

curtains, etc.

84. Smack: single-masted sailing boat for coasting or fishing.

85. The 'disturbance' was the general election in December 1834 at which Wellington and Peel failed to obtain a majority. They clung on without adequate support from the House until April 1835 and then were forced to resign. See Briggs, *The Age of Improvement*, 273.

86. 'Irving returned to England in 1900 to live in Albury, the centre of his Church, to devote himself to its interests and support the last apostle . . .' Martin, *Martin Howy Irving*, 41.

87. *Fraser's Magazine*, January 1835.

Bibliography

Addison, Joseph. *Cato: A Tragedy as It Acted at the Theatre Royal Drury-Lane etc.* London: Tronson, 1813.

Archibald, Raymond Clare. *Carlyle's First Love: Margaret Gordon Lady Bannerman.* 2 vols. London: Haskell House, 1910.

Baxter, Robert. *Narrative of Facts Characterizing the Supernatural Manifestations in Members of Mr. Irving's Congregation and Other individuals, in England and Scotland, and Formerly in the Writer Himself.* London: Nisbet, 1833.

Bebbington, David W., editor. *The Baptists in Scotland: A History.* Glasgow: The Baptist Union of Scotland, 1988.

Beckford, William, *The History of Caliph Vathek.* London: Johnson, 1786.

Blair, George. *Biographic and Descriptive Sketches of Glasgow Necropolis.* Glasgow: Ogle and Son, 1857.

Bolitho, Hector, and Derek Peel. *The Drummonds of Charing Cross.* London: Allen & Unwin, 1967.

Briggs, Asa. *The Age of Improvement.* London: Longman, Green, 1969.

Brown, Stewart J. *Thomas Chalmers and the Godly Commonwealth in Scotland.* Oxford: Oxford University Press, 1982.

Bulteel, Rev. H. B. *A Sermon on I Corinthians II, Preached before The University of Oxford on Sunday Feb 6, 1831 by the Rev H. B. Bulteel, late Fellow of Exeter College, and curate of St. Ebbe's Oxford.* Oxford: Baxter, 1831.

Byron, Lord George Gordon. *Childe Harold's Pilgrimage, Canto the Fourth.* London: Murray, 1818.

Cameron, George G. *The Scots Kirk in London.* London: Becket, 1979.

Cardale, J. B., editor. *Two Pastoral Letters 'to the Flock of God, which the Lord Jesus Christ hath Given into My Hand.'* London: Jowett & Mills, 1835.

Carlyle, Alexander, editor. *The Love Letters of Thomas Carlyle and Jane Welsh.* 2 vols. London: Lane, 1909.

Carlyle, Thomas. *Reminiscences.* Edited by K. J. Fielding and Ian Campbell. Oxford World Classics. Oxford: Oxford University Press, 2000.

Cole, Hubert. *The Betrayers.* London: Eyre Methuen, 1972.

Davis William. *A Key to Bonnycastle's Algebra, Containing Solutions of the Questions, with the References, as They Stand in the Fifth Edition of That Work etc.* London: Printed for the Author, 1803.

Drummond, Henry. *Narrative of the Circumstances which Led to the Setting Up of The Church of Christ at Albury.* Printed for private Circulation only, n.d.

Bibliography

———. *Observations on Matthew xxiv. Papers Read before the Society for the Investigation of Prophecy.* London: Seeley & Son, 1827.

Egan, Pierce. *Boxiana; or Sketches of Modern Pugilism.* London: Smeeton, 1812.

Endelman, Tod E. *The Jews of Georgian England 1714–1836.* Philadelphia: Jewish Publication Society of America, 1979.

Erskine, Thomas. *Remarks on the Internal Evidence for the Truth of Revealed Religion.* Edinburgh: Waugh & Innes, 1820.

Fielding Henry. *The Life and Death of Jonathan Wild, Thief Taker General of Great-Britain and Ireland etc.* Northampton, UK: Dicey 1725.

Fisher, H. A. L. *A History of Europe.* London: Arnold, 1936.

Flegg, Columba Graham. *Gathered under Apostles: A Study of the Catholic Apostolic Church.* Oxford: Clarendon, 1992.

Forsyth, Robert, *The Beauties of Scotland.* Edinburgh: Sonar and Brown, 1805.

Foulkes, Richard. *Church and Stage in Victorian England.* Cambridge: Cambridge University Press, 1997.

Frey Samuel. *Narrative of Joseph Samuel Frey: with an Address to Christians of All Denominations.* London: published by the author, 1810.

Froude, James Anthony. *Thomas Carlyle, the First Forty Years of His Life.* 2 Vols. London: Longman, Green and Co., 1882.

George, Eric. *The Life and Death of Benjamin Robert Haydon Historical Painter. 1786–1846.* 2nd ed. Oxford: Oxford University Press, 1967.

Gilpin, William. *The Life of Bernard Gilpin.* Glasgow: Chalmers and Collins 1824.

Grass, Timothy. *The Lord's Watchman: Edward Irving.* Eugene, OR: Pickwick, 2012.

Hair, John. *Regent Square: Eighty Years of a London Congregation.* London: Nisbet, 1898.

Haldane, Alexander. *The Lives of Robert Haldane of Airthrey, and of His Brother, James Alexander Haldane.* London: Adams, 1852.

Hamilton, Miss Elizabeth. *The Cottagers of Glenburnie: A Tale for the Ingle-Nook Intended to Instill into the Minds of Youth the Advantages of a Tractable Disposition.* Edinburgh: Manners & Miller, 1808.

Haüy René Just. *Elementary Treatise on Natural Philosophy.* 2 vols. Translated by O. Gregory. London, 1807.

Hazlitt, William. *The Spirit of the Age or Contemporary Portraits.* London: Colburn, 1825.

Heron Robert. *Scotland Described.* Edinburgh: Brown, 1797.

Herries, Rt. Hon. Charles. *A Reply to Some Financial Misstatements, In and Out of Parliament, by J. C. H.* n.p., 1803.

Horner, Alistair. *The Age of Napoleon.* London: Orion, 2005.

Irving, Edward, *Babylon and Infidelity Foredoomed of God: A Discourse on the Prophecies of Daniel and the Apocalypse, which Relate to These Latter Times until the Second Advent.* Glasgow: Chalmers & Colling, 1825.

———. *The Confessions of Faith and the Books of Discipline of the Church of Scotland, of Date Anterior to the Westminster Confession: To which are Prefixed a Historical View of the Church of Scotland from the Earliest Period to the Time of the Reformation, and a Historical Preface, with Remarks.* London: Baldwin and Cradock, 1831.

———. *The Day of Pentecost or Baptism with the Holy Ghost.* London: Baldwin & Craddock, 1831.

———. 'Facts connected with Recent Manifestations of Spiritual Gifts.' *Fraser's Magazine* 4 (1831–32) 754–61; 5 (1832) 198–205, 316–20.

———. *Facts connected with Recent Manifestations of Spiritual Gifts*, reprinted from *Fraser's Magazine 1832*. London: Fraser, 1832.

———. *Farewell Discourse (on Cor. Xiii 11) to the Congregation and Parish of St. John's Glasgow*. Glasgow: Chalmers and Collins, 1822.

———. *For Missionaries after the Apostolic School: A Series of Orations*. London: Hamilton, Adams and Co., 1825.

———. *For the Oracles of God, and For Judgment to Come: An Argument in Nine Parts*. London: Hamilton, 1823.

———. *A Judgment, as to What Course the Ministers and the People of the Church of Scotland Should Take in Consequence of the Decisions of the Last General Assembly*. Greenock, UK: Lusk, 1832 (extracted from *Morning Watch 5, 1832*, 84–115).

———. *The Last Days: A Discourse on the Evil Character of These our Times, Proving Them to be the 'Perilous Times' of the 'Last Days.'* London: Nisbet, 1850.

———. *The Orthodox and Catholic Doctrine of Our Lord's Human Nature Set Forth in Four Parts: I. Statement of the Doctrine from Scripture. II. Confirmation of It, from the Creeds of the Primitive Church and of the Church of Scotland. III. Objections to the True Doctrine Considered. IV. The Doctrines of the Faith which Stand or Fall with It*. London: Baldwin & Cradock, 1830.

———. *A Sermon Preached on the Occasion of a Fast Appointed by the Presbytery of London, to be Held in all their Churches on the First Day of the Present Year*. London: Nisbet, 1828.

———. *Sermons and Lectures, and Occasional Discourses*. 3 vols. London: Seeley & Burnside, 1828.

Jones, M. G. *Hannah More*. New York: Greenwood, 1968.

La Place, Marquise Pierre Simon. *System of the World*. 2 vols. Translated by J. Pound. London: Phillips, 1809.

Leybourn, Thomas. *The Gentleman's Diary or The Mathematical Repository 1799–1801*. London: 1742–1840.

Locke, John. *Essay concerning Human Understanding*. 1690. Reprint. London: Penguin, 1997.

Martin John. *Martin Howy Irving: Professor, Headmaster, Public Servant*. Working Paper No. 10. The History of the University Unit. Melbourne: University of Melbourne, 2006.

McDowell, William. *History of the Burgh of Dumfries*. Edinburgh: Black, 1867.

McLagan Jennifer. *Fat: An Appreciation of Misunderstood Ingredients with Recipes*. Toronto: McClelland and Stewart, 2008.

Mechie, Stewart. *Education for the Ministry in Scotland Since the Reformation*. Records of the Scottish Church History Society, 1966.

Miles, Alfred H. *Our National Songs Collection of One Hundred and Eighty Songs of England, Ireland, Scotland and Wales*. London: Hutchinson, c 1890.

Miller, Frank. *A Bibliography of the Parish of Annan*. Reprinted from the transactions of the Dumfrieshire and Galloway Natural History and Antiquarian Society. Dumfries: n.p., 1925.

Miller, James. *The Lamp of Lothian or, the History of Haddington*. Haddington, UK: Allan, 1844.

Milton, John, 'Ode on the Morning of Christ's Nativity, The Hymn.' In *The Golden Treasury*, edited by Frances Turner Palgrave. London: Oxford University Press, 1947.

More, Hannah. *Coelebs in Search of a Wife: Comprehending Observations on Domestic Habits and Manners, Religion and Morals*. 2 vols. London: Cadell & Davies, 1809.

Bibliography

———. *Coelebs Married Being Intended as a Continuation of Coelebs in Search of a Wife*. London: Walker, 1814.

Mrs. Oliphant. *The Life of Edward Irving*. 2 vols. 2nd ed. London: Hurst and Blackett, 1862.

Palmer, H. P. *Joseph Wolff: His Romantic Life and Travels*. London: Cranton, 1935.

Paul, Fr M. R. P. A Critique of the Work Composed by Juan Josafat Ben Ezra, entitled *The Coming of the Messiah in Glory and Majesty*. 2 vols. Translated from the Spanish, with a preliminary discourse by E. Irving. Containing MS Notes by Coleridge. 2 vols. London: Seeley & Son, 1827.

Pierce, Egan. *Boxiana or Sketches of Modern Pugilism*. London: Humphrey, 1741.

'Pierre Jean George Cabanis (1757–1808).' Online: www. britannica.com.

Playfair, John. *Bija Gannita or the Algebra of the Hindus*. Edinburgh: Edinburgh Review, 1813.

Porter, Jane. *The Scottish Chiefs*. London: Longman, 1810.

Prideaux. Humphrey. *The Old and New Testament connected with the History of the Jews*. 2 vols. London: Russell, 1716–18.

Rousseau, Jean-Jaques. *Eloisa: A series of Original Letters*. 3 vols. London: Harding, 1810.

———. *Letters sur les spectacles*. Basel: Revis, 1758.

Sanders, Charles Richard, general editor. *The Collected Letters of Thomas and Jane Welsh Carlyle*. Durham, NC: Duke University Press, 1970.

Saunders, Laurence James. *Scottish Democracy 1815–1840: The Social and Intellectual Background*. Edinburgh: Oliver and Boyde, 1950.

Scott, Thomas, *The Force of Truth*, London :,Printed by C.Watts, sold by Bellamy and Roberts and the author, 1789.

Schiller, Johann Christoph Friedrich von. *The Maid of Orleons*. 1801.

Scott, Hew. *Fasti Ecclesiae Scoticanæ*. 9 vols. Edinburgh: Oliver & Boyd, 1915–2000.

Scott, Sir Walter. *Tales of My Landlord*. Edinburgh: Murray, 1818.

Scott, Thomas, *The Force of Truth*, London: Keith and Johnson, 1789.

Shaw, P. E. *The Catholic Apostolic Church*. New York: King's Crown, 1946.

Stewart, Dugald. *Outlines of Moral Philosophy, for Use of Students in the University of Edinburgh*. Edinburgh: n.p., 1801.

Story, Rev. R. Herbert Story. *Memoir of the Life of the Rev Robert Story*. London: McMillan, 1862.

Voltaire. *Histoire de Charles XII of Sweden*. Basel: Nevis, 1731.

Waddington, Barbara. *The Rev. Edward Irving and the Catholic Apostolic Church in Canden and Beyond*. London: Camden History Society: 2007.

Walton, Isaak. *The Compleat Angler*. London: n.p., 1750.

Wilson, D. A. *A Life of Thomas Carlyle*. 6 vols. London: Kegan Paul, 1923–34.

Wilks, Washington. *Edward Irving: An Ecclesiastical and Literary Biography*. London: Freedman, 1854.

Newspapers Used

Literary Gazette
New Monthly Magazine
The Christian Instructor
The Christian Review
The Crisis
The Morning Watch

The Pulpit
The Review
The Revivalist
The Scotsman
The Scottish Guardian
The Times

Magazines Used

Blackwood's Edinburgh Magazine
Blackwood's Magazine
Christian and Civic Economy
Christian Weekly
Fraser's Magazine
Quarterly Review
The London Magazine

Electronic Resources

Biography of Charles Augustus Coulomb, St Andrews University, www.britannica.com. accessed November, 2008, 18.

Index

Aiken, Hugh, 63.
Ainslie, Mr of Begbie, 33, 48.
Alexander, Mr 422, 435.
Alexander, Mrs, 417.
Allen, Matthew, 73, 73n, 96n, 98, 98n, 178, 178n.
Anderson, Mr, 204.
Anderson, Mr (of Catholic Apolstolic Church), 369, 399.
Armstrong, Rev Nicholas, 322, 322n, 370, 382, 393.

Badams (Badomer), Dr John, 201, 201n.
Baldwin and Craddock, 278.
Banks, George, 7.
Banks, Misses, 290.
Barclay, Archibald, 333, 336, 342, 369, 375, 376, 389, 391, 397.
Baring, Sir Thomas, 180, 180n, 209n.
Baxter, Mrs, Edinburgh confectioner, 15.
Baxter, Robert of Doncaster, 293, 294, 295, 300, 300n, 301n, 302n, 303, 356, 367.
Bayford, Mr, 335, 403, 414.
Begg, Mr, 329.
Bell, Mr and Mrs, 36.
Beveridge, George, 63.
Bishop, Mrs, 359.
Blair, Dr, 26.
Blinny, Lady, 5.
Blinny, Miss, 5.
Blyth (see Blythe), Dr of Woolwich, 221, 221n.
Blyth, David, 197, 235, 277.
Blythe (Blyth), Dr of Woolwhich, 221, 221n.
Bonar, Rev Dr, 310.
Borthwick, Mr T, 256, 256n.
Boyd, Rev James, 129n, 130.
Brame, Miss, 4, 5, 6, 12, 15, 40, 41, 49.
Bridges, James, 210, 210n, 245.
Brodie, Mr, 9.
Brodie, Mr James, 254.
Brodribb, John, Henry, (the actor Henry Irving), 55.

Brough, Thomas, 48.
Brougham, Henry Peter, lst Baron Brougham and Vaux, 79n, 245, 246, 249, 251.
Brown, David, 71n, 271, 271n, 272, 277, 283, 382, 393.
Brown, Dr. (Adam Hope's brother), 88
Brown, James, 13, 13n, 15, 16, 17, 34, 35, 45, 47, 52, 73, 80, 83, 144, 144n, 191.
Brown, Mr, 257.
Bruce, Mr, (innkeeper at Haddington), 27.
Brydgeman, Mr, 405.
Brydon, Tranent, 25, 25n, 27.
Buchan, Charles, 345, 410, 411, 420.
Buller Family, 245.
Buller, Arthur, 126n.
Buller, Charles, 126n.
Buller, Mrs Isabella, 125, 125n, 126, 128, 132, 132n 173n, 189. 190.
Buller. Charles, Snr, 125n, 128, 132, 132n, 135, 251n.
Bulteel, Henry Bellenden, 363, 363n.
Burder, George, 120, 120n.
Burn, Adam (James Burn's son?), 29.
Burn, James, 29.

Caird (see Campbell), Mary, 270, 279, 285, 290, 299, 300, 301, 302, 304, 305, 306, 314, 315, 320, 322, 330, 335, 337n, 357, 360, 363, 365, 369, 370, 374, 375, 377, 381, 391n, 401, 407, 411, 412n, 413, 413n, 414.
Caird, (the Caird's baby), 371n.
Caird, W.R, (Mary's husband), 279, 285, 319, 322, 337n, 357, 360, 369, 371, 372, 375, 376, 377, 378, 386, 402, 407, 411, 413.
Campbell (see Caird), Mary, 270, 279, 391n, 412n.
Campbell, Isabella, (Mary Caird's sister) 377, 413, 413n.
Campbell, John McLeod, 272, 391, 411, 415, 416.
Campbell, Mrs, 365, 377, 375.
Canning, George, 124, 124n.

443

Index

Cannon, Mr, 383.

Cardale, Miss Emily, 286, 290, 291, 295, 300, 301, 302, 305, 307, 314, 315, 317, 319, 373, 377, 392.

Cardale Family, 259, 292, 293.

Cardale, John, 329, 335, 358, 362, 363, 363n, 372, 273, 373, 374, 376, 378, 382, 386, 387, 388, 389, 391n, 392, 393, 394, 395, 400, 409, 418, 420, 425, 426, 432, 435.

Cardale, Mrs John, 291, 406, 414.

Carlile, John, (an Apostle), 333.

Carlile (see Carlyle and Irving), Agnes (known as Nancy), 92n, 94, 100, 100n, 191.

Carlile (see Carlyle), Thomas, 72, 72n.

Carlile (see Carlyle), Warrand, (Edward Irving's brother-in-law), 91, 92, 92n, 93, 94, 100, 100n, 143, 353.

Carlisle, Rev James of Paisley, 89, 89n.

Carlisle (see Carlyle), John (also called Jack), (Thomas Carlyle's younger brother), 132n, 152n, 172, 176, 176n.

Carlisles' (see Carlyles), 109.

Carlyle (see Carlile and Irving), Agnes (known as Nancy), 92n, 94, 100, 100n, 191.

Carlyle, Alexander, (Sandy), Thomas Carlyle's brother, 72n, 98n, 100n, 108n, 139, 156n.

Carlile (see Carlyle), John, (Warrand Carlile's cousin), 353.

Carlyle (see, Carlisle), Thomas, 54, 59, 66n, 70, 71n, 72n, 73, 73n, 75n, 76, 77n, 78, 80, 81, 83, 85, 85n, 86, 87, 89n, 90, 90n 91, 92, 92n, 93n, 94, 94n, 96, 96n, 98, 98n, 99, 99n, 100, 100n, 102, 105, 105n, 107, 107n, 108n 109n, 110, 110n, 111n, 112n, 113, 114, 121, 123, 124, 124n, 125, 125n, 126, 126n, 128, 131, 132n, 133, 135n, 140, 143, 144n, 145, 146, 146n, 150, 150n, 152n, 161, 161n, 162, 168n, 170, 173n, 174, 174n, 175, 175n, 176, 177, 178n, 179n, 180n, 181, 181n, 183n, 189, 189n, 190, 190n, 196, 200, 201n, 203n, 204n, 205, 208n, 209n, 223, 223n, 232, 241, 241n, 243, 245, 246, 246n, 247, 248n, 249, 251, 251n, 254n, 260, 262n, 293, 358n, 379, 436.

Carlyle, Thomas, an Apostle of the CAC, 367, 369, 374, 375, 376, 383, 398, 399.

Carlyle (see Carlile), Warrand, (Edward Irving's brother-in-law), 91, 92, 92n, 93, 94, 100, 100n, 143, 353.

Carlyle (see Welsh), Jane, 54, 61n, 94n, 109, 109n, 110n, 111, 111n, 112, 122, 124, 125n, 126, 131, 133, 139, 140, 152n, 159, 160, 161, 167, 168, 169n, 172, 173, 182n, 183n, 195, 196, 203, 204n, 223, 223n, 241n, 259n, 260n.

Carlyle, James, Snr, 73, 96n, 100n.

Carlyle, James, Jnr 107n.

Carlyle, Janet, 72n.

Carlyle, John (also called Jack), (Thomas Carlyle's younger brother), 132n, 152n, 172, 176, 176n.

Carlyle (see Carlisle), John, (Warrand Carlile's cousin), 353.

Carlyle, Margaret, 251n.

Carlyle, Richard the Atheist, 162, 162n.

Carré, Collinge, Manger, 329, 329n, 331, 335.

Carswell, Thomas, 277.

Cary, Henry Francis, 175n.

Cathcart, (see Elliott) Countess Lady Elizabeth, 4, 5, 5n, 6.

Cathcart, Lord William Schaw, 1st Earl, 4, 5, 14.

Cathcart, Miss, 5, 15, 23.

Chalmbers (see Chalmers), Thomas, 114.

Chalmers, Ann, 150.

Chalmers, Eliza, 150, 202, 382.

Chalmers, Dr Thomas, 59, 76, 76n, 82, 84, 89, 89n, 91, 95, 102, 105, 114, 117, 118, 119, 131, 141, 149, 151, 152, 153, 155, 158, 161, 163, 169, 169n, 179, 180n, 201, 204, 222n, 230, 230n, 232, 233, 234, 236, 237, 240, 244, 245, 246, 252, 266, 271n, 279n, 284.

Chalmers, Mr Robert the Antiburger, 9, 9n

Chalmers, Mrs Thomas, 103, 106, 150, 154, 169, 202, 239.

Charteris, Mr, 22.

Christison, Alexander, 71, 71n.

Clark, Mrs (Mrs Martin's sister), 183.

Clarke, Mr William, (Edward Irving's private pupil in Haddington), 17, 23, 24, 26, 30, 35.

Cleaver, Rev Mr of Dalgany, 282.

Cockburn, Mr and Mrs of Haddington, 48.

Cole, Rev of Clare College, Cambridge, 232.

Coleridge, Samuel Taylor, 175n, 209, 209n, 230n, 241n, 248.

Collins, William, 76n, 120, 149, 155, 158, 163, 168, 169, 169n, 193, 212, 219, 219n.

Cornwall, Barry, (see Procter), 175, 175n.

Costobadie, Jacob, 185n.

Cowper, Mr A. of Bridgenorth, 404.

Cowper, William, 97, 97a.

Cragcroft, Miss, 402.

Crombie, John, 153, 153n.

Crosbie, John Geddes, 150, 150n, 180, 207, 222, 240.

Cunningham, Alan, 171, 172n, 175, 218.

Cunningham, Mr, of Haddington, 15, 16.

Cunninghame, 256.

444

Index

Dalgleish, Rev William, 3n, 27n.
Dalton, Henry, 386, 387, 388, 389, 405.
Darling, Dr, 242, 395n, 403.
Declaration on the Divinity of Christ, 275n, 276.
Dewar, Dr, 77.
Dickson, Alik, Tom, 170.
Dickson (see Dixon), Francis, 71, 71n, 73, 73n, 83n, 87, 93, 163.
Dickson, Janet (also known as Jenny), (see Irving) (Edward Irving's sister), 7, 7n, 27n, 88n, 191, 192, 417, 435.
Dickson, Mrs, 421.
Dickson, Robert, (Edward Irving's brother-in-law), 7n, 27n 88n.
Diddep, Mr, 34, 36, 50.
Dinwiddie, Mrs William, 131, 187.
Dinwiddie, William, 116, 116n, 117, 119, 121n, 123, 129, 135, 141, 143, 147, 153, 186, 195, 197, 203, 206, 216, 222, 235, 255, 275.
Dixon (see Dickson) Francis, 71, 71n, 73, 73, 73n. 83n, 87, 93, 163.
Dixon (see Dickson), Mr and Mrs (David Dow's in-laws), 383.
Dobbie, 123.
Dodds (see Dods), Rev Marcus, 266, 272, 326, 327. 327n.
Dods, (see Dodds), Rev Marcus, 266, 272, 326, 327, 327n.
Dods, Mr and Mrs Peter of Clerkingtown 25, 25n, 49
Dodsworth Rev Mr, 290, 359, 359n.
Dornford Miss, 255.
Douglas, William, 63.
Dow, Rev David, 282, 336, 337, 348, 359n, 360, 367, 383, 383n, 391, 398, 399.
Dow, William, 399.
Downie, Bryce, 3.
Drummond, Henry, xi, 209, 209n, 228, 228n, 230, 256, 256n, 257, 261, 264, 268, 271n, 279, 319, 320, 321, 329, 331, 332, 334, 335, 336, 347, 354, 356, 358n, 359n, 361, 362, 364, 365 367, 368, 368n, 369, 371, 371n, 372, 374, 375, 377, 377n, 379, 385, 386, 388, 390, 391n, 393, 396, 398, 400, 401, 403, 405, 410, 413, 413n, 414, 416n, 417, 418, 423, 424, 431.
Drummond, Lady Henrietta, 256, 256n, 257, 164, 265, 270, 280, 330, 335, 337, 348, 357, 360, 363, 365, 369, 374, 377, 386, 401, 405, 407, 411, 434.
Duff, Mrs, 68, 76, 80, 83, 84, 85, 102.
Duffle, David, 154.
Duke of York, 120n, 122, 130n, 134.
Dukron, David, 117.

Duncan, Dr Henry, 72n 77n.
Duncan, Mr, 60, 192.
Duncan, Mrs, 192.

Elders of St. Cuthberts, Edinburgh, 213.
Elders of the Caledonian Church, 135, 140, 142, 147, 150, 152, 205, 213, 220, 223n, 240n, 250, 253, 274, 296.
Elliott (see Cathcart), Elizabeth, 4,5, 5n, 6.
Elliott, John, 161.
Ellister, 278.
Erskine, Thomas of Linlathlin, 40, 140n 391, 391n, 423.
'Ettrick Shepherd,' (see Hogg), 74, 74n.
Evill, Thomas, 344, 353.

Farish, Mr, 9, 12, 22, 35, 47.
Farmer, Miss, 263.
Farrer, Mr D, 348.
Ferguson (see Fergusson), John, 75, 75n, 90n, 260, 260n.
Ferguson of Annan, 85.
Fergusson (see Ferguson), John, 75, 75n, 90n, 260, 260n.
Fergusson, Dr John Lowther, (Edward Irving's brother-in-law), 88n, 158.
Fergusson (see Irving), Mrs, (Edward Irving's sister Margaret), 88n, 221, 221n.
Ferrar, Miss, 268.
Finch, Mr, 8.
Fisher, Mr, (one of Edward Irving's teachers), 27.
Fleming, Dr Thomas, 107,107n, 117, 126, 126n, 127, 128, 129, 130, 132, 132n, 133, 140, 163.
Foggus, Mr, 43.
Foley, Mr, 294, 302.
Foulkes, Richard, 55, 55n
Fraser, James, 291, 436n.
Frere, Hatley, 209, 209n.
Frey, Joseph, Samuel, 32n, 41, 41n, 42, 49, 50, 50n.

Galloway, Mr, 71, 71n, 74.
Gambier, Capt, 343, 359, 359n, 363, 365, 369 371, 377, 405.
Gardener, Mr of Southampton, 372.
Gardiner, Samuel, Rawson, (Isabella Irving's daughter's huband), 436.
Gillespie, Alexander, Jnr, 277.
Gilpin, Bernard, 194, 194n.
Godden, Mr, 386, 402, 403.
Goodson, Dr, 252.
Gordon, Margaret, 85, 85n, 93, 94, 94n, 95, 98n,122.

Index

Gordon, Mrs of Islington, 229.
Gordon, Mrs, 137, 138.
Gordon, Rev Dr Robert, 107, 107n, 108, 109, 117, 137, 169, 180, 221, 222, 228, 235, 238, 239, 240, 253.
Gordon, Rev Robert, 107, 107n, 117n 137, 180, 190.
Graham, Mr William, (teacher at the Haddington Grammar School), 8, 16, 22, 25, 26, 38, 48, 50.
Graham, Mrs, of Haddington, 25, 48.
Graham, William of Burnswark, 92, 92n, 100, 100n, 102, 109, 112, 137, 140, 144, 156, 163, 165, 188, 274.
Green, Mr of Chelsea, 382.
Greig, Mr, 64, 65, 67.
Grey Mr 117, 329.
Grierson, Mr, of Dumfries, 15.

Haldane, Alexander, 253.
Haldane, James, 36n.
Haldane, Robery, 36n, 209n.
Hall, Miss Elizabeth, 290, 290n, 302, 302n, 308.
Hall, Mr, 223, 223n, 226, 275.
Hall, Mrs, 226.
Hamilton (see Martin) Elizabeth, Edward Irving's sister-in-law, 227, 328n, 329, 395n, 417, 422.
Hamilton, Alexander, 261.
Hamilton, Dr, 51.
Hamilton, William, 116n, 131, 135, 136, 143, 155, 156, 161, 187, 197, 199n, 223, 224, 228, 232, 235, 236, 237, 242n, 243n, 254n, 261, 265, 266, 277, 280, 281, 284, 326, 327, 328, 328n, 329, 417, 420, 422, 434, 436.
Haydon, Benjamin, painter, 102n.
Hazlitt, William, ixi, 54, 54n, 175, 175n.
Heath, Christopher, 333, 392.
Henderson Mr, (Printer), 258, 277, 278, 348, 350, 351.
Henschell, Ridley, 348.
Henslow, Rev Prof, 276, 276n.
Herbertson, Mr, 77, 77n.
Hershall, Joseph, Irving, 281.
Hill, James, first pastor of The Congregational Church, Haddington, 36, 36n, 37, 43.
Hinton, Mr, 363.
Hitchens, General, 26.
Hogg, (Ettrick Shepherd), James, 74, 74n.
Holliday, John, 23.
Hollis, Thomas, 72, 73n.
Honer, Mr, 89.
Hood, Thomas, one of Edward Irving's pupils in Haddington, 27.
Hope, Adam, brother to Dr Brown, 100, 100n.

Hope, David, 3, 3n, 27, 33n, 82, 100, 100n, 109, 109n, 149, 152n, 164, 188, 254, 254n.
Hope, James, 30,
Hope, Miss, 221.
Horn (see Horne), Archibald, 197, 235, 277, 339, 348, 435.
Horne, (see Horn) Archibald, 197, 235, 277, 348, 435.
Horner, Leonard, 249, 249n.
Howden Mr, Elder of St.Cuthberts, 214, 217.
Hunter, Mr of Gloucester, 158.

Ingles, Frederick, 333.
Irving (see Carlisle and Carlyle), Agnes (known as Nancy), (Edward Irving's sister), 92n, 94, 100, 100n, 191.
Irving (see Martin), Isabella, 54, 61, 85n, 88n, 94n, 116n, 124, 125, 152n, 182n, 183, 183n, 189n, 190, 190n, 191, 194, 195, 196, 200, 207, 208, 209, 211, 212, 216, 217, 218, 219, 219n 220, 227, 232, 234, 240, 241n, 242, 243n, 249, 252, 259n, 260n, 271, 289, 302n, 328n, 335, 360n, 370, 374, 375, 376, 382, 404, 405, 406, 410, 416, 417, 419, 421, 422, 423, 425, 433, 435, 436.
Irving, (see Kennedy), Elizabeth, (Edward Irving's sister), 88n, 105n, 107.
Irving, (see Fergusson), Margaret, (Edward Irving's sister), 28n.
Irving, Ebenezer, (Edward Irving's son), 293, 337, 337n 354, 354n, 371n.
Irving, Edward, ix, 3, 3n, 4, 7n 12n 16n, 26n, 27n, 32n, 37n, 54, 55, 60n, 67n, 68, 85n, 90n, 94n, 111n, 116n, 124, 130n, 175n, 179n, 183n, 189n, 194n, 198n, 209, 209n, 210, 212, 224n, 232, 241n, 251n, 254n, 255n, 258, 259, 275n, 279n, 291, 293, 328n, 371n, 423n, 436.
Irving, Edward, Jnr, 202, 225n, 234n.
Irving, Elizabeth, 7, 107.
Irving, Gavin, (Edward Irving's son), 259, 268n.
Irving, Gavin, (Edward Irving's father), 3, 26n, 223n, 419.
Irving, George, (Edward Irving's brother), 3, 157, 172, 176, 187n, 245, 246, 293, 357n, 360n.
Irving, George, (Edward Irving's uncle), 90n, 180n.
Irving, Mrs George, (Edward Irving's aunt), 180n.
Irving, Henry, born John Henry Brodribb, actor, 55.
Irving, Isabella, daughter, 395n.

Index

Irving, Janet (also known as Jenny), (see Dickson) (Edward Irving's sister), 7, 7n, 27n, 88n, 191, 192, 417, 435.
Irving, John Lowther, (Edward Irving's brother), 3, 26n, 178,179n, 218n, 262.
Irving, Margaret, (Edward Irving's daughter), 210, 211, 218, 248, 401, 436.
Irving (see Fergusson), Margaret, (Edward Irving's sister), 88n, 221, 221n.
Irving, Martin, Howy, (Edward Irving's son), 259, 283n, 405, 435, 436, 436n.
Irving, Mary, (Edward Irving's daughter) 236n.
Irving, Mary, (Edward's maternal grandmother, married to Bryce Johnstone), 28n.
Irving, Mary, (Edward's mother), 3, 191, 419, 421.
Irving, Mr G, (Mr Graham's assistant at Haddington), 38
Irving, Mr G, Edward was mistaken for him, 38.
Irving, Mr of Dumfriesshire, 38.
Irving, Mrs George, 180n.
Irving, Samuel, (Edward Irving's son), 268n.
Irving, William, (Edward Irving's cousin), 28.

Jackson, Mr, 411.
Jackson, Rev Mr, 9.
Jameson, Mr, 'young man at the Book,' 50.
Jameson, Prof. Robert, 74. 74n.
Jamieson, Mr, of Haddington, 48.
Jaspet, Mr, 407.
Jeffrey, Lord Francis, 25, 79n, 245, 246n, 247, 260, 260n, 261n, 246, 24n, 247, 260, 260n, 261n.
Johnston, Baillie, 26, 35, 36, 37.
Johnston, Mr and Mrs, 102, 109, 413, 413n.
Johnstone, Bryce, Edward Irving's mother's uncle, 28, 28n.
Johnstone, James, ("Targer"), 72, 72n, 102, 133, 144n, 163, 174, 174n, 178, 179.
Johnstone, Miss of Dumfries, sister to Dr Bryce Johnstone, 25n, 28, 90, 190, 191.
Johnstones re 'rise of the Church at Albury,' 413, 413n.
Joplin, Mr, 382.

Kelly, Francis Maria, (known as Fanny), 173, 173n.
Kemp, Robert, 174.
Kennedy (see Irving), Elizabeth, (Edward Irving's sister), 88n, 105n, 107.
Ker (see also Kerr), David, 277, 348, 350, 352, 353, 411.
Ker Mr of Edinburgh, 13, 18.
Ker, Mr, 8.

King, Mr, 328.
Kirk, Robert, 63.
Knox, Boy, 257.
Knox, Sir John, 220, 220n.

Laing Dr, 421.
Lamb, Charles, 173n, 201n.
Lamb, Mr (Alexander Reddoch's landlord), 6, 38, 39.
Lang, Edward, 18,63.
Lauderdale, James Maitland, 8th Earl of, 52, 71, 71n.
Laurie, James, 116, 116n, 117, 121, 135, 150, 155, 163, 423, 424.
Laurie, Mrs, 423.
Leslie, Sir John, 4, 16n, 54.
Lewis, Mr of Leith, 329.
Little, George, 23, 88, 88n, 123.
Lockhart (see Lockheart), John Gibson, 74, 74n, 326, 327.
Lockheart (see Lockhart), 74, 74n, 326, 327.
Lorimer, Dr Robert, 11, 11n, 12n, 16, 17, 18, 23n, 29, 30, 32, 37, 43, 46, 47, 50, 51.
Lowrie, Mr from Dunbar, 6.
Lumsden, Mr, 51.
Lundie, Mrs, 77.
Lundie, Rev Robert, 77, 77n.

M'Kenzie, (see MacKenzie), Duncan, 235, 348, 359n, 383.
Mcdonald Family, 259, 279n.
Macdonald, Mr, 270, 277.
Macdonnald, Matthew, 369.
Macfarlane, Patrick, 272.
Mackenzie (see M'Kenzie), Duncan, 235, 348, 359n, 383.
MacLean, Rev Hugh, 285, 327, 384n.
Magus, Simon, 268. 356.
Malcolm, Alexander, 63.
Mandeville, Lord, 285.
Mann, James, Hargrave, 278, 279, 279n.
Manuel, Dr, 153, 153n.
Marshall, Mr, 90, 153, 153n.
Marchbanks, Mrs, 24.
Martin, Margaret, 200, 212, 225, 226.
Martin (see Hamilton), Elizabeth, 227, 328n 329, 329n, 395n, 417, 422.
Martin (see Irving), Isabella, 54, 61, 85n, 88n, 94n, 116n, 124, 125, 152n, 182n, 183, 183n, 189n, 190, 190n, 191, 194, 195, 196, 200, 207, 208, 209, 211, 212, 216, 217, 218, 219, 219n 220, 227, 232, 234, 240, 241n, 242, 243n, 249, 252, 259n, 260n, 271, 289, 302, 328n, 335, 360n, 370, 374, 375, 376,

Index

382, 404, 405, 406, 410, 416, 417, 419, 421, 422, 423, 425, 433, 435, 436.
Martin Family, 59, 152n, 191.
Martin, Mrs John, 182, 183, 192, 194, 200, 395n.
Martin, Rev John, father of Isabella Irving, 34, 54, 60, 64, 66n, 67, 68, 70, 169, 190n, 191, 192, 199, 211, 227, 242, 255, 280, 293, 317, 371n, 402, 416, 420, 424, 434.
Martin, Samuel, (Isabella Irving's brother), 183n, 221n, 271, 326, 328, 328n, 381, 423.
Mary, (Irving's servant), 208, 220.
Mason, Dr John Mitchell, 135, 135n.
Maxton, Miss of Alloa, 85.
McCall, Mrs, 76.
Mclean, Archibald, 24, 24n.
McGie (Ann Paul), Jenny, 18.
McGregor, Major, 103.
McIntyre's shop in Haddington, 48.
McLean, (a piper), Allan, 39.
McLean, Colonel, 39.
McLean, Rev Hugh B, 281, 384.
McNeil, Jnr, 271.
McNeill, Rev Hugh, 365, 365n.
McNicolson of Paisley, 435.
McWhir, John, (of the Chapel of Ease at Dunfermaline), 28, 28n.
Millar, Miss Emma Margaret, 304.
Millar, Mr (Parish Priest of White Kirk), 8.
Millar (see Miller), Rev J.R, 289, 389, 356, 356n 359, 361, 371, 376, 377, 389, 397.
Millar, Rev James, (presenter of a protest at Edward Irving's trial in Annan), 303.
Miller, (see Millar), Rev. J.R, 289, 389, 356, 356n 359, 361, 371, 376, 377, 389, 397.
Mitchell, Robert, 71n, 72, 72n, 77n, 174n.
Moderator of the Presbytery of Annan, (see Moncrieff), Moderator of the Presbystery of Annan, 105n, 152n.
Moncrieff, Sir Henry, 117.
Moncrieff, William Hardie of Annan, 105n, 152n.
Montague, Basil, 183, 209n, 241n, 242, 244.
Montague, Charles, 193, 202.
Montague, Mrs, 111n, 183, 191, 240, 240n.
Morton, Mr, Edward Irving's landlord in Haddington, 26, 33.
Mudie, Mr of Dundee, 200, 200n, 201.
Murat, Joachim, 68, 68n.
Murray, Mr, 207.

Neil, Mr. of shop and lending library, 25.
Nisbet, James A, 235, 258n 277, 277n, 283.
Norbet, Mr, 435.

North, Christopher (see Prof. John Wilson), 102n, 103.

Oliphant, Mrs Margaret, 4n, 22n, 59, 61n, 65n, 67n, 111n, 116n, 124n, 133n, 143n, 149n, 156n, 164n, 165n, 179n, 187n, 188n, 193n, 199n, 207n, 208, 208n, 210, 216n, 218n, 221n, 223n, 223n, 224n, 227n, 242n, 254n, 260n, 274n, 277n, 279n, 293n, 304, 317n, 335n, 371n, 385n, 391n, 402n, 405n.
Orpen, Dr C.E.H, 281, 282.
Orr, Mr, 330.
Owen, H.J, 367, 389, 389n, 397.

Paine, Peggy, 3.
Panton, Andrew, 235, 265.
Parker, James, 201, 201n, 226.
Patterson, Mr of Leith, 329.
Paul, Ann, (Jenny McGie), 18.
Paul, Henry, 70, 211, 319, 321, 322, 323.
Paul, Mr, Elder at St.Cuthbert's Church, 214, 217.
Paul, Mrs, 155.
Pears, John, 66, 66n, 70, 74.
Perceval (see Percival), Spencer, 302n, 320, 337, 346, 363, 337n, 374.
Percival J, 291.
Percival (see Perceval), Spencer, 302n, 320, 337, 346, 363, 337n, 374.
Petrie, Peter, 326, 326n.
Piers, (see Pears), John, 66, 66n, 70, 74.
Pit[t], William, the Younger, 8, 8n.
Pitcairn, Mr, 383.
Playfair, Prof. John, 60n, 74.
Preacher, Mr, 38.
Pringles, Mr of Haddington, 34.
Probyn, Rev Edward, 286, 290.
Procter, Brian Waller, (see Cornwall), 175, 175n.
Provand, Mrs, 414.

Reddoch, Alexander, 6, 7, 8, 9, 10, 15, 17, 18, 23, 24, 25, 33, 34, 36, 37, 38, 39, 40, 42, 43, 45, 46, 50.
Rede, William, Leman, 54, 55, 55n.
Richardson, Mr, Surgeon, 283.
Richmond, Mr, 131.
Ridick, Mrs, 25.
Riely, Miss, 109.
Ritchie, Mr, 51.
Robertson, Andrew, artist, 131, 134, 135, 138, 141, 141n, 142.
Robertson, James, bookseller of Edinburgh, 7, 41.
Robertson, Jas, 41, 42.

Index

Robertson, Mr, wine merchant, 103.
Robertson, Thomas, 41, 42.
Robinson, Henry Crabbe, 201, 201n.
Rook (see Rooke), Miss, 405, 422.
Rose, Mr, 207.
Rutherford, Ebenezer, 63.
Ryder's Company, 54, 55.
Ryerson, George, 402, 402n.

Samuel, Mr, 23.
Scott, James, 266, 266n.
Scott, John, 175, 175n.
Scott, Thomas, 168, 168n.
Shepherd, Mr, 382.
Sheriff, Mr, (of Mungo's Wells), 34.
Sheriff, Mr, of Drem, 16, 50.
Sibbald, Dr William, 9n, 10, 10n, 15, 19, 24n, 28, 44, 45, 50, 51.
Sibbald, James, Hope, 18, 22, 22n 27, 35, 44, 44n.
Sibbald, Mrs, 15.
Simpson, James, Gilliland, 197, 197n, 217n, 293, 299, 299n, 310, 310n, 311, 326.
Simpson, Mrs Jane, 293, 299, 304, 308, 312, 313, 314, 316, 317, 319, 325, 326.
Simpson, Robert, 129, 129n, 130, 131, 135.
Sitwell, Frank, 425n, 434, 434n.
Skinner, Mr, 256.
Smith, Mr, 276, 322, 356, 367, 398.
Sober, Mrs of Brighton, 364.
Sparrow, Lady Olivia, 264, 264n, 265, 284.
Stevenson, Charles, 333, 353.
Stevenson, Jas, 91.
Stewart, Dr Andrew of Bolton, 22, 22n, 23, 23n, 40, 47, 51, 88, 90, 138, 407.
Stewart, Mr and Mrs, 406, 407.
Stewart, Mr, (principal waiter at Laing's Inn), 39.
Stewart, Prof Dugald, 37n, 107, 107n, 244, 248.
Story, Mrs, 412.
Story, Robert, 59, 61n, 375n, 412, 412n, 413n.
Strachey, Edward, 128.
Stratchey, Mrs Julia (aka Kitty), 173, 173n, 204, 245.
Strutt, Hon J.J, 229, 229n, 252, 289, 290
Swan William, 108, 108n.
Symes, Miss J, 405.
Symes, Mr, 363.

Tait (see Tate), Rev Walter, 199, 199n, 277, 375, 375n, 378.
Tait, Archbishop, 434n.
Tait (see Tate), William, 378, 378n, 383, 393, 414, 415, 419, 425.

Taplin, E.O, 286, 299, 302n, 319, 330, 334, 337, 357, 358, 359, 360, 361, 367, 372, 374, 391n, 392, 395.
Tate (see Tait), Mrs, 199.
Tate (see Tait), Rev Walter, 199, 199n, 277, 375, 375n, 378.
Tate (see Tait), William, 378, 378n, 383, 393, 414, 415, 419, 425.
Taylor, John, Editor of *London Magazine*, 175, 175n, 177, 181.
Taylor, Mr 414, 422, 433.
Tennant, Hugh, 170.
The Congregation, Dear Beloved Members and Office Bearers of the Caledonian Church, 214.
The Members and Elders of the Presbytery of Annan, 324.
The Trustees of Regent Square Church, 287, 289, 290, 296, 298, 303n, 435.
Thompson Mrs, 435.
Thompson, Andrew, 86, 90, 107, 107n, 117, 137.
Thompson, Dr James, 253, 315, 359, 359n, 390, 391n, 435.
Thompson, James, 169, 212, 213, 221.
Trimer, Mr, 351, 352, 353.
Tudor, John, 220n, 256, 341, 348, 360, 360n, 375, 376.

Unknown Recipient, 234, 254, 261, 385.

Vaughan Rev E.T, 256, 256n.
Vertue, Charles, 277, 289.

Wales Rev William, 365, 382.
Wales, Mrs, 381.
Walker, John, 12, 13, 18, 35, 68.
Wallis, Charles 333, 342, 352
Waugh, Dr Alexander, 120, 120n.
Waugh, John Baillie, bookseller, 108, 108n.
Waugh, Robert, 13.
Welsh (see Carlyle) Jane, 54, 61n, 94n, 109, 109n, 110n, 111, 111n, 112, 122, 124, 125n, 126, 131, 133, 139, 140, 152n, 159, 160, 161, 167, 168, 169n, 172, 173 182n, 183n, 195, 196, 203, 204n, 223, 223n, 241n, 260n.
Welsh, David, 28n.
Welsh, Mr, 110n.
Welsh, Mrs, 165, 169n.
Whytt, Ebenezer, 197, 279.
Wickham, Lieutenant, 25.
Wilberforce, William, 180.
Wilkie, Sir David, 1, 218, 218n.
Wilkinson, Mr, 414.

449

Index

Williams, Dr, 36.
Wilson, Prof John (see Christopher North), 102n, 103.
Wirgman, Rev Dr, 282.
Woodhouse, Francis, 333, 333n, 414, 415, 416, 417, 418, 422, 424, 431, 432, 433.

Woodrow, Mr, 221, 221n, 240, 240n.
Woods, Mr and Mrs, 103, 155.
Woods, Mr Walter, 103, 154, 155.
Wolf, Joseph, 233, 233n, 255, 255n, 287, 367.

Young, Mr, 207.